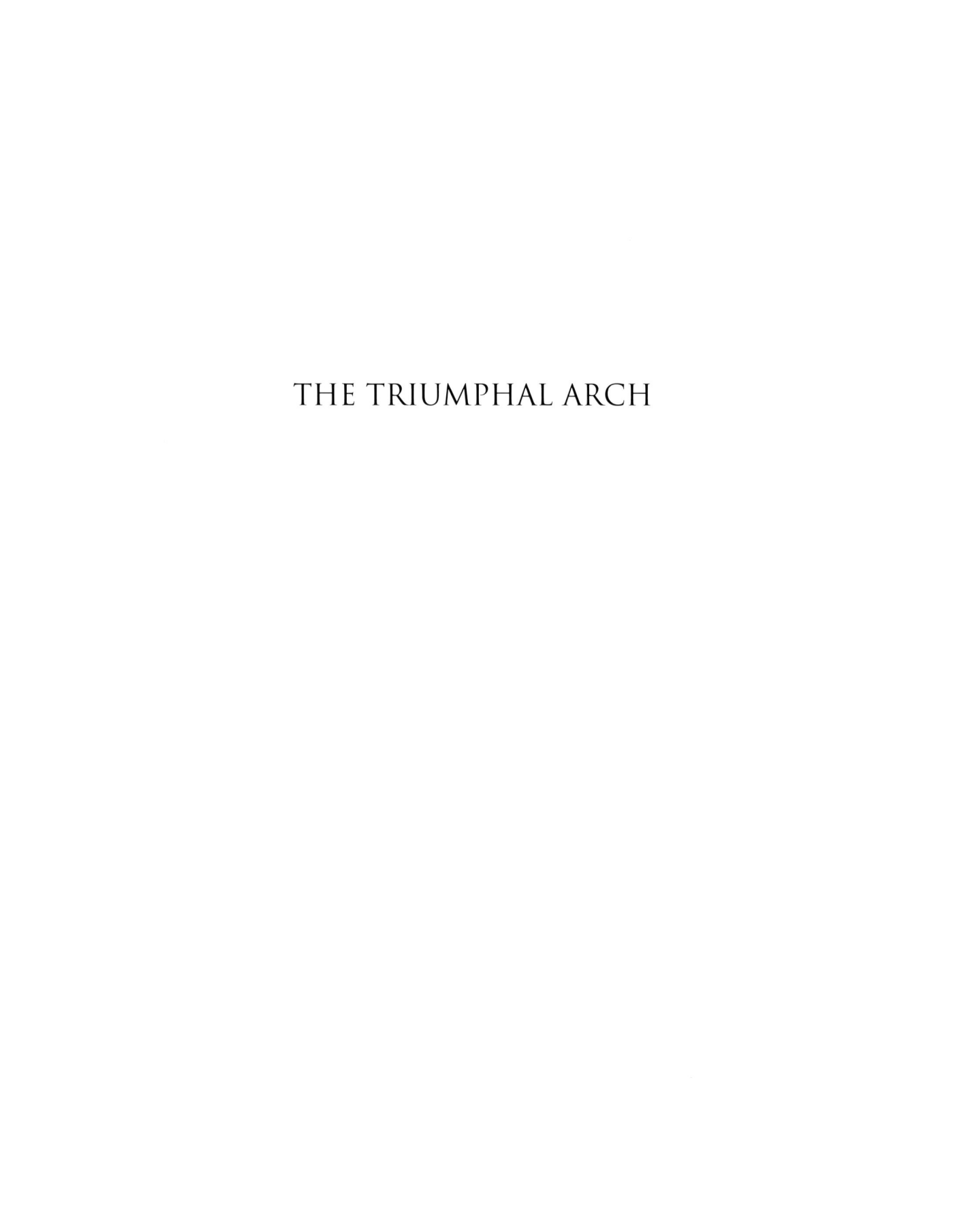

THE TRIUMPHAL ARCH

THE TRIUMPHAL ARCH

PETER HOWELL

UNICORN

To Edward, after 42 years

Published in 2021 by
Unicorn, an imprint of Unicorn Publishing Group LLP
5 Newburgh Street
London
W1F 7RG
www.unicornpublishing.org

© Peter Howell

All rights reserved. No part of the contents of this book may be reproduced, stored in or introduced into a retrieval system, or transmitted, in any form or by any means (electronic, mechanical, photocopying, recording or otherwise), without the prior written permission of the copyright holder and the above publisher of this book.

Every effort has been made to trace copyright holders and to obtain their permission for the use of copyrighted material. The publisher apologises for any errors or omissions and would be grateful to be notified of any corrections that should be incorporated in future reprints or editions of this book.

ISBN 978 1 913491 40 6
10 9 8 7 6 5 4 3 2 1

Index by Nicola King
Design by newtonworks.uk
Printed by Finetone

ABBREVIATIONS

AA	Archäologischer Anzeiger
ADAJ	Annual of the Department of Antiquities, Jordan
AJA	American Journal of Archaeology
ANRW	Aufstieg und Niedergang der römischen Welt
BICS	Bulletin of the Institute of Classical Studies
CIL	Corpus Inscriptionum Latinarum (Berlin, 1862–)
CRAI	Comptes Rendus de l'Académie des Inscriptions et Belles Lettres
IGR	Inscriptiones Graecae ad Res Romanas Pertinentes (ed, R. Cagnat, Paris 1906–27)
ILAlg	Inscriptions Latines de l'Algérie (ed. R. Cagnat, Paris 1922)
ILS	Inscriptiones Latinae Selectae (ed. H. Dessau, Berlin, 1954–5)
IRT	Inscriptions of Roman Tripolitania (ed. J.M. Reynolds and J.B. Ward Perkins, London 1952)
JRA	Journal of Roman Archaeology
JRS	Journal of Roman Studies
JSAH	Journal of the Society of Architectural Historians
LTUR	Lexicon Topographicum Urbis Romae (ed. E.M. Steinby, Rome, 1993–)
NACF	National Art Collections Fund
ODNB	Oxford Dictionary of National Biography (Oxford, 2004)
PBSR	Papers of the British School at Rome
PIR	Prosopographia Imperii Romani
ZPE	Zeitschrift für Papyrologie und Epigraphik

Frontispiece: Susa (Segusio), in the Alps: the arch dedicated to Augustus in 9/8 BC by M. Julius Cottius (see figure 2.4).
Page vii: Turin, Arco in onore all'Artigliere d'Italia, 1930. Pietro Canonica (see figure 33.13).

CONTENTS

PREFACE   *viii*

1 THE ROMAN TRIUMPHAL ARCH: ORIGINS   *1*
2 ARCHES OF THE TIME OF AUGUSTUS   *7*
3 FROM TIBERIUS TO NERO   *29*
4 AFTER NERO IN ITALY   *36*
5 AFTER NERO IN EUROPE OUTSIDE ITALY   *71*
6 AFTER NERO IN ASIA MINOR   *90*
7 NORTH AFRICA   *107*
8 FROM ANTIQUITY TO THE RENAISSANCE   *130*
9 RENAISSANCE ITALY   *137*
10 PAPAL ARCHES   *169*
11 ARCHES FOR CELEBRATIONS IN ITALY   *191*
12 ENGLAND AND SCOTLAND IN THE SIXTEENTH AND SEVENTEENTH CENTURIES   *202*
13 FRANCE IN THE SIXTEENTH AND SEVENTEENTH CENTURIES   *221*
14 FRANCE FROM LOUIS XIV TO THE REVOLUTION   *229*
15 THE LOW COUNTRIES FROM THE SIXTEENTH TO THE NINETEENTH CENTURY   *246*
16 ARCHES AS FEATURES OF PARKS AND LANDSCAPE GARDENS   *262*
17 ENGLAND, SCOTLAND AND IRELAND IN THE EIGHTEENTH CENTURY   *291*
18 ARCHES IN BRITAIN AND IRELAND FOR ROYAL OCCASIONS   *304*

19	NAPOLEONIC ARCHES	*316*
20	ARCHES IN FRANCE AFTER NAPOLEON I	*325*
21	LONDON – THE MARBLE AND WELLINGTON ARCHES	*329*
22	GERMANY AND AUSTRIA FROM THE SIXTEENTH TO THE NINETEENTH CENTURY	*334*
23	CENTRAL AND EASTERN EUROPE	*348*
24	RUSSIA AND MOLDOVA	*355*
25	SCANDINAVIA	*363*
26	SPAIN AND PORTUGAL	*368*
27	MALTA	*374*
28	AMERICA, 1758–1939	*377*
29	MEXICO, SOUTH AMERICA, CUBA	*381*
30	AUSTRALIA	*388*
31	INDIA	*393*
32	THE FAR EAST	*396*
33	ARCHES AS WAR MEMORIALS	*401*
34	TWENTIETH- AND TWENTY-FIRST-CENTURY ARCHES	*425*

BIBLIOGRAPHY *440*

PICTURE CREDITS *441*

ACKNOWLEDGEMENTS *443*

INDEX *444*

PREFACE

Everyone is familiar with the phrase 'triumphal arch', which is the one commonly used in English, and the one used in this book [0.1]. The truth is, however, that this architectural form, invented by the Romans, had in its origin no real connection with the 'triumph' as celebrated by them. This means that the German term *Ehrenbogen* and the Italian *arco onorario*, both meaning 'honorary arch', are more correct. It is true that the Latin phrase *arcus triumphalis* is found a few times, but this is something of a mystery (as discussed later).

0.1 A Roman Triumph, engraving from Jacques Grasset de Saint Sauveur, *L'Antique Rome*, 1795. The traditional idea of the arch and triumph.

How then are we to define the phenomenon? Clearly there must be an opening (though in some cases the opening may not be round-headed) through which people can pass. There must be some way of distinguishing the 'triumphal arch' from a mere gateway, and the answer must be that some kind of commemorative function is required. The supposed connection with the triumph meant that arches were often erected in later times to commemorate military successes, or the 'entries' of rulers or powerful individuals to towns or districts. Many of these were temporary constructions, often made of timber and canvas, or plaster. Some were made from scratch, while others reused materials stored from previous arches. They were frequently designed by architects or artists, and incorporated paintings or statues, often by distinguished painters or sculptors. In the nineteenth century it became quite common for arches to be decorated with materials representing relevant trades or products, and occasionally even the form of the arch might be symbolic. Sometimes the arches were so much admired that permanent versions were erected.

However, the classic form of 'triumphal arch' became commonly used as an architectural motif, in many different contexts, and these also need to be considered.

The history of arches extends from Roman times to the present day, with barely a hiatus, and their geographical spread is astonishing. One of its most curious manifestations is the gateways set up in China to honour individuals, though any connection of these with the Roman arch is unlikely.

This book would appear to be the first to cover the whole history of the 'triumphal arch'. Obviously it can make no claim to be complete and comprehensive, but it is hoped that it will give an idea of the altogether remarkable influence of an architectural type sometimes denounced as a regrettable example of Roman pomposity. For example, D.S. Robertson, in his *Greek and Roman Architecture* (Cambridge, 1969) described 'monumental arches' as 'typical of the rather pretentious magnificence of the Empire', 'another individual and unattractive Roman invention'.

The basic synoptic account of Roman arches is still that of Heinz Kähler, in A.F. von Pauly and G. Wissowa, eds, *Real-Encyclopädie der classischen Altertumswissenschaft*, s.v. Triumphbogen (Stuttgart, 1939). Arches in Italy are discussed in more detail in Sandro De Maria, *Gli archi onorari di Roma e dell'Italia romana* (Rome, 1988). For the arches erected for the papal *possesso* the only complete account is still that of Francesco Cancellieri, *Storia de' solenni possessi de' sommi pontifici* (Rome, 1802), though there is also an article by Hans Martin, Freiherr von Erffa, 'Die Ehrenpforten für den Possess der Päpste im 17. und 18. Jahrhundert', *Festschrift Harald Keller* (Darmstadt, 1963, pp. 335–70). There are many accounts of arches erected for 'entries' in the Renaissance and later, particularly important ones being Jean Jacquot and Elie Konigson, eds, *Les Fêtes de la Renaissance* (Paris, 1956–75), J.R. Mulryne and Helen Watanabe-O'Kelly, eds, *Europa Triumphans: Court and Civic Festivals in Early Modern Europe* (Aldershot, 2004), Marcello Fagioli, *La Festa a Roma: dal rinascimento al 1870* (Turin, 1997), and Maurizio Fagioli dell'Arco, *La Festa Barocca* (Rome, 1997). There are important monographs on individual arches, including Giovanni Voghera, *Illustrazione dell' Arco della Pace in Milano* (Milan, 1838), Thomas W. Gaehtgens, *Napoleons Arc de Triomphe* (Göttingen, 1974), and Isabelle Rouge-Ducos, *L'Arc de Triomphe de l'Étoile* (Dijon, 2008).

1
THE ROMAN TRIUMPHAL ARCH: ORIGINS

The Latin term *arcus triumphalis* is not used before the second or third century AD, when it occurs in the inscriptions on two arches in North Africa – one at Cirta, erected under Caracalla, and one at Cuicul, erected under Severus Alexander. It is also used once by the fourth-century historian Ammianus Marcellinus (XXI 16.15). Whatever the explanation for this, it shows that a connection between the arch and the triumph was established in some men's minds, even though under the Empire, from the reign of Augustus, only emperors held triumphs, and they were only held at Rome.

Despite some attempts to find Greek forerunners, there can be no doubt that the 'triumphal arch' was a Roman invention. The elder Pliny, writing at the end of the first century AD, tells us (XXXIV 27): *columnarum ratio erat attolli super ceteros mortales, quod et arcus significant nouicio inuentu* ('the reason for erecting columns was so that men should be lifted up above the rest of mortals, something which arches also signify with their new invention'). Pliny calls them 'new' by comparison with columns to support statues, already familiar in Rome and in the East. He makes no mention of triumphs.

The most substantial study of the arch was published in 1939 in the great German encyclopedia, the *Realencyclopädie der classischen Altertumswissenschaft*. Its author, Heinz Kähler, attached great importance to Pliny's statement, arguing that the chief function of the arch was to support statuary – generally, though not exclusively, a *quadriga* (a chariot drawn by four animals and driven by the person commemorated). Our earliest evidence bears out the correctness of Pliny's claim. The first known arches are the three which Livy tells us were erected by L. Stertinius in 196 BC, when he returned to Rome from his proconsular command in 'Further Spain' (the south-east): *L. Stertinius ex ulteriore Hispania, ne temptata quidem triumphi spe, quinquaginta milia pondo argenti in aerarium intulit et de manubiis duos fornices in foro boario ante Fortunae aedem et Matris Matutae, unum in maximo circo fecit et his fornicibus signa aurata inposuit* (XXXIII 27.3–4): 'L. Stertinius, coming from Further Spain, without even attempting to fulfil his hope of celebrating a triumph, put 50,000 pounds of silver into the treasury, and out of the booty erected two arches in the Forum Boarium in front of the temples of Fortuna and Mater Matuta, and one in the Circus Maximus, and on the arches he placed gilded statues'). The gilded statues (whether of Stertinius himself or of deities, we cannot say) must have been of bronze, but what the arches looked like is unknown. The Forum Boarium was between the Tiber and the Palatine, south of the Capitoline. The sites of the temples mentioned by Livy have been identified with those in the 'Area Sacra di Sant'Omobono', just south-west of the Capitoline. The foundations of arches have been identified there, between the temples, but these date from the imperial period. As the Circus Maximus was during the Republic (before the reign of Augustus) mainly an open space, with no permanent seating, it is not known how the arch there related to it, though Francesco Marcattili argues that it must have stood at the northern end of the *carceres*, the starting boxes at the north-west end of the circus. He illustrates a relief and coins showing an arch with *quadriga* on top in this position.[1] It is interesting that the arches were paid for from the booty, which bears out the supposition (suggested by the case of Stertinius) that they were a kind of substitute for a triumph. It is also relevant that both the Forum Boarium and the Circus Maximus were on the traditional triumphal route. However, this seems to have passed behind the temples, whereas the arches stood in front of them.

It is again Livy (XXXVII 3.7) who tells us of the next arch, erected in 190 BC by P. Cornelius Scipio Africanus, who owed his last name to his victory over the Carthaginians under Hannibal, for which he celebrated a triumph in 201. He erected an arch *aduersus uiam qua in Capitolium escenditur* ('opposite the road by which one climbs onto the Capitolium'), with seven gilded statues, two horses, and two marble basins (the earliest known use of marble at Rome). He put up the arch before setting out to assist his brother in the campaign against Antiochus of Syria, presumably wanting to ensure his own commemoration before he left Rome.[2] It is interesting that the arch was not over the road but 'opposite' it. Sandro De Maria suggests that it might have been sited at the point where the Clivus Capitolinus (the road up the Capitoline hill) entered the sacred area, 'constituting a sort of monumental entrance'.[3] As with Stertinius's arches, we do not know whether the statues represented divinities (the horses might suggest the Dioscuri) or members of Scipio's family.

The next known arch is a mystery. Orosius tells us that Tiberius Gracchus was killed in 133 BC 'on the steps which are above the Calpurnian arch'.[4] It is not known where this stood. More is known about the Fornix Fabianus (*fornix* is another word for 'arch'), which is important for two reasons: it is the first arch definitely associated with a triumph, and it spanned the Sacra Via at the point where that entered the Forum Romanum from the east. A passage of Seneca shows that it was regarded as marking the eastern boundary of the Forum.[5] It was erected, probably in 121 BC, by Q. Fabius Maximus, who in that year received a triumph for his great victory over the Allobroges – a victory which brought the Romans the territory of Gallia Narbonensis (the area of Gaul around Narbonne). However, we do not know for certain that he erected it himself. Cicero refers to it three times, once recalling a joke made by Crassus in a public speech, to the effect that Memmius thought himself so great that when coming down into the Forum he lowered his head at the arch of Fabius.[6] It is thought to have been a *quadrifrons* (an arch with four openings) placed over the crossroads at the north-east corner of the Regia (the seat of the Pontifex Maximus), between that and the later Temple of Antoninus and Faustina. Various architectural and inscriptional fragments have been discovered, and they suggest that it was simple in form, built of travertine, peperino and tufa, with openings almost 4 m wide. It had a Doric frieze on top, above an inscription. The sixteenth-century excavators apparently saw what were presumably reliefs of 'shields and symbols of victory' (trophies?). The fragments of inscriptions show that this was the first arch we know for certain to have borne portraits (presumably statues, but conceivably busts within niches): two represented L. Aemilius Paulus and P. Cornelius Scipio Africanus, both ancestors of the later Q. Fabius Maximus, nephew of the founder, and curule aedile, who restored the arch in 57 BC. These decorative elements probably derive from that date. There must surely have been an image of the elder Fabius. The arch's restoration must reflect the intense competition between aristocratic families at this period, each anxious to emphasise its historic services to the Republic, and it shows the importance attached to such family monuments.[7] A later repair may have been responsible for the fluted column of green Carystian marble on a red granite base, probably belonging to the brick wall behind it, on the corner of the Regia.[8]

In one of his famous speeches against Verres, the rapacious governor of Sicily, Cicero tells us (*In Verr.* II 2.154) that 'this man has an arch in the forum at Syracuse, on which his son stands naked, while he himself looks from his horse at the province which he had stripped naked'. This is the first certain example of an arch commemorating a living person (since we cannot be sure about the original Fornix Fabianus); however, if it actually was the first, Cicero would probably have reproached Verres with the fact. We do not know who was responsible for its erection, but there is likely to have been at least a pretence that it was done by the local community.

At this point the evidence so far adduced may be summarised. It has been seen that the sources do not refer to any actual triumphs held, but they do emphasise the role of arches as bearers of statuary or trophies, so corroborating Pliny's statement. Although triumphs were, as Mary Beard has shown, rare under the Empire, they were regular occurrences under the Republic.[9] What then was the connection between these arches and triumphs?

There is general agreement that there was a 'triumphal route' up to the Capitolium, by way of the Forum Boarium, Circus Maximus, Forum Romanum and Sacra Via, but considerable disagreement about its exact course.[10] Even more disputed is the site of the *Porta Triumphalis* referred to by Josephus in his description of the triumph of Vespasian and Titus in AD 71. He calls it 'the gate which took its name from the fact that triumphs always pass through it'. T.P. Wiseman suggests that by 'always' Josephus means 'always in living memory', and that Vespasian and Titus's procession formed up on the Campus Martius and passed under the arch of the Aqua Virgo (brought to the Campus Martius in 19 BC by Marcus Agrippa) over the Via Flaminia. He argues that the fact that it had become the formal entry-point into the city explains why it was transformed in AD 51 into a *monumentum* of Claudius's conquest of Britain.[11]

Wiseman goes on to consider what might have been the equivalent under the Republic. He suggests that there was no fixed 'triumphal gate', and that the general could choose which gate he wanted to use. That gate would then be decorated. He explains the only contemporary evidence for the gate, Cicero's jibe at L. Piso's return to Rome in 55 BC, *quasi ... ad rem pertinet qua tu porta introieris, modo ne triumphali* (*In Pis.* 55), by translating it as 'it doesn't matter what gate you entered by, so long as it wasn't triumphal'. If the general wanted to start his procession from the Campus Martius or Circus Flaminius, he would choose the Porta Carmentalis, as was the case in 187 and 63 BC (Liv. XXXIX 5.17; Plut. *Lucullus* 37.2). However, if his procession started elsewhere, he might choose (for example) the Porta Capena or Porta Collina.

Whatever may be the truth regarding the triumphal route and gate, there seems to be little to connect them with the erection of arches. The chief criterion for the siting of an arch was no doubt its visibility in a much-frequented place, a point stressed by the description of the arch for Gaius Caesar at Pisa (see p. 14) as *celeberrimo coloniae nostrae loco* ('in the busiest place in our colony').[12] Hence the locations in forums, beside or over streets, on bridges, and so on.

The earliest surviving arches are outside Rome. Substantial fragments of one are to be seen at Cosa, a town picturesquely situated on top of a coastal promontory at the southern corner of Tuscany. It formed the entrance to the forum from the north-west, and was linked to buildings on either side. Built of rubble with stone facings, it had three openings, of which the central one was 3.84 m wide, and the side ones 0.96 m – the first example of the type which was to become common. The arch has been dated to *c.* 175–150 BC. Whether it had a commemorative function is debatable. The two 'statue-bases' attached to the outer side have been cited as evidence that it had, but it is now thought that they may have been basins (as on the arch of P. Cornelius Scipio Africanus – see above).[13]

In view of this uncertainty, it is more reasonable to regard the arch at Aquino as the earliest [1.1]. The Roman Aquinum, best known as the birthplace of Juvenal and St Thomas, is at the southern end of Lazio. Now no more than a village, it has picturesque Roman remains that include a charming, if ruinous, arch. This suffered the curious fate of being utilised as a sluice-gate on the leet supplying a paper factory, and is now in a private vegetable garden (near the church of Santa Maria della Libera). The arch, built of local travertine, has a single opening. On the outer sides of the piers are pairs of three-quarter columns, attached to the corners, with Corinthian capitals. The semi-columns flanking the opening have Ionic capitals. The lower part of the arch is buried, and the trabeation missing, but sixteenth-century drawings show it projecting over the

1.1 Aquinum, the arch used as a sluice on a water-channel.

4   THE TRIUMPHAL ARCH

corner three-quarter columns. They also show a pediment above the attic, not placed in front of it, but this is likely to be imaginary. The arch was situated outside the town, spanning the Via Latina to Cassino (Casinum). It may well have marked the point where the road entered the *pomerium*, the sacred boundary of the town. There is not even a fragmentary inscription, but the form and architectural details suggest a date of about 40–30 BC, or perhaps a decade later.[14] As the triumviral colony was founded in 41 BC, the arch may possibly have commemorated the event.

At this point further discussion may be attempted of the origin and early development of the triumphal arch. We know little of the appearance of most of the Republican examples. De Maria rightly argues that the arched openings of some of them may well have been flanked by attached semicolumns, as this motif is already found at the sanctuary at Palestrina, dated to *c*. 120–100 BC. The fact that the arches of Stertinius in the Forum Boarium and that of Africanus on the Capitoline were situated in association with temples can hardly be coincidental. Those of Stertinius were erected 'out of his booty', and must have been dedicatory. He dedicated them as a private citizen, not as a magistrate, and the same applied in the case of Africanus. The arch of Verres represented merely the glorification of an individual provincial governor, and may have been erected in his honour by the Syracusans (though he ought not to have agreed to it).

What then was the origin of the monumental, freestanding arch? This is an extraordinarily difficult question, and it has been answered in many different ways. The most obvious comparison is with town gates. Arched gates are found at Etruscan cities such as Volterra and Perugia from *c*. 300 BC onwards. The gates of Falerii Novi (near Civita Castellana), dated to *c*. 240–200 BC, take the form of stone arches, and later on the type with a larger arch for wheeled traffic, flanked by smaller arches for pedestrians, becomes common. Much has been made of the monumental gate to the Agora at Athens, next to the Stoa Poikile. Pausanias tells us that on it was a trophy celebrating the Athenian victory over Pleistarchos, in 303/2, and some have speculated (without certainty) that it may have been erected in honour of Demetrios Poliorketes, who had helped the Athenians to defeat his fellow Macedonian. A bronze equestrian statue supposed to be of Demetrios, of which fragments have been found nearby, might possibly have been associated with the gate. The foundations have been excavated, but there is no way of knowing whether the opening had an arch or a straight lintel.[15]

The use of an arch to support statues has led some scholars to see a connection with Greek monuments consisting of not just one column but a pair, but there is no evidence for such monuments in the Roman world, except perhaps in rural sanctuaries shown in wallpaintings. Other attempts have been made to find precedents in the Greek world, but none is very convincing, although the Hellenising atmosphere of second-century-BC Rome makes it reasonable to suppose that there might have been some kind of Greek influence on the development of this type of honorific structure.

Also relevant is the so-called 'Janus'. Janus was an ancient deity whose function was to carry a road over a river, though he later developed many others.[16] Cicero (*De Natura Deorum* II 67) defines *iani* as *transitiones peruiae*, or 'thoroughfares'. Because a gate faces, and can be passed through, in two directions, the god Janus, who is protector of the gate and of the house-door (*ianua*), is the god of beginnings (hence January), and is represented with faces looking both forwards and back. In the Forum Romanum there were three *iani* – *summus* (highest), *medius* (middle) and *imus* (lowest), probably crossing-places on the stream that became the *cloaca maxima*.[17] Livy tells us that in 174 BC porticoes, shops, and three *iani* were constructed in the forum of Sinuessa (a town on the coast of Campania, modern Mondragone). These works were presumably based on the model of Rome, but we have no idea what the *iani* looked like. It is reasonable to assume that they were similar to the earliest *fornices*. It is interesting that ancient sources sometimes call the same structure either *ianus* or *arcus*. The latter word came to be used in the Augustan period instead of *fornix*, perhaps because by then *fornix* had acquired a secondary meaning of 'brothel'. The fact that two of the earliest known arches (the Fornix Fabianus and the arch at Cosa) and also possibly the arch of Verres formed the entrances to *fora* supports the connection with these *iani*.

Notes

1. F. Marcattili, *Il Circo Massimo* (Rome, 2009), 180–87. For the coin, see Sabine Fähndrich, *Bogenmonumente in der römischen Kunst* (Rahden, 2005), 38–9. (The illustrations collected in her book could not more strongly support the idea that the purpose of arches was to support statuary.) Others think that the arch was at the south, curved, end of the Circus, where an arch was built by Titus: see Anne Hrychuk Kontokosta, 'Reconsidering the arches (*fornices*) of the Roman Republic', *JRA* 26 (2013), 13–14.
2. Marion Roehmer, *Der Bogen als Staatsmonument* (Munich, 1997), 11, finds it surprising that the arch was erected before Africanus set out for Syria. Kontokosta (cit. in the preceding note) argues that Republican arches were not so much 'votive' as publicity gestures to boost the credit of individuals and their families.
3. Sandro De Maria, *Gli archi onorari di Roma e dell'Italia romana* (Rome, 1988), 263.
4. Orosius, *Adv. Pag.* V 9.2.
5. Seneca, *Dial.* II 1.13
6. Cicero, *De Orat.* II 66.267.
7. This makes it likely that the arch is what Cicero was referring to at *Vatin.* 28.
8. Amanda Claridge, *Rome: An Oxford Archaeological Guide* (2nd edn, Oxford, 2010), 103, 111.
9. Mary Beard, *The Roman Triumph* (Cambridge, Mass., 2007), 69–71.
10. T.P. Wiseman, 'Three Notes on the Triumphal Route', *Res Bene Gestae: Ricerche di storia urbana su Roma antica in onore di Eva Margareta Steinby* (Rome, 2007), 445–9; Maggie L. Popkin, *The Architecture of the Roman Triumph: Monuments, Memory and Identity* (Cambridge, 2016).
11. T.P. Wiseman, 'Rethinking the Triumph', *JRA* 21 (2008), 389–91.
12. *CIL* XI 1421; De Maria, 250–51.
13. F.E. Brown, *Cosa: The Making of a Roman Town* (Ann Arbor, Mich., 1980), 43.
14. Roehmer 1997, 55–6. Claridge 2010 prefers the dates given here.
15. John M. Camp, *The Athenian Agora* (Athens, 1992), 64–5, 162–5.
16. L.A. Holland, *Janus and the Bridge* (Rome, 1961); see especially ch. 17, 'Survival of the arch at the crossing'.
17. Professor Wiseman pointed out in an email that there is no evidence that these *iani* were entrances to the Forum.

2
ARCHES OF THE TIME OF AUGUSTUS

Pliny's statement about the function of arches as supporting statuary is borne out by the evidence for arches erected in honour of Octavian – soon to be Augustus – and his family. After his naval victory over Sextus Pompeius at Naulochus in 36 BC, Octavian was granted various honours (presumably by the Senate), including a 'trophy-bearing arch'. As we know nothing of its location or appearance, it is possible that he declined the honour. However, the arch which the Senate decreed should be erected in the Forum Romanum after the battle of Actium (31 BC) certainly was erected, along with another at Actium itself. A series of *denarii* issued at Rome between 29 and 27 shows what must be that arch. This is the first occasion when numismatic evidence provides our only visual source for the appearance of an arch. The structure (shown in very summary form) has a single opening, with what may be shields on the piers, winged victories in the spandrels, and a *quadriga* above. On the attic are the words 'IMP[erator] CAESAR'. It seems likely that the consular *fasti* (lists of consuls) were set on this arch. The crucial question of where the arch was situated has been furiously discussed for over a hundred years. The most authoritative recent investigation, by Elisabeth Nedergard, has concluded that it cannot, as things stand, be answered.[1] Of the arch at Brindisi (Brundisium), the port from which the fleet set sail for the campaign which culminated at Actium, we know nothing at all with regard to its location or appearance.

In 27 BC Octavian was granted the title Augustus, and in effect became emperor. At the battle of Carrhae in 53 BC the Parthians – Rome's most troublesome enemy – had defeated Crassus, and the recovery of the lost standards and prisoners of war had become an increasingly insistent demand. In 20 BC Augustus at last obtained their return, by diplomatic rather than military means. Nevertheless, the Senate decreed that he should enter the city on horseback (a kind of lesser version of a triumph), and that an arch should be erected. An ancient commentary on Virgil's *Aeneid* tells us that the arch was beside the Temple of Divus Julius, and the discovery of the foundations of a triple arch immediately south of the temple, between it and the Temple of the Castors, was inevitably associated with this information. The side openings were evidently set back. Evidence for the appearance of the structure comes from two series of coins. The first series, issued in the provinces in 18–17 BC, shows a triple arch, of a very simple form, with a *quadriga* over the central opening. Over the side ones stand figures, obviously Parthians (one has a bow, their characteristic weapon), offering standards to the *triumphator*. The coins bear an inscription which records the

2.1 The Parthian arch of Augustus, shown on a coin of 16 BC.

dedication by the Senate to 'Imperator Caesar' for his having recovered the citizens and standards. The second series, coined in Rome in 16 BC, shows the structure in more detail [2.1]. The taller central section has pilasters supporting the arch, and columns on the corners bearing the attic, on which is the inscription *SPQR IMP. CAE.* (the beginning of the full inscription). Above is the *quadriga*. The flanking sections have columns supporting flat architraves (not arches). Above are pediments with pedestals above, which support standing figures, shown slightly differently from those on the earlier coins, though their wild gesticulations presumably have the same function of offering standards.[2]

The position of the arch alongside the Temple of Divus Julius, which had been begun by the triumvirs in 42 BC and completed by Octavian in 29, and whose podium was decorated with the *rostra* of ships taken at Actium, was clearly intended by Augustus to provide a further new element to the southeast of the Forum, equally celebrating his new regime.[3] Various fragments of the arch survive, including a Doric capital and parts of a Doric architrave, frieze and cornice, and parts of a Corinthian capital, cornice and coffering, all closely comparable with details of the Temple of Apollo Sosianus (rebuilt in 32 BC). According to the most up-to-date reconstruction of the arch, the side elements used the Doric order, and the central arch the Corinthian.[4] Despite various alternative suggestions, it seems most likely that the consular *fasti*, transferred from the Actian arch, were framed by the Corinthian aedicules on either side of the central passageway, while the triumphal *fasti* (lists of those who had held triumphs) were inscribed on the inner faces of the Doric pilasters which supported the arch. Whether various figurative elements, including a fragment of a trophy-bearing winged Victory, really belonged to the arch is disputed: Renaissance antiquaries say that they included trophies, shields and helmets. The excavations which discovered the *fasti* in the mid-sixteenth century were continued by the scholar Onofrio Panvinio. At first he thought that the arch was a *quadrifrons*: hence the elaborate reconstruction made by his friend Pirro Ligorio.[5]

For an arch erected by Augustus himself, in honour of his father Octavius, we have the evidence of Pliny. He tells us (*NH* XXXVI 36) that it was on the Palatine, and that on top was an 'aedicule' ornamented with columns, in which stood a *quadriga* with figures of Apollo and Diana, carved out of a single block by the sculptor Lysias. The purpose of the arch links it to Republican arches such as the Fornix Fabianus, intended to honour the dedicator's family. The siting of the arch on the Palatine, and the figure of Apollo, make it natural to associate it with the lavish Temple of Apollo, adjacent on the west, which Octavian vowed during his campaign against Sextus Pompeius in 36 BC, and dedicated in 28. He regarded Apollo as his patron. Part of an inscription block, a semi-engaged fluted column, and other fragments now set on either side of the western entrance to Domitian's palace may have belonged to the arch.[6] No other arch is known to have had an aedicule on top, and there is no way of knowing whether it was circular or rectangular. The date of Lysias is uncertain, but he probably worked in the second century. It is odd that an arch in honour of Octavius should have featured Apollo so prominently.[7]

In the same year that Octavian made his political 'settlement', and was granted the title Augustus, 27 BC, he initiated a programme for the rebuilding of the main roads leading from Rome, undertaking the Via Flaminia himself. In return, the Senate decreed the erection of arches bearing his image on the Milvian Bridge, where the road crossed the Tiber just north of Rome, and at Rimini (Ariminum), where it ended on the Adriatic coast. The arch at Rimini survives (see below), but nothing else is known of the Milvian one. Its position on the bridge, which would have made it particularly conspicuous, and would have marked an obvious boundary, looks forward to a long series of similar arches.[8]

Arches were also erected at Rome to members of Augustus's family. The first was in honour of Nero Claudius Drusus, younger son of Augustus's wife Livia by her first husband, and brother of the future emperor Tiberius. He had been a distinguished general, and on his death in 9 BC the Senate voted him, along with the hereditary name Germanicus and other honours, 'a marble arch with trophies on the Via Appia' (Suet. *Claud.* 1.3). De Maria argues for its location near the Temple of Mars, just outside the Porta Appia (now called the Porta San Sebastiano), pointing out that this location was traditionally associated with ceremonies connected with departure to and return from war. The so-called 'Arch of Drusus', just inside the gate, was in fact part of the Aqua Antoniniana built by Caracalla to take water to his Baths, and is misnamed. Evidence for the appearance of the real arch comes from coins datable between AD 41 and 45, which show a single arch, flanked by pairs of semicolumns, on top of which is a statue of a horse being ridden at a gallop towards the right, its rider holding a lance, to left and right of which are trophies above crouching captives. On the arch are the letters *DE GERM*.[9]

Among the remains of the Basilica Paulli (formerly known as the Basilica Aemilia), which runs along the north side of the Forum Romanum, is a large and beautifully cut inscription, recording a dedication by the Senate to Lucius Caesar, grandson and adopted son of Augustus, when he was fourteen years old: in that year, 2 BC, he was given the title *Princeps Iuventutis* and made consul designate, as his older brother Gaius had been three years before. The inscription must come from the Porticus Gaii et Lucii referred to by Suetonius (*Aug.* 29.4). This has been identified with the portico added in front of the Basilica; an arch (apparently commemorative) seems to have linked the projecting bay at the southeast corner across the Sacra Via with the flank of the Temple of Divus Julius. It would have replaced the Fornix Fabianus as the feature closing this side of the Forum.[10]

Arches in Italy of the Augustan period

The arch at Rimini (Ariminum), mentioned above, replaced the eastern gate in the town walls, which had been built in the third century BC between two rectangular towers. (These were rebuilt in hexagonal form in the third century AD.) The arch was of travertine. The external face is well preserved. The large opening (10.23 m high and 8.84 m wide) is framed by attached Corinthian columns [2.2]. These support an entablature and modillioned cornice, which projects over the columns. A low pediment is placed against the lower attic. Within the spandrels are four *clipei* (circular shields), containing heads of deities (Jupiter and Apollo on the outer face, Neptune and Roma on the inner one). The keystones have bulls' heads. A second attic (now mostly lost, and replaced by medieval brick battlements) extended only as far as the centre line of the columns. On each side, just below the level of the attic, were rectangular plaques which partly

2.2 Rimini (Ariminum), the arch erected to mark the building of the Via Flaminia.

2.3 Aosta (Augusta Praetoria). The colony was founded in 25 BC, and the arch was dedicated to Augustus.

survive. Parts of the inscription (originally with inset bronze letters) survive, recording the dedication of the arch to Augustus, to commemorate his having brought about the rebuilding of the Via Flaminia and other principal roads of Italy. Sculpture, probably in bronze, must have surmounted the attic, since Cassius Dio tells us that the arch bore a statue of the emperor (LIII 22). It may have taken the form of a *quadriga*, and at the lower level on either side there may have been trophies.[11] Shortly before reaching the arch the road crossed a stream, and this recalls the function of the *ianus*.[12]

A river-crossing is also close in front of the arch at Aosta, which otherwise could hardly have a more different situation from Rimini, with the Alps as backdrop [2.3].[13] The colony of Augusta Praetoria was founded in 25 BC, after the Salassi had submitted to Augustus, and this must surely be the 'trophy-bearing arch in the Alps' whose erection Cassius Dio tells us was voted by the Senate (LIII 26.5), after Augustus had refused a triumph. Aosta is a textbook example of a new town planned within rectangular walls: the arch is situated outside these, about 350 m from the eastern gate, on the road leading towards Rome. It may have marked the *pomerium*, the sacred boundary of

ARCHES OF THE TIME OF AUGUSTUS 11

the city. Built of local grey stone (called in Italian *puddinga*), it is of imposing size and articulation. Each of the two piers has a tall plinth, above which rise pairs of attached Corinthian columns (one beside the opening, the other on the corner). The entablature is Doric (the mixture with Corinthian is mentioned by Vitruvius), and breaks forward over the opening and the corner columns. On each side elevation there is a central attached column. Shallow rectangular niches between attached columns on the front and back possibly contained the reliefs for which there is some evidence. Within the opening, between plinth and cornice, there is a pilaster on each side, corresponding to those on each front corner. The attic has disappeared, along with the inscription, of which two bronze letters have been found. A hipped roof dates from 1912–13, and within the opening a fifteenth-century wooden crucifix set on a cross-bar adds to the picturesque effect. The arch may well have been surmounted by a *quadriga*.

The arch at the famous Greek city of Syracuse in Sicily is sometimes claimed to have been erected to commemorate the founding of the colony. The bases of the piers are visible southeast of the amphitheatre. It stood over an important street running east-west, and may have marked the division between two districts of the city. Its closeness to the amphitheatre may also have been significant. It seems to have been very plain, the most remarkable feature being its rusticated masonry, though its east front may have had an applied order. Syracuse was given the status of *colonia* by Augustus in 21 BC. It is possible that the arch was erected by the town's citizens to express their thanks for this, and for the repaving of the streets which was probably contemporary with it.[14] The arch was altered in about AD 200, and again in the seventh century.

At Spello (Hispellum) in Umbria a few fragments survive of an arch, including enough letters of an inscription to suggest that it was erected by Augustus himself. The town was an Augustan colony, and one might have expected its citizens to have been responsible for its erection, as at Syracuse.[15] Also in Umbria is another arch, at Spoleto (Spoletium), whose structure survives. It marked the southern entrance to the forum. The inscription (between archivolt and entablature) records its dedication by the local senate to Germanicus and Drusus Minor, the sons of Tiberius, either at or soon after the death of the latter in AD 23 (Germanicus having died in 19). However, it has been proved by Henner von Hesberg that the arch itself must have been erected in the early Augustan period (*c.* 25 BC). The arch of the single opening is supported on Corinthian pilasters, and similar pilasters at the corners support the Doric entablature and frieze. Above this must have been an attic, with inscription and statue, no doubt honouring Augustus. It is likely that, when the second inscription was added, statues of Germanicus and Drusus were added on either side of Augustus.

Another well preserved arch in the foothills of the Alps, at Susa, was built under rather different circumstances from the one at Aosta [2.4]. Susa (ancient Segusio) is on the road leading westwards from Turin to the pass of Mongenevre. The elegant arch, dramatically sited on the hillside to the west of the town, is built of honey-coloured local stone, and is complete except for the upper cornice of the attic. Each side of the attic bore an inscription in bronze letters (legible, despite their loss) recording its erection in 9/8 BC, in honour of Augustus, by M. Iulius Cottius, son of King Donnus, who was *praefectus* of the fourteen *civitates* (tribes) of the western Alps whose names are listed. Cottius's new role, like the arch, was a sign of loyalty to Rome, after he came into its *amicitia* following the submission of the last of these tribes in 14 BC. The arch

2.4 Susa (Segusio), in the Alps: the arch dedicated to Augustus in 9/8 BC by M. Julius Cottius.

is situated on the new route of the main road over the Alps, which Cottius caused to curve westwards through Susa. The structure is simple: the arch is supported on Corinthian pilasters, while on each corner there is an attached Corinthian column. Between the entablature and the modillioned cornice a frieze runs all the way round. The reliefs on the two principal fronts show the *suovetaurilia* – the sacrifice of a pig, a sheep and a bull – to Mars, over which preside Cottius and a Roman representative.[16] In the southern relief the Dioscuri appear: they were the patrons of the equestrian order, to which Cottius now belonged. The frieze on the west side shows Cottius and the Roman holding the treaty document, which the fourteen tribes are signing. Little is left of the eastern frieze. The quality if the sculpture is not high: it has been suggested that the sculptor was more used to working in wood.[17] There may well have been more sculpture above the attic.[18]

The Augustan colony of Pisa decreed various honours, known from an inscription, for Augustus's grandson Gaius Caesar after his death in Lycia in AD 4. One of these was to take the form of an arch 'in the most frequented place' in the town – presumably the forum. It was to be adorned with the spoils of conquered peoples; above was to be a statue of Gaius in triumphal dress, and on either side gilded (bronze) equestrian statues of Gaius and his brother Lucius (who had died two years earlier). The presence of two statues of the same person is odd, but the equestrian statues probably honoured the two brothers (the *principes iuuentutis*) as patrons of the colony. We cannot be certain that the arch was ever erected.

An even more remarkable example of a 'dynastic' arch was set up in AD 8/7 at Pavia (Ticinum), further north. Its existence is only known from a ninth-century traveller, whose manuscript, at Einsiedeln, records the inscriptions, of which there were no fewer than ten. Each presumably related to a statue. Augustus and Livia were no doubt in the centre. On one side were Tiberius, Germanicus, Drusus (son of Tiberius), and Nero (son of Germanicus). On the other side were Gaius and Lucius Caesar, Drusus (son of Germanicus), and Claudius (perhaps surprising, but no doubt as another son of Germanicus). It has been guessed that the arch was a triple one, to accommodate such a crowd, and that it might have served as the eastern gate to the city. The arch must have demonstrated loyalty to the Augustan family, at a time when the succession was a matter of concern, and may reflect the new prosperity of the city after the province of Cisalpine Gaul became part of Italy.[19]

Arches of the Augustan period outside Italy

The earliest arches known from Gallia Narbonensis (southern France) are the pair at either end of the bridge which forms such an impressive crossing over the little river Touloubre near St-Chamas, on the Via Iulia Augusta from Marseilles to Arles (just northwest of the Étang de Berre) [2.5]. The road was built in 13/12 BC, and it is likely that the bridge was built in connection with it, according to the will of L. Donnius Flavos, *flamen* of Rome and Augustus; the inscriptions on the arches tell us that his executors built it. Each arch has Corinthian pilasters, which support a frieze on which the central inscriptions are flanked by carved tendrils. Above the pilasters are reliefs of eagles holding wreaths. There is no attic, but on each corner stands a lively lion, possibly pouncing on a man's head. Only the northern lion on the eastern arch is original; the rest date from a restoration of 1763–4. The western arch is largely modern, its most recent repair having been necessitated by an accident with a German tank in the last war. Some have argued that the arch had a funeral purpose, like those of Aix-les-Bains, Pula and Verona that we shall meet, but Annette Küpper-Böhm prefers to see its symbolism as representing the *flamen* Donnius's loyalty to the victorious emperor.[20]

The erection of arches in connection with road-building recalls the arches of Augustus at the Milvian Bridge and Rimini, described above. A series of coins minted in Spain in 17–16 BC bears variations on the inscription *SPQR CAESARI AUGUSTO QUOD UIAE MUN[ITAE] SUNT* (some add *EX EA P[ECUNIA] Q[UAM] IS AD A[ERARIUM] DE[TULIT]* ('the Senate and People of Rome to Caesar Augustus, because roads have been built ... out of that money which he put into the treasury'). Four different types of arch are shown. One has a single opening, apparently forming

2.5 The twin arches on the bridge at St Chamas, near Arles, on the road built in 13/12 BC.

the central section of a bridge, on which is a chariot drawn by two elephants. In this stands the emperor, with a Victory behind, crowning him. Another has a two-bay arch on a bridge, with a similar elephant-drawn chariot. On the third the chariot is drawn by four horses, and the two-bay arch has projecting *rostra* (ship's rams – another triumphal symbol). On the fourth series there is an arch at each end of a bridge, each surmounted by an equestrian statue and a trophy. This latter type is an interesting parallel for St-Chamas, though the arches there are too shallow to have supported statuary.[21]

The fact that these coins were struck in Spain is interesting, since two examples of such bridge-arches are known there. One is known only from milestones on the Via Augusta, which refer to it as Ianus Augustus, and locate it on the river Baetis (Guadalquivir), where it marked the boundary between the provinces of Hispania Citerior and Hispania Baetica. It probably stood near the modern Mengíbar (north of Jaén) in the vicinity of the Roman Iliturgi, where a few archaeological remains have been attributed to it. The arch must have stood at one end of, or even on, the bridge, and was presumably erected in connection with the building of the road; the earliest milestone mentioning it dates from 2 BC, and the *terminus post quem* is probably Agrippa's campaign in Spain of 19 BC.[22]

The other Spanish example is at Martorell, where the Via Augusta crossed the river Llobregat, 30 km west of Barcelona [2.6]. As at St-Chamas, an arch stood at each end of the bridge; only one survives, in the form of a rough mass of masonry. Legionary

ARCHES OF THE TIME OF AUGUSTUS **15**

2.6 The surviving arch on the bridge at Martorell, near Barcelona, of c. 10 BC.

masons' marks have been found on the sides of the bridge, from which it has been dated around 10 BC.[23]

Another arch which may well have been erected in connection with the building of the Via Augusta (or rather with the repair of the Via Herculea and its renaming) is the one at Roda de Berà, 20 km northeast of Tarragona (Tarraco). It stands on an island, on either side of which the main road runs. 'Berà' is a corruption of 'Sura': the inscription tells us that the arch was 'consecrated according to the will of L. Licinius Sura'. Until recently this was assumed to be the man who was three times consul under Trajan, and died in 110, but Xavier Dupré i Raventos has proved that the Corinthian capitals and other elements of this plain but well-proportioned arch date from the early Augustan period. He identifies its builder with a L. Sura who was *praefectus* of the Colonia Victrix Iulia Lepida, known from a coin of 39 BC, who might have been transferred later to Tarraco. The arch stands at the point where the Via Augusta enters the *ager Tarraconensis*, but as this was not significant for Roman administration, Dupré suggests that the location may relate to Sura's own property. As for the question of the 'consecration' of the arch, the obvious explanation would be that it was dedicated to Augustus himself. There was probably another inscription on the missing attic, and possibly statuary above.[24]

Tarragona itself had an urban arch, standing in the forum near the basilica. It is known only from fragments of its reliefs, which include heads of a bearded man and a woman, and the lower parts of two men, shown as barbarians by their dress. This may be the same arch shown on a coin minted at Tarraco to commemorate Galba's revolt against Nero in 68; three prisoners with hands bound are led through it.[25]

The Tarraco fragments have interesting similarities with the reliefs for which the arches of Gallia Narbonensis are particularly noteworthy, and these will be dealt with as a group. The bridge arches of St-Chamas have already been described. The most prosperous Roman city in the district was Arles (Arelate), and it had two arches. The earlier, the 'Arc du Rhône', dated from about the same time as St-Chamas, *c.* 0 BC. It was destroyed in 1684, but is known from descriptions and drawings. It seems to have had pairs of attached Corinthian columns, with the archivolt decorated with tendrils, and a tendril frieze, but no attic. The entablature was Doric, with kneeling oxen between the triglyphs. Each narrow side had a single attached column in the centre, and might have had relief sculpture. The chief peculiarity of the arch was that the interior space had a flat ceiling, like that of the Arch of the Gavii at Verona. It stood in the northern part of the town, at the approach to the bridge over the Rhône. Roehmer suggests that it might have been a private dedication. An inscription was carved on it later, probably to honour Constantine, who favoured the city.[26]

The arch at Carpentras survives, but in a sadly mutilated form, having been adapted as a porch to the Romanesque Cathedral, and then (after the church collapsed) as the corn-store, and later kitchen, of the bishop's palace [2.7]. After the Revolution, this became the Palais de Justice, and the arch was hemmed in by prison buildings. These were demolished in 1950, but the arch still looks as if pushed into a corner, with the

2.7 Figures of captives on the arch at Carpentras, of the early C1 AD.

ARCHES OF THE TIME OF AUGUSTUS 17

Palais de Justice close up on two sides. The upper part is largely destroyed, but the channelled pilasters with their decorative capitals and one archivolt with tendril frieze survive. Little is known about the Roman colony of Carpentoracte Meminorum, but it appears that the arch stood somewhere in its centre. What makes the arch remarkable is the reliefs on the ends. Each shows a large trophy, beneath which stand two men with their hands bound behind their backs. The eastern side is better preserved: a beardless Oriental wears a Persian cap, and a bearded German wears an animal-skin and has a hair-knot. At their feet appropriate weapons are presented by means of incised outlines (a technique found on other Gallic arches).[27] The figures on the western side are identified by Küpper-Böhm as coming from Asia Minor and Thrace. She argues that the four figures represent the geographical range of the Roman Empire, such as would have inspired the citizens with pride.[28]

The arch at Carpentras has usually been dated later than the one at St-Rémy (see below), but Küpper-Böhm dates it earlier, to the first decade AD, slightly earlier than the arch at Cavaillon (Cabellio), a town 20 km southeast of Avignon. This is the only *quadrifrons* among the early imperial arches of Gaul [2.8]. It has suffered even worse than the arch at Carpentras. Already at least partially rebuilt in the Middle Ages, it served as the crypt of a chapel attached to the bishop's palace. In 1880 it was moved to a new site about 200 m southwest. All that survives are the four piers and two of the archivolts, together with the spandrel blocks of the east side, which show flying Victories. The finest feature of the arch is the decoration of the pilasters, which here form the piers: their rich acanthus and vine scrolls, with occasional birds, recall the Ara Pacis at Rome. The archivolts are decorated with anthemia, and the undersides of the arches have an unusual arrangement of square coffering. It seems likely that the arch had a flat roof. Careful study by Annette Küpper-Böhm has shown that in the course of medieval rebuilding some missing blocks were replaced with others which appear to have come from an identical arch. The surviving arch's western side is blank, which suggests that it stood up against a portico: she considers that each arch stood at the eastern end of one arm of a three-sided portico that enclosed two temples which stood on the site of the present Cathedral, and just south of it, and faced onto the *cardo maximus*.[29]

2.8 The arch at Cavaillon, early C1 AD, has fine acanthus and vine decoration.

18 THE TRIUMPHAL ARCH

The Arc du Rhône at Arles has already been described. It has recently been supposed that there were two other arches in the town, but Küpper-Böhm argues that the so-called 'Arc Admirable' was not in fact a Roman arch, as sometimes supposed. A considerable number of fragments, discovered when part of the eighth- or ninth-century walls near the Porte de l'Aure were demolished in 1902, were at one time attributed to the 'Arc Admirable', but are now reckoned to come from an arch near to where they were found. It may well have spanned the Via Aurelia, which led to Marseilles. The fragments include a Corinthian capital, tendril-decorated voussoirs, coffering, a relief of a trophy of shields and arms, and another with the jumbled-up arms characteristic of South Gaul, and a severed head. Similarities with the decoration of the Cavaillon arch suggest a contemporary date.[30]

Just south of St-Rémy stands a pair of Roman monuments, traditionally known as 'Les Antiques'. The earlier is the splendid mausoleum of the Julii, and only a little later (perhaps built about AD 10) is the arch. A short distance further south is the town of Glanum, a Celtic settlement which around the second century BC was rebuilt in the Hellenistic manner. In the second half of the first century BC it was again rebuilt as a Roman town (possibly a colony). The arch stands on the principal northern approach to the town, possibly marking the *pomerium*. The mausoleum, placed just outside the *pomerium*, is sited in relationship to the road. The link between the two monuments was emphasised when the surrounding area was laid out with a wall and benches to mark a visit in 1777 by the comte de Provence (later Louis XVIII). At the same time the arch, of which nothing except the spandrels survived above the level of the tops of the columns, was given the present gabled 'roof' [2.9]

2.9 'Les Antiques' near St-Rémy: the Mausoleum of the Julii and the slightly later arch.

ARCHES OF THE TIME OF AUGUSTUS   19

The structure itself is fairly simple, with a pair of attached columns standing on bases which break forward, on either side of the opening. What makes the arch chiefly noteworthy is its rich decoration. Each archivolt bears an elaborate and beautifully carved garland of leaves and fruits. The spandrels contain winged Victories. On the face of each of the piers, on both sides, is a pair of figures in relief. As at Carpentras, they are on either side of trophies. Each arch-soffit is carved with 'candelabrum-tendrils'. The vault is decorated with hexagonal coffers containing rosettes. Beneath it runs a narrow frieze of sacrificial and musical instruments. The ends of the arch have flat niches between tendril-pilasters, in which further reliefs or inscribed tablets may have been fixed.

The significance of the pairs of figures has been much discussed. It is important to distinguish between the two sides of the arch. On the northwest side, which is the one seen by those approaching the Romanised town, the left-hand relief shows a Gaul wearing a fringed *sagum* (cloak), with one hand on the shoulder of a huge chained barbarian, while the right-hand one shows a woman seated on a pile of weapons, to whom a male captive turns his back. The woman has been identified as triumphant Rome, but her Gallic dress does not support this. The archivolt on this side shows ripe and partly open fruit, while the Victories in the spandrels hold laurel garlands and palm branches. On the southeast side, facing those who travel towards the less Romanised areas further north, the two piers each have a group of male and female captives, the archivolt frieze shows unripe fruit, and the Victories hold standards. So one side represents the state of peace and prosperity, while the other represents the ongoing process of 'pacification'.[31]

The arch at Orange, about 25 km north of Avignon, is a prodigy [2.10]. It is huge, proudly situated on the main road running north from the town. It may mark the *pomerium*. Apart from the gate at Cosa (see above, p. 4), it is the earliest triple arch known outside Rome (presumably taking its cue from the Parthian arch). It is lavishly decorated with relief sculpture, and its architectural form has many striking features. The arch is 20 m wide, 8 m deep, and 19 m high. The central opening is flanked by half-columns, which support a projecting entablature, above which is a gable attached to the lower attic. Half-columns at the corners also support projections in the entablature, with corresponding pilasters above. The arch pilasters are decorated with tendrils, and the archivolts with fruits. The spandrels are blank, but holes show that bronze ornaments were attached, as on the attic above. The spaces over the side openings are filled with reliefs of jumbled-up Gallic weapons, including shields inscribed with their owners' names, musical instruments, and torques. The narrow frieze shows a Gallic battle. Above, on the lower attic, are reliefs of naval trophies and emblems. On the upper attic, the central section has a relief of Gallic battles on either side (that on the north is a modern copy of the decayed original). The one on the south had a bronze frame. Further reliefs ornamented the sides, now cut through by the walls linking the central attic to the side ones. The only original side attic is that on the east, which has sacrificial instruments carved on one side and a female bust with cloak billowing behind it on the other. It is likely that there was statuary on top. The side elevations are articulated by four half-columns supporting a pediment, whose entablature is broken through by a semicircular recess. This remarkable motif is paralleled later in the peristyle at Split. In the spaces between the columns are trophies with bound captives

2.10 The triple arch at Orange has lavish sculptural decoration. Probably built in honour of Augustus, but with later additions.

(one of them a woman) on either side of them, very similar to those at Carpentras and St-Rémy. Within the semicircular recess on the east side (the west side has been destroyed) is a male head with rays, representing the Sun (perhaps balanced by the Moon on the other side). On either side are cornucopiae. In the spandrels over the pediment are Tritons with rudders. The vault of the central opening has hexagonal cassettes with rosettes, while the side ones have four-cornered ones arranged in star patterns.

The arch has had a chequered history. In the thirteenth century it was turned into a fortress, with an additional 8 m of battlemented masonry on top, and sloping masonry added around the base to prop it up. In the course of this work much damage was done, and it was then that the whole of the west façade was destroyed. Restoration began in 1721. The principal campaign was started in 1807–9 by Reux, and completed in 1823–5 by Auguste Caristie. Where architectural elements were missing he replaced them, but distinguished his work from the original by leaving it sharply cut and new-looking. However, twentieth-century critics disliked this effect, and in the 1950s the new elements were (ludicrously) given their complete ornamentation, and then artificially 'weathered'.

The dating of the arch at Orange is one of the most fiercely contested issues in Roman archaeology. An inscription can be reconstructed from the dowel-holes, and dates to AD 26/27, with a dedication to Tiberius. The fact that some of the shields represented bear the name Sacrovir led some scholars to assume that the arch was erected to commemorate the putting down of the rebellion of Julius Sacrovir in Gaul in AD 21, but that event was far too insignificant to warrant such a grand erection, and in any case Orange had nothing to do with it. Even the inscription fails to settle the matter, since it appears on the architrave, which would be inconceivable if it was contemporary with the building of the arch.

The author of the latest detailed study, Annette Küpper-Böhm, argues that the arch was erected in four separate stages. The first phase included the lower attic; as this had an applied pediment in the centre, it was not suitable for an inscription, and the intention was that this should go on the north frieze. Before it was carved, it was decided to add a low second attic. Later this was taken off, and a taller attic carved with reliefs was added over the main opening. Finally, matching 'bases' were added on either side, linked by walls to the central attic and the ends. On the grounds of similarities with the arches of Cavaillon and St-Rémy, she dates the first phase to the second decade of our era. The central attic she dates to the early second century, and the side sections to some time later. She associates the heightening of the upper attic with the tendency of Trajanic arches to emphasise height.

The Colonia Iulia Arausio Secundanorum had been founded by Julius Caesar, so the arch cannot have commemorated that event. Like the arches of Carpentras and St Rémy, it was probably erected by the municipality to honour Augustus, and its situation north of the town, together with its relief decoration, emphasised the might of Roman conquest over the Gallic provinces. It is less easy to explain the subsequent alterations for which Küpper-Böhm argues. As Kleiner points out, one might have thought that, if the municipality wanted to honour Tiberius, it would have been expected to build him a new arch.[32]

Arches were also erected in the eastern, Greek-speaking, part of the Empire. The earliest known was (perhaps appropriately) at Philippi in Macedonia, where a colony, mostly of Italians, was set up after the battle of Actium (Colonia Augusta Iulia Philippi). The arch stood over the principal road, the Via Egnatia, about 2 km west of the town. Little survives. Very plain, even severe, it had Corinthian pilasters and an attic.

The arch at Ephesus which served as the southern entrance to the agora was altogether exceptional, its form being closer to the propylaea of Greek tradition than to the Roman 'arch' [2.11]. Its main, southern front had three openings, the side ones set in wings which projected to double the depth of the centre. Rectangular openings led from the central passage into the side ones, with semicircular niches corresponding on the outer walls, and similar niches adorned the return walls of the wings. All these niches held statues. The corners and openings were framed by pilasters. On the central attic was an inscription in Greek, 'Mazaios and Mithradates [sic] to their fathers and the people' (slaves legally had no 'fathers'; when they were freed, their former masters took on this rôle). Longer Latin inscriptions on the wings recorded the dedication in 4/3 BC by these two to their patrons Augustus and Livia on the left, and Agrippa (who was already dead) and Julia on the right. An inscribed base reveals that the arch also bore statues of Gaius and Lucius Caesar. We know that Mithradates was a freedman of Agrippa, and it is likely that Mazaios was too, and so the primary purpose of the structure was to emphasise their wealth to their fellow-citizens (hence the dedication to 'the people').[33]

2.11 Ephesus, Gate of Mazaeus and Mithradates.

Another Augustan arch in Asia Minor had a more public character. Galatia became a Roman province in 25 BC, and the town of Antioch became Colonia Caesarea Antiochia. (Strictly speaking, this Antioch was in Phrygia. It was known as 'Antioch towards Pisidia' because it was near the Pisidian border, to distinguish it from the more famous Antioch in Syria.) The arch was probably built to commemorate the founding of the colony, in the centre of the town, as the entrance to the colonnaded precinct of the Temple of Augustus. It stood at the top of a flight of steps. Only fragments survive, but they indicate that the larger central arched opening and slightly smaller side ones sprang from the same height. Over the four Corinthian half-columns which framed the arch the entablature broke forward. There was no attic. Rich sculptural decoration included Victories and genii over the side openings, holding garlands, while over the central one was a pair of bound Pisidian captives. On the frieze of the entablature were reliefs of a Capricorn (symbol of Augustus), weapons, and sea-trophies. Over the columns were busts of deities, including Neptune and Ceres. What statuary surmounted the arch is unknown. It also bore a copy of Augustus's *Res Gestae* (the account of his achievements best known from the copy at Ancyra, modern Ankara), probably set within the openings. The inscription dedicating the arch to Augustus is dated 2/1 BC. Roehmer suggests that it was deliberately modelled on the Parthian arch at Rome.[34]

Cassius Dio (LVI 17) tells us that, after Tiberius had put a successful end to the Illyrian war in Pannonia in AD 9, the Senate voted various honours to Augustus and him, which included 'two trophy-bearing arches in Pannonia'. There is no reason to

ARCHES OF THE TIME OF AUGUSTUS 23

believe that these were ever erected, and the obvious reason lies in the fact that almost at once, after hearing the news of Varus's disastrous defeat in Germany, Tiberius hurried off there, renouncing his triumph.[35]

A somewhat unexpected type of arch seems to make its first appearance under Augustus – that which commemorates deceased people. It is generally held that the earliest known is the one at Aix-les-Bains (Aquae), which now stands isolated in the square between the town hall and the thermal establishment (which occupies the site of the Roman baths). It is quite tall, but comparatively narrow, and extraordinarily shallow (only 75cm). Its architectural form is very simple: the Tuscan pilasters which in effect form the piers meet on the ends. The only relief decoration was on the keystone, but it is too decayed to be identifiable. The eastern side of the arch is plain, but the western side bears inscriptions and niches. The architrave has eight incised rectangles, each containing an inscription. In the frieze eight round-headed niches correspond to these. Too shallow to have contained funerary urns or busts, they presumably held portrait reliefs. On the plain attic are six more 'frames' containing inscriptions. There may have been busts corresponding to these above the attic. Across the spandrels is the inscription *L. POMPEIUS CAMPANUS VIVUS FECIT* ('L. Pompeius Campanus made this in his lifetime'). The other names (of which only twelve survive) are all in the dative, and represent three generations of his relatives. Although there may be a symbolic function, in that the arch may represent the passage from life to death, the siting of the arch also gives it the rôle of approach to the baths: this would certainly ensure that the desire of all Romans to be remembered after death would be fulfilled. Küpper-Böhm argues that a date in the second century AD fits better the architectural forms of the arch, the names of the family members, and the context (the baths were given their architectural form then), and she denies the funerary connection. However, Kleiner still prefers the traditional date and interpretation.[36]

What is now Pula, in Croatia, was formerly Pola, chief city of Istria, a peninsula which, after being part of Illyricum during the Republic, was incorporated into Italy by Augustus. It lies on the sea, around a hill. At the southeast corner of the circuit of walls (partially preserved) stands the Arch of the Sergii [2.12]. It is now free-standing, at the entrance from a piazza into a street, but it was originally built right up against a gate in the walls. This explains why the western side remains unfinished; it is assumed that the intention was that the gate would be demolished and the arch completed, but the demolition did not take place until 1827.

Although the arch is comparatively simple in form, and very shallow, its east side is richly decorated. The pairs of attached Corinthian columns are fluted, and the entablature breaks forward over them. The spandrels of the opening contain winged Victories. The pilasters have vine-reliefs. The vault has coffers containing flowers and animals, and at the centre a lozenge surrounded by four dolphins and containing an eagle with a snake in its claws. The frieze has weapons on the sides, and over the columns garlands held by putti and bucrania. The central inscription panel has on either side a chariot. The military imagery, although it might at first sight seem 'triumphal', could equally well be funerary in significance. Similarly, the eagle and snake are considered to allude 'to apotheosis and to the voyage to the Isles of the Blessed'.[37]

The inscription reads *SALVIA POSTUMA SERGI DE SUA PECUNIA* ('Salvia Postuma, wife of Sergius, [erected this] at her own expense'). The attic has three

2.12 Pula, Arch of the Sergii.

projections, two corresponding to the paired columns and a narrower one in the centre. These bear inscriptions: the central one (*L. SERGIUS L. F. LEPIDUS AED. TR. MIL. LEG. XXIX* – 'L. Sergius Lepidus, son of Lucius, aedile, military tribune of the 29th Legion') – is Salvia's husband, while the other two Sergii (both aediles and *duumuiri* – local magistrates) are related to him. Between the left-hand and central projections is a fifth inscription, *SALVIA POSTUMA SERGI*. There must have been statues of the three men on top, to which a fourth, of Salvia herself, was added after her death. The resulting asymmetry must have been odd.

The date of the arch is not certain, though the disbanding of the 29th Legion in 27 BC gives a clue. Comparison with the Temple of Roma and Augustus, also at Pula, suggests a date at the end of Augustus's reign, or early in Tiberius's. The arch was illustrated and described in Book III of Sebastiano Serlio's *Tutte l'opere d'architettura et prospettiva* (1540). Views of it were also published in the fourth (posthumous) volume of Stuart and Revett's *Antiquities of Athens*, edited by Joseph Woods (1816), but were criticised by Edward Allason, who had visited Pula in 1814, and who published his *Picturesque Views of the Antiquities of Pola in Istria* in 1819. He praised the arch as 'beautiful and elegant'. A later British architect, Thomas Graham Jackson, was more critical: 'the proportions are rather wide, and the scale is not great, but the design is good, and the arabesque ornamentation pretty, though, like all Roman work of that kind, far inferior to the similar work of the early Italian Renaissance'.[38]

The third 'funerary' arch is the best known – the Arco dei Gavi at Verona [2.13]. Originally it stood on the Via Postuma (modern Corso Cavour), 550 m outside the Porta

2.13 Verona, Arco dei Gavi.

dei Borsari. It was taken down in 1805, and reerected in 1932 in a small park just east of the Castelvecchio – slightly nearer the city than its former situation – where it is oriented north-south, instead of east-west. Not surprisingly, much of the material is modern. The main elevations are given life by projections at plinth, entablature and attic levels for each of the four half-columns. The pilasters of the arch are decorated with acanthus scrolls. Over the openings, the projections are continuous, and surmounted by a pediment in front of the attic. In the intercolumniations there are rectangular niches, which must have held statues. Beneath three of them are inscriptions with names of members of the Gavii family (two men and one woman), in the dative, indicating a dedication. Over the niches are plaques. On the frieze slight remains of another inscription again include the name *GAVI*. On the piers, within the arch, there appears twice the inscription *L. VITRUVIUS L. L. CERDO ARCHITECTUS*. This cannot be the author of the famous treatise (as Serlio already realised). The arch is technically a *quadrifrons*, as the sides are pierced by arched openings, with windows above. The internal space has a flat, coffered ceiling (as at the Arc du Rhône at Arles); in the centre is a Gorgon's head on a shield. Presumably the arch stood at a place where the Via Postuma was crossed by another road. It seems probable that it was erected by a member of the Gavii family in honour of deceased relatives. As at Aix-les-Bains, a prominent situation was chosen. The architectural details suggest a date in the Tiberian period, but its purpose makes it appropriate to discuss it here, along with the previous two arches. The arch had a great influence on Renaissance designers. It was illustrated and described by Serlio, immediately after the arch at Pula, and was drawn by Baldassare Peruzzi, Antonio da Sangallo the Younger, Palladio, and others.[39]

Notes

1 E. Nedergard, *Bulletino della Commissione Archeologica di Roma* 96 (1994–5), 33–70. For the evidence of coins, see Nathan T. Elkins, *Monuments in Miniature: Architecture on Roman Coinage* (American Numismatic Society, 2015), reviewed by F.S. Kleiner in *JRA* 29 (2016), 730–31, who thinks that representations of buildings on coins are often generic depictions.
2 A third coin type, struck at Pergamum in 19 BC, shows a single arch with a *quadriga* above, and the inscription *signis receptis*, but the representation of the structure is clearly inaccurate.
3 R.T. Scott, *JRA* 13 (2000), 183–91.
4 The most modern reconstruction of the arch is by G. Ioppolo, following the excavations of R. Gamberini Mongenet.
5 More reliable is another drawing by Ligorio of part of the arch, in the Codex Bodleianus (De Maria 1988, pl. 49). Panvinio was the author of *Fasti et Triumphi Romanorum a Romulo Rege usque ad Carolum V Caes. Aug.* (Venice, 1557) and *De triumphis commentarius* (Venice, 1571). On him see J.L. Ferrary, *Onofrio Panvinio et les antiquités romaines* (Rome, 1996).
6 F.S. Kleiner, *The Arch of Nero in Rome* (Rome, 1985), 22, associates it with Augustus's building programme in honour of Apollo after Actium. See Claridge 2010, 142–4.
7 It has been suggested that this hints at the legend that Apollo was Augustus's real father (Suetonius, *Aug.* 94.4).
8 L.A. Holland, *Janus and the Bridge* (Rome, 1961). J.B. Fischer von Erlach published an imaginary reconstruction of the arch, as a *quadrifrons* in the centre of the bridge, with a *quadriga* drawn by a pair of elephants on the city side, in his *Entwurff einer historischen Architectur* (Leipzig, 1721), bk II, pl. III. For arches on bridges, see also Fähndrich, 240–47.
9 De Maria 1988, 273. The same arch seems to appear on a fragment of a sarcophagus relief, dated to the end of the third century (now in Stockholm), which shows a carriage travelling along a suburban road. Whether the same arch is shown on coins of Claudius dated 41 and 42 is debatable: the reverses have the name of Drusus and show an arch which is similar in many respects but not all (Kleiner 1985, 34–5, with pl. VII.2; De Maria, 273).
10 *LTUR* 1996, I, 183–7 (H. Bauer); IV, 122–3 (D. Palombi).
11 In addition to De Maria 1988, see R. Angelini, *L'Arco di Augusto a Rimini* (Forlì, 1986).
12 L.A. Holland, *Janus and the Bridge* (Rome, 1961), 291–2.
13 J. Prieur, 'Les arcs d'Aoste, Suse, Aix-les-Bains', *ANRW* II 12.1 (*Festschrift Vogt*, 1982), 459.

14 R.J.A. Wilson, *Sicily under the Roman Empire* (Warminster, 1990), 55–7.
15 De Maria 1988, 226, considers that this was a town gate, with no honorary significance.
16 H. von Hesberg, *Kölner Jahrbuch fur Vor- und Frühgeschichte* 23 (1990), 109–16. Marion Roehmer, *Der Bogen als Staatsmonument* (Munich, 1997), 61–6, suggests that the sacrifice may represent the ritual purification of Cottius's army after he had handed over its command to Rome.
17 Prieur (cit. at n. 13), 459.
18 Roehmer 1997, 63–6, argues that the initiative for the erection of the arch must have come from Augustus himself, and that the reason for the delay between the reception of Cottius into the *amicitia* of Rome and its erection is that further trouble with the Alpine tribes suggested to Augustus the idea of having an arch erected which would proclaim the rewards of loyalty to Rome.
19 The existence of this arch was denied by C.R. Rose (*JRA* 3 (1990), 163–8), but reaffirmed by Roehmer 1997, 57–9.
20 A. Küpper-Böhm, *Die römischen Bogenmonumente der Gallia Narbonensis in ihrem urbane Kontext* (Espelkamp, 1996), 5–13.
21 Kleiner 1985, 30–31. This type is reproduced in Autori Vari, *Studi sull'arco onorario romano* (Rome, 1979), pl. III 3.
22 Roehmer 1997, 73–6; A. Garcia y Bellido, *Colloquio Italo-Spagnuolo sul Tema: Hispania Romana* (Accademia dei Lincei, Rome, 1974), 17.
23 G. Fabre, M. Mayer and I. Rodà, *Épigraphie hispanique* (1984), 282–8.
24 X. Dupré i Raventos, *L'Arc Roma de Berà* (Barcelona, 1994); see also A. Nünnerich-Asmus in W. Trillmich (ed.), *Denkmäler der Römerzeit* (*Hispania Antiqua*, Mainz, 1993), 137–9; Roehmer 1997, 76, n. 353.
25 E.M. Koppel, in W. Trillmich and P. Zanker (eds), *Stadtbild und Ideologie*, Bayerische Akademie der Wissenschaften, *Abhandlungen* (Neue Folge), 103 (1990), 327–32; Garcia y Bellido (cit. at n. 22), 17–18.
26 Küpper-Böhm 1996, 14–24; Roehmer 1997, 94–5; B. Fornasier, *Histoire d'art* 27 (1994), 19–29.
27 Kleiner 1985, 44, n. 115.
28 Küpper-Böhm 1996, 28–41. The weapons on the trophies have, however, been identified as both Gallic and Roman: see R. Peters, *Dekorative reliefs an römischen Ehrenbögen in Sudgallien* (Diss., Bochum, 1986). See also Roehmer 1997, 78–81.
29 Küpper-Böhm 1996, 42–62; G. Picard, *Comptes rendus de l'Académie des Inscriptions*, 1960, 13–16; R. Turcan, in *Hommages à Lucien Lerat* (Paris, 1984), 809–19.
30 Küpper-Böhm 1996, 63–76. See also M. Heijmans, in Claude Sintès and Patrice Arcelin, *Le Musée de l'Arles antique* (Arles, 1996), 47, who dates the arch to the second century.
31 Küpper-Böhm 1996, 77–85; Roehmer 1997, 76–8.
32 F.S. Kleiner, *JRA* 11 (1998), 611–12. For the arch at Orange, see Küpper-Böhm 1996, 86–109; Roehmer 1997, 81–94.
33 Roehmer 1997, 71–3. The arch has been reconstructed: see Vedat Idil in *Festschrift Jale Inan* (Istanbul, 1989), 147, with fig. 9.
34 Roehmer 1997, 68–71; S. Mitchell and M. Waelkens, *Pisidian Antioch* (London, 1998), 146–7. For the sculpture, see D.M. Robinson, *Art Bulletin* 9 (1926), 21–41.
35 Roehmer 1997, 66–7, points out that Tiberius did celebrate the triumph later, and thinks that the reason why the arches were not erected was that the Senate failed to appreciate that arches should only be erected in areas which had reached a higher degree of Romanisation than Pannonia had at that time. It is hard to believe that she knows better than the Senate.
36 Küpper-Böhm 1996, 129–35; Kleiner 1985, 612. See also Prieur (cit. at n. 13), 460–75.
37 Kleiner 1985, 37.
38 T.G. Jackson, *Dalmatia, The Quarnero and Istria* (Oxford, 1887), III, 292–3. On the arch, see De Maria 1988, 251–2.
39 Giovanna Tosi, *L'Arco dei Gavi* (Rome, 1983).

3

FROM TIBERIUS TO NERO

When we look back at the early history of the Roman Empire, it is natural for us to see Augustus, the first Emperor, as having established a dynastic autocracy. However, he himself went to great pains to ensure that although such a succession would come about it would not be blatantly obvious. Once it had happened, it was not surprising that the erection of arches in honour of the Emperor himself and of his family should continue, as a means of boosting the prestige of the dynasty.

A year after the accession of Tiberius – Augustus's stepson, son-in-law, and adopted son – in AD 15, the Senate decreed that an arch should be erected beside the Temple of Saturn, to commemorate the recovery by Germanicus, the nephew and adopted son of Tiberius, of the standards lost when Varus defeated the Romans in the Teutoburger Wald in AD 9. The arch, dedicated in 16, must have honoured both Germanicus and Tiberius himself. Two brick piers standing on either side of the Vicus Iugarius, which climbs the Capitoline Hill, between the Basilica Iulia and the Temple of Saturn, have been identified with it, and some fragments of decoration and inscriptions found nearby may belong to it. The arch is depicted on a Constantinian relief on the Arch of Constantine: quite simple, its single opening has applied Corinthian columns supporting an entablature.[1] Its occasion interestingly recalls Augustus's Parthian Arch (p. 7).

In AD 18 news reached Rome that Germanicus had pacified Armenia. The Senate decreed that he and Drusus Minor (son of Tiberius) should celebrate an *ovatio* (the lesser form of triumph – the only sort celebrated by anyone other than the emperor during the Empire).[2] At the same time, according to Tacitus, arches were built on either side of the Temple of Mars Ultor, in the Forum of Augustus, bearing their statues.[3] Remains have been found, set halfway along the *cella* of the temple, at the point where steps go down to the exits from the Forum. Each was about 8 m wide. Fragments of the marble inscription show that the northern one was that of Drusus. The position of the arches on either side of a temple recalls the arches flanking the Temple of Divus Julius in the Forum Romanum. A key feature of the Forum of Augustus was the series of statues of great men in the history of Rome: the addition of those of Germanicus and Drusus had obvious significance.[4]

In the next year, 19, Germanicus died at Antioch. Among honours voted by the Senate were three arches, one in Rome, one on the Rhine, and one on Mons Amanus in Syria. Tacitus tells us that each bore an inscription recording Germanicus's *res gestae* (his achievements) and the fact that he died for his country.[5] The text of the *senatus consultum* referred to by Tacitus survives in fragmentary form on inscriptions, the fullest of which, the Tabula Siarensis, was found in Spain in 1982. The Roman arch (described, like the other two, as a *ianus*) was to be of marble, and was to have statues of gilded bronze of defeated barbarians (perhaps in front of the attic, on either side of the inscription). On top were to be a statue of Germanicus in his triumphal chariot, along with statues of no fewer than twelve members of his family. The situation of the arch is identified as 'in the Circus Flaminius, by the place where statues of Augustus and his family were dedicated by C. Norbanus Flaccus'. This was near the Portico of Octavia, and a large single-opening arch has been identified on the Marble Plan of Rome, standing over the street which runs parallel to the south side of the Portico, at the east end of the Circus Flaminius. What may have been its foundations have been excavated, along with part of an inscription and a relief of Greek marble showing a mural crown around a club of Hercules, surmounted by a globe and eagle. This is identified by E. Rodriguez Almeida as a legionary standard, presumably one of those recovered by Germanicus.[6]

In 1986 foundations and fragments of an arch were discovered at Mainz near the right bank of the Rhine, on the axis of the road to the Roman bridge. It was a substantial triple arch, its chief peculiarity being that the side passages were rectangular, with flat roofs of hexagonal coffers. The triple form may have been a deliberate echo of Augustus's Parthian arch. Some of the stone blocks bear the builder's mark of the Legio XIV, stationed at Mainz. Fragments of relief sculpture include one with a shepherd and a dolphin with a Cupid, and another with part of a colossal river-god. A fragment of a twice-lifesize bronze statue also survives, which may have represented Germanicus on horseback, on top of the arch. The *senatus consultum* mentioned above has been restored by W.D. Lebek so as to lay down that the arch should be near the tumulus built to the memory of Drusus. This was on the left bank, where the modern city is, and that has cast doubt on the identification of the arch with the foundations on the other bank.[7] The *senatus consultum* also decreed that an annual parade should be held in honour of Germanicus.

The third arch was erected in Syria because Germanicus had died in the capital of that province, over which, as over the rest of Rome's eastern possessions, he had held *maius imperium* (complete power). One might have expected the arch to be set up at Antioch. Mons Amanus, the range between Cilicia and Syria, must have been chosen because of the important passes which crossed it.

The fact that these arches were erected in honour of a man who was dead relates them to the type of the funerary arch, already mentioned in the cases of the three arches to private families.[8]

Before he died, Germanicus had had an arch dedicated to him, together with Tiberius and Drusus Minor, at Saintes (Mediolanum Santonum), about 100 km north of Bordeaux [3.1]. It stood at the approach to the Roman bridge over the Charente, on the right bank, but was rebuilt on the left bank in 1841 after the bridge was destroyed. The inscription tells us that it was dedicated by C. Iulius Rufus, priest of Roma and Augustus at Lyon, and *praefectus fabrum* (chief engineer). His great-grandfather had the resounding Gallic name of Epotsorovidus. The chief peculiarity of the arch is that it has two openings (compare, for example, Langres). It is also unusual in having Corinthian pilasters which support a frieze at the height of the springing of the arches, with a second order of attached columns above carrying the entablature. The attic must have had on it three statues (of the dedicatees).

3.1 The unusual double arch at Saintes, Charente Maritime.

Drusus died in AD 23. As has already been mentioned (p. 12), the early Augustan arch at Spoleto was then dedicated to him and to Germanicus. That an arch was erected to him at Rome would seem to follow from Tacitus's statement that the same honours were decreed for him as for Germanicus.[9] However, nothing else is known of it, except that the *Fasti Ostienses* mention the dedication of an *arcus Drusi* in AD 30, which may be this one.

Three arches which appear also to have honoured the family of Tiberius were erected at Pompeii. One pair was built on either side of the Temple of Jupiter which occupies the north end of the Forum, over the two narrow access roads. Simple in form, they were of brick with marble revetment. The western arch, whose brick core survives, appears in the famous relief from the House of Caecilius Jucundus which shows the buildings on the north side of the Forum as affected by the earthquake of 62: it has pairs of pilasters or half-columns and a pediment against the attic. The eastern arch was probably similar, and each may have borne an equestrian statue. It is generally considered that the arches were erected soon after AD 18 in imitation of those flanking the Temple of Mars Ultor in the Forum of Augustus at Rome, and likewise honoured Drusus Minor and Germanicus.

The eastern arch was demolished so as not to block the view of another, placed further north at the north-east corner of the temple, at a crossroads. Again, the brick core (on a travertine base) survives, along with fragments of the marble revetment, which include bits of the pairs of fluted half-columns which stood on either side of the arch, on both faces. On the south side there are two round-headed niches which must have held statues. A fragment of an inscription indicates that one represented Nero,

FROM TIBERIUS TO NERO

the son of Germanicus, in which case the other surely represented his brother Drusus. An equestrian statue of Tiberius must have crowned the whole: fragments of a bronze horse were found nearby. On the north side of the arch are two rectangular niches which contained fountains, with basins in front (compare the arch of Scipio Africanus at Rome (p. 2), and Cosa (p. 4)). Steps and bollards ensure that passage through the arch was only for pedestrians. The arch must have been built after the death of Drusus Minor (son of Tiberius) in 23, when Nero and this Drusus became Tiberius's heirs.[10]

A fourth arch at Pompeii, also of brick, survives in the centre of the south side of the Forum. Almost a cube, its passageway is very narrow, and not aligned on any thoroughfare: it is therefore more of a base than an arch, and probably supported an imperial statue. Its date is uncertain, but probably not earlier than the reign of Tiberius.

The only other arch surviving at Pompeii may also date to same reign. This is the so-called 'Arch of Caligula', which spans the Via di Mercurio (on the same axis as the arch beside the Temple of Jupiter), just north of its crossing with the Via di Nola. The simple, shallow brick structure presumably had a marble revetment. It had pipes in its piers to feed fountains attached to its southern side (as on the arch to its south). Fragments of an equestrian statue of bronze, found nearby, have generally been associated with the arch. The person portrayed was formerly identified as Caligula (hence the name), but for no good reason, though it was probably a member of the imperial family.[11]

The latest Tiberian arch known is the one near the Augustan market at Lepcis Magna in North Africa. The inscription (repeated on both faces of the plain and shallow stone arch) records that it was set up in 35/36, to commemorate the paving of all the roads of Lepcis by C. Rubellius Blandus, proconsul of Africa, in honour of Tiberius (whose niece was his wife). There may be an interesting parallel for this in the arch at Syracuse (above, p. 12).[12]

Suetonius tells us (*Claud.* 11.3) that the Senate decreed that a marble arch should be erected to Tiberius at Rome 'next to the Theatre of Pompey', but it could not be carried out until the time of Claudius. Tiberius had begun a restoration of the theatre after a fire in 21. Claudius also put an inscription in his honour on the stage. Neither the site nor the appearance of the arch is known, but it probably stood in relation to the portico attached to the stage building.

The only evidence for an arch in honour of Tiberius's successor Caligula is an inscription found near the Capitolium at Thugga (Dougga, in modern Tunisia). Caligula's name was, after his assassination in 41, replaced with that of Claudius.

Claudius was keen to have the military successes of his reign suitably commemorated. Coins of 41–42 and 46–47 have his image and name on the recto, and on the verso an arch shown in schematic form. Above the attic, inscribed *DE GERMANIS*, is an equestrian statue, between trophies. Confusingly, however, a similar arch appears on coins of 41–45 which have on the recto the image of Claudius's father, Nero Drusus. These have already been mentioned in connection with his arch outside the Porta Appia. If the Claudian coins really represent a different arch, it must have commemorated the German victories for which Claudius received an imperial salutation in 41. The fact that the same design appears again on a coin of 46–50, with the inscription *DE BRITANN.*, suggests that it had become merely a numismatic symbol, and cannot be taken as a genuine record of the appearance of the arches – if they ever existed.

Several arches were certainly erected to commemorate the British victories. In 43, according to Cassius Dio (LX 22), the Senate decreed the erection of one at the place in France where Claudius took ship, Gesoriacum (Boulogne). This recalls the arch at Brindisi, from where Augustus set out for Actium (p. 7), but, as in that case, we know nothing more of it. From an inscription we know that another was erected at Cyzicus (modern Bal Kiz in Turkey), the trading city in the Propontis (Sea of Marmara), by the Roman citizens living there and the natives. It says something for Claudian propaganda that his achievements should be commemorated at the opposite ends of the Empire.

Dio tells us that at the same time the Senate decreed a triumph for Claudius, and the erection of an arch at Rome. Despite the fact that the inscription records its dedication as late as 51–52, it is likely that this was the arch which stood over the Via Lata (the modern Corso), near the Via del Caravita, close to S. Ignazio. The Via Lata continues northwards as the Via Flaminia. The site of the arch probably marked the new boundary of the *pomerium*, enlarged by Claudius to celebrate his British victories. It took the form of an elaboration of an arch of the aqueduct of the Aqua Virgo, where that crossed the street. This aqueduct was reconstructed by Claudius in 46. Many fragments attributed to the arch were discovered in the sixteenth century, and on their basis Pirro Ligorio made a reconstruction, not all of which can be correct. The single arch was built of marble. The masonry of the piers was rusticated, in the fashion of Claudius's reign (compare the Porta Maggiore). Each pier had a pair of Corinthian semicolumns, framing aedicules with pedimented entablatures.[13] The entablature broke forward over each pair, and the attic broke forward over each semicolumn. In the centre was the finely cut inscription, stating that the Emperor had received the surrender of eleven conquered British kings with no loss of men, and was the first to bring barbarian peoples beyond the Ocean (identified with the Channel) under British sway.[14] On each side was another inscription giving the names of four members of the imperial family. So there were no doubt nine statues above the attic.

It is not entirely certain which of the many fragments of decorative carving attributed to the arch – some known only from sixteenth-century drawings – really belonged to it, but it seems clear that this was the first arch at Rome to be decorated with a substantial amount of relief sculpture. One drawing (by Pierre Jacques) indicates that the frieze represented scenes of battle. The spandrels contained flying Victories. A fragment of relief at Hever Castle in Kent shows part of a triumphal procession, with two *tubicines* (trumpeters) in the background, and another in the Louvre shows a group of officers and a standard-bearer. A curious story related by Martial (IV 18) probably relates to this arch: because it constantly dripped, an icicle formed one winter, fell, and pierced the throat of a boy passing beneath.[15]

We know of only one arch certainly erected in honour of Claudius's successor Nero, but it is of particular importance. The sole literary evidence comes from Tacitus's *Annals*. In the first year of Nero's reign (54), the Parthians invaded Armenia, which was a Roman protectorate. In 58 Domitius Corbulo captured the Armenian capital Artaxata, and among numerous honours voted by the Senate to the Emperor were 'statues and arches and continuous consulships' (XIII 41.4). Whether any arches were actually erected at this date is unknown, but in 61, although the Roman troops had in fact suffered a setback in Armenia, the Senate decided to cover up the situation by voting that Parthian trophies and an arch should be set up *medio Capitolini montis* ('in the middle of the Capitoline Hill' – XV 18.1). The parallel with Augustus's Parthian Arch must have been intentional. The site was presumably between the two peaks of the hill (the Arx and the Capitolium proper), and the arch may well have spanned the Clivus Capitolinus – the final stretch of the triumphal route to the Temple of Jupiter Optimus Maximus. It is noteworthy that the arch erected in 190 BC by P. Cornelius Scipio Africanus would have stood 'opposite' this road, and the *fornix Calpurnius* probably spanned the staircase up the western side of the hill. Wherever Nero's arch stood, its design (see below) makes it clear that it must have been visible from all four sides.[16]

Since the area where the arch probably stood is now covered by the Piazza del Campidoglio it has not been excavated, but the absence of any later references to it suggests that it was destroyed as part of the unofficial *damnatio memoriae* after Nero's death in 68. Some Neronian monuments simply had his name erased, or his face replaced by a different one, but destruction is all the more likely since Domitian's arches certainly were destroyed as part of his official *damnatio memoriae* (Dio LXVIII 1).[17] The Capitoline Hill was in any case ravaged by fires in 69 and in 80.

Nevertheless, we have good evidence for the appearance of the arch from *sestertii* minted at Rome and Lyon [3.2]. Over four hundred specimens, struck over a period of four years (64–67), are known. They have been exhaustively analysed by Fred S. Kleiner.[18] He describes the representation of the arch as 'justly hailed as one of the masterpieces of Roman numismatic art'.[19] He argues that the explanation for the fact that the arch is much more realistically shown than any previous arch known from coins is largely the strikingly novel character of the arch itself, whose depiction in a three-quarters view was suggested by its having sides which were as significant as its faces, since each had a pedimented niche housing a colossal statue, and also freestanding columns on projecting bases with bracketed entablatures. Both features appear here for the first time, so far as we know, and the second was to be particularly important. Kleiner explains the unusually careful proportions of the representation as due to the need to show the abundant relief sculpture – more abundant than on any previous arch at Rome (though comparable to arches in Gaul).

The arch had a single opening, and the Corinthian columns were placed at the corners.[20] Behind them were pilasters. The entablature broke forward over them, and this

3.2 The arch of Nero at Rome, voted in 61, known only from coins.

34 THE TRIUMPHAL ARCH

projection was carried upwards through the attic, in the centre of which was a larger projection bearing the inscription (which is unknown). Above this stood a *quadriga*, driven by the Emperor, who held a sceptre in one hand and a palm-branch in the other. On one side stood Victory, holding a palm-branch and offering a garland, and on the other Peace, holding a *caduceus* and a cornucopia. Above the columns, at attic level, stood four statues of soldiers, raising their arms in salute. The niche on the visible side of the arch contained a statue of Mars (probably of bronze); its pair presumably also contained a deity.

The relief sculpture included panels showing Victories on either side of the inscription panel. There may have been reliefs on the sides of the attic (one coin shows a seated figure). The keystone of the arch, in the form of a console (another significant innovation), bore a figure identified by Kleiner as the Genius of the Roman People. The frieze seems to have been left plain. The spandrels on either side of the keystone showed reclining river-gods. Below these, between the arch pilasters and the columns, were further reliefs on two levels, each panel containing a Victory, the lower ones each crowning a trophy. The column pedestals also bore reliefs, possibly of battles. It may also have been the case that the panels on either side of these pedestals and below the aedicules on the sides were decorated with reliefs – a feature apparently without parallel. Within the arch opening the coins show hanging garlands.[21]

Apart from the *quadriga*, which was clearly based on the one on Augustus's Parthian Arch, none of these features had an exact precedent. The most influential innovation of all was the use of freestanding columns, which would be used not just for arches but for other buildings (for example, Hadrian's Library at Athens), and provide a striking motif for architects throughout many centuries. Such an innovation comes as no surprise in the reign of Nero, whose Domus Aurea revealed spectacular new developments in architecture and decoration.

Notes

1 E. Nash, *Pictorial Dictionary of Ancient Rome* (London/New York 1961–2), I, 131–2.
2 Mary Beard, *The Roman Triumph* (Cambridge Mass., 2007), 62–3.
3 Tacitus, *Annals* II 64.1.
4 *LTUR* II, 292 (V. Kockel).
5 Tacitus, *Annals* II 83.2.
6 *LTUR* 1996, I, 270 (A. Viscogliosi); see also *Bollettino d'Archeologia*, 7 (1991), 1–4.
7 H.C. Frenz, *JRA* 2 (1989), 120–25; also 416, where he quotes the dissenting view of H. Bellen.
8 For the arches of Germanicus, and the honours decreed to him and Drusus, see W.D. Lebek, *ZPE* 67 (1987), 129–48; 78 (1989), 42–91; 86 (1991), 47–78; *Antike und Abendland*, 36 (1990), 93–102.
9 Tacitus, *Annals* IV 9.2.
10 Henner von Hesberg in V.M. Strocka, ed., *Die Regierungszeit des Kaisers Claudius* (Mainz, 1994), 250, thinks that the architectural form of the arch suggests a Claudian date.
11 Von Hesberg (cit. in the preceding note), 252, thinks that this arch too may be Claudian.
12 P. Romanelli, *Africa italiana*, 7 (1940), 87–96.
13 According to von Hesberg (cit. at n. 10), 250, 258. See his reconstruction on p. 251.
14 *CIL* VI 920 = *ILS* 216. See P. Salway, *Roman Britain* (Oxford, 1981), 86.
15 On the epigram see R. Moreno Soldavila, *Martial, Book IV, A Commentary* (Leiden/Boston, 2006).
16 A military diploma of AD 74 refers to two arches on the Capitoline, but whether these were the Republican ones or different ones is unknown – *CIL* III, p. 852; XVI, p. 18.
17 On the subject of *damnatio memoriae* (which is not an ancient term) see E.R. Varner, ed., *From Caligula to Constantine: Tyranny and Transformation in Roman Portraiture* (Leiden/Boston, 2000).
18 F. S. Kleiner, *The Arch of Nero in Rome* (Rome, 1985).
19 ibid., 73.
20 The coins show the columns on the corners. Kleiner's reconstruction shows them set in from the corners, but in his text (ibid., 88) he describes them as being 'at the ends of each façade'.
21 Strangely these are not mentioned by Kleiner.

4

AFTER NERO IN ITALY

Rome

After the turmoil of the 'year of the four emperors', following the death of Nero in 68, Vespasian re-established peace. His principal military achievement had been the suppression of the Jewish rebellion. In 70, the year after his accession, his son Titus captured Jerusalem. Cassius Dio tells us that, among other honours, arches were decreed by the Senate to the two of them together. It is not known for certain that any arch was in fact erected, but Kleiner has argued for the existence of three.[1]

The first of these is shown on the famous relief panel within the passageway of the surviving Arch of Titus, where the procession carrying the spoils is about to pass under an arch. Of this one pier is shown, and one spandrel of the opening, with the flying Victory which was by now usual. On top of the arch are two *quadrigae*, between which are a man on horseback and a female figure, larger than lifesize. No other Roman arch had two *quadrigae* on it, and the obvious explanation is provided by the double triumph which Vespasian and Titus celebrated in 71. Josephus tells us that they were accompanied by Titus's younger brother Domitian on horseback. The female figure may well be Minerva, regarded by Domitian as his patron.

The problem with Kleiner's interpretation is that the arch bearing two *quadrigae* cannot actually have been built by the time of the triumph, so that its appearance here is an anachronism. He claims, however, that the fact that on the arches of Titus in the Campus Martius and in the Forum only Titus appears (see below) supports the idea that this particular arch must date back to Vespasian's reign. There is no evidence to suggest its location.

Kleiner's second arch is the one he interprets as a *quadrifrons*, shown on a rare series of *sestertia* minted in 71. This would have been the first *quadrifrons* erected at Rome (for the one at Cavaillon see above, p. 18). The 'arch' appears behind the figure of Vespasian, who is making a sacrifice while being crowned by Victory, with the legend *VICTORIA AUG. S.C.* The peculiar feature of the 'arch' is that on top are just two standing figures, identified by Kleiner as the Genii of the Senate and the Roman People (found later on a relief on the Arch of Trajan at Benevento). Kleiner suggests that the absence of a *quadriga* may represent a deliberate revival by Vespasian of the Republican type of votive arch. However, the image is so sketchy that its interpretation can only be hypothetical.

Kleiner's third 'Vespasianic' arch is the one shown on the Haterii relief (below, p. 42).

Vespasian died in 79. His elder son Titus was not only popular, but enjoyed the credit of military success in Judaea, which culminated in the destruction of Jerusalem. He was honoured with two arches at Rome. The first was erected in 81, the year of his untimely death. It occupied a position of great prominence, at the curved southeastern end of the Circus Maximus (and so presumably, as mentioned above (p. 2), replacing one of Stertinius's arches). It is shown on a fragment of the Marble Plan, with three intercommunicating openings; on various coins; and on mosaic and relief representations of Circus scenes. Excavations have produced fragmentary remains of its cladding of Luna (Carrara) marble, and, in 2015, the bases of the columns and their plinths and parts of the travertine pavement.

Two particularly interesting architectural features can be noted. On each front there were four columns, detached from the structure, but on bases which were attached, as were their entablatures. This arrangement, which represents a development from the corner columns of the Arch of Nero, has come to be associated especially with arches, because of its appearance on the arches of Septimius Severus and Constantine, though it had also appeared on the façade of Vespasian's Forum Pacis. The Marble Plan shows that the arch was approached up steps on the outer side, while mosaics show that the same was the case on the inner side. This feature, which occurs on some later arches, indicates that the function of an arch as a processional passageway was not critical.

The inscription of the arch was transcribed in the ninth century by the 'Anonymus Einsiedlensis'. It makes clear its commemorative purpose, recording its dedication to Titus in 81 by the Senate and People, 'because, acting on his father's precepts and advice, he conquered the Jewish people and destroyed Jerusalem, a task either attempted in vain, or not attempted at all, by all previous commanders and peoples'.[2] Coins show that it had a *quadriga* on top, and reliefs relating to the Jewish war. A fragment in Pentelic marble survives, showing the head of a soldier whose helmet bears a thunderbolt, symbol of the Twelfth Legion, which fought in Judaea.[3]

Titus's second arch is one of the most celebrated in Rome, because of its prominent position at the south-east end of the Forum, and its completeness [4.1]. It has, however, to be remembered that its prominence would originally have been less striking, when it was surrounded by other buildings, and its completeness is due to early nineteenth-century restoration. The arch stands on the saddle of a hill which links the Palatine to the Velia ridge. It used to be believed that it stood on the Sacra Via, but it did not, though it did stand on what is called the *via triumphalis* leading to the Forum from the Colosseum. It stood near the atrium of Nero's Domus Aurea, hated for its overbearing size, and marked the approach via the Clivus Palatinus to the Domus Flavia, the new imperial residence on the Palatine.

There is no reference to it in ancient literature (though Martial, at *Spect.* 2.2, may refer to its scaffolding), but the original inscription on the eastern side makes it clear that it was dedicated by the Senate and People *divo Tito*, in other words after the deification which immediately followed Titus's death. Its erection is usually dated to the early years of the reign of Domitian. He is said to have jealously detested his brother's memory, but this was doubtless exaggerated by hostile propaganda. The natural assumption is that the arch was intended to commemorate the deification, and it is even possible that Titus was buried here, until 94, when Domitian built a family mausoleum on the Quirinal (compare Trajan's burial beneath his column).

4.1 The Arch of Titus in the Roman Forum, built soon after his death in 81.

    The arch of Titus has a single opening. Its concrete core is faced with Pentelic marble up to the capitals, and with Luna marble above. It is 14 m wide and 14.5 m high. On each side there were four attached columns, fluted, and with Composite capitals (one of the earliest uses of this type on a public monument).[4] It is likely that there was a bronze *quadriga* on top. The sculptural decoration of the exterior consists of winged Victories in the spandrels that carry a trumpet, a standard, a crown of laurel and a palm-branch, and a trophy; figures on the keystones (Virtue on the east, and Honour on the west, or, according to others, Rome and the Genius of the Roman People); and a narrow frieze showing the triumphal procession of Vespasian and Titus. The spaces between the columns on the fronts contain blind arches below blank panels.

    The richest decoration is found within the archway. On either side are the two great reliefs showing the triumph of 71. On the northern one Titus is shown on his *quadriga*, being crowned by Victory, while on the south are shown the men carrying the spoils of the Temple of Jerusalem – the seven-branched candlestick, the table with the sacred vessels, and the silver trumpets. The procession is approaching an arch, described above [4.2].[5] The vault is richly decorated with square coffers framing rosettes. In the centre is a panel which shows Titus being carried up to heaven by an eagle.

In the Middle Ages the arch was incorporated into the fortress of the Frangipane family, and was reduced to the archway with its flanking columns; of the attic almost nothing except the eastern inscription survives. This was the state in which so many artists, including Piranesi and J.M.W. Turner, represented it, after the fortress had given way to the monastery of Santa Francesca Romana.[6] Renaissance artists made attempts at reconstruction, of which the most accurate was by the so-called 'Master C of 1519', whose notebook is in the Albertina. He was a member of Raphael's circle.[7] The first proposals for restoration were made during the French occupation. In 1810 Auguste-Jean-Marie Guénepin submitted as his Envoi de Rome drawings of the arch as it was and as it should be.[8] In 1813 the matter was discussed between the French administrators and architects and a delegation from the Accademia di San Luca, headed by the sculptor Antonio Canova. The latter proposed mere consolidation, whereas the former preferred a 'restoration'. After Pius VII had returned to Rome he entrusted the task of restoration to Raffaele Stern (architect of the Braccio Nuovo of the Vatican Museum, and restorer of the Colosseum). After Stern's death in 1820, his project was carried out (in 1822–4) by Giuseppe Valadier. The missing parts were executed in travertine, not marble. This is generally said to have been due to a laudable intention to differentiate new from old, but Valadier's own account shows that (like the absence of fluting on the new columns) it was due to lack of money. An inscription on the west side of the attic records the restoration.[9]

4.2 Relief on the Arch of Titus showing the spoils of Jerusalem.

AFTER NERO IN ITALY 39

Suetonius (13.2) tells us that Titus's brother Domitian (who reigned 81–96) erected so many and such large arches (described as *ianos arcusque*) with *quadrigae* and symbols of triumph throughout the city that a clever graffitist wrote on one of them *arkei*. This Greek word means 'that's enough', but could be mistaken for a solecistic plural of *arcus*. Cassius Dio (LXVIII 1.1) tells us that more arches were erected to Domitian than to any other man, and that they were destroyed after his death. Their disappearance made their exaggeration by historians sharing in the senatorial hostility to the dead 'tyrant' all the easier. We have evidence for four, at most, in Rome, together with perhaps as many as three elsewhere. It will be seen that they were in any case not all destroyed.

One particularly important arch was described by Martial in an epigram (VIII 65) published in about 93, soon after the Emperor's return from his campaign against the Sarmatians, when he celebrated not a triumph but an *ovatio* (he had, after all, lost a legion):

> *Hic ubi Fortunae reducis fulgentia late*
> *templa nitent, felix area nuper erat:*
> *hic stetit Arctoi formosus puluere belli*
> *purpureus fundens Caesar ab ore iubar;*
> *hic lauru redemita comas et candida cultu*
> *Roma salutauit uoce manuque ducem.*
> *grande loci meritum testantur et altera dona:*
> *stat sacer et domitis gentibus arcus ouat;*
> *hic gemini currus numerant elephanta frequentem;*
> *sufficit immensis aureus ipse iugis.*
> *haec est digna tuis, Germanice, porta triumphis:*
> *hos aditus urbem Martis habere decet.*

('Here, where the Temple of Fortuna Redux [Fortune who brings people home] gleams, shining far and wide, was recently a favoured place: here stood Caesar, handsome in the dust of northern war, spreading bright light from his face. Here Rome, her hair wreathed in laurel, and dressed in white, greeted the leader with voice and hand. Another gift also bears witness to the great merit of the place: there stands a sacred arch, which rejoices over the defeated peoples. Here twin chariots count frequent elephants, and he himself, all golden, suffices to control the immense yokes. This gate is worthy of your triumphs, Germanicus: it is right that the city of Mars should have such an approach.')

What must be the same arch is shown on sesterces minted at Rome in 85, 90–91 and 95–6 [4.3]. The date of the earliest of these shows that the occasion for the erection of the arch must have been Domitian's return in 83 from defeating the Chatti, a German people (hence the title 'Germanicus'). He celebrated a triumph, and the arch must have been voted then, and built by 85. The coins show a *quadrifrons*: on each side pairs of detached Corinthian columns stand, one beside the opening, the other on the corner. Their plinths and entablatures break forward. Much sculptural decoration is shown. There are reliefs on the column plinths, and over the opening on each side is

4.3 Lost Arch of Domitian, (?) 85, shown on a coin.

what appears to be an *imago clipeata* (a shield-shaped image). The centre of each side of the attic contains a relief, one recognisable as a scene of sacrifice. Over each column is a standing figure, probably Roman soldiers or German prisoners. Above the attic are two chariots, facing in opposite directions, each drawn by four elephants. This corresponds with Martial's description, but whereas his words might be taken to imply that there was just one gilded statue of the Emperor driving both chariots, the coins more plausibly show two statues.[10]

Unfortunately it is not known for certain where the arch, and the Temple of Fortuna Redux, stood.[11] Some have argued that the arch was a reconstruction of the Porta Triumphalis, on the southern side of the city (see p. 3), and that the temple was one of the two in the so-called 'Area Sacra di Sant' Omobono'.[12] However, the Porta Triumphalis must have been set in the city wall, whereas Domitian's *quadrifrons* must have stood at a crossroads. In any case it is far more likely that a general returning from the North would have been welcomed north of the city, not south. The most plausible theory is that of Helge Lyngby, who places the arch on the Via Lata (the modern Corso) at the point where it was crossed by the *pomerium* (as renewed by Vespasian in 75), near the present church of San Lorenzo in Lucina.[13]

What must be the same arch is shown on three works of art dating from the reign of Marcus Aurelius. Two are reliefs reused on the north side of the attic of the Arch of Constantine [4.4]. One, probably showing an *aduentus*, or arrival, has in the background a tetrastyle temple, identifiable as dedicated to Fortuna by the reliefs in the pediment, and a *quadrifrons*, while the other, identified as a *profectio*, or departure, shows the arch with four elephants on top. Beside these is a group consisting of a trophy, a seated female figure, and a standing chained barbarian (compare the reliefs on the arches of South Gaul, pp. 17–20). The spandrel reliefs are clearly represented, and garlands hang within the opening (as on the coin depictions of the Arch of Nero, p. 34). The third Aurelian artefact is a bronze medallion commemorating an *aduentus*, dating from 173–4: it shows both temple and arch. It seems that the arch is also shown on a Constantinian relief on the Arch of Constantine, representing the Emperor's entry into Rome. The reason why this arch survived, when most of Domitian's other arches were destroyed, is presumably that it played a ceremonial role: no doubt all references to Domitian himself were erased.

AFTER NERO IN ITALY 41

4.4 Profectio relief from the Arch of Marcus Aurelius, reused on the Arch of Constantine.

A second arch which may have been spared is known from a pair of foundations visible on the Clivus Palatinus, the road leading up to the eastern end of the Palatine Hill. Presumably it marked the entrance to the piazza in front of the Domus Flavia, whose building was one of Domitian's greatest achievements.

Another arch almost certainly built by Domitian, early in his reign, is shown on a famous relief in the Vatican Museum, showing buildings erected by the family building firm of the Haterii. It comes from a family tomb, and dates from *c.* 100. The arch is identified as *Arcus ad Isis*, and must be the one shown on the Marble Plan as the eastern entrance to the Iseum Campense – the temple precinct of Isis in the Campus Martius. This arch remained standing until its demolition *c.* 1595, and part of its north pier has been excavated. It site was just west of the Piazza del Collegio Romano. The Temple of Isis was destroyed in the great fire of AD 80, and rebuilt by Domitian. The Haterii relief shows the arch with three openings, and four detached Composite columns. Statues of deities appear within the openings, but these must just refer to the arch's location. On top is a *quadriga*, with palm-trees, kneeling captives and trophies on either side: these suggest that the arch commemorated the Jewish triumph. On the attic there are three garlands, which might refer to the three Flavian emperors. The reliefs over the side openings have Isiac significance.

A second arch on the same relief could date from Domitian's reign. This one has a single opening, with pairs of Composite columns on either side. Apart from the garlands in the frieze of the entablature, the only sculptural decoration is the *quadriga* on top, driven by an Emperor holding a sceptre, while a Victory crowns him; in front is a trophy. The *quadriga* is shown in profile, which may indicate that the arch was a *quadrifrons*. The only clue to its whereabouts is provided by the figure of the Magna Mater, on an altar with a staircase, shown within the opening. This may represent the Temple of the Magna Mater on the Palatine.[14]

After Domitian was assassinated in 96 he was succeeded by Nerva, who reigned for only two years; no arch is known to have been erected for him. However, the efficient and well-regarded Trajan (98–117) had a good ten or so put up in his honour at Rome and elsewhere. Granted his military career, and particularly his conquest of Dacia, this is not surprising.

Two are known only from coins. One, shown on sesterces of AD 100, has three equal openings; apart from this, its most remarkable feature is that above the attic stand, in some versions, a *quadriga* with Trajan crowned by Victories between trophies, but in others two chariots each drawn by six horses, with six statues at the sides. It may have celebrated Trajan's German campaign in 99. A quite different arch appears on two series of sesterces of Trajan's fifth consulate (103–11); the obvious occasion for this arch would be the triumph at the end of the first Dacian War in 102. Although it is quite wide, there is only one opening, and this has an architrave with a blind lunette above. The fact that this might indicate that it was fitted with doors, and the letters *IOM* (*Ioui Optimo Maximo*) on the upper of two attics (the lower has a pediment over the opening), have suggested that the arch might have formed an entrance to the precinct of the Temple of Capitoline Jupiter – the final goal of the triumphal procession. The coins show elaborate relief decoration, and a chariot drawn by six horses on top.

A third arch, known only from the Regionary Catalogue (a late fourth-century list of buildings in each region of the city) is described as *arcus diui Traiani*, and so is probably posthumous. Apart from its location in the first Region, nothing else is known. The so-called *Arcus Pietatis*, known only from medieval documents, survived until the fifteenth century. The name came from a relief (now lost) with a scene of clemency which was the source of the legend about Trajan's justice which appears in Dante's *Purgatorio* (X 73–93). It stood north of the Pantheon, and may also have been posthumous.

Until recently it was thought that Trajan's magnificent new Forum, dedicated in 112, incorporated two arches, one forming the principal entrance, set in the curved south-eastern side, while a second arch, which Cassius Dio (LXVIII 29.3) tells us was decreed by the Senate in 116 to celebrate Trajan's Parthian victories, might have taken the form of a remodelling of one of the two arches which flanked the central arch. However, excavations in 1999–2006 revealed that the monumental entrance from the Forum of Augustus into the Forum of Trajan, shown on coins, was not in fact an arch, but a columnar backdrop to his equestrian statue, and that there were no flanking arches.[15]

Although numerous arches were erected by or to Hadrian (117–38) throughout the Empire, at Rome only one or two at most can be attributed to his reign (unless one accepts the theory that the Arch of Constantine is in fact Hadrianic – see below). The Arcus Pietatis has already been mentioned, as has the arch built by Domitian as the eastern entrance to the Iseum Campense. The western entrance also took the form of an arch, and this is dated by brick-stamps to 123. It was set within the Porticus Meleagri, which formed the eastern side of the Saepta Julia (the voting enclosure); these were restored by Hadrian (*SHA* 19.10). This part of the Marble Plan is missing, but a plan was made after 1515 by Antonio da Sangallo the Younger. What remained of the arch was destroyed in 1872–3. A reconstruction has been made by G. Gatti, and suggests that it was highly unusual. It was a *quadrifrons*, of brick faced with marble. Its east and west faces had three openings, while the north and south faces had only one. The central openings on east and west were much wider than the side ones. If Gatti's reconstruction is correct, the entablature of the porticoes on either side continued across the piers; both below and above them were smaller arches flanked by detached columns on pedestals. The central space had a cross vault. Nothing is known of any sculptural decoration, nor is there any clue to a commemorative purpose.

Hadrian's successor Antoninus Pius (138–61) erected a large temple in his honour, dedicated in 145. It stood north of the Iseum, and most of its north side still stands, on the Piazza di Pietra, having been converted into the Stock Exchange. It was set within a large precinct, surrounded by a colonnade. The entrance from the east (from the Via Lata) was through a triple arch, which is mentioned by fifteenth- and sixteenth-century authors, and shown on Pirro Ligorio's pictorial map of 1561 as *Arcus Veri Parthici* (wrongly identified as an arch for Lucius Verus). What may be a fragment of one corner was recently discovered close to the Corso. It seems likely that the arch stood separate from the eastern colonnade of the precinct. Ligorio tells us that it had four detached columns, with Composite capitals. Two of its relief panels survive. One was taken in 1573 to the Palazzo dei Conservatori, and set above the stairs. It shows an imperial *aduentus*, probably on Hadrian's return from Illyria in 118. The Emperor's head is a restoration, and the same is the case on the other relief, now in the Torlonia collection, where the head is a portrait of Lucius Verus. This shows an act of submission to the Emperor by some barbarians.[16]

No arch is known to have been erected in honour of Antoninus Pius. The Regionaries tell us that one in Regio I commemorated *divus Verus*. This was presumably put up by Lucius Verus's colleague and father-in-law Marcus Aurelius (161–80) after his death and deification in 169, but nothing else is known of it. Of the arch erected by the Senate in 176 to commemorate the military successes of Marcus himself, we possess a transcript of the inscription (made in the ninth century by the Anonymus Einsiedlensis), and eleven and part of a twelfth of its relief panels. Eight of these were reused on the Arch of Constantine, and three have been preserved since the sixteenth century in the Palazzo dei Conservatori. Only a fragment of the twelfth, with the Emperor's head, survives in the Ny Carlsberg Glyptotek in Copenhagen. The reliefs can be divided into two series, the differences in style being due to their authorship by different workshops.

If there were originally only twelve reliefs, there could have been six on each side of the arch – two on each pier, and one on each side of the inscription on the attic, as on the Arch of Trajan at Benevento. However, E. Angelicoussis has argued that it may have been a *quadrifrons*, with four panels on the attic of each side, and eight panels on the sides of each of the four passages, giving a total of twenty-four. She points out that nine of the eleven reliefs preserved show the Emperor turned towards the right, whereas it is usual (as e.g. at Benevento) to have the principal figures on reliefs arranged mirror-wise. The missing panels may have celebrated Commodus, whose role as Marcus's successor was especially prominent in the years 175–6. Certainly a figure, probably of Commodus, has been chiselled off the scenes of triumph and of *liberalitas* (generosity), presumably after his *damnatio memoriae*. On her theory, the scenes would begin with Marcus's departure for the German wars in 169, and conclude with the *liberalitas* of Marcus and Commodus in 177. This creates a problematic conflict with the date 176 recorded for the triumph, but she suggests that this date might have been an error. Torelli, on the other hand, dates the first series of reliefs to 173, date of the abortive return of Marcus, and the second to 176, when his triumph was decreed. The location of the arch is far from certain. Some have identified it with an *Arcus Panis Aurei in Capitolio* (arch of golden bread on the Capitoline), but this is doubtful. The reuse of the reliefs on Constantine's arch might suggest that that of Marcus Aurelius had for some reason been dismantled.[17]

Whatever the form and location of the arch, the series of reliefs is of great interest and value. Nothing could demonstrate this more clearly than the reuse of eight panels by Constantine. The first series shows a *profectio* (the Emperor sets out from Rome), *lustratio* (ritual purification of the army at the camp), *adlocutio* (address by the Emperor before battle), *captivi* (presentation of prisoners to the Emperor), *clementia* (pardoning of prisoners by the Emperor), *rex datus* (the appointment by the Emperor of a king to rule over the defeated), *aduentus* (return of the Emperor to Rome by the *Porta Triumphalis*), and *liberalitas* (granting of largesse to the people in the Forum of Trajan). The second series shows *deditio* (surrender of an enemy), *triumphus* (triumphal entry of Marcus and Commodus on a chariot through an arch), and *sacrificium* (sacrifice by the Emperor on the Capitoline at the end of the triumph).

The energetic Septimius Severus, who was born at Lepcis Magna in North Africa, became emperor in 193, and died at York in 211, is commemorated in Rome by two surviving arches. The larger and more prominent one closes off the north-east corner of the Forum Romanum [4.5]. The huge inscription (which originally had gilded bronze letters) is repeated all across the attic of each face: it records the dedication of the arch by the Senate and People in 203 to Septimius Severus and his sons Marcus Aurelius Antoninus, nicknamed Caracalla, and Lucius Septimius Geta, to commemorate their 'restoration of the republic' and extension of the Empire. The former refers to Severus's defeat of his rivals for the throne, while the latter refers to the victories over the Parthians in two campaigns, the first in 195 and the second ending in victory in 203. It was to these that the decoration of the arch was

4.5 The Arch of Septimius Severus in the Roman Forum, dedicated in 203.

devoted. Geta's name was replaced with superfluous verbiage after his murder by his brother in 212. The arch was the first major monument built in the Forum for eighty years, and represents the Severan dynasty's desire to make its mark. The relationship with Augustus's Parthian arch, across the Forum, may well have been significant.[18]

The arch stood at the western end of the Sacra Via, but no road actually went through it: it stood on a travertine platform, which could only be reached by steps. It has three openings, and is 21 m high and 23 m wide. It is built mostly of travertine and marble, with some brick and concrete in the attic. Most, and possibly all, of the marble is Proconnesian.[19] The four detached columns on each side are fluted, with Composite capitals.

The principal sculptural ornament takes the form of four large panels over the side arches. They show episodes from the Parthian wars, in chronological order from the left side of the Forum façade to the right side of the Capitoline façade. Herodian tells us that after his final victory, the taking of Ctesiphon, Septimius Severus sent back to Rome large paintings illustrating the campaigns: these probably served as models.[20] Each panel represents a series of events shown one above the other. The technique is closely related to that of the reliefs on the Column of Marcus Aurelius. In the spandrels of the central

4.6 Giovacchino & Pietro Belli (1756–1822 and 1780–1828), Arch of Septimius Severus, c. 1808–15. Marble and gilt bronze, 63 × 57 × 27.5 cm (whole object).

46   THE TRIUMPHAL ARCH

openings there are the usual flying Victories, beneath which stand figures of the Genii of the seasons. The spandrels of the side openings contain figures of river-gods on rocky backgrounds. On the keystones are various deities. Beneath the large panels are narrow strips, with scenes of procession (either Severus's triumph or his return to Rome). The plinths have reliefs of Roman soldiers and barbarian captives. From coins, and recent investigations, we know that on top of the arch there was a chariot drawn by six horses; on either side was an equestrian statue (Caracalla and Geta ?), and there may well have been standing figures between these and the chariot [4.6].

The ground level around the arch gradually rose until it almost reached the side keystones. A medieval street ran through it, and a tower (or possibly two towers) was built on top. That is how Marten van Heemskerck represented it in 1535; the tower was taken down soon afterwards. The lower part of the arch was excavated from 1802 under the direction of Carlo Fea by Giuseppe Camporese and T. Zappati. It has suffered badly from atmospheric pollution, and efforts have been made recently to restore it.[21]

The second surviving 'arch' in honour of Septimius Severus and his family is only slightly later than the Forum arch. This is the so-called Arcus Argentariorum, of which one of the piers was incorporated in 683 into the side of the church of San Giorgio in Velabro [4.7]. There are two particularly remarkable features. One is that it is not strictly an arch, as it consists merely of two piers (whose plain travertine lower parts are

4.7 Arch of the Argentarii, or Goldsmith's Gate, Rome, 1860s. Albumen silver print from glass negative.

AFTER NERO IN ITALY   47

now buried for over half their height) supporting an architrave. The piers are articulated by pilasters which are decorated with foliage and candelabra motifs, military emblems, and Composite capitals. The other peculiarity is that the monument was erected by a private 'guild'. The inscription identifies its members as *argentarii et negotiantes boari huius loci qui inuehent* ('bankers and cattle-dealers of this place who are importers'). This explains the arch's location on the final stretch of the Vicus Iugarius, where some argue that it must have served as the monumental entrance to the Forum Boarium, the cattle market. Others doubt this, not least because the northern side of the arch was blank. Another suggestion is that it was the entrance to the collegiate *schola*. It is likely that it was intended to thank the Emperor for favours granted.

The inscription records that the arch was built between December 203 and December 204. It was originally intended to honour Severus, Caracalla, Geta, Severus's wife Julia Domna, Caracalla's wife Plautilla, and the latter's father, the powerful Praetorian Prefect Plautianus. However, after the fall of Plautianus and the deaths of Plautilla and Geta their names had to be removed from the inscription (and again replaced with verbiage), and their images had to be erased from the reliefs. These are executed in the Hymettian marble which clothes the whole monument. The two principal reliefs are on either side of the passageway. Both show scenes of sacrifice. On the east side are Septimius Severus and Julia Domna, who holds a *caduceus*; another figure, probably Geta, has been erased. On the west is Caracalla, and here it seems that two figures, perhaps Plautilla and Plautianus, have disappeared. Above each relief is a panel with two Victories holding a garland; below are a narrow band of sacrificial instruments and a panel with on the east the sacrifice of a bull, and on the west another sacrifice. On the architrave the inscription is flanked by reliefs of Hercules and a Genius. The reliefs on the south front of the western pier are much worn, but include another sacrifice of a bull. The only surviving panel from the eastern pier is now set on the northern side of the western pier. On the west side of the western pier the principal relief shows Roman soldiers and Parthian prisoners, an allusion to the Parthian victories celebrated by the Forum arch. Above is a panel with four men and an incense-burner, a scene relating to the imperial cult, while the surviving part of the frieze below shows animals led by a man (perhaps booty). There may have been an attic above the surviving cornice, and there were probably gilded bronze statues of the members of the imperial family commemorated on top. Jas Elsner draws attention to the curious fact that whereas this arch bears scenes of sacrifice, the Forum arch has none. There is no obvious explanation for this.[22]

Caracalla as emperor (211–17) was responsible for building an arch to carry the new aqueduct which fed his great bath-complex over the Via Appia. Known traditionally as the 'Arch of Drusus', because of its mistaken identification with the arch erected in honour of Drusus on the Via Appia (see p. 9), it stands a short way north of the Porta San Sebastiano in the Aurelianic Walls. It has one opening, and is built of rubble and travertine, originally clad in marble. On the south side the applied order survives – a pair of detached columns of yellow Numidian marble, on attached bases, which, like the Composite capitals, are of white marble. The entablature breaks forward over these. The attic had a marble pediment attached on each side. On either side of the arch broad, plain arches carried the aqueduct. There is no evidence for any sculptural decoration, nor for any commemorative purpose, and it may simply have formed a decorative entrance to the city, until the construction of the Aurelianic Walls.[23]

Renaissance sources refer to an 'Arcus Gordiani' to the south-west of the Castra Praetoria. This presumably commemorated Gordian III, acclaimed emperor by the Praetorian guards in 238, when he was thirteen. Various fragments have been attributed to it, but we have no certain information about its appearance or location. It might have been erected in connection with the triumph held in 242 to celebrate victories over the Parthians. It was demolished by Cardinal Riario so that the materials could be used for the construction of the Palazzo della Cancelleria, completed in 1517.[24]

The so-called Arch of Gallienus is now recognised as having originally been built in the late Augustan period as a gate (the Porta Esquilina) in the Servian Walls [4.8]. It now consists of a single arch in travertine, with Corinthian pilasters, but was originally triple. The association with Gallienus (emperor 253–68) derives from an inscription

4.8 The Arch of Gallienus at Rome, late Augustan but dedicated to Gallienus after 253.

AFTER NERO IN ITALY   49

which appears on both sides, not on the frieze but on the architrave below it. This records a dedication to Gallienus, described as *princeps*, and his mother Salonina, described as *Augusta*, by the unknown Aurelius Victor, described merely as *uir egregius* ('a distinguished man'). It seems that the original Augustan inscription on the friezes was chiselled off, and strips of marble were fixed over the friezes. Emilio Rodriguez Almeida argues that these must have borne the principal part of the new inscription dedicating the arch to Gallienus's father (and co-emperor from 253 to 260) Valerian, in anticipation of his triumphal return from his eastern expedition of 259; when this ended in disaster, with Valerian's capture, the marble strips were removed. There is, however, a certain implausibility in the idea of the inscription being set up in advance. Whether any other minor additions were made to the arch (for example, sculpture on the attic) is unknown.[25]

Diocletian became emperor in 284, and in 293 set up the tetrarchic system, with pairs of Augusti and Caesares in both west and east. What the Regionary Catalogues and the so-called 'Chronographer of the year 354' call the Arcus Novus dates from this period. They tell us that it was on the Via Lata (the modern Corso), and was erected under Diocletian and Maximian. It must have been the arch destroyed in 1491 for the construction of the new church of Santa Maria in Via Lata. Parts of its relief sculpture were discovered in excavations in 1523, 1923 and 1933. The reliefs found in 1523 were transferred in 1584 from the Palazzo della Valle to the Villa Medici, where they remain, built into the rear façade. They all come from monuments of the Claudian period, with the figures of important men altered in the 'tetrarchic' style. Some of them, including a relief showing a sacrificial procession to a temple, come from the altar known as the *Ara Pacis* (or *Ara Gentis Iuliae*), while four other fragments are probably also Claudian.[26] These show the Emperor with the figure of Virtus-Roma; the personification of a barbarian race; and Venus Genetrix between a flying Eros and two kneeling personifications of cities, writing on a shield the imperial victories. This has been reworked with the words *VOTIS X ET XX* so as to commemorate the recurrence of the Decennalia of the Augusti in 293–4 (the celebration held every ten years – the 'ten' looking back to the previous ten years, and the 'twenty' looking forward to the next ten).

The proximity of the Arcus Novus to the Arch of Claudius, and the reuse of Claudian reliefs, have suggested that it may have been intended to celebrate the tetrarchic victory of 293 over Carausius in Britain – the province whose conquest was commemorated by the Arch of Claudius. In fact, it even appears from fragments discovered in 1933 that architectural elements of the Arch of Claudius were reused, as well as other elements from a building of the second century AD. From the fragments it can be deduced that the Arcus Novus had three openings, half-columns with Corinthian capitals, and flying Victories in the spandrels.[27]

The tetrarchic system eventually collapsed, and Constantine became sole emperor in 324. A crucial stage in the process was his victory over Maxentius, who ruled Italy, at the battle of the Milvian Bridge in 312. The victory was commemorated by the Arch of Constantine at Rome, the most celebrated of all ancient arches, and the one which has most often served as model for later ones [4.9]. As with the Arcus Novus, its decorative elements were largely reused from earlier monuments. In his novel about Constantine's mother, *Helena* (1950, chapter 8), Evelyn Waugh provides an amusing idea of the reason for this. Constantine asks why his arch is not yet finished, and complains that

4.9 The Arch of Constantine at Rome, (?) 315.

the sculpture is 'atrocious': 'Your figures are lifeless and expressionless as dummies ... Why, damn it, there's something there that looks like a doll that's supposed to be Me.' He wants sculpture like that on 'the arch of Trajan', but is told that no contemporary could match it. 'Then, God damn it, go and pull the carvings off Trajan'a arch, and stick them on mine. Do it at once. Start this afternoon.' 'Spoken like a man, my son, said Helena.'

The question of the reused materials has recently been assumed into a much more fundamental debate about the origin of the arch itself. In 1912 A.L. Frothingham advanced the theory that it was one of those erected in honour of Domitian (see p. 40).[28] This is improbable, as it is unlikely that such an arch could have survived between his *damnatio memoriae* and the time of Constantine. In 1994 A. Mellucco Vaccaro and A.M. Ferroni claimed, on the basis of archaeological investigations around the base of the arch, and study from scaffolding erected for its restoration, that it dated from the time of Hadrian. However their arguments were refuted by Patrizio Pensabene and Clementina Panella.[29]

The arch is situated on the *via triumphalis*, on the axis of the stretch which runs between the Palatine and Caelian Hills (the modern Via San Gregorio), and south-west

AFTER NERO IN ITALY

of the Colosseum. The inscription which appears on both sides of the attic records its dedication by the Senate to Constantine: *quod instinctu diuinitatis mentis magnitudine cum exercitu suo tam de tyranno quam de omni eius factione uno tempore iustis rem publicam ultus est armis arcum triumphis insignem dicauit* (*CIL* VI 1139: 'because, as a result of divine inspiration and his greatness of mind, together with his army he avenged the republic with just weapons, over both the tyrant and his whole party at one time, [the senate] dedicated this arch made remarkable by triumphs'). Further inscriptions describe Constantine as 'liberator of the City' and 'bringer of peace', and also record *votis X votis* and *votis XX*. These references to the Decennalia and Vicennalia may refer (as in the case of the Arcus Novus – see above) back to the previous ten years, and forward to the succeeding ten, in which case the arch would have been erected in connection with the Decennalia of 315.

The overall form of the arch was modelled on that of Septimius Severus. It is interesting to note that the earlier arch is actually represented in the *adlocutio* relief (see below). One notable difference is that the vaults of the passageways in the Arch of Constantine do not have the coffering which is found on that arch and most earlier ones. Its dimensions are closely similar to those of the Arch of Septimius Severus, though it is somewhat wider (21 m high, 25.7 m wide, 7.4 m deep). The central openings are of identical width. The proportions have been analysed by Mark Wilson Jones, who suggests that they are based on a modular system deriving from the height of the four detached giallo antico columns on each side. He comments that this is all the more remarkable considering that the columns, like every single other marble structural part (as is now recognised), were reused from an earlier building.[30]

The base of the arch is of travertine, the piers are of white marble, and the attic is of brick faced with marble slabs. The white marble Corinthian capitals, like the fluted columns of giallo antico, date from the first or second century AD. The column on the north-east corner is a replacement of 1732–3 for that used for the organ gallery of St John Lateran in 1597. Corresponding to the columns are fluted pilasters, also of giallo antico, only one of which is ancient. The architrave projects over the columns. Colour was provided, not just by the yellow columns and pilasters, but by slabs of porphyry (mostly gone) above the side openings and in the recessed panels on the flanks, framing the circular reliefs, and also by the statues at attic level, mostly of pavonazzetto (purplish), but with hands and heads in white marble, and bases of cipollino (green). It seems that on top of the attic there was a kind of parapet, which would rule out the possibility of freestanding sculpture there: this is certainly surprising.[31]

On the other hand, there is a remarkable quantity of figurative sculpture on the arch itself. Most, but not all, comes from earlier monuments. The eight circular reliefs on the principal fronts come from an unidentifiable Hadrianic building. They are arranged in pairs over the side openings, alternating scenes of hunting with scenes of sacrifice, in what cannot have been their original sequence. The heads which formerly represented Hadrian were remodelled to represent Constantine or his father, Constantius Chlorus. They were restored in 1498–9.

The eight statues above the columns, at attic level, have often been said to come from the series of Dacian prisoners in the Forum of Trajan, but it is now considered that they may have been made earlier but not used, and were stored in a depot.[32] Their heads were stolen in 1534 by Lorenzino dei Medici. One statue is modern, and the heads and arms of the rest were made by Pietro Bracci as part of the general restoration of the arch carried out in 1732–3 under Clement XII.[33]

On each side of the inscription in the attic is a pair of relief panels, which come from the arch of Marcus Aurelius (see p. 42). The original portrait heads of Marcus Aurelius must have been replaced with heads of Constantine, though the present heads, mistakenly representing Trajan, are by Bracci. On the flanks of the attic, and at the sides within the central passageway, are four sections of the so-called 'great frieze of Trajan'. In each case the Emperor's head has been reworked to represent Constantine. Although it is assumed that the frieze came from Trajan's Forum, it is not known for certain where it was placed. It is possible that these reliefs, like the statues of Dacians, were retrieved from a store. One of the two panels within the passageway shows the Emperor welcomed by a helmeted female, perhaps Virtus or Dea Roma, and crowned by a winged Victory, with a battle scene behind, while in the other he is on horseback charging the enemy. The attic panels have scenes of battle.

The remaining sculpture is Constantinian. The circular reliefs on the flanks of the arch show, on one side, the rising Sun on a *quadriga*, with a putto above holding a torch and Oceanus below, and on the other the setting Moon [4.10].[34] The plinths of the columns have, on the front, Victories with kneeling barbarians, and on the sides soldiers with prisoners, and trophies with captive families. The spandrels of the central opening on either side have flying Victories, with the Genii of the seasons below, while the side openings have river-gods – as on the Arch of Septimius Severus. The six keystones, much decayed, had allegorical figures or deities. Within the side openings are eight busts. Constantine appears twice, while the others represent imperial personages and deities.

Most important are the reliefs above the side openings, and on the flanks at the same level. The series begins on the west flank, with the departure of the army from Milan; then on the south front come the siege of Verona and the battle of the Milvian Bridge. On the east flank is Constantine's entry into Rome, and finally on the north front come the *adlocutio* of Constantine in the Forum Romanum, and the *congiarium* (distribution of largesse) held on 1 January 313. The *adlocutio* scene shows the Basilica Iulia, the Arch of Tiberius, the Rostra, with the Decennial Monument behind, and the Arch of Septimius Severus.

The idea that these reliefs demonstrate a decline in artistic quality goes back at least to the early sixteenth century. A letter written to Pope Leo X in about 1512–13, attributed to Raphael, gives the

4.10 The Arch of Constantine at Rome, (?) 315.

AFTER NERO IN ITALY 53

arch as an example of how the arts deteriorated in the time of the Late Empire: it praises the architecture and the reliefs dating from the times of 'Trajan and Antoninus Pius', but denounces those of Constantine as insipid and worthless.[35] The same contrast was used by Vasari to indicate the decline in Roman sculpture.[36] It is hardly surprising that Winckelmann agreed, and Sir John Soane called the arch 'the daw dressed in the feathers of the peacock'.[37] The most recent and celebrated instance of the tendency is Bernard Berenson's book *The Arch of Constantine, or The Decline of Form* (1954).

Now, however, it is considered that, although the reliefs cannot be claimed as masterpieces, they reveal an interesting style of their own, possibly based on popular art, and possibly showing oriental influence, with their formal rows of hieratically arranged figures, and – especially in the *adlocutio* and *congiarium* scenes – a preference for frontality. The contrast of styles on the arch would not have caused surprise, as it was traditional in Roman art: Diana Kleiner points out that it goes back at least as far as the Republican so-called Altar of Domitius Ahenobarbus.[38]

The prominent situation, fine state of preservation, and historical importance of the arch ensured that it was a favourite subject for artists and engravers. One of its earliest and most splendid representations is as the principal background feature to one of the frecoes which Sandro Botticelli executed for the Sistine Chapel in 1481–3. It shows the punishment of Korah, Dathan and Abiram, who rebelled against Moses. The reliefs are not depicted with absolute accuracy, and the attic has been provided with a Latin inscription referring to the biblical incident.[39] The arch appears again, twice over, in Perugino's fresco on the opposite wall, which shows the Delivery of the Keys to St Peter. In the background is an octagonal building, intended to represent Solomon's Temple, flanked by identical arches. They are reasonably accurate depictions of the Arch of Constantine, apart from their fanciful attics. The inscription panels bear an elegiac couplet in honour of the Pope.[40] Presumably both Botticelli and Perugino included this particular arch because it was erected by the first Christian Emperor.

A second arch which may have been built by Constantine is the *quadrifrons* known as the Arch of Janus, which stands near Septimius Severus's Arcus Argentariorum (see above), between the Velabrum (on the west) and the Forum Boarium (on the south) [4.11]. The fact that the Cloaca Maxima runs beneath it has suggested that an earlier *ianus* may have stood on the site. Around it was a paved square, but the arch must have been placed in relation to the streets. The structure is square in plan, 16 m high and 12 m wide. The four openings are each 10.6 m high and 5.7 m wide. The arch is built of concrete, covered with marble slabs, many of them taken (as on the Arch of Constantine) from earlier buildings.

Each pier has a plain base with a projecting cornice, while the rest is covered by two tiers of three niches, separated by a cornice. The niches on the east and west fronts are real, as is the central niche of each triplet on the north and south fronts, but the remainder are fictive. The real niches have shell-shaped half-domes. Originally the niches were flanked by small columns resting on the cornices.[41] Another cornice ran along the top. It seems likely that each of the thirty-two real niches contained a statue. The only surviving sculptures are the four keystones – Roma on the eastern one, and on the others perhaps Juno (west), Minerva (north), and Ceres (south).

The concrete vault within the arch incorporates storage jars, to lighten it. Until 1830 there was a brick structure on top: this was removed by Valadier as it was considered to

4.11 The Constantinian Arch of Janus in the Forum Boarium at Rome. Arch of the Argentarii beyond.

be medieval, but it appears that it contained a square chamber surrounded by a passage whose vaulted roof was similar to that below, and so may have been original.[42] Hülsen proposed a restoration with a plain attic slightly set back, with a tall pyramid on top, but there is no good evidence for that. Parts of what may have been the inscription on the attic survive, built into the nearby church of San Giorgio in Velabro. The arch seems to be referred to in the Regionary Catalogues as *arcus Constantini*, and situated in the Velabrum. Its architectural character suits such a date, but nothing else is known of its purpose or occasion. Very much a one-off among surviving arches, it is, as it stands, rather cumbersome in its proportions.

Remains of an arch standing at an ancient bridgehead were discovered in 1878 beneath the Ponte Sisto, which crosses the Tiber south of the Campus Martius. There are remains of another ancient bridge a short distance upstream. In the vicinity an inscription was found referring to the restoration of a *pons Agrippae* by Antoninus Pius in 147. The bridge on the site of the Ponte Sisto was traditionally identified with the Pons Aurelius, and the other with the Pons Agrippae, but Coarelli argues that it is the other way round.[43] One of the surviving fragments is the base of a detached column, bearing a dedication by the Senate to the Emperor Valens, and recording the fact that the bridge was rebuilt by the *praefectus urbis* L. Aurelius Avianus Symmachus (father of the celebrated author). The other base must have borne a dedication to his co-emperor Valentinian I, and the date must have been between 365 and 367. Other fragments were reused from earlier buildings, and the bronze statue, of which parts including the

AFTER NERO IN ITALY 55

feet survive, dated from the first century AD, though its head, and that of its matching twin, must have been replaced with those of Valens and Valentinian.[44]

The arch has generally been reckoned to date from their time, but Coarelli argues that this was the Pons Agrippae, and that the arch is of Augustan date; he suggests that the statues may have represented Augustus and Agrippa. The arch had a single opening, and was linked to the bridge parapet. Covered in white marble, it had detached columns of violet granite (unlikely to be Augustan). The substantial attic had projections corresponding to the projections of the entablature over the columns: the statues stood above these. Coarelli suggests that the bridge linked Agrippa's properties on either side of the river, but he fails to explain why such a bridge should have been marked by such a grandiose commemorative monument.

Another arch at the approach to a bridge, not far away, was built by Valentinian's sons Gratian and Valentinian II and their co-emperor Theodosius in about 380. The inscription, recorded by the Anonymus Einsiedlensis (*CIL* VI 1184), as well as relating to the Pons Aelius (the Ponte Sant'Angelo) states that the Emperors built it to provide a monumental ending to the Porticus Maximae, which ran along the street which led north to the bridge from what was probably the Via Triumphalis (now the Corso Vittorio Emanuele). It stood near the church of San Celso. It collapsed in the fourteenth century, and nothing is known of its form. Its situation is interesting, as it marks the new emphasis in the Christianised city on roads leading to the shrines of martyrs – in this case, of course, St Peter's.[45]

An arch built to commemorate the general Stilicho's suppression of an African revolt in 397–8 is mentioned in Claudian's Panegyric for the sixth consulate of Theodosius's son Honorius (AD 404).[46] Nothing else is known of it. Another arch celebrating a victory of Stilicho, in this case over the Getae, was dedicated by the Senate (the last dedication of an arch by the Senate known to us) to the Emperors Arcadius, his brother Honorius, and Arcadius's son Theodosius II. Its inscription was again transcribed by the Anonymus Einsiedlensis (*CIL* VI 1196). It must have dated from between 402 and 408. Like the two bridge-arches mentioned above, it was situated in the Campus Martius, at the western end, perhaps north of San Giovanni dei Fiorentini. Another medieval source tells us that the arch had lost its marble revetment. The inscription indicates that it was decorated with statues of the Emperors and trophies. It is amusing to recall that Theodosius had only been born in 401.

The so-called Arco di Portogallo has generally been considered to be the last arch built at Rome in antiquity [4.12]. It stood over the Corso – the Via Lata – at the level of the Via delle Vite, opposite the Palazzo Fiano, where the Cardinal of Portugal used to live. It was demolished in 1662 on the order of Alexander VII, as part of his regularisation of the Corso. A marble tablet records its site. Its appearance is known from various drawings, including one in the Codex Destailleur in Berlin, in which the plan is inaccurate, since it shows identical articulation on both sides, whereas the southern side was in fact absolutely plain and smooth. More accurate drawings were made as part of the study of the arch with which Carlo Fontana was entrusted prior to its demolition: his mistaken conclusion that it was not in fact ancient persuaded the Pope that it could be demolished.[47]

The arch had a single opening. Its structure consisted of a travertine core covered in peperino blocks. The attic was of brick. At the sides of each pier were pairs of columns of green marble, with Composite capitals. Their bases were of 'cushion' type. Both the plinths on which they stood, and the projections of the entablature above them, were continuous. The entablature had on it a frieze with spiral foliage. The keystone represented a flying Victory. Columns and entablatures were reused from earlier buildings, and Fontana noted that much of the structural material was also reused. The vault of the opening was smooth. On each pier was a large relief, taken from some other (unknown) monument, and these alone survive, placed, on the Pope's orders, in the Palazzo dei Conservatori. One shows an *adlocutio*, with the bearded Emperor on a podium and a temple to the right, while the other shows the seated Emperor watching the figure of Eternity carrying a woman up into heaven from a blazing pyre. The figure seated on the ground represents the Campus Martius, where members of the imperial family were traditionally cremated. The reliefs are much restored. The Emperor is usually identified as Hadrian, and the woman as his wife Sabina, but Torelli identified them as Antoninus Pius and his wife Faustina (who died in 141).

The arch has usually been dated to the late fifth century. The fact that only its northern side was decorated has suggested that it might have commemorated an imperial *aduentus*. Torelli, however, thinks it might have been erected in connection with the Temple of the Sun built nearby by Aurelian (who ruled from 270 to 275), and intended to mark the line of the *pomerium*

4.12 Giovanni Battista Piranesi, Arco di Portogallo, print, 1762.

which was now superseded by the Aurelianic Walls further north. The *adlocutio* relief would have alluded to Aurelian's wisdom in choosing his successor, while the other would have celebrated the imperial *consecratio* marked nearby by the *ustrina* (places of cremation) and temples of the imperial cult (starting with that of Hadrian).[48]

Italy

It is perhaps surprising that the number of later Roman arches in Italy is comparatively small, but the explanation may lie in the fact that imperial propaganda was considered to be less necessary in Italy than in the Empire.

The only evidence for Flavian arches concerns Domitian, as might be expected, granted his fondness for them (see p. 40). However, of these the only certain example is one near Minturno (Minturnae), on the Campanian coast. This is known from a poem by Statius (*Silvae* IV 13), which celebrated the completion in AD 95 of the Via Domitiana, which ran along the coast from Sinuessa to Puteoli, and so avoided the inland detour of the Via Appia. The situation of the arch has been the source of disagreement, because of the geographical inexactitude of Statius's poem. He introduces the river Volturnus as speaking, while leaning on an arch of Caesar's bridge, and then describes the road as rising up on its 'huge back' (the agger or dyke on which it was raised above the marshy country). 'The gate and prosperous threshold of this [road] is an arch, gleaming with the warlike trophies of our leader, and all the quarries of Liguria [i.e. Luna], as great as that with which Iris crowns the clouds [the rainbow]. There the hurrying traveller turns his journey, there the Appia grieves to be abandoned' (lines 97–101). It seems clear that the arch is situated at the place where the Via Domitiana branches off from the Via Appia. This is some 26 km north of the river Volturnus: the reason why the river is made to speak is no doubt because it was the principal obstacle which the new road had to cross.[49] The use of arches to commemorate road-building has been mentioned several times before (see pp. 9, 11). The trophies presumably celebrated the victories over the Chatti and the Dacians for which Domitian held a double triumph in 89.[50]

It has been suggested that two other arches adorned the Via Domitiana, but there is no evidence that the so-called Arco Felice, just east of Cumae, had any commemorative function: it was intended to protect the road from landslides and link the two sides of the hilltop.[51] The arch at Puteoli, of which fragments survive, is attributed by De Maria to the time of Trajan (see below).

It is possible that two arches honouring Domitian stood on the harbour moles at Ostia, the port of Rome at the mouth of the Tiber. Two reliefs showing harbour scenes include an arch surmounted by a chariot drawn by four elephants. One, in the Museo Torlonia, was found near Trajan's harbour at Ostia, and dates from the Severan period; it shows the arch in profile, with the chariot driven by the garlanded Emperor holding a sceptre and (perhaps) a palm-branch. The other relief is a sarcophagus-front in the Vatican Museum, datable to about the mid-third century. This shows the arch from the front. The single opening is flanked by half-columns. To the right is another arch, this time a *quadrifrons*, apparently astylar, with a *quadriga* drawn by four hippocamps or tritons.

Apart from the find-spot of the Torlonia relief, the identification of the scene as the Portus of Ostia is assured by the representation of its lighthouse in the centre. Neither relief was intended as an accurate topographical picture. In the mid-nineteenth century two quadrangular foundations were discovered in corresponding positions at the points where the harbour-moles started to curve towards the lighthouse. It is likely that these were for the arches. It is odd that their architectural forms do not correspond, but these may have been less interesting to the artists than the elephants. These suggest a comparison with the *quadrifrons* of Domitian near the temple of Fortuna Redux (see p. 41); possibly this one, or these two, also date from his reign, in which case they were obviously not destroyed at his *damnatio memoriae*, but must have been adapted.[52]

An arch at Verona is datable on stylistic grounds to the end of the first century AD. All that survives is a keystone showing the head of Jupiter Ammon, after which the arch is called, but there are a number of Renaissance drawings and engravings of it. These differ from one another, because already in the late fifteenth century the

58 THE TRIUMPHAL ARCH

structure was ruinous. The most reliable reconstruction is by Palladio. This shows a narrow *quadrifrons*, with a very unusual articulation. Each pier, on the principal fronts, has a half-column with spiral fluting on either side, supporting a pediment applied to the attic. The side passageways have architraves supported on pilasters, the space above being occupied by a rectangular frame decorated with foliage and heads. The narrow sides also had passageways with architraves supported on pilasters. The arch stood at the crossroads of the *decumanus maximus* (the Corso Porta Borsari) and one of the *cardines* (Via Quattro Spade).

The several arches erected in Italy in honour of Trajan include two of the most celebrated arches of Roman times – those at Benevento and Ancona. They were almost contemporary, but the one at Beneventum (Benevento) in Campania was marginally

4.13 Arch of Trajan at Benevento, dedicated in 114.

AFTER NERO IN ITALY 59

the earlier [4.13]. The inscription makes clear that it was dedicated by the Senate and People between August and December 114, but gives no reason for its erection. However, the description of Trajan as *fortissimus princeps* (most strong emperor) suggests a connection with his Dacian triumph of 107, and the situation of the arch must be explained by the inauguration of the Via Traiana from Benevento (where it diverged from the Via Appia) to Brindisi, dated to 109 by its milestones.[53] The arch may well have stood on the *pomerium* of the ancient city. Its form is very similar to that of the Arch of Titus at Rome. It has a single opening and piers with half-columns (fluted, with Composite capitals) on either side, and three-quarter columns on the corners. The columns rest on continuous bases. The entablature and the attic break back over the piers. The structure is built is local stone, with Parian marble revetment.

The most remarkable feature of the arch is its lavish sculptural decoration. The reliefs are particularly notable, but their interpretation is much debated. On each pier there is a pair, one above the other, and there is a third at attic level, making a total of twelve large panels. Between the main panels on the piers are narrow ones, each representing two Victories killing bulls, on either side of a candelabrum. Above the upper reliefs are panels showing pairs of young men on either side of incense-burners. The frieze (which runs round all four sides) shows a triumphal procession, presumably that of 107. The spandrels contain, on the town side, two flying Victories, and on the outer side either Oceanus and Tellus (Earth) or two river-gods. On the keystones are unrecognisable female figures. The richly coffered vault of the passageway has in the centre a panel showing Trajan, in breastplate, crowned by Victory, while the cornice has a frieze of weapons. On either side of the passageway are large reliefs. The pilasters which support the archivolt are plain on the outside, but on their inner sides have friezes of tendrils surmounted by eagles. The inscriptions on the central panels of the attic are the same on each side. There was presumably a bronze *quadriga* with a figure of the Emperor on top.

The quality of the principal reliefs is very high, and their state of preservation on the whole excellent, but it is unfortunate that there is so little agreement about what they represent [4.14]. Interpretations have not been assisted by attempts to insist on 'reading' them in some particular order. One of the biggest problems is the generally accepted appearance of Hadrian in one, or possibly two, of the attic reliefs: in 114 he was not yet recognised as Trajan's successor. His adoption is supposed to have taken place on Trajan's deathbed in 117. The simplest explanation is that these reliefs were put up after that event, although the inscriptions remained unaltered (after Trajan's death one would have expected *DIVO TRAIANO OPTIMO PARTHICO*).

The scenes on the reliefs show various military and political aspects of Trajan's rule, including (on the outer side) the making of a pact with German peoples, a visit to a military camp, a recruiting scene, Trajan with two children in the presence of Mars (perhaps a reference to the *alimenta* system, for the upbringing of poor children), Trajan with various divinities, the submission of Mesopotamia, and (on the inner side) the first arrival of Trajan in Rome in 99, Trajan with veterans (perhaps alluding to the foundation of new colonies), Trajan with three merchants in the presence of Portunus (the harbour god), Hercules and Apollo (perhaps alluding to the Emperor's improvements to Italian harbours), and a *profectio* (departure) of Trajan in the presence of various divinities, and also of Hadrian. The background to the latter scene includes an

4.14 Relief of Trajan with barbarian princes on the Benevento arch.

arch with winged females in the spandrels: this was identified by Hassel and Rotili as the Porta Triumphalis, but this seems unlikely (see p. 3). The reliefs within the passageway show Trajan presiding over a sacrificial scene (possibly at the inauguration of the Via Traiana), and a scene almost certainly alluding to the institution of the *alimenta* system, including several children.[54]

The arch was frequently drawn and studied in the Renaissance and later. Giuliano da Sangallo visited it between 1488 and 1490, and several of his drawings survive, as do others from the same period. It was the subject of engravings by Piranesi, Rossini, and others. Nineteenth-century views show it used as a city gate, set between iron railings.[55] In the Fascist era the Comune decided that the arch should be given more 'breathing space'. A first plan was made in 1932, but in 1934 Mussolini gave a copy of the bronze statue of Trajan erected in Rome on the Via dei Fori Imperiali, and a second scheme followed in 1935. Demolition began, and marble statues of Trajan and Plotina (wrongly supposed by some to have stood on top of the arch) were found. In 1938 the creation of a new 'Via Traiana' leading to the arch was approved, but progress was halted by the war. After the town was severely bombed, the reconstruction plan of 1947 finally made the 'Via Arco Traiano' a reality.[56]

By contrast with the arch at Benevento, that at Ancona is almost devoid of sculptural decoration [4.15]. What gives it its distinction is its remarkably tall and narrow proportions, though this elegance is primarily the result of its position on a harbour mole. In this, the arch is comparable to those of Ostia (see above) and Puteoli (see below), and here the occasion for its building is made clear by the inscription, which records its dedication to Trajan by the Senate and People of Rome some time between

AFTER NERO IN ITALY   61

4.15 Arch of Trajan at the harbour of Ancona, dedicated in 114/115.

December 114 and December 115, *quod accessum Italiae hoc etiam addito ex pecunia sua portu tutiorem nauigantibus reddiderit* ('because he made the approach to Italy safer for those travelling by sea by adding this harbour at his own expense'). Subsidiary inscriptions to left and right record dedications to Plotina and Marciana, the Emperor's wife and sister.

The arch originally stood on an octagonal sloping base, lower than the present tall travertine one. The arch itself, built of marble from Hymettus (near Athens), is 14 m high, but only 10 m wide. Its basic form is similar to that of the Benevento arch, though here the order is Corinthian, and the columns stand on articulated podia. The piers are subdivided into three sections by two slender cornices, one at the height of the springing of the arch, the other lower. Below each is a rectangular framed panel. The vault of the passageway is smooth. The only figurative sculpture in marble takes the form of busts on the keystones (perhaps Neptune, on the sea side). There were certainly statues of Trajan (on horseback, or on a *quadriga*(?)), Plotina and Marciana on top, facing the land (the inscriptions only occur on this side), probably in bronze. There was further bronze decoration: on the face of each pier, and also on the sides, appear sets of holes linked by grooves, forming triangles, which may well have held prows of bronze, and holes in the spandrels were perhaps fixings for flying Victories.

Investigations in the 1950s revealed that the arch had an earlier phase, in which three statues on the attic faced the sea, and there were marble acroteria on the corners, but no bronze decoration, and no inscription. This has naturally been related to the arch on a harbour-mole which is shown on Trajan's Column: the scene (no. 79) is usually identified as Ancona. The arch has statues, facing seawards, identified as Portunus, Neptune and Mercury. The event depicted on the Column (dedicated in 113) is Trajan's departure for the Second Dacian War, which took place in 105. There are problems in the identification: for example, Trajan's arch stands at the landward end of the mole, but the arch on the Column at the seaward end. Whether the arch was really in existence in 105 is hard to say: it could have been merely projected. That arch was presumably not dedicated to the Emperor, and had the function simply of marking the 'approach to Italy'. At any rate, it is certainly more economical to assume that the arch shown on the Column is the same as the one dedicated to the Emperor in 115.[57]

The present high base dates back to the arrangement made in the later fifteenth century, though the steps were remade in 1857–9. Pope Sixtus V (1585–90) enlarged the harbour, and the architect Giacomo Fontana proposed to commemorate this by adding Sixtus's symbols on top of the arch.[58] Trajan's arch was joined in 1735–6 by a new arch, in honour of Clement X, who had abolished the port taxes in 1732, and had the harbour enlarged by Luigi Vanvitelli (see p. 184). In 1936 a scheme was drawn up by Edoardo Galli for tidying up the surroundings of the arch, which would be approached by a long ramp flanked by trees and bushes.[59] This never happened, and the arch's surroundings, within the restricted port area, are appealingly workmanlike – even if not quite so melodramatic as when it was flanked by a dry dock used for large vessels, shown in the painting by Sir Frank Brangwyn in Wolverhampton Art Gallery [4.16].

The existence of an arch in honour of Trajan at Puteoli (Pozzuoli) has been deduced from two marble reliefs found there, now in Berlin and Philadelphia (at the University Museum). The latter shows a soldier standing within a rectangular niche, holding

4.16 Frank Brangwyn, Arch of Trajan at Ancona.

a lance and shield. The Berlin relief, which fits onto the other at right angles, has a similar figure on the right, and remains of two marching soldiers on the left. It has been argued that they decorated the base of one of the piers of an arch, similar in form to that at Ancona. The Philadelphia relief is carved out of a block of marble on the other side of which is an erased inscription in honour of Domitian, dated to 95–6.[60] The style of the sculpture suggests an attribution to the reign of Trajan. The find-spot of one relief is unknown, and the other was among reused material. Kähler suggested that the arch might have commemorated the completion of the new road from Pozzuoli to Naples, in 102, and might have stood at its beginning.[61]

It is perhaps surprising that only one arch in Italy can be dated, though without certainty, to the reign of Hadrian. This is the so-called 'Arco del Sacramento' at Benevento. It stood free at the south-west edge of the Forum (now occupied by the Duomo). On travertine bases stand piers of brick-faced concrete containing niches: the southern ones presumably held statues, but the northern ones are too shallow. The attic has a large arched opening in the centre, corresponding to the opening beneath. Of the marble revetment there survives merely the cornice below the vault of the passageway.[62] The piers probably had pairs of freestanding columns. The only argument for dating the structure is the similarity of its building techniques to those of the nearby theatre, inaugurated in 126: the arch would have provided an entrance to the Forum from the theatre.[63]

It seems likely that two towns honoured Antoninus Pius with arches. Evidence for a pair on the harbour mole at Puteoli comes from two unusual sources – first, a series of late third–fourth-century glass bottles preserved in various locations, and, second, a painting found on the Esquiline at Rome in 1668, now lost, but known from drawings.

It is not easy to reconcile the various representations, but it seems that one arch stood at the seaward end, and the other towards the landward end. Whether they were double or triple arches is unclear, and they may have been *quadrifrontes*. The seaward arch appears to have had a *quadriga* of hippocamps, drawn by Neptune, facing the sea, while the landward arch had four tritons, holding tridents and blowing trumpets. Despite this mythological ornamentation, the most probable occasion for their erection is provided by two inscriptions (*CIL* X 1640–41) recording a dedication to Antoninus Pius in thanks for his restoration of the mole, which had been destroyed by the sea.[64]

There were three other arches at Puteoli, of uncertain date. One, near the Forum, is known from two sculpted marble voussoirs (now lost): it seems to have given its name to the *regio portae triumphalis*. Two triple arches are known to have stood on the quay north of the mole, from remains of their piers which were visible until the early nineteenth century. The existence of four arches connected with the harbour makes an interesting comparison with Ostia and Ancona (see above).

The other town which may have honoured Antoninus Pius is Capua, also in Campania (now Santa Maria Capua Vetere). Part of an arch still stands over the main road (the former Via Appia), south-west of the amphitheatre, at the western approach to the Roman town. What survives is only the southern opening of a triple arch. Built of brick-faced concrete, on tall travertine plinths, it has niches on either side of the opening, presumably for statues, and shallow rectangular niches, presumably for reliefs, within. Given the substantial size of the surviving part, the whole must have been very large. The structural technique suggests a date *c.* 160, which would coincide with the dedication of the amphitheatre by Antoninus Pius.

Capua was also the site of an arch which may have honoured Septimius Severus. Beloch saw the remains of the piers of an arch near the sanctuary of Diana Tifatina, about 3 km north of the town, and associated them with an inscription of 196 dedicated by the Colonia Capua to that Emperor.[65] His son Caracalla was certainly honoured by an unusual pair of arches at Ostia. These stood over the *decumanus* at a distance of about 13.5 m from each other, between the curved outer wall of the theatre and the portico in front of the houses opposite. Each seems to have been decorated only on the outer side. Parts of the piers survive. From these it appears that freestanding columns, with Composite capitals, flanked the opening, and supported an articulated entablature in Luna marble. The attics had inscriptions, on panels of Proconnesian marble, the surviving one of which (the eastern one) is a dedication to Caracalla of the year 216. The effect of the arches would have been to emphasise the intervening space, presumably as the principal entrance to the theatre, which was enlarged by Septimius Severus and Caracalla. It has been suggested (without evidence) that this space might have been covered.

Two Italian arches were erected in honour of Constantine. The massive structure of the first still stands at Malborghetto, about 19 km north of Rome, on the Via Flaminia [4.17]. The constructional technique suggests a date in the early fourth century, which makes it likely that the arch was built to commemorate Constantine's victory over Maxentius in 312 at Saxa Rubra, on the site of his camp before the battle – the place where he had his vision of the *signum Christi*. The structure survives because it was adapted as a farmhouse; to its south stands a small chapel of 1742–4. Built of brick-faced concrete, the *quadrifrons* is 15 m wide on its north and south fronts, and 12

4.17 Arch at Malborghetto commemorating Constantine's victory over Maxentius in 312.

m wide on its east and west fronts; its original height was probably just under 18 m. Another road crossed the Flaminia at this point. Within, the crossing is vaulted. Stone blocks run around the structure at the height of the springing of the arches, and marble blocks of the architrave remain on the corners. Other marble fragments have been discovered. As one would expect at this date, some of the marble blocks are reused (inscriptions or the like). The attic has been raised in modern times, and now has a gabled roof. Within are three rooms, reached by a staircase in the south-east pier. An inscription on glazed tiles records a restoration in 1567, under Pius V.

A drawing by Giuliano da Sangallo provides a lavish reconstruction of the arch, with freestanding columns on two sides and pilasters on the others, large relief panels of weapons on each pier, and three relief panels at attic level. Above is a pediment, and over that a conical superstructure. Curiously this is shown as ruinous, and it may relate to a reference to the arch in a thirteenth-century document as a *trullum* (a circular structure). There is no other reason to suppose that Sangallo had any real evidence for any of this, except that another drawing shows a relief of weapons like that drawn by him. It seems that the arch had a pair of freestanding Corinthian columns on either side of each pier, on the main fronts; at the sides their bases were shared by corner pilasters. There was a tall attic, articulated above the columns by pilasters.[66]

The other arch honouring Constantine was in fact erected as the eastern gate of Fanum Fortunae (Fano), on the Adriatic coast south of Pesaro, when Augustus built the walls, as its inscription of AD 9/10 records (*CIL* XI 6218–19) [4.18]. Only the external side survives, the inner side having been remodelled in 1625. The gate faced the 3-km road which linked the town to the Via Flaminia. Built of stone, it has a large central opening and smaller side ones. The only architectural decoration consists of mouldings around the central archivolt, running back under the vault, and a keystone decorated with an animal head. Above are an architrave, a plain frieze on which the Augustan inscription was set in bronze letters, and a dentilled cornice. Only fragments survive of the original upper stage, which consisted of seven small arches set between Corinthian semicolumns; it was destroyed in 1493 by the artillery of Federico da Montefeltro.

Two further inscriptions recorded the dedication of the 'gate-arch' to Constantine (described as *pater dominorum*) under the agency of L. Turcius Secundus Asterius, who was *praefectus Urbis* in 339 (Constantine had died in 337). Only one word survives of the upper inscription, but it is reproduced in a relief showing the gate which is built into the façade of the little church of San Michele (completed in 1504) which stands to the south of the gate. It is possible that the dedication to Constantine also involved the addition of a statue. It is not known whether it was made in gratitude for a favour conferred by him on the town.

The last ancient arch in Italy stood at Mediolanum (Milan), where in the mid-fourth century the *decumanus maximus* was lined, where it ran south-east beyond the

4.18 Gate at Fano built in 9/10 but later dedicated to Constantine, with the relief on S. Michele.

walls, with porticoes 600 m long. At the end stood a *quadrifrons*. In this way the approach from Rome was monumentalised. The foundations of the arch (11 × 13 m) have been excavated. Medieval texts add little to our knowledge of its form. It survived until the siege by Federico Barbarossa in 1162. The arch seems to have stood apart from the porticoed street. It is considered to have been erected under the Emperor Gratian, who resided at Milan from 381.[67]

Notes

1. *Mitteilungen des deutschen archäologischen Instituts: Römische Abteilung*, 97 (1990), 127–36.
2. *CIL* VI 944.
3. Some scholars have argued that the arch originally had only one opening, and can be identified with that on the Haterii relief, which has a *quadriga* on top and a statue of the Magna Mater in the opening, but this is denied by De Maria 1988, 285–7, 292–3. Circuses throughout the Roman Empire regularly had a monumental arch set in the semicircular end, either single or triple, but none has an inscription, or sculptural decoration, so no commemorative purpose can be ascertained. See John H. Humphrey, *Roman Circuses* (London, 1986), 36 (Lepcis Magna), 308 (Cherchel), 311 (Sétif), 357 (Toledo), 368–9 (Mérida), 451 (Antioch), 469 (Tyre), 592–3 (Rome, Circus of Maxentius).
4. J.B. Ward-Perkins, *Roman Imperial Architecture* (Harmondsworth, 1981), 73.
5. John Evelyn was so impressed with this relief as a link between ancient Rome and Christian scripture that in 1645 he commissioned a drawing of it from Carlo Maratti (Antony Griffiths, *NACF Review* (1992), 35–7). See also L. Yarden, *The Spoils of Jerusalem on the Arch of Titus* (Stockholm, 1991).
6. Repairs had been carried out under – among others – Sixtus IV (1472–84). The standard work on the arch is M. Pfanner, *Der Titusbogen* (Mainz am Rhein, 1983).
7. Ian Campbell, *The Codex Stosch* (Lyon and Turnbull sale catalogue, Edinburgh, 2005), 13–14, 46).
8. *Roma Antiqua: Envois des architectes français (1788–1924) – Forum, Colisée, Palatin* (Rome/Paris, 1985), 292–303.
9. Olivier Poisson, 'Caristie et Valadier', *Bull. de la Société d'histoire de l'art français* (1991), 187–94.
10. Alexander the Great was sometimes shown in a chariot drawn by elephants. Later Dionysus is shown returning from India in one. Pompey tried to enter Rome in one after his African victory of 81 BC, but it could not pass through the gate. Coins show Augustus, Caligula, Claudius and Vespasian similarly. Several later emperors did the same, Caracalla being said to have deliberately imitated Alexander. Elephants had a complex symbolism, including a reputation for piety, but their size and exotic origin were obviously important factors (H.H. Scullard, *The Elephant in the Greek and Roman World* (London, 1975), 254–8.
11. The temple seems to have dated back at least to the time of Tiberius (*CIL* VI 8705), and was probably only restored by Domitian. See *LTUR s.v.* Fortuna Redux, Templum.
12. Coarelli is of the opinion that the temple must have been the Temple of Fortuna in the Area Sacra of Sant' Omobono (*LTUR* 1996, II, 275–6. He refers there to an *LTUR* entry on the Porta Triumphalis, but there is none).
13. H. Lyngby, *Opuscula Romana*, 8 (1974), 44–5. On Martial's epigram, see Christian Schöffel, *Martial, Buch 8* (Stuttgart, 2002), 541–53. He considers that the arch was an enhancement of the Porta Triumphalis.
14. Excavations carried out in 1992 around the Arch of Constantine revealed a large foundation in conglomerate which the excavators identified as the base of one of Domitian's arches, dismantled after his death (M.L. Conforto et al., *Adriano e Costantino: le due fasi dell'Arco nella Valle del Colosseo* (Milan, 2001), 112.
15. James E. Packer, *The Forum of Trajan in Rome* (Berkeley, Calif./London, 1997), 85–95; James E. Packer in *LTUR* II, 350; R. Meneghini, *Mitteilungen des deutschen archäologischen Instituts – Römische Abteilung*, 108 (2001), 245–64.
16. *LTUR* III, 8 (M.Cipollone).
17. De Maria 1988, 303–5; E. Angelicoussis, *RM* 91 (1984), 141–205; M. Torelli in *LTUR s.v.*. Torelli suggests that Marcus's arch might have stood on the site of the Arch of Constantine, who put the inscription and four unused panels on a new arch (the one known as *Panis Aurei*), sited on the Clivus Argentarius, on the slopes of the Capitoline.
18. The principal account of the arch is R. Brilliant, *The Arch of Septimius Severus in the Forum Romanum, Mem. Amer. Acad.*, 29 (1967). The first scholarly monograph on it was by Bishop Joseph-Marie Suares, *Arcus Septimii Severi Aug. Anaglypha cum Explicatione* (Rome, 1676), with plates by Pietro Santi Bartoli: it commemorated a restoration by Cardinal Francesco Barberini. For recent investigations, see R. Nardi, *Monumentum*, 27 (1984), 343–61; Soprintendenza archeologica di Roma, *Roma, Archeologia nel Centro*, I, *L'area archeologica centrale* (Rome, 1985), 34–55.
19. Brilliant describes it as mostly of Pentelic, with Proconnesian columns, and the relief panels probably of Luna (Carrara), but see M. Bruno, C. Gargoni and P. Pallante in P. Pensabene and C. Panella, eds, *Arco di Costantino* (Rome, 1999), 164.

20 Herodian III 9.12: τὰς μάχας τε καὶ τὰς νίκας δημοσίαις ἀνέθηκε γραφαῖς.
21 On the disinterment of the arch see M. Jonsson, *La Cura dei monumenti alle origini* (Stockholm, 1986), 21–4.
22 Jas Elsner, 'Sacrifice and Narrative on the Arch of the Argentarii at Rome', *JRA* 18 (2005), 83–98. There are two monographs on the arch: D.E.L. Haynes and P.E.D. Hirst, *Porta Argentariorum* (London, 1939); and M. Pallottino, *L'Arco degli Argentari* (Rome, 1946).
23 *LTUR* 1996, I, 93 (C. Pisani Sartorio); De Maria 1988, 272–4, 309.
24 *LTUR* I, 95 (M. Torelli).
25 *LTUR* I, 93–4 (E. Rodriguez Almeida); De Maria 1988, 191, 311–12.
26 *LTUR* I, 101–2 (M. Torelli); De Maria (1988, 312–4) and others think that they are second-century, probably Antonine.
27 Plinths with reliefs of Victories, barbarian prisoners and the Dioscuri, now in the Boboli Gardens in Florence, used to be attributed to the Arcus Novus, since they also came from the Palazzo della Valle, but they are now thought to come from a different monument.
28 *AJA* 16 (1912), 368–86.
29 Mellucco Vaccaro and Ferroni first published their argument in *Rendiconti della Pontificia Accademia di Archeologia*, 66 (1993–4), 1–60, and it was reaffirmed in the exhibition catalogue *Adriano: Architettura e Progetto* (2000), 107–55, and in M.L. Conforto, A. Mellucco Vaccaro, P. Cicerchia, G. Calcani and A.M. Ferroni, *Adriano e Costantino: le due fasi dell'arco nella valle del Colosseo* (Milan, 2001). Pensabene and Panella first published their view in the same journal, 111–283, and later edited *Arco di Costantino tra archeologia e archeometria* (Rome, 1999). F.S. Kleiner's supportive review of this book in *JRA* 14 (2001), 661–3, usefully summarises the arguments.
30 Mark Wilson Jones, *Principles of Roman Architecture* (New Haven/London, 2000), 123–6. See also his contribution to *Arco di Costantino tra archeologia e archeometria* (cit. in the preceding note), pp. 75–99.
31 Some reconstructions of the arch have understandably included a *quadriga*: an example is the model made in 1808–15 by Giovacchino and Pietro Belli in the Royal Collection (Jane Roberts, ed., *Royal Treasures: A Golden Jubilee Celebration* (London, 2002), 139–40).
32 Pensabene and Panella (cit. at n. 29), 33. Pensabene claims that the inscription AD ARC[UM] ('for the arch') on the base of one of the statues supports this argument.
33 This is commemorated by an inscription on the west flank; see also Giambattista Gaddi, *Roma nobilitata nelle sue fabbriche dalla Santità di N.S. Clemente XII* (Rome, 1736).
34 Quarter-size versions of these reliefs were modelled by Thomas Banks during his stay in Rome (1772–9). In 1801 John Soane commissioned copies of them to be set above the side openings of the triumphal arch which framed the entrance to Bullion Court in the Bank of England. Casts of them were also set on the pendentives of the Old Dividend Office (1818–23). These parts of the Bank have been demolished, but Thomas Banks' original terracottas survive in the Soane Museum. See C.F. Bell, ed., *Annals of Thomas Banks* (Cambridge, 1938), 147.
35 For this letter see M.L. Conforto et al., *Adriano e Costantino* (cit. at n. 29), 11–14; I.D. Rowland, *The Culture of the High Renaissance* (Cambridge, 1998), 229.
36 G. Vasari, *Le Vite* (Florence, 1967), II, 14, in the *Proemio delle Vite*.
37 Sir John Soane (ed. D. Watkin), *Sir John Soane: Enlightenment Thought and the Royal Academy Lectures* (Cambridge, 1996), 549.
38 Diana E.E. Kleiner, *Roman Sculpture* (New Haven/ London, 1992), 454–5.
39 Ronald Lightbown, *Sandro Botticelli: Life and Work* (London, 1989), 102–11. An arch, less closely based on that of Constantine, appears in the *History of Lucretia* (ibid., 261–9; P. Hendy, *Catalogue of the Exhibited Paintings and Drawings: Isabella Stewart Gardner Museum* (Boston, 1931), 66–9.
40 P. Scarpellini, *Perugino* (Milan, 1984), 77.
41 An engraving of 1560 shows the arch with the columns restored. It is based on a drawing of c. 1550 (in the Victoria and Albert Museum), ascribed to an unknown French engraver called Flaminio.
42 Giovanna Tedone, 'La fabbrica superiore dell'Arco di Giano', *Bollettino di archeologia*, 23–4 (1993), 195–202. Early sixteenth-century artists included the attic in their reconstructions (Campbell [cit. at n. 7], 15–16, 46–7).
43 F. Coarelli, *LTUR* IV, 107–8.
44 For the bronze fragments see M.R. Di Mino and M. Bertinetti, eds, *Archeologia a Roma: la materiale e la tecnica nell'arte antica* (Rome, 1990), 107–10.
45 *LTUR* s.v. Porticus Maximae (F. Coarelli).
46 Claudian, *Paneg. De VI cons. Honori Aug.* 369–73.
47 A. Angelini, M. Butzek and B. Sani, *Alessandro Chigi (1599–1667): Il Papa Senese di Roma Moderna* (Siena, 2000), 307–8.
48 M. Torelli, *LTUR* I, 77–9; see also his article in *Ostraka*, 1 (1992), 105–31. For engravings of the arch see E. Nash, *Pictorial Dictionary of Ancient Rome* (London/New York 1961–2), I, 83–4. De Maria reproduces the Destailleur drawing and a reconstruction by S. Stucchi.
49 The Volturnus bridge is described by M.W. Frederiksen in *Campania* (British School at Rome, 1984), 18, as 'a great piece of engineering', not replaced until the 1950s. He also points out (p. 20) that Volturnus's speech emphasises the amount of land reclamation which the road must have required.
50 On the passage of Statius, see *Statius Silvae IV*, ed. by K.M. Coleman (Oxford, 1988), *ad loc*. De Maria 1988, 239, follows Kähler 1939 (col. 413) in locating the arch at the bridge, at the modern Castel Volturno. A. Maiuri, *I Campi Flegrei* (4th edn, Rome, 1963), 104, rightly locates it at the deviation.

51 P. Amalfitano, G. Camodeca and M. Medri, *I Campi Flegrei* (Venice, 1990), 308–9. See also M.E. Blake, *Roman Construction in Italy from Tiberius through the Flavians* (Washington, D.C., 1959), 142.
52 De Maria 1988, with pls 25–6 and fig. 26: R. Meiggs, *Roman Ostia* (2nd edn, Oxford, 1973), 150, 159. For harbour arches see S. Fähndrich, *Bogenmonumente in der römischen Kunst* (Rahden, 2005), 229–40.
53 Another arch which may have been built to commemorate the opening of the Via Traiana is that at Canusium (Canosa). Built of brick and concrete, it has a single opening flanked by pairs of plain pilasters. Situated outside the town, to the north-west, it was certainly on the line of the road. However, it could also have been erected to mark the *pomerium* when the town became a *colonia* under Antoninus Pius, or it could be a private monument.
54 The most substantial monograph on the arch is M. Rotili, *L'arco di Traiano a Benevento* (Rome, 1972). For much good sense on the interpretation of the reliefs, see F.A. Lepper's review of F.J. Hassel, *Der Trajansbogen in Benevent* (Mainz, 1966), in *JRS* 59 (1969), 250–61. On them see also K. Fittschen, 'Das Bildprogramm des Trajansbogen zu Benevent', *AA* 87 (1972), 742–88; Erika Simon, *Die Götter am Trajansbogen zu Benevent* (Mainz, 1981).
55 See Rotili (cit. in the preceding note).
56 S.A. Muscettola et al., eds, *Benevento: L'Arco e la Città* (Naples, 1985).
57 On the relationship between the arch shown on Trajan's Column and that at Ancona, see F.A. Lepper, *JRS* 59 (1969), 255–7.
58 W.E. Stöpfel, *Römisches Jahrbuch für Kunstgeschichte*, 12 (1969), 211.
59 *Boll. d'arte*, XXX (1936), 321–35; the article gives an interesting history of the arch since the fifteenth century.
60 On this see *Année épigraphique* (1973), no. 137: it recorded the town's gratitude for the building of the Via Domitiana.
61 Kähler 1939, col. 410. On this road see Amalfitano (cit. at n. 51), 21–3.
62 Architectural fragments attached to the north side do not in fact belong to the arch. On it see F.J. Hassel, *Jahrbuch des römisch-germanischen Zentralmuseums Mainz*, 15 (1968), 95–7.
63 The pair of arches at either side of the Temple of Rome and Augustus at Ostia may go back to the systematisation of the Forum, whose south side they close off, which took place under Hadrian. Only remains of the brick piers survive. There is no indication that they had any commemorative purpose.
64 On the mole, now encased within the modern one, see Amalfitano (cit. at n. 51), 122–3.
65 J. Beloch, *Campanien* (2nd edn, Breslau, 1890), 308, 365.
66 The second drawing is in the Codex Escurialensis (Real Biblioteca del Monasterio de El Escorial, MS 28-I-11), f. 18. The sensitive restoration which took place after the acquisition of the arch by the State in 1982 was followed by the publication of G. Messineo, *Malborghetto* (Rome, 1989), which supersedes F. Töbelmann, *Der Bogen von Malborghetto* (Heidelberg, 1914).
67 Gemma Sena Chiesa, *Milano capitale dell'impero romano 286–402 d. C.* (Milan, 1990).

5
AFTER NERO IN EUROPE OUTSIDE ITALY

France, Germany, Switzerland, Austria

After the remarkable number of arches built in the southern part of Gaul during the early Empire, there are only a few subsequent ones in the north-west part of the Roman Empire which require mention.

One was erected at Vindonissa (Windisch, 27 km north-west of Zurich) in AD 79, by the local inhabitants, in honour of the gods Mars, Apollo and Minerva. The use of an arch for such a purpose is curious, but can be compared with the arch of Dativius Victor at Mainz, and one at Geneva (see below). The Vindonissa arch is known only from an inscription (*CIL* XIII 5195).

Several arches appear to date from the second half of the second century. One at Trier is known only from some carved stones, whose findspot is unknown. They come from a shallow triple arch. The spandrels of the larger central opening had flying Erotes on one side, and, on the other, a half-naked youth and a woman being approached by Eros with a torch. On the smaller archivolts are a flying Victory and a seated woman. Kähler suggests that it might have been a funerary arch.[1]

The so-called 'Porte Noire' at Besançon (Vesontio) is comparatively well preserved, standing over the road which leads up to the cathedral, wedged between later buildings [5.1]. It owes its name to the darkening of the stone (which has now been cleaned). It is tall, measuring 12.36 m, without the attic which surely crowned it. The bases of the piers are medieval. The single opening has pairs of attached half-columns on either side, the cornice of whose articulated entablatures is at the level of the springing of the arch. Each has a corresponding pair of smaller half-columns above. The relationship between the articulation of the piers and the pilasters and archivolt of the arch is most uncomfortable. The upper entablature is continuous between the inner columns; the frieze projects correspondingly, and originally bore the inscription. In the Middle Ages the arch, which had already partially collapsed, was incorporated into a tower where the cathedral sacristan lived. The opening was walled up, leaving only a small arch for access. The arch was restored in 1825 by the town architect, P. Marnotte, but the south side has never been completely revealed.

The arch was covered with elaborate relief sculpture, of which about half is now lost. It is as idiosyncratic as the form of the structure, paying little attention to relative proportion, and showing a distinct *horror vacui*. It has been analysed by Theodor Kraus.[2] The only decorative elements which correspond to what is normally found on an arch

5.1 The Porte Noire at Besançon, of the late 2nd century.

are the Victories (which hold garlands) in the spandrels, and the three historical reliefs set one above the other on either side of the opening. These include battles between Romans and barbarians, the defence of a city, and captives begging the emperor for mercy. Each of the pilasters supporting the archivolt is divided into six rectangles, containing figures which probably represent divinities. On the archivolt is a series of fighting giants; Jupiter may have been shown on the keystone as their conqueror. The left-hand pier on the town side retains its decoration. Between the columns are five bands, showing mythological scenes. The inner column is decorated with rich tendrils. However on the country side of the arch the corresponding column bears six reliefs. Again, on this side one of the surviving pair of upper columns is decorated with bands of figures, the other with leaves.

Kraus points out the peculiarity of reducing the columns to fields for ornament, which negates the architectonic articulation still dominant on a comparably decorated arch such as that of Trajan at Benevento. The nearest parallel he can suggest on an arch is the Porte de Mars at Reims (for which see below), but for this kind of *horror vacui* he cites also the façade of the thermae at Sens, while, for the strange proportional relationships of figures, and the treatment of niches as flat canopies, he compares grave-reliefs from Gaul and Germany, such as those from Neumagen.

As for the significance of the iconography, there is little which relates to the usual 'triumphal' themes. Otherwise, the scenes are taken from Greek mythology, and are again comparable with those on grave-reliefs, on relief-series from the temple precincts

72 THE TRIUMPHAL ARCH

of Yzeures and Champlieu, and on Gallic *terra sigillata*. In the absence of the inscription it is impossible to tell what the occasion and function of the arch were, but it certainly formed a monumental entry between the town and the citadel. It has generally been dated to the later second century.

The so-called 'Porte de Mars' at Reims (Durocurtorum) is dated to the same period [5.2].[3] The most remarkable feature of the arch is its bizarre architectural form. It is 32 m wide (7 m wider than the Arch of Constantine at Rome), and 6.5 m deep. Its height, without the missing attic, is 11 m. It has four piers, of equal width, and three openings; what is peculiar is that the side ones (10 m high and 3 m wide) are so big in proportion to the central one (10.5 m high and 4.5 m wide). Picard suggests that it could be considered as two single arches linked by a central vault. Presumably the intention was to provide a grandiose northern entrance to the town, with generous passageways.

The arch stands on the *cardo maximus* at the north-western limit of the town. After being incorporated into the ramparts, it was disengaged and restored in 1844 by the local architect Narcisse Brunette. The west end of the north side is entirely his, and seems to have been faithfully restored. On each pier are two attached Corinthian columns, on projecting bases. Between the columns are pedimented aedicules, above which are *imagines clipeatae* (shield-shaped reliefs portraying figures). This is the same arrangement shown on coins representing the so-called 'arch' at the entrance to the Forum of Trajan (now thought to have been an internal façade – see p. 43). That may have served as the model.[4]

5.2 The Porte de Mars at Reims, also late 2nd century.

AFTER NERO IN EUROPE OUTSIDE ITALY 73

The decoration has been described as 'baroque'. The capitals are of an unparalleled type, and the column bases are elaborately decorated. On each pediment stands a pair of putti, holding the *imagines clipeatae*. Above these another pair of putti holds up drapery, in the centre of which are pairs of crossed *caducei*. Unfortunately the state of preservation of the monument only permits the identification of a limited amount of its sculpture. The aedicules contained reliefs. Some have been identified as representing Mars and Rhea Silvia; Aeneas, Ascanius and Anchises; Venus; Dea Roma; and Bacchus leaning on a satyr. The jambs of the aedicules were also decorated with figures. The most significant reliefs, and the best preserved, are those on the vaults of the passageways. That on the east represents the wolf suckling Romulus and Remus, and that on the west Leda and the swan. The friezes around these show piled-up arms, and, at the corners, Victories writing on shields. The central relief has a male figure holding a cornucopia, identified as either the genius of the year or Tellus (Earth), with the four seasons. The surviving parts of the surrounding frieze show the occupations of the months. At the level of the imposts of the central arcade runs a frieze where winged genii hold draperies, on which are flowers, baskets of fruit, and birds. Within the central passage were reliefs on the piers, one of which may have shown an emperor crowned by a winged Victory.

The scene with Leda reminds the viewer that her sons Castor and Pollux, in their alternation of life and death, symbolise eternal renewal, and the eternity of Rome's victory must have been the principal theme of the arch's decoration. Picard points out that this was particularly current after Hadrian's dedication of the Templum Urbis at Rome. The *caducei* symbolise peace, and the *imagines clipeatae* may have shown either deities or members of the imperial family, as guarantors of Rome's eternity. The late twelfth-century builders of the great abbey church of St Rémi seem to have modelled the fluted columns under the upper flying buttresses of the chevet on those of the Porte de Mars.[5]

At the opposite end of the *cardo maximus* stood another arch of similar character, though with only one opening. It was known as the Porte Bazée. One pier survives, built into a house. A relief from its vault showed a triton carrying a nymph and a winged Eros.[6]

Remains of a very curious arch were found in the medieval walls of Mainz (Mogontiacum) [5.3]. It was comparatively small – only 6 m

5.3 Arch of Dativius Victor at Mainz. Cast.

high and 4.6 m wide, and very shallow (0.7 m). Pilasters supported the archivolt, and also stood at the corners, supporting the entablature, above which was a low attic. The whole of the front is covered with relief sculpture, but the back is partly blank.[7] The inscription on the attic (*CIL* XIII 11810) is on a *tabula ansata* supported on either side by an Eros. It records the dedication of the arch and 'porticoes' to Jupiter Conservator by Dativius Victor, a magistrate of Civitas Taunensium (Heddernheim, just west of Frankfurt), and former priest of the imperial cult, whose promise to the citizens of Mainz was fulfilled by his sons and heirs. Von Gall suggests that Dativius might have taken refuge at Mainz in the face of some danger on the other side of the Rhine.

The one feature, apart from the architectural form and the inscription on the attic, which links this arch with the general type of commemorative arches, is a pair of figures representing two of the seasons (autumn, and perhaps spring), not in the spandrels (as on the Arch of Trajan at Benevento, and the Arches of Septimius Severus and Constantine at Rome) but on the pilaster capitals. Above these are scenes of sacrifice, presumably representing Dativius himself. The outer pilasters are decorated with vines, and the inner ones with stylised tendrils. The most remarkable part of the decoration is that on the archivolt and keystone. On the former appear the signs of the zodiac; on the latter are Jupiter and Juno, with other deities above the archivolt on either side. For the combination of the zodiac and several deities von Gall compares a Mithras relief from Osterburken (north-east of Heilbronn), seeing in it possible Oriental influence. He points out that a symbolic doorway appears in Mithraic iconography, including a curious triangular relief found at Heddernheim itself.

A few other arches are known to have existed in these regions. One at Geneva, again dedicated to Jupiter, is known from an inscription referring to *arcum cum suis ornamentis* ('an arch with its ornaments' – *CIL* XII 2590). Ammianus Marcellinus tells us (XXI 16.15) that Constantius *magis quam recto vel usitato triumphalis arcus ex clade provinciarum sumptibus magnis erexit in Galliis et Pannoniis, titulis gestorum adfixis se –quoad stare poterunt monumenta – lecturis* ('erected triumphal arches, as a result of the disaster suffered by the provinces, to a greater extent than was right or customary at great expense in Gaul and Pannonia, fixing to them inscriptions which will be read as long as the monuments are able to stand'). One of these may well have been the 'Heidentor' ('Heathens' Gate') at Carnuntum, near Petronell on the Danube 40 km downstream from Vienna. This was a *quadrifrons*, about 20 m high, built of limestone and concrete, with columns and sculpture of Slovenian marble. Two piers linked by a cross-vault survive. It was situated outside the town in a cemetery. The piers were plain, apart from a bold moulding projecting at the height of the arch springing, and a dentilled cornice above. On the attic groups of three niches, framed by projecting colonnettes, flanked the inscription panel. Fragments survive of the statues which stood in the niches, apparently representing rulers. At the centre of the interior a circular pedestal must have carried a statue of the emperor. An inscription of the time of Caracalla was built into the upper part of the arch, but coins date the construction to the reign of Constantius II (353–61). The purpose of this huge structure is unknown. It seems far too big to have been a funerary arch.[8] We know nothing else about the other arches. The passage of Ammianus is interesting as the only occasion in Latin literature (as opposed to epigraphy) in which the phrase *arcus triumphalis* appears (used here no doubt with heavy irony).

Britain

When Heinz Kähler published his list of Roman arches in 1939 no British examples were included, but six are now known. The earliest may have been the one built into the Balkerne Gate on the eastern side of Colchester (Camulodunum) in Essex. This may have been erected to commemorate the foundation of the colonia in AD 49 – the first *colonia* in Britain.[9] The arch has been hypothetically reconstructed with a pair of openings framed by pilasters, and an attic above the entablature. This double-arched form is found in Gaul at Saintes and Langres. The combined width of the two carriageways was 7.8 m. If the arch was erected at this period, when there were no masonry defences, it must have been incorporated into the walls when they were built in about 70. On the other hand, the fact that the arch is built several metres east of the line of the walls has suggested that it may postdate them, to around 100.[10]

A particularly remarkable arch stood on the south-east coast at Richborough (Rutupiae) in Kent. Here a supply base for the invasion of AD 43 was laid out. In about 85 (during the reign of Domitian) most of its buildings were removed to make way for a *quadrifrons*. This was sited on a flint platform 38 × 25 m, and over 9 m deep. All that survives is this platform, and a cruciform mass of concrete on top which marks out the site of the passageways [5.4]. The form of the arch was comparatively plain. Its main elevations had single openings 7 m wide; each pier had a pair of half-columns or pilasters (the relationship between these is unclear), standing on continuous bases. It is assumed that the order was Corinthian. Above the cornice was a substantial attic. The narrow side elevations were articulated in the same way [5.5]. The paved passageways within the opening were at a higher level than the surrounding area (hence the concrete 'cross'), and were reached by steps outside each opening. The height of the arch is estimated as 26 m.

5.4 Richborough, Kent, foundations of arch, *c.* 85.

5.5 Richborough, model of arch.

The structure was of masonry, faced with marble imported from Luna (Carrara). Many fragments have been found, including architectural details of cornices, mouldings, facing slabs, half-columns and pilasters, and remains of three inscriptions. The scantily carved ornament included astragals with bead-and-reel mouldings, and probably decorative keystones. Bronze fragments have been interpreted as coming from a gilded equestrian statue, presumably of the Emperor, wearing a cuirass: it must have stood on the attic.

The dating of the arch is particularly interesting, as it was in 84 that Domitian recalled Agricola, the legate of Britain: he had decided that the conquest of Britain had gone far enough. Donald Strong suggested that the arch was intended to symbolise the *accessus Britanniae* ('the approach to Britain' – the phrase borrowed from the inscription on Trajan's arch at Ancona, the *accessus Italiae*). It stood at the beginning of Watling Street, the Roman road running to London, and was highly visible from the sea. Domitian's fondness for arches was notorious (see p. 40). Presumably his statue will have been removed after his *damnatio memoriae*. In the third century the monument was enclosed within an earth fort, and used as a lookout against Saxon pirates. It was demolished when the Saxon shore fort was constructed.[11]

No other arch is known to have been erected before the third century.[12] In 1975 remains of an arch were discovered in Upper Thames Street, London. Reused in the fourth-century river wall were fifty-two blocks of limestone, mostly carved in relief, which were recognised as belonging to a monumental arch, at least 6 m high and 7.5 m wide, and a screen over 6 m wide. The form of the arch was simple, with plain piers and a low attic. All four sides, above the springing of the arch, were covered with rich architectural and figurative sculpture. There were at least four full-length figures, including

AFTER NERO IN EUROPE OUTSIDE ITALY 77

Minerva and Hercules: these stood framed on either side of the opening. Within the spandrels were busts in roundels, perhaps including the Seasons, and sea monsters below. Above ran, on one side, a row of seven busts, probably representing the days of the week. On the other side was probably an inscription panel, supported at each end by a flying Cupid. The short sides were decorated with vine scrolls rising from *canthari* (urns); on each side there is a bust above the *canthari* (one representing Apollo). Above the frieze of busts the cornice was decorated with acanthus leaves.

It is not known where the arch originally stood, though it may have formed the entrance to a precinct. Its character is religious rather than military. Although the upper part is carved on all sides, and must have been freestanding, we cannot be sure that its lower part was not incorporated into, say, a precinct wall. It is uncertain whether it had any commemorative function. Its date is reckoned to be early in the third century, and it is considered to be the work of Romano-British masons.[13]

Unfortunately far less is known of the appearance of the three arches which stood at St Albans (Verulamium). The town was founded at about the same time as Camulodunum, but as a *municipium*. The earliest seems to have been the Southern Arch, which stood at the point where three other streets met Watling Street. The foundations measure about 14 × 4.5 m, and the plan suggests a double arch like the Balkerne Gate at Colchester, with openings about 3 m wide. Fragments of marble (probably from Luna) may come from the arch. It has been dated *c.* 250–75.[14] The Northern Arch also stood on Watling Street, as it headed westwards out of the town. Its foundations measure 12.5 × 3 m. Unlike the Southern Arch, it stood in a built-up street – hence its narrowness. Whether it was single or double is unknown. Frere suggests that the purpose of both of these arches may have been similar, since the Southern Arch lies just outside the first-century defence ditch, and the Northern one just inside it. Assuming that the ditch marked the original *pomerium* of the town, the arches may have been erected to commemorate Claudius's original foundation, on the occasion of the building of the new city wall *c.* 265–70.[15] The third arch, which may be slightly later (*c.* 300) also stood on Watling Street, close to the theatre. Each pier of the single arch was probably 4 m wide. Plinths projecting on each side probably bore columns. A fragment of carved cornice was found.[16]

In 1998 it was reported that what might be the foundations of an enormous triple arch had been discovered just inside Newgate, London, but subsequent excavations disproved this idea.

Spain and Portugal

There are not a great many arches in Spain and Portugal: Kähler lists a total of eighteen. Of these, several have already been discussed – Roda de Bera (Torredembara), Martorell, Mengíbar, and Tarragona. Only one of the others is securely dated, but the earliest may well be the granite arch at Medinaceli, about halfway between Zaragoza and Madrid [5.6]. It is particularly remarkable for its situation. The town stands on top of a steep hill (at a height of 1,200 m above sea level), and the arch is set at the edge of a precipitous drop, so that it is visible from far off. It stands on the line of the town walls, which were partially demolished for its erection, but it is very shallow, and was never usable by traffic, despite the fact that it is a triple arch (the only one in the

5.6 Arch at Medinaceli, at a height of 1,200 m, dedicated to Domitian.

Iberian Peninsula). It may have served as a boundary arch between the territories of the *conventus Caesaraugustiensis* and the *conventus Cluniensis*.[17] The central opening is much larger than the lateral ones, which are set above the plinth. A cornice runs all round the monument, and above each opening is a blind aedicule with fluted pilasters supporting a pediment. At this upper level there are also pilasters on the corners, supporting the entablature, above which there is a low attic. On both sides of this are holes for bronze letters. The inscriptions have been reconstructed as on the north side *NUMINI AUGUSTO SACRUM* (sacred to the divinity of the emperor), and on the south *NUMINI IMP[ERATORIS] DOMITIANI AUG[USTI] GER[MANICI]* (sacred to the divinity of the Emperor Domitian Augustus Germanicus), modified in 98 to read *TRAIANI*. The second line on each side is illegible, but has been suggested to read *OCILITANI ARCUM EREXERUNT* (the Ocilitani erected the arch).[18]

Another very unusual arch survives in a reasonably good state at Cáparra, west of Madrid. It is a *quadrifrons*, built of concrete faced with granite, and stood over the crossing of two of the main streets of the town of Capera, near the forum. There are four equal openings, and tall podia, the archivolts supported on pilasters with Corinthian capitals. Each of the two principal faces had attached three-quarter columns at the corners, supporting the entablature. What makes the arch exceptional is the plinths for sculpture which project from, and rise higher than, the podia; on the north side these extend almost 3 m, while those on the north are much shorter. It is suggested that the larger ones must have supported equestrian statues, and the shorter ones standing figures. This is very curious, since one would expect the sculpture to be on top of the arch. The explanation might lie in the fact that the arch was tightly packed in by houses, so that sculpture at a lower level would be more easily seen.

An inscription on one of the shorter plinths records that the arch was erected according to the will of M. Fidius Macer, in honour of his mother and father (or son).[19] Garcia suggests that it might have commemorated the family's achievement of full Roman citizenship. The plinth perhaps bore statues of the mother and father (or son). It hardly seems likely that the equestrian statues would have represented Macer and another member of his family; perhaps they honoured the emperor and another. The only evidence for the date of the arch is provided by another inscription erected by M. Fidius Macer, whose magistracies give a date of about AD 100. The structure has one other bizarre feature: the masonry of the arrises of the vault is of extremely irregular blocks. Garcia can provide no explanation for this, and the only parallel is the Mausoleum of Theodoric at Ravenna, of AD 526.[20]

Garcia draws attention to the fact that the famous bridge at Alcántara, with its arch set on the central span, is only 75 km from Cáparra, and suggests that both monuments could be the work of the same architect [5.7]. Built of granite, the bridge has

5.7 Bridge over the Tagus and arch at Alcantara, dedicated to Trajan in 105/6.

80 THE TRIUMPHAL ARCH

six arches, and crosses the deep, wide valley of the river Tagus, covering a length of 192 m. The bridge has been much damaged and repaired, including works by Charles V in 1543, and by 'Queen Elisabeth' (Isabella) in 1858–60. The arch (10 m tall) is very simple. It probably had a Doric cornice. A marble tablet on the attic records the dedication of the bridge to Trajan in 105/6, and a marble tablet on one of the piers (the other is missing) records that it was paid for by thirteen local *municipia*. There is also a small temple in honour of Trajan at the head of the bridge, and this bears an inscription in elegiac couplets informing travellers that both temple and bridge were built by Lacer, further identified by a (perhaps dubious) inscription as C. Iulius Lacer.[21]

Three arches possibly erected in connection with the building of the road have already been mentioned. Remains of another arch which has often been associated with the road stand at Cabanes, some 150 km south of Tarragona. So little remains of this granite arch – simply the piers, with moulded bases and cornices, and the voussoirs of the opening – that it is almost impossible to date, though a recent study by L. Abad Casal and F. Arasa i Gil suggests the first decades of the second century AD. They argue that the arch is unlikely to have been erected in connection with the building of the road as it stands not across it but parallel to it, nor do they accept that it might have been a territory marker. They suggest that it was a private monument, like the arches of Pola, Verona, Aix-les-Bains, Zadar, and, of course, Cáparra. The arch stands on a plain, where it would have been visible from afar.[22]

A further parallel with the arch at Cáparra is provided by the location of the arch in the important town of Mérida (Colonia Augusta Emerita). Known as the Arch of Trajan, it spans the *cardo maximus*, and it seems likely that it formed the entrance to the forum. There is no evidence for any commemorative purpose, but one seems very likely. A large ashlar structure with a single opening, it was clad in marble some time after it was built. The earlier mouldings were cut off where necessary, and the marble attached with dowels.[23]

Several other Spanish arches are known from fragments of evidence. Two, which probably date from the late second century, are known only from keystones with winged Victories: these were found at Málaga (Malaca), and at Itálica (near Seville). Garcia relates them, as victory arches, to the Moorish invasions between 172 and 176.[24] We know of the existence of an arch at Sádaba, a small town north-west of Zaragoza, only from a sketch made in 1610: it shows an arch with the odd feature of double podia supporting the piers. The opening has pilasters, and there are columns on the corners, with a low attic above. The overall height was some 18 m.[25] There is evidence of several arches in the district of Valencia, in addition to that at Cabanes already mentioned. At Liria (north-west of Valencia) one marble pier survives of an arch, about 3 m high.[26] At least two more arches are known from inscriptions. One (now lost) was found at Elche (Illici), or perhaps Alicante: only the words *PORCIO RUFINO … ARCUM FECIT* survived.[27] Another inscription, found at Jérica, north-west of Segorbe, reads as follows: *QUINTIA PROBA / SIBI ET PORCIO / RUFO ET PORCIO / RUFINO ARCUM / FECIT ET STATUAS / SUPERIMPOS. hs. n. XL* (Quintia Proba erected this arch to herself and Porcius Rufus and Porcius Rufinus, and put statues on top of it, at a cost of 40,000 sesterces).[28] A third inscription, from Viver (close to Jérica), appears to record the burial of two men called M. Porcius, son of Marcus, one with the *cognomen* Rufinus, the other Rufus, and of Quintia Proba, daughter of Marcus.[29]

These are the three people to whom the arch mentioned in the Jérica inscription was erected. The arch cannot therefore have been the actual tomb, but must have been a monument erected by Quintia to her husband Porcius Rufus and son Porcius Rufinus, as well as to herself. The names are common in the area. The design of the inscription tablets suggests a date in the second century. Abad points out that these arches make an interesting comparison with the arches mentioned above, and especially with that at Zadar (see below, p. 87), which also records the erection of an arch with statues above by a woman in memory of her husband, and gives the cost.[30]

A relief in the museum at Mérida celebrates the victory of an emperor over barbarians. J. Arce identifies him as Maximianus Herculius, who in 296–7 fought in Spain and Mauretania, and suggests that the relief might have come from an arch erected *c.* 300 to commemorate his victories, in the town which under Diocletian had become capital of the Diocesis Hispaniarum.[31] Another relief, showing a row of dignitaries, who probably accompanied the Emperor, in the museum of Cordoba, has been attributed to an arch near Espiel, on the Sierra de Chimorra north-west of Cordoba. It may have marked the boundary of the territory of the Colonia Corduba, on a road which branched off northwards from the road to Emerita (Mérida).[32]

As far as Portugal is concerned, Kähler lists four arches, none of which survives, nor is anything known of the dates or purposes of their erection.

Greece and the Balkans

The arch at Philippi has already been referred to (p. 22). The next datable arch is reckoned to be the large triple one at Olympia, forming the south-east entrance to the Altis, the sacred precinct of Zeus. Only the foundations survive. The arch has been associated with Nero's visit in AD 66. He also visited Isthmia, in 67, and it is possible that this led to the erection of another large triple arch, which marked the eastern approach to the sanctuary of Poseidon. It was about 16 m wide, but only 2 m deep, and was built of limestone covered with white stucco. It was very simple, the only decoration consisting (so far as the evidence goes) of the traditionally Greek mouldings of the pilaster bases (raised on top of a podium, these had simple Ionic capitals), the entablature above, and the top of the attic. The arch could be a little later than the time of Nero: it may be significant that Vespasian refounded the colony of Corinth (which had control of the Isthmian games). It is not clear why the arch was placed where it was, except to mark the approach to the sanctuary; it certainly stood over one of the main roads into the Peloponnese, and may have marked a boundary. In about AD 400 it was built into the Hexamilion fortress.[33] A third arch which has been connected with Nero's visit is the one at the south-west corner of the Forum at Corinth. Its eastern pier abutted the South Stoa, and its opening had a span of about 4.5 m.[34]

A much more remarkable arch stood over the Lechaion road which entered the Forum from the north. It was described by Pausanias, in the second century (2.3.2), as *propulaia* with gilded chariots on top, one bearing the Sun, the other his son Phaethon – the gods of Acrocorinth. Presumably the chariots faced in opposite directions. Excavation has revealed the foundations, from which it appears that the first phase, when it was a triple arch, may have dated from as early as the reign of Augustus. The central bay, flanked by columns, had on the north a projecting architectural framework. At this stage the arch was not big enough for two *quadrigae*. Later it was rebuilt as a single arch, but on a larger scale.[35] There is little evidence for its form, but Edwards suggests that attached half-columns might have stood in pairs on the piers. An interesting point is that the paved area on the north side of the arch was reached by an ascending flight of steps. In the second phase the stone arch was covered with marble revetment. A considerable number of fragments of relief sculpture have been found in the area, and Edwards suggests that a weapons frieze may have run around the upper part of the arch, and panels showing a sacrifice, in the presence of Hercules and a statue of Athena, and (probably) a submission scene (apparently including Parthian captives) may have stood on either side of the passageway. He dates the second phase towards the end of Trajan's reign, commemorating his eastern victories. It must have been this arch that was shown on coins of Hadrian.[36]

An arch which was certainly dedicated to Trajan, in 113, stood at Podgrade (the ancient Asseria), near Benkovac in Croatia, some 32 km south-east of Zadar. It replaced the north-west gate of the town. Its inner side had pairs of half-columns on the piers, with statue niches between them, but on the outer side the outer half-columns were (most unusually) replaced by freestanding columns. Over the archivolts were pairs of keystones: two survive, representing the forepart of an animal and the bust of a human-headed animal. Apart from the dedicatory inscription on the attic, the central part of the architrave and frieze bore a second inscription giving the name of the dedicator.

Several arches are shown on Trajan's Column at Rome. The wooden bridge which Apollodorus of Damascus built over the Danube (dedicated in winter 105–6) is shown in two scenes. In the first, two stone flood-arches at one end support a tall arched gateway; it has no statues or trophies on top (there is no room). The arch at the other end is shown in the neighbouring scene, and this does have trophies on top. In fact there must have been statues and trophies on the arch at each end, as shown on coins.[37] This is how they have been reconstructed on the model of the bridge in the museum at Turnu-Severin in Romania.[38] On the Column two arches appear on a lower scene, one above the other. The upper one is plain, but the lower one has a *quadriga* on top, and stands in water. Cichorius thought that they stood on either side of the river Save where it entered the Danube, but Lepper and Frere suggest that the scene may represent a riverside harbour somewhere in the Danube catchment area (possibly Drobeta or Sirmium on its north bank, or Viminacium or Siscia on its south bank).[39]

An arch in honour of Hadrian still stands at Athens, in virtually the same state as when it was illustrated by James Stuart and Nicholas Revett in the third volume of their *Antiquities of Athens*, published in 1795 [5.8]. It is situated south-west of the Acropolis, across the road whose line was cut, further on, by the precinct wall of the Olympieion, the temple of Olympian Zeus, which was completed and dedicated by Hadrian in 130.[40] The form of the arch is unusual. Built of Pentelic marble (of poor quality), its single opening has an archivolt supported on pilasters with Corinthian capitals. There are further pilasters at each end. The marble between is coursed. Freestanding columns with freestanding bases stood near the ends, placed so as to conceal the joints in the coursing. The freestanding columns are similar to those on the Library of Hadrian, also at Athens. The attic is particularly curious. In the centre is an aedicule, with freestanding columns supporting a pediment, on which is an acanthus acroterion. This aedicule

5.8 Arch of Hadrian at Athens.

was originally filled in with marble slabs. On either side is a pier, linked to the aedicule by an entablature. Originally these piers had in front of them columns, which stood free above the freestanding columns of the lower stage. Another odd feature is the way in which the archivolt cuts into the architrave, which is without parallel in Roman architecture (though sometimes shown on coins). The central aedicules have often been supposed to have held, on either side, statues of Hadrian and Theseus, but some argue that they are too shallow, and may have contained painted pictures.[41]

The architectural form of the Athens arch is obviously indebted to Asia Minor. The most similar example is the Trajanic arch at Ephesus, which had three open bays below, and an attic of six bays, with a pediment over the four central ones. Various details also have parallels in Asia Minor. Post sees in the arch a mixture of western (in the lower part) and eastern (in the attic) elements, which corresponds to the message of the inscriptions. Ward-Perkins writes that 'it betrays the working of a thoroughly baroque mentality operating within the conventions of rather formal classicism'.[42] On either side of the arch, on the architrave, is an inscription, consisting of an iambic trimeter in Greek. That on the west side reads: ΑΙΔ' ΕΙΣΙΝ ΑΘΗΝΑΙ ΘΗΣΕΩΣ Η ΠΡΙΝ ΠΟΛΙΣ ('This is Athens, the former city of Theseus'), while that on the east reads: ΑΙΔ' ΕΙΣ' ΑΔΡΙΑΝΟΥ ΚΟΥΧΙ ΘΗΣΕΩΣ ΠΟΛΙΣ ('This is the city of Hadrian, and not of Theseus'). According to the *Scriptores Historiae Augustae* (Hadrian 20.4) Hadrian called part of Athens 'Hadrianopolis': if this can be believed, it presumably refers to the suburb around the Olympieion, which is hyperbolically called a *polis*. The arch must certainly have been intended to mark the approach from the Acropolis to the Olympieion, and honour the Emperor who completed the temple, and who made the city head of the Panhellenic League. Presumably it was erected by the people of Athens, or perhaps (as Post suggests) by the Panhellenes, who erected the similar arches at Eleusis (see below). Similarities with Hadrian's Library suggest that the same workmen may have been used here. Stuart used the arch as his model for the one he erected in the park of Shugborough in 1761–6 (see p. 274).

Another Attic town which benefited from Hadrian's generosity was Eleusis. He took part in the famous mysteries at the sanctuary of Demeter and Kore each time he visited Athens. On either side of the Greater Propylaea, which led into the sanctuary, is a pair of arches, one over the road to the sea, and the other over the road to Megara. They were identical, and were almost exact copies of the arch at Athens. Each bore, on both faces, the inscription: τοῖν θεοῖν καὶ τῶι Αὐτοκράτορι οἱ πανέλληνες ('the Panhellenes to the two goddesses and the Emperor'). The Panhellenic League was created by Hadrian in 131/2. A statue base survives with a dedication to Hadrian: as he is called *theos* (a god), it must date from after his death. Near the southern arch were found five more statue bases inscribed to the deified Marcus Aurelius, his wife Faustina, and three of their daughters. There seems to have been a similar set at the northern arch. The statues may have stood on the upper stage of the arches, six on each; the likelihood is that three faced one way, and three the other. There seem to have been screen walls between the columns (not just the central ones, as at Athens).[43]

An arch honouring Hadrian at Corinth is known only from coins: it had a single storey, on which stood a *quadriga*.[44] Another is shown on coins of Bizya, near the Black Sea coast in Thrace. It is actually a town gate, with a tower on either side and a portcullis in the opening, between reliefs showing the Dioscuri. Above are seven niches with busts. On top is a *quadriga*, apparently driven by Zeus, with Victory hovering above and Artemis hastening in front.[45] Whether the arch had a commemorative function is unknown. The same is true of a gate at Patras, known only from Pausanias (7.20.7), which served as the entrance to the forum. It had on it gilded statues of the legendary founders of the city, and may have dated from the time of Herodes Atticus (mid-second century). He may also have been responsible for a triple arch at Delphi, at the south-east entrance to the Stadion, which he remodelled. Surviving remains show that there were rectangular statue-niches on each of the middle piers. Yet another arch at Corinth, this time a triple one bearing a *quadriga* (shown in profile), appears on coins of Antoninus Pius. Coins of Commodus seem to show a different arch, whose central part has a raised attic, again with a *quadriga* shown in profile. Coins of Pagai (a port on the Gulf of Corinth), of the reign of Septimius Severus, show a very plain triple arch with three statues on it.[46]

A triple arch shown on coins of Markianopolis (Prawady-Devno) in Moesia (Serbia), of the time of Macrinus and Diadumenianus (217–18), bears four statues on pedestals, one of them female: if these represent Septimius Severus, Iulia Domna, Caracalla and Geta, the arch must date from the reign of Septimius Severus, or immediately after his death, as otherwise Geta's statue would not have been included.[47]

On Thasos, the northernmost island of the Aegean, remains survive of a triple arch known as the 'Arch of Caracalla'. This is because an inscription on the architrave of the central opening records that the city of the Thasians honoured Caracalla, his mother Iulia Domna, and his deified father Septimius Severus. However it has been pointed out by Jean-Yves Marc that the inscription must have been added later, as the fascias of the architrave have been chiselled off to make a space for it. Furthermore, the names appear in the accusative, not the dative, as one would expect if the arch was dedicated to the Emperor. No doubt three statues were placed on top.[48] Marc dates the arch to the last third of the second century. There is no evidence for any commemorative function, and Marc emphasises the important role that the arch plays in the planning of the city, where it forms the monumental termination to the marble-paved main street which runs south-west from the agora to the Herakleion, beside which the arch stands. Its form was curious: the central opening and its entablature were higher and wider than the side openings with their entablatures. The larger and smaller pilasters, which have Corinthian capitals, were placed virtually side by side, but at the outer ends were broad sections of masonry. There was no attic.

5.9 Arch of Galerius at Thessalonika, after 297.

86 THE TRIUMPHAL ARCH

Coins of Tomis on the Black Sea (now Constanta in Romania), minted under Maximinus (235–8), show a triple arch, while a second arch at Markianopolis is shown on coins of Gordian III (238–44): it is a triple arch bearing three male statues. An arch partially survives at Zadar (Iader), on the Croatian coast. It forms the inner side of the Porta Marina (Lucka vrata). It stood over the principal approach to the town from the south-east (the only land approach), and was erected to the memory of Q. Laepicius Bassus by his wife. The inscription (*CIL* III 2922) states: *emporium sterni et arcum fieri et statuas superponi test. iussit ex hs. DC d XX p. [R.]* ('she ordered in her will that the marketplace should be paved and an arch erected and statues placed above it at a cost of 600,000 sesterces (less the twentieth part which went to the Roman people)'). It has a single opening, and from the form of its Corinthian capitals and entablature cannot be earlier than the third century. For this type of private funerary arch one may compare Pola, Verona, Aix-les-Bains, Caparra and Cabanes. A particularly interesting comparison is with the arch mentioned in the inscription from Jérica in Spain (see p. 81).[49]

The latest arch to survive in Greece is an extraordinary monument by any standards. Galerius had been chosen as Caesar of the East by Diocletian in 293, and established his capital at Thessalonika (Thessaloniki). He won a great victory over the Persians in 297. It must have been to commemorate this that he built an immense arch north-east of his palace, where a colonnaded street was crossed by another which led from the palace to the rotunda which was intended to be his mausoleum (now the church of St George) [5.9]. It was begun as a *quadrifrons*, with four immense piers supporting a dome on pendentives. Before it was finished, further piers were added on either side, corresponding to the colonnades of the main street; their passageways were also vaulted with cupolas. They linked the arch to the palace vestibule on one side, and the stoas flanking the axial street on the other. Of the eight piers only three survive, on the north-west side, with the vaults above. Originally the whole structure was about 37 m long, and the main opening was 10 m wide and 12.5 m high. The piers are 4 m thick. Over each pier, on either of the main fronts, was a niche: these may have held statues of Diocletian and Galerius on the south-east side, and Maximian and Constantius Chlorus (the other members of the Tetrarchy) on the north-west, facing their respective provinces.

The structure is of brick and concrete, but the main piers are faced with marble blocks carved with reliefs arranged on three levels. The iconography and arrangement of these reliefs have been much discussed, most recently by Margret S. Pond Rothman.[50] Unfortunately they are much damaged, and their condition has deteriorated seriously over the last century. Rothman argues that the reliefs on the outer faces of the surviving piers are comparatively conventional representations of triumphal imagery, while those on their inner sides are more specific, and are deliberately arranged. They should be read downwards. Those on the east face of the north pier show Galerius leading a cavalry charge; the capture of the Persian harem; and the pursuit of the Persians across the river Tigris (which is identified by an inscription). Those on its south face show what Rothman calls 'the last battle', with Galerius on horseback triumphing over a pile of Persians; a female figure on an elephant *quadriga*; the submission of the Persian captives, who include women riding dromedaries; and the *aduentus* of the triumphant Emperor. She interprets the corresponding reliefs on the south pier (nearer to the palace) as 'moving from the historical record to a paraphrase of history to a-historical imperial dogma'. Those on its east face include Galerius's *adlocutio* (address to the troops); his reception of a Persian delegation; a sacrifice by Galerius and Diocletian; and a procession of Persians bringing gifts, which include elephants and lionesses. On the north face are the Emperor's *aduentus*; a fight between Galerius and the Persian king Narses (who never in fact met on the battlefield); and the enthroned Emperors Diocletian and Maximian with Constantius Chlorus and Galerius standing on either side, all raising up personifications of Persia and Britain, in the presence of various deities. The other surviving scenes show symbols of victory, clemency and virtue, and a triumphal procession. One particularly significant scene (on the south face of the south pier) shows Victories holding a shield, between trophies and figures of Mars and Virtus: it probably refers to Galerius's *decennalia* in 303. Rothman suggests that the arch might have been dedicated during Diocletian's visit in that year. Most of the lowest registers of the piers show a parade of animals.

Notes

1. Kähler 1939, col, 423. Further carved keystones seem to belong to two other arches.
2. *Römische Mitteilungen*, 72 (1965), 171–81.
3. G. Picard, 'La "Porte de Mars" à Reims', *95e Congrès national des sociétés savantes, Reims 1970, archéologie* (Paris, 1974), 59–84; F. Lefèvre, 'Réflexions à propos des sculptures de la "Porte de Mars" à Reims', *Caesarodunum*, 23 (1988), 149–60.
4. Compare the arch at Volubilis (in modern Morocco), which dates from AD 217 (pp. 118–20).
5. C. Wilson, *The Gothic Cathedral* (London, 1990), 61.
6. E. Espérandieu, *Recueil général des bas-reliefs, statues et bustes de la Gaule romaine*, V (1913), no. 3680.
7. H. von Gall, 'Bemerkungen zum Bogen des Dativius Victor in Mainz', *Jahrbuch des römisch-germanischen Zentralmuseums Mainz*, 15 (1968), 98–119. A cast of the reconstructed arch stands in front of the museum. See also Kimberly Cassibry, 'Provincial patrons and commemorative rivalries: rethinking the Roman arch monument', *Mouseion*, 8 (2008), 417–50.
8. E. Swoboda, *Carnuntum* (4th edn, Graz/Cologne, 1964) 170–73: Klaus Müller, 'Der Quadrifrons von Carnuntum – Wissenschaftliche Untersuchung und Neupräsentation', *Architectura*, 33 (2003), 123–34.
9. Tacitus, *Annals* 12.32.
10. P. Crummy, *Colchester Archeological Report 3: Excavations at Lion Walk, Balkerne Lane and Middleborough* (Colchester, 1984), 121–3.
11. D.E. Strong, 'The Monument', in B.W. Cunliffe, ed., *Fifth Report on the Excavations of the Roman Fort at Richborough, Kent* (Oxford, 1968), 40–73; J.S. Johnson, *Richborough and Reculver* (English Heritage, 1997). Sheppard Frere, *Britannia* (London, 1974), 138, suggests that it was Agricola himself who erected it, but if so one might have expected his son-in-law Tacitus to have mentioned it in his biography.
12. In *Roman Bath* (Oxford, 1969), 20, B.W. Cunliffe suggested that the main entrance to the precinct of the Temple of Sulis Minerva might have taken the form of a double arch like that at Colchester, but this is doubtful.
13. C. Hill, M. Millett and T. Blagg, *The Roman Riverside Wall and Monumental Arch in London* (London and Middlesex Archaeological Society, 1980); R. Merrifield, *London, City of the Romans* (London, 1983), 167–81. Parts of the arch are on view in the Museum of London.
14. R.E.M. and T.V. Wheeler, *Verulamium* (Oxford, 1936), 76–7.
15. S.S. Frere, *Verulamium Excavations*, II (London, 1983), 75–82.
16. K. Kenyon, 'The Roman Theatre at Verulamium', *Archaeologia* 84 (1934), 238; Wheeler (cit. at n. 14), 129. The cornice fragment is illustrated in Rosalind Niblett, *Verulamium* (Stroud, 2001), 124; for the arches see also 84–5, 122, and for a plan of the town 90.
17. J. Arce, *Arcos romanos en Hispania: una revision*, Archivo Español de Arqueología 60 (1987), 82.
18. Juan Manuel Abascal and Géza Alföldy, *El Arco Romano de Medinaceli (Soria, Hispania Citerior)* (Madrid, 2002). See especially pp. 71–115 on the inscription, and pp. 117–28 (by L. Abad Casal) on the monument. On the arch, see also A. Garcia y Bellidos, 'Arcos honoríficos romanos en Hispania', *Colloquio Italo-Spagnuolo sul Tema: Hispania Romana* (Rome, 1972), 22–3. See also B. Taracena Aguirre, *Carta arqueológica de España: Soria* (Madrid, 1941), 95; M. Pfanner, in W. Trillmich and P. Zanker, eds, *Stadtbild und Ideologie*, Bayerische Akademie der Wissenschaften, *Abhandlungen* (Neue Folge), 103 (1990), 88–9.
19. *CIL* II 834.
20. Garcia (cit. at n. 18), 8–16; A. Nünnerich-Asmus, *El arco cuadrifonte de Cáparra*, Anejos de Archivo Español de Arqueología XVI (Madrid, 1996). For a plan of the town, see *Excavaciones arqueologicas en España*, 34 (1965), fig. 7; and for Laborde's view of it (1811) ibid., 54 (1966), pl. VIII.
21. Garcia (cit. at n. 18), 19; A. Nünnerich-Asmus, in W. Trillmich, ed., *Hispania Antiqua* (Mainz,

1993), 136–7; G.M. Leather, *Roman Bridges in Iberia* (Garstang, 2006), 34–8, 128. The inscriptions are *CIL* II 759–61. Arce (cit. at n. 17), 85, suggests that the plural *templa* in the inscription indicates that there might have been a temple at each end of the bridge.

22 L. Abad Casal and F. Arasa i Gil, *Archivo Español de Arqueología*, 61 (1988), 81–117; F. Arasa i Gil and L. Abad Casal, *L'arc romà de Cabanes* (Castelló, 1989). See also Garcia (cit. at n. 18), 20–21; Nünnerich-Asmus (cit. at n. 21), 139.

23 I.A. Richmond, *Archaeological Journal*, 87 (1930), 108–9; M. Almagro Basch, *150 Jahre Deutsches Archäologisches Institut* (Mainz, 1981), 161–2; Pfanner (cit. at n. 18), 102; Arce (cit. at n. 17), 82, 85 (where he suggests a date *c.* 300); L. Berrocal Rangel, *Boletín de la Asociación Española de Amigos de la Arqueología*, 29 (1990), 62–6.

24 Garcia (cit. at n. 18), 24.

25 ibid., 23–4; Arce (cit. at n. 17), 79.

26 Garcia (cit. at n. 18), 21–2.

27 *CIL* II 3558.

28 *CIL* II 3997.

29 *CIL* II 4011.

30 *CIL* III 2922. On these inscriptions, and the arches, see L. Abad Casal, *Lucentum* 3 (1984), 193–200. An inscription said to have been recorded at Petrel by Canon Montesinos, referring to an arch erected by Quintia Rufa to herself and 'Malcus Pambinus', with statues above, at a cost of 24,000 (or 29,000?) sesterces, may be a forgery (ibid., 195).

31 J. Arce, *Madrider Mitteilungen*, 23 (1982), 359–71.

32 R. Nierhaus Baedro, *Madrider Mitteilungen*, 5 (1964), 199–205.

33 T.E. Gregory and H. Mills, 'The Roman Arch at Isthmia', *Hesperia*, 53 (1984), 407–45.

34 C.K. Williams and J.E. Fisher, 'Corinth, 1975: Forum Southwest', *Hesperia*, 45 (1976), 135–7.

35 C.M. Edwards, 'The Arch over the Lechaion Road at Corinth and its Sculpture', *Hesperia*, 63 (1994), 263–308.

36 Coins of Domitian show a roughly similar arch, and Edwards' study of the remains of the arch's structure suggested to him a date around that time, but the style of the reliefs points to a Trajanic date.

37 H. Mattingly and E.A. Sydenham, *Roman Imperial Coinage* II (London, 1926), 284, no. 569.

38 F. Lepper and S. Frere, eds, *Trajan's Column: a New Edition of the Cichorius Plates* (Gloucester, 1988), 150. For the arches, see pp.148–50 and pls LXII and LXIV.

39 ibid., 81–3, pl. XXV. For arches at harbours, compare Ostia and Puteoli.

40 On the arch see A, Adams, 'The Arch of Hadrian at Athens', in S. Walker and A. Cameron, eds, *The Greek Renaissance in the Roman Empire*, BICS Supplement, 55 (1989), 10–16; A. Post, 'Zum Hadrianstor in Athen', *Boreas*, 21/22 (1988/9), 171–83.

41 For a restoration with a statue, see J.B. Ward-Perkins, *Roman Imperial Architecture* (Harmondsworth, 1981), 269; also Stuart and Revett, III, 65.

42 Ward-Perkins (cit. in the preceding note), 269.

43 G.E. Mylonas, *Eleusis and the Eleusinian Mysteries* (Princeton, 1961), 166–7; K. Clinton, 'Hadrian's contribution to the Renaissance of Eleusis', in Walker and Cameron (cit. at n. 40), 56–68. On the dating of the arches, see also Post (cit. at n. 40). On the Panhellenes, see A.J. Spawforth and S. Walker, 'The World of the Panhellenion', *JRS* 75 (1985), 78–104.

44 Some argue that these coins show the arch over the Lechaion road: see C.M. Edwards (cit. at n. 35), 272, n. 20.

45 M.J. Price and B.L. Trell, *Coins and their Cities* (London, 1977), figs 24 and 497.

46 W.L. MacDonald assumes that the arch stood either on a mole or on the shore (*The Architecture of the Roman Empire*, II (New Haven/London, 1986), 262).

47 Price and Trell (cit. at n. 45), fig. 85.

48 J.-Y. Marc, 'Der sogenannte Caracalla-Bogen in Thasos und die Funktion monumentaler Bögen in der griechischen Städten der römischen Kaiserzeit', in H. Friesinger and F. Kringinger, eds, *100 Jahre österreichische Forschungen in Ephesos: Akten des Symposions Wien 1995* (Vienna, 1999), 707–11.

49 L. Abad Casal, *Lucentum*, 3 (1984), 196. For an ill. of the Zadar arch see C.M. Ivekovic, *Dalmatiens Architektur und Plastik* (Vienna, 1910–27), III, pl. 112.

50 'The Thematic Organisation of the Panel Reliefs on the Arch of Galerius', *AJA* 81 (1977), 427–54. On the arch see also C.J. Makaronas, *The Arch of Galerius at Thessaloniki* (Thessaloniki, 1970).

6

AFTER NERO IN ASIA MINOR

Turkey

The most celebrated monument of Xanthos in Lycia is the Nereid Monument, of the fifth century BC: it is now in the British Museum. Below it stood a small arch with a Doric entablature. Two of its metopes, with busts of Apollo and Artemis, are also in the British Museum. An inscription recorded that it was erected by the people, through the agency of Sextus Marcius Priscus, who was Vespasian's legate in Lycia.

Iznik (Nicaea), in Bithynia, is remarkable for its grand late Byzantine walls. Between the projecting semicircular towers of the Lefke Kapi (the east gate) is a Roman arch, with a broad central opening and pilasters at either end supporting a substantial entablature. Over the rectangular side openings are round-headed niches framed by pilasters, which presumably contained statues. On the architrave and frieze, on both sides, is an inscription dedicating the gate to the imperial house and to Nicaea, chief city of the *eparcheia* (province), by M. Plancius Varus. Plancius, who came from Perge in Pamphylia, was proconsul of Pontus and Bithynia under Vespasian.[1] On the frieze over the northern opening on the town side is an inscription put up by Ti. Claudius Quintianus to honour M. Plancius Varus, patron of the city and his friend, and over the southern opening is a similar inscription set up by C. Cassius Chrestus. Clearly Plancius paid for the gate, and he was presumably honoured with statues by his friends, who were citizens of the town (the Cassii were a well-known family, which included the historian Cassius Dio). On the architrave of the town side is a dedication to Hadrian, which must have been added when he visited Nicaea in 123, and helped with its reconstruction after a recent earthquake. On the lower part of the south side is an inscription put up by the city to honour C. Iulius Bassus, who was made proconsul of Bithynia by Nerva and governed in 97/8 or 98/9.[2]

Another Roman arch is embedded within Istanbul Kapi, the northern gate of the city. This is better preserved, though its lower part is buried. It is very similar to the Lefke Kapi arch. Each side bore an inscription in metal letters honouring the *Autokratores* (Vespasian and Titus), but not mentioning the proconsul. The arch was 10 m wide, 7 m high and 3.5 m deep, and was built of greyish-black marble, with the projecting mouldings in white marble. There was an upper storey, of which little survives.[3]

At the main crossroads of the colonnaded streets of Perge (near the Pamphylian – southern Turkish – coast, north-east of Antalya) stands an arch whose inscription records its building under Titus. Enough survives for a rebuilding to be possible.[4]

A monumental gateway at Hierapolis (near Pamukkale, east of Aphrodisias in Caria – western Turkey) was erected under the supervision of Sextus Julius Frontinus, some time between 84 and 86, in honour of Domitian. Frontinus, who is best known for his book on aqueducts, was proconsul of Asia in 82/3. The gate stands on the line of the main street, some 155 m north of the walls. There are three openings, of which the central one is slightly larger than the others, and the gate is flanked by round towers (mentioned in the inscription), which had no defensive purpose. The structure is of limestone, apart from the marble blocks bearing the inscription, on both sides, which run above the archivolts. There was originally a more ornate upper storey, of marble; pilasters and columns on a parapet supported an entablature. Another gate stood outside the walls on the south; it seems to have been identical, apart from the fact that the flanking towers were square.[5]

At the north-east corner of Patara, in Lycia, stands a well-preserved arch with three vaulted openings, the central one the largest, below a Doric entablature and frieze. On both faces, beside the openings, are six consoles which carried busts. Inscriptions identify these as the family of Mettius Modestus, who was legate of Lycia under Domitian (and later, under either Trajan or Hadrian, proconsul of Asia). The three large niches – rectangular ones within the openings, and a square one over the central opening – perhaps held imperial statues. An inscription on each side records that the arch was built by 'the people of Patara, metropolis of the Lycians'.[6]

A second arch at Perge stands across the end of the horseshoe-shaped court which forms the inner side of the Hellenistic south gate. It was similar to the gate at Antalya (see below), with three openings. It was built by Plancia Magna, daughter of M. Plancius Verus (see above). In its niches stood statues of emperors and empresses, and other members of the imperial family, from the reign of Nerva to the reign of Hadrian; the titles on the bases (inscribed in both Greek and Latin) give a date between 119 and 122. Plancia also decorated the court with marble revetment and a two-storey Corinthian colonnade, whose niches also contained statues. The surviving ones are now in the museum at Antalya.[7]

The much earlier arch of Mazaeus and Mithradates at Ephesus has been described (above, p. 22). Close to it, between the Library of Celsus and the Heroon, stood a striking gate which was probably erected in honour of Trajan, to celebrate his Parthian victories. It may have been dedicated during his lifetime, or after his death, either on Hadrian's accession in 117 or at the time of his visit in 123. The remaining fragments of the inscription could refer to either emperor. The form of the gate was remarkable. Pairs of freestanding Corinthian columns supported entablatures, between which rose an arch, flanked by pilasters. These did not correspond to the two central columns, but freestanding piers on either side stood over the outer columns below. Above a second entablature stood a smaller Corinthian order, with one column at either end and four over the opening. The entablature over all these columns was broken in the centre, where a smaller arch was framed by a pediment corresponding to the four central columns.[8] The gate has been described as 'a unique combination of half and three-quarter columns and pilasters. The second storey had a delicate columnar structure comparable to the nearly contemporary Gate of Hadrian in Athens.'[9]

Along the south-east curve of the harbour at Ephesus stood three more 'gates', whose dating is uncertain; it will be simpler to discuss them together here. The middle one may date to the reign of Hadrian.[10] It was articulated on each side by four pairs of freestanding Ionic columns, with projecting bases and entablatures. The end bays, and the third and fifth bays, were open, whereas the second, fourth and sixth were solid, with a rectangular opening in the middle one, and lower arched openings on either side. No inscription has been found, though a statue-base nearby names Septimius Severus and his family, while two others, erected by named Eirenarchoi ('justices of the peace'), honoured L. Egnatius Victor Lollianus. He was proconsul of Asia three times, the last under Philippus (244–7).[11]

The southern gate bore an inscription recording that it was set up by the city with money left to 'the goddess' (Diana) by M. Fulvius Publicianus Nicephorus. Its form, known from fragments, was truly bizarre. Its east façade was curved, and had two storeys, each consisting of six Corinthian columns or pilasters. Over the central pair of the lower order was a pediment. The west façade was similar, but straight, and set at an angle, so that the southern façade, which had two arched openings between pilasters, was wider than the northern one.

The northern gate was the simplest. Four attached columns framed three arches, of which the central one was the largest. Over it the entablature broke forward. The date is unknown, as only odd letters survive of the inscription. Near it was another inscription honouring L. Egnatius Victor, erected by the same two Eirenarchoi.[12]

West of Antioch in Pisidia stands a monumental gate, with three equal openings. Its form echoed that of the Augustan gate in the same city (see p. 23). In the spandrels were reliefs showing (as on the earlier arch) Victories and genii of the seasons. Over the central opening two barbarians with standards flanked a trophy, and on the frieze were weapons and pairs of tritons beside trophies. The holes for the inscription have been read as indicating a dedication to Hadrian in 129.[13]

At Antalya (Attaleia), in Pamphylia, stands the impressively restored Gate of Hadrian [6.1]. It has three large openings, of equal size, and on each front are four freestanding Corinthian columns. The openings have coffered vaults, with rosettes. There was an upper storey, of which only two column bases survived until the nineteenth century. They did not correspond to the columns below. The gate forms the eastern entrance to the town, and is flanked by Hellenistic towers. On the attic over the entablature was an inscription recording the dedication of the gate by the council and people to Hadrian, who is described in eulogistic terms that culminate in the phrase 'saviour of the world'. A second inscription on the upper fascia of the architrave, in gilded letters, recorded another dedication to Hadrian, perhaps of a statue. The gate was probably erected to celebrate the Emperor's visit in 130. The freestanding columns and bases (which stand well clear of the piers) recall the Library and Arch of Hadrian at Athens.[14]

Ariassos (Pisidia) in the Taurus mountains has a simple arch, also in honour of Hadrian, with three equal openings. In the spandrels on either side are consoles, and on top three bases survive; the inscription refers to four statues.[15]

Yet another arch honouring Hadrian stands at Isaura, also up in the Taurus Mountains. It has a single opening, 5.5 m high. Its archivolt rises from a cornice which runs all round the piers. The upper part, including the entablature, is missing. The keystone was originally carved in some form, but later worked into a cross. On the architrave of the upper cornice was the inscription, which, as at Antalya, recorded the dedication of

6.1 Antalya, Turkey, Gate of Hadrian, probably after 130.

the arch by the council and people. It stands at the north end of the square below the acropolis.[16]

A second arch at Isaura stands at the end of a street crossing into the same square from the west. It bears an inscription dating it to 166–9, in the reign of Marcus Aurelius. In size and form it is roughly similar to the arch of Hadrian, but it is much shallower and the back is plain. At the corners are raised bands like pilasters. The bases of the piers project as benches. The lengthy inscription is carved on the left pier below the cornice. It records the benefaction of M. Marius Pius Flavianus, a former high priest, who built a stoa with twenty-five columns, and workshops in it with a vault, at his own cost, and dedicated the arch to good fortune, on behalf of the Emperor, the senate, and the Roman people.[17]

A single arch at Tarsos in Cilicia is dated to the early second century by the character of the ornament on the archivolt, but nothing else is known about it. At Korykos, also in Cilicia, a monumental gate stands near the east corner of the walls. It was freestanding, and may have marked the beginning of a colonnaded street from the harbour. It is almost 14 m broad, but shallow, and its single opening is 6 m wide. There are four pilasters, with 'rustic' acanthus capitals, supporting a richly decorated cornice. On each pilaster is a console, at the same level as the projecting bases of the two rectangular pedimented niches which occupy the centre of each side space. No doubt both consoles and niches supported statues, which indicates the commemorative function of the arch. The architectural details suggest a date in the later second or third century.[18]

The spectacular tetrapylon at Aphrodisias, re-erected in 1991, probably dates from the middle of the second century or soon after. It stands in front of the precinct of Aphrodite, to which it served as the entrance. It is not known whether it had a commemorative purpose. It consists of four rows, each of four columns, those in two of the rows with spiral fluting. On each of the main fronts was a pediment, broken by an arch (as on the sides of the arch at Orange – p. 20). The pediments are decorated with the rich and elegant sculpture for which Aphrodisias is famous.[19]

Part of an arch survives at Kilikiai Pylai (Cilician Gates), or Kodrigai, south of Issos, on the border between Cilicia and Syria. From its inscription we know that it was erected in honour of Septimius Severus, near the site of his defeat of his rival Pescennius Niger in 194. It has been suggested that the place was chosen partly to associate his victory with Alexander the Great's famous defeat of the Persians at Issos, and partly because of its proximity to the arch honouring Germanicus on Mons Amanus (see p. 29), on a spur of which it stands. Only the stump of the west pier now survives; much of the rest was used after 1902 for a railway cutting. The arch was made of limestone, faced with marble. There were pilasters at the corners, and probably half-columns on either side of the opening. The name Kodrigai suggests that there was a *quadriga* on top. References to the arch go back to the thirteenth century, and it seems that it was originally a comparatively lavish structure.[20]

A particularly remarkable arch stands largely intact at Anazarbos (Anavarza), northeast of Adana in Cilicia [6.2]. It marked the southern approach to the city, and originally stood on its own, though a fortification wall with a gate between square towers, parallel to it but not axial with the arch, was built in front of it, probably in the fourth century. The arch is triple. The south side is the principal front. Above the side arches

6.2 Anazarbos (Anavarza), Turkey, C2 or C3.

runs an entablature, which curves up over the taller central opening. This is flanked by pilasters. On the piers between the openings are pairs of freestanding columns of black granite. On the end piers are single freestanding columns, with, on the outer corners, short walls which project at right angles. These had fluted pilasters on their outer corners, with pediments facing inwards, and segments of pediments facing south. There appears to have been an upper storey, with aedicules over the side openings, and pairs of freestanding columns supporting pediments over the paired columns and at the ends. Whether there was an upper storey over the projecting walls is uncertain. The inner side of the arch was much plainer, and articulated with pilasters, but on either side of the central opening were richly decorated consoles, probably surmounted by aedicules. An interesting feature of the arch is that its concrete core was faced with a variety of stones, to produce an effect of polychromy. The decoration of the arch suggested to Verzone a date in the third quarter of the second century, but Louis Robert pointed out that coins of Anazarbos from the reign of Macrinus (217–18) commemorated Macrinus's Parthian 'triumph', which suggests an earlier date.[21]

A third arch at Isaura was built by the council and people in honour of Severus Alexander, 'lord of land and sea and the whole race of men'. The occasion may have been his triumph in 233 after the recovery of Mesopotamia. Parts of its piers survive, built of reused material. Similar to the arch of Hadrian at Isaura, though slightly smaller, its proportions were clumsy.[22]

A coin of Severus Alexander's successor Maximinus, minted at Alexandria Troas (on the coast south-west of Troy), shows an arch (apparently single, but it could be triple) with a chariot drawn by two oxen, the driver of which holds a standard; there are also four legionary eagles. Another coin, inscribed *IMP. MAXIMUS CAE.*, shows an arch with three openings, on top of which a Victory stands on a globe between two trophies. She holds a shield over her head. The two coin types may show the same arch.[23] An arch which may have been of similar date is shown on a coin of the Empress Otacilia Severa (244–9) from Olba-Diokaisareia (Uzuncaburç) in Cilicia. The arch is supported on columns, and has figures on top. Within the opening the columns have consoles attached, which bear statues.[24] An arch at the end of a bridge appears on the coinage of Antiochia ad Maeandrum, in Caria, dating from the reigns of Decius, Valerian and Gallienus (249–68). The arch is triple, the central opening much higher than the side ones, above which are niches. A river-god reclines on the bridge.[25]

Coins of Mopsuestia (Misis), in eastern Cilicia, show an arch on a nine-arched bridge over a river which is identified as the Pyramus. The city is given the additional name Hadriana, and A.L. Frothingham suggested that the arch might have commemorated the territorial reorganisation under Hadrian. The coins, however, date from the reign of Valerian, who built the bridge (rebuilt under Justinian).[26] The same arch appears on contemporary coins of the nearby Aigai, which led Frothingham to suggest that it might have marked the boundary between the two cities and the mountain tribes across the river.[27]

Two other Cilician arches may be mentioned here. A very plain one stands over a Roman road at Bayramli, about 16 km north of Tarsos, whose territorial boundary it may mark.[28] Another stands over the road between Mopsuestia and Issos, near Myriandos. This too is plain, and built of black basalt, which may have been used to face an earlier arch of marble. It stands within a narrow defile where the road comes out of the Amanus mountains into the plain of Issos, and may have marked the territory of Mopsuestia or Aigai.[29] Coins of the reign of Gallienus from Parion, a port on the Hellespont near Lampsacus, show a triple arch of masonry blocks with four columns; on top is a chariot drawn by elephants. It seems that the arch formed the entrance to the tomb-shrine of the city's founder, Parios.[30]

Three arches date from the period of the Tetrarchs. In the fifteenth century, Cyriacus of Ancona saw a marble *quadrifrons* at Mytilene on the island of Lesbos, and recorded its inscription, which stated that it was dedicated by Aurelius Agathus Gennadius, governor of the province of the Islands.[31] Four reliefs found at Iznik (Nicaea) may come from an arch. They show scenes from the war against the Alamanni, defeated by Constantius Chlorus in 298, and are similar to the reliefs on the arch at Thessaloniki (see p. 87). At Antioch in Pisidia an arch fronted the tunnel under the *cavea* of the theatre. Simple in form, it was built on the initiative of Valerius Diogenes, governor of Pisidia: references to Maximinus, Licinianus and Constantine date it between 311 and 313. On the cornice is the dedication *CONCORDIAE AUG[USTORUM]*.[32]

A few other arches are known, whose dates cannot be established. At Assos, on the Turkish mainland north of Lesbos, a simple arch stood over the street west of the agora. At Celenderis, on the south coast of Cilicia, are remains of a *quadrifrons*, which had a pyramid in place of an attic (comparable perhaps with the Arch of Janus at Rome – see p. 54). It stood beside the sea. At Labraynda, in Caria (north-east of Halicarnassos), another simple arch stood at the entrance to a bridge. At Sagalassos, north of Antalya, are remains of a 'gate-arch'; surviving fragments of its inscription record that it was built by the city.[33] A large triple gateway stands at Uzuncaburç (Olba-Diokaisareia) [6.3]. The central opening has a moulded archivolt, supported on Corinthian pilasters. The masonry over the side openings reaches the tops of these capitals. Bases for statues remain on the cornice above the main opening, and probably existed also on the side

6.3 Uzuncaburç (Olba-Diokaisareia), Turkey, date unknown.

walls. In addition there are consoles for statues or busts on either side of the main opening, on both fronts. The date and commemorative purpose (if any) are unknown; the inscription of the time of Arcadius and Honorius (*c.* 400), on the outer front, refers to a restoration.[34] At Side, on the Pamphylian coast east of Antalya, the inner city was entered by a monumental gate in the fourth-century walls. This once had an attic, probably surmounted by a *quadriga*, since the area was known, according to inscriptions, as the Quarter of the Quadriga. The gate is still over 12 m high. When it became the main entrance to the city, a smaller gate was set within it (now dismantled).[35]

Constantinople

A number of arches were erected at Constantinople in the period between Constantine (reigned 306–37) and Theodosius I (reigned 379–95). The site and form of only two are known. The so-called Milion, built in the first half of the fourth century, was the equivalent of Rome's Milliarium Aureum, and stood at a bend in the main street next to the Augusteion (south-west of Haghia Sophia). It took the form of a *quadrifrons*, and probably had a cupola. It was crowned by statues of Tyche (Fortune), and of Constantine and Helena with the cross, as well as equestrian statues of Trajan, Hadrian and (?) Theodosius II, together with a *quadriga* driven by Helios. Further statues were added later – for example, of the wife, daughter and niece of Justin II.[36]

Theodosius I (379–95) began the building of a new forum, generally known as the Forum Tauri. It was based on Trajan's Forum at Rome, and had a basilica, a column, and an equestrian statue. There was a freestanding arch at the west end [6.4]. On either

6.4 Arch in Forum of Theodosius, Constantinople, *c.* 380.

AFTER NERO IN ASIA MINOR 97

side of the central opening were groups of four freestanding columns, each group on a rectangular base. The columns were of Proconnesian marble, and were decorated with leaf patterns. They supported a plain upper stage, crowned by a dentilled cornice. The vault was coffered. The lower side openings had masonry above reaching up to an entablature at the same height as that above the central columns. The restoration of the arch by R. Naumann shows a group of four columns at each end, matching the central ones, but there is no certain evidence for these. The site of the Forum is now Beyazit Meydaní; the podia of the central opening and other fragments can be seen there. One of the columns was reused in the sixth century in the Yerebatan (the Basilica Cistern).[37]

Descriptions of triumphal routes, particularly that of 879, mention other arches, including two on the street called Xerolophos, an 'Arch of the Artopolia', and an 'Arch of the Portico', but of these nothing else is known.[38]

Syria, Jordan, Palestine and Lebanon

As in Turkey, the 'arches' of this area show significant differences from those in the West. They relate to the Hellenistic building type of 'propylon', or entrance gateway, and it is not always easy to distinguish between a 'gateway' and an 'honorific arch'. Few of the arches have inscriptions, and the sort of sculptural decoration so often found in the West is for the most part lacking. There are, however, a certain number of monuments which, either by their commemorative purpose or their architectural form, or both, need to be considered in this study. The rarity of inscriptions frequently makes their dating uncertain.

It has been argued recently by Ingeborg Kader that the tetrapylon of Latakia (Laodicea ad Mare), on the Syrian coast east of Cyprus, dates from the time of Augustus or the early Empire; others, however, still prefer a date in the second century [6.5]. The larger arches, on the north–south axis, have attached half-columns on either side. A low pediment stands in front of the tall attic. The smaller arches, on the east–west axis, have rectangular attached piers on either side. The interior is roofed with an octagonal vault. The lowest course of the cupola bears a weapon-frieze. Kader suggests that the arch was the entrance to a sacred precinct, perhaps dedicated already to a Hellenistic ruler-cult, and later adapted to the Roman imperial cult. Apart from this purpose, there is no reason to assume a commemorative function.[39]

6.5 Tetrapylon at Latakia (Laodicea ad Mare), Syria, C1 or C2.

6.6 Temenos Gate at Petra, Jordan, C1.

As its name makes clear, the 'Temenos (sacred enclosure) Gate' at Petra, in Jordan, marked the entrance from the colonnaded street which formed the principal axis of the city to the precinct of the temple known as Kasr el Bint. This was built in the late Nabataean period (roughly corresponding to the reign of Augustus), but the gate must be later [6.6]. Kader suggests that it was built early in the first century AD, but remodelled after the annexation of Nabataea in 106. Built of ashlar faced in pink sandstone, it stands up against buildings on either side. The central opening is much higher than the side ones. On the eastern side (the front) there are freestanding columns, behind which are pilasters. These had floral capitals of Nabataean type. The south pilaster of the southern arch retains the three lower blocks of a floral frieze rising from acanthus leaves. The pilasters of the central opening were decorated with square panels carved alternately with busts and floral motifs. The west side has half-columns on either side of the central opening, and quarter-columns at the ends. Fragments of sculpture from the gate include a bust of a god (possibly Serapis), a winged head, a relief bust of Hermes and a winged Tyche. As Kader points out, these do not suggest a monument dedicated to the imperial house. The three openings were fitted with doors.[40]

There used to be another arch at Petra, generally known as the Monumental or Triumphal Arch, just inside the entrance to the Siq, the great gorge through which the city is approached. The actual arch collapsed in 1895; on either side survive the remains of pilasters flanking podia with apsidal niches above. It must have dated from the second half of the first century AD at the earliest.[41]

The 'town gate' of Tyre stood on the only approach road to the island town, from the east, and formed the monumental end to a Roman colonnaded street, dominating the necropolis to its east. Only the central part survives, but it was originally triple, with four attached Corinthian columns on either side. There was a pediment over the central opening. At the sides were low rectangular openings, beneath round-headed niches set in pedimented aedicules. The gate was flanked by round towers, and was freestanding. It was dated by M.-H. Chehab to the time of Hadrian, who visited Tyre, or Septimius Severus, who made it a colony, but Kader dates it to the early Empire on stylistic grounds.[42]

The Nabataean Gate, or East Arch, of Bostra stood at the east end of the Decumanus Maximus, at the entrance to the Acropolis. It has only one large opening, and each pier is pierced by a narrow barrel-vaulted passageway. Each pier on the main sides is divided into two horizontal registers. The lower has entablatures at the level of the arch imposts; these are supported on pilasters, repeated at the corners. Between are rectangular niches, with half-columns on either side. Each pier in the upper register is pierced with semicircular niches between pairs of smaller rectangular ones. A broad pediment takes the place of an attic, ruling out the possibility of statuary. There was no inscription. The side façades were similarly articulated. The capitals are all of Nabataean type. The arch has been dated, after recent investigations, to the second half of the first century AD.[43]

At Dura Europos, far off to the east on the river Euphrates, remains of an arch survive, which include parts of the inscription repeated on both sides. These show that it was built by the Legio III Cyrenaica in honour of Trajan. The date is almost certainly 115/16. The arch seems to have been 13.4 m wide, and had three openings, of which the central one was 8.4 m high, and the side ones 4 m. These are unusually narrow in relation to the central one, and – even more unusually – the arches are pointed, a feature which occurs in other buildings in the town. The materials were brick and ashlar. Of the decoration, only fragments of mouldings, from a column, survive. The arch stood 1,800 m outside the town gates, near the point where the roads to Palmyra and to Soura and Antioch diverged. The occasion for its erection is not entirely clear. Trajan had been in the East since 113, and spent the winter of 115–16 at Antioch. Baur suggests that the sailing of the Roman fleet down the Euphrates in 115 or 116 might explain the arch, though it is not known whether Trajan accompanied it. It is the easternmost arch in the Roman Empire.[44]

Another arch with an inscription stands 460 m south of the city of Jerash – Gerasa – in Jordan. A substantial amount of the structure survives [6.7]. Each side had four attached Corinthian half-columns; the base of each has acanthus-leaf decoration – a rare feature of Hellenistic origin. Above the low side-arches were semicircular recesses within pedimented aedicules. The principal entablature is decorated with a rich floral frieze. The double attic had an attached pediment over the central opening, and an inscription in the upper register that records the dedication of the arch by the city in honour of Hadrian in 130. He had visited it two years before. The money came from the will of Flavius Agrippa. He may be the M. Flavius Agrippa known from an inscription of Caesarea, and may also be the youngest son (born 77/8) of the historian Flavius Josephus.[45] The word used for the structure is πύλη (gate), and it is remarkable that the side openings had wooden doors, and the central one a door lowered from above. One may compare Petra (above), where the doors make sense at the entrance to a sanctuary. At Gerasa, however, the arch is freestanding. It appears that it may have been intended to be a new gate for the city, whose southward expression would commemorate the Emperor's visit. A further puzzle in the inscription is the phrase σὺν θριάμβῳ. θρίαμβος is the word generally used to translate *triumphus*: suggested explanations

6.7 Arch at Jerash (Gerasa), Jordan, dedicated to Hadrian in 130.

include ceremonial pageantry accompanying the dedication, or a triumphal statue of the Emperor crowning the arch. Yet another peculiarity of the arch is the fact that it was flanked by 'pavilions' articulated by pilasters, which had round-headed niches below and pedimented rectangular ones above. Their entablatures linked up with that of the arch. They extended its original width of 22.25 m to 37.45 m.[46]

Another remarkable feature of the arch at Gerasa is its close similarity to the south gate of the city, outside which it stands. Restored in 1988–90, that too had three openings, the central one wider than that of the arch, the side ones narrower. The articulation was almost identical. The attached half-columns have leaf decoration on the bases, and had Corinthian capitals. Above the side openings were niches within aedicules. On either side was a narrow 'pavilion', decorated with a round-headed niche between Corinthian pilasters. The appearance of the upper part of the gate is unknown. The quality of the carved detail is superior to that of the arch. The gate is dated to the first quarter of the second century, and it is suggested that the arch may have been copied from it. When first built the gate was freestanding, though before long the city was fortified and walls were built on either side. Seigne and Wagner think that it was built at the same time as the Hadrianic arch.[47]

The north gate of Gerasa was also of monumental form, with a tall central opening set between giant aedicules; pairs of Corinthian columns framed round-headed niches, one above the other, and supported pediments. The plan of the gate was triangular, to disguise the change in axis of the street, as at Palmyra, though here the piers were solid. An inscription indicates that the gate was erected in 115 by Trajan's legate Claudius Severus.[48]

Yet another arch stood at the south entrance to the Cardo Maximus from the 'Oval Plaza'. It was a single arch spanning 11 m. It could not have been vaulted, and it was probably similar to the Arch of Hadrian at Athens and the Trajanic gate at Ephesus. It seems to have dated from the second century.[49]

The 'Damascus gate' at Jerusalem is now dated to the time of Hadrian, and reckoned to define the northern limit of his new Colonia Aelia Capitolina. It consisted of a triple gateway set between towers, not connected with fortification walls; these towers are canted outwards. The openings were decorated with half-columns and pilasters.[50]

A third arch with an inscription is known from Umm-el-Jimal (south-west of Bostra), but the inscription, which honours Marcus Aurelius and Commodus, is the only feature distinguishing this gate, the northern one of two in the west wall, from other gates. It was the main entrance to the city, but was very plain, the arched opening set between projecting towers.[51]

An arch in Jerusalem is known as the 'Ecce Homo arch' because of the tradition that this was where Pontius Pilate showed Christ to the people [6.8]. It is now hidden by other buildings, and only partially visible. It seems to have acted as the gate to the area in the northern part of the town occupied by the Roman legion, and is dated to the second half of the second century. Comparatively plain, it had three openings, whose archivolts rested on pilaster capitals; there were, however, no pilasters. On the west side there were semicircular niches between the arches, and round-headed niches (or possibly openings) above the side arches.[52]

6.8 'Ecce Homo' Arch at Jerusalem, C2.

A monumental arch at Apamea (east of Latakia), which survives in a collapsed state, also probably dates from the second century. It stood about 50 m outside the North Gate – not an uncommon position for an arch (compare e.g. Gerasa). In the Byzantine period a new rear façade was applied to the arch, which was linked by thick walls to the gate.[53]

A second arch at Bostra, known as the Central Arch, is dated to the second or third century. Its form and placing are most unusual. It stood on the south side of the *decumanus maximus*, over the street leading to the theatre. It was presumably incorporated into the colonnade running along the street, which explains why it was built not with solid piers, but with two groups of four small square piers linked by arches, so that the length of the structure can also be traversed. The north façade was more richly decorated than the south. Each pier had a pilaster attached with a Corinthian capital, and halfway up the piers were corbels to support statues. The upper part of the arch was rebuilt in the Byzantine period. Butler suggests that there was originally a pediment across the whole structure, with the central arch rising up into it.[54]

The arch at Palmyra is celebrated both for its rich decoration and for its ingenious plan, elegantly illustrated in the plates of James Dawkins and Robert Wood's *Ruins of Palmyra* (1753) [6.9]. It stood at the east end of the great colonnaded street, at the point where the road bends to the south-east, towards the Sanctuary of Bel. In order to disguise the change of axis, the arch was triangular in plan, with each façade properly aligned to the street it faces. On the west the side openings were within the colonnades, which attached themselves to the arch. The colonnade entablature was supported at the junction with the arch by a Corinthian capital above a console supported on a lion's head. On the east side, the colonnades were attached to the arch's extremities. The pilasters and pilaster capitals, and the archivolts, were richly decorated with varied floral ornament, while the soffits of the arches were coffered in geometric patterns. Within the structure, above the arches which open at the sides of the central passageway, were niches, one on the north, and two on the south. These had pedimented aedicules with freestanding columns between projecting bases and entablatures. Inscribed blocks found beneath the arch may have come from it: if they do, they provide a *terminus post quem* of 212. The decoration might suggest a slightly earlier date. The arch was destroyed by ISIS in 2015.[55]

A freestanding arch was identified at Gadara, in the Decapolis (group of ten cities), in 1974, and excavation began in 1990. The arch has three openings, the central one much taller and wider than the side ones. On each side were freestanding columns with Corinthian capitals and attached Attic bases. Above the side openings were niches framed by pedimented aedicules. It is assumed that there was an attic. The arch is flanked by towers, which are flush with the east side but project in semicircular shape towards the west – the outer side. A peculiarity is that the openings are arched on the east side, but rectangular on the west, perhaps to suggest their role as gates. The structure was mostly built of basalt, but the columns, niches and aedicules were of limestone. The arch stood 360 m west of the city wall, on the line of the main street, and so is comparable with the monumental gateway at Hierapolis in Asia Minor, erected in 84–86: that has a round tower on either side, and it too is freestanding (see p. 91). The closest parallel nearby is the Arch of Hadrian at Gerasa, and there is a curious further

6.9 Arch at Palmyra, Syria, c. 200, destroyed 2015.

AFTER NERO IN ASIA MINOR 103

parallel in that in each case the arch stands close to a hippodrome. The Gadara arch is dated on stylistic grounds to the early third century.[56]

The so-called Nabataean Sanctuary at Sî (north-east of Bostra) was entered by a gate in the form of a triple monumental arch. Known as the 'Roman Gate', it was comparatively wide, and it was exceptionally richly and finely decorated. The eastern (outer) façade was the more elaborate. Between the openings were pairs of pilasters, flanked by fluted quarter-columns, and on the outer sides of the side openings the same arrangement was halved. All these pilasters, and the pilasters supporting the archivolts, were carved with vine branches and other decorative motifs. The entablature was equally richly ornamented. The west façade had plain pilasters with Ionic capitals. There may have been a pediment over the central opening on each side. The arch was dated by Butler to the first half of the second century; however, remains of inscriptions indicate that it was built at the expense of Julius Heraclitus, equestrian governor of Arabia (it is described as πύλος and as θύραι), which would indicate a date in the second half of the third century.[57]

A fragment of a much later arch stands at Der Sim'an, in northern Syria. The piers are T-shaped. The arch voussoirs spring from freestanding columns, and the pilasters, in front of which they stand, have carved foliated capitals running round the arms of the T. Oddly, the projecting arms of the T stop at a height of about two thirds of the total height, to carry freestanding colonnettes, above which the main cornice springs forward. The arch is dated to the late fifth or early sixth century. It stood above the sacred road leading from Der Sim'an to Kal'at Sim'an.[58]

Two plain arches are undatable. One is the so-called Bab il-Hawa, at Djebel Halaka, over the road from Antioch to Chalkis. It is simply a plain wall pierced by a wide arch, with a plinth below and a stringcourse at the level of the springing.[59] The other is at es-Suweda, north of Bostra. Two piers bear an arch, which had an attic above it. Nineteenth-century travellers recorded 'finely wrought profiles' on one of the façades. The arch stands at the upper end of the main street, and may have formed the entrance to the acropolis.[60]

In this area there were a number of examples of *quadrifrontes*, called in Greek τετράπυλα. One of the most striking stood at Gerasa, towards the north of the city, at the point on the *cardo maximus* where the 'north *decumanus*' went off towards the theatre. The plan is a square of 12.5 m. The openings to north and south were flanked by freestanding columns, which may have borne pediments. The arches to east and west had niches on either side (which may have been framed by aedicules). The entablature has a frieze of pulvinated 'continuous triglyph' motif, found also at the Temple of Bacchus at Baalbek. The cornice breaks up into a segmental pediment over the arch. Within the western one was a small relief of the moon, to which the sun corresponded on the east. A peculiarity of these two sides is that the pilasters near the corners project more at the top than at the bottom; the difference may have been made up with plaster (certainly used on the inside of the structure). The piers are concave on their inner sides, which suggests that the arch may have been roofed with a dome. It must date from before the widening of the south *cardo c.* 180, and may have been erected in connection with the building of the theatre in 165/6. On the north-west pier there is an inscription in honour of Decimus Junius Arabianus Socrates, who must have been equestrian procurator: it dates from the reign of Severus Alexander (222–35).[61]

Another tetrapylon stands at the crossing of the main streets of the so-called 'Camp of Diocletian' in Palmyra. The western end of the city was transformed into a camp some time in the reign of Diocletian (284–305). The structure had solid piers at the corners; pairs of columns between these supported pediments. The colonnades of the principal street abutted it at the outer corners, but those of the cross street abutted the intercolumniations. There were no arches.[62]

A related structure, known as the tetrakionion, is found in several places in the area. Here the four podia are not connected, and each bears four freestanding columns. The best-known example is at Palmyra, which has been fully restored. It stands in an oval piazza at the point where the colonnaded street makes a slight bend.[63] Similar monuments stood in circular piazze at Bostra (late second or third century) and Gerasa (late second century), and at the intersection of the main streets of Philippopolis (dating from the mid-third century). There was a smaller one at Antipatris.[64]

Notes

1 *PIR* VI (1998), no. 443.
2 Sencer Sahin, *Bithynische Studien: Inschriften griechischer Städte aus Kleinasien* 7 (Bonn, 1978), 8–28.
3 A.M. Schneider and W. Karnapp, *Die Stadtmauer von Iznik*, Istanbuler Forschungen 9 (Berlin, 1938), 22–5.
4 J. Wagner, *Turkei: Die Südküste von Kaunos bis Issos* (Munich, 1988), 170.
5 D. De Bernardi, *Annuario della scuola archeologica di Athene*, 41–2 (1963–4), 391–407; G. Monaco, ibid., 409–10 (on the inscription); D. De Bernardi Ferrero, in F. Berti et al., *Arslantepe, Hierapolis, Iasos, Kyme: Scavi Italiani in Turchia* (Venice, 1993), 110, 128.
6 G.K. Sams, *Archaeology* 28 (1975), 203–4; G.E. Bean, *Lycian Turkey* (London, 1978), 86; Wagner (cit. at n. 4), 77; V. Idil, *Festschrift für Jale Inan* (Istanbul, 1989), 356 and ill. 12; C. Arnold, *Les arcs romains de Jérusalem* (Göttingen, 1997), 132–3. On Mettius Modestus, see *PIR* V,1 (1970), no. 568.
7 G.E. Bean, *Turkey's Southern Shore* (2nd edn, London, 1979), 31; E. Akurgal, *Griechische und Römische Kunst in Turkei* (Munich, 1987), 449–50; Wagner (cit. at n. 4), 169.
8 Hilke Thür, *Das Hadrianstor in Ephesos*, Forschungen in Ephesos XI/1 (Vienna, 1989).
9 R. Stilwell (ed.), *The Princeton Encyclopaedia of Classical Sites* (Princeton, 1976), 308.
10 E. Weigand ('Propylon und Bogentor in der Östlichen Reichskunst, ausgehend vom Mithridatestor in Ephesos', *Wiener Jahrbuch für Kunstgeschichte* V (1928), 75) prefers a date in the late first century BC.
11 *PIR*² III (1943), no. 36.
12 Kähler 1939, 455, mistakenly describes this as being on the frieze. On the three gates see *Forschungen in Ephesos* III (Vienna, 1923), 169–223. Nothing is visible of them on the ground.
13 S. Mitchell and M. Waelkens, *Pisidian Antioch* (London, 1998), 96–9; H. Bru, in T. Drew-Bear (ed.), *Actes du premier Congrès International sur Antioche de Pisidie* (Lyon, 2002), 359–68; A. Ossi, *Bull. of the University of Michigan Museums of Art and Archaeology* 16 (2005–6), 5–28.
14 K. Lanckoronski, *Städte Pamphyliens und Pisidiens* II, *Pisidien* (Vienna, 1892), pl. XXII (as 'Kretopolis'); Idil (cit. at n. 6), 357.
15 K. Lanckoronski, *Städte Pamphyliens und Pisidiens* I, *Pamphylien* (Vienna, 1890), 20–26; Bean (cit. at n. 7), 22.
16 H. Swoboda, J. Keil and F. Kroll, *Denkmäler aus Lykaonien, Pamphylien und Isaurien* (Prague, 1935), II, 131–2.
17 Swoboda et al. (cit. in the preceding note), 125–7; also (for the inscription) 73, n. 147.
18 E. Herzfeld and S. Guyer, *Monumenta Asiae Minoris Antiqua* II (1930), 173–6; Wagner (cit. at n. 4), 222; F. Hild and H. Hellenkemper, *Kilikien und Isaurien* (Vienna, 1990), 317.
19 The arch is dealt with by Kähler 1939, cols. 455 and 457, at both VII 15 (under the name Merkes Kalesi) and VII 28. See also A.L. Frothingham, *AJA* 19 (1915), 168–9; R. Heberdey and A. Wilhelm, *Reisen in Kilikien* (Vienna, 1896), 19; Hild and Hellenkemper (cit. in the preceding note), 302, with fig. 232; E. Winter, *Staatliche Baupolitik und Baufürsorge in den römischen Provinzen des Kaiserlichen Kleinasien*, Asia Minor Studien (Bonn, 1996), 133. The inscription *IGR* III 927 may come from the arch.
20 Kenan Erim, *Aphrodisias City of Venus Aphrodite* (London, 1986), 60–61, 181; R.R.R. Smith, *Aphrodisias, City and Sculpture in Roman Asia* (Istanbul, 2008), 33.
21 P. Verzone, *Palladio* 7 (1957), 15–22; L. Robert, *Comptes rendus de l'Académie des Inscriptions* (1961), 176–7 = *Opera Minora Selecta* III (Amsterdam, 1969), 1463–4. See also M. Gough, *Anatolian Studies* 2 (1952), 110–13; Wagner (cit. at n. 4), 236–7; Hild and Hellenkemper (cit. at n. 18), 181.
22 Swoboda et al. (cit. at n. 16), 129–30, and 74, no. 150.

23 F. Imhoof Blumer, *Kleinasiatische Münzen* (Vienna, 1901–2), II, 507 (with pls) XIX, 12–13; M.J. Price and B.L. Trell, *Coins and their Cities* (London, 1977), figs 325, 324.
24 Price and Trell (cit. in the preceding note), fig. 507.
25 G.F. Hill, *Catalogue of the Coins of Caria, etc.* (London, 1897), 22–3; Frothingham (cit. at n. 19), 163; Price and Trell (cit. at n. 23), fig. 82.
26 Wagner (cit. at n. 4), 230–31. On the form of the arch, see Weigand (cit. at n. 10), 96–7.
27 G.F. Hill, *Catalogue of the Coins of Lycaonia, Isauria and Cilicia* (London, 1900), cxii, cxv; Frothingham (cit. at n. 19), 163.
28 Frothingham (cit. at n. 19), 162, 169. C. Mutafian, *La Cilice au carrefour des Empires* (Paris, 1988), 232. Mutafian reproduces (pl. 80) an engraving published in 1852; the arch shown in pl. 81, as 'l'Arc à Sagliki, entre Tarse et les Pyles', is presumably the same one.
29 Frothingham (cit. at n. 19), 169–70. Mutafian (cit. in the preceding note), 325, identifies the place as Karakapi (black gate); he reproduces an engraving published in 1836 (pl. 32).
30 Mitchell and Waelkens (cit. at n. 13), 107–9.
31 Price and Trell (cit. at n. 23), 117–18, fig. 211.
32 *CIL* III 450; A.H.M. Jones and J.R. Martindale, *Prosopography of the Later Roman Empire*, I (Cambridge, 1971), 390.
33 Lanckoronski (cit. at n. 15), II, 134, 228.
34 J. Keil and A. Wilhelm, *Monumenta Asiae Minoris Antiqua* III (1931), 53–4; Idil (cit. at n. 6), 358–9.
35 Bean (cit. at n. 7), 64; Idil (cit. at n. 6), 354–5, with pls 5 and 6.
36 R. Guilland, Études de *topographie de Constantinople byzantine* (Berlin, 1969), II, 28–31; W. Müller-Wiener, *Bildlexicon zur Topographie Istanbuls* (Tübingen, 1977), 216–18; M. McCormick, *Eternal Victory: Triumphal Rulership in Late Antiquity, Byzantium and the Early Medieval West* (Cambridge, 1986), 134 etc.
37 Guilland (cit. in the preceding note), II, 56–9; Müller-Wiener (cit. in the preceding note), 258–63 (illustrating Naumann's reconstruction); McCormick (cit. in the preceding note), 214–15.
38 McCormick (cit. at n. 36), 215–19.
39 I. Kader, *Propylon und Bogentor: Untersuchungen zur Tetrapylon von Latakia und anderen frühkaiserzeitlichen Bogenmonumente im Nahen Osten* (Mainz, 1996).
40 G.R.H. Wright, *Revue biblique*, 73 (1966), 404–19; Iain Browning, *Petra* (London, 1977), 141–7 (the reconstruction on p. 145 is erroneous); Judith McKenzie, *The Architecture of Petra* (Oxford, 1990), 132–4; Kader (cit. in the preceding note), 108–44; Arthur Segal, *From Function to Monument* (Oxford, 1997), 106–8.
41 Browning, *Petra* (cit. in the preceding note), 111–13; McKenzie (cit. in the preceding note), 37, 131; Kader (cit. at n. 39), 171–4.
42 M.-H. Chehab, *Bull. du Musée de Beyrouth* 33 (1983), 1–132; Kader (cit. at n. 39), 165–9.
43 H.C. Butler, *PUAES* II.A (1919), 240–43; J.-M. Dentzer, *Berytus* 32 (1984), 163–74; *CRAI* 1986, 62–87, 1993, 117–47; Kader (cit. at n. 39), 144–58; Segal (cit. at n. 40), 133–5.
44 P.V.C. Baur, ed., *The Excavations at Dura-Europos – Fourth Season 1930–31* (New Haven, 1933), 3–4, 56–68; M.I. Rostovtzeff, ed., *The Excavations at Dura-Europos – Sixth Season 1932–3* (New Haven, 1936), 480–82; F.A. Lepper, *Trajan's Parthian War* (Oxford, 1948), 123–5.
45 *PIR*[2] III (1943), 198.
46 C.H. Kraeling, *Gerasa, City of the Decapolis* (New Haven, 1938), 78–83; Segal (cit. at n. 40), 131–3. D.J. and C.M. Watts (*JSAH* 51 (1992), 306–14) argue that the placing of the arch relates to 'the geometrical ordering of the Roman master plan of Gerasa', and so helps to prove its intended rôle as lynchpin of a new urban quarter. They lay great emphasis on the fact that the arch frames the view of the Temple of Artemis – the most important in the city.
47 Kraeling (cit. in the preceding note), 140–52; I. Browning, *Jerash and the Decapolis* (1982), 112–14; J. Seigne and C. Wagner, *ADAJ* 36 (1992), 241–54; Segal (cit. at n. 40), 100–101.
48 Kraeling (cit. at n. 46), 117–23; Browning, *Jerash* (cit. in the preceding note), 170–73; Segal (cit. at n. 40), 90–94.
49 Kraeling (cit. at n. 46), 155–7; Browning, *Jerash* (cit. at n. 47), 133–4; Segal (cit. at n. 40), 133, argues that the arch was not a triple one.
50 Caroline Arnould, *Les arcs romains de Jérusalem* (Göttingen, 1997), 150–249.
51 H.C. Butler, *PUAES* II.A (1913), 156–8; Segal (cit. at n. 40), 87–8.
52 Arnould (cit. at n. 50), 136–8.
53 J.C. Balty, *CRAI* 1994, 77–101.
54 Butler (cit. at n. 43), 243–7; Segal (cit. at n. 40), 135–6.
55 The arch had been restored in 1930–31 by Robert Amy: *Syria* 14 (1933), 396–411. On the date see D. Schlumberger, *Berytus* 2 (1935), 151. See also I. Browning, *Palmyra* (London, 1979), 130–34.
56 A. Hoffmann, *Archäologischer Anzeiger* (1990), 216–38; Segal (cit. at n. 40), 95–6.
57 H.C. Butler, *Architecture and the Other Arts* (New York, 1903), 363–5; *PUAES* II.A (1919), 395–8; *PIR* IV (1952–66), 351.
58 Butler (cit. at n. 57), 268.
59 ibid., 267.
60 R.E. Brunnow and A.von Domaszewski, *Die Provincia Arabia*, III (Strassburg, 1909), 90; Segal (cit. at n. 40), 130–31.
61 Browning, *Jerash* (cit. at n. 47), 85, 168–70; F. Zayadine, ed., *Jerash Archaeological Project 1981–3* (Amman, 1986), 351–409; Segal (cit. at n. 40), 142–4.
62 D. Krencker (ed.), *Palmyra* (Berlin, 1932), 89–90; Browning, *Palmyra* (cit. at n. 55), 185; Segal (cit. at n. 40), 149.
63 Browning, *Palmyra* (cit. at n. 55), 84–5.
64 Segal (cit. at n. 40), 141–8. See also J.-C. Balty, '*Tetrakionia* de l'époque de Justinien sur la Grande Colonnade d'Apamée', *Syria* 77 (2000), 227–37.

7
NORTH AFRICA

North Africa is especially rich in arches – more so, taken as a whole, than any other part of the Roman Empire. There were well over a hundred of them. The reason for their popularity seems to have been fashion: once they became regular features of towns, and regular objects of private benevolence and public patronage, they proliferated. On the whole, the arches are fairly simple, and only a few attempt architectural elaboration. It is notable that sculptural decoration is rare: only the *quadrifrontes* of Septimius Severus at Lepcis Magna, and of Marcus Aurelius at Oea, have substantial amounts of relief sculpture. Even the arch at Volubilis, whose decoration is sparse by comparison with Roman or Gallic arches, is exceptional for Africa.

The principal function of the arches is urbanistic. More often than not they stand over important streets, or form the entrance to a forum or temple precinct. The inscriptions show that the most common occasion for their erection was as a public benefaction on the part of individual citizens, in return for election to a priesthood or magistracy.[1]

The earliest known arch stood in Lepcis Magna in Libya at the intersection of the *cardo maximus* (the so-called Triumphal Way) with the coast road, at the point where the Arch of Septimius Severus was later built. It is known as the 'Augusta Salutaris arch', as these words occur in the surviving fragment of the inscription, which records its dedication by C. Vibius Marsus, proconsul of Africa in AD 27–30.[2] It is appropriate that the earliest known arch should be at Lepcis, on the coast of Tripolitania, as that city was richest of all in arches. The next two known arches are also there, and date from a few years later. The better preserved one spans the *cardo maximus* at the corner of the market. It helps to disguise the slight bend in the road just south of it. It is of limestone, and absolutely plain except for the cornice at the top. The inscription, simply carved on the plain stone, is repeated on both sides, and states that the arch was dedicated to Tiberius in 35/36 by C. Rubellius Blandus, proconsul of Africa, to commemorate the paving of all the streets with *silex*, here used not in the sense of flint but of cut stone. This was done through the agency of M. Etrilius Lupercus, patron of the city, out of the income from the land which Rubellius had restored to the citizens (presumably after the rebellion of Tacfarinas). The contract was let by means of an auction. Remains of a similar arch, with identical inscriptions, were found on the street parallel to the *cardo maximus*, running along the north-west side of the theatre, a short distance north-east of the latter.[3]

Arches erected at Thugga (Dougga, in modern Tunisia), in honour of Tiberius and Caligula, are known only from inscriptions found near the Capitolium. On the latter, after Caligula's death the name of Claudius was substituted. The arch was built by a local magistrate and a priest who was *patronus* of the town.[4]

An arch at Lepcis Magna was dedicated to Vespasian and Titus in 77/78 on behalf of the proconsul C. Paccius Africanus: parts of its inscription survive. It seems to have stood at the entrance to the old Forum, and may have celebrated the granting of the status of *municipium* to the town.[5] Only 40 m south-west of the arch of Tiberius at Lepcis stands the arch of Trajan. Also built of limestone, this is a *quadrifrons*, set over the junction of the *cardo maximus* with the road to the theatre. It forms a perfect square. The openings were flanked by fluted Corinthian pilasters. At each corner, on all four fronts, were freestanding Corinthian columns on tall bases. On the inner side of each pier was a Corinthian column, its base at the same level as that of the pilasters. There were three inscriptions. On the south side (facing those coming from outside the town) the principal one recorded the building of the arch in honour of Trajan in 109/10 by the colony of Lepcis, at public expense. The phrase *cum ornamentis* ('with its ornaments') must have referred to statuary on top. The second inscription commemorated the rôle (probably as dedicator) of Q. Pomponius Rufus, proconsul of Africa: this is a regular feature of African arches. The inscription on the north side recorded the name of C. Cornelius Rarus Sextius, also proconsul, who may have begun the construction of the monument. Although simple, the arch must have been an elegant and pleasing feature of the city.[6]

Another arch erected in honour of Trajan forms the southern entrance to the Eastern Forum of Mactar (Mactaris) in Tunisia. It has a single opening framed by half-columns, entablature and pediment. Higher half-columns on either side support another entablature with low attic. The schema is similar to that of the Arch of the Gavii at Verona (p. 26). On the frieze over the opening is an inscription which records the dedication of the arch to the Emperor in 116 by the proconsul Caecilius Faustinus.[7]

An arch at Medeina (Althiburos), also in Tunisia, may well commemorate the granting of the status of *municipium* by Hadrian on his African journey of 128. The single arch stands over the road leading along the south-west side of the forum. The inscription appeared on both sides between entablature and frieze, enclosed within consoles. The arch is dedicated to Hadrian by the decurions (magistrates) as *conditor municipii* (founder of the *municipium*). The consoles are decorated with acanthus, and the attached columns beneath them had Corinthian capitals.[8] An inscription of the same year from Pont du Chelif (Quiza) mentions an arch.[9]

A very remarkable structure, erected perhaps the late Trajanic period, is the so-called *Praetorium* which stands over the crossing of the main streets of the great legionary camp at Lambaesis in Algeria [7.1]. Like an enormous rectangular *quadrifrons*, its north side, which faces the 143 m-long Via Praetoria, has the schema of a triumphal arch. Both the very wide central opening and the smaller and lower side ones are flanked by pairs of freestanding columns on tall bases (six in all). Between the arches are round-headed niches. The keystones are carved with various symbols. The other sides are articulated with four columns each. The east and west sides have an additional small opening on their south sides. Strictly, the structure can hardly be defined as an arch. An inscription of Gallienus, recording its restoration in 268, calls it a *groma* (a structure set over a crossroads).[10]

An inscription found at a road junction 3 km from Zama Maior (in Tunisia) records that L. Ranius Felix gave additional money so that an arch could be made bigger.

7.1 'Praetorium' at Lambaesis, Algeria, of uncertain date.

Hadrian founded the colony, and the arch may well have marked the boundary of its territory. Ranius Felix was the *flamen Augustalis* (priest of the imperial cult): Frothingham points out that the ceremony of consecrating a boundary was a religious one.[11] An arch from Hadrian's third consulate stood at Gafsa (Capsa, in Tunisia). The inscription recorded that it was built from the ground up, together with a statue and a *quadriga*, at the expense of P. Aelius Papirius to commemorate his duumvirate (a magistracy), a further sum being added to celebrate his holding the post of *flamen perpetuus*. The arch was dedicated by permission of the proconsul, who was also *patronus* of the *municipium*.[12] Another town founded as a *municipium* by Hadrian, Avitta Bibba (now Henchir Bu Ftîs), erected an arch in his honour and that of Aelius Caesar and Sabina in 137. It is divided into two storeys by an entablature at the height of the abutment. In the lower part are statue niches on either side of the opening.[13] Two other arches in honour of Hadrian are known from inscriptions. One was a single arch at El Gouléa (Arsacal) in Algeria, built by Q. Potitus.[14] The other was at Ain Golea: it was paid for and dedicated by Philoxenus to commemorate his sons' *adlectio* (co-option) to the decurionate.[15]

Hadrian's successor Antoninus Pius was honoured with six arches in North Africa. The first, at Sbeitla (Sufetula) in Tunisia, dates from 139–140 [7.2]. It forms the entrance to a temple precinct in the southern part of the town. The arch is not situated exactly on the central axis of the precinct, presumably so that it would face down the street opposite. On the outer side the triple arch is reached by a flight of five steps. It is articulated with half-columns, and above the side openings are rectangular niches for statues. On the attic are three inscriptions, the central one honouring Antoninus, while the others honour Commodus and Marcus Aurelius.[16] Two of Antoninus's arches took the place of gates at Timgad (Thamugadi, Algeria). That on the north, a remodelling of a Trajanic arch, was dedicated in 149 by L. Novius Crispinus, the proconsul, who was *patronus* of the city. It has inner columns and outer pilasters of the Corinthian order.

NORTH AFRICA   **109**

7.2 Sbeitla (Sufetula), Tunisia, entrance to temple precinct, 139–40.

The piers contained accessible spaces, and the opening could be closed with gates.[17] A similar arch stood at the entrance to the forum from the *decumanus maximus*. Each pier had (as on the north gate) a half-column and a pilaster. Behind stretched a platform, with two side entrances flanked by pilasters.[18] Remains survive of another arch east of the town; the fragmentary inscription recorded its dedication by a patron of the colony (presumably a proconsul), in this case unknown.[19]

On the main road leading north-west from Lepcis Magna stand the remains of an arch of 163 in honour of Antoninus. Originally freestanding, it is a deep single arch, built of stone, but originally clad in Pentelic and Proconnesian marble (the earliest masonry building at Lepcis intended to be treated in this way). The openings had on either side freestanding columns of *cipollino*, with white marble bases and Corinthian capitals, and projecting entablatures. Further decoration included winged Victories and panels on the arch coffering with the head of Medusa on an aegis. Some parts were reused in a nearby madrasa. The arch was incorporated into the west gate of the later defences.[20]

It used to be thought that the arch at Volubilis was the only one in modern Morocco, but remains of another have been found at Sala, near Rabat. It was a large (17 m wide) but comparatively simple triple arch, standing in a square formed by the widening of the principal *decumanus*. On the east side (alone) were bases which must have supported columns or pilasters. Fragments of the inscription suggest that it was built by C. Fabius Modestus, which would date it to the reign of Antoninus.[21] In the year of Antoninus's death, 161, an arch was set up at Djemila (Cuicul), in Algeria. It stood over the road to the theatre. Only the bases and other fragments survive, but the inscription records that it was built with 15,000 sesterces left in the will of

110   THE TRIUMPHAL ARCH

C. Iulius Crescens, the first *flamen sacerdotalis* of the province to come from Cuicul. The arch was dedicated to the Fortune of the Emperor and to Mars, genius of the colony. Crescens ordered statues of Fortune and Mars to be placed on it. His grandson gave more money and a statue of the Emperor. The arch was dedicated by the imperial legate, patron of the colony.[22]

Even more arches were erected in honour of Marcus Aurelius (and – until his death in 169 – to his colleague Lucius Verus) than to Hadrian. One at Markouna (Verecunda) stands south-west of the town over the road from nearby Lambaesis. It was erected by the *res publica* and dedicated in 162 by D. Fonteius Frontinianus, legate of the Emperor. Pilasters with Corinthian capitals flanked the opening.[23] Ten years later the *res publica* built another arch, over the road to Timgad in the north-east part of the town. It was dedicated in 172 by M. Aemilius Saturninus, legate of the Emperor. A single arch, like the other, it could be closed off (compare the northern arch at Timgad (above), and some of the Syrian arches, e.g. Gerasa). Here freestanding columns stood on either side of the opening, with pilasters behind; pilasters also stood at the extremities of the piers. Above the entablature was an attic.[24]

An inscription from Municipium Aelium Sua (Schauwasch, in Tunisia) records the building of 'a temple with an arch and porticoes and gates and stucco work', in honour of Marcus Aurelius and L. Verus. The inscription was brought to Tunis by scouts sent out by Giovanni Pagni, of Pisa, when he stayed there in 1666–7, so it is not known where it was found.[25]

At Tripoli (Oea), in Libya, the well-preserved *quadrifrons* is the most conspicuous surviving relic of the Roman town [7.3]. It stood where the *cardo* crossed the northernmost *decumanus*, near the harbour. The north-east side (facing the harbour) and

7.3 Quadrifrons at Tripoli (Oea), Libya, dedicated in 163/4 to M. Aurelius and Lucius Verus.

NORTH AFRICA **111**

south-west side were decorated with pairs of freestanding Composite columns, with rectangular niches for statues between them. One statue (probably of Lucius Verus) survives: the arch may have commemorated his victory over the Armenians in 163. Over the niches are tondi with busts, and above these are Erotes holding garlands. There are Victories in the spandrels, and below them are attributes of the patron gods of the city, Apollo and Minerva. On the north-west and south-east sides are reliefs of barbarian captives and trophies; in the spandrels are Apollo and Minerva. The arch is roofed with an octagonal cupola, formed of blocks with floral motifs, acanthus and shields. On each side an identical inscription appeared on the architrave and frieze. That on the frieze recorded the dedication of the arch in 163/4 to Marcus Aurelius and Lucius Verus by the proconsul and legate, while that on the architrave recorded that C. Calpurnius Celsus, magistrate and priest, built the arch out of solid marble at his own expense. The marble was imported from Proconnesus (Marmara).[26]

Zana (Diana Veteranorum), between Lambaesis and Cuicul, in Algeria, was founded for the veterans of the Third Legion. An arch was set up there in 164/5 in honour of Marcus Aurelius and Lucius Verus, and dedicated by C. Maesius Picatianus, legate and patron of the *municipium*. It has freestanding columns on either side of the opening, whose soffit is richly decorated with coffering, with a relief of Diana on the keystone. The arch imposts and archivolts are also richly decorated. The frieze is pulvinated.[27] Part of an arch erected in 164/6 has been rebuilt at Cyrene. It was a triple arch, articulated by projecting fluted pilasters, which had Corinthian capitals of unusual type.[28]

In the western part of Timgad a single arch stood over the road to Lambaesis, 350 m from the Arch of Caracalla. Fragments of its inscription record its dedication to Marcus Aurelius and Lucius Verus in 167/9. It had freestanding fluted columns, with Corinthian capitals, and could be closed off. Another arch stood 200 m east of the east gate, on the road to Khenchela. It had the same articulation. Remains of two inscriptions have been found, recording its dedication to Marcus Aurelius in 171 by C. Modius Iustus, legate and patron of the colony. It was built at public expense. It is referred to as *arcus triumphalis cum statuis et ...* . This is the earliest known use of the term *arcus triumphalis*. It is interesting that it is associated with an emperor renowned for his military achievements. In addition to these two arches, an inscription from the time of Marcus Aurelius mentions a statue of Mars set up *ad arcum pantheum*, possibly the south gate. The expense was borne by a *flamen*.[29] An arch at Henchir Bu Ftîs (Avitta Bibba) honoured Lucius Verus alone (161–8). Erected by the *municipium*, it stood at the opposite end of the town from Hadrian's arch.[30]

At Lepcis Magna beyond the arch of Antoninus Pius stands a small *quadrifrons*, erected in honour of Marcus Aurelius. All that survives are the stone bases of the piers and corner columns, which had grouped pilasters on their inner sides, a Corinthian capital, and some fragments of the marble revetment. These include two white marble architraves, bearing inscriptions which record that the arch and its statues were mostly paid for by a private individual in 173/174, and give the names of the proconsul C. Septimius Severus and his legate, L. Septimius Severus – the future emperor, and possibly his nephew.[31] An inscription from Bordj el Arbi (Saltus Massipianus) records the rebuilding by the *coloni* of various collapsed buildings, and the building of two arches, on the orders of the imperial procurator, who also dedicated them on behalf of the health of Marcus Aurelius and his sons. One partially survives.[32]

The Third Legion Augusta had been based at Lambaesis, an important crossroads, since the time of Augustus. East of the camp the civilian town grew up, and here an arch stood over the road leading from the east gate of the camp towards Verecunda. The single opening had a pair of pilasters on either side. According to the inscription it was erected in honour of Commodus in 183–5 by C. Pomponius Maximus, a former centurion of the Third Legion who was now a decurion of Timgad.[33] Another arch for Commodus was built for the *municipium* by the Third Legion on the road leading east of the forum, some way to the south-east of the camp. The piers are articulated with pairs of pilasters. On the inner ones are carved consoles, which may have borne statues, or – if the outer pilasters had matching consoles – colonnettes framing niches. On the keystone one side is a bust of a female with a turreted crown.[34] A third arch for the same emperor is known from a long inscription found at Henchir el Ust, near Assuras. This states that the arch was built in 188 by C. Ortius, a priest, who increased the sum available because of his piety and patriotism. It refers to a statue of *Ianus pater*, which may have stood on the arch. Frothingham thought that it might have marked the boundaries of the territories of Henchir el Ust and Assuras.[35]

It is hardly surprising that there should be a considerable number of arches (a dozen are known) in honour of Septimius Severus, who came from Lepcis Magna. The earliest dated example, completed in 195, is at Haïdra (Ammaedara, or Colonia Flavia Augusta Emerita) in Tunisia. Well preserved, it has a single opening with two pairs of projecting columns on each face. The pairs of columns have plain, linked bases, and linked entablatures. It stands east of the town, outside it, over the road from Carthage. The inscription, on the east side, is on the very high frieze between the projections of the entablature. Whether there was an attic is uncertain. In Byzantine times the arch was transformed into a bastion.[36] A single arch at Teboursouk (Thubursicum Bure), south-west of Tunis, is dated by an inscription to 196.[37] Khamissa (Thubursicum Numidarum, south of Hippo Regius, in Algeria) had no less than three arches dedicated to Septimius Severus and his family. One stands over the street east of the Forum Novum; it bears no inscription, but is attributed to this period. Not far away remains of another arch have been discovered, including a lengthy inscription recording its building in 198 by the priest Pomponius Quirinus Tertullus. As usual the murdered Geta's name has been removed.[38] The third arch stands on a hill south-west of the town, within the precinct wall of a temple of Saturn. The inscription records its erection for 'the ornament of the temple of Saturn' by the priest M. Fabius Laetus and his family.[39] An inscription found at Aïn el Bordj (Tigisis), south-east of Cirta, records the dedication of an arch in honour of Septimius Severus, Geta and the rest of the imperial family in 198. The dedicator, Titus Flavius, gave the *legitima summa* due from a decurion, together with additional money about which he boasted.[40]

Dougga (Thugga), in Tunisia, has an arch dated to 205. It stands south-west of the town over the road to Khamissa. On each side are niches for statues between pairs of pilasters, which had columns standing in front of them. There were inscriptions on the attic on each side, one honouring Septimius Severus and Julia Domna, the other Caracalla and Geta. That on the east recorded the erection of the arch by the *res publica* to the founders of the *municipium*.[41] The survival of an inscription at Béja (Vaga), north of Thugga, indicates that an arch was built there in 209 to celebrate the foundation of a colony by the proconsul T. Flavius Decimus.[42] At the northern entrance to Sbeitla

(Sufetula) an arch was dedicated some time between 209 and 211 (the year of Septimius's death); parts survive. The word *VICTORIAE* must refer to Septimius's victory in Britain.[43] At Lambaesis an arch marked the northern end of the civilian town, standing over the Via Septimiana which led to the camp. No inscription was found, but it is generally reckoned to have been built by the legionaries under Septimius Severus. A triple arch, it had freestanding columns on attached bases, and pairs of pilasters on the sides of the piers.[44]

The grandest of all the arches erected in Africa to Septimius Severus stood in his birthplace, Lepcis Magna, over the intersection of the *decumanus maximus* and the *cardo maximus* (the so-called *Via Triumphalis*) [7.4]. The arch has been almost entirely re-erected since 1970. Its restoration has been the subject of much discussion, and may not be correct in every detail. By a strange anomaly, traffic cannot pass through

7.4 Arch of Septimius Severus at Lepcis Magna, Libya, (?) 206–9, re-erected since 1970.

the *quadrifrons*, as its central area is raised on steps. It used to be thought that this was because the arch incorporated the lower part of an earlier *quadrifrons*, possibly Trajanic or Hadrianic, but it now appears that the road level was deliberately lowered in order to make the arch more conspicuous. As a result, the foundations of the earlier arch had to be clad in marble, to match the rest of the basically limestone structure. The weight of the marble (said to be about 2,000 tons) required the reinforcement of the foundations with a concrete platform.

Each face of the arch was identical. Freestanding Corinthian columns flanked the openings. The entablatures projected over the columns, and, as restored, support slices of pediment, whose width is that of the entablatures, but whose sharp points jut above the level of the principal cornice. This means that not only do they stand free in front of the foliage-decorated frieze, but they also (perhaps mistakenly) obstruct oblique views of the long relief panels which, as restored, decorate the otherwise plain attic.

The sculptural relief decoration of the arch is exceptionally rich – richer than on any other African arch. The pilasters supporting the archivolts, and the corner pilasters, were decorated with foliage. In the spandrels of the openings are naked Victories holding garlands and palm branches. Between the corner pilasters and the columns were trophies with captives standing at their bases. Further reliefs ornamented the inner faces of the arches, and above these – as over the attic reliefs – were lines of putti holding garlands. Within the *quadrifrons*, the spandrels of the cupola were carved with eagles, with outstretched wings. The vaulting of the openings was coffered, with a rosette to each coffer.

Most important of all were the historical reliefs. It is not certain how they were arranged, but the four main panels (now in the Tripoli Museum, with casts set up on the monument) must have been placed high up on the outer sides. Two of them (those on the north-west and south-east) have been interpreted as showing triumphal processions, but Strocka argues that their iconography is symbolic rather than historical.[45] In the better preserved north-west one, Septimius Severus's *quadriga* is going from left to right, but he stands in it facing to the front, with his sons at his sides. Their faces were mutilated in antiquity. Left of the chariot are men on horseback, right of it men on foot, including the town magistrates in togas. The chariot itself is decorated with reliefs showing the Fortuna of the city, with its patrons Liber Pater and Hercules on either side, and a winged Victory. In the upper right hand corner is the lighthouse of the Severan harbour. Strocka sees the scene as the triumphal manifestation of the Gloria of the Augusti in the Emperor's native town, and thinks that it commemorates the imperial visit.

In the south-east relief Strocka argues that the participation of deities in the procession suggests that here the Virtus of the divine house reveals itself in victory by the will of the gods. The north-east frieze shows a scene of sacrifice, with the Emperor in the centre, Julia Domna and Geta on his right, and the consul and the victim ox on his left. Strocka sees this as a sacrifice offered to the Capitoline Triad at Rome, emphasising the *pietas* of the imperial family.

The south-west relief is known as the *Dextrarum Iunctio*, as it shows Septimius Severus shaking hands with his son Caracalla. Between them is Geta, later murdered by his brother; the figure's sawn-off head was found buried nearby. The other figures include Fortuna, Hercules, Liber Pater, Minerva and Julia Domna. According to

Strocka, here the Concord of the Augusti, the bringer of peace, as guaranteed by the gods, reveals itself at Lepcis – a curious irony.

The minor panels that flanked the passageways are poorly preserved, but one shows the siege of a Parthian city (comparable with that on Severus's arch at Rome), while another shows Africa personified with Julia Domna as Juno and Severus as Jupiter. A third shows Hercules, Severus and Caracalla, with a scene of sacrifice below.

The date of the arch is uncertain. Some have associated it with the Emperor's visit in 203, but Strocka maintains that the absence of Plautianus, the Praetorian prefect put to death in 205, and his daughter Plautilla, who had married Caracalla, together with Caracalla's hairstyle, suggest a date between 206 and 209.

The quality of the sculptures is variable, but they show interesting signs of being on a cusp: the hieratic frontality of the figures looks forward to the late Empire, while the use of the drill is characteristic of the period. They are considered to be the work of artists from Asia Minor.[46]

Septimius Severus was succeeded in 211 by Caracalla, who had several arches erected in his honour in North Africa. One was built in 212 (the year of Geta's murder) to Caracalla and his mother as the entrance to the sanctuary of Mercury at Henchir Aïn Bez (Vazi Sarara) in Tunisia. The inscription tells us that the priest of Mercury at his own expense built the *arcum cum gradibus suis* (with its steps), and gave a bronze statue of Mercury *in petra sedentem* (sitting on a rock), and also, doubling his expenditure, a statue of Septimius Severus.[47]

A remarkable *quadrifrons* still stands at Tébessa (Theveste), in Algeria, where it was incorporated into the Byzantine fortifications in the sixth century [7.5]. On each side

7.5 Tébessa (Theveste), Algeria, 214. Photo *c.* 1860–1890.

the central (re-entrant) part of the attic bears an inscription, that on the east honouring the Divine Severus (and giving the date 214 for the dedication), that on the south the Emperor Caracalla, and that on the west Julia Domna. On the north side a Byzantine inscription was set up in the nineteenth-century restoration. An inscription within the opening quotes the will of C. Cornelius Egrilianus, prefect of the Fourteenth Legion, according to which the arch was built. The total sum of his bequests was 700,000 sesterces – the fourth largest individual benefaction known in Africa. Of this the arch, *tetrastyla*, and statues were to cost 250,000 sesterces.[48]

The arch, which is 11 m square, has on either side of each opening pairs of Corinthian columns, above which the entablature projects. The frieze of the entablature is decorated with foliage and rosettes. The soffits of the projections have heads of Oceanus amid foliage. On each keystone is a medallion with a bust, representing Minerva (E), Hercules (S), and the Fortune of the city (W). The northern one is destroyed. The space within the arch has corner niches and cross-beams which may have supported a cupola, as at Tripoli.

Above the attic on the south side is an aedicule of polychrome marble containing a niche. This has provoked much discussion, but it likely that Bacchielli is right to argue that there were originally four of these, linked by balustrades rising to the height of the capitals, and that they are anticipated by the will of Egrilianus, which runs: *arcum cum statuis … item tetrastylis duobus cum statuis … et Minervae, quae in foro fieri praecepit …* ('an arch with statues, also with two four-column structures with statues … and of Minerva, which he ordered to be set up in the forum'). It had previously been assumed that the *tetrastyla* were separate from the arch, but the sense of the passage seems against this. As we do not know where the forum of the ancient town was, this cannot affect the argument. There are two problems: first, the aedicules are not in fact *tetrastyla*, and second, there are four of them, not two. Bacchielli argues that although Egrilianus in his will stipulated two statues of divinities in *tetrastyla* (which would appropriately suggest *tempietti*), together with two statues of living members of the imperial family, the architect wanted to achieve symmetry, and so provided four aedicules instead. The statues must have corresponded to the inscriptions below, which means that the surviving south aedicule would have held a statue of Caracalla. The east and west ones commemorate the deified Septimius Severus and Julia Domna; as she was alive, she was represented by Minerva. The words before *et Minervae* were presumably *Divi Severi*. The north side would have had a statue of Geta, but he was assassinated before the arch was completed. Bacchielli suggests that a statue of the Virtus of Caracalla was substituted, citing a female torso in marble found under the arch. Another headless statue found in the upper part of the arch represents a male figure, nude apart from a cloak: Bacchielli suggests that this might be the image of Septimius Severus. For the general appearance of the arch, with aedicules above the attic, he suggests the Arch of Hadrian at Athens. It has to be said that the latter is more harmonious than the Tebessa arch, on his reconstruction.[49]

Zanfour (Assuras), in Algeria, had three arches, but only one survives, whose inscription dates it to 215. It was built by the Colonia Iulia Assuras.[50] At Djemila (Cuicul), also in Algeria, the area outside the south gateway to the main street was laid out in the early third century as a new forum. Up at its western end an arch was erected by the community in 216 in honour of Caracalla and Julia Domna, and the deified Septimius Severus [7.6]. The inscription describes it as *arcus triumphalis*, once again appropriate for a military commander. On either side of the opening are pairs of Corinthian columns, with shell-headed niches between them. Their entablatures break forward, and over them are aedicules with pediments. Above the attic are three bases for statues. On the forum side there are small heads over the springing of the arch. It is 12.6 m high. It was linked to other structures by an angled wall on the south and an arch on the north.

The arch has had two lucky escapes. Ahmed, last bey of the province, who was dispossessed by the French in 1837, thinking that it was made of marble, sent men to dismantle it so that he could use the materials for his new palace at Constantine. Only after part of the attic had fallen did they realise it was not solid marble, and give up. Further collapse resulted.[51] Then, in 1839, the duc d'Orléans, in command of an expeditionary force, saw the arch and decided to have it taken to Paris and set up in a square with the inscription 'L'armée d'Afrique à France' [*sic*]. Fortunately this had not yet happened when he died in 1842, but the monolithic columns were later cut up to support the posts of a shed in the camp. The arch was restored in 1921–2.[52]

The second of the two Moroccan arches, and much the better preserved, is the one at Volubilis [7.7]. Before the excavations it was the only standing monument there, although, since the collapse of the vault in 1755, only partially standing. It was rebuilt in 1931–2. It has a number of peculiarities. The whole structure is 19 m wide. The piers

7.6 Djemila (Cuicul), Algeria, Arch of Caracalla.

7.7 Volubilis (Morocco), Arch of Caracalla, dedicated 216–7, wrongly rebuilt 1931–2.

are exceptionally broad, so that the pairs of freestanding columns are widely spaced. The arch is built of grey local limestone. Unfortunately its restoration was erroneous, as it took no account of the drawing made by John Windus in 1721.[53] Between the columns are triangular-headed niches, an oriental motif not previously used on any official Roman monument. Beneath the niches there were fountain basins. There are parallels for this: the arch of Scipio on the Capitoline at Rome had 'basins', and two arches at Pompeii have fountains. Domergue suggests that, as water was so important in Africa, there may have been some symbolic intent here. Above each niche was, on the west side, a rectangular relief panel representing a hexagonal shield. Corresponding to these on the east were reliefs of standing Victories, each holding a crown and a palm. Above the architrave was a tall frieze, which bore the inscription in the centre. Above the columns were narrow relief panels showing *signa*, *vexilla*, stylised lotus flowers, and Victories above acanthus plants. Between these were rectangular reliefs of weapons. There was a cornice, bolder than the one restored, and an attic above, lower than the frieze. This was decorated with narrow reliefs, showing lozenges with bucklers, which corresponded to the columns below, between which were medallions. The three surviving ones represent summer, autumn and winter: their representations are similar to those found on mosaics at Volubilis and elsewhere. The total height of the arch was probably 13.75 m.

The inscription tells us that the arch was dedicated by the imperial procurator, M. Aurelius Sebastenus, in 216/217, on behalf of the *res publica* of Volubilis, to Caracalla and Julia Domna, because of his recent generosity, exceeding that of all previous emperors, along with the six-horse chariot and 'all the ornaments'. Fragments of the *sestiga* survive, namely two hooves and a hock, of bronze. Caracalla's generosity is explained by another inscription, of 215/216, from Banasa, which tells us that he remitted all outstanding debts to the imperial treasury. The arch forms the entrance to a piazza where the streets leading to the forum meet. It seems that it was intended to be seen from far off by the inhabitants of the surrounding district, not yet subjugated by the Romans.[54]

A single arch in honour of Caracalla stood at Constantine (Cirta) in Algeria. It bore the same inscription five times – once on the attic, while the other, smaller, versions were presumably on both sides of the piers. They recorded the building of the *arcus triumphalis*, together with a bronze statue of the Virtus of the Emperor, by the magistrate M. Caecilius Natalis, together with previous manifestations of his generosity. Fortunately the arch was recorded by Ravoisié and Delamare before its destruction. Its oddest feature was that each pier had only one freestanding column, with pilaster behind. The bases of the columns had sunken panels on each side, and the pilasters cut through the impost cornice. The arch stood at the southern end of the town (the principal approach).[55] Another Caracallan arch stands at Ksûr Abd el Melek (Uzappa) in Tunisia, towards the east of the town. The attic has an inscription recording its erection by the town, and its dedication to the *Genius civitatis Uzappae*.[56]

The splendid arch at Timgad (Thamugadi) in Algeria is known as the Arch of Trajan, but is a remodelling as a triple arch, perhaps in 203, of a single one built as the west gate of the Trajanic colony [7.8]. It was described by Ballu as the most

7.8 'Arch of Trajan', Timgad (Thamugadi), Algeria, Trajanic arch remodelled (?) 203.

120   THE TRIUMPHAL ARCH

elegantly proportioned arch in Africa.[57] It is built of local sandstone, white limestone, and coloured marble, which produce a pleasing effect of polychromy. Each face had a pair of fluted Corinthian columns, with eagles and serpents in the capitals of the inner columns on the east side. Their projecting entablatures support segmental pediments – a most unusual feature. Above the side openings were rectangular niches in aedicules, whose red marble columns stood on consoles. The arch provided a grand entrance to the town from the direction of Lambaesis. It stood at a slight angle to the *decumanus*, so as to face more in the direction of the *decumanus* of the suburb, which bends northwards.[58] The structure was 12 m high. On the west side, in front of the columns flanking the central opening, are octagonal bases which supported statues of Mars and Concord, dated by their inscriptions to the reign of Caracalla. What may be the inscription from the arch itself was published by H. Doisy in 1953: it records a dedication by the *res publica* of the *colonia* to Septimius Severus, along with Caracalla, Geta and Julia Domna, in 203 – the year in which the Emperor visited Africa to inspect its provinces.[59]

Also in Algeria a triple arch at Zana (Diana Veteranorum) was erected in 217 by the *res publica* in honour of Macrinus and Diadumenianus, as the northern entrance to the forum. It had four freestanding Corinthian columns on each side. The architrave and frieze are insignificant, especially when compared with the elaborate cornice. The inscription is on the north side. The arch was incorporated into a Byzantine fortress.[60] At Announa (Thibilis), east of Cirta, in Algeria, an arch over the principal street has the usual pairs of columns (of poor marble), between which bases for statues were added later. There is no inscription, but the character of the capitals suggests a date not before the beginning of the third century.[61]

In Tunisia, an arch was built at Dougga (Thugga) north-west of the town in 231–2 to honour Severus Alexander for the privileges which he granted to the *municipium*. The opening (4 m wide) is flanked by pairs of fluted pilasters, framing rectangular niches. In front of each pilaster stood a Corinthian column. Above the opening, which has plain voussoirs, runs a frieze with alternating paterae and lozenges.[62] An arch was erected for Gordian in 239 at Henchir Mest (Mustis, Tunisia). Parts of the inscription survive, and record the dedication of the arch by the magistrate C. Cornelius, together with statues of the Emperor, the Genius of the city, and a personification of Carthage (presumably on the attic), along with other public benefactions.[63] Another inscription refers to an arch, possibly this one or the next.[64] There was another arch on the opposite side of the town, attributed to Constantius II, which I.A. Peyssonel described in 1724–5 as 'un peu près dans le goût de la porte St Denis de Paris et de la même hauteur'.[65]

A single arch at Henchir ed-Douâmis (Uchi Maius), also in Tunisia, near the temple of Aesculapius, dates from 230. It commemorates the acquisition of the status of colonia from Severus Alexander.[66] Another arch was erected there in 241 for Gordian and his wife Sabina Tranquillina. The donor adorned it with statues, according to a lost inscription. It stands at the western limit of the built-up area. Much of the south-east pier stands. It has a rectangular niche, and remains of fluted pilasters. It may stand on the *pomerium*, a position known from other countries, but not from elsewhere in Africa.[67]

Two arches survive at Besseriani Negrin (Oasis Nigrensium Maiorum, or Ad Maiores) in Algeria, south-west of Tebessa. A small one 300 m north of the fortress was built in 286–7 in honour of Diocletian and Maximianus. According to the inscription, and the similar one on the second arch, it had been promised to the *municipium* by Clodius Victor and Pomponius Macianus to commemorate their election to the duovirate, after an earthquake had occurred during the night in 267. The arch was only built, by their heirs, in 286/7 – a delay due to the disorder prevailing in the area before the reign of Diocletian.[68] Each pier has a Corinthian half-column; these support a simple cornice. The second arch stands 110 m west of the west gate.[69]

One of the few arches with two openings in Africa stands at the south end of the main street of Announa (Thibilis) in Algeria. Made of sandstone, and dating from the late third or early fourth century, it has a fluted Corinthian pilaster at each corner of each pier, up to the level of the springing of the arches. The arch may have commemorated the granting of the status of *municipium* at the end of the third century. Parts of two marble inscription tablets bearing the words *Augusti nostri* may belong to it. Originally freestanding, the arch was later incorporated into the Byzantine fortifications.[70]

Again in Algeria, a triple arch at Bêdja (Vaga) is presumed to have had an inscription recording its dedication by Aelius Helvius Dionysius, who was proconsul between 296 and 300, under the Tetrarchs. He was later involved in a senatorial conspiracy, which would explain why his name was removed. The structure may be identical with one to Septimius Severus known from an inscription.[71] An inscription found at Ksûr el Ahmar (Macomades), near Constantine (Algeria), records the building of an arch to commemorate the Vicennalia of Diocletian and his colleagues (the Tetrarchs) in 303. It was erected by the *municipium* at the expense of two citizens, both priests. It had a statue of Victory.[72] Another arch honouring Diocletian and his colleagues stands at a road junction, on the bank of a stream, a few kilometres from Thebursuk, near Dougga (Tunisia). It was dedicated by the colony of Thugga. Frothingham argues that its situation shows that it was a boundary arch, and suggests that it might have commemorated a territorial redistribution by Diocletian.[73] An arch at Henchir Midid (Mididi), in Tunisia, known only from an inscription, was also erected in honour of the Tetrarchs, some time in 293–4. It was built along with a *porticus* around the forum, presumably as its principal entrance. It was dedicated by the proconsul.[74] At Sbeitla (Sufetula), also in Tunisia, a large arch at the entrance to the town from the south-east has pairs of columns, with linked bases and entablatures, on each pier, framing rectangular niches. On the attic on the outer side is an inscription recording its dedication to the Tetrarchs. The attic is articulated with a short pilaster over each pier pilaster.[75]

At Henchir Gasrîm, or Kasserine (Cillium), in Tunisia, a single mostly plain arch has a tall attic articulated by four small pilasters on each side. The inscription records its building in the third century by Q. Manlius Felix, with his usual liberality to his fatherland, describing it as *arcum ... cum insignibus coloniae*. These *insignia* probably included a she-wolf, a symbol of Roman citizenship. A second inscription, probably later, commemorates the restoration of its *ornamenta libertatis* and *insignia*, in the time of Constantine and Licinius.[76]

In about 360 a large *quadrifrons* was erected at Constantine (Cirta), together with a basilica and porticoes, by the *comes* Claudius Avitianus. It was destroyed in the French siege of 1837. The architecture was simple, but each side measured 14.3m. There were no pilasters. The inscription contains the first known use of the word *tetrapylum*. It stood near the arch of M. Caecilius Natalis (see above).[77] A second arch at Ksûr el

Ahmar (Macomades), in honour of Valentinian I and Valens, is known from an inscription. It was built by a priest to mark his holding of the office.[78] Another arch probably erected in their honour survives in a ruinous state at Henchir Bu Arada, in Tunisia. It was built with 'voluntary contributions from the citizens'.[79] An inscription found at Ghardimaou (also in Tunisia) comes from an arch restored in honour of Gratian, Valentinian and Theodosius some time between 379 and 383. It is said to have been an *arcus triumphalis*, built from the foundations up in squared stones, but later allowed to fall apart; the restoration was paid for by a priest and his son.[80] At El Gussa, or Henchir Gouçat (Leges Maiores), south-east of Khenchela (Algeria), are two simple arches, one or both erected in honour of Valentinian, Gratian and Valens.[81]

A third arch at Announa (Thibilis) stands at the east end of a colonnaded street which runs from the main street between the other arches, described above. An inscription probably belonging to it would date it between 375 and 378, a time that suits the debased forms of the mouldings. It records the dedication of the *porticus cum area*, built by the duumviri. Each pier has a pair of unfluted Corinthian pilasters, which rise to the height of the openings.[82] Three arches in honour of Septimius Severus at Khamissa (Thubursicum Numidarum) have been mentioned. Two more seem to date from the fourth century. One simple arch without an inscription stands over the road to Tebessa, to the south-east of the town. Quite well preserved, it lacks entablature and attic.[83] Remains of a simple triple arch stand north of the Forum Novum. Parts of a frieze bear an inscription, which records the remodelling of the forum. The central opening is 3.4 m wide, the side ones 2.3 m. The arch stands at the top of six steps.[84] A second arch at Medeina (Althiburos, see above) formed the north-west entrance to the town. Quite well preserved, it appears to date to the fourth or fifth century. It is 11 m wide, and the opening is 7 × 5 m. It has only a single half-column on each pier, up to the first cornice; above is a pilaster (compare the arch of M. Caecilius Natalis at Constantine, above).[85]

So far only those arches whose dates can be established with some certainty have been discussed, but there are a considerable number of arches (more than forty) of unknown date. The functions of some are known. One at Gigthis in Tunisia (possibly of 138–61) formed the entrance to the forum, by way of a short paved street on to which the porticoed precinct of a temple opened by way of three doorways. The fragmentary inscription shows that the paving and the arch were paid for by the *flamen perpetuus* M. Iulius Mandus, who was rewarded when the council of the town erected a statue of him. The arch, which is not freestanding, has fluted pilasters with Corinthian capitals, supporting a moulded archivolt. There was an attic, bearing the inscription.[86] Two arched gates in enfilade may have stood at either end of the forum of Kuch Batia (Thimida Bure). They are very simple, but the better preserved one has its entablature and cornice.[87] A simple arch at Henchir Kissa (north of Tebessa, in Algeria)) may have served as the entry to a square or sanctuary. It has no archivolt or entablature, apart from a cornice.[88]

Several arches certainly did form the entrances to sanctuaries. One survives at Sidi Amara, in Tunisia, with niches on the outer sides of the piers.[89] A second arch at Gigthis, known only from an inscription, stood in front of the sanctuary of Concordia Panthea. The temple had been promised by M. Ummidius Quirinus Sedatus to commemorate his son's decurionate, and he added an image of Concord, a *pronaus* (porch), and an arch.[90] A third arch at Zana (Diana Veteranorum) formed the entrance to the

Temple of Diana. The opening was only 2.5m wide, and the piers were plain. It could be closed with doors. Remains of the inscription show that a *pronaus* and porticoes were added by the priest and magistrate Saturio.[91] An inscription found 500 m northwest of Tebessa (Theveste) reveals that there was a sanctuary of the goddess Caelestis, which was adorned by Coronatus, an *adiutor tabularii* (assistant to the registrar): he added *antae* (pilasters) and an arch.[92] At Schauwasch (Sua) an arch stood in front of a nymphaeum, and may have served as entrance to the sacred precinct. It was 8 m high and 8.5 m wide, and stood over the stream, which was lined with broad black stones. An inscription on the side away from the spring, of only one line, referred to it as *arcum triumphalem*. Hülsen considered that the arch dated probably at the earliest to the fourth century, but it may have been dedicated to Caracalla.[93] Another arch connected with water stood at the approach to a bridge at Mses el Bab (Membressa, in Tunisia). It was dedicated to Gratian, Valentinian and Theodosius. This seems to be the only instance in Africa of this location – common elsewhere. Frothingham held that it marked the boundary between the province of Africa and the kingdom of Numidia.[94]

There appears to be only one arch in Africa for which a funerary significance is likely, because of its small size and location, and that is at Haïdra (Ammaedara), where an arch stands outside the town by the side of the ancient road. On each pier there is a niche, which had an aedicule resting on consoles.[95]

Several further examples are known of towns with groups of arches. In some cases these were of varying dates. At Mdaurusch in Algeria (Madauros, the home town of Apuleius) there were possibly four or five. Three are known from inscriptions that record their erection, in each case with a statue, in return for the office of *flamen*.[96] A fourth inscription refers to *porticus novae ... ab arcu ad forum*: this could be one of the preceding. A (possible) fifth probably commemorates the dedication of an arch.[97] Remains of one arch survive, at the angle of the *decumanus* and the *cardo* leading to the forum. Only marks on the paving remain *in situ*, but there are fragments of cornice, entablature, columns, a base, and capitals. The columns seem to have projected in the middle of each pier (compare Constantine, p. 120).[98] Three towns had sets of arched gateways. At Thuburbo Maius (Tunisia) there are gates at the north, east and west, apparently contemporary. They were built of stone and covered in stucco, parts of which remain, including rosettes from the coffering of a projecting cornice. The north gate had two semicircular niches with shell heads. Although of different dimensions, the arches have similar proportions. Nothing survives of their inscriptions.[99]

An inscription found at Ain Melluk (Vicus Phosphorianus, in Algeria) reveals that four arches stood presumably at the entrances to the roughly square town (*vicus*) which lay below the sanctuary of the goddess Caelestis. They were built by Phosphorus, along with the temple, the buildings of the *vicus*, and its columns and porticoes. He also set up a market.[100] Even more remarkable is the insignificant village of Um el Abuab ('the town with the gates') in Tunisia, where four arches stood at the entrances to the town. By 1904 only two remained. The northern one, with fluted pilasters, has an inscription within the opening which records the building of the arches according to the will of the equestrian Felix Armenianus, aided by the generosity of his mother and sister. The *municipium Seressitanum* (whose name is otherwise unknown) provided a *quadriga*. The idea of entering this remote and obscure town through one of four arches, crowned with a *quadriga* (presumably driven by the emperor), is extraordinary.

Frothingham thought that the finer of the surviving arches dated from the reign of Caracalla.[101] At Tiddis (Castellum Tidditanorum, Algeria) the principal north–south street passed under two arches at right angles to each other, at the lower end of the forum. The eastern one had a keystone carved with a crown.[102]

Finally, there are a fair number of undated arches that survive, or survived until comparatively recent times; they may be briefly mentioned. These include a large triple arch at Constantine (on the east bank of the river) and an arch with two openings at Tipasa in Algeria (possibly second century).[103] Other arches include Igibba, Lambiridi (west of Lambaesis), Mactaris, Meschta Nehar, Rapidum (south of Algiers), Tebessa and Uzelis.[104] Two further arches stand at Lambaesis, both with three openings; one formed the entrance to a temple near the forum. An inscription recording the erection of an arch by a *flamen ob diem festiuissimum* (to celebrate a most festive day) may have belonged to any of the five arches (not including the so-called Praetorium) at Lambaesis.[105] The well preserved second arch at Ksûr Abd el Melek (Uzappa in Tunisia) has interesting peculiarities. It stands east of the town, and was dedicated to the *genius* of the *civitas Uzappa*. Its form is similar to that of the Trajanic arch at Mactaris, but between the entablature and the taller half-columns are consoles, decorated with eagles on the front and with bearded, horned heads on the sides.[106]

Egypt

It is noteworthy that in the areas described in the last sections no coins have been found showing arches. A considerable number of coin-issues of Alexandria do so, but the significance of this is a matter of dispute. The earliest example is a coin of Augustus, showing a simple arch with horses above; it is a copy of Pergamene *cistophori* celebrating the return of the Parthian standards in 19 BC. As Kleiner says, it is not surprising that Parthian matters should interest the inhabitants of the eastern part of the Empire.[107] Next comes a coin of Galba, which shows a tall triple arch, with pilasters (or columns) rising to support a pediment, above the centre of which is a small attic with a chariot on top. This peculiar arrangement has been attributed to lack of space for representation of an attic extending right across the width of the arch.

Another arch is first seen on a coin of the sixth year of Domitian (86/87) that continued to be issued up to the seventh year of Hadrian. The three openings are flanked by columns rising as high as the imposts of the central arch, which bear statues of figures with spears. Above the side openings are relief panels. Again there is a pediment over the whole width; this contains a disc or globe in the centre between flying Victories. The attic supports a chariot drawn by six (or four) horses, on either side of which is a trophy with a bound captive seated on either side. The figure of the Emperor in the chariot holds a palm and a sceptre. Some examples have a Doric frieze below the pediment. A variant of this type shows a pair of horizontal bands in place of the pediment.

A third type of arch appears on coins of Trajan. Here four columns support a pediment, with no indication of any arched openings. The pediment is again decorated with a disc. The sculpture above is as on the previous type.

It is the fourth type which has led to so much argument, as this one (also issued under Trajan) clearly represents the Arch of Nero at Rome, and is based on a Roman sestertius of 64–8. Kleiner argues from this, and also from the fact that various features

7.9 Arch at Antinoë. Hadrianic, from the Napoleonic *Description de l'Égypte*.

of the arch (he takes it that the second and third types represent only one arch) are characteristic of the West, that it is in fact an arch set up at Rome to celebrate Domitian's German triumph. He attributes the lack of evidence for it to that Emperor's *damnatio memoriae*, and supposes that the Alexandrian mint officials were unaware of its disappearance, and continued to illustrate it. De Maria, however, maintains that the arch, which he describes as 'singular' because of the statues on columns, was indeed at Alexandria: he suggests that it might have been the gateway (*propylon*) to a sacred area, identifying the disc in the pediment as the image of the sun god Re.[108]

Until the nineteenth century an arch stood at Antinoe (Antinoopolis), at the western end of the main street, facing the Nile [7.9]. It is known from engravings in the Napoleonic *Description de l'Égypte*.[109] It had three openings, and was articulated with pilasters supporting a Doric entablature, with pediment above. The side arches were framed by freestanding columns with acanthus capitals, supporting entablatures which projected over the columns. Above each of these was a rectangular window lighting upper rooms (reached by spiral staircases within the piers). It is assumed that the arch was associated with the foundation of the city by Hadrian.[110]

Notes

1 For a general account of African arches, see the catalogue in Giuseppe Mazzilli, *L'Arco di Traiano a Leptis Magna* (Rome, 2016); P. Romanelli, *Topografia e archeologia dell'Africa Romana*, Enciclopedia Classica, sez. II, vol. X, tom. VII (Turin, 1970), 131–45.

2 Mazzilli 2016, 249. It is now suggested that the arch may relate to a new water supply. See also J.M. Reynolds and J.B. Ward-Perkins, *Inscriptions of Roman Tripolitania* (Rome/London, 1952), 308; A. Di Vita, G. Di Vita-Evrard and L. Bacchielli, *Libya* (Cologne, 1999), 98.

3. Mazzilli 2016, 249; P. Romanelli, *Africa Italiana*, 7 (1940), 87–96, 105; D.J. Mattingly, *Tripolitania* (London, 1995), 56, 118. For an illustration, see Di Vita et al. (cit. in the preceding note), 65. For the purpose of commemorating street paving, compare the arch at Syracuse (p. 12).
4. Mazzilli 2016, 280–81; *CIL* VIII 26519.
5. Mazzilli 2016, 249; Reynolds and Ward-Perkins (cit. at n. 2), 342. One block is at Virginia Water. See also M. Floriani Squarciapino, *Leptis Magna* (Zurich, 1966), 15, 57, 88.
6. Mazzilli 2016, 250; Reynolds and Ward-Perkins (cit. at n. 2), 353; P. Romanelli, *Africa Italiana* 7 (1940), 96–105. For a reconstruction, see R. Bianchi Bandinelli et al., *Leptis Magna* (Verona, 1964), 73.
7. Mazzilli 2016, 256; G. C. Picard, 'Civitas Mactaritana', *Karthago* 8 (1957), 148.
8. Mazzilli 2016, 237; *CIL* VIII 27775; A. Merlin, *Notes et Documents* 6 (1913), 22–4.
9. *CIL* VIII 9637.
10. Mazzilli 2016, 223–6; F. Rakob and S. Storz, *Mitteilungen der deutschen archäologischen Instituts: Römische Abteilung*, 81 (1974), 253–80; on the inscription, see H.-G. Kolbe, ibid., 282–300; J.-M. Blas de Roblès and C. Sintès, *L'Algérie* (Aix-en-Provence, 2003), 179–82.
11. Mazzilli 2016, 284; *CIL* VIII 16441; A.L. Frothingham, *AJA* 19 (1915), 164–5.
12. Mazzilli 2016, 243–4; *CIL* VIII 98.
13. Mazzilli 2016, 242–3; *CIL* VIII 799, 12266. Frothingham (*AJA* 8 (1904), 8) claimed that the arch was not dedicated until the reign of Antoninus Pius.
14. Mazzilli 2016, 216; *CIL* VIII 6047.
15. Mazzilli 2016, 236; *CIL* VIII 25955.
16. Mazzilli 2016, 269–70; *CIL* VIII 228, 11319; A. Merlin, *Notes et Documents*, 5 (1912), 16–17; R. Wood and M. Wheeler, *Roman Africa in Colour* (London, 1966), 98.
17. Mazzilli 2016, 227; *CIL* VIII 17852. R. Cagnat (*Bull. archéologique* (1915), 240) claimed that the arch originally bore an inscription recording Trajan's foundation of the colony, which was found nearby (*CIL* VIII 17843). See also S. Gsell, *Les monuments antiques de l'Algérie* (Paris, 1901), I, 162–3.
18. Mazzilli 2016, 227; Gsell (cit. in the preceding note), 163.
19. Mazzilli 2016, 227; *CIL* VIII 2376 (which wrongly says that it was found in the forum).
20. Mazzilli 2016, 251–3; Mattingly (cit. at n. 3), 118; Di Vita et al. (cit. at n. 2), 98–9, 102.
21. Mazzilli 2016, 207; L. Chatelain, *CRAI* 1930, 336–40; idem, *Le Maroc des romains* (Paris, 1949), 86–8.
22. Mazzilli 2016, 217–18; *CIL* VIII 8313=20136, 8335=20142, 10898=20141; E. Albertini, *Bull. archéologique* (1924), CLIX; Blas de Roblès and Sintès (cit. at n. 10), 110.
23. Mazzilli 2016, 235; *CIL* VIII 18510; Gsell (cit. at n. 17), 159, 161.
24. Mazzilli 2016, 235; *CIL* VIII 18947–8; Gsell (cit. at n. 17), 165–7.
25. Mazzilli 2016, 269; *CIL* VIII 1310.
26. Mazzilli 2016, 263–6; Reynolds and Ward-Perkins (cit. at n. 2), 232; S. Aurigemma, *L'arco quadrifronte di Marco Aurelio e di Lucio Vero a Tripoli* (Tripoli, 1970); P. MacKendrick, *The North African Stones Speak* (London, 1980), 157–8; Mattingly (cit. at n. 3), 123–4; Di Vita et al. (cit. at n. 2), 8–9. A. Lézine (*Libya Antiqua* 5 (1968), 58–9) argues that the use of marble indicates the wealth of the city, and points out that the arch may not have been the only one at Oea, which was probably larger and more important than Sabratha, the third city of the Libyan *tripolis*.
27. Mazzilli 2016, 220; *CIL* VIII 4591–2, 18648; Gsell (cit. at n. 17), 164–5; Blas de Roblès and Sintès (cit. at n. 10), 191–2.
28. Mazzilli 2016, 285; R.G. Goodchild, *Cyrene and Apollonia: A Historical Guide* (3rd edn, Tripoli, 1970), 93; idem, *Kyrene und Apollonia* (Zurich, 1971), 137; MacKendrick (cit. at n. 26), 127–8.
29. Mazzilli 2016, 229–30; *CIL* VIII 2372.
30. Mazzilli 2016, 242–3; *CIL* VIII 801.
31. Mazzilli 2016, 253–4; *AE* 1967, no. 536; G. Di Vita Evrard, *Mélanges de l'École française de Rome* 75 (1963), 389–414 (see p. 394 for a reconstruction by C. Catanuso); Di Vita et al. (cit. at n. 2), 102–6; Bianchi Bandinelli (cit. at n. 6), 101; Floriani Squarciapino (cit. at n. 5), 62–3; G. Ioppolo, *Libya Antiqua* 6–7 (1969–70), 231–6. One of the capitals is in Virginia Water, Surrey.
32. Mazzilli 2016, 267–8; *CIL* VIII 587.
33. Mazzilli 2016, 222; *CIL* VIII 2699–2700, 18112, 18246; Gsell (cit. at n. 17), 160–62; Blas de Roblès and Sintès (cit. at n. 10), 182. See also Kimberly Cassibry, 'Provincial patrons and commemorative rivalries: rethinking the Roman arch monument', *Mouseion* 8 (2008), 417–50.
34. Mazzilli 2016, 223; *CIL* VIII 2698, 18247; Gsell (cit. at n. 17), 159–60.
35. *CIL* VIII 16417; A.L. Frothingham, *AJA* 19 (1915), 166.
36. Mazzilli 2016, 237–9; *CIL* VIII 306–7; R. Cagnat, *Carthage, Timgad, Tebessa* (Paris, 1909), 131, 134; F. Baratte and N. Duval, *Les ruines d'Ammaedara-Haïdra* (Tunis, 1974), 26–8.
37. Mazzilli 2016, 278; *CIL* VIII 1428, 1444.
38. Mazzilli 2016, 279; S. Gsell, *Bull. arch.* (1917), 316; S. Gsell, ed., *Inscriptions latines de l'Algérie* (henceforward *IlAlg*), I (Paris, 1922), 1255.
39. Mazzilli 2016, 278–9; S. Gsell, *Bull. arch.* (1917), 316; *IlAlg* I, 1256.
40. Mazzilli 2016, 234; S. Lancel and P. Pouthier, *Libyca* 4 (1956), 133–6: MacKendrick (cit. at n. 26), 218.
41. Mazzilli 2016, 280–81; *CIL* VIII 26539, 26540; A. Golfetto, *Dougga* (Basel, 1961), 24.
42. Mazzilli 2016, 283; *CIL* VIII 1217. This arch may be identical with the arch dedicated to the Tetrarchs (see below).
43. Mazzilli 2016, 270; A. Merlin, *Bull. arch.* (1913), CLXXXII.
44. Mazzilli 2016, 226; Gsell (cit. at n. 17), 176–7; Blas de Roblès and Sintès (cit. at n. 10), 183–4. M. Janon (*Antiquités africaines* 7 (1973), 2-5-8) points out that it is very difficult to make sense of the placing of the various arches at Lambaesis. He also doubts whether this arch does date to the reign of Septimius Severus.
45. M. Strocka, *Antiquités africaines* 6 (1972), 147–72.

46 Mazzilli 2016, 254–6; R. Bartoccini, *Africa Italiana* 4 (1931), 32–152; Bianchi Bandinelli (cit. at n. 6), 25–48, 67–70; Floriani Squarciapino (cit. at n. 5), 63–9; A. Di Vita, *Quaderni di archeologia della Libya* 7 (1975), 3–26; MacKendrick (cit. at n. 26), 159–61; L. Bacchielli, *L'Africa Romana: Atti del IX Convegno di Studio, Nuoro 1991* (Sassari, 1992), 763–70; Di Vita et al. (cit. at n. 2), 112–16. On the reliefs, see I.S. Ryberg, *Memoirs of the American Academy at Rome*, 22 (1955), 134–6; Strocka (cit. at n. 45), 147–72.

47 Mazzilli 2016, 284; *CIL* VIII 23749.

48 R. Duncan-Jones, 'Costs, outlays and *summae honorariae* from Roman Africa', *PBSR* 30 (1962), 57–8, 80.

49 Mazzilli 2016, 231–3; *CIL* VIII 1855–9; Gsell (cit. at n. 17), 180–85; Cagnat (cit. at n. 36), 135–6; MacKendrick (cit. at n. 26), 273–5; L. Bacchielli, in A. Mastino, ed., *L'Africa Romana: Atti del IV Convegno di Studio: Sassari 1986* (Sassari, 1987), 295–321 (for his reconstruction see p. 310); Blas de Roblès and Sintès (cit. at n. 10), 225–6. On the inscription, see also *IlAlg* I, 3040. A further inscription (*CIL* VIII 1860=16505) records the rebuilding in 361, from the ground up, of *frontes duas*, presumably two façades of the arch, which were 'full of endless ruins'. There was another arch, west of the town, of which only part of one pier survived: this has now disappeared (Blas de Roblès and Sintès, 223).

50 Mazzilli 2016, 241; *CIL* VIII 1798.

51 A. Ravoisié, *Exploration scientifique de l'Algérie pendant les années 1840, 1841, 1842* (Paris, 1846–53), I, 53–6; pls XXXIV–XXXVIII.

52 Mazzilli 2016, 218–20; *CIL* VIII 8321; A. Delamare, *Exploration scientifique de l'Algérie – Archéologie* (Paris, 1850), pls 101, 104; with S. Gsell, *Exploration scientifique … Texte explicatif* (Paris, 1912), 103, 105; Gsell (cit. at n. 17), 167–9; Blas de Roblès and Sintès (cit. at n. 10), 108–10.

53 J. Windus, *A Journey to Mequinez, the Residence of the Present Emperor of Fez and Morocco, on the Occasion of Commodore Stewart's Embassy thither for the Redemption of British Captives in the Year 1721* (London, 1725), 87–8.

54 Mazzilli 2016, 208–12; *CIL* VIII 21828; Chatelain, *Le Maroc* (cit. at n. 21), 193–8; R. Thouvenot, *Volubilis* (Paris, 1949), 39–40; C. Domergue, *Bull. arch. du comité des travaux historiques et scientifiques*, Années 1963–4 (1966), 201–29; idem, in R. Chevallier, ed., *Mélanges d'archéologie et d'histoire offerts à André Piganiol* (Paris, 1966), I, 463–72; MacKendrick (cit. at n. 26), 301.

55 Mazzilli 2016, 217; *CIL* VIII 7095–8; Ravoisié (cit. at n. 51), I, 19, 35–6, pls XIV, XVII–XIX; Delamare (cit. at n. 52), pl. 123; Gsell (cit. at n. 17), 164; S. Gsell, *Atlas archéologique d'Algérie* (Alger/Paris, 1911), Feuille 17, p. 7.

56 Mazzilli 2016, 283; *CIL* VIII 11924; A.L. Frothingham, *Revue archéologique* (1923), 52.

57 A. Ballu, *Les ruines de Timgad* (Paris, 1897), 108, with photographs of the arch before restoration.

58 A. Lézine, *Bull. d'archéologie algérienne* 2 (1966–7), 123–7. He points out that the porticoes in front of the buildings east of the arch did not abut it (as sometimes claimed).

59 Mazzilli 2016, 230–31; Gsell (cit. at n. 17), 174–6; H. Doisy, *Mélanges d'archéologie et d'histoire, École française de Rome*, 65 (1953), 125–30, incorporating *CIL* VIII 2368 and 17872; MacKendrick (cit. at n. 26), 237; Blas de Roblès and Sintès (cit. at n. 10), 159–60.

60 Mazzilli 2016, 220–22; *CIL* VIII 4598; Gsell (cit. at n. 17), 177–9.

61 Mazzilli 2016, 273–4; Gsell (cit. at n. 17), 167; S. Gsell and C.A. Joly, *Khamissa, Mdaourouch, Announa* (Alger/Paris, 1914–22), pt III, 51; MacKendrick (cit. at n. 26), 204.

62 Mazzilli 2016, 281; *CIL* VIII 1485, 26551; Golfetto (cit. at n. 41), 59.

63 Mazzilli 2016, 261–2; *CIL* VIII 1577, 15572.

64 Mazzilli 2016, 263; *CIL* VIII 15578.

65 Mazzilli 2016, 262; *CIL* VIII 1579.

66 Mazzilli 2016, 282; *CIL* VIII 26262.

67 Mazzilli 2016, 282; *CIL* VIII 26264; M. Khanoussi, A. Mastino and A. Ibba, *Uchi Maius* (Sassari, 1997), 29.31.

68 Mazzilli 2016, 214–5; *CIL* VIII 2480.

69 Mazzilli 2016, 215–16; *CIL* VIII 2481=17970; Gsell (cit. at n. 17), 172; C. Lepelley, *Les cités de l'Afrique romaine au Bas-Empire*, I (Paris, 1979), 87–8.

70 69 Mazzilli 2016, 274; Ravoisié (cit. at n. 51), II. 10–11; Delamare (cit. at n. 52), pls. 164, 166; *CIL* VIII 5527, 18861; Gsell (cit. at n. 17), 172–3; Gsell and Joly (cit. at n. 61), III 48; Lepelley (cit. at n. 68), I 197.

71 Mazzilli 2016, 283.

72 Mazzilli 2016, 226; *CIL* VIII 4764=18698.

73 Mazzilli 2016, 281–2; *CIL* VIII 15516; A.L. Frothingham, *AJA* 19 (1915), 165.

74 Mazzilli 2016, 259; *CIL* VIII 608=11772.

75 Mazzilli 2016, 270–72; *CIL* VIII 11326.

76 Mazzilli 2016, 246; *CIL* VIII 11299; A.L.Frothingham, *Revue archéologique* (1905), II, 221 (he claims that the arch was built under the Flavians, and dedicated to the colony); Groupe de recherche sur l'Afrique antique, *Les Flavii de Cillium* (Rome, 1993), 8.

77 Mazzilli 2016, 217; *CIL* VIII 7037–8; Gsell (cit. at n. 17), 179: Gsell (*Atlas* (cit. at n. 55), Feuille 17. 6. 16.

78 Mazzilli 2016, 217; *CIL* VIII 4767, 18701.

79 Mazzilli 2016, 241; *CIL* VIII 23863.

80 Mazzilli 2016, 247; *CIL* VIII 14728.

81 Mazzilli 2016, 226; *CIL* VIII 10702=17616; Gsell (cit. at n. 17), 171–2.

82 Mazzilli 2016, 274–5; *IlAlg* II, 4677; Delamare (cit. at n.52), pls 164, 166; Gsell (cit. at n. 17), 158.

83 Mazzilli 2016, 279; Gsell (cit. at n. 17), 156.

84 Mazzilli 2016, 279–80; *IlAlg* I, 1275; Gsell (cit. at n.17), 174.

85 Mazzilli 2016, 237; *CIL* VIII 1832=16471 (a fragment); V. Guérin, *Voyage archéologique dans la Régence de Tunis* (Paris, 1862), II, 84; A. Merlin, *Notes et documents* VI (1913), pl. I.

86 Mazzilli 2016, 247; *CIL* VIII 22694; L.-A. Constans, *Gigthis* (Paris, 1916), 39–41.

87 Mazzilli 2016, 276; L.B.C. Carton, *Découvertes épigraphiques et archéologiques faites en Tunisie*

88 (*région de Dougga*) (Paris, 1895), 286. Kähler (col. 428) and Mazzilli suggest that because of their small size and location they may have had a funerary purpose.
88 Mazzilli 2016, 222: Gsell (cit. at n. 17), 157–8.
89 Mazzilli 2016, 235–6.
90 Mazzilli 2016, 247: *CIL* VIII 22693.
91 Mazzilli 2016, 220; *CIL* VIII 4585,18647; Gsell (cit. at n. 17), 157.
92 Mazzilli 2016, 234; *IlAlg* I, 2997.
93 Mazzilli 2016, 269; *CIL* VIII 1314=14817; M. Bouyac, *Bulletin archéologique* 1894, 319–20; C. Hülsen, *Festschrift zu Otto Hirschfelds sechzigsten Geburtstage* (Berlin, 1903), 425, n.4. For the position of the arch over the stream, Bouyac compares the gates at Henchir Sidi Khalifa and Bulla Regia. He also (p. 322) mentions another monumental gate which had a sculptured keystone. Another inscription (*CIL* VIII 1309) records the dedication of *arcuus* (more than one arch?) to his fatherland by Fabius Larinus Stachumelis. The inscription begins *Herculi Augusto sacrum*.
94 Mazzilli 2016, 259; *CIL* VIII 1296=14798; A.L. Frothingham, *AJA* 19 (1915), 165.
95 Mazzilli 2016, 239; Baratte and Duval (cit. at n. 36), 26–8.
96 Mazzilli 2016, 258; *CIL* VIII 4679; 4684; *IlAlg* I, 2130.
97 Mazzilli 2016, 258; *IlAlg* I, 2086.
98 Mazzilli 2016 258; Gsell and Joly (cit. at n. 61), II 20, 56; E. Babelon, *Bullletin archéologique* 1921, LXVI.
99 Mazzilli 2016, 277–8; A. Lézine, *Architecture romaine d'Afrique*, Publications de l'Université de Tunis, 1 sér., IX (1961), 134–6. Frothingham (*AJA* 8 (1904), 1) suggests that the arches must date from the time between Marcus Aurelius and Commodus.
100 Mazzilli 2016, 235; *IlAlg* II, 6225; J. Carcopino, *Bulletin archéologique* (1914), 566–70, who suggests that the inscription may come from the principal arch.
101 Mazzilli 2016, 268; Guérin (cit. at n. 85), II 354–5; *CIL* VIII 937; A.L. Frothingham, *AJA* 8 (1904), 12.
102 Mazzilli 2016, 216; A. Berthier, *Tiddis* (Alger, 1972), 41–2.
103 Mazzilli 2016, 217 (Cirta); 213 (Tipasa).For the latter, see Romanelli, *Topografia* (cit. at n. 1), 135. Only the foundations survive. The foundations of the piers of a second monumental arch have been found on the *decumanus* further south-west.
104 On Rapidum, see MacKendrick (cit. at n. 26), 250.
105 Mazzilli 2016, 226; *CIL* VIII 2723.
106 Mazzilli 2016, 283 (who dates it to 161–9); *CIL* VIII 11924.
107 F. S. Kleiner, *Numismatic Chronicle*, 149 (1989), 69–81.
108 S. Handler, *AJA* 75 (1971), 70–71; De Maria 1988, 62–3; Kleiner (cit. in the preceding note). Some have identified the arch as the entrance to the Iseum Campense at Rome, but this is impossible. Others have assumed that an arch was erected to commemorate the suppression of a revolt by the Jews of Alexandria in 117, under Trajan, but this is equally implausible. Handler quotes Dio Chrysostom (3.265), who tells the Alexandrians (under Trajan) that they have not the energy to erect 'stately portals', but it seems perverse of her to argue from this for the erection of an arch.
109 (Paris, 2nd edn, 1822), ch. 15, most easily accessible in C. C. Gillespie and M. Dewachter, eds, *Monuments of Egypt: the Napoleonic Edition* (Princeton, 1987), vol. IV, pls 55–7.
110 See also Edmund Weigand, 'Propylon und Bogentor in der östlichen Reichskunst', *Wiener Jahrbuch für Kunstgeschichte,* V (1928), 98–100. The east gate of the town had a pair of Corinthian columns, but the Napoleonic investigators could not provide a reconstruction.

8
FROM ANTIQUITY TO THE RENAISSANCE

The last arch built in the classical period seems to have been the Arco di Portogallo in Rome, dated to the late fifth century. The concept of triumph was certainly familiar, at least from the seventh century onwards, in the East, as references exist to such ceremonies for emperors (see the section on Constantinople). It is likely that the West also retained this consciousness, although there it had a religious connotation. This can be clearly seen in a remarkable piece of evidence from the time of Charlemagne. His counsellor and biographer Einhard (*c.* 770–840) left to the church of St Servatius at Maastricht a reliquary in the form of a triumphal arch [8.1]. Unfortunately it was destroyed, probably at the end of the eighteenth century, but a seventeenth-century drawing survives, as well as a written description. Made of silver and 38 cm high, it served as the base for a cross, and bore the inscription on an ansate panel on the attic:

8.1 Reliquary of Einhard, *c.* 840, in a C17 drawing.

130 THE TRIUMPHAL ARCH

Ad tropaeum aeternae victoriae sustinendum Einhardus peccator hunc arcum ponere ac Deo dedicare curavit ('The sinner Einhard had this arch set up to support the trophy of eternal victory and dedicated to God'). The arch had a single opening. On the attic were represented Christ and the apostles; the spandrels showed the Evangelists with their symbols in tondi; the narrow sides had the Annunciation and the witness of John the Baptist; the piers showed men with haloes bearing lances and the *vexillum* (standard); and the inner walls of the opening had men on horseback (possibly Constantine and Charlemagne, or symbols of Eastern and Western Rome), piercing dragons with lances. Einhard described a similar work in ivory as *ad instar antiquorum operum* ('on the model of ancient works'), and the reliquary shows the same awareness.[1]

It is interesting that about the same time the term *arcus triumphalis* is first used in post-Roman times, for the great arch leading into the apse of a basilica, in the Life of Pope Paschal I (died 824). As it is most unlikely that the rare earlier uses of this term (pp. 75, 112, 118) would have been known at this time, it was probably a new coinage.[2]

Some scholars have seen another Carolingian reminiscence of the Roman triumphal arch in the gateway to the monastery of Lorsch, in Hessen, which dates from *c.* 774–90

8.2 Monastery gateway at Lorsch, Germany, *c.* 774–90.

[8.2]. It stands free within the court in front of the church, near the entrance. It has three equal openings, and there is a room above (later made into a chapel). The most direct model seems to be the *propylaeum* of old St Peter's at Rome, but the most remarkable feature here is that the structure is isolated, and its only purpose can have been to be passed through. Krautheimer compared its function, and its form, to that of a Roman triumphal arch. Even the upper storey is compared with the vaulted attics of some arches (the steep-pitched roof dates from the fourteenth century). He argues that the model must have been the Arch of Constantine, whose Christian associations would have given it special significance.[3] The upper room has been identified as the *palatium regale*, or *Königshalle*, reserved for the use of the sovereign or his representative. Its painted decoration (a dado with Ionic pilasters and entablature above) has been compared with Roman fresco schemes.[4] Conant points out that Richbod, a member of the Palatine School at Aachen, was Abbot of Lorsch from 784 to 804, during Charlemagne's campaign against the Saxons, and that Tassilo, Duke and King of the Bavarians, died a monk there *c.* 797: 'it is easy to see how the idea of a triumphal arch could arise under these circumstances'.[5] However, Conant's suggestion that the gatehouse was 'like a Roman triumphal arch in its forum' is less convincing: it was not a regular practice to have an arch standing in a forum – least of all in an axial position.

An illumination in the first Bible of Charles the Bald (mid-ninth century) shows a town, in front of which stands a plain and simple arch, astylar, but with a cornice at the level of the springing running around the piers.[6]

The west front of Lincoln Cathedral was built by Bishop Remigius from *c.* 1072/5 to 1092. This huge and powerful structure, still visible within the Gothic remodelling, had three deeply pierced arches, the central one taller than the side ones. Peter Kidson suggested that the front was related to the monumental architecture of ancient Rome, claiming that 'what is required is a triumphal arch like the Porte de Mars at Reims', and that there might have been such an arch in England. The Porte de Mars is an odd choice, since its three openings are of equal height, but Anthony Quiney has proposed that the source for Lincoln was the Arch of Constantine at Rome, the proportions of whose openings are remarkably similar. Remigius had visited Rome in 1071 and 1076, and the symbolism of that arch, celebrating the victory of Constantine over paganism, might have suggested to him that such a building would celebrate both his ecclesiastical authority and the reality of the Norman conquest. It is possible that the west front was originally freestanding, and served as both vestibule and fortified palace, which might support the argument – and provide a parallel with Lorsch. It is a fascinating speculation, but it may be wondered how many of those who saw it could possibly have appreciated the symbolism.[7]

A less obvious connection has been proposed with the façade of the Romanesque church of Ripoll in Catalonia (eleventh–twelfth centuries). There is only one large arched opening in a broad and richly decorated front, which is divided into three zones by cornices.[8]

The interest in the antiquities of Rome shown by many people in the twelfth century is well known. Poems praising ancient Rome were written; statues were collected; a decree was promulgated in 1162 for the protection of Trajan's Column; and guidebooks began to be published, the earliest and best known being the *Mirabilia Romae*.[9] It was presumably as a result of this interest that it became customary for the new pope, after his coronation, to process back from the Vatican Basilica to the Lateran Palace. This symbolised his taking power over the city of Rome, and was known as the *possessio* (*possesso* in Italian).[10] In the account of the procession of Pope Callixtus II, in 1120, it is stated that arches were prepared on the route. This is the first time that such arches are mentioned, but the phrase *de more* ('according to custom') indicates that their erection was already customary. The subsequent history of these 'possessi' is dealt with in the chapter on papal arches (pp. 169–82).

In 1122 Callixtus II achieved a significant diplomatic victory when he settled old disputes with the Emperor by the Concordat of Worms. In the next year he made a triumphal entry into Rome. One of his chief allies was Cardinal Johannes von Crema, who in the same year began to rebuild the church of San Crisogono. It broke with tradition by having an architrave above the granite columns of the nave, instead of arches. The Ionic capitals were ancient. The chancel arch is an *arcus triumphalis* supported on huge porphyry columns with Corinthian capitals. P.C. Claussen sees the nave as a triumphal street leading by way of the triumphal arch to the altar and papal throne.[11]

The significance of the Arch of Constantine was recognised by John of Salisbury, who quotes its inscription in the prologue to his *Policraticus* of 1159.[12]

Romanesque Italy provides some parallels with arches. Three examples of a particular type of pulpit are found in Campania in the later twelfth century: the box-like upper part is supported by four columns, above which are spandrels. The most notable instance is in the Duomo of Salerno, where the spandrels contain reliefs of angels, but others are found at Teano and at Sessa Aurunca [8.3]. The type occurs nowhere else in Europe.[13] At Città Castellana, in Lazio, the west front of the cathedral is preceded by a colonnade, which is interrupted in the centre by a very tall arch, with moulded archivolt, set into a rectangular frame which has a Cosmatesque frieze dated 1210. The spandrels are plain apart from small eagles on consoles. The inscription, *Gloria in excelsis Deo*, etc. (Luke 2.14), explains the triumphal theme.[14]

The medieval topographers of Rome took particular interest in the reliefs and inscriptions on triumphal arches. The twelfth-century *Descriptio Lateranensis Ecclesiae* refers to the relief on the Arch of Titus.[15] In his *Narratio de Mirabilibus Urbis Romae* of *c*. 1200 the Englishman Magister Gregorius pays particular attention to the reliefs on arches and columns. Curiously enough, none of the three arches he describes is easy to identify. The first, of which he records an implausible inscription stating that it was built by Augustus, was near the Pantheon, and, according to him, its reliefs included the battle of Actium and the suicide of Cleopatra. This may be the so-called Arcus Pietatis, of the fourth or fifth century. The second, described as *arcus triumphalis Magni Pompeii*, must be the one also seen by Petrarch on the Campus Martius, but it is not known which is the arch in question. Gregorius claimed that his third arch was erected to celebrate Scipio's victory over Hannibal. It has been suggested that he was referring to the Arch of Constantine, but this would have been an unlikely mistake.[16]

The Emperor Frederick II was obsessed with the idea of himself as a Roman *triumphator*. For example, after his victory over the Lombards in 1236 he held triumphal parades, with booty, trophies and prisoners, at Cremona, and later at Rome. In a letter to the Roman Senate he boasted that he had enhanced its ancient triumphal monuments by new achievements. The most striking physical sign of his obsession was his

8.3 Pulpit in the Duomo of Salerno, late C12.

great gateway at Capua, built between 1234 and 1240 at the head of the bridge where the Via Appia from Rome crossed the river Volturno [8.4]. It was destroyed in 1557, apart from the rusticated bases of the polygonal towers which flanked it, but its appearance is known from drawings, the best of which is by Francesco di Giorgio Martini. The arched opening had tondi above it and on either side, containing busts. The two stages above were articulated by pilasters in four unequal sections, supported on corbel busts. The first stage had three statues in niches, the central niche (with the statue of Frederick) taller than the others. It has been suggested that the model for the gate was the arch at Rimini, erected to commemorate the rebuilding of the Via Appia (p. 10). Similarly, Frederick's gate marks the original terminus of the Via Appia.

8.4 Gateway of Frederick II at Capua, 1234–40, destroyed 1557. 19th-century drawing.

The sculpture on it, some of which survives in the Museo Campano, is of especial interest, as the gate is claimed to have been the first medieval monument with a secular programme of decoration, and to have borne the first lifesize portrait of a seated ruler since antiquity. It is furthermore remarkable in incorporating ancient sculpture, as was noted by the sixteenth-century chronicler Scipione Sannelli. The figure in the niche on the left of the Emperor's statue seems to have been a second-century AD statue of Diana, and the figure on the right may have represented Apollo: the two torsos survive. They would have symbolised hunting and the arts – two pursuits very important to Frederick. The busts that occupied the tondi around the opening were new, and represented leading members of Frederick's court, but their technique recalls a bust of Jupiter which was formerly the keystone of one of the external arches of the Roman amphitheatre at Capua Vetere. The head of the bust over the arch survives, and recalls the bust of Diana still at the amphitheatre: it may have symbolised Custodia, the protecting deity of the Sicilian state, or perhaps Capua itself. Sannelli relates that 'above the arch' (presumably within it) were marble victories and trophies. A second-century AD fragment of a relief survives, showing the spoils of victory, including weapons, standards, prows of ships, and so on – a type of relief commonly found on Roman arches. This (together with two similar reliefs now lost) may well be one of the sculptures referred to by Sannelli, and may conceivably have come from the surviving Roman arch at Capua Vetere (see p. 65). The iconography of the gate must have served to identify Frederick with the Roman emperors whom he sought to emulate.[17]

In 1375 Giovanni Dondi, a Paduan doctor, wrote to his friend Petrarch about the antiquities still visible at Rome, whose inscriptions and reliefs recorded patriotic deeds: he particularly specified 'i grandiosi archi trionfali e le colonne'.[18] Early in the next century (about 1411) the celebrated Greek scholar Manuel Chrysoloras wrote in a

FROM ANTIQUITY TO THE RENAISSANCE 135

letter to the Byzantine Emperor John VIII Palaeologus that he saw the ruins of Rome as evidence for the Roman cast of mind, and particularly the triumphal arches, whose reliefs showed the military and civilian customs of the inhabitants of different parts of the empire. He was obviously thinking especially of the Arch of Septimius Severus. The letter became widely known, and must have served to draw attention to the arches.[19]

Notes

1. B. Montesquiou-Fezenzac, *Cahiers archéologiques*, 4 (1949), 79–103, 8 (1956), 147–74; H.M. von Erffa, *Reallexicon zur deutschen Kunstgeschichte*, IV (1958), s.v. *Ehrenpforte*, 1448–9; A. Grabar, *Cahiers archéologiques*, 27 (1978), 61–83; M. Imhof and C. Winterer, eds, *Karl der Grosse* (2nd edn, Petersberg, 2013), 114–16.
2. R. Krautheimer, *Rome: Profile of a City, 312–1308* (Princeton, 1980), 114; H.L. Kessler and J. Zacharias, *Rome 1300: On the Path of the Pilgrim* (New Haven/London, 2000), 114.
3. R. Krautheimer, 'The Carolingian Revival of Early Christian Architecture', *Art Bulletin*, 24 (1942), 32–4; Imhof and Winterer (cit. at n. 1), 174.
4. M. D'Onofrio, *Roma e Aquisgrana* (Rome, 1983), 55–83.
5. K.J. Conant, *Carolingian and Romanesque Architecture* (3rd edn, Harmondsworth, 1973), 18, 297, n. 21.
6. B. Montesquiou-Fezenzac, *Cahiers archéologiques*, 8 (1956), 157–9.
7. P. Kidson, in D. Owen, ed., *A History of Lincoln Minster* (Cambridge, 1994), 20–21; A. Quiney, *Architectural History*, 44 (2001), 162–71.
8. Y. Christe, *Cahiers archéologiques*, 21 (1971), 39–40; A. Pinelli, in S. Settis, ed., *Memoria dell'antico nell'arte italiana*, II (Turin, 1985), 287.
9. James Bruce Ross, 'A Study of Twelfth Century Interest in the Antiquities of Rome', in J.L. Cate and E.N. Anderson, eds, *Medieval and Historiographical Essays in Honor of James Westfall Thompson* (Chicago, 1938), 302–21; R.L. Benson and G. Constable, eds, *Renaissance and Renewal in the Twelfth Century* (Oxford, 1982).
10. Francesco Cancellieri, *Storia de' solenni possesi dei sommi pontifici* (Rome, 1802). This is still the standard work.
11. P.C. Claussen, in B. Schimmelpfennig and L. Schmuzze, eds, *Rom in höhen Mittelalter* (Sigmaringen, 1992), 99.
12. Johannes Sarisberiensis, *Policraticus*, ed. C. Webb (Oxford, 1909), I, 13.
13. D. Glass, 'Romanesque Sculpture in Campania and Sicily', *Art Bulletin*, 56 (1974), 318–24; C. Frugoni in S. Settis, ed., *Memoria dell'antico nell'arte italiana* I (Turin, 1984), 21, n. 63 (she illustrates the Salerno pulpit as fig. 10).
14. Touring Club Italiano, *Attraverso l'Italia: Lazio* (1967), fig. 217; E. Kitzinger in Benson and Constable (cit. at n. 9), 649–50.
15. R. Valentini and G. Zucchetti, *Codice topografico della città di Roma*, III (Rome, 1946), 341; G. Seibt, *Anonimo romano: Geschichtsschreibung in Rom an der Schwelle der Renaissance* (Stuttgart, 1992), 167.
16. Valentini and Zucchetti (cit. in the previous note), III, 159–63; C. Nardella, *Il fascino di Roma nel Medioevo: Le Meraviglie di Roma di Maestro Gregorio* (Rome, 1997), 96–102. See also J. Osborne, *Master Gregorius: The Marvels of Rome* (Toronto, 1987), 79–82.
17. J. Meredith, 'The Arch at Capua: the strategic use of *spolia* and references to the antique', in W. Tronzo, ed., *Intellectual Life at the Court of Frederick II Hohenstaufen, Studies in the History of Art*, 44 (1994), 109–26. She points out that Frederick actually owned the arches of Titus and Constantine in Rome, then converted into fortresses – another parallel with the gate at Capua.
18. Frugoni (cit. at n. 13), 22–4; R. Weiss, *The Renaissance Discovery of Classical Antiquity* (Oxford, 1988), 52. Petrarch's own interest in triumphs is shown by his famous *Trionfi*.
19. M. Baxandall, *Giotto and the Orators* (Oxford, 1971), 80–81. See also P. Bober and R. Rubinstein, *Renaissance Artists and Antique Sculpture* (London, 1986), 210–11.

9
RENAISSANCE ITALY

Arches

Frederick II's triumphal entries have been described (p. 133). Occasional examples are known in the next couple of centuries from Flanders, including that of Philippe le Bel into Ghent in 1301; that of Comtesse Marguerite, again into Ghent; and those of Philippe le Bon into Bruges in 1440, and into Ghent in 1458. For these events scaffolds were set up with 'tableaux vivants' or paintings, but arches do not appear until the entry of Charles V into Bruges in 1515 (see the discussion of the Low Countries, pp. 246–61).

Arches had, however, played an important role in the renaissance of classical architecture in fifteenth-century Italy. It has been shown that medieval topographers and antiquarians were fascinated by their reliefs and inscriptions, but now it was their architectural form that aroused most interest, although their purpose (whether actual or supposed) was by no means forgotten.

The most important architectural theorist of the century was Leon Battista Alberti, whose *De re aedificatoria libri decem*, written in about 1450–52, was published in Florence in 1485, after Alberti's death in 1472. The work was dedicated to Lorenzo de' Medici in words composed by Angelo Poliziano, a striking sign of its significance. Alberti deals with arches in the sixth chapter of the eighth book. He considers them the greatest possible ornament to squares or to crossroads, and defines the arch as 'a gate standing continually open'. He claims that their origin was due to the extension of city boundaries, which left the gates freestanding; later they were adorned with the spoils of victory. They should have three openings, the central one for the triumphing soldiers, and the side ones for the citizens to go out and welcome them. He then gives details of the proper proportions for arches. The columns standing in front of the piers should have Corinthian or Composite capitals. Statues should stand above them. On top of the structure should stand 'larger Statues, triumphal Cars, Animals and other Trophies'. Reliefs and inscriptions should occupy 'convenient Places'.[1] It is obvious that Alberti's principal model is the Arch of Constantine.

The fact that so many arches were visible and comparatively easily accessible meant that they were bound to be among the most studied of all ancient monuments. In an essay called 'Antitheses of the Quattrocento' Sir John Summerson contrasted Alberti's book with another which showed an 'entirely different aspect of the Renaissance attitude to Roman architecture', the *Hypnerotomachia Poliphili* of Francesco Colonna, completed in 1467 and published in 1499 [9.1]. In his dream-wanderings, Poliphilus comes upon an 'ancient portal of splendid workmanship, marvellously constructed and with exquisite regularity and art, and magnificently decorated with sculpture and varied lineaments'. It took the form of a triumphal arch, with pairs of Corinthian columns of porphyry, serpentine, Cariatic marble, and Laconic stone, and bronze bases and capitals, on either side of the opening. The entablature projected above. The opening had a pilaster on either side. Each spandrel contained 'a noble sculpture of Victory'. On the frieze were carved trophies and weapons, and a dedication to Aphrodite and her son. Above the attic was a pediment. Poliphilus gives a detailed account of the proportional system on which the design of the arch is based, and draws from it a lesson in the art of the architect. The illustration of the arch is much simplified and shows little of the sculptural decoration.[2]

Alberti made a more extensive and remarkable use of the triumphal arch as a model than any other architect except Lutyens. His first important work was the remodelling of San Francesco at Rimini into a dynastic memorial for Sigismondo Malatesta, which he began in the early 1450s, but which was left unfinished when Malatesta died in 1466. Rudolf Wittkower pointed out that for the façade – 'the first façade in the new style' – Alberti used the triumphal arch motif, which 'from then on ... was repeatedly used for church façades and remained for some time one of the few effective ideas in this context'. Some details were taken from the Arch of Augustus at Rimini itself, but the Arch of Constantine was, as Wittkower puts it, 'the prototype for the whole system'.[3] In the lower part of the façade a tall central arch frames the doorway, while on either side lower blank arches stand on a high base, each flanked by Corinthian half-columns, and with *clipei* (shields) in the spandrels. These arches were intended to be deeper, and to contain the sarcophagi of Sigismondo and his mistress Isotta (the arches along the side of the church do contain sarcophagi). Wittkower saw the arches as symbolising triumph over death.

In Alberti's last work, the church of Sant'Andrea at Mantua (designed in 1470, and begun in 1472, the year of his death) the triumphal arch provides the model for both the façade and the internal articulation, though here the source is not the tripartite form of arch but the single one such as those of Titus at Rome and Trajan at Ancona [9.2]. A further striking difference is that instead of half-columns Alberti uses pilasters. In the façade he blends the triumphal arch theme with that of the temple front, not only by placing a pediment above the entire entablature, but by carrying the moulding on which the central archivolt rests across the side bays, so that it seems that the large order breaks into it. This, writes Wittkower, 'strengthens the impression that the giant pilasters belong both to the triumphal arch and to the temple front', so marrying the two classical systems 'in an unprecedented way'. The articulation of the front is repeated inside along the sides of the nave, with the arches framing the chapels. Wittkower comments that 'in repeating the same articulation inside and outside Alberti was giving visual evidence of the homogeneity of the wall structure'.[4]

9.1 'Ancient portal' from Hypnerotomachia Poliphili, 1499.

9.2 Mantua, S. Andrea, designed 1470 by L. Alberti.

    A small arch at Ferrara has been attributed to Alberti [9.3]. In 1443–4 he was asked by Lionello d'Este to arbitrate in a competition for an equestrian monument to Lionello's father, Niccolò III. The commission for the statue went to Antonio di Cristoforo, and that for the horse to Niccolò Baroncelli. The monument was inaugurated in 1451,

9.3 Ferrara, Palazzo Comunale: equestrian statue of Niccolò III, 1451, on base by Alberti.

and stood on the corner of the Palazzo di Corte (now Palazzo Comunale) opposite the cathedral. The base takes the form of an arch, at a right angle to the building, resting on a half-column attached to the wall and a freestanding column (the latter renewed).

140 THE TRIUMPHAL ARCH

Adolfo Venturi suggested that this might have been designed by Alberti himself, pointing out that the *clipei* in the spandrels, the garlands in the frieze and other details are paralleled in the Tempio Malatestiano at Rimini. He also notes that Donatello's statue of Gattamelata had not yet been set up at Padua, and that its base is modelled on funerary monuments, whereas the Ferrara 'triumphal arch' is a more up-to-date idea.[5]

In 1452 Alberti showed a copy of his treatise to the humanist Pope Nicholas V, a great patron of the arts. Nicholas's biographer Gianozzo Manetti tells us that he proposed to add to the Vatican two great towers, and between them a *porta cum fornice triumphali*, as the entrance to the palace. This was presumably intended to commemorate the reunification of the church, celebrated by the jubilee of 1450, or the peace agreed by all the powers of Italy except Genoa in 1455 – the year of his death.[6]

Nicholas's project was remarkably similar to the one executed by the Aragonese Alfonso I after he established his rule at Naples in 1442. In the next year he entered the city in triumph. The idea of a triumphal procession must have been due to the interest in antiquity of Alfonso and the humanists in his entourage, and was probably influenced by the triumphal entries of Frederick II into Jerusalem (1229) and Rome (1237).

9.4 Castelnuovo, Naples, 1452–71.

Details of the procession are known: it entered through a breach in the walls, and on the Piazza del Mercato an arch of gilded wood, decorated with heraldry and inscriptions, was erected. It was also adorned with trumpet-players and angels.[7]

The Neapolitans began to erect a marble arch in front of the Arcivescovato, to the design of Pietro di Martino of Milan. However, Alfonso, who was rebuilding the damaged Angevin Castel Nuovo as his principal residence, asked them to use instead the narrow space between a pair of new round towers for a magnificent triumphal arch gateway, erected between 1452 and 1471 – an interesting comparison with the more or less contemporary project of the Pope [9.4].[8] Alfonso was, like Nicholas V, a leading humanist, a collector of coins, medals and books. His circle of scholars, including Lorenzo Valla, was the first 'academy' of the Renaissance. This helps to explain the remarkable use of archaeological detail in the arch. The two chief models were the arches at Pula and Benevento. Pietro di Martino, traditionally regarded as the arch's designer, was working at Ragusa (Dubrovnik) when summoned to Naples, and might have seen Pula en route, though this has been doubted. Benevento

RENAISSANCE ITALY 141

(its arch important also as a model for the sculptural decoration) had been taken by Alfonso in 1440, and was in the centre of his South Italian kingdom. Other details came from imperial temples and from sarcophagi.

Pietro di Martino was identified on his tomb in Santa Maria la Nova, Naples (now lost), as having been responsible for the arch. However, C.L. Frommel has argued that it must have been Alberti who produced the design. Alberti had designed the Tempio at Rimini for Alfonso's rival Sigismondo (see above), and Frommel suggests that Alfonso proposed to trump him with an even grander arch. A question which has aroused much discussion is the relation between the executed structure and a drawing in the Museum Boijmans Van Beuningen in Rotterdam, signed by the unknown 'Bonams de Ravena'. It has been wrongly attributed to Pisanello. It shows an arch very similar to that of Alfonso, though more Gothic (with its pointed arch and twisted columns), and incorporating arms and emblems. The chief difference from the arch as built is the absence of the triumph frieze. Frommel considers that the drawing probably depicts a wooden model for the arch.[9] The arch was completed after Alfonso's death in 1458 by his illegitimate son Ferrante. Its erection, with its iconographic emphasis on Ferrante as Alfonso's successor, was a vital piece of propaganda. It was not intended, however, as a military monument. The only actual scenes of warfare are on the inner bronze doors added by Ferrante. The emphasis throughout is on legitimate rule as the guarantee of peace, and the placing of the arch on the castle, far from being paradoxical, was intended to identify it as the palace of a king rather than the castle of a tyrant (a distinction drawn by Alberti). Alfonso must also have had Frederick II's gate at Capua in mind (see pp. 133–5).

As well as Pietro di Milano, the outstanding group of artists involved included Francesco Laurana, from Dalmatia; Paolo Romano; the Tuscans Isaia da Pisa and Antonio di Chellino; the Lombard Domenico Gagini; Andrea dell'Aquila; and the Catalan Pere Johan. The marble structure is 35.7 m high and 9.2 m wide. On the lower stage the opening is flanked by elegant pairs of fluted Corinthian columns, whose entablatures project (as at Pula). The spandrels contain bold griffins supporting the coat of arms. On the frieze above is the inscription *Alfonsus Rex Hispanus Siculus Italicus pius clemens invictus* ('Alfonso, King of Spain, Sicily and Italy, pious, clement, unconquered'). At the sides within the arch are reliefs. The right-hand one shows Alfonso and Ferrante, probably at the conquest of Naples, and the left-hand one shows Ferrante as commander, perhaps in the Tuscan campaign of 1452–4; they are based on ancient *adventus* and *profectio* (arrival and departure) reliefs. On the column-base of the left-hand relief is a medallion portrait of Ferrante. The vault has hexagonal coffers with rosettes and winged heads of putti.

The attic stage shows the triumphal procession in high relief, with Alfonso under a canopy on a carriage drawn by horses. The projecting pedimented end sections show Tunisian ambassadors and other dignitaries on the left, and musicians on horseback on the right. On the frieze is the inscription: *Alfonsus regum princeps hanc condidit arcem* ('Alfonso, chief of kings, founded this citadel'). Above a second entablature is another arch, flanked by pairs of fluted Ionic columns; it is open, and was intended to contain a bronze equestrian statue of Alfonso, never executed. Donatello was given the commission, but died before he had made much progress. A bronze horse's head in the Museo Nazionale in Naples is thought to have been intended as part. In 1466 Ferrante hung here a gilded vessel containing his father's heart. The spandrels of this arch hold winged Victories and putti with cornucopia and torch. In front of the left-hand columns stands a figure usually identified as warlike Virtue, to which another figure must have been intended to correspond. Above the third entablature are shell-headed niches containing statues of the four virtues. Then comes a segmental pediment, in which are a pair of reclining river gods with cornucopiae. At the very top is a statue of St Michael, traditional protector of the southern regions. Originally it was flanked by statues of SS. George and Anthony.[10] The proportions of the arch are in effect late Gothic, but the articulation and the elaborate decoration are in Venetian-Lombardic Renaissance. It represents the crucial stage in the introduction of the Renaissance into South Italy.

At Venice the new entrance to the Arsenale, dated 1460, was an obvious place for triumphal imagery, and its design (no longer attributed to Antonio Gambello) is based on the arch at Pula [9.5]. The paired cipollino columns with Veneto-Byzantine capitals are twelfth-century (possibly from Torcello). Above the cornice is the winged Lion of St Mark, in a pedimented aedicule. The winged Victories in the spandrels were added after the Battle of Lepanto. Fortini Brown describes the gate as 'the first serious attempt to give monumental Venice a plausible Roman presence'.[11]

9.5 Arsenale gateway, Venice, 1460.

The most remarkable use of the triumphal arch motif by Donato Bramante was in the Cortile del Belvedere of the Vatican, but Arnaldo Bruschi has identified earlier examples. In 1492–4 the Piazza Ducale at Vigevano was built to his design, for Duke Ludovico il Moro of Milan. The piazza is surrounded by arcades. Two main streets lead into it, from the west and north-west, and these entries were emphasised by the curious device of painting giant arches to frame them. The western one had two orders of pilasters. In the spandrels of the painted arch are tondi with heads in profile, and above is a huge coat of arms. The north-western 'arch' created the impression of a triple arch, with a pair of pilasters on either side of a central opening. The first 'arch' established an axis with the cathedral, and the second with the castle tower.[12]

Bramante used a similar idea at the Canonica di Sant'Ambrogio in Milan, probably around 1492. Here the centre of the arcade surrounding the courtyard is marked by a much taller arch, supported on piers with attached pilasters. In the spandrels are circular openings.

RENAISSANCE ITALY **143**

Bruschi sees the idea, both here and at Vigevano, as coming from Alberti, who suggested that the entrances to a 'forum' should be marked by triumphal arches.[13]

Julius II was elected Pope in 1503, and within a year Bramante made a design for the Cortile del Belvedere in Rome. Julius was determined to establish the power and prestige of the popes, and – like Nicholas V – he regarded the rebuilding of both St Peter's Basilica and the palace as essential to this purpose. Bramante proposed to link the Belvedere, a villa built by Innocent VIII, with the palace by means of loggias 300 m long, with terraced gardens between them. The plan derived from the imperial villas of ancient Rome. For the loggias of the upper (eastern) court, Bramante used a series of interlocking triumphal arches. On the sides, pairs of pilasters have rectangular panels, one over the other, between them. They flank the arches, which were originally open. On the end wall the arches were always closed, and here round-headed niches appear between the pilasters. (The upper storey above the arcades was added later.) The triumphal arch motif was anticipated in the nymphaeum on the staircase that leads up from the lower court.[14]

Bramante's use of the triumphal arch formula as a means of articulation was highly influential. One example is the Palazzo Bevilacqua at Verona by Michele Sanmicheli (1530), where the upper part of the façade consists of three overlapping arches. The effect is much richer than at the Vatican, with half-columns (fluted vertically or spirally), arched windows below pediments in the intercolumniations, and rich sculpture which includes allegorical figures in the spandrels. The Villa Giulia at Rome is attributed to Giacomo Vignola (1551–3). The semicircular loggia within the courtyard has 'triumphal arches' in the centre and at either end (though these curiously lack the end pier), linked by colonnades. At the ends the 'arches' have pairs of pilasters.[15] At Vignola's Palazzo Farnese at Caprarola (1559–75) the circular central courtyard has overlapping triumphal arches at both levels. The lower one is simply rusticated, while the upper one has half-columns with rectangular openings between them.[16]

It is not surprising that city gates should sometimes (as in antiquity) adopt the scheme of the triumphal arch. Two elegant examples at Padua were designed by Giovanni Maria Falconetto.[17] The Porta San Giovanni (1527–8) recalls the Arch of Titus, with Corinthian half-columns whose entablatures project (the central ones linked). The side openings are framed by Corinthian aedicules. On the attic coats of arms, and (originally) the Lion of St Mark, in white Istrian stone, contrast with the grey stone of the rest. At the Porta Savonarola (1529–30) the columns are of white stone, and over the side openings are *clipei* with busts.[18]

Falconetto's celebrated Loggia Cornaro in Padua (1524), built for the great humanist Alvise Cornaro, also recalls the triumphal arch. The arcade has Doric half-columns. The larger central arch has winged Victories in the spandrels. (The upper storey was added in 1537, after Falconetto's death.)[19] His grandest triumphal arch is the one he built in 1532 to replace the Gothic entrance archway to the Palazzo del Capitanio (or dei Camerlenghi), in the Piazza dei Signori at Padua. It has paired Corinthian half-columns, and winged Victories in the spandrels. On the attic is the Lion of St Mark.[20]

Sanmicheli's Palazzo Bevilacqua has already been mentioned. He was also responsible for three magnificent gates at Verona, but none is clearly of triumphal arch type, though the Porta San Zeno follows the overall scheme, with the curiosity of rusticated pilasters at the corners and surrounds to the openings. Other works by Sanmicheli derived from the triumphal arch type include the Altare dei Magi in the Duomo of Orvieto, designed in 1514, and richly carved by Simone Mosca, which is articulated with pilasters and a pediment, and frames a large relief.[21] The portal he added in 1530–31 to the Palazzo del Capitano (or del Podestà) in Verona is handsomely proportioned, with Ionic columns supporting a pediment over the central arch, and pilasters at the sides.[22] Even the curved screen of the presbytery of the Duomo at Verona (the 'pergula' or 'tornacoro', 1534) has winged figures in the spandrels, and coffering under the arch.[23] Similarly, in Sanmicheli's superb Cappella Pellegrini at San Bernardino (1556), the lower elevation of the interior is like overlapping arches formed into a circle.[24] Much more 'architectural' is his altar of 1523 on the south side of the church of San Fermo Maggiore, with its huge pairs of freestanding Corinthian columns and enormous attic. Its arch frames a painting by Francesco Torbido.[25] Finally, in Sanmicheli's magnificent Palazzo Grimani, on the Grand Canal in Venice, the central part of the ground floor is based on the triumphal arch [9.6]. Here the winged Victories in the spandrels were carved by Alessandro Vittoria.[26]

Jacopo Sansovino was born in Florence in 1486, but moved to Rome. After the Sack in 1527 he took refuge in Venice, where he soon became chief architect to the Procurators of St Mark's. They were responsible for the scheme for remodelling the Piazza San Marco. As part of this, he replaced the old Loggetta at the base of the campanile with a new one, in 1537–49. This splendidly ornamental structure – intended

9.6 Palazzo Grimani di San Luca (Venice).

to hold its own in the Piazza despite its comparative smallness – has a principal façade which reads like three overlapping triumphal arches. The Composite columns and their entablatures project. In the intercolumniations are four bronze statues, while the tall attic has panels in bold relief, with a crowning balustrade. Until 1663 the side openings were windows, not doors. The end elevations (which were of brick until the reconstruction of the Loggetta after it was destroyed in the collapse of the campanile in 1902) repeat the formula as a single triumphal arch. Until the eighteenth century the attic did not extend over the intercolumniations at each end; as it was believed to be incomplete (a supposition supported by the beautiful drawing made in 1540, when the building was indeed incomplete, by Francisco d'Ollanda), it was then extended.[27] The statues are by Sansovino himself, while the reliefs are by Gerolamo Lombardo, Tiziano Minio and Danese Cattaneo. The front of the Loggetta is faced in carefully chosen stone – red Verona marble for the framing elements, white Carrara for the pilasters, frieze and capitals, *verde antico* for vertical strips, Istrian stone for the reliefs, and rare oriental marbles for the columns. The elaborate polychrome effects provide a rare example of an actual triumphal arch structure as colourful as a painted temporary arch. The iconography provided a celebration of Venice's power and majesty. Deborah Howard describes it as 'the most complete surviving visual representation of the "myth of Venice" – that is, the Venetian view of their own state as the perfect republic'.[28]

Two of Sansovino's other architectural works in Venice are clearly based on the triumphal arch scheme. One is the façade of the church of San Giuliano (San Zulian), begun in 1553. This can only be seen as a whole at close quarters. The use of the 'triumphal arch' to frame the doorway is effective. It has pairs of fluted Doric half-columns, with reliefs between them. The central arch contains the rectangular door, above which is Sansovino's seated bronze statue of the patron, Tommaso Rangone. At the upper level smaller Ionic pilasters of a curious shape, above the half-columns, flank niches.[29]

Sansovino's huge Scuola Grande della Misericordia, begun in 1532, never received its stone façade, but a drawing, attributed to Palladio, is apparently based on one of Sansovino's designs. It shows the same arrangement of three overlapping arches that he had used at the Loggetta, but here on two levels. There is rich sculptural decoration, including superimposed niches, containing statues, between the lower pairs of columns, while above are single niches with statues and reliefs. The triumphal arch formula was also used for the executed decoration, in three dimensions, of the *androne* (entrance hall) on the ground floor, and for the painted decoration of the upstairs *salone* (begun in 1588, but probably following Sansovino's intentions).[30]

Similar use of the motif was made by Giulio Romano in his rebuilding of the Benedictine abbey church of San Benedetto Po, near Mantua (1524–47) [9.7]. For the façade he uses three interlocking 'arches', with fluted Corinthian pilasters. The repeating pilasters help to disguise the asymmetry which required the addition of an extra pair at the right-hand end. Above the central 'arch' is placed a second one, slightly less tall, and with plain pilasters. The side elevation is articulated with the same system: three intersecting 'arches' (blank, of course) are flanked by further arches and pilasters.[31]

The two great architectural writers of the sixteenth century were Sebastiano Serlio and Andrea Palladio. Serlio was born in Bologna, studied in Rome under Baldassare Peruzzi, and lived in Venice from 1527 until he moved to Rome in 1541. His treatise

9.7 S. Benedetto Po, abbey church, 1524–7. Giulio Romano.

Tutte l'opere d'architettura e prospettiva was published in six books between 1537 and 1575 (a seventh book was never published). Book III, on antiquities, was published in Venice in 1540. It covers a group of arches. The first is the Arch of Janus at Rome, which Serlio did not consider to be a 'triumphal' arch. He continues with the Arch of Titus, whose original form he restores; the Arch of the Argentarii; the Arch of Septimius Severus; the Arch of Trajan at Benevento (included with the arches in Rome because 'very well known, complete and an impressive sight'); the Arch of Constantine; the Arch of Trajan at Ancona; the arch at Pula; the Arch of the Gavii at Verona; and the Porta dei Leoni in the same city. He did not include the Porta dei Borsari, also in Verona, because it was 'so barbarous'. Interestingly, he goes on next to the Cortile del Belvedere of the Vatican, starting with the elevation of the upper part, though he does not explicitly associate it with the triumphal arch. Of each arch he discusses and illustrates both the overall form and the details of its ornamentation.[32] Serlio's principal work of architecture is the Château of Ancy-le-Franc in Burgundy (begun in 1546) [9.8]. Here the ground-floor elevation of the courtyard is articulated as a series of interlocking 'triumphal arches', whose close derivation from Bramante's Cortile del Belvedere is demonstrated by Sabine Frommel.[33]

The importance attached to arches by Andrea Palladio is shown by his intention to devote a separate book to them. He refers to this several times in his *Quattro libri dell'architettura*, published in 1570.[34] He had made several visits to Rome to study the

RENAISSANCE ITALY 147

9.8 Courtyard of château of Ancy le Franc, begun 1546 by S. Serlio.

ancient remains between 1541 and 1554, and in the latter year published his guide to them, *L'antichità di Roma raccolta brevemente de gli auttori antichi e moderni*. In 1556 his patron Daniele Barbaro published an edition of Vitruvius, for which Palladio provided the illustrations, including the title page. This shows an elegant triumphal arch, with pairs of Corinthian columns on either side of the opening. Between the columns are niches containing statues, with reliefs above. The imposts of the arches are continued sideways as stringcourses. In the opening, which has winged Victories in the spandrels, is a statue of Architecture. Above the projecting entablatures, at attic level, are statues, and the book's title appears in the centre.

In the same year an arch was erected at Udine to commemorate the ending of a plague, and the relief work of Domenico Bollani, the Venetian governor. (The occasion for the arch's erection interestingly anticipates that of the arch at Gatchina in Russia for Prince Orlov (see pp. 281–2).[35]) It is highly likely that it was designed by Palladio. It is heavily rusticated, with a Doric entablature, above which stands the Lion of St Mark. Some twenty years later a much grander arch was erected in Vicenza, and this too is based on a design by Palladio. Known as the Arco delle Scalette, it serves as the entrance to steps which lead up to the Sanctuary of the Madonna on Monte Berico [9.9]. The project probably dates back to 1574, but the arch was only built in 1595. It has pairs of columns. The sculptural decoration consists of winged Victories in the

148 THE TRIUMPHAL ARCH

9.9 Arco delle Scalette, Vicenza, 1595 after a design by A. Palladio.

spandrels, coats of arms at the sides of the attic, and the Lion of St Mark between pairs of statues on top: these are by Giovanni Battista Albanese, who was responsible for the erection of the arch, Palladio being dead. A drawing by him in the Devonshire collection, itself based on the arch at Ancona, seems to have provided the model. The niches added later within the opening contain statues of the Annunciation by Orazio Marinali.[36]

RENAISSANCE ITALY 149

9.10 Loggia del Capitaniato, Piazza dei Signori, Vicenza, 1572. Palladio.

There is no doubt about Palladio's authorship of the Loggia del Capitaniato in the Piazza dei Signori at Vicenza, built in 1572 [9.10]. The principal façade, with its giant Corinthian order, and arches to the lower storey, relates to the triumphal arch model, and the side elevation was actually intended to commemorate the victory at Lepanto of October 1571. Its lower storey is formed like a triumphal arch, with statues of Peace and Victory on bases between the Corinthian columns, and relief panels of trophies above. Over the central opening (which has female figures in the spandrels) is a 'Serlian' window, with a balustrade below it which interrupts the parapet. At either side of this are statues, with large reliefs over the intercolumniations. The sculpture is by Lorenzo Rubini.[37]

Another building in Vicenza for which Palladio is suggested as architect has a façade based on the triumphal arch: this is the small church of Santa Maria Nuova, founded by a will of 1578, and built in 1585–94. The entablature is recessed over the central archway, which frames the door, and there is a pediment above.

In his church of Il Redentore at Venice (1576–80) Palladio uses the triumphal arch motif to articulate the nave arcades. Between pairs of Corinthian columns are two tiers of niches containing statues. This form of articulation recalls Alberti's at Sant' Andrea in Mantua, and looks forward to Lutyens's design for Liverpool Roman Catholic Cathedral.

The use of the side elevation of the Loggia del Capitaniato to commemorate the battle of Lepanto has been mentioned. It has been suggested by Hanns Gabelmann that the Portale of the Palazzo Rospigliosi at Zagarolo in Lazio was also erected to mark that victory, despite the inscription suggesting that it dates from 1670–1722. The upper part of the gate is decorated with a comparatively flat articulation clearly intended to recall a triumphal arch, and it reuses pieces of ancient sculpture, including a relief of horses incorporated in the triumph frieze.[38]

An arch was built in Vicenza on the Campo Marzio (now Piazzale Roma) in 1608 by Pier Paolo Battaglia, Capitano di Vicenza. Formerly attributed to Scamozzi, it is now thought to have been by Ottavio Bruto Revese. A triple arch, it had banded rustication. The side openings were rectangular. Above the centre was a pedimented attic, with a pinnacle on either side. The arch was unfortunately demolished in 1938.[39]

The usefulness of the triumphal arch scheme to designers in the sixteenth century is shown by several structures at the Villa d'Este at Tivoli, constructed for Cardinal Ippolito d'Este after he became governor of the town in 1550, under the direction of the antiquarian architect Pirro Ligorio. In the villa itself, the loggia that projects from the centre on the garden side (1566–7) uses the scheme in a simple pilastered form, while the dining loggia on the south-west corner (1566–8) has columns; its niches once held ancient and modern sculpture. Two fountains just to the north-west of this have more elaborate versions of the arch motif. The Fontana della Civette (1566–8), by Giovanni del Duca and Raffaello Sangallo, has single Ionic columns entwined with garlands of golden apples, from the cardinal's arms, which appear in full on the attic, between statues above the projecting entablatures. The Fontana degli Imperatori (now called the Fontana di Proserpina after the seventeenth-century stucco group in the niche) has pairs of Salomonic columns. Again their entablatures project against the double attic. The fountain was built in 1569–79 to the design of Alberto di Galvani. It is suggested that the form of these two fountains recalls the arches of ancient Rome, and also perhaps the triumphal welcome given to the Cardinal on his arrival in Tivoli in 1550.[40] The Fontana dell'Organo, begun in 1566, also has the form of a triumphal arch, with pilasters in the form of atlantes, a broken pediment above, and a kind of 'kiosk' for the organ in the centre.

The elegant arch at Chieri in Piedmont was built in 1580 in honour of Duke Emanuele Filiberto of Savoy, who had crushed the Reformation in the area. It has four freestanding Corinthian columns, obelisks on the corners of the attic, and a taller pedimented central attic. The architect was Giovanni Battista Riva, who also designed the fairly conventional arch at Savigliano, also in Piedmont, built in 1585 to commemorate the visit of Carlo Emanuele I of Savoy on the occasion of his marriage to Caterina of Austrian Spain. In 1965 a Latin inscription was added to dedicate the arch to Liberty, on the twentieth anniversary of the Resistance. Pieve del Cairo (Pavia) has an arch which commemorates the stay of Margarita of Austria in 1598, on her way to marry Philip III of Spain. Of brick, it has a Doric pilaster on either side of the opening, and an attic with inscription tablet. The side openings are much lower, beneath curving projections.

At Lecce, in Puglia, the Porta Napoli is also known as the Arco di Trionfo [11/ 9.11]. Until 1934 it formed part of the city walls, but is now isolated. It was built in 1548 in honour of Charles V, to the design of Gian Giacomo dell'Acaja, a local military architect who worked for the Emperor. It is over 20 m high, with pairs of attached Corinthian columns on either side of the opening supporting a triangular pediment containing the Emperor's arms. The back of the arch is completely flat.[41]

Another town gate in Puglia, rather late to be described as Renaissance, is the Porta del Carmine at Francavilla Fontana, built in 1640. It take the form of a triple triumphal arch, with attached Corinthian columns. Over the side openings are rectangles of white stone with decorative frames.

Charles V entered Palermo after his conquest of Tunis in 1535. He used the fifteenth-century gate, which the senate decided to rebuild in his honour. This was done in 1583–4. The façade of the Porta Nuova to the Cassaro has four Corinthian pilasters and busts in tondi above the entablature. The outer side is more remarkable, with chunky rustication and four telamones representing the defeated Moors. The upper part, added by Gaspare Guercio when he restored the arch in 1667 after an explosion, has elegant colonnades and a pyramidal roof.

9.11 Porta Napoli, Lecce, for Charles V, 1548. Giovanni dell'Acaja.

Altars, tombs, etc.

In the late fifteenth and early sixteenth centuries a number of altarpieces were made whose form clearly echoes the standard type of triumphal arch. One of the earliest is the marble one now in the Salviati Chapel of San Gregorio al Celio in Rome [9.12]. Made in 1469 for the high altar, it is attributed to Andrea Bregno and his school. The central arch, recessed in false perspective, shelters a Virgin and Child with angels.[42] On each side attached Corinthian columns frame niches containing statues of saints. Above each column stands an angel, and over each niche is a tondo relief. Above this level runs the inscription, and over that a frieze represents the procession of St Gregory to the Mausoleum of Hadrian. At the top, over the central arch, is a relief of God the Father.[43]

There are two similar altarpieces in Naples, in the church of Monte Oliveto. One, in the Piccolomini Chapel, is by Antonio Rossellino (c. 1475).[44] The other, in the Correale Chapel, is by Benedetto da Maiano (1489). The Corbinelli Chapel in Santo Spirito, Florence, has a fine marble example by Andrea Sansovino (1492). It is very like that in San Gregorio al Celio, though here the central arch shelters a tabernacle, and the richly ornamented pilasters (rather than columns) stand on plinths between which are reliefs. On top of the plain entablature and dentilled cornice is a central semicircular relief, later framed in an aedicule with broken pediment. Angels carrying torches stand at either side.[45] Another altarpiece, though with a crucifix in place of the tabernacle, is one by Andrea Ferrucci, from San Girolamo, Fiesole, now in the Victoria and Albert Museum in London.[46] There are two similar altarpieces in terracotta. The one now at San Medardo, Arcevia, which is dated 1513, has been reduced in size. It is by Giovanni della Robbia, as is the one at San Lucchese, Poggibonsi, of 1514 (or 1517).[47]

Freestanding wooden altarpieces could take the same form. One was commissioned for the altar of the Tornabuoni Chapel in Santa Maria Novella, Florence, to contain paintings by Ghirlandaio and his workshop, and was executed in 1491–6 by Baccio d'Agnolo. It was gilded, and had four columns at front and back, supporting an entablature on which stood a central arch flanked by candelabra. It was destroyed in 1804.[48] Another frame, more richly decorated, was made, also by Baccio, for the high altar of Santissima Annunziata in Florence. It contained a painting by Perugino, but was destroyed in 1655.

9.12 S. Gregorio al Celio, Rome, Cappella Salviati, altar of 1469, attributed to Andrea Bregno.

RENAISSANCE ITALY 153

9.13 S. Giovanni Laterano, Rome, organ case, 1577–9, designed by Giacomo della Porta, executed by Giovan Battista Montano. One column to gallery from the Arch of Constantine.

Baccio's assistant, Nanni Unghero, made an organ-case for the Annunziata in 1509–11, which was inspired by the high altar.[49] He also made a frame – also lost – for the altar of San Nicola da Tolentino in Santo Spirito, Florence (finished by 1518). Its central niche contained the statue of the saint, and on either side was a niche with a panel above, each housing an angel; on top was an urn, between putti and candelabra.[50] A similar frame of gilded wood seems to have been designed by Bernardo Buontalenti for the high altar of Santa Croce at the end of the sixteenth century, to contain the tabernacle designed by Giorgio Vasari.[51] A drawing in the Uffizi by the younger Vasari shows a similar altar, described as under the organ of the Annunziata.[52]

A particularly grand organ-case in the form of a triumphal arch was executed in 1597–9 for the north transept of St John Lateran in Rome by Giovanni Battista Montano [9.13]. It was commissioned by Pope Clement VIII. The gilded wooden case has spirally fluted Composite columns, with a segmental pediment above. The lavish decoration includes erotes and putti.[53] Other fine organ-cases of this type include that by the younger Vasari at Santo Spirito in Rome, dating from 1547, and one at Santa Maria della Scala in Siena, the work of Ventura di ser Giuliano Turapilli.[54]

To these pieces of church furniture in wood may be added a splendid prie-dieu of walnut, dating from the first half of the sixteenth century, now in the Museo dell'Antica Casa Fiorentina in the Palazzo Davanzati, Florence. It is articulated by four fluted Corinthian pilasters, with a tall opening in the centre and niches on either side. Palladio is known to have designed medal cabinets in the form of a triumphal arch for Ludovico Mocenigo.

The Renaissance development of the wall-monument not surprisingly produced numerous variations on the triumphal arch theme. Two monuments in Santi Giovanni e Paolo, Venice, are examples. On the entrance wall is the tomb of Pietro Mocenigo, who died in 1476, by Pietro Lombardo [9.14]. Mocenigo was celebrated for his military exploits against the Turks. The composition is framed by an arch on richly decorated pilasters. This breaks forward, and on either side are three niches containing statues, one over the other. Above the central entablature is a relief, with statues above. The sarcophagus on which Mocenigo's figure stands, with a shield-bearing page on either side, is

9.14 SS. Giovanni e Paolo, Venice, monument to Pietro Mocenigo, died 1476. Pietro Lombardo.

RENAISSANCE ITALY 155

supported by three warriors. Even more clearly indebted to the triumphal arch is the monument to Doge Andrea Vendramin (d. 1478) in the presbytery. It formerly stood in the Chiesa dei Servi. It is probably the work of Pietro Lombardo and his son Tullio, and work was still in progress in 1493. It differs from Mocenigo's tomb in various ways. Particularly striking is the use of freestanding columns, with projecting entablatures, to support the central arch. Here the figure is recumbent. On either side is a niche with a statue, and above each of these is a circular relief. Above the entablature are rectangular panels, with kneeling statues in front.[55]

The monument to Doge Nicolò Tron, in the Frari at Venice, the work of Antonio Rizzo (begun in 1476), is not so obviously related to the triumphal arch, but the three equal arches at the lowest stage, and the large arch crowning the whole, together with the statues and reliefs, have triumphal resonances. It is interesting to compare these with a painting installed in the Magistrato di Cattaver of the Ducal Palace during Tron's term of office (1471–3): it shows a simple, unornamented triumphal arch in a landscape setting. The frieze bears a Latin inscription, and on top are Tron's arms, supported by putti. In front of the arch stand three more putti, holding shields.[56]

More clearly derived from the triumphal arch are the magnificent pair of tombs on opposite sides of the choir of Santa Maria del Popolo in Rome. Both are signed by Andrea Sansovino, but the work may well have been directed by Bramante, who designed the sanctuary in 1505–7.[57] One commemorates Bramante's patron, Cardinal Ascanio Sforza. He was a bitter enemy of Julius II, who nevertheless erected the tomb, as well as the matching one to Sforza's cousin Cardinal Girolamo Basso della Rovere (1507) [9.15]. Preliminary drawings for the monuments survive in the Victoria and Albert Museum and in Weimar; they differ from each other, and neither presents a form so close to the triumphal arch as what was erected.[58] Each tomb has a central arched opening, whose imposts are at the level of the entablatures of the side sections, which have pairs of half-columns flanking niches. The central arch is framed by short pilasters supporting entablature and cornice. Within it is a sarcophagus, on which the deceased sleeps with his head supported on his arm. Above is a circular relief. Statues stand in the niches, while others are seated above. Over the topmost cornice are three more statues. The central one is seated above a coat of arms set in a bizarre arrangement of volutes. All of the architectural elements are decorated with the utmost elegance.[59]

Clearly based on these tombs is one designed by Baldassare Peruzzi for Pope Adrian VI (d. 1523) in Santa Maria dell'Anima, Rome. The architecture is heavier and the detail more sparse, with coloured marble used for the columns, pulvinated frieze, and upper pilasters. Between the columns are pairs of niches containing statues, but there are none above, and the central arch is crowned by a pediment. Below the sarcophagus bearing the Pope's effigy is a relief showing his entry into Rome. This is attributed to Niccolò Tribolo; the statues are by Michelangelo Senese.

A drawing for this tomb (in the Rijksmuseum, Amsterdam) shows pairs of columns flanking niches at the upper level, making a more unified composition.[60] This is closer to a second pair of tombs which face each other across the sanctuary of Santa Maria sopra Minerva in Rome. These commemorate Popes Leo X (d. 1521) and Clement VII (d. 1534), and were executed in 1536–41. They were designed by Antonio da Sangallo the Younger, and the architectural form is yet more severe and grandiose than in Adrian VI's tomb. Of four attached Composite columns, the central pair frame a tall,

9.15 S. Maria del Popolo, Rome, Tomb of Girolamo Basso della Rovere. Andrea Sansovino.

broad arch, containing the seated statue of the Pope, while at the sides are lower arches containing statues, below blank panels. The linked projecting entablature in the centre supports the projecting centre of the attic, on which is a large relief, with a broken pediment above. The recessed sections on either side also contain reliefs. According to Vasari, Baccio Bandinelli was supposed to execute the project, but decamped to

Florence before it was complete, so that Raffaello da Montelupo was called in to make the statue of Leo X, and Nanni di Baccio Bigio that of Clement. The principal reliefs show the meeting of Leo and François I in Bologna, and the coronation of Charles V by Clement. The smaller reliefs show scenes in the lives of the saints represented by the statues. Vasari professed to be shocked by the 'lack of religion, or excess of adulation, or both together', shown in the larger reliefs, which were by Baccio.[61]

The monument to Gerolamo Andreasi (d. 1524), now in Sant'Andrea, Mantua, stood originally in the church of the Carmine, but was moved here in 1785 [9.16]. It now stands against a wall, raised on an incongruous base, but was presumably intended to be freestanding. A drawing in Hamburg by its designer, Giulio Romano, shows it next to a column, whose plinth is of the same height as the wider lower sections of the richly decorated piers. The central opening is void. There is no attic, and only a thin cornice. Above it is the splendid sarcophagus, based on a famous Roman one which used to stand in front of the Pantheon at Rome, and on top of this is the figure of the deceased, reclining, his elbow propped on a cushion.[62] Another monument by Giulio Romano, in this case based on the arch at Pula, frames the inner doorway to the north aisle of San Francesco, Bologna. It commemorates the philosopher Lodovico Boccadiferro, who died in 1545. The sarcophagus forms the centre of the attic, and a bust stands against a tympanum within the opening. The sculptor was Girolamo Coltellini.[63]

Palladio used the triumphal arch scheme in his design for a church monument, probably for the Grimani tombs in San Francesco della Vigna, Venice, possibly dating from the 1560s. It shows a triumphal arch covering the west wall of the nave, with the doorway framed in the central arch. The two sides present alternative possibilities, one with sarcophagus and recumbent figure on a high base between the columns, the other with the recumbent figure at the level of the column bases and the sarcophagus rising from the ground. In the centre of the attic is a large sarcophagus with a figure sitting on it, and on either side are statues and reliefs. The monument seems to have been built, but later demolished. The figures in the drawing are by Federico Zuccaro.[64]

A drawing in the Chinnery Album in Sir John Soane's Museum in London shows a large wall-monument in the form of a triple arch. The central opening is walled up to the height of the column bases, and three steps appear below; presumably an effigy would have been placed here. The sides are open, not niches. Above the projecting entablatures of the freestanding Corinthian columns four statues stand in front of the attic. The drawing of these and the four reliefs over the side openings and on the attic

9.16 S. Andrea, Mantua, tomb of Gerolamo Andreasi, died 1524. Giulio Romano.

is attributed to Alessandro Vittoria, while the architectural drawing is attributed to Vincenzo Scamozzi. The date 1583 appears on the attic, and the day of the month over a side arch; this is oddly specific. The commissioner is perhaps indicated by the initials 'F.P.'. Fairbairn compares the drawing to the monument to Doge Nicolò da Ponte in Santa Maria della Carità in Venice, of 1582–5, which included a bust by Vittoria. The architect was Vincenzo Scamozzi, and the other sculpture was by Girolamo Campagna. The monument was destroyed in 1807; only the bust survives, but the form of the rest is known from engravings.[65] The bust stood within the central arch, above a sarcophagus on a tall podium. Above this arch is a pediment, set against the attic. The principal difference between this monument and the one in the drawing is that it is completely solid, with niches containing statues at the sides, whereas the other has three openings, suggesting that it was freestanding. Charles Davis suggests that the similar monument in Santa Maria dei Gesuiti to Doge Pasquale Cicogna, of 1595–1604, where the figure on the sarcophagus was again by Campagna, and the monuments on either side of the high altar of San Francesco della Vigna, to Doge Andrea Gritti and Triodano Gritti, to the same schema but with pilasters and no effigies, are also by Scamozzi.

Arches in Renaissance paintings

9.17 Jacopo Bellini, *Christ Before Pilate*, Book of Drawings, fol. 35, Louvre.

An interesting change in attitude towards the remains of ancient Rome took place in the mid-fifteenth century. At some time between 1451 and 1454 the ruined Arch of Gratian, Valentinian and Theodosius in Rome was destroyed. The Pope, Nicholas V, was a scholar and a builder (see p. 141), but did not consider the preservation of such remains important. On the other hand, Paul II, who became Pope in 1464, was the first to restore ancient remains, including the Arch of Titus.

In the second half of the fifteenth century painters liked to include real or imaginary Roman buildings in their compositions. Arches were sometimes used for their associations, sometimes for their suitability as framing devices, and often for both reasons. An example is the drawing of Christ before Pilate in Jacopo Bellini's sketchbook, now in the Louvre, whose contents date from between the 1440s and the 1460s [9.17]. The tiny figures are dwarfed by the extraordinary setting, where a pair of freestanding columns appear on either side of a narrow arched opening. The archivolt rests on a massive entablature, and has a figure of Amor on the keystone. In the spandrels flying Victories hold palm branches. The frieze on the entablature shows scenes of equestrian warfare. The arch shows similarities with the Roman arch at Pula (p. 24). A Bellini drawing known as 'Flagellation by Torchlight' has a similar arched opening.[66] The architecture must be intended to contrast the might of Roman paganism with the Christian scenes acted out within it.[67]

The use of a large arch as a framing device appears in a work of art with which Jacopo Bellini was involved – the mosaic of the Dormition of the Virgin on the vault of the Cappella dei Mascoli at San Marco, Venice. This was designed by the Florentine Andrea del Castagno, probably in 1442. The richly decorated single arch, with Corinthian pilasters, frames a view of a street. The cartoon seems to have been completed by Michele Giambono, and the figures of the three Apostles were designed by Bellini, who was also responsible for the adjoining scene of the Visitation, also framed in elaborate architecture based on the form of a triple arch.[68]

A comparable effect of architecture taking precedence over the scene played out is found in the painting of the Presentation of the Virgin in the Temple by Fra Carnevale (Museum of Fine Arts, Boston). This dates from *c.* 1466. The entrance to the basilica consists of a huge triple arch; freestanding columns with Composite capitals and projecting entablatures support kneeling figures of the Virgin and the angel Gabriel. Over the side arches are large reliefs.[69]

Andrea Mantegna was celebrated for his knowledge of antiquity. The fragmentary ruins to which his two Sebastians are bound (Kunsthistorisches Museum, Vienna, 1459; and Louvre) both have freestanding columns and decorative pilasters supporting broken archivolts. The first also has a spandrel relief with a woman holding a trophy. In the second scene there is a complete triumphal arch in the background, as gate of the town. Mantegna's fresco of Herod's interrogation of St James, in the Eremitani Chapel at Padua (completed by 1457), shows the action taking place in front of a handsome arch, with a single opening and four attached columns [9.18]. On the visible pier are a square relief above two circular ones, and an inscription, taken from a funerary monument, which also appears in Bellini's sketchbook.[70]

One of Mantegna's fellow-pupils at Padua was Marco Zoppo. His drawing of St James on the way to execution (in the British Museum) is based on Mantegna's painting of the subject in the Eremitani series. The structure which forms the background to the scene in the latter is only vaguely reminiscent of a triumphal arch, but Zoppo's is much more obviously one, although very bizarre. It has pairs of columns on two levels projecting from the piers, and a throng of combative putti, one riding a horse like Gattamelata.[71]

Mantegna's most striking use of an arch is in his great series of paintings of the

9.18 Andrea Mantegna, *Interrogation of St James*, Ovetari Chapel, Eremitani, Padua.

9.19 Botticelli, *The Punishment of Korah*, Sistine Chapel, Rome.

Triumphs of Caesar, at Hampton Court. This was begun in the 1470s, and completed by his death in 1506. The arch appears behind the *triumphator*'s chariot. The most likely model for it is the arch at Pula (p. 24), which Mantegna might have known from drawings. The frieze is probably based on a famous one which in his time was in San Lorenzo fuori le Mura in Rome. The sculpture on top of the arch includes flanking groups based on the Horse Tamers, which the painter would have known from drawings. The inscription on the arch reveals that it commemorates Caius Marius, also a great general, and uncle to Caesar. The central group on top, of captives and trophy, may be based on coins, but the best-known trophy groups surviving at Rome were thought to have commemorated Marius's victory over the Cimbri, and so this too may have been intended to refer to him.[72]

The use of an arch based on that of Constantine as the background to Pinturicchio's fresco of the disputation of St Catherine in the Borgia Apartment of the Vatican, and its symbolic link with Alexander VI, are discussed in the context of papal arches (p. 170). An even more celebrated depiction of the same arch is the accurate one by Botticelli in the Sistine Chapel, where it forms the background to the scene of the punishment of Korah, Dathan and Abiram, who rebelled against Moses and Aaron (Numbers, 16) [9.19]. The arch bears the inscription *nemo assummat* [sic] *honorem nisi vocatus a Deo tamquam Aron* ('let no one assume this honour unless he is called by God as was Aaron'). Ettlinger argues that this text from the Epistle to the Hebrews (5.4) is crucial: the Papacy had overcome the crises of the fifteenth century, and the punishment of Korah and the others had more than once been compared with disobedience to the Pope. The Arch of Constantine was chosen for its Christian significance.[73]

In the same chapel, Perugino's scene of the handing of the keys to Peter has in the background a large octagonal building, on either side of which is an arch like Constantine's, though each has a tall attic, curiously decorated with a frieze of lozenges

RENAISSANCE ITALY **161**

and squares and crowned by garlands of foliage hanging from candelabra [9.20]. The inscription on each arch forms an elegiac couplet:

> I[M]MENSV[M] SALAMO TEMPLVM, TU HOC, QUARTE, SACRASTI, SIXTE, OPIBUS DISPAR, RELIGIONE PRIOR
>
> ('Solomon consecrated an immense temple; you, Sixtus the Fourth, consecrated this one, inferior to him in wealth, but superior in religion').

9.20 Perugino, *Handing of the Keys to St Peter*, Sistine Chapel, Rome.

The placing of the two frescoes opposite each other emphasises their interrelationship. Christianity triumphs over Judaism, and the Papacy over its enemies. According to Ettlinger, the central building represents the church.[74]

Dominico Ghirlandaio used a triple arch decorated with reliefs as background to his fresco of the Massacre of the Innocents in Santa Maria Novella, Florence (1485–90). Aby Warburg claims that he also borrowed 'formulae of pathos' for the struggling figures in the foreground from triumphal arch reliefs.[75] In the background of his Adoration of the Shepherds in the Cappella Sassetti of Santissima Trinità, also in Florence, the procession of the three kings approaches through a single arch, with pilasters, whose frieze bears the inscription *GN. POMPEIO MAGNO HIRCANUS PONT. P.* Hircanus was high priest of the temple in Jerusalem: the idea must be that, after being reinstated in office after the capture of Jerusalem in 63 BC by Pompey, he erected the arch in gratitude. The inscription on the sarcophagus in front of which the child Jesus lies also refers to Pompey, claiming that a Roman augur killed in the attack prophesied that a divinity would be born out of his tomb. Saxl argues that the inscription must have been invented by Sassetti's friend the scholar Bartholomaeus Fontius (Fonza), and that 'if the first inscription indicated … the triumph of paganism over Judaism, the second signifies the victory of Christianity over the heathen world'.[76] Saxl also claims that the tombs of Francesco and Nera Sassetti, on either side of the chapel, which are attributed to Giuliano da Sangallo, 'seem to have been conceived as triumphal arches'. Their form (a sarcophagus within an arched recess) bears only a faint resemblance to an arch, but the paintings in the spandrels, copied from Roman coins, include scenes of triumph and an *adlocutio*.[77]

A curious arch appears in the background of the painting of the Martyrdom of Sebastian, attributed to Antonio and Piero Pollaiuolo, in the National Gallery, London (*c.* 1475?). The single arch, with pilasters, has a large relief within the opening. Another relief, this time circular, appears in the tall square attic, above which is a ruinous pediment. Ettlinger argues that both the arch and the distant soldiers 'indicate the time and place of Sebastian's martyrdom, reminding us that he was an officer in the Roman praetorian guard'.[78] Poletti draws attention to the reliefs within and above the arch, in which the men fighting on horseback (which recall the reliefs on the Arch of Constantine) and the man brought before an emperor suggest Sebastian's life as a soldier and condemnation by Diocletian.[79]

The arch that appears with other Roman monuments in the background of Sodoma's fresco of St Benedict receiving the Roman youths Maurus and Placidus, at Monte Oliveto Maggiore (after 1505?), is there to provide geographical context. Similarly, an arch figures in the background of Carpaccio's Preaching of St Stephen (Louvre, 1514). The town must be intended to represent Jerusalem, but the arch is clearly based on the one at Ancona, that Carpaccio must have known. Two figures appear in relief on each pier, between the columns, one above the other.[80] A more precise reference is natural in Giulio Romano's painting of the Triumph of Titus and Vespasian, of c. 1537, painted for the Camera dei Cesari in the Palazzo Ducale at Mantua, but now in the Louvre. The arch through which the *triumphatores* are about to pass is intended to represent the Arch of Titus, though not with precision.[81]

For the background of his painting of the Nativity in the church of San Domenico, Siena (datable to 1485–90), Francesco di Giorgio Martini uses an arch with four freestanding columns of which two survive and a projecting entablature but only a single opening with coffered vault [9.21]. The arch is in a state of ruin, and a sloping roof fitted roughly into the archway provides the stable for the ox and ass.[82] This is a variation on a familiar motif, which symbolises the triumph of Christianity, as seen in the humble circumstances of Christ's birth, contrasted with the collapse of luxurious paganism. It relates to the myth, found in the Golden Legend of Jacopo da Voragine, according to which the new Temple of Peace at Rome fell in ruins on the night of the Nativity. The pair of square columns supporting a rough timber roof in Ghirlandaio's Adoration of the Shepherds (see above) relate to this. The use of a ruinous triumphal arch, which is found in the late fifteenth and early sixteenth centuries, especially in Siena and Emilia, is a variation on the idea, the 'triumphal' connotations adding an extra twist. Pinelli relates it to another story in the Golden Legend, according to which the Sibyl warned Augustus that another man, soon to be born, would erase the memory of his power, whereupon he refused the divine honours offered by the Senate. Pinelli illustrates a curious painting by the Bolognese Amico Aspertini, in which an

9.21 Francesco di Giorgio, *Nativity*, 1485–90, S. Domenico, Siena.

overgrown arch serves as entrance to a vaulted temple, behind a scene of the Adoration of the Shepherds.[83]

Drawings of arches

These fall into four categories. First, there are 'antiquarian' drawings of existing Roman arches. Second, there are designs for permanent arches intended for execution. These have been dealt with above. Third, there are designs intended purely as 'fantasies'. Fourth, there are designs for temporary arches erected for commemorative purposes. These will be dealt with in the relevant chapter. The first and third categories will be briefly discussed here.

The 'Codex Coner' in the Soane Museum, compiled *c.* 1515 by Bernardo della Volpaia – a cousin of Giuliano da Sangallo – contains reconstructions of the principal arches at Rome (including the Arco di Portogallo), and also details.[84] Cassiano dal Pozzo owned three volumes of drawings by Giovanni Battista Montano, a woodcarver and architect from Milan who moved to Rome in the 1570s. (These are also in the Soane Museum.) One of the drawings is a fanciful reconstruction of the Arch of Janus in the Forum Boarium, showing Ionic and Composite orders on the two levels, all the niches filled with statues, and a pedimented tempietto on top.[85] Another is a reconstruction of the tomb of 'Publius Minacius' on the Via Appia. The façade has the form

164 THE TRIUMPHAL ARCH

of an arch, with Corinthian half-columns, the central ones supporting a pediment. The opening is a rectangular doorway, with a relief panel above. The side niches contain a statue on one side and a relief on the other. Above the attic are statues, the central ones set against a higher attic, above which is a segmental pediment.[86]

Cassiano dal Pozzo is famous for his 'Museo Cartaceo' or 'Paper Museum' (in the Royal Collection), never published, but much used by other scholars.[87] The drawings include another reconstruction of the Arco di Portogallo, by Pirro Ligorio. A number of drawings of arches outside Rome are copies after Giuliano da Sangallo; they include Malborghetto, Benevento, Ancona, Fano, Orange, and also the Arch of Gallienus at Rome.[88] There are two drawings by Francesco di Giorgio of the arch at Benevento; drawings by Bernardo della Volpaia of the keystones of the arches of Titus and Septimius Severus; one by Battista Franco of the cornice of the Arch of Constantine; drawings of the arches of Ammon and of the Gavii which are copies from Giovanni Francesco Caroto's *Le antichità di Verona* (Verona, 1560); and an anonymous drawing of the arch at Susa. Engravings from Antoine Lafréry's *Speculum romanae magnificentiae* include the arches of Titus, Septimius Severus, Gallienus and Constantine. As Campbell points out, 'the most obvious absence is the Arch of Augustus at Rimini'.[89] In 1638 Cassiano asked the painters Jean Saillant and Nicolas Mignard to draw the arch at Orange, but Saillant sent back an engraving of it by a local artist. In the same year Cassiano wrote to someone called Giovanni Sommai about drawings of the arch at Benevento.[90] Seventeenth-century drawings include a view of the Arch of Constantine and views of the arches of Janus and Drusus by an artist from the circle of Nicolas Poussin. Cassiano's drawings of inscriptions include that from the Arch of Claudius in Rome, made at the time of its discovery in 1641, and that on the arch at Susa.[91] The drawings mentioned so far were reconstructions or measured drawings of details, but there were also numerous *vedute*, including important early examples by Giovanni Antonio Dosio.[92]

Other collections include numerous views by artists from the Low Countries who worked in Rome in the sixteenth and seventeenth centuries. Notable among them is Maarten van Heemskerck, the Dutch painter and engraver who lived in Rome between 1532 and 1536 or 1537. The collection of his drawings in Berlin known as the *Römische Skizzenbücher* contains views of the arches of Titus, Septimius Severus and Constantine, as well as a sketch of an ephemeral arch, identified as one erected for Charles V's entry to Mantua in 1530.[93] Gerard ter Borch the Elder drew the arches of Septimius Severus and Constantine in 1609.[94] A later view of the Arch of Constantine by Jan Asselyn is in the Chinnery Album in the Soane Museum, and there is another in the Louvre.[95]

The third category listed above is of 'fantasy' designs. A particularly striking group of these is found in the 'North Italian Album' in the Soane Museum, described by Lynda Fairbairn as 'designs for ornament by a Lombard artisan c. 1500'.[96] Four are identified by her as designs for triumphal arches. One (No. 43) is based on the Arch of Constantine, while two others (Nos 7 and 22) are much more fanciful, lavishly decorated with coloured stone and sculpture. Fairbairn notes similarities between No. 7 and the drawing for the Arch of Alfonso at Naples formerly attributed to Pisanello (p. 142). The fourth (No. 14) is more like a Roman town gate, though the decoration includes trophies and weapons which Fairbairn identifies as quoted – like some of the architectural details – from Mantegna's fresco of St James in the Eremitani in Padua. Several of the other drawings have similarities to the triumphal arch formula.

Another remarkable set of fantasy designs, of the sixteenth century, is in the Rothschild Collection in the Louvre. They too are attributed to a North Italian artist, and some twenty-three represent variations on the theme.[97] Many of them are triple arches, taking their basic idea from the Arch of Constantine. They are characterised by tall, narrow proportions, but this is probably due to the formula of the sketchbook. Many are decorated with figurative and ornamental reliefs. Some experiment with openings with triangular tops. The whole series gives a wonderful idea of the possibilities of the formula in the hands of an inventive and playful artist. It was suggested by Margherita Licht that the drawings in the Soane and Rothschild albums were made as designs for temporary arches, to be constructed in wood and canvas, but it seems more likely that they are simply *jeux d'esprit*.[98]

Notes

1. The translation is that of 1726 by James Leoni.
2. F. Colonna, *Hypnerotomachia Poliphili*, transl. by Joscelyn Godwin (London, 1999), 42–54. Summerson's essay was published in his *Heavenly Mansions* (London, 1949), 29–50.
3. R. Wittkower, *Architectural Principles in the Age of Humanism* (3rd edn, London, 1962), 39, 37, n. 3.
4. Wittkower (cit. in the preceding note), 53–5. Summerson (cit. at n. 2), 41, describes the triumphal arch motif as 'cruelly ironed out on the façade', but 'rather more gently used in the bay design of the interior'.
5. A. Venturi, *L'Arte*, 17 (1914), 153–6. The equestrian statue was destroyed in 1796, but a replica was set up in 1926.
6. T. Magnuson, *Studies in Roman Quattrocento Architecture* (Stockholm, 1958), 355; see also 157f.
7. A relief over the door of the Sala dei Baroni inside the Castel Nuovo showed the procession. Executed in about 1457 by Domenico Gagini, it was destroyed by fire in 1919 (H.-W. Kruft and M. Malmanger, *Institutum Romanum Norvegiae: Acta ad Archaeologiam et Artium Historiam Pertinentia*, 6 (1975), 221, fig. 98.
8. Kruft and Malmanger (cit. in the preceding note), 213–306; G. L. Hersey, *The Aragonese Arch at Naples 1443–1475* (New Haven/London, 1973); Christoph Luitpold Frommel, 'Alberti e la porta trionfale di Castel Nuovo a Napoli', *Annali di architettura*, 20 (2008), 13–36.
9. For the attribution to Pisanello see D. Cordellier, *Pisanello* (Paris, 1996), 418–19. Rosanna Di Battista (*Annali di architettura*, 10–11 (1998–9), 15–16) argues that the drawing was made for a temporary structure, probably for the wedding in 1450 of Alfonso's niece to Frederick III.
10. The attribution of the sculptural elements is fully discussed by Frommel (cit. at n. 8).
11. P. Fortini Brown, *Venice and Antiquity* (New Haven/London, 1996), 108–10. R. Lieberman (*Renaissance Architecture in Venice* (London, 1982), pl. 2) sees the influence of the arch at Pula also in 'the paired columns supporting a broken entablature with a vine-pattern decoration' of the portal of Santi Giovanni e Paolo, erected in 1459–63 to the design of Bartolomeo Buon.
12. A. Bruschi, *Bramante* (London, 1977), 64–5. The arcades were carried across the openings of the arches some two hundred years later by Bishop von Lobkowitz.
13. ibid., 59–64.
14. ibid., 87–108. He analyses the subtle devices by which Bramante produces the illusion of greater depth in the Cortile.
15. R. J. Tuttle et al., *Jacopo Barozzi da Vignola* (Milan, 2002), 163–95.
16. ibid., 210–33.
17. The drawings of Roman arches in Palladio's collection which were attributed to Falconetto by G. Zorzi (*I Disegni delle Antichità di Andrea Palladio* (Venice, 1959), 48–62) are now ascribed to Palladio himself (L. Puppi, *Andrea Palladio* (London, 1975), 10–11).
18. L. Capellini, *Guide di Architettura: Padova* (Turin, 2000), 129–30; *Padova: Guida ai monumenti e alle opere d'arte* (Venice, 1961), 594–6, 449–51. The earlier Porta Santa Croce and Porta Portello (Capellini, 126–8) are much less elegant. The former (1517, attributed to Sebastiano Mariani) has pseudo-Ionic pilasters, with small pedimented doorways between them, while the Porta Portello (1519–35, probably by Guglielmo de' Grigi) has pairs of Corinthian columns framing the large central opening and excessively small side ones; the clumsy great projections of the attic over the columns support stone cannonballs (Capellini, 128).
19. Capellini (cit. in the preceding note), 98–9.
20. ibid., 139; *Padova: Guida* (cit. at n. 18), 500–501.
21. L. Puppi, *Michele Sanmicheli, architetto di Verona* (Padua, 1971), 14–15. He reproduces a drawing for the same altar by Antonio da Sangallo the Younger, so similar that it appears to be based on Sanmicheli's.
22. ibid., 46.
23. ibid., 71–3.

24 ibid., 41.
25 Accademia di agricoltura, scienze e lettere di Verona, *Michele Sanmicheli* (Verona, 1960), fig. 230.
26 Puppi (cit. at n. 21), 132–3.
27 E. Tormo, ed., *Os Desenhos das antigualhas que vio Francisco d'Ollanda* (Madrid, 1940), ff. 42–3.
28 D. Howard, *Jacopo Sansovino: Architecture and Patronage in Renaissance Venice* (New Haven/London, 1975), 34. W. Lotz (*JSAH* 22 (1963), 3–12) argues unconvincingly that the design of the Loggetta does not derive directly from Roman triumphal arches, though his comparison with Giuliano da Sangallo's design for a façade for San Lorenzo, Florence, is interesting. Howard points out that the drawing by Francisco d'Ollanda referred to above 'omits the Campanile and portrays the Loggetta itself as a triumphal arch'.
29 Howard [cit. in the preceding note], 84–7.
30 ibid., 96–112.
31 M. Tafuri et al., *Giulio Romano* (Cambridge, 1998), 266–75. The volutes at the top of the façade are not by Giulio.
32 Books I–V are translated, with a commentary, by Vaughan Hart and Peter Hicks, as *Sebastiano Serlio on Architecture*, I (New Haven/London, 1996).
33 S. Frommel, *Sebastiano Serlio architetto* (Milan, 1998), 145–70.
34 A. Palladio, *I quattro libri dell'architettura*, ed. L. Magagnato and P. Marini (Milan, 1980), 11, 34, 66, 188. Palladio is said to have left material for a volume which would have included arches ready for printing, but this never materialised. The drawings probably intended to form the basis of that book are collected by Zorzi (cit. at n. 17), 47–64.
35 The similarity of the arch to the documented gate of San Daniele del Friuli supports the attribution: H. Burns et al., *Andrea Palladio 1508–1580* (London, 1975), 246–7.
36 Franco Barbieri, Renato Cevese and Licisco Magagnato, *Guida di Vicenza* (Vicenza, 1953), 404–5.
37 Burns et al. (cit. at n. 35), 31–3; A. Venditti, *The Loggia del Capitaniato, Corpus Palladianum*, IV (University Park, Pa./London, 1971).
38 H. Gabelmann, *Der Triumphbogen in Zagarolo: Antiken in einem Bildprogramm des Manierismus* (Vienna, 1992).
39 Barbieri (cit. at n. 36), 12–13.
40 M. Fagiolo and M.L. Madonna in I. Barisi et al., *Villa d'Este* (Rome, 2003), 111–14. See also D.R. Coffin, *The Villa d'Este at Tivoli* (Princeton, 1960).
41 Two other gates at Lecce take the form of triumphal arches. The Porta Rudiae, of 1703, by Giuseppe Guidi and his sons, has four attached Corinthian columns and a curved attic bearing a statue of St Oronzo, patron of the city. The Porta San Biagio of 1774 has four Doric columns and a statue of the saint.
42 For the arch with false perspective, flanked by pilasters, compare the celebrated tabernacle in San Lorenzo, Florence, by Desiderio da Settignano, of c. 1460–61 (I. Cardellini, *Desiderio da Settignano* (Milan, 1962), 220).
43 V. Moschini, *S. Gregorio al Celio (Le Chiese di Roma Illustrate)* (Rome, n.d.).
44 L. Planiscig, *Bernardo and Antonio Rossellino* (Vienna, 1942), pl. 80.
45 G. Hayden Huntley, *Andrea Sansovino* (Cambridge, Mass., 1935), 14.
46 J. Pope-Hennessy, *Catalogue of Italian Sculpture in the Victoria and Albert Museum* (London, 1964), I, 179–81, pl. 173.
47 Allan Marquand, *Giovanni della Robbia* (Princeton, 1920), figs 28 and 43; G. Gentilini, *I Della Robbia: l'arte nuova della scultura invetriata* (Florence, 1998), 251–2; idem, *I Della Robbia: la scultura invetriata del Rinascimento* (Florence, 199-), 284–5, 297, 321.
48 Alessandro Cecchi, *Antichità viva*, Anno XXIX, no. 1 (1990), 34.
49 J. Balogh, *Az Országos Magyar Szépmuvészeti Múzeum Évkönyvei*, 4 (1927), 94–5.
50 Cecchi (cit. at n. 48), 39–40.
51 There is in the Vatican a drawing identified by Josephine von Henneberg as a study for the arrangement of the Santa Croce tabernacle and altar (*Master Drawings*, 30, no. 2 (1992), 208, n. 9). For the Santa Croce altar, see F. Moisé, *Santa Croce di Firenze* (Florence, 1845), 173f.; von Henneberg, 201–9. The tabernacle survives, but not the frame. Von Henneberg identifies a drawing in the same collection as a project by Vasari for a similar altar with tabernacle at Santo Stefano dei Cavalieri at Pisa. A drawing by Teofilo Torri, after the younger Giorgio Vasari, which may be connected with the Santa Croce project, is in the Soane Museum, London. Pairs of Doric columns frame niches with roundels (L. Fairbairn, *Italian Renaissance Drawings from the Collection of Sir John Soane's Museum* (London, 1998), II, no. 664).
52 See F. Borsi, ed., *Il disegno interrotto: trattati medicei d'architettura* (Florence, 1980), II, pl. 83. Other altars in this collection include those for 'S. Gerolamo nella Canonica di Fiesole' (pl. 82) and for the 'Badia di Firenze' (pl. 87). Fairbairn (cit. in the preceding note) also illustrates a drawing by Orazio Porta for another altar, deriving from Buontalenti's 'frame' for the tabernacle at Santa Croce (II, no. 714, see also p. 511).
53 Fairbairn (cit. at n. 51), II, 452. For the column from the Arch of Constantine used to support the gallery, see p. 154.
54 For Vasari's 'ornamento dell'organo di Santo Spirito di Roma' see Borsi (cit. at n. 52), pl. 97.
55 For illustrations of these tombs see J. Burckhardt, ed. P. Murray, *The Architecture of the Italian Renaissance* (Harmondsworth, 1987), 206–7. See also G. Lorenzetti, *Venezia e il suo Estuario* (Trieste, 1963), 341, 347.
56 P. Fortini Brown, *Venice and Antiquity* (New Haven/London, 1996), 113–15.
57 Bruschi (cit. at n. 12), 163–6. See also Lara Langer, 'The *maniera moderna* and Andrea Sansovino's Cardinal tombs at Santa Maria del Popolo', *Sculpture Journal*, 28.1 (2019), 75–102.
58 Johannes Myssok, *Bildhauerische Konzeption und plastisches Modell in der Renaissance* (Münster, 1999), 179–84.

59 For possible involvement by Jacopo Sansovino, see Bruce Boucher, *The Sculpture of Jacopo Sansovino* (New Haven/London, 1991), II, 314. Benedetto da Rovezzano may also have assisted. See also Lara Lanyer, 'The *maniera moderna* of Andrea Sansovino's cardinal tombs at Santa Maria del Popolo', *Sculpture Journal*, 28 (2019), 75–102.
60 André Chastel (transl. by B. Archer), *The Sack of Rome, 1527* (Princeton, 1983), 140.
61 ibid., 227–31: G. Vasari, *Le Vite*, ed. R. Bettarini, V (Florence, 1984), 255–8.
62 E. Gombrich et al., *Giulio Romano* (Milan, 1989), 564–5; M. Tafuri et al., *Giulio Romano* (Cambridge, 1998), 292–5. The monument makes an interesting comparison with the Jervoise tomb in All Saints' Church, Chelsea (after 1563: see p. 207).
63 Tafuri (cit. in the preceding note), 302–4.
64 H. Burns et al., *Andrea Palladio 1508–1580* (London, 1975), 135–6.
65 Fairbairn (cit. at n. 51), I, 260, no. 367; T. Martin, *Alessandro Vittoria and the Portrait Bust in Renaissance Venice* (Oxford, 1998), 122; Charles Davis, 'Vincenzo Scamozzi progettista di monumenti commemorativi?', in Franco Barbieri and Guido Beltramini, *Vincenzo Scamozzi* (Venice, 2003), 89–109. It was the first ducal monument to feature a portrait bust. See also A. Zorzi, *Venezia scomparsa* (2nd edn, Milan, 1977), 104, 527.
66 Colin Eisler, *The Genius of Jacopo Bellini: The Complete Paintings and Drawings* (New York, 1989), pls 194–5, also pp. 104, 327. At p. 452 Eisler describes Bellini as 'the first known Venetian master of classical architecture'.
67 According to F. Saxl (*Lectures* (London, 1957), I, 155) 'the classical details are there to remind us that we are in front of the palace of a man living in the age of classical antiquity, and the life of Christ is represented as an event in the historical past. This is the essentially new feature.' He describes the figure of Amor as 'somewhat unclassical, and quite out of place' (p. 154).
68 Patricia Fortini Brown, *Venice and Antiquity* (New Haven/London, 1996), 106–8.
69 Carlo Prosperi, ed., *Fra Carnevale* (Milan, 2004), 261–3.
70 Saxl (cit. at n. 67), I, 158.
71 Hugo Chapman, *Padua in the 1450s: Marco Zoppo and his Contemporaries* (London, 1998), 51–4.
72 Andrew Martindale, *The Triumphs of Caesar by Andrea Mantegna* (London/New York, 1992), 371.
73 L.D. Ettlinger, *The Sistine Chapel before Michelangelo* (Oxford, 1965), 104–13.
74 Ettlinger (cit. in the preceding note), 91
75 A. Warburg, *Gesammelte Schriften* (Leipzig, 1932), I, 157.
76 F. Saxl, *Journal of the Warburg and Courtauld Institutes*, 4 (1940–41), 28.
77 For an illustration of the tomb of Francesco Sassetti see A. Busignani and R. Bencini, *Le Chiese di Firenze: Quartiere di Santa Maria Novella* (Florence, 1979), opp. p. 144.
78 L.D. Ettlinger, *Antonio and Piero Pollaiuolo* (Oxford, 1978), 50.
79 F. Poletti, *Antonio e Piero Pollaiuolo* (Milan, 2001), 162, 171.
80 V. Sgarbi, *Carpaccio* (New York, etc., c. 1994), 175.
81 F. Hartt, *Giulio Romano* (New Haven, 1958), I, 174–5, II, 37.
82 R. Toledano, *Francesco di Giorgio Martini, pittore e scultore* (Milan, 1987), 102. The drawing in Turin to which he refers does not show an arch. See also L. Bellosi, ed., *Francesco di Giorgio Martini e il Rinascimento a Siena* (Milan, 1993), 478–81.
83 A. Pinelli, in S. Settis, ed., *Memoria dell'antico nell'arte italiana*, II (Turin, 1985), 288–91.
84 T. Ashby, 'Sixteenth Century Drawings of Roman Buildings attributed to Andreas Coner', *Papers of the British School at Rome*, 2 (1904), 52–4, 56, 60, 87–8, 95, 97, 134, 137, 144, 147. The Codex also contains a drawing of a section of the Cortile del Belvedere by Bramante (44).
85 L. Fairbairn, *Italian Renaissance Drawings from the Collection of Sir John Soane's Museum* (London, 1998), II, no. 1028. See also pp. 737–8 for other depictions of the arch by (among others) Baldassare Peruzzi, Antonio da Sangallo the Younger and Raffaello da Montelupo.
86 Fairbairn (cit. in the preceding note), no. 1214.
87 Ian Campbell, ed., *The Paper Museum of Cassiano dal Pozzo: Series A – Antiquities and Architecture*, pt 9, *Ancient Roman Topography and Architecture* (London, 2004).
88 Giuliano da Sangallo's own drawings were published as *Il libro di Giuliano da Sangallo* (Leipzig, 1910).
89 Campbell (cit. at n. 87), I, 58.
90 ibid., 59.
91 W. Senhouse, ed., *The Paper Museum of Cassiano dal Pozzo: Series A – Antiquities and Architecture*, pt 7, *Ancient Inscriptions* (London, 2002), 324, 337.
92 Röll and I. Campbell, in Campbell (cit. at n. 87), I, 236–7. Drawings by Dosio of reliefs on the arches of Titus, Septimius Severus and Constantine are in Berlin: C. Hülsen, *Das Skizzenbuch des Giovannantonio Dosio* (Berlin, 1933).
93 C. Hülsen and H. Egger, *Die römische Skizzenbücher von Marten van Heemskerck im königlichen Kupferstichkabinett zu Berlin* (1913, repr. Soest, 1975); E. Filippi, *Maarten van Heemskerck – Inventio Urbis* (Milan, 1990). While in Rome van Heemskerck contributed to the paintings on the arch set up for Charles V's entry to Rome in 1536.
94 M. Fagiolo, ed., *Le Feste a Roma* (Turin, 1997), I, 54–5.
95 Fairbairn (cit. at n. 85), I, no. 317.
96 ibid., I, 13–51. She disputes attempts to attribute the album to Nicoletto da Modena or Gherardo Costa.
97 They occur within the sequence 1407–1441 DR. They were attributed by Margherita Licht (*Arte Lombarda*, 38–9 (1973), 91–102) to Baldassare Peruzzi.
98 Licht (cit. in the preceding note), 91.

10

PAPAL ARCHES

From the perspective of our modern understanding of the papacy, it might seem surprising that triumphal arches should be erected in honour of popes. However, it has to be remembered that until 1870 the pope was the ruler of a temporal dominion. Since that dominion was centred on Rome itself, popes with political aspirations wished to be seen as successors of Roman emperors. For example, Boniface VIII (1294–1303) sometimes dressed in the imperial insignia, and boasted *ego sum Caesar, ego sum imperator*.[1] It is notable that in some cases arches are particularly associated with popes who wished to emphasise their temporal power, or whose temporal power was under threat. However, this should not be exaggerated, as there was a strong element of tradition.

The interest in the antiquities of Rome shown by many people in the twelfth century is well known. Poems praising ancient Rome were written; statues were collected; a decree was promulgated in 1162 for the protection of Trajan's Column; and guidebooks began to be published, the earliest and best known being the *Mirabilia Romae*.[2] It was presumably as a result of this interest that it became customary for a new pope, after his coronation, to process back from the Vatican Basilica to the Lateran Palace, riding a white horse. This symbolised his taking power over the diocese of Rome, and was known from 1471 as the *possessio* – *possesso* in Italian.[3]

Arches for the new pope's procession

In the account of the procession of Pope Callixtus II in 1120, it is stated that arches were prepared on the route. This is the first time that such arches are mentioned, but the phrase in the description *de more* ('according to custom') indicates that their erection was already customary.[4] The individual arches were erected by different groups of people: thus, for the *possesso* of Celestine II, in 1143, the Jews (at pains to demonstrate their loyalty) erected an arch representing 'the law', and the Roman clergy one representing 'thuribles' (incense-burners). It seems to have been normal for the pope to reward those who erected the arches with sums of money. In the description of the *possesso* of Boniface VIII in 1295, the arches are called *arcus triumphales*. Nothing is known of the appearance of these medieval arches.[5]

In 1309 Clement V took up residence at Avignon: the 'exile' of the popes was to last until 1377. When they returned, the custom of erecting arches seems not to have been revived until the coronation of Alexander VI (Borgia) in 1492. However, it is interesting that the great project for the Vatican of Nicholas V, *c.* 1450, included, at the south-west corner, two great towers, and between them a *porta cum fornice triumphali* ('gate with triumphal arch').[6] In honour of Alexander VI more than fourteen arches were erected, described as 'in the likeness of ancient triumphs'. In his *Historia di Milano* of 1554 Bernardino Corio gives a description of some of them. The first, in front of the church of San Celso, just south of the Ponte Sant'Angelo, was 'like that of Octavian near the Colosseum', which must mean the Arch of Constantine. It had four large columns supporting figures of armed men 'in the manner of ancient barons, with drawn sword'. Above these were the papal arms, flanked by cornucopias and garlands. On the second arch, behind the church, stood girls who recited verses in Latin and Italian. The position of these arches, which deliberately recalled the situation of the Arch of Gratianus, Valentinianus and Theodosius (379–83), at the head of the Pons Aelius, the Ponte Sant'Angelo, was to become traditional.[7] The arch 'at the palace of Naples' was 'worked with plants' (i.e. made of foliage). Other arches were decorated with paintings, marine monsters, and 'a spring with an ox' (Alexander's emblem was a bull). The lack of any religious imagery is noteworthy.[8]

Alexander's fondness for triumphal imagery is shown by a fresco by Pinturicchio and his assistants (begun in 1492) in the Sala dei Santi of the Borgia Apartment in the Vatican Palace. The scene of the disputation of St Catherine of Alexandria with the philosophers before the Emperor Maximian has in the background an arch based on that of Constantine, with Alexander's bull on top of it. Since the Arch of Constantine commemorates the defeat of Maxentius, and so symbolises the triumph of Christianity over paganism, its inclusion is presumably intended to emphasise that Catherine's cause will be victorious. It was in the fifteenth century that the Arch of Constantine was first restored, which shows the attention paid to its significance.[9] The arch in the fresco is also linked to papal propaganda by the inscription *PACIS CULTORI* ('to the advocate of peace'): it was a regular feature of such propaganda that a pope should be represented as a peace-maker.[10]

For Alexander's successor (after the very brief reign of Pius III), Julius II, who had himself described on a medal as 'Iulius Caesar II', no less than eighteen arches were erected, but, although we have some evidence on where they stood, we have no evidence for their appearance.[11] Four years after his *possesso*, in 1507, Julius made his entry into Rome after his victory over Bologna, in a campaign which he had led himself, wearing full armour. Designed to evoke an ancient triumph, its decor included eighteen arches. One, in front of the Vatican, was modelled on the Arch of Constantine, and bore reliefs showing events in the campaign. The arch erected by Antoninus Pius at the entrance to the Temple of Hadrian, on the Corso, then identified as built by Domitian, was so richly decorated with statues and pictures that it was said to look as if Domitian was triumphing again.[12]

Julius was the last pope whose *possesso* formed part of the coronation ritual, involving a religious procession in Mass vestments, preceded by the Eucharist. He was succeeded in 1513 by the Medici Leo X (second son of Lorenzo the Magnificent), and from then on the *possesso* was simply 'a solemn cavalcade'. We have detailed descriptions of the buildings erected for Leo, written by the Florentine doctor Giovanni Giacomo Penni.[13] No illustrations survive, but Fagiolo and Madonna have reconstructed the first three *apparati* on the basis of his account.[14] The imagery and inscriptions made much reference to the beginning of a golden age, and to peace. The first arch, at the head of the Ponte Sant'Angelo, was set up by Bishop Petrucci of Siena. Similar to ancient triumphal arches, it differed in the unusual feature of concave façades. Apollo and a woman holding a book were represented among the sculptures and painted figures. The capitals of two pilasters produced on one side wine and on the other water. A little further south, Agostino Chigi erected an 'arch' in front of his house. It had a rectangular opening, and in the niches were statues of Apollo (again) and Mercury. A woman dressed as a nymph recited verses. The Sienese connection of both Petrucci and Chigi leads Fagiolo and Madonna to attribute these two *apparati* to Baldassare Peruzzi, and two drawings by Peruzzi for arches in honour of Leo survive.[15] The Chigi *apparato* provided a frame for the next one, at the junction by the Zecca. Not really an 'arch', though the arched openings had figures in the spandrels and sculptures above, it had gilded reliefs. Another *apparato* had a 'portico' in front, and yet another was made of foliage. There were also two arches set up in front of the palazzo of the de' Rossi and della Valle families, on which were displayed some of the ancient statues from their collections. The latter incorporated two lifesize statues of Pan.[16] The return from the Lateran was by a different route. Near the Cancelleria was an arch set up by the Genoese merchants: as the pope rode through it, a sphere appeared out of its vault, opened up, and revealed a putto who recited Latin verses. Von Erffa points out that in this *possesso* no mention is made of the two places which were to be particularly important later on, the Campidoglio and the Forum (then known as the Campo Vaccino), and that the Roman Senate had no involvement.[17]

There is no evidence for the erection of arches at *possessi* between that of Leo X in 1513 and and that of Gregory XIV in 1590, and this does not seem to be owing merely to defective information. The austere Dutchman Hadrian VI was scorned by the Roman people as a Northern barbarian: one arch was set up when he entered Rome in 1522, but he appears to have had his *possesso* performed by a procurator. The Medici (bastard) Clement VII, elected in 1523, intended to hold a splendid *possesso* in 1525, but his plans were probably disrupted by the troubles following the battle of Pavia. (For his arches outside Rome, see below.)

Von Erffa points out that it is particularly surprising that no arches were erected for *possessi* between 1513 and 1590, considering that between those years so many temporary arches were erected throughout Europe. However, when Paul III returned to Rome in 1538 from Nice, where a conference had been held to make peace between François I and Charles V, various *apparati* were erected, including an arch at the Porta del Popolo, the decoration of the Arco di Portogallo (see pp. 56–7), and an arch (unfinished) at San Marco.[18] No illustrations survive, and it is not known who the artists were.[19] It is easy to understand why the harsh reformer Pius V would not have wanted arches: immediately after the closing of the Council of Trent, he is said to have put forward a proposal to demolish the surviving ancient arches as pagan relics.[20] However, an important change took place at his *possesso*: from now on the procession went up onto the Campidoglio, where the city magistrates made a demonstration of their loyalty.

That a pope of this period might be willing to call on the symbolism of the arch is shown by the decoration of the Sala Regia in the Vatican, executed in 1573 for Pius's successor Gregory XIII by Giorgio Vasari and his workshop. One panel represents Gregory XI's return to Rome from Avignon in 1377: the papal procession is shown as having passed through an arch. The pope has the features of Gregory XIII, and the architecture is of his time rather than of the fourteenth century. Partridge and Starn see the arch as associating Gregory XIII, through Gregory XI, with the triumphs of ancient Rome, so that the arch is 'a kind of time machine generating perpetual victory'. Another panel depicts the wounding of Coligny on 22 August 1572: a triumphal arch appears in the background, to represent Catholicism's triumph over Protestantism.[21]

The *possesso* of Gregory XIV, in 1590, was the first when the display of the so-called 'Apparati, Livree et Ceremonie' (structures, liveries and ceremonies), which were to become customary, took place. The route from the Vatican to the Arch of Titus was hung with tapestries, paintings, etc. The grocer Marcantonio Ciappi erected in front of his shop an arch of aromatic herbs, on which stood three boys representing Pax, Caritas and Abundantia, the last of whom threw confectionery to the procession. More significantly, the Senate set up an arch on the Campidoglio, between the statues of the Dioscuri: this was to become a regular custom. As so often happened, it was not finished in time. It was designed by Gabriele Cesarini.[22] The Arch of Septimius Severus was decorated by the Jews with Hebrew inscriptions, for which Latin translations were supplied.

Leo XI, another Medici, was elected in 1605, and his is the first ceremony for which we have illustrations of the arches. His fellow Florentines set one up just south of the Ponte Sant'Angelo [10.1]. It was designed by Donato Frosini, of Pistoia. The single opening was flanked by marbled Corinthian columns; between them on the front side niches held statues of Liberality and Justice, painted to look like metal, and over these were reliefs showing the coronation and *possesso*. On the back were statues of Magnanimity and Religion, below reliefs showing Leo's election and installation as Archbishop of Florence. Below were reliefs showing Leo's two outstanding achievements as Cardinal Legate of Clement VIII in France – the conclusion of peace between Henry IV and Philip II, and the reconciliation of Henry IV with the Church. The Pope's emblem, a garland of roses, was represented many times. Above the archway was a tall attic with a dedicatory inscription, surmounted by a pediment with Leo's arms.[23]

At the top of the steps to the Campidoglio, the seat of the government of the City, the Senate and people erected an arch

10.1 Florentine arch for Leo XI, 1605. Donato Frosini.

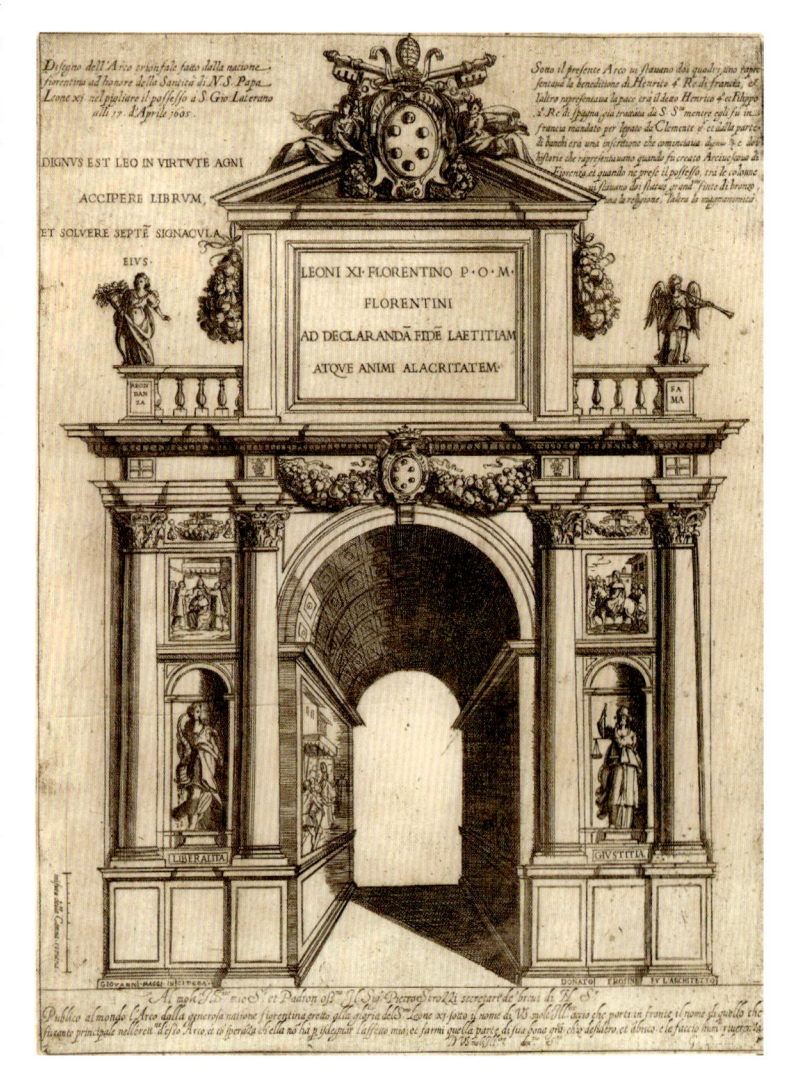

so similar to the Florentine one that von Erffa thinks this must have been deliberate, although there was a different architect involved, Giovan Paolo Maggi, from Como.[24] The statues represented Liberality and Magnanimity (again), and Magnificence and Strength. On the balustrade were Religion and Justice (again), and Charity and Prudence. The order was Ionic. The inscription was placed in a panel which interrupted the entablature, and the attic panel was painted with the papal arms, in gold, by the Cavalier d'Arpino.[25] The arches of Septimius Severus and Titus were also decorated with inscriptions and the papal arms. Ranuccio I Farnese, Duke of Parma, had the walls of his gardens, on the Palatine Hill on the south side of the Forum, covered in costly tapestries, and erected an *apparato*. Von Erffa suggests that this may have been designed, in the form of a triumphal arch, by Buontalenti.[26] Decorating this wall became a tradition.

Leo had the misfortune to catch a chill during his *possesso*, and died only twenty-six days after his election. Later in the same year (1605) his successor, Paul V (Borghese), held his *possesso*. Various *apparati* were built, including an arch at the Gesù built by the Jesuits: it bore the arms of the city of Rome, no doubt because Paul was a Roman.[27] For the same reason, the principal arch was the one on the Campidoglio, the seat of Roman government. It was very like the one for Leo, though here the order was Composite, and the attic covered the whole width. The positions of the arms and inscription were the reverse of those on Leo's Capitoline arch. The statues on the front represented Strength and Prudence, and on the back Peace and Religion. On the attic stood Justice and Abundance. Above the pediment were figures of Fame with trumpets. The columns were marbled, with gold capitals, and the statues of white stucco imitating Carrara marble. The Borghese emblem, the dragon, appeared frequently. The designer was Antonio Tempesta, who published an engraving of it.[28] Again, the arches of Septimius Severus and Titus were decorated.

For the *possesso* of Gregory XV (Ludovisi) in 1621, the arch on the Campidoglio had twelve fluted columns (perhaps four each on front and back, and two on each side), twenty stucco statues, and many reliefs in white and gold.[29] The next pope was Urban VIII (Barberini), celebrated for his patronage of Bernini and Borromini. Perhaps surprisingly, he at first forbade any expenditure on decorations for his *possesso*, but later yielded to the entreaties of the people. In 1624, the year after his coronation, a work was published by Agostino Moscardi describing *Le pompe del Campidoglio per la Santità di Nostro Signore Urbano VIII*. The arch was a *quadrifrons*, designed by Antonio de' Battisti. The order was Corinthian. There were the usual statues and inscriptions, together with paintings showing scenes from Urban's career. The statues on top included Rome, Romulus, the younger Cato, Caesar and Marcus Aurelius (or Trajan). The cupola within the archway was dotted with Barberini bees. The steps leading up to the arch were lined with more stucco statues, and the black marble lions at the bottom spouted wine.[30] There was another arch in the Piazza Sant'Angelo, erected by the Florentines, with statues simulating gilded bronze.

Even more detailed descriptions survive of the arches erected for the *possesso* of Urban's successor, Innocent X (Pamphili), in 1644.[31] The printed descriptions do not correspond accurately with the various engravings, but, according to the diary of the Conservatore Giacinto Gigli, this was because the latter were prepared before the event (this was usual, so that they could be sold on the day). In any case, neither of the two arches was ready on time. The Senate's arch on the Campidoglio was designed by Carlo Rainaldi. Framed by the principal Composite order were eight large allegorical statues: the sculptors included Domenico de' Rossi, Angelo Pellegrini and Nicolas Cordier the younger. After the *possesso*, the arch was sold off (presumably for scrap) for only 100 *scudi*.[32]

An important novelty for this *possesso* was the erection of an arch in the Forum by Odoardo Farnese, Duke of Parma. This became a tradition, continued later by the kings of the Two Sicilies.[33] The arch was designed by Girolamo Rainaldi (father of Carlo).[34] It stood in front of the wall of the Farnese Gardens and on the axis of the Arch of Titus. As has been mentioned above, it had been customary in the preceding century for this wall to be decorated with tapestries, coats of arms and the like. The regular practice now was for the duke's agent and the architect to offer the pope 'the drawing for the arch' (*il disegno dell'arco*): in this case Rainaldi had to apologise for its incomplete state. Innocent took it well, and ordered that the arch should be completed: he came back a fortnight later to see it. It won high praise because of its *artis novitas*. It is not easy to appreciate from the descriptions and differing engravings in what this consisted. It had a gilded Ionic order, and the decoration included Farnese lilies and Pamphili doves. As usual, there were statues in the niches, and on the arch and in the passageway were paintings. The part of the papal route between the arches of Septimius Severus and Titus was, according to custom, decorated by the city guilds, and that between the Arch of Titus and the Colosseum by the Jews, with a series of pictures of Old Testament scenes. The choice of the Arch of Titus, with its reliefs celebrating the destruction of Jerusalem, must have been cruelly deliberate.

Alexander VII (Chigi) expressly forbade the erection of arches for his *possesso*. For his successor, in 1667, Clement IX (Rospigliosi), the Senate was again forbidden to set up an arch, but the Duke of Parma erected one, to the design of Carlo Rainaldi, within four days. Pairs of apparently freestanding Composite columns flanked it, and in front of each was a statue on a base. Above the lower order stood a second one, also gilded, supporting a pediment with the papal arms and trumpeting Fames above it. There was no attic. On the back, two more statues framed a large inscription.[35] The design differed significantly from the fairly standardised type that had been customary for the senatorial arches. This standardisation has led many scholars to suspect that the basic framework of an arch may often have been re-used. There is evidence for this in

10.2 Capitoline arch for Clement X, 1670. Carlo Rainaldi.

174   THE TRIUMPHAL ARCH

the case of earlier Parma arches, whose parts were kept from one *possesso* to the next in the *grottoni del Palatino*, to be re-used or hired out for other festivities, including the *Quarantore* (the forty hours' devotion before the exposed Blessed Sacrament) at the Gesù (for example, in 1652).[36]

Both the arches erected for Clement X (Altieri) in 1670 were designed by Carlo Rainaldi, and fine engravings of both were made by Giovanni Battista Falda.[37] The senatorial arch was a richer version of the conventional type [10.2]. At the front, the plinths were linked with those of the statues of the Dioscuri which stand on either side at the top of the steps. Above pairs of freestanding Corinthian columns both entablature and attic broke forward. The sculpture between the columns was set within niches. Above the attic the papal arms were flanked by two standing Fames, statues of Charity and Religion, and kneeling atlantes bearing the globes of heaven and earth. On each narrow side was a single freestanding column. The back matched the front. The painter Giovan Battista Magni was in charge of the decoration.

This arch had an interesting fate. As the Holy Year of 1675 approached, the authorities of the church of Gesù e Maria (on the Corso) were concerned about the fact that it had no proper high altar, and asked the Conservatori if they could buy the components of the 1670 arch. They took four columns of painted cloth on a wooden framework, and medallions (which were repainted). These pieces so impressed a donor that he offered to pay for a permanent version, also by Rainaldi, which is still *in situ* [10.3].[38]

10.3 Church of Gesù e Maria, Rome.

PAPAL ARCHES 175

The arch erected in 1670 by Ranuccio Farnese, Duke of Parma, was far less conventional. Descriptions rightly speak of its *forma scenografica*. Strictly speaking, there was no arch. The rectangular opening was flanked by Composite pilasters; at angles to these were pairs of freestanding columns, each pair flanked by statues on bases. The columns imitated *giallo antico*. The entablature had triglyphs. Above the attic were double broken segmental pediments, framing the papal arms. One statue surmounted each projecting section.

In 1676 the austere Innocent XI (Odescalchi) held that the secular pomp of triumphs was unsuitable for the *possesso*, and that the money spent on decoration would be better given to the poor.[39] The Duke of Parma nevertheless began to erect an arch, but when only the framework had been set up the Pope forbade its completion. Innocent's successor in 1689, Alexander VIII (Ottoboni), was a completely different character. Once again the Duke of Parma commissioned an arch from Carlo Rainaldi.[40] It was more conventional than Clement X's. Von Erffa suggests that the cartouche with the stemma (coat of arms) and its supporting angels, and also the statue of Charity below, may have been re-used from the 1670 arch.[41] The Senate did not build an arch (though the Campidoglio was decorated), and this was to be the case from now on, with the single exception of 1721, when Innocent XIII (Conti) held his *possesso*: he was a Roman by birth, and so the Senate had a special interest in him.

When Innocent XII (Pignatelli) held his *possesso* in 1692, Raimondi was dead, and the Parma arch was designed by Carlo Fontana [10.4].[42] It was so similar to the 1689 arch that it must have re-used many of its components. The new statues were modelled by the Lombardic *stuccadore* Lionardo Retti. The arch was extremely colourful, imitating different marbles – the plinths white-blue Bardiglio, the columns and frieze Sicilian diasper (a black and yellow stone), and the pilasters *verde antico*. The capitals were gold-bronzed. Clement XI (Albani) was elected in 1700. Fontana was again commissioned to design the Parma arch [10.5]. His first sketch is dated October 1700 – before the conclave. The result was grander than ever. From each side projected triple plinths, supporting freestanding columns between statues. Above the entablatures of these side-pieces were the sections of a broken segmental pediment, each bearing a reclining figure holding a version of Trajan's Column. On top of the large attic was a huge globe: it was intended that this should open, revealing choirs and instrumentalists representing the four continents, but that was forbidden in case it endangered the procession.[43]

As mentioned above, Innocent XIII was the last pope to receive the honour of an arch from the Senate and people, in 1721. It was designed by Alessandro Specchi, a pupil of Fontana, who a few years before had made a survey of the Arch of Septimius Severus for the Senate.[44] Fairly conventional, the papal arch was given movement by the projection of the columns flanking it and by plinths at the sides, with

10.4 Farnese arch for Innocent XII, 1692. Carlo Fontana.

10.5 Farnese arch for Clement XI, 1701. Carlo Fontana.

10.6 Farnese arch for Innocent XIII, 1721. Pompeo Aldrovandini.

pairs of freestanding columns supporting large scrolls on either side of the bulky attic. The Duke of Parma's arch, designed by the Bolognese architecture-painter Pompeo Aldrovandini [10.6], was also rather conventional, but enlivened by some up-to-date touches, such as bracketed side-entablatures and a fancifully Baroque attic.[45] The humble Dominican Benedict XIII forbade any decoration of the Campidoglio for his *possesso* of 1724; the Parma arch, again by Aldrovandini, made use of the 1721 framework, with a few changes.[46]

Although Clement XII was a Florentine, no arch was erected in 1730 in the Piazza Sant'Angelo as had become traditional. The Duke of Parma's, yet again by Aldrovandini, was old-fashioned in its use of niches containing statues, but more up-to-date in its use of oval reliefs in the attic side-panels, with a broken pediment above flanking a coffered semidome.[47] It was Clement XII who erected a building which is one of the most remarkable applications of the triumphal arch formula to a solid building, namely the Trevi Fountain, erected in 1732–51 to the design of Nicola Salvi. Here elements copied from the arches of Titus and Constantine – the latter restored by Clement XII in 1732–3 – articulate the solid façade.[48]

During the same reign, Lione Pascoli (1674–1744), a lawyer best known for his *Vite de' Pittori, Scultori ed Architetti Moderni* (Rome, 1730 and 1736), published a work called *Testamento politico d'un Accademico Fiorentino* (Cologne, 1733), in which he proposed ways of improving the commerce of Rome.[49] One suggestion was the establishment of an exchange (a *borsa*) on the Campidoglio, where he further suggested

PAPAL ARCHES 177

improving the approach stairs, with a majestic triumphal arch at the bottom.[50] As Stöpfel points out, this is hardly consistent with his stated intention to avoid unnecessary expense in erecting structures *per pura pompa* (purely for show).[51]

By 1741, when Benedict XIV (Lambertini) held his *possesso*, the Farnese Gardens, and consequently the duty of providing the arch, had passed to the Infante Carlos of Spain, in his role as King of the Two Sicilies [10.7]. The design was provided by the well-known architect Ferdinando Fuga, and was on a grand scale. Large sculpture groups filled the spaces between the repeated pairs of columns on either side of the archway.[52] Fuga also designed (in collaboration with Giuseppe Panini) the arch for Clement XIII (Rezzonico) in 1758: this was grander still, the archway flanked by deep aedicules, their paired columns having sculpture groups projecting between them. The same feature was repeated on the sides.[53] For Clement XIV (Ganganelli) in 1769 exactly the same arch was used. It was supervised by Giuseppe Panini. As the Pope passed under the Arch of Septimius Severus, his horse reared and threw him. Although he injured his shoulder, he joked that he had thought he was the successor of St Peter, not St Paul.[54]

The extravagant and worldly Pius VI (Braschi) held his *possesso* in 1775. King Ferdinand entrusted the design of his arch to the superintendant of royal buildings in the papal kingdom, Francesco Milizia, who is best known as a writer on architecture.[55] As one might expect, at a time when Neoclassicism was fashionable, the arch is simpler than its predecessors, and more closely modelled on antiquity. The sculpture, however, was re-used from the 1758/69 arches. On top was an elongated octagonal pedestal to support the papal arms. There was no inscription, but there were numerous bas-reliefs. (The Pope had himself represented on horseback at his *possesso* in a bronze statuette by Lorenzo Weber.)[56]

In 1782 Pius went to Vienna to try to persuade the Emperor Joseph II to adopt an attitude more favourable to the Vatican. The Venetians proposed to hold a regatta in his honour, with an arch designed by Giannantonio Selva. Based on the arch of Septimius Severus, with a lion on top, it would probably have risen from the water like the later arch for Napoleon. Pius's journey was a failure, so there was no celebration.[57]

On 15 February 1798 General Berthier entered Rome, on the orders of the Directoire, and proclaimed the Roman Republic. Pius had to leave, and on 20 March a *Festa della Federazione* was held in the Piazza S. Pietro. A large triple arch was erected at the south end of the Ponte Sant'Angelo. It was comparatively simple in form, with four Doric columns on the front and a plain attic, but there was rich relief decoration over the side arches and on the entablature. The architect was Giuseppe Barberi.[58]

10.7 Farnese arch for Benedict XIV, 1741. Ferdinando Fuga.

Pius died in France in 1800. His successor, Pius VII (Chiaramonte), was elected in Venice in March 1800. In July he entered Rome, and the nobility welcomed him with an arch in the Piazza del Popolo, designed by the Capitano Ingegnere Benedetto Piernicoli. It linked the twin churches of Santa Maria dei Miracoli and Santa Maria di Montesanto, framing the entrance to the Corso, and was designed to harmonise with them. Above the inscribed attic was a group by Luigi Acquisti, representing Religion with Error and Deceit prostrated on either side. This was flanked by genii carrying golden crowns, alluding to the double power of the Pope. In the intercolumniations of the arch were four colossal statues: towards the Piazza, SS. Peter and Paul were by Monti, while on the Corso side SS. Gregory and Pius V were by Francesco Barberi. At the sides were two chiaroscuro reliefs, painted by Liborio Coccetti, showing the Pope embarking at Pesaro, and meeting the ambassador of King Ferdinand. Beyond each church the streets (Via di Ripetta and Via del Babuino) were spanned by porticoes. The sides of the Piazza were transformed into a sort of circus.[59] Pius celebrated his *possesso* in 1801 in a modest manner, and no arches were erected.

In 1804 Pius tried to win the favour of Napoleon by giving him a splendid clock, chosen by Canova. In the form of a triumphal arch, it was designed by Giacomo Raffaelli, with mechanism by Breguet. It is in the Gilbert Collection at the Victoria and Albert Museum. However, in 1809 Pius was forced by Napoleon to leave Rome. He returned in 1814: the Piazza del Popolo was decorated, to the designs of Giuseppe Valadier, and these temporary decorations were later made permanent. An arch was erected on the Piazza Venezia by the *mercanti di campagna* (country merchants). Designed by Clemente Folchi, it was of the Greek Doric order. On top was a group of statues showing Religion giving peace to the nations, who were represented by two kneeling kings. These figures were said to be by Canova, but this probably only refers to the figure of Religion, which was copied from the famous one on the tomb of Clement XIII. On the base two statues showed Fame crowning the *trionfatore*. Within the arch were reliefs of Christ giving the keys to Peter, and Rome praying for the return of Pius. A relief on the exterior showed 'agricultural and pastoral operations', to symbolise the donors. On either side stood candelabra producing incense, and fulsome inscriptions. At the crossroads known as 'Cesarini' (the present Largo Argentina) stood another arch, very simple, with a variant of the Doric order. There were many other *apparati*, including arches over the streets formed of myrtle, with garlands of roses hanging from them, and in the centre 'vases of Etruscan form'. The Jews erected an *apparato* resembling a synagogue.

Yet another arch was set up in the middle of a temporary bridge of boats across the Tiber, intended to facilitate the movement of the crowds wishing to welcome the Pope [10.8]. It was paid for by the merchant Giovanni Rotti.[60] The architect was Paolo Provinciali, and the *macchinista* was Giuseppe Argomenti. The arch was quite simple, astylar, with statues in niches and reliefs above, and an inscription on the attic, above which was a group showing Religion trampling on the vices. The idea of the arch on a boat was to symbolise the ship of St Peter, remaining afloat in every weather. Over 60,000 people crossed the bridge, 'to join in a spectacle more splendid than any given to ancient conquerors'. After dark the arches were lit up with torches.[61]

Pius VII died in 1823. No arches were erected at Rome for his successors, Leo XII and Pius VIII. In 1835 Gregory XVI (Cappellari, elected in 1831) visited Fiumicino, to inspect the proposed river works. In his honour the Marchese Domenico Pallavicini

10.8 Arch in the Tiber for the return of Pius VII, 1814. Paolo Provinciali.

erected an arch on his property near Trajan's Harbour. Designed by Pietro Holl, it was simple and astylar, with statues of Fame standing on bases against the side elements, Victories in the spandrels, and, on top, a sculpture group representing Christian Rome triumphing over Pagan Rome.[62]

When Pius IX (Mastai-Ferretti) was elected in 1846, he declared a political amnesty. Two months before his *possesso*, on the feast of the Birth of the Virgin, an arch was erected on the Piazza del Popolo, in front of the twin churches. It was a triple arch, after the model of that of Constantine, and was decorated with garlands, painted reliefs and statues. On top were statues showing the Pope accompanied by allegorical females. The architect was Felice Cicconetti, and the arch was paid for by the people.[63]

The events of 1848 forced Pius to leave Rome, but he returned in 1850. This was celebrated by a firework display symbolising the Triumph of Religion, whose statue surmounted a triumphal arch set in a semicircular arcade. It was designed by Luigi Poletti (who had rebuilt San Paolo fuori le Mura after the fire there).[64]

In May 1857 Pius IX left Rome for a tour of the Papal States. Politically, this was a critical moment for the temporal power of the Pope. Various Roman bodies decided to erect a monument to welcome him when he returned. The lead was taken once again by the *mercanti di campagna*, and they were joined by the Chamber of Commerce, the Pontifical Bank, and two railway companies (the Pio Centrale and Rome–Naples). The site chosen was the open ground on the other side of the Ponte Molle (the northern approach to the city), which the sponsors preferred for three reasons: they could leave the decoration of the streets to the Municipio; as farmers they liked the open country; and the Pope would see their monument first. They chose Virginio Vespignani as their architect, partly because he was known to be a quick worker – the Pope was due back in September. The structure took the form of a combined arch and circus, on the model of the Circus of Maxentius on the Via Appia (excavated in 1825) [10.9]. At the northern extremity was the arch, set in the curved end of the circus, which was open at the other end, towards the bridge. Around the interior ran banks of seats, with porticoes behind

10.9 Arch and amphitheatre for Pius IX, 1857. Virginio Vespignani.

and above them, fronted by Doric colonnades. The eastern side was interrupted by an exedra roofed with a coffered half-dome. The stairs up to it were flanked by statues of Agriculture and Commerce, by Stefano Galletti. The arch itself was of the Corinthian order, a little bigger than the Arch of Titus. It was modelled on the arch at Benevento, which Pius had restored in 1856. The archway was flanked by freestanding columns; at the corners were pilasters. On top of each column was a statue – on the outer face, Justice and Charity; on the inner, the Genius of the Arts and Trades, and Public Prosperity. These were by Giuseppe Baini. The Latin inscriptions were composed by Father G. Marchi, S.J. The list of those who erected the arch included 'Societates Viis Ferratis instruendis agendis, altera Roma ad mare ad Padum, altera Roma ad Lirim' – the two railway companies. There were also bas-reliefs painted in tempera by Francesco Grandi. These represented various achievements of the Pope: on the outer face, the newly rebuilt basilica of San Paolo fuori le Mura, the definition of the Immaculate Conception, the Concordat with Austria, and the new Commission for Sacred Archaeology; on the inner, gas-lighting of the streets, the electric telegraph, railways, and the arts of wool, linen and silk. The Pope had already indicated that he would stop here and give his apostolic blessing. The seats held over three thousand people, bands played, and speeches were made. A few days later the Pope came back to have another look.[65] The event was also celebrated by the Senate and people, who employed Luigi Poletti both to decorate the Porta del Popolo and to erect an arch between the twin churches. It was a *quadrifrons*, harmonising with the churches. Within was a hemispherical cupola, and paintings by Gioacchino Altobelli. On each side of the arch was a pair of freestanding columns, and above was a statue of the Pope giving his blessing, by Carlo Chelli.[66]

From 1860 onwards, the anniversary of Pius's return to Rome on 12 April 1850 was celebrated. The decorations became more elaborate each year, involving temporary structures, paintings and statues. A detailed description survives of those of 1867. The many *apparati* included some in the classical style, some Gothic, and even a Chinese pavilion. There were two arches, a simple one in the Via dei Serpenti, and a more elaborate one in the Piazza Santi Apostoli. This was again designed by Vespignani, and had a Corinthian order on the front, with a Tuscan order for the flanking porticoes. A coloured statue of Our Lady, lit by gas, stood below the arch.[67]

For the anniversary in 1868 the *apparati* again included two arches. One, in the Piazza Pia (by the Castel Sant'Angelo), had four Corinthian half-columns, and an attic with scrolls and flaming urns. It was designed by Francesco Azzurri, and commemorated the Pope's 'reform of hygiene in hospitals'. Another, in Via Pia, was designed by Filippo Martinucci to frame the Porta Pia, and honour the Virgin. It was fairly similar to the other one.[68] The 'arch' erected by the Barone Visconti 'sulla Ripa Mastai all'Emporio' for the 1869 celebration was a feeble affair.[69]

It is hardly surprising that once the papacy had lost its temporal power, at the unification of Italy in 1870, the association of arches with triumph should cause them to disappear from the scene.

Temporary arches for popes outside Rome

When popes travelled outside Rome, they might be greeted with 'entries' like those provided for secular rulers. Naturally the sixteenth century was the period when this happened most often. After Julius II recovered the city of Bologna in 1506, he was received with thirteen arches. It is not known who the artists were, but their iconography was straightforward.[70]

After François I defeated the Emperor Maximilian and his allies at Marignano in 1515, Leo X decided to go to meet the French King at Bologna. He was received in his native Florence with a magnificent entry. The seven arches (together with a temporary façade for the Duomo) were designed and decorated by many of the most celebrated artists in the city, including Baccio da Montelupo, Antonio da Sangallo the Elder, Granacci, Pontormo, Rosso, Andrea del Sarto, Sansovino, Bandinelli and Piero di Cosimo. The specification survives, as do several descriptions, and Vasari gives further information, but sadly no illustrations are known.[71] Each of seven *apparati* (including the Duomo façade) celebrated one of the canonical virtues, while on the eighth all the virtues appeared together. The procession lasted seven hours, as the Pope had to listen to songs at each arch. One commentator thought that Vitruvius would have awarded the prize to Rosso for his *quadrifrons* with twenty-seven Doric pilasters imitating porphyry, and gilded garlands.[72] There had been other papal visits to Florence, most recently by Pius II in 1459, but the explanation for the lavish *apparati* at Leo's may be (as suggested by Shearman) that the Florentine merchant colonies in Lyon and Bruges would have sent back news of the entries in the same year of François I at Lyon and Prince Charles at Bruges. At Bologna arches were erected to greet both Leo X and François I, but little is known about them.[73]

In 1530 Clement VII marked his reconciliation with the Emperor Charles V by crowning him at Bologna (the last time a Holy Roman Emperor was crowned by a Pope). Both rulers were greeted with arches.[74] Etiquette required that the superior person should arrive first, which in this case meant the Pope (23 October 1529). There was little time for preparation, but the streets were decorated with 'temporary galleries and arches', and the same arches were used afterwards for the Emperor. The procession after the coronation was shown in engravings by Nicolas Hogenberg, but only one includes an arch, and that is comparatively simple.[75]

In 1543 Paul III was greeted on his entry to Ferrara with five arches, but no description survives.[76] The duchy of Ferrara 'devolved' to Clement VIII because there was no legitimate heir; Cesare d'Este tried to take it over, but Clement both threatened war and excommunicated him. On the day Clement left Ferrara, in January 1598, his nephew, Cardinal Aldobrandini, made a triumphal entry, for which arches were erected. In the same year Clement himself made a triumphal progress to inspect the duchy. Arches were erected by numerous towns: there were, for example, six at Ancona, and single arches at smaller towns like Senigallia and Macerata. At Ferrara itself the principal arch was designed by the local painter Domenico Mona, and there were two others, and a copy of Trajan's Column. While Clement was at Ferrara, he was visited by Margaret of Austria, and two arches were erected for her, both celebrating her forthcoming marriage to Philip III. She and her brother had earlier been welcomed on crossing the Adige with a triumphal arch on a specially erected bridge.[77] On his way back to Rome, Clement was given a splendid entry to Bologna, with some substantial *apparati*. These are represented in a series of engravings after Guido Reni.[78] There were four arches. The first, outside the town, was made of foliage, while the other three were of brick. The second, 11 m high, had a statue of Bologna on top, within a broken pediment. The third was surmounted by a statue of Moses, to represent the good government of the Pope. The fourth and grandest was a *quadrifrons*, at the entrance to the Piazza. Each side corresponded to a point of the compass, and over each attic was a broken pediment containing a female statue representing a continent, to show that the Pope's fame was universal. Africa sat on a crocodile, Asia on a camel, Europe on a globe, and America on 'an animal of that country'. The inscription tablets were in Latin, together with Arabic, for Africa; Hebrew, for Asia; Greek, for Europe; and 'Indian', for America.

A striking painting of 1786 by Louis Ducros in the Museo di Roma shows Pius VI on his way to the Pontine Marshes, which he proposed to drain. The Pope is shown on horseback, coming from a large triumphal arch in the Doric order, but this is a fiction of the artist.[79]

In 1841 Gregory XVI made a pilgrimage to the sanctuary of Loreto, and was greeted at Assisi and Camerino by triumphal arches designed by Luigi Poletti.[80]

On his tour of the Papal States in 1857, mentioned above, Pius IX was greeted at Bologna by a large freestanding arch, with a statue of the Pope above the attic, and the usual allegorical figures, coats of arms, and flagpoles.[81] At Viterbo two arches were designed by Virginio Vespignani. A triple one was set against the back of the Porta Fiorentina, and was based on the Roman arch at Fano. Four freestanding Corinthian columns supported symbolic statues by Stefano Galletti. The other arch, similar but with only one opening, stood at the end of the Via della Svolta, on the axis of the first.[82]

Permanent arches for popes

So far as Rome is concerned, no permanent arch was erected simply to honour a pope, but some structures were erected or adapted in the sixteenth and seventeenth centuries which have both the form of a triumphal arch and a commemorative function.

The earliest is the Porta Santo Spirito, begun by Paul III *c.* 1540 to span the principal approach to the Vatican from the south, and soon afterwards incorporated into the fortifications of Pius IV (1564). The powerful composition by Antonio da Sangallo the Younger, with four attached columns, was never completed.

It was also Pius IV who had the grandiose external facade added to the Porta del Popolo (the principal approach to Rome from the north) in 1562–3. It was designed by Nanni di Baccio Bigio. The inner façade was later altered by Bernini to celebrate the triumphal entry of Queen Christina of Sweden in 1655: to the order of pilasters which already existed he added an attic with an inscription (originally painted, subsequently carved) reading *FELICI FAUSTOQ. INGRESSUI* ('for a happy and fortunate entry'). Above this are garlands of oak leaves, ears of corn, and roses (referring to the arms of both Christina and Alexander VII), below the papal (Chigi) arms.[83]

In the first year of his pontificate, 1585, Sixtus V launched his outstanding contributions to the city of Rome by bringing in a new aqueduct, the Acqua Felice. This made use of the Aurelianic Wall, but left it at the Porta Tiburtina. A gateway over the modern Via Marsala took the form of a plain triumphal arch, of grey tufa and white travertine, with three openings and an attic bearing inscriptions. On one side this commemorates the aqueduct, on the other the opening up of Sixtus's new streets. The arch is now uncomfortably huddled against the side of the Stazione Termini.[84]

During the eighteenth century there was a fashion for building arches in honour of popes in the Marche and Romagna. The first was at Jesi, in 1734, and honoured Clement XII, who had abolished the port taxes at Ancona, reduced other taxes, and built a new road from Nocera to Ancona. The tall brick arch, simple but stately, was designed by Domenico Valeri, and spans the south-west end of the main street.[85] Clement's creation of a free port, which took place in 1732, was also commemorated by an arch at Ancona itself. The harbour was enlarged and modernised by Luigi Vanvitelli from 1733. In about 1735–6 he built an arch out on the mole, within an earlier fortification, not far from the Arch of Trajan, but at a lower level. Although simple in form, it makes use of the Doric order in a sophisticated and ingenious way. Carved ornament (including seashells in the metopes) is sparingly used. It was intended that a lavish cartouche with the papal arms should surmount it, but this was never executed, nor was the attic inscribed. An engraving of the harbour by Vasi, after Vanvitelli, shows the arch with a seated statue of the Pope on top of it. The city authorities had decided in 1735 to erect a statue, and in 1737 the Pope, at the suggestion of Sir Thomas Dereham (a Norfolk Jacobite resident in Rome), gave the city a seated statue of himself, executed by Agostino Cornacchini, which had been set up in the narthex of St John Lateran, but which he had replaced with the statue of Constantine from the Capitoline. Despite what must have been Vanvitelli's intention, the statue can never have been set up on the arch, and when it arrived in 1738 it was put in the Piazza del Plebiscito.[86]

Another arch to commemorate papal beneficence was erected at Senigallia, further up the coast from Ancona, in 1750. Benedict XIV (Lambertini) had had the market area newly laid out beside a canal. Closing the view down the street which leads from the town centre over a bridge is the Porta Lambertina, which also functions as a town gate for those approaching from the north. Built of travertine, it has a broken segmental pediment at attic level, and pretty cornucopias flank the stemma on top. An inscription records that it was designed and built by Cardinal Giuseppe Ercolani, who

10.10 Santarcangelo di Romagna, arch for Clement XIV, 1772–5. Cosimo Morelli.

was in charge of the papal works here, but the architect Alessandro Rossi (from Osimo) was also involved.[87]

Further north again, and inland from Rimini, the insignificant town of Santarcangelo di Romagna was the birthplace of Clement XIV (Ganganelli), and capitalised on this claim to fame by erecting an arch in his honour in the main square [10.10]. Begun in 1772, it was completed in 1775, the year after the Pope's death. The architect was Cosimo Morelli, from Imola, whose best-known work is the Palazzo Braschi at Rome. The mixture of brick and Istrian stone produces a festive effect, and the papal arms on top are backed by bronze leaves. Stöpfel finds the result reminiscent of an ephemeral arch translated into permanent materials.[88] An inscription was added within the opening in 1860, which states that in suppressing the Society of Jesus Clement had benefited both religion and civilisation.

Pius VI was honoured with two permanent arches. The Porta Pia at Ancona, of 1787–9, stands near the southern end of the harbour, close to the Mole Vanvitelliana, or Lazzaretto. It was intended to thank the Pope for opening up a more convenient access to the city along the sea, and was designed by Filippo Marchionni the Younger.[89] Pius was also honoured as a benefactor in his old diocese of Subiaco, where his visit in 1789 to consecrate the church of Sant'Andrea (designed by Pietro Camporese) was initially commemorated by four temporary arches, erected by the nobility. One, at the border of the abbey lands, was decorated, along with the usual statues and reliefs, with trout, to commemorate Pius's works to make the river Aniene navigable. Another, designed by Benedetto Piernicoli, had on top an equestrian statue of the Pope crushing rebellion, avarice and pride. After the visit, a permanent arch, of comparatively simple Ionic form, designed by Giulio Camporese, was set up at the entrance to the town [10.11].[90] A proposal to honour the fifteenth anniversary of Pius's reign, in 1790, by means of an arch of travertine and Carrara marble, to be erected at Rome (the first permanent arch since ancient times), was made by Giuseppe Valadier. His elegant, if rather conventional, design was intended to combine elements of Roman imperial arches, and recalls the arches of Titus and of Trajan at Ancona. On top a seated statue of the Pope is set on a fluted drum, beside which sit allegorical figures.[91]

Another pope honoured in his birthplace was Pius VIII, who came from Cingoli in the Marche. He reigned for only eighteen months (1829–30), and the Porta Pia was not erected until 1845. It was designed by Ireneo Aleandri (best known for the remarkable Sferisterio, the ball-game court, at Macerata).[92] Forming the principal gateway to the hilltop town, it is of rusticated brickwork, with Doric pilasters and entablature of stone. The papal stemma surmounts a fulsome inscription.

Pius IX shared with Pius VI the honour of an arch in the city of which he had previously been bishop, namely Imola. The tall single arch was flanked by Corinthian pilasters, and bore a substantial attic. On the inner side it stood between guardhouses, and on the outer side were iron gates, between stone pylons pierced by arches and bearing stemmata.[93] The arch no longer exists.

10.11 Arch at Subiaco for Pius VI, after 1789. Giulio Camporese.

Pius also rebuilt two of the gates of Rome. The first was the Porta San Pancrazio, up on the Janiculum, which had been built by Urban VIII, but was badly damaged in the bombardments of 1849. Pius had a new gate built in 1854, to the design of Virginio Vespignani. Its inner facade takes the form of a substantial but relatively simple triumphal arch, while the powerful outer side has rustication around the single opening, and on the quoins.[94] In 1851 the Porta Pia was severely damaged by lightning. The inner side had been built by Michelangelo in 1561–4. His gate, erected for Pius IV, was remarkable in several ways. It faced inwards, down the new Via Pia (now Via XX Settembre), which linked the Quirinal to the Via Nomentana, and not outwards. It was described by J.S. Ackerman as 'pure urban scenography – a masonry memento of the temporary arches erected in the Renaissance to celebrate the arrival of princes, though without their triumphal connotations'.[95] The idea of a street terminating in an arch goes back to Vitruvius's account of the ancient theatre, and was recommended by Daniele Barbaro in his edition of Vitruvius. The design of the gate itself is highly original, and does not refer either to Roman gates or to triumphal arches; the crenellations recall rather medieval gates.[96] At the other end of the street Sixtus V set up the magnificent group of the Dioscuri (or 'Horse Tamers') found in the nearby Baths of Constantine. Bernini produced a splendid, but unexecuted, design for a concave arch, facing down the Via Pia, on which the Dioscuri would stand diagonally on tall plinths in front of the paired columns. Above the entablature dolphin-like scrolls flank the 'mountains' and star of the Chigi Alexander VII.[97] Vespignani ingeniously repaired Michelangelo's inner façade. In 1861 he designed a new external façade. It is based on the Arch of Titus, but has freestanding columns on either side of the opening, supporting a pediment. Beyond these are niches containing statues of SS. Alexander and Agnes (supposed to have been martyred on the Via Nomentana) by Federico Amadori (1864). If the arch had a triumphal message, this was tactfully ignored in the inscription.[98] In 1863 its impending completion was celebrated by the incorporation of a reproduction of its façade as part of the huge pyrotechnic *macchina* designed by Vespignani for the customary illumination on Easter Sunday. The arch was set against a battlemented wall, above which rose two temples in front of a long portico.[99] Only a couple of years after its completion, in 1870, the new Porta Pia suffered minor damage in the attack by Garibaldi's troops which breached the wall just to its north, an event recalled in (obviously staged) photographs, and by the monument to the Bersaglieri set up opposite the arch in 1932.

Notes

1. J.N.D. Kelly, *The Oxford Dictionary of Popes* (Oxford, 1986), 209. This is the most convenient history of the papacy.
2. James Bruce Ross, 'A study of twelfth century interest in the antiquities of Rome', in J.L. Cate and E.N. Anderson, eds, *Medieval and Historiographical Essays in Honour of James Westfall Thompson* (Chicago, 1938), 302–21.
3. Francesco Cancellieri, *Storia de' solenni possessi dei sommi pontifici* (Rome, 1802). This is still the standard account.
4. When the antipope Gregory VIII was handed over to him in 1121, Callixtus humiliated him by making him 'traverse Rome in mock triumph, mounted backwards on a camel and exposed to the jeers and peltings of the populace' (Kelly, cit. at n. 1, 164).
5. Hans Martin, Freiherr von Erffa, 'Die Ehrenpforten fur den Possess der Päpste im 17. und 18. Jahrhundert', *Festschrift Harald Keller* (Darmstadt, 1963), 335–70. This is the basic account of these arches.
6. Torgil Magnuson, *Studies in Roman Quattrocento Architecture* (Stockholm, 1958), 129–30, 355.
7. Marcello Fagiolo, ed., *La Festa a Roma* (Turin, 1997), I, p.43.

8 Bernardino Corio, *L'Historia di Milano* (Venice, 1514). For a useful plan showing the development of the route of the *possesso*, see Fagiolo (cit. in the preceding note), II, p.13.
9 Eva Brües, *Raffaele Stern* (diss., Bonn, 1958), 132.
10 See e.g. J. Shearman, *Raphael's Cartoons in the Collection of H.M. The Queen* (London, 1972), 14–17. Also Sabine Poeschel, *Alexander Maximus: Das Bildprogramm des Appartamento Borgia im Vatikan* (Weimar, 1999).
11 Cancellieri (cit. at n. 3), 58; von Erffa (cit. at n. 5), 336; Bonner Mitchell, *Italian Civic Pageantry in the High Renaissance* (Florence, 1979), 114–15. For the *possessi* of Julius and his successors, see Irene Fosi, 'Court and city in the ceremonies of *possesso* in the sixteenth century', in G. Signarotto and M. A. Visceglia, eds, *Court and Politics in Papal Rome 1497–1700* (Cambridge, 2002), 31–52.
12 Mitchell (cit. in the preceding note), 114–15. For the arch at the Vatican, see Werner Weisbach, *Trionfi* (Berlin, 1919), 14, and for the 'Arch of Domitian' see Francesco Albertini, *Mirabilia Romae* (Lyon, 1520), 45v.
13 William Roscoe, *The Life and Pontificate of Leo the Tenth* (Liverpool, 1805), II, 174–6, Appendix, 39–56 (Penni's description); Mitchell (cit. at n. 11), 117–19.
14 M. Fagiolo and M. L. Madonna, in Fagiolo (cit. at n. 7), I, 42–9.
15 ibid., 49; Ingrid D. Rowland, *The Culture of the High Renaissance: Ancients and Moderns in Sixteenth-Century Rome* (Cambridge, 1998), 212.
16 Kathleen Wren Christian, *Empire without End: Antiquities Collections in Renaissance Rome* (New Haven/London, 2010), 156–7, 361–3, 383–7.
17 Von Erffa (cit. at n. 5), 336.
18 ibid., 337.
19 Mitchell (cit. at n. 11), 129–30.
20 According to Nicolas Cusano, the agent of Maximilian II (N. Lemaitre, *Saint Pie V* (Paris, 1994), 222).
21 Loren Partridge and Randolph Starn, 'Triumphalism and the Sala Regia in the Vatican', in *'All the World's a Stage …': Art and Pageantry in the Renaissance and Baroque*, ed. Barbara Wisch and Susan Scott Munshower, *Papers in Art History from the Pennsylvania State University*, VI (1990), pt 1, 26. The Coligny painting is illustrated at 1-28; Gregory XI at 1-23.
22 Maurizio Fagiolo dell'Arco, *Corpus delle Feste a Roma*, I, *La Festa Barocca* (Rome, 1997), 181. (This work replaces M. Fagiolo dell'Arco and S. Carandini, *L'Effimero Barocco* (Rome, 1977).)
23 ibid., 204. On p. 203 he reproduces three projects for the arch.
24 Von Erffa (cit. at n. 5), 338.
25 Fagiolo dell'Arco (cit. at n. 22), 202. The Cavalier d'Arpino is said to have designed several whole arches for the Campidoglio, but nothing is known of them: Herwarth Röttgen, *Il Cavalier Giuseppe Cesari d'Arpino* (Rome, 2002), 508.
26 Von Erffa (cit. at n. 5), 365, n. 35.
27 In the Blunt Collection (at the Courtauld Institute in London) there is a drawing for an arch with the arms of Paul V and Franciscan symbols (ill. in F. De Leva, 'La collezione Anthony Blunt a Londra', *Il disegno di architecttura*, 8 (Nov. 1993), 19.
28 Von Erffa (cit. at n. 5), 365, n. 38; Fagiolo dell'Arco (cit. at n. 22), 202.
29 Fagiolo dell'Arco (cit. at n. 22), 231; G. L. Masetti Zannini, *Capitolium* (1966), no. 6, p. V.
30 Fagiolo dell'Arco (cit. at n. 22), 252–3.
31 Von Erffa (cit. at n. 5), 344–6; J. Montagu, *Roman Baroque Sculpture* (New Haven/London, 1989), 182–3; Fagiolo (cit. at n. 7), II, 19; Fagiolo dell'Arco (cit. at n. 22), 330–34.
32 Montagu (cit. in the preceding note), 183.
33 For the Parma arches see Montserrat Moli Frigola, 'Teatro, musica y fiestas en las residencias Farnesianas', in G. Morganti, ed., *Gli orti Farnesiani sul Palatino* (Rome, 1990), 464–79. See also Fagiolo dell'Arco (cit. at n. 22), 359; Giuseppe Morganti, *Gli Orti Farnesiani* (Milan, 1999).
34 A project for the arch by Giovan Battista Mola (father of the painter Pier Francesco Mola) survives in the Prado (Fagiolo dell'Arco (cit. at n. 22), 333–4; *Il disegno di architettura*, 6 (Nov. 1992), 42). Interestingly, it incorporates the Dioscuri within its side niches.
35 Fagiolo dell'Arco (cit. at n. 22), 452–3.
36 Moli Frigola (cit. at n. 33), 469. On the *apparati* erected for the Quarant'Ore see Mark S. Weil, 'The Devotion of the Forty Hours and Roman Baroque Illusions', *Journal of the Warburg and Courtauld Institutes*, 37 (1974), 218–48. Some made use of the triumphal arch motif, for example the design by Andrea Pozzo of 1685 (pl. 56c).
37 Fagiolo dell'Arco (cit. at n. 22), 482–3.
38 Montagu (cit. at n. 31), 184–5.
39 Von Erffa (cit. at n. 5), 350.
40 Fagiolo dell'Arco (cit. at n. 22), 551–2. The first caption on p. 552 wrongly locates the arch 'in Campidoglio'.
41 Von Erffa (cit. at n. 5), 351–2.
42 Fagiolo dell'Arco (cit. at n. 22), 561–2. On Fontana, see A. Braham and H. Hoger, *Carlo Fontana: The Drawings at Windsor Castle* (London, 1977).
43 Maurizio Fagiolo dell'Arco, *Corpus delle Feste a Roma*, II, *Il Settecento e l'Ottocento* (Rome, 1997), 6–7. For a temporary arch designed in 1716 by Giuseppe Marchetti, to stand on the Capitoline and commemorate 'a victorious prince', clearly celebrating Clement's role in the great victory over the Turks of 1715, see Christopher M. S. Johns, *Papal Art and Cultural Politics – Rome in the Age of Clement XI* (Cambridge, 1993), 190–94. He also illustrates the 'triumphal arch portico' designed by Alessandro Specchi for the courtyard of the Palazzo dei Conservatori, to celebrate the same victory. It has the Cesi *Roma* as its centrepiece.
44 Thomas Ashby and Stephen Welsh, 'Alessandro Specchi', *The Town Planning Review*, 12 (1927), 237–48.
45 Fagiolo dell'Arco (cit. at n. 43), 39–42.
46 ibid., 50.
47 ibid., 80–82; Fagiolo (cit. at n. 7), II, 22; see also Cancellieri (cit. at n. 3), 370–73.
48 John A. Pinto, *The Trevi Fountain* (New Haven/London, 1986), 239–40. For the Arch of

Constantine, see the inscription on its western side.
49 See P. Sohm in *Dictionary of Art*, s.v. Pascoli.
50 Lione Pascoli, *Testamento politico*, 188. See also E. Battisti, 'Lione Pascoli, Luigi Vanvitelli e l'urbanistica italiana del settecento', *Atti del VIII Convegno Nazionale di storia dell'architettura, Caserta 1953* (Rome, 1956), 51–64; fig. 2 on p. 59 shows a reconstruction of the Campidoglio scheme. According to Battisti, the claim that the *Testamento politico* was published in Cologne was fictitious.
51 Pascoli (cit. in the preceding note), 177–8; W. Stöpfel, 'Triumphbogenentwürfe des 18. Jahrhunderts im Archiv der R. Accademia di S. Luca in Rom', in *Kunstgeschichtliche Studien für Kurt Bauch* (Munich, 1967), 241–52.
52 Fagiolo dell'Arco (cit. at n. 43), 119–20; Roberto Pane, *Ferdinando Fuga* (Naples, 1956), 74–5, figs 52–3.
53 Fagiolo dell'Arco (cit. at n. 43), 163–4. The sculptors were Tommaso Righi and Andrea Birganti (Cancellieri (cit. at n. 3), 391).
54 Fagiolo dell'Arco (cit. at n. 43), 195–7; Fagiolo (cit. at n. 7), II, 21.
55 Fagiolo dell'Arco (cit. at n. 43), 163–4; Fagiolo (cit. at n. 7), II, 23; Jeffrey Collins, *Papacy and Politics in Eighteenth-Century Rome: Pius VI and the Arts* (Cambridge, 2004), 39–42. Milizia had encouraged the building of arches in his *Principii di Architettura Civile*, *Opere Complete* (Bologna, 1826–7), vol. VII, II 407).
56 Ill. by von Erffa (cit. at n. 5), 362. For the arch, see Fagiolo dell'Arco (cit. at n. 43), 219–20 (reproducing an engraving which copies that for Clement XIII).
In 1790 Giuseppe Valadier dedicated a design for an arch to Pius VI, offering to build it for 20,000 *scudi* (W. Stöpfel, 'Der Arco Clementino Vanvitellis und die Statue Cornacchinis: ein Ehrenbogen für Clemens XII in Ancona', *Römisches Jahrbuch fur Kunstgeschichte*, 12 (1969), 221; see also Paolo Marconi, *Giuseppe Valadier* (Rome, 1964), 105, 118, fig. 38.
57 Elena Bassi, *Giannantonio Selva* (Padua, 1936), 47.
58 C. Pietrangeli, *Il Museo di Roma* (Bologna, 1971), fig. 159 – a painting by Felice Giani, reproduced by Fagiolo (cit. at n. 7), I, 144. For a painting by Sebastiano Ittar see Luciana Gallo, *Lord Elgin and Ancient Greek Architecture* (Cambridge, 2009), 39.
59 Cancellieri (cit. at n. 3), 470–72; Fagiolo dell'Arco (cit. at n. 43), 261–2; Anon., *Descrizione dell'Arco Trionfale ed altre decorazioni architettoniche inalzate a Roma nella Piazza del Popolo per solennizzare nel di 3 luglio MDCCC il primo glorioso ingresso nella dominante della santità di Nostro Signore Papa Pio VII felicemente regnante* (Rome, 1800). What appears to be a project by Valadier for the same occasion is illustrated by E. Debenedetti, *Valadier* (Rome, 1985), nos 38, 39. The lavish design includes much sculpture (including huge trophies). Debenedetti points out that no. 38 is stylistically close to a remarkable group of 23 arch designs in Valadier's *Secondo taccuino* (nos 381–404 in her catalogue), though she suggests that the impulse for these came from the Festa della Federazione. For the 1800 and 1814 celebrations, see Luciano Nasto, *Le feste civili a Roma nell'Ottocento* (Rome, 1994), with illustrations of the arches.
60 See the inscription on his monument in the north nave aisle of San Carlo al Corso.
61 For the 1814 celebrations, see Erasmo Pistolesi, *Vita del Santo Padre Pio VII* (Rome, 1824), III, 194–202; Gaetano Giucci, *Storia della vita e del pontificato di Pio VII* (Rome, 1857), II, 101–9. The attribution of the Piazza Sant'Angelo *apparato* to Zappati is made by Pistolesi, but he may be wrong: a view of it in the Praz Collection is signed 'Antonio Luigi, disegnatore; Zappati Tommaso, incisore'. A watercolour in the same collection, also by Luigi Antonini, shows the arch on the bridge of boats: Christophe Beyeler, ed., *Pie VII face à Napoléon* (Château de Fontainebleau, 2015), 218–19.
62 Fagiolo dell'Arco (cit. at n. 43), 236.
63 Fagiolo (cit. at n. 7), I, 151, 175, II, 20; Fagiolo dell'Arco (cit. at n. 43), 355–8; Uwe Westfehling, *Triumphbogen im 19.und 20. Jahrhundert* (Munich, 1977), 35. See also Anon., *Il Trionfo della Clemenza di N. S. Papa Pio IX* (Rome, 1846).
64 Fagiolo (cit. at n. 7), II, 268.
65 Anon., *Descrizione del circo e dell'arco onorario eretti di là da Ponte-Molle pel fausto ritorno in Roma del Sommo Pontefice Pio IX il 5 settembre 1857* (Rome, 1858); Fagiolo dell'Arco (cit. at n. 43), 375–8; Clementina Barucci, *Virginio Vespignani* (Rome, 2006), 224–6.
66 On Poletti, see M. Vaccari et al., *Luigi Poletti architetto* (Bologna, 1992); C. Huemer, 'Rome ca. 1820: An Album of Drawings by Luigi Poletti', *Memoirs of the American Academy at Rome*, 45 (2000), 185–216.
67 Fagiolo dell'Arco (cit. at n. 43), 391; Nasto (cit. at n. 59), 70, n. 33, 98.
68 Fagiolo dell'Arco (cit. at n. 43), 399–400.
69 ibid., 401–3.
70 Mitchell (cit. at n. 11), 15–17.
71 John Shearman, 'The Florentine Entrata of Leo X', *Journal of the Warburg and Courtauld Institutes*, 38 (1975), 136–54. See also D. Moreni, *De ingressu summi pontificis Leonis X Florentiam descriptio Paridis de Grassi* (Florence, 1793); Mitchell (cit. at n. 11), 39–43.
72 Shearman (cit. in the preceding note), 32.
73 Mitchell (cit. at n. 11), 17–19.
74 ibid., 19–25.
75 *The Procession of Pope Clement VII and the Emperor Charles V after the Coronation at Bologna on the 24th February 1530 designed and engraved by Nicolas Hogenberg and now reproduced in facsimile, with an historical introduction by Sir William Stirling Maxwell, Baronet* (Edinburgh, 1875). To the Italian artists said to have worked on the *apparati* (Amico Aspertini, Alfonso Lombardi and Giorgio Vasari) can be added the Flemish Peeter Kempeneer (Pedro de Campaña): Nicole Dacos in *Dictionary of Art*, 17, 895–7.
76 Mitchell (cit. at n. 11), 32–4.

77 Bonner Mitchell, *1598: A Year of Pageantry in Late Renaissance Ferrara*, Binghamton (1990), 38. See also Bonner Mitchell, 'A Papal Progress in 1598', in Wisch and Munshower (cit. at n. 21), I, 119–36; Angelo Rocca, *De Sacrosancto Christi Corpore Romanis Pontificibus iter conficientibus praeferendo Commentarius … Clemente VIII P. M. Ferrariam proficiscente* (Rome, 1599).
78 *The Illustrated Bartsch*, 40 (1982), 175–83, Commentary, pt I (1987), 292–5. For illustrations of the engravings: Anon., *Descrittione de gli apparati fatti in Bologna per la venuta di N. S. Papa Clemente VIII, con gli disegni de gli archi, statue e pitture* (Rome?, 1598).
79 Collins (cit. at n. 55), 46–7.
80 *Luigi Poletti architetto* (cit. at n. 66), 137.
81 *Albo a memoria dell'augusta presenza di Nostro Signore Pio IX in Bologna l'estate dell'anno 1857* (Bologna, 1857); engraving reproduced in *Musei d'Italia – Senigallia: Museo Pio IX e Museo Diocesano* (Bologna, 1991), no. 317b.
82 Barucci (cit. at n. 65), 304–5.
83 Anthony Blunt, *Guide to Baroque Rome* (London, 1982), 253. The old attribution to Michelangelo is discredited: the attribution given here comes from *Guida d'Italia del Touring Club Italiano: Roma e dintorni* (Milan, 1962), 185. On Christina's entry, see Carlo Festini, *I Trionfi della Magnificenza Pontificia celebrati per lo passaggio nelle città e luoghi dello Stato Ecclesiastico e in Roma per lo ricevimento della Maestà della regina di Svetia* (Rome, 1656), 147.
84 The Fontana Paola built on the Janiculum in 1612 to commemorate Paul V's restoration of an ancient aqueduct has been described as a triumphal arch, but with little justification.
85 Wolfgang E. Stöpfel, 'Der Arco Clementino Vanvitellis und die Statue Cornacchinis: ein Ehrenbogen fur Clemens XII in Ancona', *Römisches Jahrbuch fur Kunstgeschichte*, 12 (1969), 216–17.
86 Stöpfel (cit. in the preceding note), 203–21. See also Fabio Mariano, *Architettura nelle Marche dall'età classica al Liberty* (Fiesole, 1995), 446 (with ills 540–41 and 550), who argues that the original intention of the arch was more functional than commemorative.
87 Stöpfel (cit. at n. 85), 215–16; *Guida d'Italia del Touring Club Italiano: Marche* (Milan, 1979), 142; Mariano (cit. in the preceding note), 396 (with ill. 559).
88 Stöpfel (cit. at n. 85), 216–17.
89 ibid., n. 60; Mariano (cit. at n. 86), 396 (with ill. 561). The rear façade, in tufa, was added by Scipione Daretti (1742–92). The papal stemma and inscription were removed during the upheavals of 1799.
90 Stöpfel (cit. at n. 85), 217; S. Andreotti and G. Sbraga, *Subiaco nella seconda metà del settecento* (Subiaco, 1975), 169–70; Collins (cit. at n. 55), 43–6.
91 P. Marconi, *Giuseppe Valadier* (Rome, 1964), 105, 118; E. Debenedetti, *Valadier* (Rome, 1985), 41–2; Collins (cit. at n. 55), 45–6. A much more elaborate arch, with a statue of the Pope on the top, was designed in 1795 by Giovanni Campana, but this was merely a *prova* for the Accademia di San Luca: see Frank Salmon, *Georgian Group Journal*, 1995, 27–8.
92 Stöpfel (cit. at n. 85), 215, n. 60. Aleandri's design is said to have been modified by the *ingegnere* Giuseppe Bertolini.
93 ibid.; for the engraving, see *Musei d'Italia – Senigallia* (cit. at n. 81), no. 361.
94 Barucci (cit. at n. 65), 84–8.
95 J.S. Ackerman, *The Architecture of Michelangelo* (London, 1961), 253. See also G.C. Argan and B. Contardi, *Michelangelo architetto* (Milan, 1990), 350–53.
96 Elisabeth MacDougall, 'Michelangelo and the Porta Pia', *Journal of the Society of Architectural Historians*, 19 (1960), 97–108.
97 F. Borsi et al., *Il Palazzo del Quirinale* (Rome, 1973), 118.
98 Fagiolo dell'Arco (cit. at n. 43), 386; Barucci (cit. at n. 65), 90–98.
99 Barucci (cit. at n. 65), 98.

11

ARCHES FOR CELEBRATIONS IN ITALY

In Rome for persons other than popes

Naturally these were not common. Far the most splendid entry into the city was that of the Emperor Charles V in April 1536. Planning began the previous November. The *via triumphalis* would lead from the so-called Porta Capena (the Porta San Sebastiano), since Charles would approach from the south (after his victory at Tunis), by a new road from the Circus Maximus to the Arch of Constantine. The arches of Constantine, Titus and Septimius Severus were further opened up, and linked by a new avenue, for which many buildings were destroyed (though probably not as many as the 'two hundred' referred to by Rabelais).[1] Vasari tells us a good deal about the decorations, which were supervised by Antonio da Sangallo the Younger, and were largely the work of Florentine artists. The first arch stood at the Porta San Sebastiano: it had chiaroscuro paintings of scenes from Roman history, by Battista Franco, and a giant Romulus. The most splendid was a *quadrifrons* of wood in the Piazza San Marco. Vasari says that he never saw a more superbly proportioned arch. It had four Corinthian columns of silver, with gilded capitals, and eight paintings, which were the work of Francesco Salviati and some young 'Germans' – in other words, Netherlanders. Vasari particularly notes that the pictures by the 'Germans' were ready on time, and attributes this to the copious amounts of wine with which they fired themselves up. On top of the arch a giant figure of Rome was surrounded by the Habsburg Emperors Albert, Maximilian, Frederick and Rudolph, and at the corners were trophies with prisoners.[2] The third arch stood at the entrance to the Borgo.[3]

After the great naval victory over the Turks at Lepanto in 1571, the commander Marcantonio Colonna was welcomed at Rome with a triumph. The Porta San Sebastiano was decorated with coats of arms, festoons, trophies with stucco figures of bound prisoners, and pictures of the battle, and the arches of Constantine, Titus and Septimius Severus were given new inscriptions. The ceiling fresco of the Salone in the Palazzo Colonna, executed in 1675–8 by Giovanni Coli and Filippo Gherardi, shows Colonna's entry into Rome: he is pictured in front of an arch.[4]

As part of the celebrations to welcome Queen Christina of Sweden in 1656, the Barberini family put on a magnificent spectacle in front of their palazzo. Called the *Giostra delle Caroselle*, and held after dark, this included a procession of triumphal chariots, a mock battle, and a fire-breathing dragon. A rectangular area was surrounded with galleries and stands, and the entrance to it was formed by a triumphal arch, which had a single opening flanked by pairs of pilasters, painted decoration simulating reliefs, and statues on the attic.[5]

The 'Chinea'

A speciality of Rome was the annual festivity of the 'Chinea'.[6] The word refers to a white horse or mule. Regarded as a symbol of royal power, this was reputed to have been part of the famous 'Donation' made by Constantine to Pope St Silvester. The gift was repeated annually, on the vigil of the feast of SS. Peter and Paul (28 June), by the Grand Constable of the Kingdom of Naples, who was always a member of the Colonna family. It symbolised the king's obedience to the pope. The festivities always included fireworks, for which magnificent *macchine di gioia* were designed. From 1722 until the ritual was abolished in 1788, it was regularly held in either the Piazza Santi Apostoli (where the Palazzo Colonna is situated) or the Piazza Farnese.

The *apparati* sometimes took the form of triumphal arches. In 1722 the *seconda macchina*, designed by Alessandro Specchi, was an arch in honour of Carlo VI.[7] In 1732 a huge arch was surmounted by a lofty representation of Parnassus, with the Muses surrounding Apollo (compare the Paris arch for the wedding of Louis XIV). An opening in the mountain below framed a Bacchanal. It was intended to symbolise the felicity of the peaceful times provided for Europe by the prudence of the King.[8] In 1745 an arch celebrated the return to Naples of Carlo di Borbone.[9] Between 1751 and 1775 Paolo Posi, who was architect to the Colonna family, designed new *apparati* every year. The first was an arch for 'Ruggero il Normanno' (Roger of Sicily).[10] In 1756 an arch appeared between Etna and Vesuvius.[11] The arch that Posi designed in 1767 is shown in an engraving by Giuseppe Vasi: richly adorned with sculpture, it stood on a stepped podium.[12]

Outside Rome before 1700

In 1494 Charles VIII of France, on his way to the kingdom of Naples, was greeted with arches in various cities. At Pavia several were built, while in Florence an arch at the Palazzo Medici was designed by Pietro Perugino. At Siena one showed the city as belonging to the Virgin Mary, and another showed Charles and Charlemagne. He entered Pisa both in that year and in the next, when an arch and an equestrian statue were erected. Also in 1495 some kind of arch was put up in Milan for the investiture of Ludovico Sforza as Duke.[13]

In 1506 two arches were erected in Naples for Ferdinand of Spain and Germaine of Foix. One showed Mars, Janus and Jacob, and had men tossing coins. However, nobles jealous of those who commissioned them got the route of the procession changed, so they were not properly seen. In the next few years several cities erected arches for Louis XII of France, on his Italian campaigns. For that at Genoa in 1502, see below. In 1507 Milan put up three, one with a Jove who spoke verses to the King. Both Cremona and Milan welcomed Louis with arches in 1509, after his victory over Venice. At Cremona there were five, the principal one having statues of the King's virtues. The four at Milan were left unfinished, though that at the Piazza del Castello had an equestrian statue and paintings of the King's battles. After the expulsion of the French in 1512 Milan welcomed Duke Massimiliano Sforza with an arch which had figures of the four cardinal virtues and Fortune, who recited verses. The entry of Leo X into Florence in 1515 is described in the discussion of papal arches (p. 182).

The Emperor Charles V was honoured with arches by several cities. Those erected at Bologna in 1530 for his coronation by Clement VII feature among papal arches (see pp. 182–3), and those erected for his entry into Genoa in 1529 and 1533 are considered below (p. 196). At Mantua in 1530, where Giulio Romano was in charge, there were two wooden gateways 'in the form of arches' (according to Luigi Gonzaga), decorated with the arms and banners of the Emperor, at the bridgeheads. The first arch in the city, 'in antique form', had eight columns with six statues between them, representing Charles, other Habsburg emperors, and Mantua, the city's mythical founder. The second arch was dedicated to Charles as restorer of peace and justice: Iris (as goddess of war) was put to flight by Mercury.[14] At Messina in 1535 Charles was welcomed after his conquest of Tunis. The artist in charge was Polidoro da Caravaggio. Vasari wrote that he *fece archi trionfali bellissimi* (made most beautiful triumphal arches). A particularly splendid arch stood outside the walls. It is recorded in a detailed description, and two sketches by Polidoro survive. It had eighteen columns, imitating marble, with gilded Tuscan, Ionic and Corinthian capitals and bases. Most unusually, these were arranged in three parallel rows, and supported an entablature which rose into an arch over the centre, surmounted by the royal arms with a huge double eagle held up by winged Victories. On the ends were putti holding the arms of the city. It is suggested that the design shows a reminiscence of the Classical temples of Sicily. Another sketch shows the 'arch' on the Ponte della Dogana: this consisted of four Ionic columns supporting a bold cornice on which is a pedestal supporting a figure of Neptune on a chariot. On pedestals beside the column bases are tritons. Here Siculo-Arab influence is detected. Yet another drawing is identified as 'for the triumphal arches' on this occasion: on the left caryatids hold up the architrave on either side of an opening where a figure sits in front of a perspective of arches, while on the right a putto with a garland and another caryatid flank a niche containing a seated figure.[15]

At Naples, also in 1535, there was an arch dense with statues and paintings, some showing Charles's Turkish victories. Siena put up an arch in 1536, with statues of Faith and Charity (there was also a separate huge equestrian statue by Domenico Beccafumi), and Florence did the same. The arch erected at Rome that year is considered with papal arches (p. 191). In 1541 Milan welcomed Charles, on his way to meet Pope Paul III in Lucca, with four arches, with statues and paintings. Giulio Romano was again in artistic charge. The arches are shown in rather schematic form in engravings in a book by Giovanni Alberto Albicante. The emphasis was on Charles as restorer of the Golden Age. The arch in the Piazza del Duomo, of the Doric order, had an equestrian statue of him trampling a Moor, a Red Indian and a Turk, and reliefs of Habsburg sovereigns. A fragmentary drawing by Giulio shows part of the arch outside the Porta Romana, which was heavily rusticated, with pairs of columns on the piers, flanking niches containing statues; eight more statues on the bridge in front represented the cities of the Milanese state.[16] Charles was also honoured by the Porta Napoli at Lecce, built in 1548 (see p. 152).

Other arches in these years included three at Milan in 1534 for the entry of Christina of Denmark, bride of Duke Francesco Sforza, and one at Florence in 1536 for the marriage of Alessandro de' Medici and Margaret of Austria which had painted buildings in perspective and a gallery for musicians. In 1539 Il Tribolo designed an arch for the wedding of Cosimo I and Eleonora of Toledo, at the Porta del Prato in Florence. It had sculptures and paintings, and a box for musicians who sang the motet *Ingredere* by Francesco Corteccia.[17] A more unusual occasion for such celebration at Florence was the feast of St John the Baptist in 1545, when two arches were erected beside the Arno.

In 1543 Palladio designed two arches at Vicenza to welcome Cardinal Nicolò Ridolfi, appointed Bishop in 1524, but only now making his first visit. The first was in front of the Porta del Castello, and had panels representing the patron saints of the city. The space between the arch and the gate was made to resemble a cave, with statues of rivers. At the end of the street there was another arch, 'bellissimo … con sue architetture', with two similar faces, decorated with statues. No illustrations survive, but there is a description by Donato Giannotti. Zorzi suggests that the second arch was inspired by one designed by Serlio.[18]

In 1548–9 it was Philip of Spain, the son of Charles V, who was greeted with arches in Italian cities. That at Genoa is described below (p. 197). Three went up at Pavia, and four in Milan, with the usual mixture of religious and mythological and historical figures, together with statues of Philip and Charles. In 1549 Cremona and Mantua put up three, and Trent six. In the same year Mantua greeted Catherine of Austria, bride of Duke Francesco Gonzaga, with arches.

In 1556 Bona Sforza, the widow of King Sigismund I of Poland, was welcomed at Padua with an arch designed by Michele Sanmicheli, erected by the Signoria of Venice. It was based on the Arco dei Gavi at Verona – admired at the time not least because of the assumption that it was designed by Vitruvius himself – and was constructed by Alessandro da Bassano, an expert on numismatics and friend of Cardinal Bembo. He designed the 'many varied figures with their motifs', some of which were criticised for lack of historical justification, but the architecture was praised. On either side of the opening were pairs of striated Corinthian columns, the two middle ones supporting a pediment above which was the Lion of St Mark with wings that were some 2 m tall.[19]

For the entry of the Dogaressa Zilia Dandolo Priuli to the Palazzo Ducale at Venice in 1557 the Macellai (butchers' guild) built in the Piazzetta San Marco an arch decorated with pilasters, festoons, trophies, and meat cleavers. Over the opening was the Lion of St Mark; on top on one side were the four theological virtues, and on the other four giants holding swords. The arch was a response to accusations of incongruity aimed at the prominent situation of the Beccaria, the butchers' stalls, alongside.[20]

In 1565 the new Bishop of Vicenza, Matteo Priuli, entered the city through an arch, on each side of which were pairs of Corinthian columns framing paintings, while the attic had pilasters and statues. This arch was designed by Palladio.[21] Two arches were erected at the Rialto in Venice in 1571 to celebrate the victory of Lepanto, but we know little about them.[22] For the arches on the journey of Henri III of France from Poland in 1574, see below (pp. 195–6). For the entry of Maria of Austria in 1581 Vincenzo Scamozzi built two arches at Vicenza. One was based on the Arch of Constantine, the other, at a crossroads, on the *quadrifrons* Arch of Janus at Rome. The first had eight statues above the columns and eight more on top, and the other had eight in niches and eight above. The Janus arch had a vault with a translucent rosone. Both had paintings by Alessandro Maganza.[23]

At Florence elaborate *apparati* continued to be erected for Medici weddings – for Francesco I and Joanna of Austria in 1565, and for Ferdinando I and Christina of Lorraine in 1589. For each an *antiporto* stood before the Porta al Prato. Alessandro Allori was involved in both. In 1565 he designed the architecture, the statues and the paintings, and himself executed three statues, four paintings, and all the ornament. The arch was of the Corinthian order. All the works are lost. Allori was responsible for the arch in 1589 and executed one of the paintings, which survives. The arch was similar to the 1565 one. In front was an open hexagonal courtyard: like the arch this had pilasters with blocky rustication, statues in niches on either side of the opening, and statues above. The large paintings depicted the history of Florence from Roman times to the Medici. The arch and other temporary structures were illustrated in the souvenir book by Raffaello Gualterotti, and in separate engravings.[24]

For the visit of Henri III, en route from Poland to assume the throne of France in 1574, Palladio was commissioned at short notice to design the *apparati*. At the Lido, where the King would disembark, an arch was built, with a loggia on the axis behind it [11.1]. The arch was described as 'in imitation' of that of Septimius Severus. It is best represented in the set of reconstruction drawings made in 1756 for Consul Smith by Antonio Visentini. It was made of wood, covered in canvas painted to imitate marble. Over the inner columns were statues of Victory and Peace, between which was the inscription, with the French royal arms perched above. Over the side openings, on the end, and within the openings were large rectangular paintings to a scheme by Veronese. The loggia (based on the Portico of Octavia at Rome) had ten columns, with

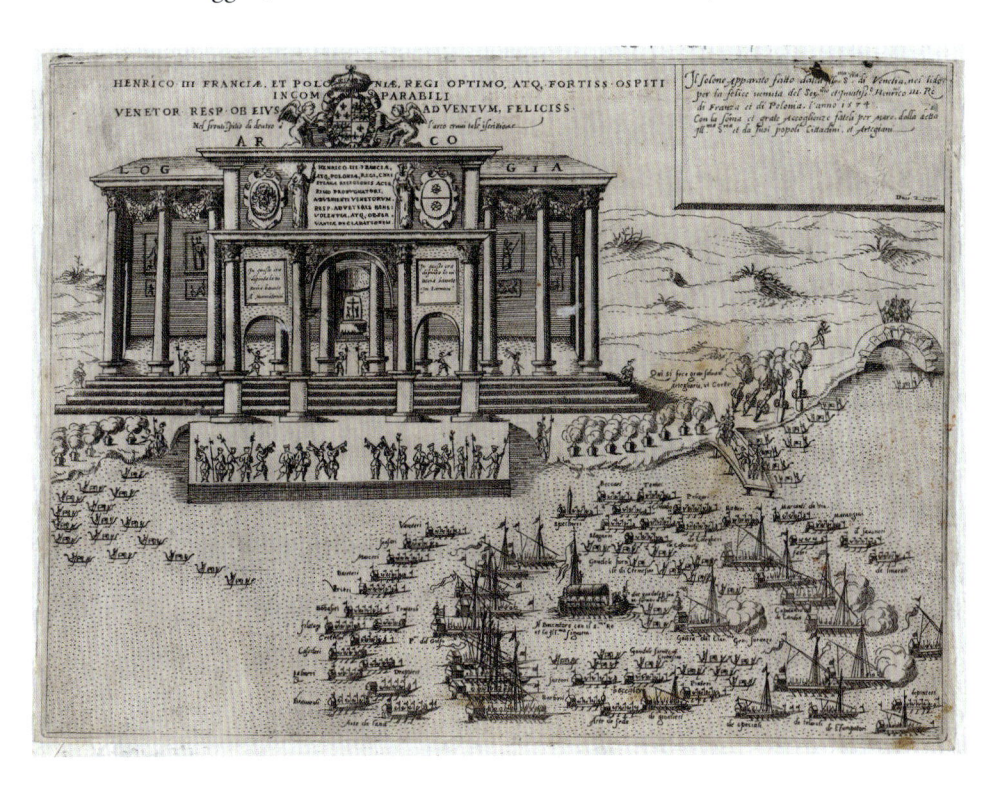

11.1 Arch for visit of Henri III, Venice, 1574. Palladio.

a pediment extending between the second and eighth bays. The end elevations had arches between paired columns.[25]

There were other arches to welcome Henri on this journey. At Treviso three bore symbols and mottoes referring to the King's life. A grandiose one at Padua had representations of his victories in France. There were two at Ferrara, with 'many stucco statues and beautiful pictures'. The arches at Mantua were said to be less fine than those at Ferrara. One was linked to the gallery of the Palazzo Guerrieri, and was crowned with a balustrade on which putti of wood played various instruments. Meanwhile in the gallery real musicians sang and played. Turin suffered from a shortage of money, and the arches had festoons of flowers and foliage with coats of arms.[26]

In 1595 Marino Grimani was elected Doge of Venice. Two years later his wife Morosina Morosini was crowned as Dogaressa. Elaborate decorations included an arch on the Molo at the entrance to the Piazzetta. This too was built by the butchers' guild, to the design of the miniaturist Bernardo Fogari, who consulted the humanist lawyer Attilio Facio. On the outer front there were pairs of Corinthian columns on the piers, framing statues on pedestals of the deities Neptune and Ops. Above were pairs of Composite columns. A statue of Venice on a chariot, other allegorical statues, and paintings of Venetian dominions featured over the opening. Other paintings celebrated the nobility and virtues of the couple. On top, obelisks stood on the corners, and in the centre was a statue of Fame, with two winged Victories. The inner front was similar.[27]

In 1621 Federigo Ubaldo della Rovere, son of Duke Francesco Maria, entered Urbino with his bride Claudia de' Medici. A *theatrum* was built on the Pian del Mercato, incorporating two arches over streets. One had four Corinthian columns, imitating Breccia di Tivoli marble, with capitals and bases imitating bronze. The rest imitated black marble veined with white. On each side was a pedestal, bearing statues of women, one with cornucopia and the other with serpent wand and wheel. The second arch had groups of putti on the pedestals, and four statues. The celebration centred on hopes for an heir, but Federigo died in 1623 leaving only a daughter. The canvas from one arch was stolen for use as mattresses, while the wood served for furniture and even coffins.[28]

Temporary arches in Genoa

Genoa was known in the sixteenth century as 'the painted city' because of its lavishly painted façades, and this liking for display led to equally lavish decorations for entries.[29] In 1502 an arch was erected for Louis XII of France in 'Lombard Early Renaissance style', with an 'arcade of columns' and foliage. Charles V made two entries, in 1529 and 1533. For both Perino del Vaga was commissioned to design the arches. His drawings for the first include two designs. One has a single opening flanked by pairs of attached Doric columns, with a huge double-headed eagle above. The other is a triple arch, of the Ionic order. Over the rectangular side openings are paintings, and above the central opening is a tall attic panel, on either side of which are scrolls with urns on the corners. For the second entry a fine drawing of 1533 shows an arch with two openings, again of the Ionic order. Between the openings is a painting showing the coronation of a warrior (which recalls that of Charles in 1530), and on the attic are three more, separated by terms. The side ones show battles, while in the centre is an enthroned woman with a tiara, representing papal Rome receiving the homage of the faithful. On top is an eagle, flanked by reclining figures with cornucopiae.[30]

When the future Philip II, the son of Charles V, visited Genoa in 1548 the arch at San Siro was adorned by Gian Giacomo Della Porta with sculptures of Philip, Jupiter and Apollo. For Margaret of Austria, in 1599, on her way to marry Philip III of Spain, an arch near the Capo di Faro had a colourful structure imitating marble and bronze, and monochrome paintings, some feigning sculpture. It celebrated the ancestry and achievements of the Habsburgs, with at least thirty statues, fourteen of family members and sixteen of virtues and allegories. The sculptor was Taddeo Carlone, of Genoa, and the designer was Giacomo Mancini, from Montepulciano.

On his way from Madrid to Brussels, in 1633, the Cardinal-Infante Ferdinand was greeted with an arch on the Strada Balbi. It had to be built in less than a month. It was designed by the architect Rocco Pellone, who built a model, while Giovanni Angelo Falcone used workers in *papier mâché* to make moulds for the plaster ornamentation. The principal painter was Domenico Fiasella. The sculptors who made the plaster statues included Martino Rezi. The theme on one side was the greatness of the house of Austria, while the other related to the dispute between the Genoese Republic and the Duke of Savoy, which Fernando resolved in the next year. Within the opening fictive bronze reliefs showed Christopher Columbus, the hero of the Republic, planting the cross in 'India', and presenting a globe and gifts to Ferdinand and Isabella. After the entry these paintings were placed in the Audience Chamber of the Palazzo Ducale.[31]

In the eighteenth and nineteenth centuries

The entry of Charles III into Palermo in 1735 was the occasion of great festivity. The city architect, Niccolo Palma, was mainly responsible for the large and elaborate arches.[32]

The Arco di Lorena in the Piazza dell Libertà in Florence was erected in 1738–40 for the arrival of Franz Stefan of the Habsburg-Lorraine dynasty [11.2]. The architect was Jean-Nicolas Jadot, from Lorraine. The sculptural decoration was added in 1739–59. There are ten Corinthian columns and reliefs of the imperial rule in Italy. On top is an equestrian statue of Franz Stefan by Vincenzo Foggini. With its two colours of stone and elegant detail this arch is outstandingly fine.[33]

In 1768 an unusual arch was built at Alessandria in Piemont to record the visit three years earlier of the King of Sardinia Vittorio Amedeo III and his wife. Designed by Giuseppe Caselli, it is of red stone. The single opening is flanked by attached pilasters, beyond which are freestanding square piers supporting urns. There is a broken pediment, and a tall attic with inscription panel and segmental pediment.

In the same year an exceedingly jolly arch was erected at Catania in Sicily, to celebrate the marriage of Ferdinand I and Maria Carolina of Austria [11.3]. Its name, Porta Ferdinandea, was changed in 1862 to Porta Garibaldi. The arch is built of alternating stripes of black lava and white stone. Curving side projections end in piers crowned with trophies. Over the opening is a pedestal incorporating a clock, which replaced a medallion of Ferdinand and his wife. It is supported by a youth riding a black elephant – the symbol of the town. On either side is a trumpeting angel.

198   THE TRIUMPHAL ARCH

11.2 Arco di Lorena, Florence, 1738–59. Jean Nicolas Jadot.

11.3 Porta Ferdinandea (Garibaldi), Catania, 1768.

11.4 Teatro Politeama, Palermo, 1867–91. G.A. Almeyda.

A splendid arch forms the entrance to the Teatro Politeama in Palermo, also in Sicily, built in 1867–91 by Giuseppe Damiani Almeyda [11.4]. It is fairly plain, but has a magnificent *quadriga* on top, driven by Apollo and Euterpe (1867–74). This is by Mario Rutelli, a pupil of Rodin best known for the fountain in the Piazza dell'Esedra in Rome. The horsemen on either side are by Benedetto Civiletti. The frieze of putti on the attic is also by Rutelli.[34]

Notes

1. For a bird's-eye view, taken from Falda's 1667 plan of Rome, see Marcello Fagiolo (ed.), *La Festa a Roma* (Turin, 1997), II, 20. On the entry, see Maria Luisa Madonna, 'L'ingresso di Carlo V a Roma', in ibid., I, 50–65, who quotes Rabelais.
2. G. Vasari, *Lives of the Painters, Sculptors and Architects* (transl. by Gaston de Vere, London, 1996), II, 111–12. For the 'German' painters, see the Life of Battista Franco, II, 498–9.
3. Roy Strong, *Splendour at Court: Renaissance Spectacle and Illusion* (London, 1973), 94–5. Various drawings of arches have been associated with the entry of Charles V. Some of those in the so-called *Taccuino Senese* were attributed by Hermann Egger to Baldassare Peruzzi, on the assumption that he was involved in designing *apparati* during his mortal illness (*Jahrbuch der kunsthistorischen Sammlungen des allerhöchsten Kaiserhauses*, 23 (1902), 1–44). Egger's theories were taken further by Guglielmo de Angelis d'Ossat, *Capitolium* (1943), 287–94. The attribution to Peruzzi has been refuted by Mircea Toca (*Annali della scuola normale superiore di Pisa* (1971), 161–79): she argues that the drawings of triumphal arches in the *Taccuino* are sketches by Iacopo Meleghino of the *apparati* erected for Charles V. A drawing for an arch in another Sienese sketchbook, attributed by Lynda Fairbairn to Orazio Porta, may be connected with the entry (*Italian Renaissance Drawings from the Collection of Sir John Soane's Museum* (London, 1998), 529). A number of drawings in the Uffizi by Antonio

da Sangallo have been identified as preliminary sketches for the *apparati* (G. Giovannoni, *Antonio da Sangallo il Giovane* (Rome, 1959), 309–12, with figs 327–31). On the inscriptions, see Florence Vuilleumier Laurens and Pierre Laurens, *L'Age de l'inscription: la rhétorique du monument en Europe du XVe au XVIIe siècle* (Paris, 2010), 130–37.
4   On the entry, see Francesco Cancellieri, *Storia de' solenni possessi dei sommi pontifici* (Rome, 1802), 112–18.
5   Fagiolo (cit. at n. 1), I, 70–71.
6   Mario Gori Sassoli, 'La cerimonia della Chinea', in Fagiolo (cit. at n. 1), II, 42–55; see also I, 89–90. The Chinea was important as the occasion for avant-garde Neoclassical architectural designs: see John Harris, 'Le Geay, Piranesi and international neoclassicism in Rome', in D. Fraser et al. (eds), *Essays in the History of Architecture Presented to Rudolf Wittkower* (London,1967), 189–96.
7   Sassoli (cit. in the preceding note), 46.
8   L. Fiorani et al., *Riti, cerimonie, feste e vita di popolo nella Roma dei Papi* (Bologna, 1970), 249, with fig. 106.
9   Fagiolo (cit. at n. 1), I, 18.
10 Sassoli (cit. at n. 6), 46; M. Fagiolo, 'Tra melodrama ed eclettismo: "Macchine" di Paolo Posi, 1751–5', *Psicon*, I (1974), 91–104.
11 Sassoli (cit. at n. 6), 50.
12 Marcello Fagiolo, *Corpus delle Feste a Roma*, II, *Il Settecento e l'Ottocento* (Rome, 1997), 181; Barbara Wisch and Susan Munshower (eds), *'All the World's a Stage…': Art and Pageantry in the Renaissance and Baroque* (University Park, Pa., 1990), pt 2, pl. opp. contents page.
13 For these arches and all erected until 1549 see Bonner Mitchell, *Italian Civic Pageantry in the High Renaissance: a descriptive bibliography of triumphal entries* (Florence, 1979). For most there are neither detailed descriptions nor illustrations, nor are the artists known.
14 M. Tafuri et al., *Giulio Romano* (Cambridge, 1998), 222–3.
15 Strong (cit. at n. 3), 92–4; Lanfranco Ravelli, *Polidoro Caldara da Caravaggio* (Bergamo, 1978), 192–8, 276–8; for other drawings related to triumphal arches, see his nos 209–11 and 213.
16 Tafuri (cit. at n. 14), 224–5.
17 Henry W. Kaufmann, 'Art for the wedding of Cosimo de' Medici and Eleonora of Toledo (1539)', *Paragone* 243 (1970), 52–67.
18 G. Zorzi, *Le opere publicche e i palazzi privati di Andrea Palladio* (Venice, 1965), 167–9. Serlio's design is in his Book IV, published in 1537.
19 Lina Padoan Urban, 'Apparati scenografici nelle feste Veneziane cinquecentesche', *Arte veneta*, 23 (1969), 148; Maximilian L. S. Tondro, 'The first temporary triumphal arch in Venice (1557)', in J. R. Mulryne and Elizabeth Goldring (eds), *Court Festivals of the European Renaissance* (Aldershot, 2002), 335–62.
20 Eric Langenskjöld, *Michele Sanmicheli* (Uppsala, 1938), 30; Luigi Cini, 'Passaggio della regina Bona Sforza per Padova nell'anno 1556', in *Relazioni tra Padova e la Polonia: Studi in onore dell'Università di Cracovia nel VI centenario della sua fondazione* (Padua, 1964), 27–65; Paul Davies and David Hemsoll, *Michele Sanmicheli* (Milan, 2004), 303–4, 374–5.
21 Zorzi (cit. at n. 18), 170–71.
22 Padoan Urban (cit. at n. 19), 148.
23 Franco Barbieri and Guido Beltramini, *Vincenzo Scamozzi* (Vicenza, 2003), 252–3. The arches are known from a contemporary description. An arch of 1608 on the Campo Marzio has been attributed to Scamozzi, but is now attributed to Ottavio Bruto Revese (ibid., 542).
24 Raffello Gualterotti, *Descrizione del regale apparato per le nozze della serenissima Madama Cristina di Lorena Moglie del serenissimo Don Fernando Medici* (Florence, 1589); Simona Lecchini Giovannoni, *Alessandro Allori* (Turin, 1991), 64, 76, 223–4, 273–5; James Saslow, *The Medici Wedding of 1589: Florentine Festival as Theatrum Mundi* (New Haven/London, 1996); Andrea Daninos, *Firenze 1589: un modello ritrovato per gli apparati delle nozze di Ferdinando I de' Medici e Cristina di Lorena* (Florence, 2000); Henri Zerner, 'The visual experience of Renaissance festivals', in J. R. Mulryne et al. (eds), *Europa Triumphans* (Aldershot, 2004), I, 84–91. Saslow (191) is mistaken in saying that 'the only original arch decoration to survive' is the painting of Christina welcomed aboard the ship *Capitana* by Don Pietro de' Medici, by Giovanni Cosci.
25 H. Burns et al., *Andrea Palladio 1508–1580* (London, 1975), 149–50; P. de Nolhac and A. Solerti, *Il Viaggio in Italia di Enrico III, re di Francia, e le feste a Venezia, Ferrara, Mantova e Torino* (Turin, 1890), 98–9; L. Puppi, *Andrea Palladio* (London, 1975), 406–8; Wolfgang Wolters, 'Le architetture venete erette al Lido per l'ingresso do Enrico III a Venezia nel 1574', *Boll. del Centro Internazionale di Studi di Architettura Andrea Palladio*, 21 (1979), 273–89; Egon Verheyen, 'The Triumphal Arch on the Lido: on the reliability of eyewitness accounts', in Karl-Ludwig Selig and Elizabeth Shears, *The Verbal and the Visual* (New York, 1990), 213–23.
26 De Nolhac and Solerti (cit.in the preceding note), 86, 161, 172–3, 181–2, 195–6.
27 Padoan Urban (cit. at n. 19), 145–55; Edward Muir, *Civic Ritual in Renaissance Venice* (Princeton, N.J., 1981), 293–8.
28 Peter Davidson, 'The Theatrum for the entry of Claudia de' Medici and Federigo Ubaldo della Rovere into Urbino, 1621', in Mulryne and Goldring (cit. at n. 19), 311–34.
29 George L. Grose, 'Between Empire and Republic: triumphal entries into Genoa during the sixteenth century', in Wisch and Munshower (cit. at n. 12), I, 188–256; Maria Ines Aliverti (ed.), 'Festivals in Genoa in the sixteenth and seventeenth centuries', in *Europa Triumphans* (cit. at n. 24), 217–370.
30 Elena Parma, *Perino del Vaga: tra Raffaello e Michelangelo* (Milan, 2001), 200–203, 328.
31 For these entries, see Lauro Magnani, 'Temporary architecture and public decoration: the development of images', in *Europa Triumphans* (cit. at n. 24), 250–52. For the 1633 arch see *idem*, '*Novus orbis emergat*: iconografie columbiane per un arco trionfale', *Columbeis* 3 (1988), 203–14.

32 Pietro La Placa, *La reggia in trionfo* (Palermo, 1736), with engravings by Giuseppe Vasi.
33 Roberta Roani Villani, 'La decorazione plastica dell'Arco di Porta San Gallo a Firenze', *Paragone* 37 (1986), 53–67. Franz's entry was commemorated by a medal by Lorenzo Maria Weber, and a lead relief by Balthasar Moll (in the Unteres Belvedere, Vienna).
34 Rutelli, whose father was British, did the war memorial at Aberystwyth.

12

ENGLAND AND SCOTLAND IN THE SIXTEENTH AND SEVENTEENTH CENTURIES

England

The earliest arches erected in England since the departure of the Romans seem to have been the two which formed part of the decorations of buildings put up at Greenwich in 1527. These were to house the entertainment which Cardinal Wolsey arranged to welcome the French ambassadors who came to negotiate a marriage between Princess Mary and either François I himself or his son. They consisted of a banqueting hall and a 'disguising theatre' (for masked revels), and stood in the tiltyard. Unfortunately no illustrations survive, but there are several descriptions. At the end of the banqueting hall, leading to the theatre, stood a triumphal arch, 'fatto a l'anticha', with three entrances. Above it was a gallery for musicians. The decoration of the arch (which was of timber and canvas) included, along with 'Gargills and Serpentes', the royal arms, Greek words, and busts of emperors. The last must surely be the 'vj antique hedds gilt silveryd and paintyd' for which Giovanni da Maiano was paid. They were presumably similar to the terracotta roundels of emperors that he did for Hampton Court. The builder of the arch was George Lovekin, who had been involved with the decorations of the Field of Cloth of Gold in 1520. As Giovanni da Maiano was also paid 'for drawing the pictures', it seems likely that he was responsible for the overall design.[1] The painting and gilding were in the hands of John Browne (also involved at the Field of Cloth of Gold) and the Italian Vincent Volpe. On the back of the arch was a large painting of the siege of Thérouanne by Hans Holbein.

A second arch stood in the disguising theatre. It had a single opening, and was also painted by Browne and Volpe. Above the opening were busts of 'Hercules, Scipio, Iulius, Pompei and other such conquerors' – more of Giovanni da Maiano's 'antique hedds'. Inside the opening were several figures 'de mezzo rilevo', apparently in papier maché. The Venetian Gasparo Spinelli was amazed that so splendid a 'machina' could have been put up so quickly. The arches were repaired (by artists who included Giovanni da Maiano) in October 1527, in preparation for the reception of another French embassy.[2]

A drawing by Holbein survives which shows Apollo and the Muses seated above a triumphal arch, and this has been associated with the 'marvellous cunning pageant' of Apollo and the Muses commissioned by the Hanseatic merchants for the entry to the

City of London of the coronation procession of Anne Boleyn in 1533. The drawing may just be a record of the pageant, but it is possible that Holbein himself designed it. Only the upper part of the arch is shown. It has three openings, with flattish arches, the central one higher, separated by pilasters. The vault is coffered, and all surfaces are elaborately decorated. There is no entablature, and the nine Muses sit or stand above a cornice, with Apollo seated in a central tabernacle above a fountain of white marble which ran with wine, against a backdrop of the twin peaks of Helicon. The figures were real, and greeted Anne with poetry, but the rest (except perhaps the fountain) must have been, as usual, painted canvas on a timber frame.[3]

A drawing in the Victoria and Albert Museum shows an arch which seems to be an allegory of the apotheosis of Henry VIII [12.1]. Dated to not long before his death in 1547, it is signed by Robert Pyte, an engraver to the Royal Mint. It has a rectangular opening, receding like a stage set, and two storeys above. The frieze of the second storey and the panelled attic above are copied from Book IV of Serlio's treatise, published in 1537. The drawing was probably intended to be engraved.

The coronation procession of Queen Mary in 1553 passed through 'very high [and] stately gates'.[4] It was agreed that the finest arch was that put up by the Genoese merchants in Fenchurch Street. No illustrations survive, but the arches were described by Giulio Raviglio Rosso. The Genoese arch was in the Corinthian order, and was painted with 'Sacrifices, Battles, History and Architecture … as if in marble', together with festoons of foliage, fruit and flowers, and figures. On each side was a Latin inscription. Rosso's comparison of the arch with ancient Roman ones led Colvin to suggest that it may have been tripartite. He refers to Perino del Vaga's designs for the arches erected at Genoa for Charles V in 1529 and 1533, pointing out that it was at Genoa that 'the transformation of the late medieval joyeuse entrée … into the revived trionfo romano can be observed' (see p. 196). Rosso's description of the arch of the Florentines refers to 'the column', which caused Colvin to compare the arch erected for the entry of the Archduke of Austria to Antwerp in 1594, in which a single column stood on the attic. He concluded that these two arches 'must have provided thousands of Englishmen with their first sight of the classical orders properly handled in the Italian manner'. Four of the 'pageants' set up for the coronation of Elizabeth in 1558 took the form of arches. One had

12.1 Robert Pyte, design for an arch to Henry VIII, not long before 1547 (Victoria and Albert Museum).

ENGLAND AND SCOTLAND IN THE SIXTEENTH AND SEVENTEENTH CENTURIES 203

columns, capitals and groups of young people. The fourth, at Cheapside, had two 'mounts', each with a youth sitting on it, and labels to explain the difference.[5]

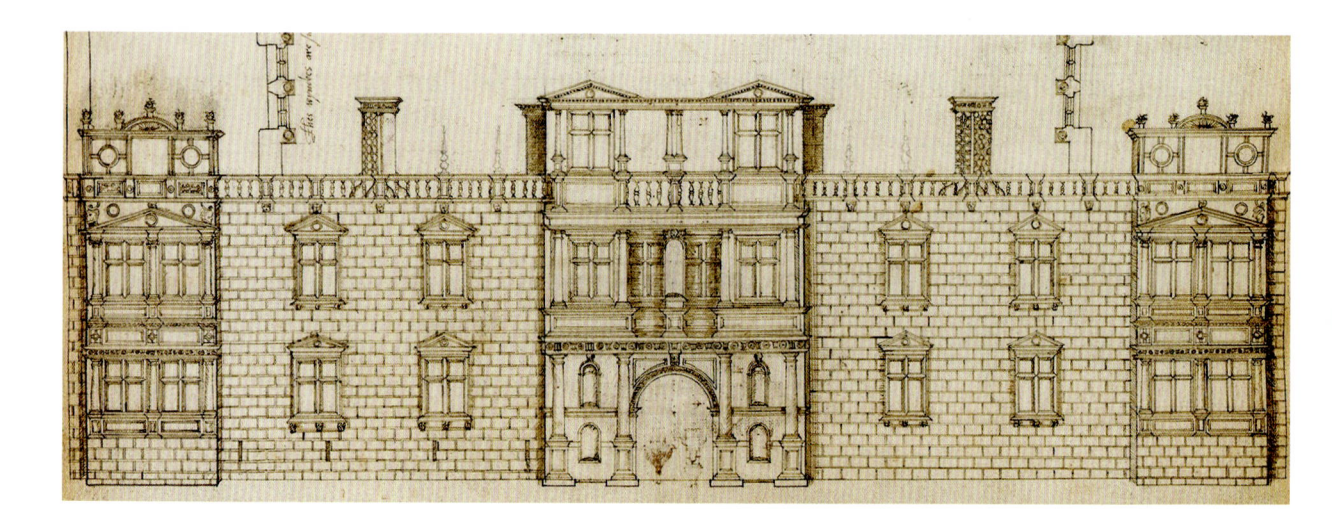

The first permanent building to show the influence of the triumphal arch was Somerset House in London, built for Protector Somerset in 1547–52 [12.2]. Summerson described its gateway as 'a development of the triumphal arch theme, somewhat on the lines of the temporary structures built for state entries on the continent', and compared the arch erected by the English merchants at Antwerp for the entry of Prince Philip (the future Philip II) of Spain in 1546, published by Cornelius Grapheus in 1550. Girouard points out that 'the classical features of the gatehouse were inspired by, but did not copy, Roman triumphal arches as recorded in Serlio's third book', but the Victories in the spandrels must derive from the Antwerp arches, as Serlio did not show them. Similarities of detail even led him to suggest that the designs might have had 'a common source', though we do not know who was responsible for either. Somerset House was demolished in 1776, but John Thorpe's drawing shows three superimposed orders. At the lowest level the central arched opening was set between wide expanses of wall which were flanked by Doric columns, and between these were niches placed one above the other. The upper storeys were much less purely classical. Summerson claims that the gatehouse was 'unquestionably one of the most influential buildings of the English Renaissance'.[6]

The motif of superimposed orders on a frontispiece to emphasise the entrance was particularly popular. The earliest example after Somerset House was Kirby Hall, Northamptonshire, where the porch, dated 1572, has Ionic pilasters on the ground floor and Corinthian half-columns above [12.3]. The third storey oddly has seven small Corinthian columns below a curved gable. Other sixteenth-century examples include Burghley House (1583), Cobham Hall (1591–4) and Stonyhurst (*c.* 1595).[7]

Examples of the use of triumphal arch type gateways of especial interest are the Gates of Virtue and Honour at Gonville and Caius College, Cambridge.[8] The college was refounded in 1558 by John Caius, a physician who had taught Greek at the University of Padua and travelled in Italy and the Netherlands. He devised the scheme by which the student entered the college by the simple Porta Humilitatis (subsequently moved), then passed through the Porta Virtutis (1565–9) into the court, dedicated to

12.2 Somerset House, 1547–52, drawing by John Thorpe (Sir John Soane's Museum).

12.3 Kirby Hall, Northamptonshire, 1572.

Sapientia, before going out to the Schools, and graduation, through the Porta Honoris (1573–5) [12.4]. We are told that Caius himself dictated the *forma et effigies* of the Gate of Honour to the *architectus*. This was presumably the same man who made Caius's tomb in the college chapel, Theodore Haveus (Theodor de Have), a native of the Duchy of Cleves, who may (like so many others) have come to England as a Protestant refugee. The gate is set into the wall on the south side of the court. Its north (inner) side has pairs of attached Ionic columns on either side of the opening, which is four-centred (a curious Gothic reminiscence, which suggests that a local mason was responsible). Between the columns are blank perspectival niches with tondi above. The southern (outer) side is similar, except that the order is Doric, and has pilasters rather

12.4 Gonville and Caius College, Cambridge, Gate of Honour, 1573–5. John Caius and Theodore de Have.

THE TRIUMPHAL ARCH

than half-columns. Above the arch is a miniature temple front, with four Corinthian columns supporting a pediment, on top of which is a hexagonal, domed structure bearing a sundial. On the corners are obelisks. Nickson suggests that the form of the gate may be based on the arch erected by the Spanish merchants for the entry of Prince Philip into Antwerp in 1549 (see above). This also has a temple-like structure over the central opening, and obelisks on the corners, but the similarity is not close. Girouard sees possible influence also from the design for a Corinthian temple in Serlio's Book IV. He points out that the temple fronts on the arch are the only known examples in Elizabethan architecture.[9]

The Gate of Virtue is described by Girouard as less inventive and accomplished than the gate of Honour. Its lower part has an arch, round-headed this time, with Victories in the spandrels, one holding a wreath and palm branch, the other a money-bag and cornucopia.[10] On either side pairs of Ionic pilasters frame plain stonework. The effect is more correctly classical than that of the other gate. The mason was probably Humfrey Lovell, who had worked for the Duke of Somerset in 1551 and became Master of the Royal Works in 1564.[11] Nickson analyses Caius's symbolic scheme in terms of Roman, Christian and contemporary moral pedagogy. Although there is no direct evidence for Caius's knowledge of the symbolism of contemporary 'joyous entry' arches, the dedication of his gates to Virtue and Honour clearly echoes their eulogistic programmes, although in this case with hortatory rather than celebratory purpose.[12]

Other architectural examples of the use of the triumphal arch motif dating from around the 1570s include the enclosed garden seat built for the visit of Queen Elizabeth to Kenilworth Castle in 1575, which has Doric pilasters on either side of the opening, with niches between them; the loggia at Slaugham Place, Sussex, with its three equal coffered openings, the central one projecting; and the arch at Winwick Manor House, Northamptonshire, whose opening is flanked by pairs of Roman Doric freestanding columns.[13]

At about this time the triumphal arch became a frequent model for church monuments. It is remarkable that what must be one of the earliest is also unique in England, and paralleled only by Giulio Romano's monument at Mantua to Gerolamo Andreasi, who died in 1534 (see p. 158). This is the monument to Richard Jervoise in All Saints' Church, Chelsea [12.5]. Jervoise died in 1563, aged twenty-seven. His monument consists of a freestanding arch, of painted stone, about 3 m high and 2.5 m wide. Architecturally it is quite plain, but its surfaces are covered with rather idiosyncratic decoration, in painted shallow relief, of a type associated with the French architect and sculptor Alan Maynard. Originally the monument stood within the arch between the chancel and the northeast chapel, and until 1819 it had a tomb-chest set within the opening. This bore no inscription: the Latin epitaph is on the inner side of the piers. In 1784 the tomb was moved to one side to prop up the collapsing arch. After the wrecking of the church in the Second World War it was rebuilt within the western arch of the chapel. Jervoise was a lawyer, and the reason for this type of monument is hard to guess. Adam White suggests that it might have been intended to represent the gate of heaven.[14]

Two common types of monument are based on the triumphal arch. One is placed against a wall, and has a blank arch set between attached columns and an attic above. Sometimes the columns are freestanding, and support a canopy. A more elaborate type

12.5 All Saints, Chelsea, tomb of Richard Jervoise, died 1563.

12.6 All Saints, Turvey, Bedfordshire, tomb of Lord Mordaunt, 1571–5. Theodor de Have.

has a freestanding canopy, often tripartite. A particularly fine example, though with a single arch, is the monument to the first Lord Mordaunt at All Saints, Turvey, in Bedfordshire [12.6]. Set within the arch between the chancel and southeast chapel, it has pairs of fluted Doric columns supporting a bold entablature. The spandrels contain Victories. The tall attic bears the coat of arms, and is crowned by a pediment, supported on caryatids. Beneath the opening is a sarcophagus, with the effigy on it. The monument was probably erected in 1571–5. Pevsner's attribution to 'Thomas Kirby' is now discounted, in favour of Theodore Haveus (see above).[15] The monument to Sir Christopher Hatton in Old St Paul's Cathedral, of *c.* 1591, was similar, but freestanding, with an obelisk on either side.

The first type described above is represented by several examples at Westminster Abbey, including that of John, Lord Russell (d. 1584), where the arch has a single freestanding column on either side and female figures in the spandrels holding wreaths and branches, and the even grander one to Mildred, Lady Burghley (d. 1589), and her daughter

12.7 John Bluck, active 1791–1831, St. Nicholas Chapel Westminster Abbey, 1812.

Anne, Countess of Oxford, which has pairs of columns under projecting entablatures, and pairs of columns flanking a smaller arch in the attic [12.7].[16] Adam White compares this type with similar wall-monuments in the Netherlands, of the mid-16th century, pointing out that those are usually smaller and often set high up on the wall.

The tripartite form of monument was especially useful when three figures were to be commemorated, as for example on the wall-monument in Westminster Abbey to Sir Richard Pecksall (d. 1571). Here Sir Richard kneels in the central, taller opening, while his two wives kneel in the side openings.[17]

The question arises of the source and significance of this type of monument. It seems likely that the Netherlandish examples derive from the numerous temporary arches erected in the Low Countries in the sixteenth century, whether directly or via engravings, and the English examples may derive from them in the same way. Clearly the form appealed to the spirit of the age, as it allowed for the inclusion of recumbent or kneeling figures, with conspicuous displays of heraldry and allegorical motifs, set within a framework of fashionably up-to-date classicism. What is less clear is the extent to which the 'triumphal' connotations of the form were significant to the commissioning patrons and the artists, as there appears to be a lack of any direct evidence. When a tomb commemorates a man of military distinction, one may easily suppose a connection, but these are comparatively rare. The obvious explanation is that the arch symbolises triumph over death, but this is not made explicit.

The coronation procession through the City of London was begun by Richard II in 1377. It had an important symbolic function: the new monarch was not just ingratiating himself with the City merchants, but showing himself to the common people.

Soon after James I was proclaimed King of England in 1603, the City of London decided that there should be a series of arches set up for his progress through its area. The City itself commissioned Stephen Harrison, 'Joyner and Architect', to design five arches, and two others were to be erected by the Dutch and Italian merchants. We are particularly well informed about the Dutch arch. The Dutch must have offered to help in spring 1603, and work began in April, with the entry due in July. However, an outbreak of plague caused the entry to be postponed until 15 March 1604. The incomplete arches were left in place, and work began again on the Dutch arch in February. It was completed on the day before the entry.[18]

The five City arches were in almost the same places as those put up for Elizabeth in 1559. In 1604 Harrison published a book containing engravings (by William Kip) of all the arches. The dedication is dated 16 June. In his endnote Harrison tells the reader that the purpose of the 'limmes' – the images – was to preserve the arches 'for ever', now that they were 'lately disioynted and taken in sunder'.[19] The poets Thomas Dekker and Ben Jonson were (despite their mutual hostility) responsible for the iconography and poetical tributes at the City's arches.[20]

These arches, described by Girouard as 'wild but not necessarily degenerate descendants of the Antwerp arches of 1549', incorporated plenty of classical architectural detail.[21] For example, Harrison tells us that the Londinium arch derived 'from the Tuscana', since the Tuscan column, as the strongest, was the best to support the remarkable model of the City (14 m wide) on top [12.8]. Nevertheless, the overall effect was one of characteristically 'Jacobean' surfeit of decoration. The Londinium arch stood in Fenchurch Street. About 12 m high, it had two openings, between which was a figure of 'Thamesis'. Above them were galleries, each containing three live figures in costume, and also 'loud music' of 'Waites and Hault-boyes'. The speakers were Thamesis and Genius. Ben Jonson had arranged that the arch should be covered with a silk curtain painted to represent a cloud. This was drawn at the King's approach, to symbolise his driving away the mists over the City.

In Cheapside stood two arches. The 'Nova Felix Arabia' arch had three openings, the central one square-headed. Above the side ones were tall obelisks. The 'new and happy Arabia' was Britain. On the front of the large central painting was a fountain which ran milk, wine and balm at the King's approach. Again the galleries contained musicians and singers. The 'Hortus Euporiae' (garden of plenty) arch was appropriately in the form of a summer arbour, its artificial fruits and flowers watered by a 'little Conduit'. The two cascades ran down steps. Three domes were made of trellis, bearing fruit. Here 'Sylvanus' made a speech, and nine choristers of St Paul's accompanied their singing on viols and other instruments. The arch in Fleet Street was called 'Cosmos Neos', or 'New World'. Its form was similar to that of 'Nova Felix Arabia', but here the side openings were set in semicircular turrets. Freestanding Corinthian columns flanked the main opening, and others above framed a square panel in

12.8 James I's coronation entry into London, 1604. Londinium Arch, Fenchurch Street, with model of the city (Stephen Harrison, *The Arches of Triumph …* (London, 1604)).

which was set a globe which moved. Harrison's fifth arch was near Temple Bar, and was called 'Templum Iani', 'The Temple of Janus'. About 21 m high, this had pairs of freestanding Composite columns on either side of the single opening, and four pairs of Composite columns at the level above. Harrison explained that 'as our work begun with Rusticke [i.e. the Tuscan order of the Londinium arch], so did wee think it fit that this our Temple should end with the famous Columne', viz. Composite, as on the Arch of Titus. Above the upper level were the royal arms, and higher still a four-faced head of Janus in a roundel. The walls were 'of brass', the pillars 'silver', the capitals and bases 'gold'. Within the 'temple' was an altar which the 'Flamen Martialis' (priest of Mars) censed.

Between the Londinium arch and Nova Felix Arabia arches were the Italian one, in Gracechurch Street, and 'the Pegme [pageant] of the Dutchmen … built by the Belgians', in Cornhill near the Royal Exchange. We are especially well informed about the latter.[22] It was designed by Conraet Jansen, a joiner who came to London in 1567 as a Protestant refugee, to a programme designed by the minister of the Dutch Church and others, including Jacob Cool, who had a particular interest in Roman triumphs, having written in 1589 a book (never published) with the title *Fasti Triumphorum*. Jansen considered the site offered by the City too narrow. Another problem was that the English and Italians had hired the best City painters, so the Dutch had to engage painters from Antwerp, including Daniel de Vos, whose father Martin had worked on arches for Antwerp entries in 1582 and 1594. The arch was 25 m high, 11 m broad, and 7 m deep. The lower stage at least was more classical than any of Harrison's, with its three openings and freestanding pairs of Corinthian columns, which had linked entablatures and freestanding bases. The columns on the front resembled black marble, those on the back red, and all the capitals were gold. The front was intended to show James as a Protestant ruler who owed everything to God's providence. Below a painting of the seated King was a gallery in which sat seventeen girls holding coats of arms, and also twelve trumpeters, four drummers and four flautists. The Latin inscription was based on those of the Arches of Septimius Severus and Constantine. Above the picture of the King was a 'pediment' framed by two dolphins. The reverse of the arch celebrated the partnership of the Dutch and English in crafts, navigation and trade; the main painting showed the coast from Dover to Thames, with ships. According to Gilbert Dugdale's eyewitness account, the King particularly admired the Dutch arch, and 'smilde looking toward it', which must have been a change from the grumpy silence with which he endured most of the spectacle. Dugdale wrote 'it was so goodly top and top many many stories, and so hie as it seemd to fall forward'.[23] At the arch a young scholar made a Latin speech, and the music went on all day. At night torches and braziers illuminated the seventeen coats of arms, and were also put into the four obelisks on top, behind holes covered in coloured glass.

The Italian arch, also 'of their own invention', was easily the most classical [12.9]. According to the Venetian ambassador, Nicolo Molin, it 'certainly came first, both for the excellence of its design and for the painting which adorned it', and Dugdale praised its 'hight, strength and quallitie', saying that the Italians had 'spared no spending'. Jacob Cool thought it 'on the small side', but beautiful despite there being so few Italian merchants. The single opening had pairs of Corinthian columns on either side, with linked entablatures and bases. Over the opening there was no entablature, but the spandrels housed females holding cornucopiae, and the royal arms occupied the centre. The attic above this had pairs of smaller columns on either side of a large painting which represented James on horseback, receiving a sceptre from Henry VII. The upper part of the arch was decorated with statues (not live figures) and obelisks. Virgilian quotations abounded. Harrison tells us that during the procession three of the conduits 'ran Claret wine very plenteously', and that the music helped it run down into bellies.

Ten years after James's 'entry' Christian IV of Denmark visited England, and was welcomed in the City by decorations which included a 'magnificent triumphal arch' at Old Change. It had two 'entry-ways', gilt columns, banners and shields, and maritime iconography. A figure of Concord was let down in a throne to the lower part of the arch, to address the two kings. For the expense of the entry the City companies were asked to pay £1,000.[24]

The annual Lord Mayor's Show in London involved the use of 'pageants', but there does not seem to be any evidence for these including arches.[25] We are told that an arch was put up in the Inns of Court in 1616 for the future Charles I's investiture as Prince of Wales, but we know nothing about it except the Latin inscription.[26] A list of works executed for Charles I in the year 1625 includes a payment to the German painter Francis Cleyn for 'all manner of drawings for ye Arch Triumphall', under the supervision of Inigo Jones. This may have been for the reception of Henrietta Maria, on her arrival in England.[27]

For the coronation in 1626 of Charles I five arches, described by the Venetian ambassadors as 'most superb', were erected in the City. The carver Gerard Christmas was paid for three 'pageants', which no doubt refers to three of the City's arches. Once again we are particularly well informed about the arch erected by the Dutch (assisted by the French and Italians). It had first been proposed for the entry of the King after his marriage in 1625, but the idea was then adapted for the coronation. To provide more time than they had had in 1603–4, it was decided in April to build the arch at the Dutch Church in Austin Friars. The 'concept' was the responsibility of Jacob Cool (again) and the banker Philip Jacobs; the architect was Bernard Janssen ('surveyor' of Northumberland House and Audley End); the principal painter was Francis Cleyn (see above); and the chief poet was Ben Jonson. As Grell says, 'they were going for the best that money could buy'. Plague stopped work in July, and a watchman was set to guard what had been erected in Gracechurch Street, but work resumed in January 1626. In May it was announced that the entry had been called off. Almost £1,000 had been spent. In June 1628 the canvas paintings were sold off at auction. The ones

12.9 James I's entry, Italian Arch (Harrison, *The Arches*).

intended for the front showed Britain and Neptune above, and Charles and Henrietta Maria below, while the back would have showed Sapientia. There were no longer any allusions to Protestantism, and little emphasis on Anglo-Dutch relations, which had deteriorated.[28] The official excuse for the cancellation of the procession was plague, but it was really to save money. The arches had to be taken down, to the great annoyance of all, and especially of course the City. We have no description of the City's arches, but Christmas's other work makes it likely that they were in the style of Harrison's arches.[29]

Another abortive project under Charles I was the replacement of the old gateway of Temple Bar in the Strand, proposed by the Privy Council in 1636. Inigo Jones made a remarkable design for a huge tripartite triumphal arch filling the width of the street [12.10]. Its elevation took the form of a square of 60 feet, the lower part 36 feet (11 m) high and the attic 24 feet (7 m) – a proportion of 3:2. The height of the columns was also 24 feet. Harris and Higgott point out that by improving the proportions of his models, the Arches of Septimius Severus and Constantine, 'Jones has exercised himself as the modern Vitruvius'.[30] Jones's elevational drawing shows the spaces over the side arches completely filled with rectangular reliefs showing a seated emperor with a captive brought before him, and a standing emperor above a river god, in front of an arch, while a hovering winged figure holds a wreath over his head. In the spandrels of the central opening are flying Victories holding wreaths. Above the columns, at attic level, are statues. The blank central panel would have been for the inscription; on either side of it are circular reliefs with symbolic features labelled *LAETITIA PUBLICA* and *HILARITAS PUBLICA* ('Public rejoicing' and 'Public hilarity'). A note by Jones indicates that these were based on Roman coins.

12.10 Arch for Temple Bar, proposed 1636, drawing by Inigo Jones.

Jones also made drawings for the other two circular reliefs, one showing men rowing two boats and the other showing goods being unloaded, to represent shipping and commerce. On top of the arch stood four more statues, with an elaborate coat of arms in the centre. A further drawing shows an equestrian statue in profile, presumably an alternative proposal. Jones also made a drawing of the brick structure of the arch, and this has a shaped pedestal on top, obviously for the equestrian statue. This drawing, dated 1638, corresponds in its proportions not with Jones's elevation but with one by his pupil John Webb, where the proportions between the lower part of the arch and the attic are not 3:2 but 2:1. The order is now Composite rather than Corinthian. This elevation shows circular panels over the side arches and rectangular ones on the attic, all blank. On the corners of the attic stand male figures

12.11 Charles II's coronation entry into London, 1661, painting by Dirck Stoop (Museum of London).

holding a trident and a rudder, and the central pedestal has the equestrian statue. Webb's design is less elegant than Jones's. Harris and Higgott suggest that Jones might have handed the project over to Webb. Had the new Temple Bar been built in this form, it would have been an astonishing assertion of the King's absolutist magnificence, right at the western entrance to the City of London.[31]

It is not surprising that the coronation of Charles II in 1661 should have been celebrated with the greatest splendour. The King himself decided to have the traditional 'entry' procession on the previous day, 22 April [12.11]. On that day the spectators were able to buy a sort of 'souvenir programme', in the form of John Ogilby's *The Relation of His Majesty's Entertainment passing through the City of London to his Coronation*. Later Ogilby published a more substantial account, in which he wrote that the City imitated the ancient Romans, who on the return of emperors erected arches of marble, 'which though we by reason of shortness of Time, could not equal in Materials, yet do ours far exceed theirs in Number, and stupendous Proportions'.[32] There were four arches, and Ogilby tells us that they were designed jointly by Peter Mills (formerly Bricklayer to the City of London) and 'another Person, who desired to have his name conceal'd'. This is generally identified as Sir Balthasar Gerbier, son of a Huguenot émigré to Holland, who, as well as working as an architect, was a courtier, diplomat and miniature painter.[33] Gerbier was in Antwerp in 1634 when his friend Rubens must have been making his designs for the 1635 'Pompa Introitus' (see pp. 250–5), and in a letter written in the next year he referred to the 'many triumphant arches' erected for it. Four drawings for the arches in the RIBA collection are attributed to him. These were engraved (with more elaborate detail) by David Loggan for Ogilby's book.[34] Gerbier's desire for anonymity might be explained by the fact that he was excluded from the Court because he had been willing to work for Parliament. In his *A Brief Discourse concerning the three chief principles of Magnificent Building* (1662) he wrote 'that divers judicious persons will not deny, that the excellency of the several Triumphal Arches Erected in the City of London consist not in their bulk' (p. 42). This has been taken as covert self-congratulation.

The first arch stood in Leadenhall Street, and represented 'The Return of the Monarchy'. It had Doric columns on either side of the opening, and the attic had in the middle an arch of the same size as the one below, containing a figure of the King, between figures of James I and Charles I. Smaller arches at the sides of the attic revealed glimpses of ruins, to show the disorder of the kingdom. At the top were the royal arms. The associated 'pageant' showed Charles putting Usurpation (i.e. Cromwell) to flight. The second arch stood near the Exchange in Cornhill, and represented 'Loyalty Restored' [12.12]. It was also known as the 'naval' arch. It had figures standing at the corners of the low attic representing Europe, Asia and Africa, while the panel on the taller central section represented the marriage of Thames and Isis. At the top Atlas supported a globe. The lower part of the arch had four Ionic columns, and was very classical in its articulation, complete with projecting entablatures and river gods in the spandrels. The inscription dedicated the arch to Charles as 'British Neptune'; he was encouraged to strengthen the Royal Navy to support commerce. As Samuel Pordage wrote, in his *Heroic Stanzas on His Majesties Coronation* (London, 1661):

> The Citie rich holds up her head on high,
> And with her Ships sucks both the Indies dry;
> This by their stately Arches they would shew,
> All by the blessing comes of having You.

The third arch, in Cheapside near Wood Street, was the 'Temple of Concord'. The single opening had pairs of Corinthian columns on either side supporting a segmental pediment. Above was a circular tempietto, with Composite pilasters and a dome on top. Bases and columns imitated brass, and the columns steel. A statue of Concord stood above the dome. The fourth arch stood in Fleet Street, near Whitefriars, and represented the 'Garden of Plenty'. It was more classical than the similarly named arch for James I. The central opening had a Doric column on either side, wreathed in vine-leaves. This central section was rusticated. The sides stepped back, with small arches below, and there were volutes above the entablature at the level of the springing of the central arch. Above a segmental pediment was an open tempietto, square, with three Ionic columns at front and back, and a swept-up roof supporting a statue of Plenty. Ogilby commented that 'the capitals have not their just Measure, but incline to Modern Architecture'. The Dutch were expected by the City to build an arch, but by the time they found the money there was no longer a site available, and they refused to take over one of the City's arches. Instead, they and the French gave £400 towards the overall cost.[35]

12.12 David Loggan, Triumphal arch at the Royale Exchange, Cornhill. Plate from a suite of four entitled 'The four triumphal arches erected for the coronation of Charles II'. London, 1662.

Each arch had musicians on galleries within. The music was composed by Matthew Locke, England's leading composer, who set four songs, and wrote pieces to be played at Cornhill by wind instruments (it is likely that his well-known pieces 'For his Majesty's Sagbutts and Cornetts' were played here), and at Cheapside by the King's new violin band.[36] The paintings were executed by Andrew Dacres and William Lightfoote, of the City. Their remuneration, of £1,130, was one of the principal expenses of the show. Once again the conduits ran with wine. The accounts show that the associated plumbing works cost four times as much as the wine itself.

The procession was of the utmost splendour. Samuel Pepys wrote that it was so 'glorious … with gold and silver' that his eyes were 'overcome' with looking at it.[37] It is represented in a kind of diagrammatic form, with the cavalcade passing through the four arches, in a painting by Dirck Stoop in the Museum of London.[38] Not everyone approved. The Puritan preacher Ralph Josselin thought that the arches represented 'Heathenisme', while Thomas Venner's Fifth Monarchy men planned to burn them down, but were discovered a few days before the procession. According to John Evelyn, the arches were intended to stand for a year, and we know from Pepys that the arch in Fleet Street was still there in February 1662, when 'most of it' was blown down in a great storm, and 'broke down part of several houses', which were repaired at the City's expense.[39] The storm also blew down the royal arms from the first arch – naturally taken by some as an omen. When the arches were taken down, the materials were sold to the carpenters who had built them.

The types of church monument based in the sixteenth century on the triumphal arch were further developed in the early seventeenth century. Two particularly conspicuous and grandiose examples of the freestanding canopied tomb were commissioned by James I for Westminster Abbey in 1605. That for Queen Elizabeth, by Maximilian Colt, was finished by 1606 (and engraved in 1620), while that for Mary Queen of Scots, by the Cure family, was completed in 1613. They were very influential, and both freestanding monuments like that of Elizabeth, Lady Pole (d. 1628), at Colyton, Devon, and wall-monuments like that to Sir Simon Leach (*c.* 1630?) at Cadeleigh, Devon, are clearly related to them. The wall-monuments to Sir Roger Aston (1611/12–13) at Cranford, Middlesex, and to John, Lord Petre (*c.* 1624), at Ingatestone, Essex, use the tripartite formula to frame several kneeling effigies, like that of Sir Richard Pecksall in Westminster Abbey (see p. 209).[40] An especially grand example of the wall type is the monument to Richard Boyle, Earl of Cork, erected in St Mary's, Youghal, Co. Cork in 1620. The sculptor was Alexander Hills, of Holborn.[41]

The fine freestanding canopied tomb of Sir Lawrence Tanfield at Burford, Oxfordshire, was erected in 1628. The attribution to Gerard Christmas, who was paid for three of the 'pageants' for Charles I's abortive coronation entry (see above), and who, with his sons, also made pageants for Lord Mayor's processions between 1618 and 1639, is considered doubtful by Adam White.[42] The symbolism of the figures that stand above the entablature has been discussed by Jean Wilson, who compares the mixture of history, politics and moral instruction with the programmes of the arches for James I's coronation.[43]

The remarkable house Westwood in Worcestershire was built after 1598. Its entrance 'portico' is described by Andor Gomme as 'a simplified miniature of the Arch of Constantine'. He suggests that it may have been inspired by Serlio's woodcut, though the Corinthian order may come from John Shute's *First and Chief Groundes of Architecture* of 1563. Over the side arches are cartouches with Netherlandish strapwork. The date is probably *c.* 1620.[44]

Scotland

The earliest 'entry' to a Scottish city was that of Margaret Tudor when she came to Edinburgh in 1503 to marry James IV. The eyewitness account of John Yonge, Somerset Herald, mentions two specially erected 'Yatts', or gates. The first, at the entrance to the town, was of painted wood, and had a turret on either side and a window between these. In the windows of the turrets were angels singing. At the further end of the town was another gate, on which sat the four Virtues, and 'Tabretts' (drums) were played. The fountain at the Mercat Cross ran wine.[45] Ian Campbell has claimed that these 'may have been the earliest Renaissance triumphal arches outside Italy', pointing out that the representation of the Judgment of Paris on one of the 'scaffolds' was 'the earliest appearance of classical mythology in the pageantry of Britain', and comparing the castle-style gates with the 'pageant' erected in Bruges in 1468 for the entry of Margaret of York and with the later example of a triple gate erected in Bruges in 1515 for the entry of Charles V. However, from the little we know of the appearance of the Edinburgh arches, it is hard to identify any element as 'Renaissance' apart from the device of the arch itself.[46]

At about the same time as this entry, in 1501–6, a new gatehouse was being built at the royal castle of Stirling. The round towers on either side have been much reduced in height. The central round-headed gateway is flanked by symmetrical pedestrian gateways, with square heads framing arched openings. This arrangement was most unusual for the time, and it has been suggested that the gateways of Classical and Renaissance Italy might have influenced it. It has even been identified as a triumphal arch, but that seems unjustified.[47]

Other Scottish entries in the sixteenth century included that of Queen Margaret to Aberdeen in 1511, that of Mary Stewart to Edinburgh in 1561, that of James VI to Edinburgh in 1579, and that of Anne of Denmark to Edinburgh in 1590. We have descriptions of the pageants erected for these, but the only one for which arches were erected seems to have been that in 1561. For this there was at 'Butter Trone' 'ane port made of tymber, cullorit with fine cullouris, hungin with syndrie arms'. On it a group of children sang, and as the Queen passed under it a mechanical cloud opened, and a child representing an angel came down and gave her the keys of the town, a Bible and a Psalm-book. (The latter symbolised the Reformed faith, a point made even more forcefully elsewhere by the burning of the effigy of a priest.)[48] It is also worth noting that when James V arrived in Paris in 1537, for his marriage to Madeleine, daughter of François I, he was received (according to the poet David Lindsay) 'with laud & glorie, / Solempnitlie throw arkis triumphall'.[49]

James VI and I's entry to Edinburgh in 1617 was very austere: pageants were then regarded as idolatrous.[50] Charles I was expected to make an entry into Edinburgh as early as 1628, but did not come until 1633. The city then went to great trouble and expense. Four arches were erected. The first, outside West Port, had a 'large canvas' showing a view of the city, comparable with the Londinium Arch of 1604, as was the figure of the river 'Lithus' (Leith).[51] Beneath the arch was a 'theatre', in the form of a mountain, on which stood a nymph representing the 'Genius' of the city. She gave Charles the keys, and delivered a speech of welcome. The second arch, 'towards the Gate of the old Towne', had paintings of wild country, including a mountain, and of the sea, with Roman soldiers pursuing naked Picts. A woman with coloured feathers in her black hair represented an American, one of several references to Scottish enterprise in the New World. A curtain fell from the arch and again revealed a 'theatre', with one woman representing the Genius of Caledonia, a gold crown hanging from the arch before her, and another 'new Scotland'. It was the former who made the speech here. The third arch stood 'at the west end of the Tolbooth'. Mars was accompanied by symbols of war, and Minerva by those of peace. Here the drawn curtain showed Mercury with the whole series of 107 Scottish kings, whom he had brought from the Elysian Fields. These were the work of George Jamesone.[52] A Latin speech was delivered. 'At the Cross' a pageant showed Bacchus, Venus, Ceres and attendants, and Satyrs who interrupted the intended speech, and another pageant beyond that represented Parnassus, with Apollo, the Muses, and 'ancient worthies of Scotland'. Trees and musicians adorned the mountain. The fourth arch, near the eastern gate, represented heaven, with Charles's star-sign Virgo, prostrate Titans, the three Parcae (Fates), and the seven planets. The shepherd Endymion came out of a grove and made speeches, before and after the prophetic speeches of the planetary deities. The back of the arch showed the Graces. The last pageant consisted of Fame and Honour standing on the battlements of the east gate, above a statue of James I.[53]

In the later sixteenth century, features recalling triumphal arches appear on Scottish buildings. A conspicuous example is the centrally placed doorway to the new chapel built at Stirling Castle *c.* 1590, where the arch has a pair of columns on either side, with linked bases and entablatures.

Notes

1. Susan Foister, *Holbein and England* (New Haven/London, 2004), 121–8.
2. Sydney Anglo, *Spectacle, Pageantry, and Early Tudor Policy* (Oxford, 1997), 209–31.
3. Foister (cit. at n. 1), 128–30.
4. Howard Colvin, 'Pompous entries and English architecture', *Essays in English Architectural History* (New Haven/London, 1999), 67–93.
5. ibid., 75; Sandra Logan, 'Making history: the rhetorical and historical occasion of Elizabeth Tudor's Coronation entry', *Journal of Medieval and Early Modern Studies*, 31.2 (2001), 251–82.
6. John Summerson, *Architecture in Britain, 1530 to 1830* (9th edn, New Haven/London, 1993), 43–5; Mark Girouard, *Elizabethan Architecture* (New Haven/London, 2009), 142–4.
7. Colvin (cit. at n. 4), 85.
8. Tom Nickson, 'Moral edification at Gonville and Caius College', *Architectural History*, 48 (2005), 49–68.
9. Girouard (cit. at n. 6), 160.
10. One is reminded of the dictum of Dean Gifford, of Christ Church: 'a classical education not infrequently leads to positions of considerable emolument'.
11. Girouard (cit. at n. 6), 159.
12. Nickson (cit. at n. 8), 55, notes the Arch of Virtue and Honour erected for the entry of Henri II into Lyon in 1548, published in a woodcut by Bernard Salomon.
13. Girouard (cit. at n. 6), 203–7.
14. Randall Davies, *Chelsea Old Church* (London, 1904), 220–26; *Survey of London*, VII, pt II (London, 1921), 20–22; Adam White, *Architectural Review*, 171 (1982), 55–6; Girouard (cit. at n. 6), 170–71. On Maynard, see Girouard, 163–5, 201–3.
15. Girouard (cit. at n. 6), 208–10. Jonathan Edis, 'Beyond Thomas Kirby: monuments of the Mordaunt family and their circle', *Church Monuments*, 16 (2001), 30–43; he notes (p. 38) that the female figures in the spandrels are similar to those on the Gate of Virtue at Caius.
16. This may be by Cornelius Cure: see Adam White, *Church Monuments*, 7 (1992), 38.
17. Nigel Llewellyn, *Funeral Monuments in Post-Reformation England* (Cambridge, 2000), 61.
18. Ole Peter Grell, *Calvinist exiles in Tudor and Stuart England* (Aldershot, 1996), 165–74; David M. Bergeron, *English Civic Pageantry* (Tempe, Ariz., 2003), 72–88; David Evett, *Literature and the Visual Arts in Tudor England* (Athens, Ga., 1990), 97–104; Graham Parry, *The Golden Age Restor'd* (Manchester, 1981), 1–21.
19. *The Arch's of Triumph erected in honor of the High and mighty prince. Iames. the first of that name. King, of England. and the sixt of Scotland. at his Maiesties entrance and passage through his honorable citty & chamber of London. vpon the 15th. day of march 1603* (sic – a curious error for 1604, the date of publication given on the final page).

20 Each published an account of his contribution: Thomas Dekker, 'The magnificent entertainment', in F. Bowers, ed., *The Dramatic Works of Thomas Dekker* (Cambridge, 1953–61), II, 229–309; Ben Jonson, 'The King's Entertainment', in C.H. Herford and P. and E. Simpson, eds, *Ben Jonson* (Oxford, 1925–52), VII, 65–109.

21 Girouard (cit. at n. 6), 280–81.

22 Grell (cit. at n. 18). The arch was described in *Beschryvinghe vande herlycke Arcus Triumphal … ter eeren … Coninck Iacobo* (Middelburgh, 1604): see Gervase Hood, 'A Netherlandish triumphal arch for James I', in S. Roach, ed., *Across the Narrow Seas: Studies in the History and Bibliography of Britain and the Low Countries* (London, 1991), 67–82. The engravings of the two sides of the arch are by Marten Droeshout, who worked on it as a painter. That of the front differs in details from Harrison's. One English painter worked on the arch, Rowland Buckett: see Edward Town, 'A biographical dictionary of London painters 1547–1625', *Walpole Society*, 76 (2014), 44.

23 G. Dugdale, *The Time Triumphant, Declaring in Briefe, the Arrival of our Sovereigne … King Iames into England* (London, 1604; reprinted in C.H. Firth, ed., *Stuart Tracts 1603–1693* (London, 1903), 79.

24 Bergeron (cit. at n. 18), 90. The entry was described in *The King of Denmarkes welcome: containing his arrival, abode and entertainment both in the Citie and other places* (London, 1606); also *Relatio oder Erzehlung wie … Christianus Quartus … im Königreich Engellandt angelanget...* (Hamburg, 1607; reprinted (in Danish) with John Davies's poem *Bien Venu. Greate Britaines welcome to hir greate friendes … the Danes* (London, 1606), Copenhagen, 1957). The reference to the arch is on p. 59. No illustration survives.

25 For a study of those held between 1604 and their temporary suppression in 1639, see Bergeron (cit. at n. 18), 238–62.

26 D.S. Bland, 'The Barriers – Guildhall Library MS 4160', *Guildhall Miscellany*, 6 (1956), 10.

27 David Blayney Brown in *Dictionary of Art*, s.v. Francis Cleyn; Edward Croft-Murray, *Decorative Painting in England 1537–1837* (London, 1962), I, 196–7; Howard Colvin (*Essays in English architectural history* (New Haven/London, 1999), 78) suggests that the arch might have been the one in Westminster Hall traditionally associated with coronation banquets (see p. 302), but it is perhaps unlikely that its design would have been paid for before 1626.

28 Grell (cit. at n. 18), 174–82.

29 Colvin (cit. at n. 27), 78: Bergeron (cit. at n. 18), 111–13.

30 John Harris and Gordon Higgott, *Inigo Jones: Complete Architectural Drawings* (New York, 1989), 251–3.

31 The engraving published by William Kent in *The Designs of Inigo Jones* (London, 1727), pl. 58, after a drawing by Henry Flitcroft, is based on Jones's design, rather than Webb's. For a drawing of Temple Bar 'as it might have appeared in the early nineteenth century' see Colvin (cit. at n. 27), 79.

32 John Ogilby, *The Entertainment of His Most Excellent Majestie Charles II in his Passage through the City of London to his Coronation...* (London, 1662; reprinted in facsimile, ed. R. Knowles (Binghamton, N.Y., 1988)). On the entry see also Sir Edward Walker, *A Circumstantial Account of the Preparations for the Coronation of His Majesty King Charles the Second* (London, 1820); Lorraine Medway, '"The Most Conspicuous Solemnity": the coronation of Charles II', in E. Cruickshanks, ed., *The Stuart Courts* (Stroud, 2000), 141–57; Gerard Reedy, 'Mystical politics: the imagery of Charles II's Coronation', in Paul J. Korshin, ed., *Studies in Change and Revolution* (Menston, Yorks., 1972), 19–42; Eric Halfpenny, '"The Citie's Loyalty Displayed": a literary and documentary causerie of Charles II's Coronation "Entertainment"', *Guildhall Miscellany*, 10 (Sept. 1959), 19–35.

33 Howard Colvin, *A Biographical Dictionary of British Architects* (4th edn, New Haven/London, 2008), 414–16.

34 *Catalogue of the RIBA Drawings Collection*, G–K (Farnborough, 1973), 18–19.

35 Grell (cit. at n. 18), 182–6.

36 Eric Halfpenny, *Music and Letters*, 38 (1957), 32–44. In Locke's 'semi-opera' *Psyche*, to words by Thomas Shadwell, first performed in 1675, the setting of Act III, Scene 2, is 'the principal Street of the City', in which is 'a large Triumphal Arch, with Columns of the Dorick Order, adorned with the statues of Fame and Honour, &c., beautified with Festoons of Flowers; all the Inrichments of Gold'. It was to welcome the Stranger-Princes who had slain a monster. M. Locke, *Dramatic Music*, ed. M. Tilmouth, *Musica Britannica*, 51 (London, 1986), 153.

37 *The Diary of Samuel Pepys*, ed. R. Latham and W. Matthews, II (London, 1970), 81–3.

38 M. Galinou and J. Hayes, *London in Paint: Oil Paintings from the Museum of London* (London, 1996), 26–9.

39 *The Diary of John Evelyn*, ed. E.S. de Beer (Oxford, 1955), III, 278: Pepys (cit. at n. 37), III, 32; Halfpenny (cit. at n. 32), 32.

40 Adam White, *Church Monuments*, III, 13 (1998), 16–53. Frits Scholten (*Sumptuous Memories: Studies in Seventeenth-century Dutch Tomb Sculpture* (Zwolle, 2003), 250) suggests that Hendrick de Keyser's monument to William the Silent in the Nieuwe Kerk, Delft, was influenced by English royal tombs, pointing out that de Keyser was in London in 1607, where he could have seen Elizabeth's, and possibly heard about Mary's, from Cornelius Cure, whose father was Dutch.

41 Amy L. Harris, *Church Monuments*, 13 (1998), 70–86.

42 Bergeron (cit. at n. 18), 243–50.

43 *Church Monuments*, 13 (1998), 87–105.

44 Andor Gomme, 'Revisiting Westwood', *Architectural History*, 44 (2001), 310–21.

45 Douglas Gray, 'The Royal Entry in sixteenth-century Scotland', in S. Mapstone and J. Wood, eds, *The Rose and the Thistle: Essays on the Culture of Late Medieval and Renaissance Scotland* (East Linton, 1998), 16–21.

46 Ian Campbell, 'James IV and Edinburgh's first triumphal arches', in D. Mays, ed., *The Architecture of Scottish Cities* (East Linton, 1997), 26–33.

47 Aonghus MacKechnie, 'Stirling's triumphal arch', *Welcome: News for Friends of Historic Scotland* (Sept. 1991). See also I. Campbell, 'A Romanesque revival and the early Renaissance in Scotland, *c.* 1380–1513', *JSAH*, 54 (1995), 302–25. In the *Buildings of Scotland: Stirling and Central Scotland* (New Haven/London, 2002), 675, Richard Fawcett wisely avoids any reference to triumphal arches.

48 Bergeron (cit. at n. 18), 28–9. The device of the boy emerging from a globe with keys was repeated in the 1579 and 1590 entries (Bergeron, 68–70).

49 Gray (cit. at n. 45), 22–9.

50 D.M. Bergeron, 'Charles I's Edinburgh Pageant (1633)', *Renaissance Studies*, 6 (1992), 100–101.

51 These and other similarities between the two entries may support the widely held, but not firmly attested, view that William Drummond of Hawthornden masterminded the 1633 entry: he was in addition a friend of Ben Jonson (Bergeron, cit. in the preceding note, 176, 180).

52 A number of them survive, and were sold from Newbattle Abbey in 1971 (*Dictionary of Art*, *s.v.* George Jamesone). Jamesone may also have painted the view of Edinburgh (Bergeron (cit. in the preceding note), 115); *Oxford DNB*, *s.v.* George Jamesone).

53 Bergeron (cit. at n. 51), 113–20. The entry was described in *The Entertainment of the High and Mighty Monarch Charles Into his auncient and royall City of Edinburgh* (1633) – the only printed description of a Scottish entry. It does not give the dimensions of the pageants. Bergeron confusingly refers to all seven as 'arches'.

13

FRANCE IN THE SIXTEENTH AND SEVENTEENTH CENTURIES

When Margaret of Austria entered Valenciennes in 1493 she was welcomed with 'une hautte et spacieuse porte' made entirely of bread, which was afterwards distributed to the poor.[1]

Two designs for triumphal arches appear already in 1509 in Jean Pèlerin's book *De artificiali perspectiva*, published in Toul where he was a canon. One is triple, apparently with attached Corinthian columns, and the other single, with columns supporting the archivolt and two tiers of pilasters above each. Triumphal arches built for entries, or permanent structures employing the motif, are particularly significant as marking the importation of Renaissance classical architecture into France. The earliest mention of a triumphal arch is for the entry of François I into the Italianised city of Lyon in 1515. The second arch there is described as *ung arc triumphant bien et richement painct à candélabres et fasson antique* ('a triumphal arch well and richly painted with candelabra and in the ancient manner'), but miniatures show it and the first as more like bridge arches. Similarly there is no evidence that the scaffold erected at Bordeaux in 1530 for Queen Eléonore and the Enfants de France, described as 'en fasson darc triomphant', was based on an ancient one. In 1530 the Pont Notre-Dame in Paris had 'porteaulx à l'antique', but the first triumphal arch in the ancient manner may have been that at Lyon in 1533, 'peint d'or et d'azur'. The arches erected at Poitiers and Orléans in 1539 for Charles V were the first definitely 'authentic' ones. At Poitiers one arch of verdure had medallions of Hercules and Agathyrsus, while a 'theatre' was ornamented with triumphal arches linked by 'taffetas'. Orléans had five 'porteaulx à l'antique façon'. For Charles's entry into Paris in the same year, organised by Girolamo della Robbia, a triple arch at St-Antoine, 'peint d'ouvrages antiques et moresques', had women holding coats of arms in the spandrels. The Pont Notre-Dame had two arches with double-headed eagles and a Siren.[2]

For the entry of the Emperor Charles V into Valenciennes in 1540, the decorations were designed by Noel Le Boucq, superintendant of artillery for the Spanish government. Drawings of them by Hubert Cailleau survive, and are the only more or less reliable illustrations of an entry in the provinces of the North. The arch at the entrance to the city, with four square columns supporting a large attic, bore little resemblance to an ancient one, unlike the second, 'revestu à l'antiquitez', which had pairs of Doric pilasters on either side of the opening, figures in the spandrels, and a pediment over the attic. The third arch, 'à la corinth', had pairs of Corinthian columns with projecting entablatures, a tall attic like a gallery with three coats of arms, and another section over its centre with a painting of an elm tree and vine. The fourth and grandest arch, also 'basti à la Corinth', was a triple arch, with four Corinthian columns on projecting bases; the attic was similar to that of the third arch. The fifth arch had a caryatid term on each side of the rusticated opening, and the pedimented aedicule above contained statues of the three Graces. In 1549 Charles V made another entry into Valenciennes, for which again five arches were erected. We have no illustrations of them, but we know that one was Tuscan and one triple arch was Ionic, and that they had statues on top. Their decoration mixed medieval and Renaissance themes.[3]

The crucial figures in the introduction of Renaissance architecture into France from *c.* 1540 were the sculptor Jean Goujon and the architects Jean Bullant and Philibert de l'Orme. The publication of architectural treatises played an important role: for example, in 1549 Jacques Androuet du Cerceau published at Orléans *Quinque et viginta exempla arcuum …* (with a second edition in 1560 entitled *Arcs de triomphe modernes et antiques*) [13.1].[4] His *Quoniam apud veteres alio structurae genere templa fuerunt aedificata* ('Because among the ancients temples were built with a different type of structure', Orléans, 1550) contained a reconstruction of the Arch of Titus. The magnificent monument to Louis de Brézé (husband of Diane de Poitiers) in the choir of Rouen Cathedral, dating from 1540–42, seems to have been designed by Goujon [13.2]. It has pairs of Corinthian columns flanking the sarcophagus supporting the effigy; over the columns are pairs of caryatids, and in the arched opening between them, which has flying Victories in the spandrels, is an equestrian figure; above is a niche containing an allegorical statue. For the Fontaine des Innocents in Paris, of 1548–9, Goujon collaborated with Pierre Lescot. Pairs of Corinthian pilasters with figures in relief between them flank the opening, which has reliefs below, and there are reliefs on the attic, below pediments; in the spandrels are Fames. The form of the structure is closely borrowed from the triumphal arch in Serlio's fourth book, which itself derived from the Roman arch at Ancona.[5] Lescot used the motif again in the courtyard of the Louvre, where he superimposes compositions of pairs of attached Corinthian columns, framing niches with statues. Between are either pedimented doors or tall windows.[6]

At the château of Écouen, the entrance portico, designed by Jean Bullant for the Connétable Anne de Montmorency, is dated to about 1544–5. Bullant had visited Rome. The portico (demolished in 1787) had three storeys, the lowest with pairs of fluted Doric columns flanking niches on either side of the doorway. The second storey

13.1 Jacques Androuet du Cerceau, *Quinque et viginta exempla arcuum …*, 1549.

13.2 Tomb of Louis de Brézé, Rouen Cathedral, 1540–2, attributed to Jean Goujon.

had pairs of Ionic columns, with an arched balcony in the middle, while the third had pairs of caryatid terms on either side of a tall arched opening which framed an equestrian statue. The surviving portico on the south wing has the first giant order in France. Corinthian columns covering two storeys, based on those of the Pantheon at Rome, support a decorated entablature. Between them are niches below, which originally housed two of Michelangelo's *Slaves*, and reliefs above.[7] At the end of the Cour d'Honneur is a doorway which has detached Doric columns and a decorated frieze. The Fames in the spandrels are by Jean Goujon, as is the other relief sculpture at Écouen.[8]

De l'Orme himself designed the frontispiece of the château of Anet (now re-erected at the École des Beaux Arts in Paris), *c.* 1550 [13.3]. Here each storey has pairs of columns, Doric, Ionic and Corinthian. The upper one has an arch in the centre with Victories in the spandrels, two levels of reliefs between the columns, and coats of arms above. It originally held a statue of Louis de Brézé, husband of the client, Diane de Poitiers (see above). Blunt sees the closest parallel to this frontispiece in the campanile of San Biagio at Montepulciano by Antonio da Sangallo the Elder.[9] De l'Orme was also responsible for the tomb of François I in St-Denis. Here the central section,

13.3 Château of Anet, frontispiece re-erected at École des Beaux Arts, Paris, *c.* 1550. Philibert de l'Orme.

224   THE TRIUMPHAL ARCH

which stands on a plinth and has a relief panel continuing the line of the projecting bases of the Ionic columns on either side, projects forward, and has another column on each of the return elevations, while the side sections also have pairs of Ionic columns. Kneeling statues are set on the low attic. Blunt sees the Arch of Septimius Severus as the model, with Corinthian replaced by Ionic, but also notes a similar design in Book VII of Serlio.[10]

Some other interesting examples from these years may be noted. The portal of the church of Notre-Dame at Hesdin in the Pas-de-Calais has fluted Composite pilasters, while the arched opening, whose concave form gives the impression of perspective, has coffering and winged Fames in the spandrels [13.4]. Within it was a tympanum with the Birth of the Virgin. On the attic are coats of arms. The portal was made before 1553 for the church of Vieil-Hesdin, and was moved to the new church in 1582. It can be compared with the arch at St-Jacques de l'Hôpital for the entry of Henri II into Paris in 1549 (see below).[11] The church of St-Nicolas-des-Champs in Paris has a portal built in 1576–86 to the design of an unknown architect which, apart from its triangular pediment, imitates the façade of the 'salle de triomphe' of the Hôtel de Tournelles, designed by Philibert de l'Orme in 1559. That took the form of a triumphal arch, with pairs of Corinthian pilasters flanking superimposed niches, Fames in the spandrels, and a broken pediment above the cornice, with statues and weapons. It is the only known example of a festival decoration designed by him, though there were surely many others.[12]

13.4 Notre Dame, Hesdin, portal, before 1553.

The mid-sixteenth century saw a considerable number of royal and ducal entries for which arches of classical form were erected. In 1548 Henri II had been greeted at Lyon by four arches. The first, double-fronted, had pairs of twisted columns. The second, over 15 m high, had pairs of Corinthian columns, statues in niches, and a pediment: it was built up against a city gate, and the city wall here was made to represent a Gallo-Roman one. The third was a double arch on a sarcophagus base, containing a grotto with statues of the city's two rivers, which flowed with red and white wine, though a Medusa head on the central pilaster squirted water on those trying to reach them. The fourth arch, double-fronted, was over 18 m high, with pairs of herms. On top was a platform where men played shawms, with a circular tempietto. The entry, with the usual symbolic statues and paintings, was supervised by the local poet Maurice Scève.[13]

In the same year the king entered Dijon, where the notable woodcarver Hugues Sambin worked on the decorations.[14] The entry of Charles V into Valenciennes in 1549 has already been mentioned.

In the same year Henri II entered Paris. The entry was masterminded by Jean Martin, translator of Vitruvius and Serlio. The supervising architect was Philibert de l'Orme, and the painters were Charles Dorigny and Jean Cousin. The sculpture for the decorative structures was by Jean Goujon, who also made the drawings for the woodcuts in the printed account. (Goujon also illustrated Martin's translation of the *Hypnerotomachia Poliphili*.) The arch at St-Jacques de l'Hôpital, mentioned above, had pairs of Corinthian pilasters, Fames in the spandrels, and a large female figure seated on the keystone; above, two winged figures held a crown over the royal arms; the opening was coffered and had a relief on either side. The arches of the Pont Notre-Dame, which was transformed into a decorated tunnel, were astylar, with superimposed niches on the piers; on top of one Tiphys held a sail, between the Dioscuri. The arch of the the rue St-Antoine, in the form of an H, had two equal openings, with Corinthian columns, the central one with a figure seated in front, and winged figures on top like those on the first arch.[15]

In 1550 Henri II entered Rouen. At the entrance to the bridge over the Seine was a triple arch ('le Massis du Roch') of rough masonry, with a superstructure of rocks and trees around a cave in which were Apollo, the Muses and Hercules. At the other end of the bridge was a single arch, representing the Golden Age: the opening was framed by square piers, within masonry dotted with rectangular projections, and there were winged figures in the spandrels; on top were two Sibyls holding a crescent moon on which stood Saturn. The entry was most remarkable for the spectacle of naked male and female Brazilians, brought over by local merchants (50 in one account, 300 in another): in a meadow planted with trees and shrubs, populated by birds, monkeys and squirrels, they enacted various occupations, culminating in a fight at the end of which one 'tribe' burnt the huts of the other.[16] In the next year Henri again entered Rouen, and in the same year the duc d'Aumale entered Dijon. Sambin was again involved, providing designs for the sculptor Jean Damotte.

Sambin also supervised the works for the entry of Charles IX into Dijon in 1564. In that year Charles and his wife, Elisabeth of Austria, made a tour of France. This included an entry into Lyon, supervised by the lawyer Antoine Giraud, in collaboration with the painter Maître Thomas. There were arches of Justice, Piety, Peace, and Royal Clemency.[17] The entries into Paris in 1571 first of Charles and then of Elisabeth are well documented.[18] The former was masterminded by Jean Dorat and Pierre Ronsard, who provided sonnets. Niccolò dell'Abbate (a disciple of Primaticcio) did the paintings and Germain Pilon the sculpture. The principal theme was the Trojan descent of the French kings. The astylar 'Portail à la rustique d'ouvrage Tuscan' at the Porte St-Denis had rustication swarming with snails, lizards and plants. It was dedicated to the origin of the kings of France. The niches contained armed figures, and on top were Francion (son of Hector) and Pharamond, flanking the royal arms. Leading to the gate was a 'berceau' ('arched trellis') covered in ivy. The Porte aux Peintres, dedicated to the grandeur of the king, his ancestors, and his brothers, was more classical. On each face were pairs of Corinthian columns, framing niches with statues. Over the attic on one side were Henri II between two columns, and Hercules and Antaeus. In the centre was an urn supposed to contain the ashes of the King (one of Pilon's most famous works is the urn for the heart of Henri, supported by the three Graces, now in the Louvre). On the other side were Henri II again and Charles IX, with two figures holding up a globe between them. A drawing in Stockholm for this arch, of great delicacy, is attributed to Giulio Camillo dell'Abbate (son and collaborator of Niccolò): the figure of Henri II on the first side is replaced by Hercules strangling the snakes.[19] The arch at the Pont Notre-Dame was Tuscan, but 'd'une mode qui iamais n'avoit été veue'. It appeared to be made of rocks, with snails, shells and plants as if on a river bank. An old man and woman represented the Marne and the Seine, while above was a silver ship representing France, between the Dioscuri. At the end of the bridge was an arch like the first, with Victory and Mars. The Queen had been supposed to be pregnant, and her entry postponed for a year, so the news that she was to make her entry only twenty-three days later came as a shock. Demolition of the King's arches had begun, but now the various structures were hastily altered. The first arch had Pepin and Charlemagne on top, with the nymphs Gallia and Germania holding a wreath over the arms in between. On the Porte des Peintres the rivers Rhône and Danube held up the globe between Henri II and Charles IX, while on the other side were the duc d'Anjou and the duc d'Alençon. The arch at the Pont Notre-Dame had a bull and Europa on top.

Also in 1571 Henri, duc d'Anjou, entered Orléans, and four portals were erected. In 1596 Henri IV entered Rouen: an arch was set up at the cathedral, and there were others. In 1600 Henri IV's second wife, Maria de' Medici, was welcomed at Avignon as she travelled from Italy to Paris with a 'labyrinth of Hercules': seven triumphal arches represented his labours, the King having recently been given the title of 'the Gallic Hercules'. There was also a triumphal chariot with horses dressed as elephants. The papal vice-legate at Avignon entrusted the design to the Jesuits, who also wrote seven odes.[20] In the same year Maria made an entry into Lyon: an engraving shows the structures erected, including five arches, three of them with broken pediments.

In 1622 Louis XIII entered Aix. Of the seven arches the first and last were unusual, as one consisted of a pair of palm trees meeting above, and the last of similarly posed olive trees. The King arrived unexpectedly, and so the author of the programme, Jean de Galaup de Chasteuil, could not explain the pavilion with a figure of a troubadour, nor could the troubadour greet him.[21] In 1629 Louis was welcomed back to Paris after the capture of La Rochelle: the arches included one with pairs of Doric columns, on which hung oval paintings, and a large painting above.[22] In the same year he made an entry into Troyes, where two portals were erected, one with a painting in the centre.[23]

There were several entries in Lorraine in the early seventeenth century. When Henri IV came in 1601 arches were built at Metz and at Toul, of which the latter were kept until at least 1610. For the marriage of Henri, duc de Lorraine, and Margherita Gonzaga of Mantua in 1606, at the entrance of the grand'rue of Nancy an arch over 15 m wide and 19 m high was built, decorated by painters including Jacques Bellange, the court painter. It had four Corinthian columns; on the cornice stood the nine Muses and three Graces, while on top was 'Ovid, poet of Mantua' – an unfortunate confusion with Virgil. In 1609 Henri was welcomed to Nancy with an arch. Charles IV was expected in Nancy in 1640, and the court painter Claude Déruet designed arches. The Duke failed to come, but the arches were engraved.[24]

A painter of this period who appreciated the triumphal arch as a motif suggesting Roman antiquity was Claude Lorrain: for example, in his *Seaport* in the National

Gallery (1639) a partly ruinous arch with attached Corinthian columns occupies the centre, where it projects into the sea. A painting of grotesques attributed to Jacques Callot includes a fanciful arch with pairs of Composite columns; on top a weird winged creature supports a globe, between trumpeting skeletons.[25]

Notes

1. E. Mannier, *Chroniques de Flandre et Artois par Louis Bresin* (Paris, 1880), 71. This reference is owed to Lorne Campbell.
2. Joséphe Chartrou, *Les entrées solennelles et triomphales à la Renaissance (1484–1551)* (Paris, 1928), 87f.; Antoinette Huon in Jean Jacquot, ed., *Les Fêtes de la Renaissance* (Paris, 1956), 24.
3. Yona Pinson, 'L'évolution du style Renaissant, dans les entrées de Charles Quint à Valenciennes (1540–1549)', *Gazette des Beaux-Arts*, May–June 1989, 201–13; Hugo Soly and Johan van de Wiele, eds, *Carolus: Charles Quint 1500–1558* (Ghent, 1999), 183–4.
4. Hubertus Günther, 'Du Cerceau et l'antique', in Jean Guillaume, ed., *Jacques Androuet du Cerceau 'un des plus grands architectes qui se soient jamais trouvés en France'* (Paris, 2010), 75–90.
5. Pierre du Colombier, *Jean Goujon* (Paris, 1949), 53–73; Yves Pauwels, 'The rhetorical model in the formation of French architectural language in the sixteenth century – the triumphal arch as commonplace', in G. Clarke and P. Crossley, eds, *Architecture and Language: Constructing Identity in European Architecture* c. *1000*–c. *1658* (Cambridge, 2000), 138–9.
6. Louis Hautecoeur, *Histoire de l'architecture classique en France*, I (2nd edn, Paris, 1965), 2, 277. For the sculpture by Goujon, see Du Colombier (cit. in the preceding note), 87–105, 181–2.
7. Pauwels (cit. at n. 5), 143–4. See also Hautecoeur (cit. in the preceding note), 307–9.
8. Du Colombier (cit. at n. 5), 179–80.
9. Hautecoeur (cit. at n. 6), 280–88; Philibert de l'Orme, *Le premier tome de l'architecture de Philibert de l'Orme* (Paris, 1567), in J.-M. Pérouse de Montclos, ed., *Traités d'architecture* (Paris, 1988); Anthony Blunt, *Philibert de l'Orme* (London, 1958), 34. Blunt also describes the entrance gateway at Anet as having 'three round-headed openings arranged in a free variant of the triumphal arch scheme'.
10. Blunt (cit. in the preceding note), 71.
11. Hautecoeur (cit. at n. 6), 478–9; Jacques Vanuxem, 'Aspects de la sculpture dans le Nord de France entre 1480 et 1540', in François Lesure, *La Renaissance dans les provinces du Nord* (Paris, 1956), 158–67.
12. Blunt (cit. at n. 9), 83–4.
13. *La Magnificence de la superbe et triumphante entrée de la … cité de Lyon faicte au treschrestien roy de France Henry deuxiesme de ce nom, et à la royne Catherine … le xxiii. de septembre m.d.xlviii* (Lyon, 1549); *La magnifica et triumphale entrata del christianiss. re di Francia Henrico secondo … fatta nella … città di Lyone … alla 21 di septembr.* (Lyon, 1548); Théodore Godefroy, *Le Cérémonial françois* (Paris, 1649), I, 838–41; Maurice Scève, ed. Richard Cooper, *The Entry of Henri II into Lyon: September 1548* (Tempe, Ariz., 1997).
14. Jacques Thirion in *Dictionary of Art*, 27, 681–3.
15. *C'est l'ordre qui a este tenu à la nouvelle et ioyeuse entre, que … le Roy treschrestien Henry deuzieme de ce nom a faicte en sa bonne ville et cité de Paris … le sezieme iour de Iuin MDXLIX* (Paris, 1549); V. L. Saulnier, 'L'entrée de Henri II à Paris et la révolution poétique de 1550', in Jacquot (cit. at n. 2), 31–59; Du Colombier (cit. at n. 5), 179f.; *The entry of Henry II into Paris 16 June 1549*, with introduction and notes by D. MacFarlane (Binghamton, N.Y., 1982); William Alexander McClung, 'A Place for a Time: the Architecture of Festivals and Theatres', in Eve Blau and Robin Evans, eds, *Architecture and the Image* (Montreal, 1989), 287.
16. *L'entrée de Henri II à Rouen 1550*, ed. Margaret McGowan (Amsterdam, 1979).
17. Victor E. Graham and W. McAllister Johnson, *The Royal Tour of France by Charles IX and Catherine de' Medici: Festivals and Entries 1564–6* (Toronto, 1979).
18. Simon Bouquet, *Bref et sommaire recueil de ce qui a esté faict … à la ioyeuse et triomphante Entrée de … Charles IX … en sa bonne ville et cité de Paris … avec le Couronnement de … Princesse Madame Elizabet d'Austriche …* (Paris, 1572); facsimile edn with intro. by Frances Yates (Amsterdam/New York, 1976); Victor E. Graham and W. McAllister Johnson, *The Paris Entries of Charles IX and Elisabeth of Austria 1571* (Toronto, 1974).
19. Anne-Marie Lecoq, 'La "Città festeggiante": les fêtes publiques au XVe et XVIe siècles', *Revue de l'art* 33 (1976), 83–4.
20. [André Valladier], *Labyrinthe royal de l'Hercule gaulois triomphant* (Avignon, 1600).
21. Jean de Galaup de Chasteuil, *Discours sur les arcs triomphaux dressés en la ville d'Aix à l'heureuse arrivée de très-chrétien, très-grand, et très-juste monarque Louys XIII* (Aix, 1624).
22. Jean-Baptiste de Machault, *Éloges et discours sur la triomphante reception du Roi en sa Ville de Paris après la reduction de La Rochelle* (Paris, 1629); Blau and Evans (cit. at n. 15), 96.
23. Godefroy (cit. at n. 13), 1000.
24. François-Georges Pariset, 'Le mariage d'Henri duc de Lorraine et de Marguerite Gonzague-Mantoue', in Jacquot (cit. at n. 2), 153–87.
25. On the market in 1935; photograph in the Witt Collection at the Courtauld Institute, London.

14

FRANCE FROM LOUIS XIV TO THE REVOLUTION

On 26 August 1660 Louis XIV and his newly married wife Marie-Thérèse, eldest daughter of Philip IV of Spain, made a triumphal entry into Paris, to celebrate peace in Europe and the cession by Spain of two provinces. Six arches of wood and canvas were erected by the city of Paris. All were the work of 'Sieur Cochy, Maistre des œuvres de Charpenterie de la Ville'. The first was in the Faubourg St-Antoine, at the place du Trône. Designed 'à l'antique' by Pierre Mélin, it was a triple arch, said to be far larger than any arch previously erected in France. The side openings were only slightly lower than the central one, which projected. Detached Doric columns, imitating red 'marbre jaspé', with bases and capitals imitating bronze, flanked each opening. The structure was made of pinewood. The numerous reliefs, and statues on top, which are shown in an engraving, remained unexecuted. Above the arch stood eighteen oboists, who echoed the trumpets at the nearby throne.[1]

14.1 Entry to Paris of Louis XIV and Marie-Thérèse, 1660, Parnassus arch. Pierre Mélin.

Behind the Pont Dormant was the Arc de Pierre de la Porte St-Antoine. This took the form of a renovation of the gate dating from the sixteenth century. It was rusticated, again of the Doric order, with an attached pediment between the pier niches, and a pediment on top between obelisks. Over this pediment were statues representing France and Spain united by Hymen, by Gérard Van Opstal. In the niches were statues of *Spes Gallica* and *Securitas Publica*, by François Anguier (now in the Musée Carnavalet). On each side of the arch, linked by walls, were pilasters bearing trophies by Alexandre Jacquet and Jean-Baptiste Tuby. Not far behind this arch was the fourteenth-century town gate: it was decorated with tapestries and a large painting by Henri and Charles Beaubrun.

It was again Pierre Mélin who seems to have designed the most spectacular arch, at the Carrefour de la Fontaine St-Gervais (now place Baudoyer) [14.1]. It represented Mount Parnassus, and the opening resembled a grotto, the pillars wreathed in laurels and taking the form of palm trees. On the 'mountain' above were olive trees. Over the opening was a circular portrait of the royal couple. At this level a gallery housed real people representing famous writers, while on the 'mountain' sat plaster figures of the Muses with Apollo at the top. The arch celebrated the arts of peace. Near it were twenty-four musicians playing and singing.

At the end of the Pont Notre-Dame stood an arch designed by Henri and Charles Beaubrun. The Ionic columns imitated lapis lazuli and had gilded capitals and bases. The large painting above had a lavish frame surrounded by drapery with putti and allegorical statues. The arch celebrated the peace which resulted from the marriage. Here the music was provided by 'les musettes de Poictou'.

At the end of the Marché Neuf a particularly elaborate arch was intended to look like a palace *à l'antique*. Dedicated to Hercules conquered by Minerva, it was designed by Michel Dorigny and François Tortebat, pupils of Vouet. Deeply concave in plan, the triple arch had pairs of Corinthian columns. The side openings were in fact simulated, as they concealed houses. At attic level was an enormous painting (described as a 'Tableau énigmatique'), and above that the poop of a ship with a bizarre assemblage of writhing figures and military equipment.[2]

The final arch, designed by Charles Le Brun, closed the end of the place Dauphine. About 35 m high, it symbolised royal authority with regard to the people. The arch itself represented the people, while the huge obelisk above stood for the monarchy. The opening was flanked by pairs of embracing caryatids, imitating bronze. Over it was a large simulated tapestry, showing the King and Queen in a chariot driven by Hymen, beneath a broken segmental pediment, which framed a figure of Atlas intended to symbolise Cardinal Mazarin as mediator between King and people. The obelisk was lavishly decorated with reliefs, statues and weapons. The famous 'vingt-quatre violons du Roi' played here.[3]

Lawrence Bryant sees the 1660 entry as having both 'revived and shattered' the traditional programme. It marked the end of long wars and failed revolution (the Fronde), emphasising the glory of the King, and the new forms of absolutism, and the queen as bringer of peace. The one great theme was that it was for the will of the King to make either war or peace.[4]

In 1662 Jean-Baptiste Colbert consulted the poet Jean Chapelain about ways of proclaiming the glory of the King. He mentioned the monuments built by the ancients, including triumphal arches, but said they were outside his province. In the next year Colbert set up a committee of four members of the Académie Française to make proposals: Chapelain was a member, and he recommended Charles Perrault as secretary.[5] In 1669 a permanent arch in honour of Louis XIV was proposed, to stand in the Faubourg St-Antoine, where the first of the 1660 arches had stood [14.2]. It was to celebrate the recent victories in Flanders and Burgundy, in which the King himself took part. After a competition with Louis Le Vau and Charles Le Brun, the design of Claude Perrault was chosen by Colbert (now Controller General of Finances), who had a full-scale model executed, with the sculpture apparently modelled in plaster. It was to be more than twice the height of the Arch of Constantine, and was a triple arch, but exceptionally broad, with pairs of Corinthian columns between the openings, and much sculpture, culminating in an equestrian statue of the King on a very large base whose sides curved inwards. When the model was almost complete, in 1670, the King came to see it. Work progressed on the arch for thirteen years, but when Colbert

14.2 Arch for Faubourg St-Antoine, Paris, proposed 1669. Claude Perrault.

died in 1683 it had only reached the stone pedestals. In 1685 the Académie made many adverse criticisms of Perrault's design: it was considered to be insufficiently like a gateway, too ornate, and too much like a base for the statue. Considering that the original function of the 'triumphal arch' is now thought to have been precisely this, the criticism seems misplaced, but the design was certainly not entirely satisfactory. Alternative designs were produced by Pierre Bullet and by François d'Orbay, but the project went no further, probably for reasons of cost. In 1715 Louis XIV died, and in the next year both the model and the executed pedestals were destroyed.[6] A curious footnote to this story is that in 1832 an architect called Aubert Parent proposed to build an arch of the same size and on the same site as Perrault's to celebrate the revolution of 1830.[7]

While this saga dragged on, four other gates in the form of triumphal arches were erected. The first was the Porte-St Denis, at the entrance to the rue du Faubourg St-Denis, which was the official entrance point of the kings into Paris [14.3]. The arch was erected in 1672 by the city to commemorate the victories of Louis XIV in Germany. The architect was the military engineer François Blondel. The structure, which survives, is 23 m in height and breadth, and is basically plain, but has obelisk-shaped reliefs on the piers. The slightly recessed opening has Victories in the spandrels and reliefs above – the passage of the Rhine on the city side, and the taking of Maastricht on the north. The sculpture was executed by Michel Anguier. The monument has had a troubled history. It came near to demolition in 1793, and was barricaded in 1830, 1848, 1851 and 1871. In 1861–6 Hector Horeau proposed to crown the arch with a strange sculptural composition representing a sort of tent, with statues, as part of his scheme for large matching blocks on either side.[8] It was restored many times, the most substantial work being done in 1885–7, when the sculptures were repaired by five artists.[9]

In 1670 Blondel reused the old Porte St-Antoine (already remodelled in temporary form for the 1660 entry) as the central part of a broad triple arch.[10] It honoured the king for his care for the beauty of the city. It was demolished in 1778 as an obstruction to traffic. The Porte St-Bernard on the quai de la Tournelle, built in 1674 to replace an old gate, was a tall arch with two equal openings, above which on each side was a large relief running right across. The arch celebrated the King's encouragement of trade and industry, and the reliefs, by Jean-Baptiste Tuby, showed, on the city side, Louis receiving the offerings of marine deities and passing them on to Paris, and on the river side Louis on the poop of a ship.[11]

In 1674 the city also built the Porte St-Martin, a short distance to the west of the Porte St-Denis [14.4]. The designer was Pierre Bullet. The triple arch 17 m in height and breadth is heavily rusticated, and reliefs over the side openings spread up into the spandrels of the central one. On the attic is an inscription dedicating the arch to Louis XIV for his having twice taken Besançon and Franche-Comté, and for his victories over the German, Spanish and Dutch armies. The reliefs show, on the city side, the taking of Besançon (by Desjardins) and the breaking of the triple alliance (by Marsy), and, on the north, the taking of Limburg (by Le Hongre) and the defeat of the Germans (by Legros *père*).[12]

14.3 Porte St-Denis, Paris, 1672. François Blondel.

14.4 Porte St-Martin, Paris, 1674. Pierre Bullet.

The most celebrated military engineer who worked for Louis XIV was Sébastien Le Prestre de Vauban.[13] The gates to his fortifications often had some resemblance to the triumphal arch, but the most spectacular was the Porte de Paris at Lille [14.5]. Built in 1685–92 and intended to celebrate Louis's conquest of Walloon Flanders, it was designed by the local architect Simon Vollant, in what Andrew Saint calls 'a loyal un-Flemish idiom'. Now freestanding, it is 40 m high. There is one small opening, set within a tall recessed arch. All the masonry except for the orders is rusticated. Above the Doric entablature is a group of Victory crowning a portrait of the King, between Fames with trumpets (surely dating from the 1890s). On either side are pairs of columns supporting entablatures which are set lower than the central one, also topped with trophies. Between these columns are statues of Mars and Hercules. Over the opening are the royal arms and the arms of Lille. The city side of the arch was given lavish treatment in 1895, after the removal of the remains of the ramparts in 1888. The central section is not dissimilar to the other side, but it has a segmental pediment over it. Flanking the opening, triple arcades are set below rusticated areas with windows between reliefs. Over these are dormers, set against a tall slate roof.[14] The Porte de Tournai at Lille (destroyed in 1890–95), was also designed by Vollant, and was more sober, though not dissimilar, in combining rusticated masonry with a Doric order. The two openings were set between three pairs of columns. Reginald Blomfield thought it 'simpler and better' than the Porte de Paris, suggesting 'a dim reminiscence of the Porta del Palio at Verona'.[15]

14.5 Porte de Paris, Lille, 1685–92. Simon Vollant.

Gates to other fortifications by Vauban which take a form similar to that of the triumphal arch include the Porte de Belfort at Neuf Brisach, which has attached Doric columns and a pediment, and the Porte de Colmar, also at Neuf Brisach, which has a pair of banded pilasters on either side of the opening, with a pediment over, while the sides have similar piers at the ends and recessed entablatures.[16] At Strasbourg the marquis de Louvois, the Minister of War, wanted Vauban to reduce the grandeur of the gates, but he successfully protested (in a letter of 1681) that it was only a matter of 'some triglyphs, metopes and dentils and the arms and monograms of the king'.[17] At La Rochelle, where François Ferry was in charge, the Porte Dauphine of 1694–9, designed by Jean-Baptiste Bullet, has a coat of arms on a tympanum set within the opening, and a sun carved in the pediment, while the Porte Royale, as executed, has pairs of attached Doric columns on the outer side, with a pediment but a plain triple arch on the inner face. Pierre Bullet made several grander designs for this gate, one of them a full-scale triumphal arch, triple, and in the Doric order, with reliefs over the side openings, and another in the tympanum of the central one showing a captive on either side of a bust.[18]

Another arch erected for Louis XIV is the handsome Porte du Peyrou at Montpellier [14.6]. Dramatically set at the entrance to the promenade du Peyrou, which leads past an equestrian statue of the King to the Château d'Eau, it was built in 1691–3 to a design by François d'Orbay, executed by Augustin-Charles d'Aviler. It has some resemblance to the Porte St-Martin in Paris. The surface is rusticated, and the central

234   THE TRIUMPHAL ARCH

14.6 Montpellier, Porte du Peyrou, 1691–3. François d'Orbay.

opening is flanked by blank arches, in the upper parts of which circular reliefs celebrating the King's achievements were placed in 1715. Above these are rectangular reliefs of trophies. The attic bears an inscription of 1715 praising the peace won by the King.[19]

In 1701 a temporary arch was erected at Grenoble to welcome the King's grandsons, the duc de Bourgogne and the duc de Berry. It was a simple structure with quoins, but over it was a huge inscription tablet, and above that a circular painting, while on either side trees bearing flags and drums grew out of rocks.[20] The two dukes entered Aix and Avignon in the same year. At Aix it was proposed by Pierre de Galaup de Chasteuil to erect seven arches, as 'the most perfect number', and as his father had done for Louis XIII (p. 227), but the assembly preferred five, which was just as well as there was not even enough time to build the fifth. The arches had a local flavour, the first set in a forest of oranges, lemons, pomegranates, palms, figs and olives, while the others had paintings of local subjects such as the 'Parlement d'Amour' of the Roi René (who died at Aix) and Gaius Marius, who won a great victory nearby in 102 BC.[21] In 1704 the façade of Du Cerceau's 'Grand Pavillon' of the Louvre in Paris was decorated by the sculptor François Girardon to celebrate the birth of the duc de Bretagne, the short-lived great-grandson of Louis XIV. Pairs of banded columns of the 'French Doric order' had statues between them, while above the entablature stood obelisks. In the centre was an elaborately curtained balcony.[22]

The gardens of Versailles had their own arch, in the 'Bosquet de l'Arc de Triomphe', erected by Pierre Mazeline under André le Nôtre in 1677–84, to celebrate the King's

FRANCE FROM LOUIS XIV TO THE REVOLUTION

military victories. It was of gilt iron or bronze, with three equal openings below a pediment. Each opening had an urn spouting water, and bowls along the pediment poured water down sea shell ladders. It is shown in a gouache by Jean Cotelle of 1693.[23]

It is not surprising that the reign of Louis XIV saw great interest in designs on paper for arches. In 1688 F. de Loriny, who described himself as architect to James II of England, published in Paris his *Livres de portes cochères et arcs de triomphe*. None of his designs is very obviously a triumphal arch, though the *Livre d'architecture de porte et cheminées* by D.A. Pierretz (published in Paris *c.* 1650), which is bound up with it in the British Library, contains two which are, both with military imagery (one inscribed *REGINA VICTORIARUM*). In 1703 Daniel Marot published his *Desseins d'arc de triomphe*, which include elaborate examples with columns, pediments, obelisks, caryatids, statues, reliefs and so on. In a seventeenth-century stage design in the Houthakker Collection in Amsterdam the buildings at the sides are taken from an engraving after Hans Vredeman de Vries, but a large arch has been added in the background, with groups of three Composite columns on either side, the central one standing forward, a frieze over the opening, and sculpture on the attic. An arcade runs back on each side.[24]

Louis XV was honoured with several arches. The magnificent Porte de l'Arsenal at Toulon was built in 1738, to the design of Bruno Nègre de Sainte-Croix and the sculptor Jean Maucord. The order is Doric, and the four freestanding columns of cipollino had been brought from Greece in 1686. Over the entablature seated statues of Minerva (by Maucord) and Mars (by Miguel Verdiguier) flank the inscription. Above that are the royal arms. On the piers are reliefs on two levels. The arch was moved in 1976 to form the entrance to the naval museum.[25]

At Nevers the Porte de Paris of 1746 also celebrates Fontenay. Built in 1742–6 to replace an older gate, it is very simple, the opening recessed within a rectangle, the cornice being the most prominent feature. Unfortunately the relief sculpture was destroyed at the Revolution: it consisted of trophies, coats of arms, etc. The most remarkable feature of this structure is the poem by Voltaire which is inscribed within the opening. These are five of its fourteen lines:

> *Dans ces temps fortunés de gloire et de puissance,*
> *Où Louis, répandant les bienfaits et l'effroi,*
> *Triomphait des Anglais aux champs de Fontenay …*
> *Les peuples de Nevers, dans ces jours de victoire,*
> *Ont voulu signaler leur bonheur et sa gloire.*
>
> ('In these fortunate times of glory and power, when Louis, spreading benefits and terror, triumphed over the English on the fields of Fontenay … the people of Nevers, in these days of victory, have wished to show their good fortune and his glory.') There was also a couplet on each face of the arch, but these have disappeared.[26]

At Vitry le François, the Porte du Pont formerly stood at the end of the bridge over the Marne, but was taken down in 1938, and reerected in the place du Maréchal Leclerc in 1982 [14.7]. Built in 1746–9 to the design of Jean-Gabriel Legendre, an engineer of the Ponts et Chaussées, it is charmingly small-scale and Rococo. On the principal side it curves forward between rusticated pilasters. The flat central section is also rusticated, and has a lavish coat of arms over it. On the plain curving sections on

14.7 Vitry le François, arch, 1746–9. Jean Gabriel Legendre.

either side are large reliefs of trophies. On top is a balustrade, with four trophies. The other side is flat and simpler.[27]

A magnificent arch was built at Nancy in honour of Louis XV [14.8]. It formed part of the splendid place Royale, whose design was conceived in 1752 by King Stanislas, and executed by Emmanuel Héré. The arch was built in 1753–5. It is triple, of the Corinthian order. The centre breaks forward, and it and the sides are flanked by pairs of columns. The reliefs on the attic show Apollo and the Muses; the union of Peace

14.8 Nancy, Place Royale, 1752. King Stanislas and Emmanuel Héré.

FRANCE FROM LOUIS XIV TO THE REVOLUTION   237

and Victory; and a hero with a bow killing Discord. Over the attic are statues of Ceres, Minerva, Mars and Hercules (a copy of the Farnese Hercules). These stone sculptures are by Jean-Baptiste Walnaeffer. On the top the gilded lead sculpture (by Barthélemy Guibal) represents a Victory blowing a trumpet. The reverse side of the arch is similar, but has trophies on top instead of statues.[28]

The Nancy scheme was illustrated by Pierre Patte in his book *Monuments érigés en France à la gloire de Louis XV* (Paris, 1765). He also illustrates several schemes made in 1752 for a competition for *places* in Paris where it was proposed to erect statues of the King, and some include arches. Germain Boffrand's proposal for the place Dauphine had a curving block on the east side with an arch in the centre, of the Corinthian order, with four statues on the attic. He also made a design for the area between the Louvre and the Tuileries: the space is flanked on each side by a long range with an opening for a street in the centre, and each opening has an arch similar to the place Dauphine one. Claude-Guillot Aubry proposed for the end of the Pont Royal a triple arch, again of the Corinthian order, with much sculptural decoration. For the carrefour de Buci Pierre-Noel Rousset designed a circular *place* surrounded by a colonnade, with a big arch with pairs of engaged Doric columns and plenty of sculpture, flanked by lesser arches.[29]

At Châtillon-sur-Seine the Porte de Paris was built in 1765 for the entry of Louis XV. It is a simple structure with little decoration, as is the similar Porte de Châtillon at Bar-sur-Seine.[30] Another gate in the form of a triumphal arch is the Porte St-Pierre at Pontarlier, in the Franche-Comté, built in 1738 to replace a gate in the walls destroyed by fire. Designed by the military engineer Jean-Claude Éléonor le Michaud d'Arçon, it is a plain triple arch decorated with garlands. The town asked for a clock-tower on top. The wooden construction was replaced in 1895–8 in stone to a fanciful design by Authier.[31]

On Marie Antoinette's arrival in France in 1770, coming to marry the future Louis XVI, she was greeted at Châlons-sur-Marne (now called Châlons-en-Champagne) with an arch designed by Nicolas Durand. Originally called the Porte Dauphine, it is now the Porte Ste-Croix. Elegantly simple, and 20 m high, it has a single opening set within a rusticated front, on the piers of which are inset tall panels with reliefs; the narrow sides are slightly recessed, and above the bracketed cornice is a coat of arms.[32] Another arch for someone other than the King was the Porte de Bourgogne at Bordeaux. It is situated opposite the Pont de Pierre, at the main approach from Paris. Built in 1750–55, its design was a revision by Ange-Jacques Gabriel of one by Nicolas Portier. It was dedicated to the duc de Bourgogne in 1755 by the Intendant Tourny. Very simple, but elegant, it is rusticated, with pairs of plain Doric pilasters on either side of the opening, a prominent cornice, and an attic which breaks forward over the pilasters. Originally there was a large coat of arms, flanked by trophies, on the top.[33]

The death of Louis's father in 1765 was, perhaps surprisingly, marked by the erection of the Porte Dauphine at Sens, where he was buried. It was designed by the distinguished mining engineer Charles-Axel Guillaumot. The bas-reliefs, by Antoine Léonard Pasquier, commemorated the Dauphin and his wife (who had died two years after him). Guillaumot is said to have intended a triumphal character on the outer side, and a funerary character on the inner side. The arch no longer exists.[34]

Another arch was built at Nancy in 1782–4. Formerly called the Porte Louis, it was renamed the Porte Désilles in memory of a Revolutionary hero. The architect was

Didier-Joseph-François Mélin, and the sculptor Johann Joseph Söntgen. The arch was to honour Louis XVI (Lorraine having reverted to France after the death of Stanislas), to commemorate the birth of the Dauphin in 1781 and (subsequently) the Treaty of Versailles (1783), and also the memory of the men of Nancy killed at Yorktown fighting for American independence. The central opening is matched by blank arches containing rectangular openings with circular reliefs above. The inner side has four Ionic pilasters and a relief showing the Treaty of Versailles; the outer side also has four pilasters, the whole covered in vermiculated rustication, and a relief of the Battle of Nancy (1477).[35]

At about the same time, in 1783, a plain but handsome arch, astylar, with channelled masonry, was built at Dijon in honour of the prince de Condé, Governor of Burgundy. The architect was Jean-Philippe Maret. It was later called the Porte de Liberté, and the reliefs showing the Prince's achievements by Claude-François Attiret on the upper part of the piers (the only sculptural decoration) were altered in 1792. Its current name is the Porte Guillaume.[36]

Temporary arches for Louis XV included one at Strasbourg in 1744, in front of the Zaberner Tor, which was clearly based on Perrault's design for the arch in the place du Trône in Paris, not least in the equestrian statue on a pedestal on the attic.[37] In 1745, to welcome the king to Paris after the victory of Fontenay, Jacques-François Blondel designed a lavish temporary ornamentation of the Porte St-Martin, in highly coloured wood and stucco, transforming it with Ionic columns on either side of the central opening, and in pairs at the sides, with entablatures breaking forward, statues on pedestals round the piers, and winged Victories holding the royal arms on the attic, which was crowned by a pedestal bearing a trumpeting Fame on horseback [14.9].[38] Blondel's decorations also included a triumphal arch for a firework display, a *quadrifrons* on an octagonal plan.[39] When the Dauphin married the Infanta Maria Teresa Rafaela in the same year, the city of Paris erected several pavilions for eating and dancing, and their 'frontispieces' took the form of triumphal arches. That of the Salle de la rue Sève was a double arch, with pairs of Ionic columns and a large painting above. That of the Salle de l'Estrapade was rusticated, with pairs of embracing caryatids, and above the opening another painting. That of the Salle de la Bastille had pairs of Ionic pilasters canted on either side, and masses of sculpture on top. Grandest of all was the frontispiece of the Salle de la place Dauphine, with groups of three Corinthian columns canted on either side, an arched niche over the opening full of putti, and trumpeting angels with the royal arms on top.[40]

For the laying of the foundation stone of the church of St-Sulpice in Paris in 1754

14.9 Decoration of the Porte St-Martin for the return of the King, September 7, 1745. Pieter de Swart.

FRANCE FROM LOUIS XIV TO THE REVOLUTION 239

Giovanni Niccolò Servandoni designed an arch to stand in the square in front. It was unusual, in that the opening was based on the so-called 'Serliana' or 'Venetian window', with Corinthian columns. Within the opening was a statue of the King, with a crown suspended above. On the piers were brackets supporting trophies. The medallions below these reproduced the medal struck for the occasion.[41]

In 1770 an arch was erected at Strasbourg to welcome the Dauphine, Marie Antoinette (her temporary arch at Châlons-sur-Marne has already been mentioned). Designed by Samuel Werner, it was clearly based on Perrault's arch in the Faubourg St-Antoine. An obelisk on the attic bore a statue of Mercury.[42]

Architects continued to make designs on paper. The competition for the Grand Prix of the Académie began on a regular basis in 1720. The subject of 'Un arc de triomphe' was set in 1722, 1730, 1747 and 1763.[43] The Prix de Rome was won in 1752 by Charles de Wailly with a design for a palace entered through a large triumphal arch, with pairs of Doric columns, statues on two levels between them, and a circular podium on top supporting a *quadriga*.[44] In 1746, while in Rome, Charles Michel-Ange Challe made a fantasy design, influenced by Piranesi, with a huge and elaborate arch, with projecting aedicules on the front and side, and (again) a circular podium on top with a *quadriga*.[45] A design for an even bigger arch was made by Jean-Baptiste Lallemand, probably when he was in Rome (*c.* 1751–61). Set on a terrace, it has four large astylar projections, with the central opening set on columns, and colonnades on either side.[46]

The prolific Jean-François Neufforge included designs for triumphal arches in his *Recueil élémentaire d'architecture* (as well as very similar gateways to palaces and cities, and fountains and a firework display).[47] In his book *Œuvres d'architecture* (1769) Pierre Contant d'Ivry included a design made for the city of Paris in 1739, with pairs of Doric columns on either side of the central opening, which has a pediment crowned with an equestrian statue of the King, and single columns at the sides of the piers.[48] In 1770, for the marriage of the Dauphin, Guillaume-Martin Couture produced an incredibly lavish design which is a screen rather an arch, with four pairs of Corinthian columns, lavish sculpture, and a circular tempietto above.[49] In the same year Jean-Charles Delafosse made an unusual design, with pedimented aedicules on the piers, containing sculptures, the opening rising up into the attic, which has reliefs. Above are the royal arms with flags. Side wings with windows have rusticated pilasters.[50] In 1779 Jean-Nicolas Sobre made a curious design with a central section with freestanding Doric columns, a bracketed cornice, and on top an allegory of the city of Paris with a ship (the emblem of the city). On either side, set back, is a lower rusticated pier, with a doorway, and a seated statue on a stepped base.[51]

For the Grand Prix of 1783 Jean-Charles-Alexandre Moreau won a prize for an arch to commemorate the Peace of Versailles. It was rusticated, with two cubic piers which had four Corinthian columns on each side, with statues above; the opening rose almost to the height of the bracketed cornice.[52] Two anonymous drawings in the Houthakker Collection show another project, with four projecting aedicules on each front and two on each side, each with two Corinthian columns, and an arched opening in the centre flanked by rectangular ones. It was to be sited at the entrance to the Champs-Elysées.[53] Another design, presumably again commemorating the Peace, by Charles-Jean Bénard, is dated 1784 and inscribed 'Liberté des Mers 1783'. The enormous arch has an elaborate rostral column in front of each pier, with a statue on each at attic level, and reliefs over the opening.[54]

Early in his career, in 1759, Étienne-Louis Boullée had designed scenery for a play put on by the pupils of the Jesuit Collège Louis-le-Grand which included a huge arch with aedicules projecting on all sides, and (yet again) a *quadriga* on a circular podium on top. Around 1780 he made three designs for arches in his characteristic colossal but plain style. One is a great wide severe arch, with a single opening, and no decoration except for coffering within and an inscription. A more elaborate design has the opening flanked by a colonnade of six Doric columns on either side; these form the front of further colonnades, with a total of 36 columns on each side of the opening. This idea was foreshadowed in his 1759 design. On the (somewhat narrower) attic is a frieze, and on top is a chariot drawn by eight horses. Boullée's most megalomaniac design is for an arch with sides sloping steeply above plinth level. The plinth is decorated with reliefs, and has statue groups over small doorways. On top is again a chariot drawn by eight horses.[55]

The reign of Louis XV also saw two Paris *hôtels* adorned with triumphal arch entrances. The Hôtel de Salm (now the Palais de la Légion d'Honneur) was built in 1782–87 to the design of Pierre Rousseau. The entrance to the forecourt takes the form of an elegant arch with Ionic columns recessed within the opening. Flying Victories in relief occupy the upper part.[56] More dramatic was the entrance to the Hôtel Thélusson by Claude-Nicolas Ledoux, built in 1778–81; a great plain rusticated structure, with a bracketed cornice and octagonal coffering, it was intended to look like an ancient arch half-buried. The house was demolished in 1826.[57]

The last arch of Louis XVI's reign, after the Revolution of 1789, had a sombre significance. It was built for the Festival de la Fédération of 14 July 1790, held on the Champ de Mars [14.10]. It was situated at the entrance to the field, at the end of a pontoon bridge across the Seine. In keeping with the scale of the event, it was a massive structure of wood and canvas, with three equal openings, 50 m broad and 25 m high. The lower parts of the piers and the archivolts were rusticated, and there were reliefs on the piers as well as a long narrow one below the entablature. The arch celebrated Liberty, Constitution and the Rights of Man. The design appears to have been a collaboration between Georges-François Blondel, Bernard Poyet and Jacques Cellerier.[58]

Under the new Republic designs for arches continued to be made. In 1790 the Academy held a competition for the design of a National Assembly. Pierre Rousseau proposed a vast complex on the Left Bank, entered by a high and deep arch, with Corinthian columns and a *quadriga* on top.[59] For the Fête de la Fraternité of August 1793 an arch was erected on the boulevard Poissonnière in memory of the female citizens who marched to Versailles in 1789. It was severely plain, but had trophies on pedestals against the piers, reliefs over the opening and on the frieze, and women pulling cannons on top.[60] The King had been guillotined in January 1793; the Queen would be in October. In 'l'an II' (1794) a competition was held for the design of propaganda structures, including a triumphal arch. Alexandre-Théodore Brongniart came up with a quadripartite 'Arc des Sans-Culottes': four groups of four columns (representing bundles of lances standing on cannon-balls) support entablatures with reliefs on the friezes, while above are plain surfaces with reliefs of winged females; the

14.10 Fête de la Féderation, Champs de Mars, Paris, 1790.

soffits are coffered, and in the centre is a dome. Philibert Moitte proposed a wonderful arch, quite plain in its structure, but with lavish decoration. It gained him the first prize. On the front and at the side of each pier groups of three large elephants (eighteen in all, two groups on each front, and one on each side) stand on richly carved bases and support the cornice at impost level; above that are trumpeting Victories seated on pedestals. Over the opening is a relief of a cock. Below the crowning entablature is a relief frieze of bulls' heads, while on top are eight lions below a naked male figure representing 'Le Peuple'. The elephants symbolise wisdom, the cock vigilance, the bulls strength, and the lions courage. In the same competition a prize was won by Jean-Nicolas Sobre for his design for a large arch to stand at the entrance to the Pont de la Concorde. The freestanding Doric columns in front of the piers had spiral friezes (like Trajan's Column), with winged females round their bases, and seated figures over the projecting entablatures. In the spandrels were winged Victories. Of Philippe de Lasalle's design for the same site only the plan survives, with a kind of temple incorporated on each side of the opening.[61]

For the festival for the foundation of the Republic in 1796 Brongniart designed an 'arc des Saisons', in which two large outcrops of rock were joined by an arch of cloud, with the scales of justice in the centre.[62] In the same year another competition was held, one of the projects being an arch in the place de la Concorde. The design by Athanase Détournelle and Armand-Charles Caraffe showed the chaste type of structure which had by now become standard, with reliefs of weapons on the lower parts of the piers, and, above these, on one side two male figures embracing giant fasces, and on the other two females doing the same. Both pairs trample Discord. The inscription records the decision of the government to rename the square and place in it monumental allegories of union and concord.⁶³

In the same year the government sought designs for a covered arena between the boulevard St-Martin and the rue de Bondi. The winning project by Jean-Baptiste Lahure included a large triumphal arch over the boulevard; it has four detached Ionic columns, with statues over their projecting entablatures, arched openings on two levels in the piers, and winged Victories in the spandrels.⁶⁴

Other projects of these years include an anonymous one for an arch to be set at the entrance to the Champs-Elysées, between the Chevaux de Marly. Fairly plain, it has the bizarre feature of zigzagging staircases against the piers, on which spectators could stand.⁶⁵ Brongniart made alternative designs for an arch in the place de la Bastille. One has pairs of Doric columns supporting projecting entablatures on each pier and on each side, with sculptural groups above.⁶⁶ Antoine Voinier showed in the salon of 1795 a megalomaniac arch for the western end of the Champs-Elysées. To honour the 'fourteen armies', it had enormous piers supporting groups of statuary, flanked by colonnades each of nine Doric columns. Above each end of these were circular pedestals with rostra, and Victories above surrounded by trophies. Steps rose up from these to a crowning Ionic circular tempietto.⁶⁷ A design of the 'an VIII' (1799–1800) shows a *quadrifrons* with seated figures above the impost level, supporting a very tall column with banded reliefs and a statue on top.⁶⁸

The eccentric Jean-Jacques Lequeu produced several predictably strange designs. Two were shown in the Salle de la Liberté in the 'an II' (1793–4).⁶⁹ One, labelled 'Arc Triomphal du chemin particulier des triomphateurs du cirque', has pairs of Ionic columns set against broad piers, on which are galleries faced with reliefs. The upper part is one huge segmental pediment, with a seated figure holding garlands in the middle. Another, 'érigé en l'honneur des braves de la patrie, … à l'extrémité du cours côté de l'orient' (i.e. at the Étoile) was to recall the 'événement affreux' of 1793. It has rostral columns in front of the piers, between pairs of Ionic pilasters; these columns reach above the topmost cornice, and on the attic is a group of symbolic female figures. Maddest of all is the 'Porte de Paris qu'on peut appeler l'arc du peuple', intended to form the principal entrance to the 'Palais de la République' by the place du Carrousel [14.11]. This has semicircular projections with banded rustication on the piers, while the taller central opening is surrounded by shield shapes. Above sits a gigantic Hercules, whose leg comes down on the right-hand pier, and his club on the left-hand one; he wears a lion-skin and a helmet, and holds a figure of Liberty. Lequeu noted that this design, which he described as 'composition d'architecture Indienne Orientale et architectures françaises', was 'to save myself from the guillotine'.

14.11 Porte de Paris, design by Jean Jacques Lequeu, *Architecture Civile*, 1794.

A new arch for the Arsenal of Toulon was proposed after the Revolution, to honour the heroes who died using the arms produced there. It was a bizarre design, standing over a canal, with pairs of narrow square piers, supporting statues, projecting on each side, while the upper part takes the form of a semicircle. The piers are decorated with strips of relief and garlands.[70]

Under the Directoire (1795–9) Charles de Wailly produced a scheme for a site north of the place Vendôme in Paris, for Belgian developers. An opera house would stand at the end of a square, entered by a large triumphal arch, which had pairs of Doric columns against the piers, and within the opening supporting the archivolt. On the piers were trophies, and the attic, over the opening, was crowned with a *quadriga*. The arch was intended to celebrate the victories of the French, but a committee of the Institut made the curious complaint that 'the Athenians would not have tolerated a triumphal arch in their city, and the Romans only erected them in honour of emperors'.[71]

In 1797 the government announced a competition for the site of the Château Trompette at Bordeaux, to commemorate both Victory and Peace. Louis-Pierre Baltard (father of the architect of the Halles in Paris) proposed an arch on the riverbank 'to the triumphs of the armies of the Republic'. It was a *quadrifrons*, astylar, with square reliefs on the piers, below circular ones, and a *quadriga* on top of a stepped attic. An alternative proposed a narrower arch, with a full-scale attic, again with a *quadriga*, but with men on horseback flanking it.[72]

Notes

1 On the inscription see Florence Vuilleumier Laurens and Pierre Laurens, 'Le débat sur la langue de l'inscription', *L'age de l'inscription: la rhétorique du monument en Europe du XVe au XVIIe siècle* (Paris, 2010), 233–7.
2 The drawing by Jean Marot for his engraving of the arch is in the Houthakker Collection (Amsterdam). Fuhring attributes the figures and ornamentation to Jean Lepautre: Peter Fuhring, ed., *Design into Art: Drawings for Architecture and Ornament in the Lodewijck Houthakker Collection* (London, 1989), no. 1003.
3 Jean Tronçon, *L'entrée triomphante de Leurs Majestés Louis XIV … et Marie-Thérèse d'Autriche … dans la Ville de* Paris (Paris, 1662); Karl Möseneder, *Zeremoniell und monumentale Poesie: Die 'Entrée Solennelle' Ludwigs XIV. 1660 in Paris* (Berlin, 1983), reproducing Tronçon's book in full; Christoph Frank, 'Les artistes de l'entrée de Louis XIV en 1745', *Bull. de la Soc. de l'histoire de l'Art Français*, 1989, 53–65.
4 Lawrence M. Bryant, *The King and the City in the Parisian Royal Entry Ceremony* (Geneva, 1986), 207–16. See also Jean-Marie Apostolidès, *Le Roi-machine* (Paris, 1981).
5 *Lettres de Jean Chapelain* (Paris, 1883), II, 272–7; Marc Soriano, *Le dossier Perrault* (Paris, 1972), 118.
6 Michael Petzet, 'Der Triumphbogenmonument für Ludwig XIV. auf der Place du Trône', *Zeitschrift für Kunstgeschichte* 45 (1982), 145–94; Antoine Picon, *Claude Perrault, 1613–1688, ou la curiosité d'un classique* (Paros, 1988), 228–30. Picon suggests that Charles Perrault might have helped his brother with the programme of sculpture.
7 Picon (cit. in the preceding note), 274, n. 56.
8 Françoise Boudon and François Loyer, *Hector Horeau 1801–1872* (Paris, n.d.), 86–7.
9 François Blondel, *Cours d'architecture* (2nd edn, Paris, 1698), 618–20. At p. 173 he complains that the sculptor failed to execute his idea for the Passage du Rhin, with an angry river-god and fleeing Naiads. See also Véronique Wiesinger, 'Quelques précisions sur la restauration de la porte Saint-Denis après la Commune de Paris (1885–7)', *Bull. de la Soc. de l'histoire de l'Art Français*, 1988, 185–95.
10 Blondel (cit. in the preceding note), 604–8; Louis Hautecoeur, *Histoire de l'architecture classique en France*, II (Paris, 1948), 574–5.
11 Blondel (cit. at n. 9), 614–8; Hautecoeur (cit. in the preceding note), 515–6.
12 Hautecoeur (cit. at n. 10), 516–17. For these three gates, see Wolfgang E. Stopfel, *Triumphbogen in der Architektur des Barock in Frankreich und Deutschland* (diss., Freiburg, 1964), 45f.
13 Sir Reginald Blomfield, *Sebastien Le Prestre de Vauban 1633–1707* (London, 1938); Michel Parent and Jacques Verroust, *Vauban* (Paris, 1971); Anne Blanchard, *Vauban* (Paris, 1996).
14 Hautecoeur (cit. at n. 10), 508–10; *Le siècle de l'eclecticisme – Lille 1830–1930* (Paris and Brussels, 1979), 8; Andrew Saint, *Architect and Engineer* (New Haven/London, 2007), 22.
15 Blomfield (cit. at n. 13), 55.

16 Hautecoeur (cit. at n. 10), 506–7; Blomfield (cit. at n. 13), 51–5.
17 Saint (cit. at n. 14), 18–19.
18 Monique Moulin, *L'architecture civile et militaire au XVIIIe siècle en Aunis et Saintonge* (La Rochelle, 1972); Eric Langenskiöld, *Pierre Bullet: The Royal Architect* (Stockholm, 1959), 133–43.
19 Hautecoeur (cit. at n. 10), 518–9.
20 Möseneder (cit. at n. 3), Abb. 136.
21 Pierre de Galaup de Chasteuil, *Discours sur les arcs triomphaux dressés en la Ville d'Aix à l'heureuse entrée de Monseigneur le duc de Bourgogne et M. le duc de Berry* (Aix, 1701).
22 Victoria and Albert Museum, London, Prints and Drawings 27935.
23 Ian Thompson, *The Sun King's Garden* (London, 2006), 130, 172. The bosquet was abandoned in 1774–5.
24 Fuhring (cit. at n. 2), no. 957.
25 Louis Hautecoeur, *Histoire de l'architecture classique en France*, III (Paris, 1950), 510.
26 For the inscriptions, see *Oeuvres complètes de Voltaire*, 10 (Paris, 1877), 532–3.
27 Hautecoeur (cit. at n. 25), 510; Stopfel (cit. at n. 12), 90.
28 Hautecoeur (cit. at n. 25), 493.
29 Rousset and Aubry's schemes are illustrated in Yvan Christ, *Le Paris des Utopies* (Paris, 1977), 78–9.
30 Stopfel (cit. at n. 12), 90.
31 ibid.
32 Louis Hautecoeur, *Histoire de l'architecture classique en France*, IV (Paris, 1952), 424–5.
33 Stopfel (cit. at n. 12), 90; Christopher Tadgell, *Ange-Jacques Gabriel* (London, 1978) 171–4.
34 Hautecoeur (cit. at n. 32), 426.
35 ibid., 137; Stopfel (cit. at n. 12), 90.
36 Hautecoeur (cit. at n. 32), 426.
37 Alain-Charles Gruber, *Les grandes fêtes et leurs décors à l'époque de Louis XVI* (Geneva, 1972), fig. 16; Petzet (cit. at n. 6), 193–4. Gruber illustrates three designs, one of them very simple.
38 Gruber (cit. in the preceding note), 186. Blondel's drawing is in the Centre Canadien d'Architecture, Montreal.
39 Drawing by Jacques-Gabriel de St-Aubin in the Houthakker Collection (Fuhring (cit. at n. 2), no. 1024). A *quadrifrons* also formed the centrepiece of a firework display for the inauguration of the statue of Louis XV in the place de la Couture at Reims in 1765 (Gruber (cit. at n. 37), 185, fig. 8).
40 *Fêtes publiques données par la ville de Paris à l'occasion du mariage de Monseigneur le Dauphin* (Paris, 1745).
41 Svend Eriksen, *Early Neo-Classicism in France* (London, 1974), 291–2, pl. 16. The arch with 'Serliana' opening anticipates Ledoux's arch for Cassel of 1776.
42 Gruber (cit. at n. 37), 38–9, fig. 12.
43 David Drew Egbert, *The Beaux-Arts Tradition in French Architecture* (Princeton, 1980), 168f.
44 Allan Braham, *The Architecture of the French Enlightenment* (London, 1980), 90.
45 Fuhring (cit. at n. 2), no. 770. He attributes another design, for an arch on the Campidoglio, to Challe (no. 771).
46 ibid., no. 774.
47 J.-F. Neufforge, *Recueil élémentaire d'architecture*, II (Paris, 1758), 110–11, 113–14, 117, 121–3, 125; VI (Paris, 1765), 361–3, 393.
48 Gabrielle Joudiou in Jean-Louis Baritou and Dominique Foussard, *Chevotet-Contant-Chaussard: un cabinet d'architectes au siècle des lumières* (Paris, 1987), 90–91.
49 Hautecoeur (cit. at n. 32), 423 (the name 'Contant d'Ivry' in the caption to fig. 266 must be a mistake for Couture).
50 ibid., 423–4.
51 Drawing sold at Sotheby's, Monaco, 1987.
52 Helen Rosenau, 'The Engravings of the Grands Prix of the French Academy of Architecture', *Architectural History* 3 (1960), 40, pl. 115.
53 Fuhring (cit. at n. 2), no. 803.
54 *Catalogue of the Drawings Collection of the Royal Institute of British Architects,* B (1972), 73.
55 Jean-Marie Pérouse de Montclos, Étienne-Louis Boullée (London, 1974), 28 (with fig. 1), 118 (with figs 83–6); idem, *Étienne-Louis Boullée* (Paris, 1969), pls 115–18.
56 Jean-Marie Pérouse de Montclos, ed., *Le Guide du Patrimoine: Paris* (Paris, 1994), 274–6.
57 Michel Gallet, *Claude-Nicolas Ledoux* (Paris, 1980), 195–202; Anthony Vidler, *Claude-Nicolas Ledoux* (Cambridge, Mass., 1990), 60–66.
58 Richard A. Etlin, 'Architecture and the Festival of Federation, Paris, 1790', *Architectural History* 18 (1975), 23–42; James A. Leith, *Space and Revolution* (Montreal, 1991), 43–8, illustrating the reliefs.
59 Leith (cit. in the preceding note), 101–2.
60 ibid., 118, 132.
61 Werner Szambien, *Les Projets de l'an II: concours d'architecture de la période révolutionnaire* (Paris, 1986), 58–9 (Brongniart), 54–5 (Moitte), 59–60 (Sobre), 60–61 (Lasalle); Leith (cit. at n. 58), 156–60; Monique Mosser et al., *Alexandre-Théodore Brongniart 1739–1813 – Architecture et décor* (Paris, 1986), 221–7.
62 Annie Jacques and Jean-Pierre Mouilleseaux, *Les Architectes de la liberté* (Paris, 1988), 100; Mosser (cit. in the preceding note), 231, 234.
63 Leith (cit. at n. 58), 275.
64 ibid., 189.
65 Szambien (cit. at n. 61), 54; Jacques and Mouilleseaux (cit. at n. 62), 100–101.
66 Mosser (cit. at n. 61), 234.
67 Szambien (cit. at n. 61), 57–9; Leith (cit. at n. 58), 282–4. Voinier's description is given by Jacques and Mouilleseaux (cit. at n. 62), 130–32.
68 Jacques and Mouilleseaux (cit. at n. 62), 106.
69 Philippe Duboÿ, *Jean-Jacques Lequeu – Une énigme* (Paris, 1987), 164, 240, 245; Leith (cit. at n. 58), 150, 157–60.
70 Jacques and Mouilleseaux (cit. at n. 62), 64.
71 Leith (cit. at n. 58), 288–90.
72 ibid., 299–302; Pierre Pinon, *Louis-Pierre et Victor Baltard* (Paris, 2005), 20–21.

15

THE LOW COUNTRIES FROM THE SIXTEENTH TO THE NINETEENTH CENTURY

In 1515 Charles V (aged only fifteen) made his entry into Bruges. Most of the very large number of 'echarfaults' (scaffolds) were Gothic, but a few were at least partly Renaissance. That in the Place des Osterlins was a plain arch, with an attic flanked by pilasters, an ogival frame containing the arms of the Emperor, the Archduke Charles, and the nation, and putti with garlands on top. Another scaffold had four square piers supporting flat arches; a fountain above had a hexagonal basin, which symbolised the benefits coming from Spain. At the place de la Bourse there were 'deux arches faictes chascune pour ung arc triumphal à l'anticque'. Each had square piers, with grotesque ornament, supporting an arch, in which hung garlands. On top of one arch Bellerophon and Cadmus fought dragons, while on the other were Alexander, Ulysses, Hercules and Perseus.[1] In 1519 Charles entered Antwerp: Cornelius Grapheus, who wrote an epigram of ten elegiac couplets to celebrate it, claimed that the spectacles were the most splendid put on for the new Emperor, but it is not known what they looked like.[2]

In 1549 Charles's son Philip made a progress through Flanders. He entered Ghent for recognition as Count of Flanders. The five arches were designed by the local architect Franciscus van de Velde. A printed text makes clear the intention to imitate the Roman custom of erecting arches. The decorative schemes were devised by the philologist Jan Oste, or Otho, who visited libraries in Cologne and elsewhere to do his research. The arches were of an architectural character, each using one of the five orders. Each had a gallery above, which served as a kind of stage for the *tableaux vivants* put on by the Chambre de Rhétorique. They showed David giving his sceptre to his son, Philip of Macedon giving his heart to Alexander, Vespasian's triumph with his son Titus, Charlemagne designating Louis the Pious as his heir, and Thierry d'Alsace leaving his son Philip in power on his departure for Jerusalem.[3]

Much grander was Philip's entry in the same year into Antwerp, which was publicised in texts in Latin, French and Flemish. Roy Strong points out that it had been intended that Philip should be welcomed as the next emperor, but the Electors refused to do what his father wished, and so he was received only as the future king of Spain. The citizens were determined to emphasise their privileges, and the rewards of their trade. Many of the intended structures remained unfinished. There were fifteen arches, in a variety of styles. Some followed the older tradition of having stages for *tableaux vivants*. The foreign arches were the most Classical (the English one – perhaps surprisingly

– most of all), but many included up-to-date strapwork and grotesques. This new style was spread through the entry and the book on it published by Pieter Coecke van Aelst, who also designed the woodcuts. It has been supposed that he had general direction of the decorations, but this is doubted by Georges Marlier and A.E. Popham.[4] Artists involved included Frans and Cornelis Floris, Hubert Goltzius and Vredeman de Vries. The 'Privatus Anglorum arcus' (private arch of the English) was a triple arch, 22 m high, with pairs of Corinthian columns flanking the main opening and single ones beyond, and also pairs of columns on the ends. The attic had matching columns. In the centre was an inscription panel, and on either side a niche with a statue. On top was the 'Oceanus Britannicus', a figure reclining in a shell boat drawn by Tritons. The arch was designed, along with the town arches at the rue Haute, the Palais, and the Galerie de la Grand' Place, by Lambert Van Noort (best known as a designer of stained glass). The German arch, 19.5 m high and 22 m deep, was a rectangular structure composed of two arches linked by pilastered walls. Each arch was similar to the English one, but with pilasters on the attic. On top was a pedestal supporting a globe with the double-headed eagle. The 'Triumphalis Florentinorum Porticus' was similar to the German arch, but had rectangular openings flanked by giant fluted Corinthian columns, the central ones breaking forward to support a pediment. The Genoese arch was designed by Stefano Ambrosio Schiappalari, a Genoese merchant living in Antwerp: the largest and most magnificent of all, 280 men worked on it for seventeen days, at a cost of 9,000 florins. Frans Floris was said to have painted seven lifesize figures in one day, and his overall work took seven weeks. The arched opening, flanked by niches, was set back behind a double colonnade: above the front of this was the triple attic, with paintings, another of which was on a pedimented aedicule above. William Eisler argues that the arch was based on the harmonic principles of the universe. The fact that this appealed to the Emperor, with his interest in astronomy and the like, is shown by his having been to see and discuss it more than once (according to Schiappalari).[5]

The Spanish arch, designed by Francisco Montesa, was triple, of rusticated Doric, the openings flanked by atlantes on bases, with a circular temple of Janus above, and obelisks on the corners. The temple was closed, the sign of peace, long ago by Augustus on one side, and it was now being closed by Charles V and Philip on the other. The approach was by way of two 'imperial' columns, and then a row of columns on either side with statues between them. The arch of the Golden Age was low, but crowned by a huge pedimented aedicule with a group of figures below a vast globe. Another arch, with pairs of Corinthian columns, had on top Charles and Philip supporting the world. Other arches symbolised commerce and peace and liberty. The *Monetarii*, or mintworkers, set up an arch at the mint with a representation of the goddess Moneta (money).[6] The final arch had a plain lower storey, above which was an aedicule with segmental pediment on which God the Father crowned Philip in front of the revolving and illuminated heaven. Sadly the day of the entry was marred by torrential rain.

For Philip's entry into Mons, also in 1549, the remarkable local sculptor Jacques du Broeucq was in charge, and one of his collaborators was the young Jean de Boulogne (Giovanni da Bologna). Little is known about the decoration. Du Broeucq probably designed the arch for Philip's entry into Brussels in that year. Quite unknown is the artist responsible for the arches at Tournai, which were said to combine all the Vitruvian orders. One had seven girls, naked apart from their *parties secrètes*, who represented the seven Virtues; the other showed scenes from the Old and New Testaments, as well as Neptune with a girl equipped as a mermaid.

The celebrations in 1549 included a *fête* at the palace of Binche, put on by Mary of Hungary in honour of Philip and Charles. Du Broeucq designed the decorations. A triple arch stood before the entrance, described as being of the Ionic order. On each side were two fluted columns imitating marble, between which were statues of Mars and Pallas, with an eagle supporting two columns above. The internal vault and side walls had paintings glorifying Charles. The reverse of the arch had statues of Hercules and Mercury. Jean de Boulogne may have collaborated again. Robert Didier suggests that the architectural effect of this arch may be suggested by the superb *jubé* at Arques-la-Bataille near Dieppe, of c. 1550, which has three equal openings, with freestanding Corinthian columns, pairs of which flank niches with statues at the ends.[7]

Marcel Lageirse and Leo van Puyvelde have drawn attention to instances where entries apparently influenced Flemish artists to include arches in their work. Lageirse cites a stained glass window in St-Jacques, Liège, by Jean de Cromois, dating from 1520–25, where the arch recalls those set up at Bruges in 1515.[8] Leo van Puyvelde cites several stained glass windows in Ste-Gudule in Brussels, of which most were designed by Bernard van Orley and made by Jean Hack. One in the north transept dating from 1537 shows Charles V and Isabella of Portugal within a triple arch whose central opening rises higher than the side ones; a similar window of 1538 in the south transept shows Louis II and Marie of Hungary. A window of 1540 in the Blessed Sacrament Chapel showing François I and Eleanor of Austria features a superimposed pair of triumphal arches. The same motif comes in another window in the same chapel, of 1542, by Jean Hack after Michel van Coxcie, which shows John of Portugal and Catherine of Aragon. A complex arch provides the structure for a painting of the life of the Virgin in Tournai Cathedral, of 1546, by Pieter Coecke van Aelst, Pieter Pourbus and Lanceloot Blondeel. A broad archway flanked by pairs of pilasters has above it a triple arch, which has single Ionic columns flanking the central opening, in front of which is a balcony supporting the figures of Our Lady and the Child. At the ends are groups of three columns, the middle one breaking forward. There are many putti and other figures. It has been seen that a few years later, in 1549, Coecke was involved with the 1549 Antwerp entry, and Blondeel was in charge of the Bruges entry.[9]

The first Dutch city to erect arches for a visiting ruler was Utrecht, for Charles V in 1540. This was also the first time a descriptive pamphlet was published. After 1549 entries ceased in Holland, owing to the poor relations with Spain. Three arches were, however, erected in 1575 for the procession at the foundation of Leiden University. One had freestanding caryatids supporting a projecting roof on each front, while another had attached caryatids on bases which projected to support pairs of columns, again with a projecting roof.[10] The tradition of the triumphal procession began again in 1580, when William of Orange entered Amsterdam. In 1586 the Earl of Leicester, appointed Governor by the States General, entered The Hague, and was greeted by two arches. One was a simple rusticated arch flanked by Doric pilasters; above was an arched frame with Corinthian half-columns. The frame contained a picture of King Arthur; the inscription suggested that Leicester was a second Arthur. The other arch was wider and had pairs of Doric pilasters. Above was a representation of the seven provinces, with small columns in front of it supporting a platform with a coat of arms.

15.1 Entry of Ernest to Antwerp, 1594. Marten de Vos.

The entry was published in a long folded etching by or after Hendrick Goltzius.[11]

William of Orange had entered Ghent in 1577, but no arch was erected as that honour was reserved for the sovereign or governor-general. In 1582 the city built one designed by Lucas de Heere for the Duke of Anjou, as Count of Flanders. In the same year as Duke of Brabant he entered Antwerp, where the three arches included one set back behind a portico with four Ionic columns. Columns on the arch piers corresponded to these, and between them were paintings.[12]

In 1594 Ernst, Archduke of Austria, entered Brussels as Governor of the Spanish Netherlands. Arches celebrated his ancestry and virtues. Several featured terms, rather than columns, and there was much strapwork. There were also pageants representing Parnassus and Etna, with Cyclopes forging armour.[13] A few months later Ernst entered Antwerp, which had suffered terribly – sacked by the Spanish in 1576, and then besieged by the Duke of Parma [15.1]. The splendour of the entry represented a brave hope for better times. Here the arches were designed by Marten de Vos, and the painters included Joos de Momper, who probably made the drawings engraved in the book of the entry. One arch had pairs of Doric columns flanking the opening, and a much bigger Doric column on top, supported by lions, symbolising Constancy. The arch erected by the merchants of Lucca had a view of their city in the solid opening, statues in niches between the columns on the piers, and naked figures on top, some supporting a globe, together with banners and cressets. The arch erected by the Antwerp authorities was also solid, and incorporated portraits of Ernst and Philip from drawings made in Madrid by Frans Francken, whose brother Ambrosius was the festival's co-designer. Arches were also erected by the Spanish, Portuguese, Genoese, Milanese and Florentines.[14]

Ernst died in 1595. In 1598 Philip II granted the Spanish Netherlands to his daughter Isabella Clara Eugenia on condition that she married Ernst's brother Albert. This took place in 1599, and in that year they entered Antwerp, Ghent and Valenciennes. Accounts of all three were published, but only the Antwerp one included illustrations.[15] Arches were again erected by the Spanish, Portuguese, Genoese and Milanese, and also by the Fugger brothers of Augsburg, as well as by the municipality. The Spanish arch had enormous dolphins on either side of the attic painting, and a gallery for trumpeters above. The 'Moles triumphalis Genuensium' was linked to an open circular tempietto on either side, and had an obelisk on top. There was an arch of the Translation of St Eugenius, with a picture of the procession with his coffin. Particularly remarkable was the 'Fortunae muliebris arcus quadrifrons', which honoured Isabella. It was a single arch with four Corinthian columns on two levels, and niches containing statues, all female, as was the statue on the gallery above a painted panel.

As in France and England, and doubtless owing much to influence from these countries, Dutch tomb design in the early seventeenth century often showed the influence of the triumphal arch. A notable example is the tomb of William the Silent, in the Nieuwe Kerk, Delft, by Hendrick de Keyser (1614–22) [15.2]. Its complex form has an effigy beneath a canopy supported on two arches, with columns, while at each end are further arches at right angles. At the front end is 'his own Statue sitting under the Triumphall Arch in Brass', as James Thornhill put it in 1711.[16] Several monuments have a tripartite arrangement, with the effigy in the centre and statues in niches on either side. The tomb of Cardinal Wilhelm von Croy (d. 1521) in the Capuchin church at Enghien (formerly at Héverlé), by Jean Mone, has a tall attic over the centre. An exceptionally grand example by the Dutch sculptor Cornelis Floris is the tomb of Duke Albrecht of Brandenburg (d. 1568) in the Cathedral of Kaliningrad [15.3]. Here there are two tiers of niches on either side, with freestanding columns, winged figures in the spandrels, and a pedimented attic over the centre with a relief of the Ascension flanked by caryatids. One of the last of these monuments was the recently restored one of Antoine de Haynin (d. 1626) in the Cathedral of Ypres, by Urbain Taillebert. The tomb of Antonius Triest (d. 1657) in Ghent Cathedral, by Jerome Duquesnoy, has projecting Salomonic columns at the ends, and a coat of arms over the centre.[17] Erik Forssmann argued that the triumphal arch motif symbolised triumph over death, but Henriette s'Jacob is cautious even about the suggestion of the fame of the man commemorated.[18]

Isabella Clara Eugenia had chosen the Cardinal-Infante Ferdinand, son of Philip IV of Spain, to succeed her as Governor of the Netherlands. She died in 1633. En route in 1634, he and his cousin King Ferdinand of Hungary (later Emperor Ferdinand III) won a victory over the Swedes at Nördlingen. In 1635 his entry to Ghent was welcomed with two arches, the finest of them a triple arch 36 m high in the Market Place, which had four pairs of columns on two levels, and a tall attic over the centre. The other arch, 18 m high, showed the events which had taken place on his journey.[19]

Even grander – in fact one of the grandest entries ever made – was the Cardinal-Infante's entry into Antwerp in the same year. The situation of the city had grown

15.2 Tomb of William the Silent, Nieuwe Kerk, Delft, 1614–22. Hendrick de Keyser.

15.3 Tomb of Duke Albrecht of Brandenburg, died 1568, Kaliningrad Cathedral.

even more miserable, so once again the entry was a brave gesture.[20] The mastermind was Jan Casper Gevaerts, scholar and city clerk, a close friend of Peter Paul Rubens. The programme for the entry was devised by Gevaerts, Rubens and Alderman Nicolaes Rockox. Rubens was commissioned with the design of all but one of the four arches and supervision of the paintings, while Gevaerts was responsible for the inscriptions. The city was to erect two arches, for Philip and Ferdinand, and there would be two others – that of the Portuguese, and that of the Mint, paid for by its officers and workmen. In addition there were four stages (*pegmata*), and the largest decoration of all, the Portico of the Emperors. Rubens made two wonderfully vigorous oil sketches for each arch, one for each face. He then brought in a team of painters which included Jacob Jordaens, Cornelis de Vos, Erasmus Quellinus II, Gerard Seghers and Theodor van Thulden, and sculptors including Hans van Mildert and Erasmus Quellinus I. The entry had been planned for January, but was postponed until April: the delay led the city to commission another arch, at St Michael's Abbey, built with a subvention from the Fuggers.

Many examples of entries were recorded in printed books, but the folio volume commemorating this one, with text by Casper Gevaerts and engravings by Theodor van Thulden, was exceptionally fine. It was commissioned by the city magistrates, and Rubens himself designed the title-page. By the time it was published, in 1642, Ferdinand had died. The dedication was dated 1641, the year of his death.

The first arch that Ferdinand saw in Antwerp was the only one not designed by Rubens. The Arch of the Portuguese was designed by Ludovicus Nonnius, a scholarly doctor of Portuguese descent. The opening was flanked by pairs of columns; in the niches on the piers of the front face were paintings of Philip III of Spain and Emanuel I of Portugal, and the painting on the attic showed Philip IV sending his brother to free Germany. On the back were the Portuguese Kings Alfonso I and John I, and on the attic Ferdinand was greeted by the kneeling figure of Belgium.

The next arch, that of Philip, was the most splendid of all [15.4]. It was more than 21 m high, 11 m wide and 6 m deep. It was a triple arch, the side openings having corbelled heads. On each side were four Composite columns imitating yellow marble, with gilded capitals carved by Erasmus Quellinus I and Adriaen de Brie. Again on both sides, the remarkable attic had a broken segmental pediment over a large painting, with a smaller one rising above. There were numerous paintings by Jordaens and de Vos, which celebrated the marriages that gave the Habsburgs of Austria rule over Spain and the Netherlands. The attic painting on the front, by Jordaens, showed the marriage in 1477 of Archduke Maximilian and Mary, daughter of Charles the Bold, Prince of Belgium and Burgundy. Over this was a painting of Jupiter and Juno, by de Vos [15.5]. Both of these paintings survive.[21] On either side of Jupiter and Juno were Providentia and Time. Below were six portraits of Maximilian and his Spanish descendants, by de Vos, some of them retouched by Rubens; five of these survive. On the rear face of the

15.4 Arch of Philip, front, engraving after Rubens.

15.5 Arch of Philip, front, painting of Jupiter and Juno by Marten de Vos (Museum of Fine Art, Antwerp).

arch, the attic painting showed the marriage of Archduke Philip the Fair, son of Maximilian, and Juana of Castile. Above was the Austrian Monarchy in majesty surrounded by the circle of the Zodiac, to whom a genius offered the globe – a design based on a coin of Hadrian owned by Rubens – flanked by the Sun (after the Apollo Belvedere) and Moon. The six portraits represented Ferdinand and Isabella, the Archdukes Albert and Isabella, Archduke Ernest and the Infante Ferdinand; three survive. The artists are as on the front.

The Portico of the Austrian Emperors ('Porticus Caesareo-Austriaca') got its name from statues of twelve Habsburg emperors. The total width was over 31 m. The centre resembled a triumphal arch, the opening flanked by pairs of Ionic pilasters, with Victories in the spandrels, below a segmental pediment on which stood an obelisk, between Salomonic columns. The golden obelisk was hollow, and lights were placed behind coloured glass in the openings. On either side porticoes curved forwards, with open arches framing gilded stone statues of the emperors, executed by a team of five sculptors, and based on oil sketches by Rubens (of which six survive). Pilasters flanking the arches were decorated with terms representing the twelve Roman deities. Ferdinand liked this structure most of all, and the statues were presented to him (they were destroyed in a fire in 1731). Martin compares the composition with the Genoese arch erected at Antwerp for Albert and Isabella in 1599.

Next came the stage, or *chapelle ardente*, in memory of Isabella Clara Eugenia, which bore some resemblance to a triumphal arch, with three rectangular openings, on the outer sides of which were pairs of Tuscan columns with Salomonic columns above. A large arched painting over the openings, by Gerard Seghers, showed Philip IV appointing Ferdinand Governor of the Netherlands, with Isabella showing her approval from heaven.

The Arch of Ferdinand was much the same size as that of Philip, and also triple. Its more Classical design is explained by Martin as being because it was 'a true arch of triumph in the antique sense', since it commemorated the victory of Nördlingen. On the front face the central opening was flanked by pairs of Doric columns, on projecting bases, while single columns stood beyond the side openings [15.6]. Over the paired columns were female statues, of Pietas and Germania, flanking the principal painting, by Jan van den Hoecke, which depicted the battle.[22] This had a pediment above. Over the end columns, at the same level, were terms. Over the side openings there were corbelled apertures framing paintings of the two Ferdinands, also by van den Hoecke.

28.4 Entry of Cardinal-Infante Ferdinand to Antwerp, 1635. Arch of Ferdinand, front, sketch by P.P. Rubens (Rubenshuis, Antwerp).

Above the pediment was a *quadriga* driven by Aurora, and on either side there were huge trophies (based, according to Gevaerts, on a coin of Trajan showing a triumphal arch), and the Dioscuri with horses.

The rear face of the arch celebrated the triumph of Ferdinand. The architecture was basically the same. The principal painting, again by Jan van den Hoecke, represented the triumph. Ferdinand rode on a golden chariot, dressed in a red cloak, while a winged Victory crowned him with a wreath, and another flew above. The statues on either side were of Honour and Virtue, and the paintings in the apertures personified the Liberality and Foresight of Philip IV. Above the pediment was Lucifer, the morning star, on a winged horse. He was flanked by winged Victories, beyond which were tall trophies. Below each was inscribed *DE MANUBIIS* ('From the spoils'). These in turn were flanked by Fames blowing trumpets. (After this arch had been dismantled, and the principal paintings removed, the rest was sold at auction, but the results were so poor that the Council decided to retain the pieces of the other structures for future reuse.) The next stage was the Temple of Janus, with open door, symbolising the hopes of peace felt by the citizens of Antwerp. Then came the Tree of Austrian Genealogy, and the Stage of the Chamber of Rhetoric, neither designed by

Rubens, though the succeeding Stage of Mercury, or 'Marina Machina', representing the formerly prosperous maritime trade of the city, was by him.

After that came the most remarkable arch of the entry, the 'Arcus Monetalis', or Arch of the Mint. In order to celebrate the gold and silver which came to Spain as a result of her South American conquests, Rubens and Gevaerts made it represent the mountain Potosí in Bolivia, the richest silver mine in the world. Martin suggests that the inspiration might have come from the rocky arch built for the entry of Henri II into Rouen in 1550 (see p. 226). Elizabeth McGrath compares other 'mint arches' such as one erected at Lisbon in 1619 for the entry of Philip III of Spain, and a bizarre triple arch representing a triple-peaked mountain, with viticulture in the centre and silver and salt mines at the sides, erected at Innsbruck in 1626 for the marriage of Archduke Leopold and Claudia de' Medici.[23]

The structure bore little resemblance to the traditional form of arch. The corbelled opening was flanked by bearded herms, while on each side the heavy stonework was pierced with a round-headed niche. Over the opening was another niche, but the rest of the upper part took the form of a rocky mountain. On the front face, the side niches contained the gods of the river Peruvius and the Rio de la Plata. Above them were two pillars (the 'Pillars of Hercules', symbol of Charles V). At the top was Jason stealing the Golden Fleece, symbolising the usefulness of money as the reward of labour, and also the Order of the Golden Fleece founded by Philip the Good, Duke of Burgundy. Jason was balanced by Felicitas, holding a ship. Below her was a rabbit (or chinchilla), a burrowing animal and symbol of Spain. The figure in the central niche, derived from Roman coins, was Moneta, goddess of coinage, holding a cornucopia. Festoons of coins flanked her, gold on the left and silver on the right. Lions peered out of caves behind these, and more lions clasped the columns. On the rear face, the side niches contained mining tools, with the gods of the rivers Condorillo and Marañon [15.7]. Over these were two pairs of miners at work, and above them were monkeys and a lizard. At the top was Hercules clubbing the dragon while Hispania stole the golden apples of the Hesperides. It would have been more logical for this scene to appear between the pillars, as on Rubens's sketch: the explanation for the reversal may be the desire to put the Golden Fleece on the front, because Philip IV was Grand Master of the Order. In the central niche was Vulcan at his anvil. McGrath points out that the arch bore no reference to Antwerp, since the mint there was entirely dependent on Spain, and sees it as a hint to Ferdinand as to how he might restore the city's prosperity. She also argues that this arch, erected by the officers and workmen of the mint, was among the last civic pageants in North Europe which were presented independently in a royal entry.

15.7 Arch of the Mint, back, Rubenshuis, Antwerp.

254 THE TRIUMPHAL ARCH

The end of the entry was marked by the arch at St Michael's Abbey. Despite the aid of the Fuggers, this arch was smaller than the others (less than 13 m high, and only about 2.2 m deep), and the four freestanding columns on each side came from the store of pieces used for previous entries. The single opening was corbelled, and the columns had Composite capitals. They supported a segmental pediment, which framed a great painting on each side. At the sides square columns supported recessed attics. On top was a coat of arms, with laurel and palms over it, flanked by winged figures holding banners. The painting on one side, by Jan van Eyck, showed Ferdinand as Hercules at the crossroads, and on the other, by David Ryckaert III, showed him as Bellerophon, mounted on Pegasus, slaying the Chimera. In St Michael's Abbey Ferdinand was addressed by Jacob Edelheer, spokesman for the magistrates: 'The magistrature of the city, kneeling humbly at the feet of Your Serene Highness, has sought to make visible, by means of triumphal arches and other signs of public joy erected in the name of the city as a whole, the incomparable greatness and splendour of the august house of Austria.'

Archduke Leopold Wilhelm von Habsburg became Governor in 1647. For his entry to Antwerp in 1648 the 'Arcus Germanicus' was designed by the sculptor Erasmus Quellinus II: his thoroughly Baroque triple arch had pairs of columns flanking the opening which supported a broken segmental pediment, below a broken triangular pediment. Beneath were painted panels, and on top lively sculpture. The crowning figure of Austria was defended by armed figures from attackers. Quellinus also designed an 'Arcus Belgicus': the lower part had columns with projecting entablatures, the central ones supporting a broken pediment, while above was a large painting in the centre flanked by statues in niches. On top over a segmental pediment was the Belgian lion.[24] A very different occasion for an arch was the funeral of the Stadhouder Frederik Henrik at Delft in 1647, where the procession passed through a simple square 'arch', with blocked pilasters, and a pedimented panel and two statues above.[25]

As mentioned above, in the northern Netherlands it was the custom to erect stages, sometimes above arches, on which allegorical *tableaux vivants* were displayed. For example, in 1613 Amsterdam erected two arches for Elizabeth Stuart, on her way to Heidelberg after her marriage in London to Frederick V, Count Palatine of the Rhine. One by the Town Hall, designed by Hendrick de Keyser, had a stage on which the marriage of Peleus and Thetis was enacted. Illusionistic architecture was painted by N. de Vries. Musicians were concealed within.[26] Arches were also erected for the visit to Amsterdam of Maria de' Medici in 1638. The first had the opening flanked by Doric pilasters, while the tall attic had Composite columns with a cartouche on top with a ship (seal of the city) and a dolphin, framing a curtained balcony – the 'theatre' – on which was represented the marriage of Maria and Henri IV. The second also had an opening flanked by pairs of Doric pilasters, while the tall attic had pairs of Ionic columns and a broken pediment: in the 'theatre' Maria was represented in a chariot drawn by lions. On an island in the river was what was described as 'new triumphal arches', but was really a tall pavilion, each of whose fronts had pairs of Ionic columns and a pediment. Within these were performed a series of allegorical scenes. The designer is not identified, but may have been Jacob van Campen.[27]

In 1660 Charles II, now restored to his throne in England, was invited to visit his sister Mary, widow of Willem II of Orange. Arches were erected at Amsterdam.

Charles failed to come, and although his sister and her son made an entry, the arches were taken down again.[28]

In 1685 Antwerp celebrated the centenary of the reestablishment of Catholicism in the city (brought about by its capture in 1585 by Alessandro Farnese, Duke of Parma). The various constructions included eight arches. One was fairly simple in its lower part, where fictive statues stood in the side openings, but over the central segmental pediment was a huge explosion of weapons, trophies and so on, with an equestrian figure of the Duke at the top, trampling the enemy. Beside this were pots of plants and two more statues. Four of the 'statues' had been designed by Erasmus Quellinus II for the *chapelle ardente* of Philip IV in 1665 (two survive in the Museum Vleeshuis). Another arch had female musicians on it, grottoes on either side with sea gods, and bowers above with more musicians. The Jesuits set up an elaborate structure, where the main opening was surmounted by two tiers of paintings, the lower one framed by pilasters and the upper by caryatids, with a dome on top. The sides were set at angles to this. They too had paintings over the pairs of smaller openings. In front of the Cathedral was a fairly simple rusticated arch, with a pilaster breaking forward on either side, and a globe, flags and plants on top. The Lievevrouwebroeders erected an arch on a curved plan, the opening surrounded with rocks and shrubs, with a pyramid above. At the top was a flying Fame.[29]

In 1691 William III of Orange, who had been appointed Stadhouder in 1672, and, after marrying Mary, daughter of James II, had become King of England in 1688, was welcomed at The Hague with three arches. The entry was supervised by Romeijn de Hooghe, who made the illustrations for the published accounts, but only designed the third arch. The first two arches were erected by the magistrates, and one at least, the one 'on the Buitenhof', was designed by Steven Vennekool. The first, on the Markt, was the highest, of two storeys. On each level were pairs of Tuscan pilasters. Over the opening, against the attic, was a pediment, and above that clouds with a globe and Pegasus. Each panel, between the pilasters, had a transparent picture on silk, lit from behind in the evening. On either side was a curving wall with panels of trophies and the like. Within the wall were obelisks ('pyramids'), supporting statues of William and Mary; these were also inset with transparent pictures.

The second arch, on the Plaats, had pairs of fluted Ionic pilasters, with a transparency on either side of the opening, and others above, and a life-size equestrian statue of the King, 'brass-like', in the centre, below a curving foliage canopy. This arch was described as 'partie à l'Antique et partie à la Moderne'. The third arch, 'voor t'Hof' (in front of the court), erected by the Estates of Holland and West Friesland, was described as 'of most curious Italian architecture' [15.8]. It took the form of a pair of single arches, with pairs of columns, the openings set in concavities. These stood on either side of a taller archway crowned with a dome on top of which was another equestrian statue. The 'Porte de la Haye' was decorated on the outside with a statue of the King in military dress between females representing public joy and public obligation, and on the other with a trophy, drums, cannons and so on.[30]

Entries in the eighteenth century were fewer and in a lower key. In 1717 the Emperor Charles VI entered Ghent. An engraving shows a rather odd double arch with five attached columns and a large painting above between massed flags. There were three arches standing in front of St Peter's Abbey.[31] In 1744 Maria Theresa was

15.8 Entry of William III to The Hague, 1691, arch 'voor t'Hof'. Romeijn de Hooghe.

received with an arch of similar outline, but in Rococo style, in front of the Town Hall, attributed to Bernard de Wilde.[32]

When the Stadhouder William IV of Orange-Nassau and his wife Anna (daughter of George II) visited Breda in 1737, a simple but jolly triple arch was erected, astylar, and with blocked courses. The central opening rose much higher than the side ones. The decoration consisted of coats of arms and an inscription, but the most conspicuous features were five trees in pots, on top, and four tilted poles carrying wreaths. At The Hague in 1747 William was greeted with an eccentric arch: the main opening was flanked by Ionic columns, and from it extended four triple arcades, at angles, reducing in height. On top was a pedestal with a crown, a female figure in front, and arms. The next year he was at Enkhuisen, where each of a long succession of wooden arches was wrapped in foliage.[33] In 1751 (the year of his death) he was installed as Markgraaf of Veere, and was welcomed with eight arches.[34]

In 1766 William's son William V was received at Veere with no fewer than nine arches. The most remarkable was 'built by the orphans'. Naturally this was a simple affair, with the opening set on narrow pilasters, and a trellis above framing the inscription, the whole covered in foliage. On top was a heart pierced by arrows.[35]

To celebrate the Peace of Aachen in 1749, a magnificent 'firework theatre' was erected at The Hague, designed by Pieter de Swart. The centrepiece was a triple arch. On either side of the central opening was a projection flanked by pairs of Ionic columns. Over the centre was a tall attic, crowned by a lavish sculptural group. Curving colonnades ended in pavilions where arched openings were surmounted by obelisks.[36]

In 1753 the 600th anniversary of St Bernard was celebrated at Ghent, and an arch was set up in front of the church of the Abbey of Baudeloo. It had banded rustication, with piers breaking forward and inset with niches containing urns. On top were statues, including Fame on a pedestal in the centre. It may have been painted by Emmanuel van Reijsschoot.[37] In 1767 it was the turn of St Macaire, whose 700th anniversary it was. There were seventeen arches, of two of which the design is known. The first stood in the Korenmarkt, and was 35 m high. It was a splendidly Rococo design. The freestanding columns were set at angles, and the side openings were in receding wings. The elaborate and curvaceous attic had a figure of the Saint between figures of SS. Peter and Paul. A drawing by Emmanuel van Reijsschoot survives. The arch in the Vrijdagmarkt was over 25 m high, and was both a little more old-fashioned and much more lavish. Pairs of columns projected from the ends of the piers, supporting statues, there was a circular space within, and the attic had many columns, the side ones on a concave plan. It housed a painting showing the reconciliation of Baudouin IV with his subjects at Tournai by the agency of the Saint. The columns imitated white and purple marble, and the draperies were green. This arch must have been a collaboration between the brothers Pieter and Emmanuel van Reijsschoot.[38]

The Delft Gate at Rotterdam was built in 1772, again to the design of Pieter de Swart. It took the form of a triple arch, with reliefs over the side doors, and more on the tall pedimented attic. There were semicircular projections at the sides. The gate was dismantled in 1939, and then wrecked by bombs. A skeleton version in steel replaced it in 1995, designed by Cor Kraat.

The versatile French architect Joseph Ramée was living in Louvain in 1793, where he designed an *entrepôt*, around a large quadrangle. In the corner of the drawing appears a design for an arch. Standing on a solid base, it is a plain structure but richly decorated with trophies on the piers, flying Victories on the spandrels, and three reliefs on the attic showing battles in which the Austrians under the Archduke Carl Ludwig (represented in profile on the keystone) defeated the French under Dumouriez, securing the Netherlands for Austria, though only for a year. Within the opening is a statue of Athena, on a base which represents another battle. It is possible that the arch, which does not appear on the plan, was intended merely as a 'title-picture'.[39] When the Austrian Emperor Franz II entered Louvain the next year, four arches were erected to welcome him.[40]

In 1781 the Revd Thomas Twining, on a tour, saw at Aalst that 'a triumphal arch erected in honour of the Archduchess, the Emperor's sister, who is appointed to the command of the Low Countries, still remained'.[41]

In the nineteenth century a few arches honoured members of the Dutch monarchy. In 1840 the Classical Willemspoort in Amsterdam was opened for the entry of the new King William II, and an arch in the Gothic style was erected alongside it. Gothic was used here and elsewhere to symbolise the restoration of the House of Orange.[42] In 1874 an arch in the Vondelstraat commemorated the Silver Jubilee entry of his son, William III: it was designed by P.J.H. Cuypers, and took the form of a medieval gate, with turrets and crenellations.[43] He was also the architect for the Gothic arch erected in 1887 over the Singelgracht, in the same street, in honour of the King's seventieth birthday.[44] This arch also symbolised 'the federative union'.[45]

A 'Rubensfest' was held in Antwerp in 1840, to commemorate the bicentenary of the painter's death, and the decorations included an arch designed by Henri Leys. It was a triple arch, with dark green piers and archivolts. The upper part was white, and was divided by pilasters supporting figures of men in the centre and mermaids at the side, holding up the Ionic capitals. Their entablatures broke forward. Between these were three paintings by Leys. On top was a pile of weapons with two seated figures and two lions.[46]

In 1853 the King of the Belgians, with the Duke and Duchess of Brabant, was welcomed at Antwerp with a large arch, designed by F. Beeckmans. It had two openings, each flanked by pairs of Corinthian columns, between which were paintings resembling Gobelins tapestries, and a taller central opening with a fanciful attic, on which pairs of caryatids flanked a large painting, above which volutes supported seated females. The personified city sat at the top. The *Builder* noted that the 'ornamental part of statues, genii, &c. are of long standing in Antwerp', and were reused.[47] In this connection it is interesting that one of the Bodleian Library copies of Bochius's *Historica Descriptio* has inserted into it a watercolour 'Drawn 1815 by Francis Cohen Esq. from the original figure in pasteboard still preserved with many others belonging to the pageant at Antwerp'. It shows a seated soldier wearing a helmet and greaves, and is annotated '5ft 8in'. He does not seem to appear in any of the plates in the book.[48]

For the entrance to the Belgian Exhibition of 1880, to celebrate the fiftieth anniversary of the country, the Brussels City Architect Gédéon Bordiau first designed a triple arch, to stand between the two pavilions. On the advice of Alphonse Balat, a single arch was approved in 1879. It was to be fairly plain, and astylar. In front of the piers equestrian figures blew trumpets, on projecting bases. On the frieze was the dedication AUX ARTS INDUSTRIELS, while on the pyramidal attic four horses reclined below a female figure held up by two companions. In 1882 it remained only half built, in wood and canvas. By 1894 the side elements, each having a projecting aedicule with pairs of Ionic columns, had been constructed in concrete, and for the 1897 Exhibition the central arch was executed in wood and plaster. In 1900 this was destroyed, and in 1904 the side elements also went, to make way for Girault's arch (for which see pp. 428–9).[49]

Notes

1. Remy du Puys, *La tryumphante et solemnelle entrée faicte sur le nouvel et ioyeux advenement de … monsieur Charles prince des hespaignes … en sa ville de Bruges* (Paris, 1515; reprinted in *Recueil de chroniques…*, 3rd ser. (Bruges, 1850; Amsterdam, 1971, with intro. by Sydney Anglo); John Landwehr, *Splendid Ceremonies: State Entries and Royal Funerals in the Low Countries, 1515–1791: A Bibliography* (Nieuwkoop, 1971), no. 2.
2. Cornelius Grapheus, *De magnificentissimis Urbis Anverpiae spectaculis, Carolo dudum Imperatore designato, aeditis*.
3. Jean Otho (Jan Oste) published a *Brevis Descriptio*, as did at least three other authors, and illustrations of the five arches were published separately. See also Marcel Lageirse, 'La joyeuse entrée du Prince Héritier Philippe à Gand en 1549', in *Anciens pays et assemblées d'états*, XVIII (Louvain/Paris, 1959), 29–46; idem in Jean Jacquot, ed., *Les fêtes de la Renaissance*, II (Paris, 1960), 297–306. For Philip's entries in 1549 see Juan Christóval Calvete de Estrella, ed. Paloma Cuenca, *El felicissimo viaje del muy alto y muy poderoso Príncipe Don Phelippe* (Madrid, 2001).
4. Georges Marlier, *Pierre Coeck d'Alost* (Brussels, 1966), 386–90; A.E. Popham, 'The authorship of the drawings of Binche', *Journal of the Warburg and Courtauld Institutes*, 3 (1939–40), 56. On the entry see Cornelius Grapheus, *Spectaculorum in susceptione Philippi Hisp. Prin. … mirificus apparatus* (Antwerp, 1550); also published as *Le très admirable, très magnifique, & triumphante entrée du Prince Philipe … en … Anvers*, and in Flemish; A. Corbet, 'L'entrée du Prince Philippe à Anvers en 1549', in Jacquot (cit. in the preceding note), 307–10 ; R. Strong, *Splendour at Court: Renaissance Spectacle and Illusion* (London, 1973), 102–5; H. Colvin, 'Pompous entries and English architecture', *Essays in English Architectural History* (New Haven/London, 1999), 67–8.

5 William Eisler, 'Celestial harmonies and Hapsburg rule: levels of meaning in a triumphal arch for Charles V and Philip II in Antwerp, 1549', in Barbara Wisch and Susan Scott Munshower, eds, *'All the World's a Stage...': Art and Pageantry in the Renaissance and Baroque* (University Park, Pa., 1990), 352–8. For the paintings by Floris, see Carl van de Velde, *Frans Floris (1519/20–1570): Leven en Werken* (Brussels, 1975), 159–85, nos 7–33; all are lost, but two (nos 11 and 30) are known from engravings.
6 On this arch see Jan van der Stock, ed., *Antwerp – Story of a Metropolis 16th–17th Centuries* (Ghent, 1993), 39.
7 Robert Didier, *Jacques Dubroeucq* (Mons, 2000), 16–17.
8 Lageirse (cit. at n. 3), 42; Yvette vanden Bemden, *Les vitraux de la première moitié du XVI siècle conservés en Belgique*, IV, *Provinces de Liège, Luxembourg, Namur* (Ledeberg/Ghent, 1981), 82.
9 Leo van Puyvelde, 'Les joyeuses entrées et la peinture flamande', in Jacquot (cit. at n. 3), 287–96; Jean Helbig and Yvette vanden Bemden, *Les vitraux de la première moitié du XVI siècle conservés en Belgique*, III, *Brabant et Limbourg* (Ledeberg/Ghent, 1974), 67–88.
10 D.P. Snoep, *Praal en propaganda: Triumfalia in de Noordelijke Nederlanden in de 16de en 17de eeuw* (Utrecht, 1975), 21–4.
11 Landwehr (cit. at n. 1), no. 48; Snoep (cit. at n. 10), 25–31, 154–5; R.C. Strong and J.A. van Dorsten, *Leicester's Triumph* (Leiden/London, 1964), 41, 47–8. The etching bears the title *Delineatio Pompae triumphalis qua Robertus Dudlaeus Comes Leicestrensis Hagae Comitis fuit exceptus*.
12 Van der Stock (cit. at n. 6), 266–7; W.H. Vroom, 'Monogrammist M.H.V.H., De Blijde Inkomste van Anjou te Antwerpen, 1582', *Bull. van het Rijksmuseum*, 37 (1989), 185–90.
13 *Descriptio et explicatio pegmatum, arcuum et spectaculorum quae Bruxellae ... exhibita fuere sub ingressum Ernesti ... Archiducis Austriae ... pro Philippo II ... Belgicae ditionis gubernatore* (Brussels, 1594). Pictures of arches sometimes differ in detail from other pictures and descriptions.
14 Joannes Bochius, *Descriptio publicae gratulationis ... in adventu sereniss. Principis Ernesti Archducis Austriae* (Antwerp, 1595); reprinted as *The Ceremonial Entry of Ernst, Archduke of Austria, into Antwerp, June 14, 1594*, with intro. by Hans Mielke (New York, 1970); Peter Davidson and Adriaan van der Weel, 'The entry of Archduke Ernst into Antwerp on 1594', in J.R.Mulryne et al., *Europa Triumphans* (Aldershot, 2004), I, 492–574. Colvin (cit. at n. 4, 72–3) suggests that the Florentine arch erected in London in 1553 may have been similar to the arch with the columns (see p. 249).
15 J. Bochius, *Historica narratio profectionis et inaugurationis ... Alberti et Isabellae ... et eorum optatissimi in Belgium adventus* (Antwerp, 1602). This incorporates *Pompae triumphalis et spectaculorum, in adventu et inauguratione Serenissimorum Principum Alberti et Isabellae, Austriae Archducum ... in eiusdam Principatus metropoli, Antwerpiae exhibitorum, graphica designatio*; *Descriptio pompae et gratulationis publicae serenissimis potentissisimisque principibus Alberto Maxaemyliani II Imp. Filio et Isabellae ... a Senatu Populoque Gandaviensi ad Inaugurationem Flandriae Comitatus decretae Maximo Aemyliano Vrientio [De Vriendt] auctore*; *Descriptio triumphi et spectaculorum ... Alberti et Isabellae ... in civitatem Valentianam ingredientibus editorum, auctore Henrico d'Oultremanno [D'Oultreman]*; Landwehr (cit. at n. 1), no. 62. Some of the plates of the Antwerp entry are appended to the 1970 reprint of Bochius's book on the 1594 entry (cit. in the preceding note).
16 Katharine Fremantle, ed., *Sir James Thornhill's Sketch-Book Travel Journal of 1711* (Utrecht, 1975), II, 40–41, no. 34. See Frits Scholten, *Sumptuous Memories: Studies in Seventeenth-century Dutch Tomb Sculpture* (Zwolle, 2003), 27, 72–8.
17 Saskia Durian-Ress, 'Das barocke Grabmal in den südlichen Niederlanden: Studien zur Ikonographie und Typologie', *Aachener Kunstblätter*, 45 (1974), 242–4.
18 Erik Forssmann, *Saüle und Ornament* (Stockholm, 1956), 34; Henriette s'Jacob, *Idealism and Realism: a Study of Sepulchral Symbolism* (Leiden, 1954), 195–6.
19 Gulielmus Becanus, *Serenissimi Principis Ferdinandi I ... Triumphalis Introitus in Flandriae Metropolim Gandavum* (Antwerp, 1636). Landwehr (cit. at n. 1, no. 96) says there were four arches, but he must include the *pegmata*, the stages.
20 *Pompa Introitus honori Serenissimi Principis Ferdinandi Austriaci Hispaniarum Infantis S.R.E. Card. Belgarum et Burgundiorum Gubernatoris, etc., a S.P.Q. Antwerp. decreta et adornata ... Arcus, pegmata, iconesque a Pet. Paulo Rubenio, Equite, inventas & delineatas inscriptionibus & elogiis ornabat, libroque commentario illustrabat Casperius Gevartius ... apud Theod. A Tulden, qui iconum tabulas ex archetypis Rubenianis delineavit et sculpsit* (Antwerp, [1641–2]); John Rupert Martin, *The Decorations for the Pompa Introitus Ferdinandi, Corpus Rubenianum*, XVI (London/New York, 1972); Larry Silver, 'The Triumphs of Emperor Maximilian I', in Wisch and Munshower (cit. at n. 5), 301–2. On the inscriptions, see Florence Vuilleumier Laurens and Pierre Laurens, *L'âge de l'inscription: la rhétorique du monument en Europe du XVe au XVIIe siècle* (Paris, 2010), 141–55.
21 The Jordaens is in the Maison pour Tous at Ste-Savine; it was shown in the Jordaens exhibition at the Petit Palais, Paris, in 2013–14. The de Vos is in the Koninglijk Museum voor Schone Kunsten, Antwerp.
22 The painting was retouched by Jordaens for presentation to Ferdinand in 1637. It is now in the Royal Collection, having been bought by Frederick, Prince of Wales, who added the frame by William Kent (Desmond Shawe-Taylor, ed., *The First Georgians: Art and Monarchy 1714–1760* (London, 2014), 262–3).
23 Elizabeth McGrath, 'Rubens's Arch of the Mint', *Journal of the Warburg and Courtauld Institutes*, 37 (1974), 191–217.

24 J.-P. De Bruyn, 'Officiële opdrachten aan Erasmus II Quellinus', *Jaarboek van het Koninglijk Museum voor Schone Kunsten* (Antwerp, 1983), 218–29. He illustrates three other designs for arches by Quellinus. See also Krista de Jonge and Joris Snaet, '*Vera simmetria*, ware proportie: "Vreemd gebouwd" in de 17de eeuw', in Stefaan Grieten, ed., *Vreemd gebouwd: westerse en niet-westerse elementen in onze architectuur* (Antwerp, 2002), 127.

25 Landwehr (cit. at n. 1), no. 114.

26 Snoep (cit. at n. 10), 34–6.

27 Caspar van Baerle, *Medicea hospes, sive descriptio publicae gratulationis qua … Mariam de Medicis excepit senatus populusque Amstelodamensis* (Amsterdam, 1638); Landwehr (cit. at n. 1), no. 108. The etchings in van Baerle's book are after Jan Martsen the Younger, Claes Moyaert and Simon de Vlieger. See also Snoep (cit. at n. 10), 39–64.

28 Jochen Becker, 'The Princess of Orange's welcome into Amsterdam in 1660', *Europa Triumphans* (cit. at n. 14), I, 575, and see p. 470; Landwehr (cit. at n. 1), no. 125.

29 Petrus Franciscus de Smidt, *Hondert-Jaerigh Jubile-Vreught bewesen in dese Stadt Antwerpen* (Antwerp, 1685); Van der Stock (cit. at n. 6), 327; Jan Grieten, 'Façades tegen ketters, heidenen en rebellen. De stadsversieringen van 1685 ter gelegenheid van de honderdjarige herdenking van de herovering van Antwerpen', in *Vreemd gebouwd* (cit. at n. 24), 157–62.

30 *Beschryving der Eerporten in 's Gravenhaage opgerecht tegen d'overkomst van Willem den III* (Amsterdam, 1691); Govard Bidloo, *Komste van zyne Majesteit Willem III, Koning van Groot Britanje … in 's Gravenhaage* ('s Gravenhage, 1691); Anon., *A Description of the … Arches* (London, 1691, republished in *A Fourth Collection of Scarce and Valuable Tracts* (London, 1751), II, 250–57); Nicolas Chevalier, *Histoire de Guillaume III … par médailles, inscriptions, arcs de triomphe et autres monuments publiques* (Amsterdam, 1692); Landwehr (cit. at n. 1), nos 143–9; Snoep (cit. at n. 10), 91–153.

31 Marie Fredericq-Lilar, *Gent in de 18de Eeuw: De Schilders van Reijsschoot* (Ruislede, 1992), 43–4.

32 ibid., 46.

33 Landwehr (cit. at n. 1), nos 205, 216, 222.

34 Andreas Andriessen, *Plegtige Inhuldigung van … Willem Karrel Henrik Friso, Prinse van Oranje en Nassau … als Markgraaf van Vere* (Amsterdam, 1751); Landwehr (cit. at n. 1), 227.

35 Landwehr (cit. at n. 1), no. 244.

36 Reinier Baarsen, ed., *Rococo in Nederland* (Zwolle, 2001), 30.

37 Fredericq-Lilar (cit. at n. 31), 52.

38 ibid., 84–6. An album of drawings by Emmanuel van Reijsschoot at Ghent University contains more designs for arches.

39 Paul Turner, *Joseph Ramée* (Cambridge, 1996), 47–51.

40 Edward van Even, *Louvain dans le passé et dans le présent* (Louvain, 1895), 81.

41 Richard Twining, ed., *Selections from Papers of the Twining Family* (London, 1887), 20.

42 Aart Oxenaar, 'Solutions to a persistent dilemma', in Bernard Colenbrander, ed., *Style, Standard and Signature in Dutch Architecture of the Nineteenth and Twentieth Centuries* (Rotterdam, 1993), 33, n. 43.

43 Hetty Berens, ed., *P.J.H. Cuypers – The Complete Works* (Rotterdam, 2007), 235, no. 166.

44 ibid., 288, no. 275.

45 Oxenaar (cit. at n. 42), 33, n. 43.

46 Alfred Willis, 'Neo-Vlaamse renaissance architectuur: eigen voor wie?', *Vreemd gebouwd* (cit. at n. 24), 440. The paintings are in the Koningklijk Museum in Antwerp.

47 *The Builder*, 11 (1853), 618–19.

48 The Bodleian book is Douce B subt. 55(1).

49 Liane Ranieri, *Léopold II: Urbaniste* (Brussels, 1973), 123–8; *The Builder*, 38 (1880), 777; 39 (1880), 110–11.

16

ARCHES AS FEATURES OF PARKS AND LANDSCAPE GARDENS

Triumphal arches as park entrances in England

The fact that the celebrated triumphal arches of the Roman Empire once spanned roadways suited them particularly as models for entrances to parks.[1] It is not surprising that a number of such arches can be found on English estates. In his *Epistle to Lord Burlington*, of 1731, Alexander Pope wrote:

> You show us, Rome was glorious, not profuse,
> And pompous buildings once were things of Use.

He went on to attack the 'Imitating Fools' who, among other mistakes,

> Turn Arcs of triumph to a Garden-gate.

It is generally held that he had in mind the entrance to the grounds of Bevis Mount, the 'little Amoret' of his friend, that extraordinary character the Earl of Peterborough, near Southampton.[2] A drawing of 1824 by John Buckler shows a plain arch with a

16.1 Entrance arch to Bevis Mount, Southampton. Drawing of 1824 by John Buckler.

262 THE TRIUMPHAL ARCH

projecting pedimented portico, supported by freestanding Corinthian columns and pilastered *antae* [16.1].³ It has been thought that Pope referred to it again in his *Epistles of Horace*, published in 1738:

> Our Gen'rals now, retir'd to their Estates,
> Hang their old Trophies o'er the Garden gates.

Buckler's view shows no sign of trophies, though it is known that at the entrance to his lawn Peterborough arranged guns and flags taken in the War of Succession.

Peterborough had settled at Bevis Mount at the earliest in 1730, so he was certainly not the first to use a triumphal arch as the entrance to a park. An outstanding example, and one whose symbolism is obvious, is the grandiose Triumphal Gateway leading from the town of Woodstock into the park of Blenheim Palace in Oxfordshire [16.2]. This was built in 1722–3, to the design of Nicholas Hawksmoor. It clearly relates to the military imagery so prominent in the house itself. Built just after the Duke of

16.2 Blenheim Palace, Oxfordshire: Triumphal Gateway from Woodstock, 1722–3. Nicholas Hawsmoor.

Marlborough's death, it bears, as Hawksmoor proposed, 'some proper Inscription to show the Succeeding Ages to whom they were obliged for defending their Liberties'. It has pairs of Corinthian columns, and the peculiarity of an attic set only above the opening itself. Kerry Downes points out that Claude sometimes shows the Arch of Titus like this; of course, he only knew the arch in its unrestored form.[4]

Much less historicist was the 'Triumphal Arch' (so called in the eighteenth century) at Holkham Hall, Norfolk. According to the 1773 edition of Matthew Brettingham's *Plans and Elevations of the late Earl of Leicester's House at Holkham*, this arch, and other garden buildings, were 'deduced from sketches by Mr Kent, with considerable alterations made in the designs, long before these works were erected'.[5] Kent's design seems to have been made in the late 1720s. The executed arch (1739–52) follows it closely (though the proportions seem a little less happy), but the attic and pediment are plain and rendered, with a wooden Diocletian window in the attic, and the pyramids over the flanking arches are missing. Narrow windows on two levels are inserted into the link walls to light the rooms within.

Similar in character to the arch at Holkham is the east gate at Studley Royal, Yorkshire, a central arch flanked by rectangular openings, surrounded by chunky vermiculated rustication forming quoins, with four ball-finials on top of the cornice. Colen Campbell was advising John Aislabie, owner of the estate, about the stables, just before he died in 1729, and Roger Morris was assisting him: the design of the gate may be due to one or the other.[6]

Another arch which uses vermiculated rustication is at Fonthill, Wiltshire. Here the rustication alternates with plain ashlar, and at the keystone forms a splendidly grotesque mask. The single opening is surmounted by a pediment, crowned by a triplet of urns, and is flanked by balustraded lodges. It is on an astonishingly grand scale. Its Palladian character led John Rutter, in his *Delineations of Fonthill and its Abbey* (1823), to attribute it to Inigo Jones, but it probably dates from some time between 1740 and 1755, shortly before the erection of Alderman Beckford's house c. 1757–60. The house was designed by a man called Hoare.[7]

The 'Folly Arch' at North Mymms, Hertfordshire, was the south entrance to the park of Gobions. It is of brick, and the tall opening is flanked by square turrets with battlements. Built c. 1740, it is attributed to James Gibbs.

On the northern approach to Appuldurcombe, on the Isle of Wight, stands the Freemantle Gate. The carriage arch is flanked by pairs of freestanding Ionic columns, and there is a lower arch on either side. It dates from about 1770. The attribution to James Wyatt is unsubstantiated.

In the sketchbook which François-Joseph Bélanger made on his visit to England, probably in 1772–4, a drawing of a grand triumphal arch gateway is labelled 'My lord Bessborough'. Presumably this was at, or intended for, his villa at Roehampton in Surrey, built in the 1760s by Sir William Chambers, to whom Bélanger seems to have had an introduction. Not known otherwise, it has a recessed central arch with a rectangular opening within it, and on either side pairs of columns or pilasters flank subsidiary rectangular openings, with roundels above. On top is some kind of animal, and at the sides are lean-to lodges whose roofs form sections of a pediment. Bélanger's sketchbook also includes a design for a lavish 'Arc de triomphe Milord Pembrook', no doubt at Wilton.[8]

It is scarcely surprising that entrance gates which play variations on the triumphal arch became more common when Neoclassicism became fashionable. Robert Adam was obsessed with the triumphal arch form. A charming drawing done in Rome in 1756 shows a pavilion (though not an entrance gate) in the form of an arch with a cascade beneath it (an idea probably suggested by the Trevi Fountain).[9] Adam's North Lodge at Kedleston, Derbyshire, designed in 1759 and executed in 1760–62, is a substantial composition. Here large Roman Doric half-columns support an entablature with triglyphs and a pediment. Lodges are attached on either side, and their roofs slope up to the arch. According to a catalogue of *c.* 1778–9, it was based on the 'Arch of Octavia', whatever that may mean.[10] At Syon, Middlesex (1773), the arch itself is simple in form, with single pilasters, but has elaborate decoration, and is linked to simple cubic lodges by rich screens of columns and entablatures. The display aptly emphasises ducal wealth on the suburban main road.[11] Adam's gateway to Croome Court, Worcestershire, of 1779 has paired Ionic half-columns. In the centre of the attic is a vertical panel with a relief. At each side is a low wall ending in a pier, on which Coade stone lions were placed in 1795.[12] A similar arch is shown in a design of 1782 at the Soane Museum. That has paired half-columns of the Tower of the Winds order, and is flanked by lodges.[13]

Much more remarkable was the slightly earlier arch at Nostell Priory, Yorkshire, shown in an elevation of 1774 and a perspective of 1776 by Adam. It stood at the crossroads north of the Obelisk Lodge, and was attached to a two-storey lodge in a self-consciously 17th-century style. The arched opening was recessed between piers on which were niches for statues. Over these were panels with bucrania and swags, and on top of the entablature were a lion and a hound (in the event two hounds were used). The entablature is partly ruinous, and the bridge in front has missing parts of the parapets filled in with cross-braced timbers. The arch was destroyed when the lodge was enlarged in 1880.[14]

The arched west gateway to the Thornton Hall estate at Thornton le Street in North Yorkshire is by an unknown architect. It is described in the *Buildings of England* as having 'pairs of Adamish columns and very good gates'.

Adam's rival James Wyatt paraphrased the Kedleston lodge at Bryanston, Dorset, in 1778, using unfluted columns and omitting the triglyphs. For the Chippenham Lodge at Dodington Park, Gloucestershire, designed in 1798, Wyatt used a remarkably strung-out composition, with a wide and flat tripartite arch linked to lodges by curved columnar screens. The arch is articulated by sunk panels, suggesting the influence of Sir John Soane, and the attic is crowned by a winged dragon, the Codrington crest.[15]

Soane himself produced a masterly variation on the triumphal arch at Tyringham Hall, Buckinghamshire. Described by Pevsner as 'in spite of its small scale, a monument of European importance', it was built in 1792–7. The arch itself is astylar, decorated only with incised lines, and is linked by recessed sections with niches to the lodges, which have pairs of recessed Greek Doric columns. Pevsner compares the gateway with the work of Ledoux and Gilly, and says that it has 'emphatically nothing of the elegance of Holland or Wyatt'.[16]

Two arches by Henry Holland are actually rather lacking in 'elegance'. The gatehouse leading from the park to the pleasure grounds of Berrington Hall, Herefordshire

(1778–81), is a large plain structure with windows on either side of the archway and cast-iron balusters over the opening itself.[17] The main entrance to Woburn Abbey, Bedfordshire, from the A5 (*c.* 1790) is tripartite, with four Ionic columns supporting an entablature which breaks forward over each of them. Over the central opening is a large attic with a huge coat of arms; at its sides and on top are scrolls. Rusticated walls flank the arch.[18]

A more successful ducal entrance than the Woburn one serves as the main (Apleyhead) approach to Clumber Park, Nottinghamshire. It was designed by the Duke of Newcastle's protégé, Stephen Wright, who appears to have been previously an assistant to William Kent. Built *c.* 1784, after Wright's death in 1780, the arch itself is slender and tall, with a niche on either side, below a triglyph frieze which runs out over flanking screens, supported on pairs of columns. Above this, on the arch, are discs set within squares (a curiously Lutyensish touch), while the balustrade on top is interrupted by a panel pierced with a coat of arms. Curved side-pieces go down over the screens. Attached to these are long curved wings containing the lodges.[19]

At Combe Abbey, Warwickshire, the park was laid out in 1771–7 by Capability Brown (Henry Holland's father-in-law), and he may have designed the West Lodge. The outer side is articulated with four pilasters, and the arched opening is flanked by round-headed windows, with blank panels above. The attic, decorated with garlands, rises only over the opening. There is a single-storey room attached on either side. On the inner face the pilasters are omitted, and the ground floor is rusticated.[20]

The Lion Gate at Ince Blundell Hall, Lancashire, is surprisingly Baroque for its date, between 1770 and 1776. The explanation for the apparent anachronism is that Henry Blundell, owner of the estate, copied the design from the background of Sebastiano Ricci's so-called *Marriage of Bacchus and Ariadne*, which he had recently acquired. The central opening is flanked by Tuscan half-columns, above which a triglyph entablature breaks forward, beneath sections of broken pediment which frame an urn on an elaborate pedestal. On either side are rusticated gateways, with garlanded plinths over them supporting lions, set in plain walls. The executant architect may have been William Everard, who designed the garden temple.[21]

The southern entrance to Chippenham Park, Cambridgeshire, is an elegant gateway designed in 1794 by James Wyatt. The triple arch is plain apart from relief panels over the side openings. The raised central attic bears a female statue.[22]

The first quarter of the nineteenth century saw the erection of a number of triumphal arch entrances. Some are of the substantial Berrington type, including that at Harewood, Yorkshire. This was not built to the design of 1800 published by Humphry Repton in his *Observations on the Theory and Practice of Landscape Gardening* (1803), which had a central opening with four freestanding Greek Doric columns, a Doric entablature, and balustrades flanking a central attic panel with arms above. On either side were long pilastered walls, curved on plan, which would have concealed buildings behind. What was actually built, *c.* 1802–5, instead of being on the main road was set back by 50 yards (about 46 m), and the design was much altered by the mason, John Muschamp. Roman Doric rather than Greek, with attached columns, it is much less elegant, and has round-headed windows on either side of the main opening. As so often the practical necessity of lighting living accommodation compromised the effect of monumentality. The flanking walls were omitted. Repton complained that his plans had been 'misunderstood and misrepresented', despite the fact that they had caused him to be 'complimented and flattered by the immortal Pitt'.[23]

A simple but elegant arch in Yorkshire has an interesting commemorative purpose. The entrance to Duncombe Park from the Thirsk road takes the form of a Doric arch, with attached columns flanking the opening and on the sides. It was built in 1806, and bears on the outer side the inscription 'To the memory of Lord Viscount Nelson and the unparalleled gallant achievements of the British Navy'. On the inner side one reads 'Lamented Hero! O! Price his conquering country grieved to pay! O dear bought glories of Trafalgar's day!'[24]

Sir Jeffry Wyatville's Horningsham Lodge to Longleat, Wiltshire, is not much more successful than the Harewood gate. As at his new stables, he borrowed his architectural details from the Elizabethan house, and the result is rather peculiar, especially since mullioned and transomed windows are introduced on either side of the arched opening, and in the flanking cubic appendages. The arch has Doric pilasters below, and Ionic above. Wyatville made his first designs for Longleat in 1800, but the work was carried out in 1806–13.[25]

Another clumsy attempt to combine lodge accommodation within an arch was made at Carden Hall, Cheshire. The south lodge (on a country lane) is remarkably grand, but its architect is unknown. It must date from the early nineteenth century. Pairs of freestanding Ionic columns support entablatures which break forward on either side of the arched opening. Tall round-headed windows provide an echo of the conventional subsidiary arches. A rather weedy attic panel surmounts the arch.[26]

Much more successful is the charming South Lodge of Tabley Hall, also in Cheshire. In this simple brick structure blank arches frame rectangular windows on either side of the opening, with circular windows above, and there is a pitched roof of slate. Mowl and Earnshaw, who rightly praise the arch, suggest that it might be by George Moneypenny, who restored the east pavilion of the house in 1819–20.[27]

A solid and handsome variant was built as the Knutsford Lodge to Tatton Park, Cheshire. In his *Red Book* of 1791, Humphry Repton illustrated a 'simple handsome arch … from a slight hint of Mr S. Wyatt's' for this entrance to the park. The existing arch was built in 1811 by Lewis Wyatt, following the design of his uncle Samuel. Stout Greek Doric columns support a pediment; on either side round-arched pedestrian openings pierce through solid walls which return towards the outer side.[28] Even more imposing, if less attractive, is Lewis Wyatt's Grand Lodge to Heaton Park, Manchester, which was built at some time between 1807 and 1824. Here the arch is flanked by pairs of attached Tuscan columns, with a stepped attic, and a cubic lodge attachment on either side, within curved flanking walls.[29]

The much daintier London Gates to Highclere, Hampshire, were described by Mark Girouard as having 'a feeling of Chambers about them', but they seem to date from *c.* 1820. The enrichments are in Coade stone. The opening is flanked by Ionic pilasters, and the keystone has a mask. Set into the bases of the pilasters are ovals within rectangles. Over the opening is a shallow attic with a large urn. On either side bays are canted forwards to form lodges.[30]

An altogether exceptional variation is the Quixhill Gate to Alton Towers, Staffordshire, built in 1822–4 to the design of J.B. Papworth [16.3]. Groups of four unfluted

Greek Doric columns flank the plain, taller opening, while the simple and severe masonry is set off by delicate iron gates and railings on either side.[31]

The gateway to the bizarre Hadlow Castle in Kent, is a triple arch in Gothic style, with pierced 'tracery' and battlements. Dating from *c.* 1820, it is probably by George Ledwell Taylor, who designed the castle.

The buildings of the Sheffield Botanical Garden were erected in 1836 to the design of Benjamin Broomhead Taylor. The solemn entrance has pairs of freestanding Ionic columns flanking the arched opening.[32]

Corporation Park in Blackburn, Lancashire, laid out by William Henderson of Birkenhead, was opened in 1857. Entrance is through a triple arch, the lower storey of rusticated stone, and the upper one of brick and stone. Over the entablature is an elaborate cartouche of arms.

The screen at the main approach to Attingham Park, Shropshire, was erected in 1862 to the design of Charles Fowler, Jun. It is a heavier version of the type of screen favoured by Adam. Attached Roman Doric columns flank the opening, on the entablature of which appears the family motto. On either side are pedestrian openings and blank-arched lodges, with urns above the channelled pilasters.[33]

A Scottish example may be mentioned here. On the axis of the fine bridge at Kelso the gateway to Springwood Park was built in 1822 to the design of Gillespie Graham. Very severe, it has pairs of attached Doric columns and an attic with coat of arms in the centre.

16.3 Quixhill gates, Alton Towers, Staffordshire, 1822–4. J.B. Papworth.

Arches as features of English gardens

The use of triumphal arches as eyecatchers in parks might seem surprising – even more so than their use for park entrances – since their original context was urban. However, their comparatively simple form, and their striking architectural and sculptural decoration, made them obvious examples for the *milordi* returning from the Grand Tour to imitate on their estates.[34] The fact that the Arches of Titus and Septimius Severus formed such well-known features of views up and down the Forum Romanum meant that, whether in actuality or in pictures, they were celebrated for their contribution to the scenery.

In his *New Principles of Gardening* (London, 1728) Batty Langley recommends that garden walks should terminate with features which include 'ruins after the Roman manner', and he illustrates a version of the Arch of Constantine, partly buried and with bushes growing on it.

The earliest arches erected as freestanding eyecatchers in English gardens are associated with the name of Roger Morris.[35] A particularly magnificent arch was designed for Eastbury Park, Dorset.[36] It may possibly have been the work of Sir John Vanbrugh, who died in 1726, but it is perhaps more likely to have been by Morris. The house at Eastbury was begun in 1718, by Vanbrugh, for George Dodington, and continued after his death in 1729 for his son George Bubb Dodington (created Lord Melcombe). Completed by Morris c. 1733–8, it was demolished in 1775. Whether the arch was built is uncertain. It is known only from a drawing by Morris in an album in the Royal Collection at Windsor which seems to have been put together in about 1733, with some involvement on the part of Dodington and Morris, apparently in connection with the series of paintings of (mostly) Palladian or neo-Palladian buildings commissioned by Consul Smith in 1745–6 from Antonio Visentini and Francesco Zuccarelli. The Eastbury arch was ornamented with seven bas-reliefs, two on either side of the single opening, and three on the attic. Above the attic was a pedestal, with curved sides, presumably intended to support a piece of sculpture. The structure was hollow, with niches in the front and back walls, a window on either side, and a narrower doorway on the axis of the arched opening. Walls are shown going off diagonally from the rear corners. It was a garden pavilion, rather than a gateway. In 1762 the Consul Smith paintings were sold to George III, and eight of the eleven remain in the Royal Collection. One shows a triumphal arch dedicated to George II (see p. 292): like the Eastbury arch, it is based on the design for Temple Bar by Inigo Jones published by William Kent in his *Designs of Inigo Jones* in 1727.

Roger Morris was the architectural collaborator of the amateur Henry Herbert, who succeeded his father as 9th Earl of Pembroke in 1733, and their names provide an intriguing link between several arches.[37] The function of eyecatcher is notable in the arch at Castle Hill in Devon, which stands on an axis with the house up on the hill across the valley. It probably dates from about 1730. Herbert, the Earl of Burlington and Roger Morris were all involved in the remodelling of the house. In effect, the arch is a large screen with three arched openings, the central one being bigger; over the centre is a raised attic, with curved sidepieces sweeping up to it. The arch was rebuilt in 1960.[38]

At Mereworth in Kent an arch, now ruinous, stands at the southern tip of the park. Colvin suggests that Roger Morris might have designed the pavilions added to Mereworth Castle c. 1740, and the church (1744–6), which might associate him with this arch.[39] It was certainly there by 1752, when Horace Walpole wrote that 'a wood that runs up a hill behind the house is broke … like an Albano landscape with an octagon temple and a triumphal arch' (by 'Albano' he means the 17th-century Bolognese painter Francesco Albani).[40] It is built of brick, faced with sandstone. The opening is flanked by coupled Composite half-columns, of which the terracotta capitals may have come from Richard Holt's artificial stone manufactory in Lambeth. The attic is pierced by three panels, now open, which suggests that there was a room above the opening from

16.4 Heaven's Gate, Highclere, Hampshire, 1737, probably by Henry Herbert.

which the prospect over the valleys in both directions could be enjoyed. John Newman suggests that the model for the arch was that at Pula, as shown by Serlio.[41] Trees now cut off the arch from the park.

The arch at Highclere in Hampshire is known as Heaven's Gate [16.4]. It looks north over the park from Sidown Hill, framing the view of the house. Surrounded by trees, it bears the inscription: *Robert Herbert hunc arcum posuit An. D. 1737* ('Robert Herbert set up this arch in 1737'). Robert was the brother of Henry Herbert, Lord Pembroke, and it is likely that Henry designed the arch. It stands on the brow of a steep hill, which may explain why it collapsed in 1739 and had to be rebuilt. A tripartite arch of brick, with a pedimented attic and stone urns, it originally had a stone seat behind the central opening, and rooms for drinking tea behind the side openings.[42]

Catherine, the sister of Robert Herbert and Lord Pembroke, married Sir Nicholas Morice. He built an eyecatcher arch on his estate at Werrington, then in Devon (now Cornwall), which Richard Pococke described as 'on the model of that … at Highcleer'. It has now disappeared.[43]

A little earlier than Heaven's Gate, a much more splendid arch, not associated with Morris and Herbert, was built at Garendon in Leicestershire (now visible from the M1) [16.5]. Ambrose Phillipps inherited the estate in 1729.[44] One of the earliest members of the Society of Dilettanti, he travelled in France and Italy, and a volume of his drawings survives in the RIBA. It includes the Roman arches at Orange and Verona, details of the Arches of Titus and Septimius Severus at Rome, and a drawing of the Porte de Peyrou at Montpellier, erected in honour of Louis XIV in 1691–3. The volume also includes 'A design of My invention for a Gate for a Park'. This was erected over a drive which led westwards towards Shepshed from the circular temple which he also

16.5 Garendon, Leicestershire, arch by Ambrose Phillipps, after 1729.

designed, on a ridge in the southern part of the park. It is elegantly articulated with four detached Corinthian columns on the east front, and a pair of attached columns supporting a pediment on the west. As Mark Girouard points out, it is in effect a reconstruction of the Arch of Titus – which did not regain its true form until the restoration by Raffaele Stern and Giuseppe Valadier in 1822 – combined with elements of the Roman arch at Orange.

Phillipps's drawing for the east front of the arch shows statues and circular reliefs between the columns, but the only sculpture executed consists of a fine relief on the eastern attic and the keystone on the west. The relief represents the story of Diana and Actaeon – appropriate for the context of hunting. Girouard notes that the coffering under the arch, the pediment on the west, and the use of a relief on the attic all derive from Orange. Although the arch has almost nothing that can be called windows, it was occupied until comparatively recently; indeed, a gamekeeper raised seven children there. Apparently Phillipps intended to build a larger arch as the main entrance to the park from Loughborough, but his death in 1737 at the age of thirty prevented it.

At Wallington in Northumberland a very curious structure stands on a hill in the park. Known as The Arches, it was built in 1735 as a screen to the Hall courtyard, but was found to be too narrow for coaches, so was used as an eyecatcher. The architect may have been Daniel Garrett. The piers have bulgy rustication. Over the central opening is a pediment, while over the side ones are rectangular recesses containing classical busts. On top are four crocketed pyramids. There are return walls with further openings.[45]

At the Vauxhall Gardens in London a series of three triumphal arches was set along the Grand South Walk. They were made of timber and painted canvas, and were there by 1751. The designer, identified as 'an ingenious Italian', was probably Giovanni Niccolò Servandoni, who was responsible for the 'Machine' set up in Green Park for the fireworks in 1749. Charmingly Rococo, the central opening was much higher than the side ones. The arches were still *in situ* in 1765, but had gone by 1786. By 1761 a Grand Portico had been built to house Roubiliac's statue of Handel. It took the form of a Doric triumphal arch, with pilasters and a pediment containing Roubiliac's cast lead group of 'Harmony'.[46]

In view of his role as a pioneer of Neoclassicism, it is not surprising that Sir William Chambers should have designed arches. In about 1758 he built an arch at Wilton, in Wiltshire, for the 10th Earl of Pembroke (son of the 9th Earl), on top of the hill on the axis of the south front of the house. A rather crude arched structure had been set up there by *c.* 1700 to support a copy of the celebrated equestrian statue of Marcus Aurelius on the Campidoglio at Rome.[47] In his Diaries, Thomas Hearne quotes a letter of 1719 in which the Hon. Francis Gwyn describes how he was shown this as a 'new Rarity' by the 9th Earl. The 'mould' had been brought from Rome in the time of Charles I, to be used for the statue of the King which is now at Charing Cross.[48] Hubert Le Sueur, who executed that statue, was sent to Italy in 1631 to buy casts of antique statues, and these must have included the Marcus Aurelius.[49] However, according to Gwyn, Lord Pembroke was the first person to make use of it. Chambers' arch was of stone, 'in the Corinthian order and in a rather Gallic taste' (John Harris), and formed a much more impressive base for the statue.[50] However, in 1790 William Gilpin denounced the placing of the arch on the hill as an 'absurd ostentatious ornament', and thought that, although 'perhaps too pompous a structure to form a part of the approach to the house, it would have been bearable there'.[51] Three years later James Wyatt did indeed move it, to form the main entrance to the north forecourt of the house.

In 1759 Chambers designed a ruined arch in the park at Kew for Augusta, Dowager Princess of Wales [16.6].[52] Already in 1728, in his *New Principles of Gardening*, Batty Langley had suggested the use of 'old Ruins' to terminate walks; his illustrations of ruins, borrowed from engravings by Jakob van Sandrart, include one of the Arch of Constantine, looking a good deal more 'ruinous' than it does today.[53] The arch at Kew was intended, according to Chambers, 'to make a passage for carriages and cattle over one of the principal walks of the garden, [and] to imitate antiquity'. The opportunity was used by him to provide a piquant element in the landscape. It appealed to the painter Richard Wilson, whose painting of it (in the Ford Collection) used – amusingly – to be known by the title 'Villa Borghese'.[54] The arch is built of stock brick, with fragments of stone capitals and cornices.

Sir Francis Dashwood, of West Wycombe, Buckinghamshire, was the nephew of the Hon. John Fane (later 7th Earl of Westmorland), who built Mereworth. Like Ambrose Phillipps, he was a member of the Society of Dilettanti, and like him he had a serious interest in architecture. At West Wycombe he built an arch near the western end of the south front of the house. Erected in about 1761, it was probably designed by John Donowell, but under Dashwood's supervision.[55] Faced with flint, with stucco

16.6 Ruined Arch, Kew, Surrey, 1759. Sir William Chambers.

dressings, it has paired attached Tuscan columns, and a plaque on the attic inscribed *LIBERTATI AMICITIAEQ[UE] SAC[RUM]* ('Sacred to liberty and friendship' – the motto of Dashwood's notorious Hellfire Club). It was intended partly as a feature to be seen from the park, partly as an entrance to the offices, but, according to dubious tradition, it had another more unusual function; the room over the arch is said to have been used to house cocks which fought in a pit beneath the arch – hence its name the 'Cockpit Arch'. Its function as an entrance was of short duration, and behind the archway is a rustic niche formed by Nicholas Revett in the wall of his stable court (1767–8). It may have been Revett who faced the arch in flint and decorated its interior. The niche now contains a lead copy of the Apollo Belvedere.

An even odder combination of arch and mausoleum, probably dating from the late 1750s, could be found in the famous landscape garden laid out by the Hon. Charles Hamilton at Painshill in Surrey.[56] Beneath a ruinous arch whose underside was ornamented with octagonal coffers was a 'columbarium' (as Horace Walpole called it), whose niches contained 'antiques' from Italy. In the walls were bas-reliefs and inscriptions, and there was a tessellated floor. Beyond the arch, and framed by it, stood an urn. Arthur Young, on his 'Six Weeks Tour', of which he published an account in 1768, admired it: 'the symptoms of decay are excellently imitated, with weeds growing from the ruined parts'.[57] However, when Walpole made a visit in 1761, especially to see 'the Gothic building and the Roman ruin', he was critical: 'you may as well suppose an Alderman's family buried in Temple Bar'.[58] The building was shown on a plate in Catherine the Great's 1774 'Frog Service', made by Wedgwood.[59] The arch itself has now vanished, leaving only the two separate masses of stone and cement-faced brick. Part of the floor (which, said Walpole, 'unluckily resembles a painted oil-cloth') also survives.

More or less contemporary with the arch at Painshill is one at Horton in Northamptonshire. Known as 'The Arches', this comparatively plain structure is set over a drive leading up from the house (demolished in 1936) towards Castle Ashby, and there are a couple of cottages behind it. Articulated by Ionic pilasters, it is a triple arch, but the side openings were presumably always blank: bay windows now project from them. The arch was probably designed by Thomas Wright at the time he worked on the house, c. 1760, for the 2nd Earl of Halifax (another Dilettante), and functioned as an eyecatcher. Horace Walpole saw it on his visit in 1763.[60]

A much more sophisticated arch was erected in 1761–6 as a feature of the park at Shugborough in Staffordshire, by Thomas Anson [16.7].[61] Anson engaged his fellow-Dilettante, James 'Athenian' Stuart, to erect various buildings there. The first of these was the Arch of Hadrian, based on the arch erected by that emperor at Athens, which had been illustrated in Stuart and Revett's *Antiquities of Athens* (1762), to which Thomas and George Anson subscribed. Elements missing in the original were restored. When Thomas Anson's brother George, the distinguished admiral, died in 1762, the arch became a memorial to him and his wife: the triple openings of the upper stage contain marble sarcophagi surmounted by busts, flanking what Stuart called an 'aplustre' – a naval trophy. These, and the relief roundels of Minerva and Neptune, were the work of Peter Scheemakers.

16.7 Shugborough, Staffordshire, 1761–6. James 'Athenian' Stuart.

What must be the largest arch erected in an English park is the Corinthian Arch at Stowe, which stands on axis with the south front of the house, a mile away across the broad valley containing the lake, and aligned on the drive to Buckingham [16.8]. It was designed by the young Thomas Pitt (later Lord Camelford) for his uncle (and fellow-Dilettante) Richard Grenville, Lord Cobham, and erected in 1765–7. Comparatively plain, it is 18 m square in height and width, and contains two houses for estate workers.[62] However, it did not please Thomas Jefferson, on his visit in 1786: 'The Corinthian Arch has a very useless appearance, inasmuch as it has no pretension to any destination. Instead of being an object from the house, it is an obstacle to a very pleasing distant prospect.'[63] A second, much smaller, arch, the Doric Arch, was erected

274 THE TRIUMPHAL ARCH

16.8 Corinthian Arch, Stowe, Buckinghamshire, 1765–7. Thomas Pitt.

between the central vista and the southern end of the Elysian Fields in 1768, to honour George III's aunt Princess Amelia.[64] Michael Bevingon has shown that the arch was built by 1724, at the north-east corner of the house, and was designed by Vanbrugh. This may have been the arch proposed to be moved to the head of the Grecian Valley.[65] In 1749 Lord Cobham wrote a Latin inscription for it to Britain's prosperity. It has been suggested by Joan Coutu that it was intended to celebrate the victories of the War of the Austrian Succession, but as Lord Cobham regarded the Peace of Aix-la-Chapelle as a sell-out, he gave up the idea of the arch.[66] In fact he died in the same year. Finally the Doric Arch was moved to its present location. It may have been 'improved' by Pitt.

In 1768 Robert Adam made an unexecuted design for a bridge at Bowood, Wiltshire, which was like a series of linked triumphal arches. It was described as 'in imitation of the Aqueducts of the Ancients'. The five openings are flanked by aedicules with pilasters and entablatures, framing niches which contain urns. The end piers have pedimented aedicules with statues of centaurs above. Like the Nostell bridge (see above, p. 265) it is partly ruinous, and has rough timbers filling gaps in the parapets.[67]

Another combination of triumphal arch and bridge is at Hartwell House, Buckinghamshire. The drive crosses a path leading from one part of the gardens to another by a bridge, whose front towards the east (the house side) takes the form of a triumphal arch. Built mainly of rough stone, the central recess (below which is the arch for the footpath) is taller than those at the sides. Between the recesses are rough pilasters, rising as far as the arch imposts. Above these are narrow vertical bands of ashlar, corresponding to which the entablature projects, with baluster-shaped finials over them. The mouldings around the recesses, and the wonderful assortment of carvings on top, were all removed from the 16th-century house which was remodelled at this time (*c.* 1760) by Henry Keene. The arch was possibly begun *c.* 1765.[68]

The unbuilt Stowe arch would have differed from the others described so far in having a commemorative purpose like its Roman models (although the Shugborough arch had been adapted to serve such a purpose). Such an arch was erected at Parlington Park, Aberford, Yorkshire, to the design of Thomas Leverton [16.9].[69] That bears the unexpected inscription 'Liberty in N. America Triumphant MDCCLXXXIII'. When the Prince of Wales visited the estate in 1806 he was so disgusted by the 'man who could thus perpetuate the memory of England's defeats' that he left at once. This man was Sir Thomas Gascoigne, Bart., a fervent supporter of American independence. On Leverton's drawing for the arch the attic is inscribed 'To that Virtue which for a series of Years resisted Oppression & by a glorious Peace rescued its Country and Millions from Slavery'. The arch, which stands on the axis of a straight avenue, is in effect a screen, with an elevation (repeated on both sides) based on the Arch of Constantine at Rome, but much simplified and flattened out.

In the same year as the Parlington arch, John Parker had an arch erected at Saltram in Devon, to form an eyecatcher from his new dining room. Both room and arch were

16.9 Parlington, West Yorkshire, arch 'Liberty in N. America Triumphant', 1783. Thomas Leverton.

276   THE TRIUMPHAL ARCH

designed by Robert Adam.[70] Known as the Boringdon Arch, it is simpler than that shown in Adam's design of 1782 at the Soane Museum. That has paired half-columns of the Tower of the Winds order, and is flanked by lodges, but is otherwise very similar to the entrance arch erected at Croome Court, Worcestershire, to Adam's design in 1779 (above, p. 265). The Boringdon Arch conceals a keeper's cottage.

In his *Architettura Campestre* of 1827, T.F. Hunt attacked the practice of building artificial ruins, denouncing even the arch at Kew ('perhaps the best of modern antiques') as exciting ridicule, and expressed satisfaction that thanks to the 'present chaste system of landscape gardening … useless masses no longer disfigure the beautiful scenery of our parks and lawns; nor ought we to "Turn Arcs of triumph to a Garden-gate"'.

So ended a chapter in the history of British gardens.[71]

Arches as entrances to Irish demesnes

According to James Howley, 'entrance gateways inspired by the triumphal arches of the Romans are very common in Ireland'.[72] His definition is, however, very loose, and the arches described here will be a narrower selection. The earliest seems to be that at Ball's Grove, near Drogheda, Co. Louth. Plain but elegant, it has an arched central opening closed by iron gates, with on either side a rectangular opening beneath an elliptical recess. Set within the pediment are the Ball arms.[73]

A more subtly articulated arch was erected by James Gandon at Carrickglass (or Carriglass), Co. Longford, along with stables and a farmyard, as subsidiary buildings to a villa which remained unexecuted. Apparently dating from some time between 1792 and 1804, the opening is flanked by round-headed niches. The cornice at impost level projects further than the plain entablature on top, and over the opening another plain course of stone suggests a vestigial cornice.[74] The Lion's Gate at Mote Park, Roscommon, is attributed to Gandon, and dates from *c.* 1787. The lion above is of Coade stone.

The grandest triumphal arch entrance in Ireland is the Dodder Lodge to Rathfarnham Castle, south of Dublin. It led into a 'densely wooded demesne', but now incongruously leads into a housing estate. The order is Tuscan, with half-columns on either side of the arched opening, and pilasters at the corners. Between these are niches below, and blank panels above. The entablature breaks forward over the opening, and is crowned by a balustrade with fancy urns. On either side walls curve out to piers, all with banded stonework. The elevation originally to the park (now facing a street) is flat, with pilasters. Here the frieze has triglyphs, and the cornice has modillions. Instead of blank panels, there are blind oculi, and the keystone represents a bearded face. Inside the arch there are doors, and in the end walls single windows light the accommodation within. The Castle was bought in 1767 by Nicholas Hume-Loftus, 2nd Earl of Ely, who was descended from Adam Loftus, builder of the Castle *c.* 1583. On his death in 1769 the estate went to his uncle, who was created Earl of Ely in 1771. The arch is said to have been built to commemorate the regaining of the estate by the family. It appears on a map of 1779 as 'new gate'.[75]

At Caledon, Co. Tyrone, John Nash altered the house in 1808–10, and made designs for a new main entrance which remained unexecuted.[76] One had pairs of Ionic columns flanking an opening, and on either side lodges with curious tripartite windows and diminutive pediments. Another had an astylar arch, though with half-pilasters above the impost level, and pairs of lodges, each with a window between pairs of Tuscan pilasters.

At Colebrook, Co. Fermanagh, the 'Triumphal Gate' on the Fivemiletown road, was built *c.* 1830, to the design of William Farrell.[77] Fairly simple, the central section, with the large opening, breaks forward and has a low attic, and there is a pedestrian opening on either side. Built of yellow sandstone, the whole is articulated by means of Tuscan pilasters.

In 1832 William Vitruvius Morrison was commissioned to remodel Oak Park, Co. Carlow. He gave it a splendid entrance gateway, on which pairs of freestanding Ionic columns, on tall projecting bases, flank the opening. The substantial entablature breaks forward over each pair. On the rear elevation the columns are Doric.[78] A couple of years later Morrison conceived a grander version of this design for the 'Dublin approach' to Castle Coole, Co. Fermanagh, where the attic sweeps up to support a coat of arms, and on each side is a screen with two Doric columns linking the arch to a niched pier.[79] The design remained unexecuted, as did a very similar design of 1838 for Baronscourt, Co. Tyrone, whose principal difference from the Castle Coole proposal is that the side screens each have two pairs of Doric columns, leading to pilastered aedicules, with walls curving out beyond these.[80]

The gateway at Bantry House, Co. Cork, is rather similar to the Rathfarnham Castle lodge, but is much cruder. It presumably dates from the time of the remodelling of the house in 1845. Here architectural effect is sacrificed to utility, with windows on two floors; plain pilasters support balls above the balustrade.[81]

An extraordinary series of designs for an entrance to the estate of Montalto at Ballynahinch, Co. Down, was commissioned *c.* 1867 by David Stewart Ker from the architects Thomas Turner and Thomas Drew.[82] One was for a lavish and ill-digested paraphrase of a triumphal arch. The opening has raised vermiculated voussoirs. The side bays are rusticated up to impost level, above which on each side pairs of Corinthian columns frame a round-headed window with a balustraded balcony. The parapet is also balustraded, with pairs of urns on the corners. Above the opening rises an attic, on which four banded Ionic pilasters frame circular windows, beneath a segmental pediment. Flanking walls are pierced with circular openings between pairs of pilasters. In the end Ker merely built gates with large piers.

The architect most closely associated with the Celtic Revival was William Alphonsus Scott. His ecclesiastical masterpiece is St Enda's Church at Spiddal, Co. Galway, built in 1904–7 for the 2nd Lord Killanin, who was one of the most important patrons of the Revival. Killanin also commissioned Scott to make alterations to Spiddal House, which included an entrance gateway in the form of a free, astylar interpretation of a triumphal arch. Of an almost Lutyensish character, this has a blocky attic rising in two stages above lower side pavilions.[83]

Arches as features of gardens outside Britain and Ireland

Marco Mantova Benavides (1489–1582) was a jurist of European reputation, who taught at the University of Padua. He was a distinguished patron of the arts, a man of vast learning, and a friend of the leading humanists of the Veneto. In 1541 he moved

16.10 Canaletto (1697–1768), *Padua: The Benavides garden, with a classical arch and a statue of Hercules,* c. 1760. Royal Collection.

into his new palazzo on the east side of the piazza behind the church of the Eremitani; it was lavishly decorated with paintings and sculpture. It is now the Albergo Mantua [*sic*] Benavides. In 1544 he employed the Florentine sculptor Bartolommeo Ammannati to carve for the cortile a colossal stone statue of Hercules, 9 m high [16.10].[84] Its octagonal base bears reliefs of seven of his labours. The idea was to celebrate Benavides's own heroic virtues, by taking up the challenge of Pliny's description of a colossal statue as an *audaciae exemplum* ('example of boldness').[85] Next, in 1545–6, Ammannati went on to design and carve a magnificent tomb for Benavides in the nearby church. Its imagery is secular, with noble figures of Wisdom, Strength, Fame and Immortality. The influence of Michelangelo is obvious.

Ammannati's third and last commission for Benavides was a 'prospetto' of stone, at the eastern end of the palazzo's cortile. Set on the axis of the vestibule, it frames the entrance to the garden and takes the form of a triumphal arch, broad and somewhat squat in its proportions.[86] It was described by Benavides as *fatto come que' di Roma* ('made like those of Rome').[87] Begun in 1545, it seems to have been complete by August 1547. The architecture shows Ammannati's debt to the architects of the Veneto, with its reminiscences of Sanmicheli, Serlio, Falconetto and Sansovino. The four fluted Doric columns support a substantial entablature, whose metopes are carved with bucrania and shields. The arch has a bold keystone, characteristic of the Veneto. In the spandrels are winged Victories which recall those on Sansovino's Library of San Marco in Venice.

On either side of the opening are niches containing statues of Jupiter, symbolising political power, and Apollo, symbolising the arts, and especially music (to which Benavides was devoted). Both statues are turned towards those passing through the arch. The niches (perhaps suggested by those of the Arco dei Gavi at Verona) have pediments supported on brackets, taken from Sanmicheli and Michelangelo, but going back to Vitruvius's Ionic *parotides* (consoles). The broad horizontal band which runs right across the arch below the impost level is a particularly striking device, also found, for example, in Ammannati's cortile of the Palazzo Pitti in Florence (though there it is confined to the niches). The attic has in its centre a panel, flanked by putti, bearing the inscription *id facere laus est quod decet, non quod licet* ('it is praiseworthy to do what is fitting, not what is permitted') – words spoken by Seneca to Nero in the tragedy *Octavia*.[88] On either side are reliefs showing events of 1545: on the left Benavides appears as ambassador of Padua to the Doge of Venice, while on the right he is created a *cavaliere* by Charles V.

The combination of the arch (which has been described as 'the most antiquarian work in North Italy') and the colossus provides remarkable testimony to Benavides' pride in his own achievements and his prospective immortality.[89] The two were drawn (on two sheets) by Antonio Canaletto. Not surprisingly, the drawings in the Royal Collection were catalogued by Sir Karl Parker among the 'purely fanciful pieces'.[90]

A particularly elegant arched entrance led to Alvise Cornaro's country estate, the Villa Cornaro at Este, near Padua. As at the Loggia and Odeon which he built in Padua, his architect was Giovanni Maria Falconetto. Only the arch survives at Este. Built of golden Pietra di Nanto, each of its piers has pairs of aedicules, one above the other, on which pairs of shell-headed niches are flanked by Ionic pilasters. In the spandrels are flying Victories, and the keystone is a bearded mask. The attic is plain.[91]

In about 1598 Tommaso Francini, a Florentine hydraulic engineer, arrived in France, probably sent by the Grand Duke Ferdinand de' Medici, and his brother Alessandro followed him. In 1631 Alessandro published a book of architectural designs for 'portiques', which include triumphal arches in a full-blown Mannerist style.[92] Kenneth Woodbridge suggests that he may have been the designer of the 'Grotte' in the garden of the Palais du Luxembourg. Originally erected at the east end of the *allée* which ran between the parterre and the palace, it was later moved further north. It is now known as the Fontaine de Médicis. Built between 1623 and 1630, it has a tall central niche, and smaller ones between pairs of flanking columns, raised above the plinth. On the attic are the arms of Marie de Médicis, between statues of the Rhône and Seine rivers by Pierre Biard. Above, three urns crown a segmental pediment. The stalactitic ornament which covers most of the stonework is similar to that on the Grotte at Wideville, built between 1630 and 1636. This has openings instead of niches, but is otherwise very like the one at the Luxembourg, and Woodbridge suggests that it too may be by Alessandro Francini.[93]

The château of Rueil, west of Paris, was bought in 1633 by Cardinal Richelieu, and became his favourite residence. He greatly improved the comparatively restricted grounds, with a splendid cascade, grottoes, fountains and statues. His adviser for these works was one of the Francinis, probably Tommaso.[94] Northeast of the château was the

16.11 Rueil-Malmaison Jardins. Israel Silvestre.

Orangerie, containing 'many exotic plants, pomegranates, lemons and orange trees'. The garden in front was flanked on its eastern side by the road to St-Cloud. As a barrier between the garden and the road, and to form a backdrop to the garden, a *trompe d'œil* triumphal arch was painted on wooden boards by Jean Lemaire, a painter of architectural perspectives [16.11]. This was done *c.* 1638. In 1644 John Evelyn visited Rueil, and described the garden in his diary. At the end of the 'Citroniere' was

> the Arco of Constantine paynted in Oyle on a Wall, as big as the real one at Rome, so done to the life, that a man very well skilled in Painting may mistake it for stone and sculpture; and indeed it is so rarely perform'd that it is almost impossible to believe it Paynting, but to be a Worke of solid stone: The skie, and hills which seem to be in between the Arches, are so naturall, that swallows and other birds, thinking to fly through have dash'd themselves to pieces against the Walls: I was infinitely taken with this agreeable cheate.[95]

Louis Huygens recorded in 1655 that the arch was seen through an iron screen at a distance of fifty or sixty paces, and that birds tried to perch on the cornices.[96] Richelieu's 'arch' naturally had less sculptural decoration than Constantine's, although it had pairs of circular 'reliefs' over the side openings, and statues at attic level over the columns. The principal difference consisted in the addition of an extra bay on each side, rising only to the level of the principal entablature. Each had a niche containing a statue, a relief above, and a lavish trophy on top. The purpose of these additions was no doubt to provide extra width.

A charming oddity is the triumphal arch constructed of trellis in the park of Schloss Schwetzingen in Baden-Württemberg, presumably in the early 18th century. Another arch stood at Zijdebalen, near Utrecht, where the silk-factory owner David van Mollem created a splendid garden. The fancifully decorated arch had a tall central opening, while the sides had pilasters with banded rustication framing magnificent marble urns, with reliefs of the seasons by Jacob Cressant, dated 1714. The arch terminated a parterre with hedges and statues.[97]

The more romantic type of landscape garden, known as 'English', became fashionable in the later eighteenth century throughout Europe, and triumphal arches were sometimes erected as features to catch the eye. Jacob Boreel, owner of Beeckestijn (Velsen-Zuid), in the Netherlands, had visited English gardens, and in 1772 had the garden laid out by Johann Georg Michael, recommending that he too should visit England. A feature of the garden was a screen in the form of a triumphal arch, with freestanding Tuscan columns, and a semicircular relief on the attic. The model was probably the Corinthian Arch at Stowe.

The Gatchina, or Triumphal, Gate at Tsarskoe Selo, outside St Petersburg, was originally intended by Catherine the Great to honour her lover Prince Grigory Orlov [16.12]. The lengthy inscription on the attic states that 'Orlov has saved Moscow from the plague': what he had actually done was to calm a revolt which had broken out there due to panic over the outbreak of plague. The Gate is situated on the southern boundary of the park, at the exit to the road to Gatchina – the estate which Catherine had given to Orlov. The arch was designed in 1771 by Antonio Rinaldi, and work began in 1778. The marble for the facing was quarried locally, and the erection was supervised by

Vasily Neelov. The iron gates, erected in 1787, were designed by Giacomo Quarenghi, and made at the State Arms Works at Sestroretsk. The arch has freestanding Ionic columns, whose volutes are linked by garlands, and the central section breaks forward. There is no sculptural decoration.[98]

In 1791, after Orlov ceased to be Catherine's favourite, she regretted that while she had honoured other military commanders she had forgotten the military hero Prince Grigory Alexandrovich Potemkin-Tavrichesky. She ordered that the Triumphal Gate should be illuminated and decorated with naval and army weapons and a banner inscribed with verses by the court poet Petrov which told Potemkin: 'You enter with splashing waves into Sophia's Temple' (in other words, to Hagia Sophia in Istanbul). This referred to the Russo-Turkish wars; Catherine wrote that after each victory she erected a suitable monument at Tsarskoe Selo, and continued: 'I have had the idea of having a Temple of Memory built in the 'little forest', the approach to which would be through Triumphal Gates where all the previous actions in the current war will be represented on medallions.' In 1792 Charles Cameron designed this arch, which was on the approach to the Baths that he had designed. A plain structure, with fluted Greek Doric columns and a triglyph frieze, it had four statues on top of the attic, and Catherine's four 'medallions' hung one above the other on each side of the opening, suspended from eagles, and framed by garlands.[99] The arch was attached to a long Ionic

16.12 Gatchina, Tsarskoe Selo, Triumphal Gates, 1771–87. Antonio Rinaldi.

colonnade, decorated with statues. This so-called 'Temple of Memory' was demolished by Catherine's son, Paul I.

In Belgium, an arch which remained unbuilt was designed by Charles de Wailly in 1782 for the 'Nouvel Herculanum' [sic] in the park at Enghien belonging to the duc d'Arenberg. De Wailly's watercolour shows a partly ruinous and overgrown arch. It is fairly plain, but each pier has an attached Doric column supporting a statue at attic level. There is a triglyph frieze. The spandrels contain swags, and the attic has an inscription panel.[100]

A Polish military hero, Prince Jozef Poniatowski, was honoured after his death in 1813 with an arch at what had been his estate at Jablonna, north-west of Warsaw. Jozef was a marshal of Napoleon, and a hero of the struggle for Polish independence. He left the estate to his cousin's daughter Anna, who had married Count Alexander Potocki in 1805, but later divorced him. Potocki had visited England in 1802–3, and studied landscape gardening, and Anna, who had artistic leanings, had remodelled the garden at Natolin (the Potocki estate). When she inherited Jablonna, she redesigned and extended its park, which had been laid out from 1783 in the English style (probably by Jakub Fontana). In it she erected a triumphal arch. Comparatively small, it spans a drive. Freestanding Ionic columns break forward on all four sides, and their entablatures are surmounted by warriors dressed as ancient Romans, armed with swords and lances. The arch bears the sole inscription *PONIATOWSKIEMU* – to Poniatowski. The architect may have been Henryk Marconi.[101]

Three other Polish parks contained triumphal arches, all apparently built in ruined form, which are known from illustrations. At the Czartoryski Palace in the Warsaw district of Powazki the garden contained a ruinous arch, with a pair of freestanding columns, built after 1774.[102] At Wilanow, where the park was laid out by Piotr Aigner *c.* 1810 for Stanislaus Kostka Potocki, there was an arch with three openings in the Ionic order.[103] Krzyztopór is famous for its vast ruined seventeenth-century house. Modern books make no mention of a landscape garden, but an engraving shows an arch built on a bridge over a stream; pairs of pilasters flank rectangular openings on either side of the central opening, and above them are elliptical openings.[104]

The park which links Lednice and Valtice, the two great houses in southern Moravia of the Princes of Liechtenstein, is on an immense scale, and the park buildings are correspondingly huge. One of these is a magnificent triumphal arch, known as the Temple of Diana or the Rendezvous [16.13]. The explanation for these perhaps surprising names, and for the arch's situation in a clearing in the forest, is that it was intended as a meeting-point for hunts. It was designed in 1810 by Joseph Hardtmuth, who had worked for the Liechtensteins since 1789, and had been given the title of *Baudirektor* by the new Fürst Johannes I in 1805. Construction began in 1811, and was more or less complete when Hardtmuth retired from the Fürst's service in 1812. The form of the arch was chosen, ingeniously, for practical reasons. The attic provides space for a large room, used both for refreshments and (through windows at the back and on the sides) as a look-out. One of the piers housed the main staircase, while the other provided a residence for a huntsman. Each side of the arch has four freestanding Corinthian columns, and there is lavish sculptural decoration, by Joseph Klieber, with circular reliefs below rectangular ones in the intercolumniations, winged figures in the spandrels, statues on the inner columns, and, on the front, a large relief at attic level. The

16.13 Lednice, Czech Republic, Temple of Diana or Rendezvous, 1810–12. Joseph Hardtmuth.

subjects predictably concern hunting and antiquity. The attic is inscribed *DIANAE VENATRICI EIUSQUE CULTORIBUS* ('To Diana the huntress and her worshippers'). The eating room was given painted decoration in 1813 by Michael Rober, to the design of Joseph Kornhäusel.[105]

Also in the year 1811 another building was begun to Hardtmuth's design, on the Reistenberg near Valtice, this time with a commemorative function. A triumphal arch in the centre, of the Corinthian order, is extended at the sides, first by open colonnades, each with a pair of freestanding columns, and then by closed bays repeating the side bays of the arch. On the front elevation it is inscribed *DER SOHN DEM VATER, DER BRUDER DEN BRÜDERN*, as Johannes intended it to commemorate his father and two deceased brothers, and the four of them are represented by statues in antique costume set within niches in the bays. Reliefs over these show their virtues. Above runs a continuous entablature, and the terrace on top is reached by spiral stairs in the end bays. The niches on the rear contain urns. When Hardtmuth retired in 1812 only the bare structure was finished, and the colonnade was completed by his successor, Kornhäusel.[106]

The château of Gaasbeek, in Brabant, came into the possession of Paul Arconati-Visconti through his Belgian wife. As a fervent admirer of Napoleon, who had appointed him Mayor of Brussels in 1800, he built an arch in the park, apparently in 1808. He intended to build a road through it leading to Paris. It is a plain structure, of brick with stone dressings, and has pairs of Corinthian pilasters on the piers.[107]

Similar hero-worship inspired the building of another arch. Not far from Valtice, across the border in Austria, the Baroque Schloss Kleinwetzdorf was bought in 1830 by Joseph Pargfrieder.[108] By profession he was an army supplier, and his origins were humble. He was obsessed with Austria's military glory, and was especially besotted with Field-Marshal Joseph Graz von Radetzky. He began to remodel the Schloss, and in 1833 built a triumphal arch in front over the main approach [16.14]. It is dedicated to Radetzky, who is symbolised by the large and fierce stone lion on top. The broad arch is supported on squat fluted Greek Doric columns, set within a frame of broad channelled pilasters and entablature.[109] In 1849 Pargfrieder decided to create his 'Heldenberg' in the park, a sort of Valhalla which commemorates Austria's military achievements by means of over 160 statues and busts of iron and zinc. The climax is the obelisk below which Radetzky, Feldmarschall Max von Wimpfen, and Pargfrieder are buried – the latter seated and wearing armour.

It is scarcely surprising that triumphal arches occur as features of Italian gardens. The grandest of all parks in Italy is the Villa Borghese at Rome. It was already mature, and well supplied with buildings, when Camillo Borghese inherited it in 1800. He acquired the land needed to enlarge the park westwards and southwards down to the Porta del Popolo, and in 1822 a project for it was produced by Luigi Canina. A problem was presented by the Via delle Tre Madonne, which ran northwards through the new property. Canina solved it by sinking the road and crossing it by means of two bridges. In front of the northern one he raised a triumphal arch. In a book on the *nuove fabbriche* published in 1823, Canina described it as *eretta secondo la maniera degli*

16.14 Schloss Kleinwetzdorf, Lower Austria, Radetzky arch, 1833.

antichi romani ('erected according to the manner of the ancient Romans'), to contrast with the Greek Ionic Propylaea at the new entrance to the Villa, and the Egyptian Propylaea at the second bridge. The first two were built in 1826–7, the third in 1827–8.[110]

Already in a volume of sketches entitled *Pensieri d'architettura*, dating from 1818–20, Canina had made various designs for arches. One, described as *Arco Trionfale semplice*, is very similar to the Villa Borghese arch – astylar, with winged Victories above impost level, and statues and reliefs below. On the stepped attic is a group of sculpture. A similar, but simpler, design appears as an alternative for the Porta del Popolo entrance to the Villa: the arch is linked by screens with pairs of Ionic columns to large bases, above which rise tapering cylinders ornamented with sculpture.[111] The arch actually erected was even more severe. Its only decoration is a pair of winged Victories in relief. On the stepped attic is a statue of the Emperor Septimius Severus, on a base, on either side of which sit bound captives. The back also has winged Victories, but the reliefs on the sides shown on Canina's engravings were not executed.

The Rotonda, the magnificent Neoclassical villa which the architect Luigi Cagnola built for himself at Inverigo, north of Milan, in 1813, had a tall and elegant arch spanning the entrance from the west. Probably about 10 m tall, it had pairs of Corinthian half-columns, above which at attic level were seated statues. It was destroyed by a cyclone in 1908.[112]

Between Inverigo and Milan, at Desio, Giuseppe Piermarini had rebuilt the Casa Cusani, and designed a fine garden for it. In the 1830s its new owner, Giovanni Traversi, commissioned Pelagio Palagi – equally remarkable as an architect, a furniture designer and a painter – to enlarge and transform it. The façade is dated 1844. The Villa is now known as the Villa Tittoni Traversi, or Antona Traversi. The park (where Bellini is reputed to have composed *La Straniera*) used to be decorated with many statues and buildings, now mostly gone. There survive an extraordinary Gothic 'oratory' by Palagi (1831–5), and a charming triumphal arch. Fluted Corinthian columns support a frieze with putti holding garlands, and on the attic is the inscription SOLLICITAE IUCUNDA OBLIVIA VITAE ('Pleasing forgetfulness of anxious life'). The quotation appropriately comes from the *Satire* in which Horace describes his delight at escaping from Rome to the country.[113]

Two of the villas in the neighbourhood of Genoa have triumphal arches in their parks. A comparatively simple one is a

16.15 Pegli, Liguria, Villa Durazzo Pallavicini, 1846. Michele Canzio.

feature of the vast Villa Duchessa di Galliera at Voltri.[114] More interesting is that at the Villa Durazzo Pallavicini at Pegli. Here the eighteenth-century house and botanic garden, formerly the property of the Grimaldi, passed in 1840 into the possession of Ignazio Pallavicini. He had a huge landscape garden laid out between then and 1846, to the design of Michele Canzio, the stage-designer of the Teatro Carlo Felice in Genoa. The park is entered from the house by a long avenue of ilex trees called the Viale Gotico. This leads beneath a Neoclassical 'Coffee House', and past a fountain pond, to the Arco di Trionfo [16.15]. It appears that this formal approach was intended to suggest an urban environment, but the inscription on the arch invites the visitor to lay aside the cares of the city – recalling the one at Desio.[115] The arch is an elegant structure of white marble, with pairs of Composite half-columns, and pretty sculptural decoration, including statues of Abundance and Joy between the columns, and winged genii and reliefs above the entablature. The sculptor was Giovanni Battista Cevasco. It comes as a great surprise to pass through the arch and find oneself in front of a 'Casetta Rustica', shaded by trees. On turning round, one sees that the back of the arch takes the form of a 'Romitaggio', or hermitage – asymmetrical, faced with rough stone, and with a pitched roof of big slates. From here onwards, the park becomes informal, laid out on the hillside and dotted with charming and remarkable features.

Notes

1. On lodges, see Tim Mowl and Brian Earnshaw, *Trumpet at a Distant Gate: The Lodge as Prelude to the Country House* (London, 1985).
2. Peter Martin, *Pursuing Innocent Pleasures: The Gardening World of Alexander Pope* (Hamden, Conn., 1984), 176–205. See also F.J.C. Hearnshaw, 'Bevis Mount', *Papers and Proceedings of the Hampshire Field Club and Archaeological Society*, 5 (1904–6), 109–25.
3. BL, Add. MS 36363, f. 88v.
4. K. Downes, *Hawksmoor* (London, 1959), 204–6, 282; idem, *Hawksmoor* (London, 1969), 182–4. The flanking walls with pedestrian gates date from before 1710, and were moved here probably c. 1773.
5. John Dixon Hunt, *William Kent, Landscape Garden Designer* (London, 1987), 138. Kent's design is also illustrated in (e.g.) M. Jourdain, *The Work of William Kent* (London, 1948), fig. 3; James Lees-Milne, *Earls of Creation* (London, 1962), 256. See also John Harris, 'Garden Buildings', in Susan Weber, ed., *William Kent: Designing Georgian Britain* (New Haven/London, 2013), 401.
6. H. Colvin, *Biographical Dictionary of British Architects 1600-1840* (New Haven and London, 2008), 217, 706; Mowl and Earnshaw (cit. at n. 1), 84–6.
7. Colvin (cit. in the preceding note), 524; Mowl and Earnshaw (cit. at n. 1), 89–91; John Harris, *Country Life*, 24 Nov. 1966, 1370–72.
8. K. Woodbridge, *Architectural History*, 25 (1982), 18, f. 102; 19, f. 144.
9. Soane Museum, London, LVI, 41; reproduced in *Country Life*, 16 Dec. 1999, 42.
10. David King, *The Complete Works of Robert and James Adam* (Oxford, 2001), 338; L. Harris and G. Jackson-Stops, *Country Life*, 5 March 1987, 99–101; L. Harris, *Robert Adam and Kedleston* (London, 1987), 77.
11. King (cit. in the preceding note), 355–6.
12. ibid., 330.
13. Soane Museum, XLIX, 62.
14. Gareth J.L. Williams, *Apollo*, 163 (April 2006), 49–53.
15. Mowl and Earnshaw (cit. at n. 1), 87; Christopher Hussey, *English Country Houses: Late Georgian* (London, 1958), 41, 48.
16. N. Pevsner and E. Williamson, *The Buildings of England: Buckinghamshire* (London, 1994), 703–4.
17. Mowl and Earnshaw (cit. at n. 1), 81–2; Dorothy Stroud, *Henry Holland* (London, 1966), 55; National Trust guidebook (1982), 34–6.
18. Mowl and Earnshaw (cit. at n. 1), 17; Stroud (cit. in the preceding note), 113.
19. The Newcastle archives refer to Wright's 'finish'd drawing for a Triumphal Arch with a cottage on each side on the hill at Normanton', which is where it was originally intended to stand: see Michael Symes, 'The Garden Designs of Stephen Wright', *Garden History* (Spring 1992), 24. It is possible that Wright's design was modified by John Simpson in the 1780s.
20. Geoffrey Tyack, *Warwickshire Country Houses* (Chichester, 1994), 61.
21. Mowl and Earnshaw (cit. at n. 1), 78; Christopher Hussey, *Country Life*, 10 April 1958, 759. The subject cannot be Bacchus and Ariadne, and the painting's whereabouts are unknown. It does not appear in Annalisa Scarpa, *Sebastiano Ricci* (Milan, 2006).

22 Jeremy Musson, *Country Life*, 1 Jan. 2004, 323–7.
23 Mowl and Earnshaw (cit. at n. 1), 80; Dorothy Stroud, *Humphry Repton* (London, 1962), 90, 100, 110–11. Muschamp's drawings for the gateway were sold at Christie's on 13 Dec. 1988.
24 T. Whellan & Co., *History and Topography of the City of York and the North Riding of Yorkshire* (Beverley, 1859), 248.
25 Derek Linstrum, *Sir Jeffry Wyatville* (Oxford, 1972), 56–7, 244–5. His design for the Lenton Lodge to Wollaton Hall, built 1823–5, is more straightforwardly Elizabethan (Linstrum, 66).
26 Mowl and Earnshaw (cit. at n. 1), 80–81; Peter de Figueiredo and Julian Treuherz, *Cheshire Country Houses* (Chichester, 1988), 223–4.
27 Mowl and Earnshaw (cit. at n. 1), 83; Figueiredo and Treuherz (cit. in the preceding note), 161–5.
28 Mowl and Earnshaw (cit. at n. 1), 87–9; National Trust guidebook (1978), 44, 46.
29 Mowl and Earnshaw (cit. at n. 1), 92–3.
30 M. Girouard, *Country Life*, 18 June 1959, 1380–81. Sir Howard Colvin owned three different sets of designs for the entrance.
31 Michael Fisher, *Alton Towers Past and Present* (Ashbourne, 2010), 24, 46. 'The arch may incorporate an existing garden feature.'
32 Colvin, *Dictionary* (cit. at n. 6), 1019.
33 J. Newman and N. Pevsner, *The Buildings of England: Shropshire* (New Haven/London, 2006), 129–30. The gateway was formerly attributed to John Nash.
34 Peter Howell, *Country Life*, 16 Dec. 1999, 36–43.
35 Steven Parissien, *The Careers of Roger and Robert Morris* (DPhil, Oxford, 1989).
36 John Harris, 'An English Neo-Palladian episode and its connections with Visentini in Venice', *Architectural History*, 27 (1984), 231–40. The arch drawing is reproduced as pl. 4a. On Eastbury, see Michael Hill, *East Dorset Country Houses* (Reading, 2013), 170–80. See also J. Martineau and A. Robinson, eds, *The Glory of Venice* (New Haven/London, 1994), 247–8, 511–12; Desmond Shawe-Taylor, ed., *The First Georgians: Art and Monarchy 1714–1760* (London, 2014), 352–4.
37 On Henry Herbert see Colvin, *Dictionary* (cit. at n. 6), 513–15.
38 Kenneth Woodbridge, *Country Life*, 4 Jan. 1979, 18–21; R. Fausset, *Garden History*, 13 (1985), 102–25.
39 Colvin, *Dictionary* (cit. at n. 6), 709.
40 *The Yale Edition of Horace Walpole's Correspondence*, ed. W.S. Lewis, XXXV (London/New Haven, 1973), 143 (to Richard Bentley, 5 Aug. 1752). There is a similar reference to 'Albano' in a letter to Chute of 4 Aug. 1753, in reference to Stowe.
41 John Newman, *The Buildings of England: Kent – West and the Weald* (New Haven/London, 2012), 418.
42 Mark Girouard, *Country Life*, 18 June 1959, 1378–81. He dates the arch to 1739, but seems to have missed the inscription. Another inscription records a restoration by George Herbert in 1896.
43 *The Travels through England of Dr Richard Pococke*, ed. J.J. Cartwright, Camden Society, I ((London, 1888), 133; D. Ellery Pett, *The Parks and Gardens of Cornwall* (Penzance, 1998), 212–15.
44 Mark Girouard, 'Ambrose Phillipps of Garendon', *Architectural History*, 8 (1965), 25–38.
45 N. Pevsner et al., *The Buildings of England: Northumberland* (Harmondsworth, 1992), 604.
46 David Coke and Alan Borg, *Vauxhall Gardens: A History* (New Haven/London, 2011), 68, 71–3, 212–13, 418. For the Grand Portico, see pp. 95, 219–20.
47 There are two drawings of the statue and its base by William Stukeley, one dated 1722, in the Bodleian Library (MS Top.Wilts.c.4, ff. 7 and 17). There is a drawing of the arch by François-Joseph Bélanger in the sketchbook he made, apparently in 1772–4: see Woodbridge (cit. at n. 8), 19, and f. 144. For the gardens at Wilton, see C. Hussey, *Country Life*, 25 July and 1 Aug. 1963, 206–9 and 164–7; John Bold, *Wilton House and English Palladianism* (London, 1988).
48 Bodleian Library, MS Hearne's Diaries, vol. 101, p. 187. I am indebted to Ruth Guilding for the reference. For the Charing Cross statue, see D.G. Denoon, *Transactions of the London and Middlesex Archaeological Society*, n.s. 6 (1933), 460–86; *Survey of London*, 16 (1935), 263–7; R.M. Ball, *Antiquaries Journal*, 67 (1987), 97–101; Margaret Whinney, *Sculpture in Britain 1530–1830*, rev. edn (Harmondsworth, 1988), 35–6.
49 Francis Haskell and Nicholas Penny, *Taste and the Antique* (New Haven/London, 1981), 31, 35, 221, 254. The 4th Earl of Pembroke had been allowed as a special favour to have a duplicate made by Le Sueur of Charles I's bronze copy of the Borghese Gladiator, to stand in the gardens at Wilton. The 8th Earl gave it to Sir Robert Walpole, and it now stands in the stairwell at Houghton.
50 John Harris, *Sir William Chambers* (London, 1970), 41, 251–2; John Harris and Michael Snodin, *Sir William Chambers* (New Haven/London, 1996), 6. A preliminary design for the arch was engraved for Chambers' *Treatise on Civil Architecture* (London, 1759).
51 W. Gilpin, *Observations on the Western Parts of England* (London, 1798), 101.
52 Sir William Chambers, *Plans, Elevations, Sections and Perspective Views of the Gardens and Buildings at Kew* (London, 1763), 7; Harris, *Chambers* (cit. at n. 50), 37–8, 213–14. Harris points out (37, n. 22) that there is a drawing for 'a more classical version of the arch' at Windsor.
53 Batty Langley, *New Principles of Gardening* (London, 1728), 195, 199, pls XIX–XXII (the latter is the frontispiece). For the Van Sandrart identification, see David Watkin in *Visions of Ruin* (London, Sir John Soane's Museum, 1999), 7–8.
54 Brinsley Ford, *The Ford Collection*, Walpole Society, 60 (1998), 16.
55 Colvin, *Dictionary* (cit. at n. 6), 326. See also A.T. Bolton, *Country Life*, 1 Jan. 1916, 50; Christopher Hussey, *English Country Houses: Early Georgian* (London, 1965), 238, 243; Giles Worsley, *Country Life*, 6 Sept. 1990, 112–17. I am indebted to Sir Francis Dashwood, Bt, for his assistance.
56 Michael Symes, *Mr Hamilton's Elysium: The Gardens of Painshill* (London, 2010), 14, 55, 81–3, 128, 133, 139. He reproduces a painting of the

arch of *c.* 1770, attributed to William Hannan, and a drawing of 1772 by William Gilpin.
57 [Arthur Young], *A Six Weeks Tour through the Southern Counties of England and Wales* (London, 1768), 189.
58 *Horace Walpole's Journals of Visits to Country Seats,* Walpole Society, 16 (1927–8), 36. He refers to his previous visit on 11 Aug. 1748 (*The Yale Edition of Horace Walpole's Correspondence,* IX (London/New Haven, 1941), 71). The arch is also referred to in descriptions of Painshill by Sir John Parnell, of 1763 (MS diaries in the British Library of Political and Economic Science, London), and by T. Whateley, *Observations on Modern Gardening* (London, 1770), 189.
59 Illustrated in Symes (cit. at n. 56), 133.
60 *Journals of Visits to Country Seats* (cit. at n. 58), 53. He was accompanied by the Revd William Cole, who also refers to the arch in a letter (*The Yale Edition of Horace Walpole's Correspondence*, X (London/New Haven, 1941), 334). For Wright's work at Horton see Colvin, *Dictionary* (cit. at n. 6), 1169.
61 John Martin Robinson, *Shugborough* (London, 1989), 23–5, 90.
62 M.J. Gibbon, 'The History of Stowe – XXI', *The Stoic* (Dec. 1974), 121–3; National Trust guidebook (1997), 19, 88. For Pitt's architectural work, see Colvin, *Dictionary* (cit. at n. 6), 806–8.
63 *Thomas Jefferson's Garden Book*, ed. E.M. Betts (Philadelphia, 1944), 113.
64 Gibbon (cit. at n. 62), 123; National Trust guidebook, 23–4. Walpole described Princess Amelia's visit to see the arch in 1770 (*Correspondence*, XXXI (London/New Haven 1961), 146–7).
65 National Trust guidebook, 46; Michael Bevington, *Architectura*, 2 (1991), 136–63; *idem, Country Life*, 24 Feb. 2000, 105.
66 Joan Coutu in Frans de Bruyn and Shaun Regan, eds, *The Culture of the Seven Years War* (Toronto, 2014).
67 *The Works in Architecture of Robert and James Adam* (London, 1778).
68 Eric Throssell, *Hartwell, Buckinghamshire*, pt I, vol. 2: *The Restoration of the Triumphal Arch* (Aylesbury, 2007); Richard Wheeler, *Garden History*, 34 (2006), 86–7.
69 T.F. Friedman, 'Romanticism and Neoclassicism for Parlington: the tastes of Sir Thomas Gascoigne', *Leeds Art Calendar*, 66 (1970), 16–24. He reproduces Leverton's elevation (Leeds City Library Archives Dept.). In the same collection there is a drawing for an arch, also based on the Arch of Constantine, whose frieze is inscribed 'SIR THOMAS GASCOIGNE, EQUES, MDCCLXXX'. Friedman attributes it to Gascoigne himself.
70 John Cornforth, *Country Life*, 14 Sept. 1967, 597.
71 T.F. Hunt, *Architettura Campestre* (London, 1827), 10, 16.
72 James Howley, *The Follies and Garden Buildings of Ireland* (New Haven/London, 1993), 77.
73 ibid.
74 Edward McParland, *James Gandon* (London, 1985), 131; Christine Casey and Alistair Rowan, *The Buildings of Ireland: North Leinster* (London, 1993), 180.
75 W. St J. Joyce, *The Neighbourhood of Dublin* (Dublin, 1939), 109; Maurice Craig, *The Architecture of Ireland* (London, 1982), 319; Mark Bence-Jones, *Burke's Guide to Country Houses*, I, *Ireland* (London, 1978), 239; Howley (cit. at n. 72), 87–8. The Revd C. Scantlebury, S.J. (*Dublin Historical Record*, 12 (1951), 27) claims that the arch was built by Henry Loftus, Earl of Ely, who died in 1783, 'to signify … the triumphal return, in his person, of the Loftuses to their hereditary establishment'.
76 J.A.K. Dean, *The Gate Lodges of Ulster* (Belfast, 1994), 138.
77 ibid., 105; Alistair Rowan, *North West Ulster* (Harmondsworth, 1979), 201.
78 Irish Architectural Archive, *The Architecture of Richard and William Vitruvius Morrison* (Dublin, 1989), 139.
79 ibid., 58; Dean (cit. at n. 76), 103.
80 *Morrison* (cit. at n. 78), 28; Dean (cit. at n. 76), 136–7.
81 Bence-Jones (cit. at n. 75), 31; Howley (cit. at n. 72), 88.
82 Dean (cit. at n. 76), 83–4.
83 Jeanne Sheehy, *The Rediscovery of Ireland's Past: The Celtic Revival 1830–1930* (London, 1980), 134–8; Jeremy Williams, *A Companion Guide to Architecture in Ireland* (Dublin, 1994), 215–16.
84 Maria Grazia Ciardi Dupré, 'La prima attività dell'Ammannati scultore', *Paragone*, 135 (1961), 20–22; L. Puppi, 'Il "Colosso" del Mantova', *Essays Presented to Myron P. Gilmore* (Florence, 1978), 311–29; C. Lattanzi, 'L'attivitá giovanile di Bartolommeo Ammannati in Veneto', in N. Rosselli del Turco and F. Salvi, eds, *Bartolommeo Ammannati, scultore e architetto* (Florence, 1995), 86–9; L. Beschi, 'L'impegno antiquario di Bartolommeo Ammannati', in ibid., 41–2; G. Morolli, 'Palazzo Uguccini e il Foro Mediceo', ibid., 123, 134; L. Attardi, 'Bartolommeo Ammannati', in A. Bacchi et al., '*La Bellissima Maniera' – Alessandro Vittoria e la Scultura Veneta del Cinquecento* (Trento, 1999), 221–3; T. Martin, 'Vittoria e la committenza', in ibid., 60. See also *Padova: Guida ai monumenti e alle opere d'arte* (Venice, 1961), 45–7; and (for the tomb) 38–40.
85 Pliny, *Natural History*, 34.18.
86 The erection of the north wing of the palazzo has unfortunately reduced the cortile from a square to a rectangle, and cramped the arch on its left. Both statue and arch have suffered greatly from deterioration of the stone. The latter was partially restored in 1920.
87 In a letter to Archbishop Altoviti of 4 Feb. 1549.
88 *Octavia*, 454.
89 The description is from L. Beschi (cit. at n. 84), 41.
90 K.T. Parker, *The Drawings of Antonio Canaletto in the Collection of H.M. The King at Windsor Castle* (Oxford, 1948), 58, with fig. 89.
91 Michelangelo Muraro, *Die villen des Veneto* (Munich, 1986), 158–9.

92 *Livre d'architecture contenant plusieurs portiques de differentes inventions, sur les cinq ordres de colonnes, par Alexandre Francini, Florentin, Ingenieur ordinaire du Roy* (Paris, 1631). Only three of the 39 designs are identified as triumphal arches, but several of the others have the same basic scheme as one or other of these. See also Kenneth Woodbridge, *Princely Gardens* (London, 1986), 124–7, 136–7.

93 Woodbridge (cit. in the preceding note), 127.

94 ibid., 148–58.

95 *The Diary of John Evelyn*, ed. E.S. de Beer, II (Oxford, 1955), 108. The story about the birds is also told in an anonymous diary of 1647 (*Francis Mortoft: his book*, ed. M. Letts, Hakluyt Society, 2nd ser., no. 57 (1925), 6, n. 2) and in the *Journals of Sir John Lauder, Lord Fountainhall*, ed. D. Crawford, Scottish History Society, 36 (Edinburgh, 1900), 6–7. A set of sixteen views of the château and gardens was published by Israel Silvestre, whose drawings were engraved by Perelle: they include two of the orangery garden and arch. See also Henri L. Brugmans, 'Châteaux et jardins de l'Ile de France d'après un journal de voyage de 1655', *Gazette des Beaux Arts*, 18 (1937), 111–12. Lemaire was the friend and collaborator of Poussin (M. Mosser and G. Teyssot, eds, *The History of Garden Design* (London/Cambridge, Mass., 1991), 169–71.

96 There is a similar trellis arch at Corbeil-Cerf in France, where the garden was laid out by Achille Duchêne at the end of the nineteenth century.

97 Reinier Baarsen et al., *Rococo in Nederland* (Amsterdam, 2001), 56–8. The urns are now in the Rijksmuseum, Amsterdam.

98 A.N. Petrov et al., *Architectural Monuments of Leningrad Suburbs* (Leningrad, 1983), 92–3; Dimitri Shvidkovsky, *The Empress and the Architect* (New Haven/London, 1996), 103–4. Isobel Rae (*Charles Cameron* (London, 1971), 63) claims that Cameron worked in the Crimea in the late 1780s, including the building of a triumphal arch, but Shvidkovsky states that Cameron never went there, and this shows a confusion with his assistant William Hastie. Rinaldi was a pupil of Vanvitelli. For Quarenghi's role in designing iron structures for the park, see John James, 'Russian Iron Bridges to 1850', *Transactions of the Newcomen Society*, 54 (1982), 82; for the situation of the arch, 83. A drawing of the Ruined Tower and Gatchina Gate by Quarenghi is reproduced in Sandro Angelini, ed., *Giacomo Quarenghi* (Bergamo, 1984), 55 (cat. no. 712). The Gatchina Gate was badly damaged in 1941–4. Peter Hayden (*Garden History*, 19 (1991), 21–7) points out that Stanislaus Augustus Poniatowski, who had visited Stowe in 1754, advised Catherine on the layout of the park at Tsarskoe Selo, and argues that the similarity of the Gatchina Gate to the Corinthian Arch at Stowe might indicate that the latter was model for the former. However, the similarity is not that close, and the Corinthian Arch was not yet built in 1754.

99 Shvidkovsky (cit. in the preceding note), 102–5. Cameron's design is ill. as fig. 114.

100 Monique Mosser and Daniel Rabreau, *Charles de Wailly: peintre architecte dans l'Europe des lumières* (Paris, 1979), 87, fig. X; Mosser and Teyssot (cit. at n. 95), 273.

101 Gerald Ciolek, *Ogrody Polskie* (Warsaw, 1954), 184; Z. Dmochowski, *The Architecture of Poland* (London, 1956), 375, 386–7, 390; Andrea Busiri-Vici, *I Poniatowski a Roma* (Florence, 1971), 80–82, 90–91. Anna Potocka also ordered statues of Jozef Poniatowski from Canova and Thorvaldsen.

102 Marek Kwiatkowski, *Palace i Wille Warszawy* (Warsaw, 2014), reproduces a watercolour of 1785 by Zygmunt Vogel.

103 Ciolek (cit. at n. 101), 174; Dmochowski (cit. at n. 101), 390.

104 Ciolek (cit. at n. 101), 50.

105 Gustav Wilhelm, *Josef Hardtmuth* (Vienna, 1990), 70–72.

106 ibid., 72–5. The colonnade recalls the Gloriette in the park of Schönbrunn, Vienna, erected in 1775 to the design of Ferdinand von Hohenberg.

107 Domaine de l'État, *Les Arconati-Visconti* (Brussels, 1967), 4–7; Herman Vandormael, *Château de Gaasbeek* (Brussels, 1988), 7, 41.

108 Laurin Luchner, *Schlösser in Österreich*, I (Munich, 1978), 144–5; Gunther Martin, *Der Heldenberg* (Vienna, n.d.). Pargfrieder's name is sometimes spelt Pargfrider or Parkfrieder (Österreichisches Biographisches Lexikon, VII (Vienna, 1978), 325).

109 The arch bears the mysterious letters VKISIPFVFE.

110 W. Oechslin in *Dizionario biografico degli italiani*, 18 (Rome, 1975), 97; Beata di Gaddo, *L'architettura di Villa Borghese* (Rome, 1997), 161–73. The bridge at the Egyptian Propylaea has completely disappeared. The Villa Borghese was bought and given to the City of Rome in 1902 by King Umberto I.

111 Augusto Sistri, ed., *Luigi Canina* (Milan, 1995), 19, 46, 88, fig. 83.

112 Augusto Merati, *Monumenti neoclassici a Monza e nella Brianza* (Monza, 1965), 181.

113 Horace, *Satires* II 6.62; Merati (cit. in the preceding note), 231–48; A.M. Matteucci in *Pelagio Palagi, artista e collezionista*, ed. R. Grandi and C. Morigi Govi (Bologna, 1976), 135–7; Roberta J.M. Olson in *Dictionary of Art*, 23, 828–30. It is not certain that Palagi designed the arch. Matteucci refers to a series of drawings which show a sort of triumphal arch, set in a wall of *opus reticulatum*, and flanked by a tower-mausoleum, but it is uncertain whether this represents a preliminary idea for the Gothic building or something different.

114 *Le Ville di Genova*, *Guide di Genova* (Genoa, 1993), 5–10.

115 Fabio Calvi and Silvana Ghigino, *Villa Pallavicini* (Genoa, 1997); *Le Ville di Genova* (cit. in the preceding note), 13–20. The inscription on the arch reads: *Valete, urbani labores; valete procul, animi impedimenta. Me supera convexa et sylvae et fonteis* [sic] *et quid quid est altiora loquentis naturae evehat ad Deum* ('Farewell, urban labours; farewell far away, impediments of the mind. May the vaulted skies and woods and fountains and whatever belongs to nature, which speaks of higher things, carry me up to God').

17

ENGLAND, SCOTLAND AND IRELAND IN THE EIGHTEENTH CENTURY

It is perhaps not surprising that no permanent arch was erected in honour of a monarch, although one was proposed in 1719 by Earl Stanhope, the Secretary of State, 'to the Honour and Immortal memory of George I', Stanhope having been a leading promoter of the Hanoverian succession [17.1]. The architect was Giacomo Leoni, who published his design in the appendix to his translation of Alberti (London, 1726). The proposed site was the centre of the Ring in Hyde Park. Its most remarkable feature was the plan: it would have been square, but enclosing a circular space, with eight attached columns. In the centre was an equestrian statue of the King, on a Baroque pedestal with reliefs of weapons and chained captives at its base. (In fact, George's military achievements were not particularly distinguished, but no doubt such a tribute was thought to be the right of a king.) At the corners were spiral staircases leading to the roof, from which the views could be enjoyed. The elevations were identical. Above the central opening the entablature broke forward, and supported a pediment with the royal arms, on top of which was a statue, and statues stood above each of the four attached Corinthian columns. The side openings were rectangular, with Ionic half-columns supporting a segmental pediment with naval trophies. Above each was a rectangular relief of a battle scene. The Corinthian columns were to be 13 m high. The arch was very broad in proportion to its height. It was to stand on a circular stylobate. Richard Hewlings rightly describes it as fairly conventional, and sees the circular interior as 'one of innumerable variants of an idea first stated in Bramante's and Sangallo's proposals for St Peter's'.[1]

17.1 Design for an arch to George I in Hyde Park, proposed 1719. Giacomo Leoni.

With his translation of Alberti's Book VIII, Chapter VI, Leoni included a design for another arch, 15 m wide. This time the plan was conventional, as demanded by the text, and clearly based on the Arch of Constantine. In the spandrels of the central opening are chained captives, and reliefs on the attic show a battle and a triumph. Four statues of deities stand on each side, over the freestanding columns,

17.2 Arch to George II, in a painting by Antonio Visentini and Francesco Zuccarelli.

and four more on top of the attic. The inscription reads *MAGNAE BRITANNIAE EUROPAE FATA IN AEQUA LANCE PONENTI* ('To Great Britain, which places the fate of Europe in an equal balance').

An imaginary arch in honour of George II appears in a painting in the Royal Collection [17.2]. This is one of a series of eleven which Joseph Smith, English Consul in Venice, commissioned in 1745–6 from Antonio Visentini and Francesco Zuccarelli. The idea was to include examples of Neo-Palladian architecture in England, based mainly on Colen Campbell's *Vitruvius Britannicus*, though here the arch is taken from William Kent's *Designs of Inigo Jones*, and reproduces Jones's design for Temple Bar (see p. 213), including the bas-reliefs. The lengthy Latin inscription purports to dedicate the arch to George, with the universal agreement of his grateful people, because of his achievements in the War of the Austrian Succession and at the Battle of Dettingen (the last at which an English king led his army). On top of the arch is his equestrian statue, between statues of Hercules and Neptune. A city in the background may be intended to represent London.[2]

An album of drawings by Visentini of buildings in the Veneto, Florence and Rome was bought from Smith by George III. In it are also some drawings by Roger Morris for Eastbury Park, Dorset, the seat of George Bubb Dodington (on whom see p. 269): the index says that they were sent to Smith by Morris. One is for a triumphal arch, and is based on the same Inigo Jones design. It has attached columns only at the front, and walls go off at angles from near each corner. The pedestal on top of the attic is also similar to Jones's. The elevation of Eastbury House is dated 1733. It is not known whether the arch was erected: Eastbury was demolished in 1775.[3]

It is not surprising that the triumphal arch so often appears as a motif in British architecture of this period. Hawksmoor's Triumphal Gate to Blenheim Palace (1722–3) has already been mentioned (pp. 263–4). He plays with the motif in unexecuted designs for two Oxford colleges. A drawing identified as 'Front for All Souls to High

Street', datable to *c.* 1708–9, shows a three-storey elevation with a Doric centrepiece of triumphal arch form, the pairs of pilasters framing round-headed windows on the ground floor, square windows above, and garlanded oculi just below the frieze. Above the tall attic are four statues, and at their level rises a large, circular Corinthian tempietto. This design is so similar to one at Queen's College, which also has Doric pilasters, that Roger White wonders if it may really have been for that college.[4] Another design for the front of All Souls, not in Hawksmoor's hand, and attributed by White to Dr George Clarke, Fellow of All Souls and amateur architect, is a bizarre variation on a design by Hawksmoor in which the medieval front is remodelled and matched by a similar front to the east, with a huge and extraordinary gatehouse between them: here this is replaced by a vast freestanding triumphal arch, based on the Arch of Constantine. The result is incongruous in both scale and style.[5] A later design by Hawksmoor (dated 1720) for the 'cloister' between his new north quadrangle and Radcliffe Square shows a screen of Corinthian columns with a centrepiece resembling a triumphal arch. The bays on either side of the central one contain open arches below round-headed niches containing statues. These bays are repeated at the ends.[6]

A most unusual use of the triumphal arch for a piece of furniture is the pedestal at Stourhead, commissioned by Henry Hoare in 1743 for his magnificent *pietra dura* cabinet, which had been made for Pope Sixtus V [17.3]. It takes the form of a *quadrifrons*, and is made of oak, veneered in mahogany. It is decorated with gilded reliefs of Roman buildings and statues, and over the opening hangs a medallion of the Pope, held by flying angels. The carver was John Boson, but the designer is unknown. The form was probably suggested by Hoare himself, who owned Filippo Rossi's *Descrizione di Roma Antica* (1739), in which the arch of Janus is illustrated, but either Henry Flitcroft or Michael Rysbrack may have been involved.[7]

Although Sir Robert Taylor never built an arch, the elevation of his Rotunda at the Bank of England, based on the Pantheon, shows the triumphal arch motif repeated and interlocking, as at Sanmicheli's Cappella Pellegrini in Verona (see p. 145), with attached Corinthian columns. In the 'centre' of the arches large niches alternate with blank spaces containing the doors.[8] The library at Harleyford (1755) is subtly articulated with recessed arches, round-headed bookcases representing niches, rectangular paintings above, and busts recessed in round openings – motifs often used by Taylor.[9] The grand façade of Heveningham (1778–80), with ten freestanding columns set on a rusticated podium pierced with arches, has a vestigial reminiscence of the triumphal arch in the larger and smaller niches set one above the other at the ends of the podium, and in the centrepiece of the attic, in three sections with four freestanding statues, described by Binney as 'on the scale of the attic of a Roman triumphal arch'.[10]

17.3 Pedestal for a pietra dura cabinet at Stourhead, Wiltshire, 1743, carved by John Boson.

Robert Adam's obsession with triumphal arches is discussed in connection with his entrance and garden arches (p. 265). He was not the first member of his family to show an interest in arches. His father William had used the motif to articulate the principal front of the House of Dun in Angus, built *c.* 1730–40 [17.4]. The central three bays are framed by four giant Ionic pilasters. The central arch rises up to the entablature, and contains a recess, while the side arches, almost equally tall, have round-headed windows above square ones. Above is a balustrade.[11] In 1753 William's eldest son John produced a design for a new Exchange for Edinburgh. His drawing also shows 'The Triumphal Arch erected on occasion of Laying the First Stone': this temporary structure is a triple arch with attached Corinthian columns, and statues in niches at the sides. The attic has relief ornament, with a coat of arms above.[12]

In 1755 Robert Adam went to Rome, and in September he went for a month's tour with his 'instructor' Charles Clérisseau, writing to his family 'we have brought home with us a portfolio loaded with Triumphal Arches, Ancient Bridges and other views'.[13] An album at Penicuik House containing some of these drawings includes arches in Rome, Ancona, Rimini and Fano.[14] An album in the Soane Museum has drawings of arch-like structures near Naples, and one or two imaginary examples.[15] Another, labelled 'Sketches done abroad', contains several designs, one with detached columns supporting entablatures on the sides of the piers, one for a Constantinian (but Doric) arch as part of a big façade, one for a plain rusticated arch with a frieze in relief, and one for a similar but extended arch, this time using columns, and so on.[16]

The entrance screen at Syon is considered in the context of gardens (pp. 263–4). Adam often used this arrangement, with the central arch flanked by colonnades. A celebrated example is the screen across the façade of the Admiralty courtyard in Whitehall,

17.4 House of Dun, Angus, *c.* 1730–40. William Adam.

dating from 1760 (his earliest public building). The order is Tuscan, and the opening is narrow, with on each side a plain pier containing a niche intended to contain a statue. Above each is a sculpture of a sea-horse. Pevsner describes the screen as having 'a gravity and simplicity which [Adam] was to lose later (cf. e.g. the Syon House screen)'.[17]

For the gateway to Portland House, the residence in Mansfield Street of the Duke of Portland, Adam designed an elegantly simple arch, using the Tower of the Winds order. In the piers are doors, and on either side of the arch curved walls contain niches with urns.[18] Blank arches appear as the pavilions at either end of the river front in a design for the Adelphi. The central opening frames an exedra with coffered ceiling, and a doorway between niches leads to a platform with an iron balcony. Delicate reliefs are set over the side niches and on the attic.[19] For Carlton House in Pall Mall Adam designed in 1767 a much more elaborate screen than the one for Portland House. It too was not executed. A Constantinian arch is flanked by walls with five bays containing niches for statues, separated by pilasters. At each end is an arched gateway with a pediment on columns.[20] A rather similar design was made for the 'illumination and transparency' put on for the King's birthday at Buckingham House in 1762. This had an arch in the centre, whose tall opening framed the transparency; paired Ionic columns on either side had urns between them, and a large coat of arms stood on top. Statues of boys and girls holding garlands linked the arch to the pedimented end pavilions.[21]

The Soane Museum sketchbooks contain numerous other designs using the triumphal arch motif, sometimes in ingenious ways – for example, a pair of arches linked by an exedra with columns, niches and sculpture relating to those on the arches; an arch surmounted by a double attic, with a circular tempietto above and sculpture on top; and a bizarre broad triple arch, articulated by four pairs of coupled columns, above which rise fat piers like altars with flaming urns on top.[22]

The elegant little mausoleum which Adam built in 1789 at Templepatrick, Co. Antrim, for the Rt Hon. Arthur Upton is another example. The rusticated centre with its large opening projects; on each side is a low niche with an urn, and a circular relief above. Over the centre is a rectangular projection, supporting an urn.[23]

Adam produced a grandiose scheme for arches and screens at Hyde Park Corner [17.5]. He was not the first to propose an impressive 'western entrance' to London. The various schemes have been described by Steven Brindle.[24] They all involved arches of some kind. The earliest dates from 1761, and its author was Thomas Robinson (later 2nd Lord Grantham). His design shows a triple arch, of the Corinthian order, with statues in pedimented niches over the side openings, winged Victories in the spandrels, and statues of captives at attic level. A Doric colonnade is linked to the arch by its triglyph frieze, which runs across the side openings. It is not a very sophisticated design. An arch was also suggested by John Gwynn in his *London and Westminster Improved* (1766). In addition to a vast new palace to go in the centre of Hyde Park, he proposed that 'it would be proper to erect a grand triumphal arch between the two Parks [Hyde and Green Parks] … Indeed, something of this kind should be erected at every principal entrance to London.' His plan shows a freestanding structure in the centre of a 'roundabout'.[25]

Adam's scheme dates from 1778: it is not known who commissioned it. The layout consisted of a grand gateway facing east and west, with attached screens running

17.5 Drawing for a proposed entrance screen at Hyde Park Corner as part of the drive to Buckingham Palace, 1778. Robert Adam.

eastwards, of which the northern one (on the site of the existing Decimus Burton screen) formed an entrance to Hyde Park, and the southern one an entrance to Green Park framing a new road to Buckingham Palace. The numerous drawings show five versions of the gateway, and five of the arches in the screens.[26] Four of the designs for the main gateway are variations on the theme of a pair of triple arches, interlocking with a taller central arch. It is not clear in what order the five designs were made. What Brindle calls the fourth may have been the first: he describes it as 'two versions of the Arch of Constantine forming the abutments of a giant central arch, its delicate ornament making a strong contrast with the boldness of its massing'. It is a remarkably lavish design with an equestrian statue, presumably of George III, on a podium over the attic.[27] Brindle's 'first version' looks like a simplification of this – ' a powerful astylar design with a pedimented centre, figures of the lion and unicorn over the wings, and aedicules low down framing the pedestrian gates and niches with statues of a king and queen'. Another drawing, which clearly refers to this last one as 'the fair Copy', is entirely rusticated. Brindle's 'third version' is like his 'first version', with the addition of freestanding Corinthian columns to support the pediment. The fifth design is rather a puzzle, as it shows a freestanding arch, with much delicate relief ornament, and statues at attic level.[28] It is not clear whether this proposal included the parks screens.

Each of the designs for the latter comprises a large central archway, with a single or double colonnade on each side. Two are comparatively plain, but with rich sculpture on top, while two are more elaborate: one has Doric columns on either side of the arch and pilasters at the outer sides, with rectangular niches between, and a figure of Britannia over the attic; the other has pairs of Ionic columns set close together, and an equestrian statue over the attic. Brindle points out the similarity to Adam's gateway at Croome Court, based on the Roman arch at Pula (p. 24). The fifth design, which goes with Brindle's 'third version', shows rather clumsy triple arches, whose side openings are large rectangles flanked by columns. Above the sides are a lion and unicorn.

Estimates for the project survive in the British Library, and indicate that the main gateway was to be built in brick, covered in Liardet's patent cement, on a stone plinth. The Green Park gateway would have the central columns and architraves in stone. The sculptures of Britannia and the rest would be of cement or lead. Nothing came of Adam's schemes: Brindle suggests that this may have been due to the success of the American War of Independence and the financial constraints it produced.

In 1794 the young Jeffry Wyatt (later Wyatville) exhibited a scheme for a gateway, but his sombre Doric design shows only a sketchy relationship to the triumphal arch, in the three large arches, with three smaller ones on each side (in one of his alternative designs), on his screens to the parks, and the large trophies above. Two years later a design was commissioned by the Surveyor General of Woods and Forests from his official architect, John Soane. The basic idea was the same as Adam's. A triple arch would stand on the main axis, with freestanding Ionic columns. The attic rises only over the central opening, and supports an equestrian statue. The side openings frame aedicules containing statues, and further statues stand on the corners. Railings flank the arch, and return to form screens to the parks. Each has in the centre another arch, this time of a more 'Soanian' character. Above a plain plinth, the main structure has channelled rustication. On each pier a pair of Corinthian columns stand *in antis*. The attic has altar-like sections over the intercolumniations; its recessed centre supports another equestrian statue. Two of the three statues would have represented the King and the Prince of Wales, but it is not clear who would have been the third. Notes on the drawing in the Soane Museum estimate the cost at £8,650, and state that, as this was too great, small lodges and side railings were put up.[29] Soane's later schemes for the 'western entrance' will be discussed later with the Marble and Wellington Arches.

Another project in which Adam suggested several uses of the triumphal arch was the scheme for the South Bridge in Edinburgh. His first version, of 1785, included the bridge over the Cowgate in the form of a rusticated triple arch, with square relief panels over the side openings. North of it, on the east side, small arched façades have niches on either side, and low attics over the centre. The new building for the College, further east, has a grand triple arch with attached Corinthian columns, and reliefs over the side openings. An attic over the centre has an elaborate coat of arms, flanked by statues, two more of which stand on the corners. The arch is linked to three-storey buildings by arcades.[30] Another design, inscribed 'Design for a Triumphal Arch for Edinburgh', shows a freestanding arch, with attached Ionic columns on each side, and an attic over the whole structure, with the City arms in the centre. The attic is inscribed 'Sacred to Science and Learning', and the circular reliefs over the side openings are inscribed 'Geometry' and 'Architecture'. This design must also have been intended for the College.[31] A drawing inscribed 'Another Design for the new Bridge…' shows the Cowgate bridge in a more elaborate form: a large astylar triple arch, on each side of which steps run up, like segments of a pediment, supports a colonnade between tall buildings at road level. Decoration is concentrated on the huge keystone and relief above.[32]

17.6 Kedleston Hall, Derbyshire, 1765. Robert Adam.

One of Adam's most celebrated uses of the triumphal arch is the south front of Kedleston Hall, Derbyshire, dated 1765 [17.6]. Above a rusticated perron, four Corinthian columns stand free and support projecting entablatures, on which stand statues. The pedimented doorway is set in a blank arch, and at the sides are niches with statues, and circular reliefs above. The attic has an inscription panel flanked by reliefs, with a shallow dome behind it. The result is an extraordinarily original front for a country house. At Luton Hoo (or Luton Park), built in 1767–74, Adam's plain north front has in the centre four freestanding Ionic columns with projecting entablatures, with statues above.[33] For the London home of the Earl of Derby, in Grosvenor Square, Adam designed an elegant screen to hide the offices at the back, in the form of a triple arch, the central opening sheltering a statue of a lion on a plinth, with a fanciful lantern above, while the side openings housed statues. Relief decoration included circular panels above these, and rectangular panels in the attic.[34] Another grandiose but abortive scheme was Adam's response to a request to submit plans for Lincoln's Inn in 1771. The main block, facing west, was linked to flanking blocks by screens which incorporated astylar arches. At a right angle, this front was linked to the north block by a full-scale arch with freestanding Ionic columns. Above the tall attic an equestrian statue is shown.[35]

Striking use of the triumphal arch was made by several eighteenth-century architects as the entrance to a stable courtyard – telling evidence of the importance attached to these apparently utilitarian structures.[36] The earliest example is William Kent's Royal Mews, of 1731–3 (demolished in 1830 to make way for the National Gallery). The centre of the composition was a rusticated triumphal arch, of the Doric order. Above the attic rose a pediment with the royal arms.[37] Colvin sees the influence of Roman and Mantuan Mannerism in the rusticated columns and the keystone breaking up into the entablature.[38] Similar influence can be seen in James Paine's entrance to the stables at Chatsworth – described by Giles Worsley as 'probably the grandest private stables ever built in Britain' [17.7].[39] Here again we have heavy rustication, also of the columns. In the centre of the attic are the ducal arms; the cornice rises up into a pediment to accommodate them. On either side are cornucopiae. The inner side of the gateway is a simplified version of the exterior.

Paine designed a much plainer, but very effective, arch as the gateway in the centre of his screen wall at Worksop Manor (1763–7). This is also Doric, and was built to screen the stable court of *c.* 1702–4. It was intended to put on top of the arch an equestrian statue of the 2nd Duke of Norfolk as victor of Flodden.[40] Another magnificent arch forms the entrance to the stables at Goodwood House. Designed by Sir William Chambers, and built in 1757, it has four Doric columns, the surface between them plain except for the entablature at impost level of the arch. Above the triglyph frieze is the attic, plain except for a wreath at either end.[41]

A very jolly arch was built *c.* 1760 as the entrance to Arno's Castle in Bristol. It is attributed to James Bridges. Moved in 1912, it has triple niches, the side ones originally containing the medieval statues from the City gates (replaced with copies in 1898). There is much fanciful Gothic decoration, including curious battlements.

17.7 Chatsworth, Stables, 1758–63. James Paine.

ENGLAND, SCOTLAND AND IRELAND IN THE EIGHTEENTH CENTURY

Towards the end of the century, architects continued to make use of the triumphal arch motif. For the entrance to his new Canterbury Quadrangle at Christ Church, Oxford, James Wyatt designed a severe gateway, to match the plainness of the rest, with fluted Doric half-columns [17.8]. The gate (1773–8) was said to have been based on 'the Arch of Claudius at Rome'; it is not clear what this refers to (see pp. 32–3 for what is known).

Notably inventive use was made by the London-born architect James Gandon, best known for his later career in Dublin. An unexecuted design for Nottingham County Hall, published in 1771, shows a centrepiece with four attached Ionic columns. Between them are statues. Over the opening stand two female figures. The executed building lacked the statues, and niches appear between the columns. Edward McParland points out the 'eccentricity' of placing a primitive entablature (with mutules) over Ionic capitals. The central section of the interior elevation is also based on the triumphal arch, with a coffered exedra set between piers with paired pilasters.[42]

Gandon's two principal buildings in Dublin are the Custom House and the Four Courts. In the former, McParland sees 'homage to Adam's conjunction of Pantheon dome and triumphal arch at Kedleston' in the early drawings for the north front, of 1780, but the dome was later dropped. Statues again stand above the columns of the portico.[43] At the Four Courts (1776–1802) an elegant triumphal arch stands in the centre of each arcaded screen on either side of the main block [17.9]. The lower part is rusticated, delicate ornament appears in the spandrels, and great coats of arms stand above. McParland points out the resemblance to Gandon's Carrickglass arch (see p. 277), the difference here being that the central opening is framed within a rectangular recession, a motif which he compares to the entrance to Ledoux's Hôtel d'Uzès in Paris (drawn by Chambers).[44] Further allusions to the triumphal arch can be found in the articulation of Gandon's interior of the Court House at Waterford (1784–7), and in the rusticated lower section of the centre of his King's Inns in Dublin (begun 1800).[45] The gateway at the King's Inns, an astylar rusticated triple arch, with the royal arms over it, is by Francis Johnston (1820).[46]

17.8 Oxford, Christ Church, Canterbury Quadrangle gateway, 1773–8. James Wyatt.

300   THE TRIUMPHAL ARCH

17.9 Four Courts, Dublin, 1776–1802. James Gandon.

A curiosity was the design for an arch to stand across Broad Street in Oxford, as a memorial to the Marian martyrs Cranmer and Ridley. This was illustrated in the second edition of *Oxonia explicata & ornata* (London, 1777), published anonymously, but by Edward Tatham (later Rector of Lincoln College). Described as 'so airy as very little to obstruct the view of the buildings', it is rather a spindly affair, with two groups of four Ionic columns, each sheltering a statue of one of the bishops, linked by a slender arch which supports a peculiar statue of Victory. Above the entablature on each side is a large urn. Across the whole runs the inscription *Christus triumphat sanguine suorum* ('Christ triumphs in the blood of his own').

In 1761 Joshua Kirby, 'Designer in Perspective to His Majesty', published *The Perspective of Architecture*. It was based on the principles of the distinguished mathematician Dr Brook Taylor, and contained a design for a Doric triumphal arch, within which was a statue of Taylor. Behind is a curved rusticated wall with medallions of Euclid and Newton. The arch is set in a wooded park. Another design, for a *quadrifrons*, 'would make an excellent piece of scenery for a theatre'.

Mention must be made of a very grand triumphal arch erected in Oxford in 1825–30 as the entrance to the University Press quadrangle. The architect was Daniel Robertson. It has freestanding Corinthian columns, with projecting entablatures which also appear on the attic. No doubt it was intended to emphasise the importance of the building in a working-class neighbourhood.

Ceremonial arches in Westminster Hall

James II did not want the procession through the City to be held at his coronation in 1685, and it never took place again. However, an arch was set up in Westminster Hall for the banquet: it had pairs of Corinthian half-columns, and a plain entablature and cornice. Above was 'a Gallery for the Trumpetts, and Kettle Drums'. The arch was painted in trompe l'œil by Robert Streater.[47] An arch must have been set up for the coronation of William and Mary in 1689, as Robert Streater made more or less the same charge 'for the ornaments about the arch'.

The same was done for the coronation of George II in 1727, which was celebrated with great splendour. The most remarkable element of the decoration supervised by the Office of Works was the arch in Westminster Hall. The design, which the King approved, was by William Kent. As usual, it was of wood and canvas. A drawing of it by Kent was engraved by P. Fourdrinier: its most unusual feature was that instead of columns it had on either side of the opening huge caryatids, supporting the entablature. On the pediment above recline Britannia and Neptune, flanking Fame. The Office of Works stated that its execution was 'in a far superior manner than was ever done on the like occasion'. The coronation of George III in 1760 followed the precedent of 1727. The arch designed for Westminster Hall by William Oram, Master Carpenter to the Office of Works, was rather tame by comparison with Kent's. It had pairs of freestanding columns, between which stood statues of Mars and Neptune. On the attic were four statues of allegorical females.

The last arch erected in Westminster Hall was for George IV, in 1821. The difference this time was that it was Gothic, to a design by William Hiort. A tall ogival arch was flanked by fancy turrets, 30 feet (9 m) high, each with a niche containing a statue of a crowned king. An engraving published in the *Gentleman's Magazine* shows the trumpeters and drummers above crowded galleries on two levels, and the King's Champion framed by the arch.[48]

Notes

1 Richard Hewlings, 'James Leoni', in Roderick Brown, ed., *The Architectural Outsiders* (London, 1985), 41, 44. See also Steven Brindle, 'The Wellington Arch and the western entrance to London', *Georgian Group Journal*, 11 (2001), 48–9.

2 Michael Levey, *The Later Italian Pictures in the Collection of H.M. The Queen* (2nd edn, Cambridge, 1991), no. 672; Jane Martineau and Andrew Robinson, eds, *The Glory of Venice: Art in the 18th Century* (New Haven/London, 1994), 247–51, 511–12.

3 John Harris, 'An English Neo-Palladian episode and Visentini', *Architectural History*, 27 (1984), 231–40.

4 Roger White, *Nicholas Hawksmoor and the Replanning of Oxford* (London, 1997), 30–31. The first drawing is no. 28 in H.M. Colvin, *A Catalogue of Architectural Drawings of the 18th and 19th Centuries in the Library of Worcester College, Oxford* (Oxford, 1964). See also H. Colvin, *Unbuilt Oxford* (New Haven/London, 1983), 38–43; H. Colvin and J.S.G. Simmons, *All Souls: An Oxford College and its Buildings* (Oxford, 1989), 27–9.

5 White (cit. in the preceding note), 33.

6 ibid., 39; Colvin, *Unbuilt Oxford* (cit. at n. 4), 41, 46. Hawksmoor's learning is shown by his annotation on a drawing for the Library at Worcester College identifying the source of the pilasters and arches as 'Arch of Saintes'. (For the arch at Saintes see above, p. 30.)

7 Simon Swynfen Jervis and Dudley Dodd, *Roman Splendour and English Arcadia* (London, 2015), 156–71. Hoare owned a second *pietra dura* cabinet, which was mounted on a pedestal made of various marbles by Benjamin Carter: this also took the form of a *quadrifrons* of 'four Pillars & four arches', as John Parnell wrote in 1769 (S. S. Jervis, *Furniture History*, 43 (2007), 247–9). Its whereabouts are unknown.

8 Marcus Binney, *Sir Robert Taylor* (London, 1984), 72–3, pl. 10. For a similar design by Adam, see Soane Museum, London, LV, 147.

9 ibid., 40–42, pl. 30.
10 ibid., 88, pl. 6.
11 This is shown on the original design, but was only carried out in 1987: David Learmont, 'The Restoration of the House of Dun', in I. Gow and A. Rowan, eds, *Scottish Country Houses 1600–1914* (Edinburgh, 1995), 98–101. See also John Gifford, *William Adam* (Edinburgh, 1989), 127–33; Margaret H.B. Sanderson, *Robert Adam and Scotland* (Edinburgh, 1992), 8.
12 Sanderson (cit. in the preceding note), 29; David King, *The Complete Works of Robert and James Adam* (Oxford, 2001), 34.
13 John Fleming, *Robert Adam and his Circle* (London, 1962), 181.
14 J. Fleming, 'An Italian Sketchbook by Robert Adam, Clérisseau and others', *Connoisseur*, 146 (1960), 186–94. More of Clérisseau's drawings are in the Hermitage in St Petersburg: they are much finer and more detailed than Adam's. Fleming illustrates his drawing of the arch at Rimini: *Robert Adam and his Circle* (cit. in the preceding note), pl. 46.
15 Soane Museum, VII, 29, 73, 144. Fleming (cit. at n. 13) illustrates a sketch of a ruined arch in the manner of Pannini (pl. 69 – Soane Museum, LVI, 30).
16 Soane Museum, LV, 122, 136, 162, 166, 171, 179.
17 *Buildings of England: London 6 – Westminster* (New Haven/London, 2003), 250–51; Soane Museum, XXXV, 1–4; *The Works in Architecture of Robert and James Adam* I (London, 1778), I, IV, I; III; XIV. The niches never received their statues.
18 Soane Museum, XXIX, 6, and LI, 98.
19 ibid., XXXII, 11.
20 *Works* (cit. at n. 17), I. V. I; Soane Museum, XXIX, 1.
21 King (cit. at n. 12), pt 2 ('Unbuilt Adam'), 269–70, pl. XI. The design shown in *Works* (cit. at n. 17), I, V, V, was more elaborate, as was the design for the firework display 'at a General Peace 1759' (Soane Museum, IX, 108).
22 Soane Museum, IX, 22; IX, 204; XXXI, 168.
23 King (cit. at n. 12), 359–61.
24 Brindle (cit. at n. 1), 47–92.
25 John Gwynn, *London and Westminster Improved* (London, 1766), p. 87.
26 The drawings are in the Soane Museum, the British Library and the Victoria and Albert Museum: see Brindle (cit. at n. 1), 51–9.
27 Soane Museum, I, 13 is a preliminary sketch for this design, lacking the equestrian statue; I, 15 is a section through the main opening, with a sketch of the vault. Neither is mentioned by Brindle.
28 A sketch for a similar arch, but with paired columns, and statues in niches over them at attic level, is Soane Museum, LIV, 168.
29 Brindle (cit. at n. 1), 61–2. Soane adds to his note a quotation from Sterne's *Tristram Shandy*: 'Now this I like'. Sterne goes on: 'when we cannot get at the very thing we wish – never to take up with the next best in degree to it, – no, that's pitiful beyond description – but instead go for something cheaper, and less good' (9th edn, London, 1773, 92).
30 Andrew G. Fraser, *The Building of Old College: Adam, Playfair and the University of Edinburgh* (Edinburgh, 1989), 67–70, 349–51; Soane Museum, XXXIV, 3 and 5.
31 Fraser (cit. in the preceding note), 71, 356–7; Soane Museum, XXXIV, 32.
32 Fraser (cit. at n. 31), 354; Soane Museum, XXXIV, 7.
33 *Works* (cit. at n. 17), I, III, V. Pevsner attributed this to Sydney Smirke, who worked at the house after a fire in 1843 (*Buildings of England: Bedfordshire, etc.* (New Haven/London, 2014), 241.
34 Soane Museum, I, 79; *Works* (cit. at n. 17), II, I, I; *Survey of London*, XL (London, 1980), 142–4.
35 Soane Museum, XXIX, 13; King (cit. at n. 12), endpapers.
36 See Giles Worsley, *The British Stable* (New Haven/London, 2004).
37 ibid., 140–41.
38 H. Colvin, *Biographical Dictionary of British Architects 1600–1840* (4th edn, New Haven/London, 2008), 613.
39 Worsley (cit. at n. 36), 140–41.
40 Peter Leach, *James Paine* (London, 1988), 78–9, 216–17. A painting of 1777 by William Hodges shows the arch with the statue (John Martin Robinson, *The Dukes of Norfolk* (Oxford, 1982), 162).
41 Worsley (cit. at n. 36), 141–2.
42 E. McParland, *James Gandon: Vitruvius Hibernicus* (London, 1985), 9.14.
43 ibid., 45–8.
44 ibid., 162.
45 ibid., 144–9, 165–70.
46 ibid., 170.
47 Francis Sandford, *The History of the Coronation of James II and Queen Mary* (London, 1687), 108, engraving opp. p. 121; H.M. Colvin, *History of the King's Works*, V (London, 1976), 454.
48 J.M. Crook and M.H. Port, *History of the King's Works*, VI (London, 1973), 647.

18

ARCHES IN BRITAIN AND IRELAND FOR ROYAL OCCASIONS

Triumphal arches might not seem to be characteristic of the period we call 'Victorian', and even less so of later times, but the tradition did not by any means die out. In fact, it might appear that the erection of arches was a way of demonstrating loyalty to the royal families of Europe, after the Napoleonic disruptions, and in defiance of the republican movements which provoked the revolutions of 1848.

In 1821 George IV visited Ireland. On his way he visited North Wales, coming ashore at Holyhead on the pier recently constructed by John Rennie. This was commemorated by a monumental gateway to the pier, of Mona marble, opened in 1824 [18.1]. It was designed by Thomas Harrison. He told C.R. Cockerell that he had thought of using the Egyptian style, but instead produced a kind of Grecianised triumphal arch. Pairs of Doric columns stand between end walls with pilasters, and support a flat entablature. Above are three stepped courses. On one side the inscription is in Latin, and on the other in Welsh.[1]

18.1 Holyhead, Anglesey, 1824. Thomas Harrison.

18.2 Dublin, arch in Sackville Street for George IV, 1821. Richard Morrison. Painting by William Turner de Lond.

18.3 Brighton, arch for William IV, *c.* 1833.

On his entry to Dublin, the King was greeted by an arch at the north end of Sackville (now O'Connell) Street [18.2]. It was built in only thirty hours, and described as 'rather the work of magic than of art'. Designed by Richard Morrison, it was said to be 'constructed in imitation of the celebrated architecture one [*sic*] of Theseus and Adrian at Athens', but it bore little resemblance to that. A painting by William Turner de Lond shows it articulated by four Ionic half-columns, the piers decorated with reliefs. Over the single opening is a semicircular pediment, with a harp inside it and a crown on top; on either side are statues of Hibernia and Britannia. However, an engraving by John Lushington Reilly published in 1823 shows a much simpler structure, covered in greenery. Over it is the inscription *CEAD MILLE FEALTACH* (for *céad míle faílte*, 'a hundred thousand welcomes'), and above that the arms of Ireland with a crown on top, beside which a uniformed figure (presumably live) played a trumpet.[2]

A few years after succeeding George IV to the throne in 1830, William IV visited Brighton. The town had suffered as a result of losing favour with George, and greeted the new King with enthusiasm. A splendid great arch was simple in form, but decorated lavishly with foliage, flags, and (appropriately for 'Sailor Bill') seventy sailors standing in rows [18.3].[3] Arches were erected at Ramsgate in 1835 for the arrival of the Duchess of Kent and her daughter

ARCHES IN BRITAIN AND IRELAND FOR ROYAL OCCASIONS   305

Princess Victoria, and for a 'grand fête' at Herne Bay in 1836. Arches may have been put up in Hyde Park for the accession of Victoria: in his novel *Henrietta Temple*, published in 1837, Disraeli refers to the pleasure of riding in Hyde Park, with 'the groves, the gleaming waters, and the triumphal arches'. Others were erected in August 1837 for her progress to Windsor at Kensington, Hammersmith, and Windsor itself, at the entrance to the Long Walk. The two last were of flowers and evergreens, but the two in Kensington were fancier, one being a triple arch surmounted by a 'magnificent imperial crown' made of variegated dahlias. A dispute between the Protestant schoolboys and the Catholic ones, thought by the Protestants to be placed too near the arch, led to an attack by thirty or forty Catholic boys, who ended up in court.[4] Victoria also made a prompt visit to Brighton, in October 1837. On the journey down from Windsor she was welcomed at Hampton Court by a floral arch, at Kingston-on-Thames by an arch with 'two bands of music', at Reigate by an arch bearing a 'floral crown', at both Crawley and Peaseporridge Gate with arches of dahlias, 'china-asters', etc., and at Albourne by a 'rustic arch with crown and stars'. At the approach to Brighton, on London Road, stood a really grand Rustic Arch, designed by George Cheesman Jun. It was 9 m high, formed mainly of evergreens, decorated with apples (on their boughs) and lemons, crowns, inscriptions, and other emblems composed of dahlias (Mr Mitchell of Piltdown, 'the most successful grower of dahlias, perhaps, in England', having presented the town with 7,000 blooms); there were also a painting of the royal arms and several flags. On one side of the road stood the bathing-women, and singers were arranged on galleries; accompanied by a concealed band, they sang the National Anthem on the Queen's approach. In front of the North Gate of the Pavilion an Amphitheatre had been erected, designed by John Fabian. It was about 90 m in circumference, and decorated with evergreens, yet more dahlias, '&c., &c.' It was entered by an arch which stood opposite the North Gate.[5] In the same month she visited the City of London; she was served with a memorial asking her to return down Piccadilly, the memorialists saying that if she did so they would erect an arch between the Green Park Hotel and Lord Ashburton's mansion.[6]

For her marriage in 1840, an arch was put up for Victoria at 'Kensington Gate' (presumably Palace Gate). It was a simple tripartite structure, decorated with garlands of evergreens.[7] While Albert was alive, the royal pair made many progresses through England and Scotland, and were frequently welcomed with arches. On their first visit to Scotland, in 1842, an arch at Perth was made of wood painted to imitate stone.[8] The year 1843 was the *annus mirabilis* for royal visits. In July Albert went to Bristol for the launch of the *Great Britain*: several arches were built, one with a musicians' gallery. The next month the royal couple, arriving in Southampton to board the new royal yacht, were greeted by an arch on the quay. When they went to Bruges, the same arch was erected as had been put up for Napoleon and Marie-Louise in 1810, but 'never used since': it was 'covered with foliage'. When they were *en route* to Cambridge in October, Royston managed to steal the show over the other arches with one 'composed of white and pink fluted columns'. In November and December Victoria visited the Midlands. Tamworth erected a big triple arch imitating stone. Lichfield – despite having only twenty-four hours' notice – put up four, two of which had illuminated transparencies (which became a regular feature of arches in this period). Melton Mowbray put up a simple arrangement of two tree-trunks decorated with foliage and garlands: framed

18.4 Dundee, 1849. John Thomas Rochead. Demolished 1964.

by the cross-pieces were a fox and hounds – appropriately for this town in hunting country. Leicester put up no fewer than seven arches, all adorned with the usual evergreens, flags, crowns and so on. Much the most remarkable was the one in 'the Tudor style': this four-centred arch, flanked by polygonal turrets, with battlements on top and inscriptions in Gothic script, was taken by two London reporters to be the medieval gate of the town.[9]

In 1844 Victoria visited Dundee. A competition for an arch at the harbour was won in 1849 by John Thomas Rochead, a pupil of David Bryce. The structure was 24 m wide, and in the Norman style, vaguely recalling a cathedral façade [18.4]. The central arch was much bigger than the side ones. There were square turrets at the ends, and over the centre an attic with the royal arms, above which rose two very fanciful turrets. The main part of the structure was covered in intersecting arches. Sadly the arch was demolished in 1964.[10]

In September 1848 Victoria and Albert made their first visit to Balmoral. They travelled in the royal yacht, and arrived a day early, taking the citizens of Aberdeen by surprise. The triumphal arch which had been erected at the entrance to the jetty was not quite finished, and the scaffolding not yet taken down. The Queen tactfully announced that she would not land until the next morning. The arch, 'in a plain, massive Roman style', was designed by 'Messrs Smith, the City Architects' (i.e. John Smith). It was 11 m high, with the royal arms and flags on top, and carved wooden festoons. Other arches were erected on the way to Balmoral.[11]

In 1861 Victoria and Albert made a clandestine visit to Fettercairn in Aberdeenshire. To commemorate this the inhabitants commissioned designs for a monument, and Victoria chose that of John Milne, a native of the town, and pupil of David Bryce [18.5]. The broad arch has a crenellated parapet above, and it is flanked by octagonal turrets with fanciful tops. The style is described in the *Buildings of Scotland* as 'triumphal Rhenish Romanesque'.[12]

After Albert's death in 1861 royal visits were mostly made by the Prince of Wales. A more special occasion was his marriage in 1863, when the many arches included a 'Grand Arch' at London Bridge, and one at Windsor. The arch at the north end of London Bridge was huge, and was lavishly decorated with a big painting over the central opening, statues on the attic, and a *quadriga* driven by Britannia in the centre. On the bridge parapets were statues of Danish kings (in honour of Princess Alexandra), and tripods burning incense.[13] In Windsor, where the wedding took place, there were two arches, of which the one 'prepared by the Eton boys' was modelled on the clock-tower in the College quadrangle; as it rained, the congratulatory speeches were not read, but 'handed in'.[14] In 1866 the Prince and Princess visited York. A wooden arch on the Ouse Bridge, 64 feet (almost 20 m) high, had a tall central opening with a dome above, and over the low side doorways were statues. The arch was built by Weatherley and Rymer. On the Prince's recovery from illness in 1872 a service was held at St Paul's Cathedral, and two arches were set up. The one at Oxford Circus was covered in laurels and other greenery.[15]

After so many rather conventional arches, the Queen must have had a great surprise when she made a rare outing to Wolverhampton in 1866. The two arches erected there celebrated local industries. One was entirely made of 'best Staffordshire coal from Lord Dudley's Round Oak Works'. It had a triangular opening, with battlements above, and was decorated with trophies of miners' pick-axes and lit Davy lamps.[16] The other arch was covered with hardware goods (Japanned tea-trays, vases, tinplate items, iron tubes, coal-scuttles and axes). This idea was taken up elsewhere: at Birmingham, to which she paid a Golden Jubilee visit in 1887, an arch was decorated with firearms. There was also a Fire Brigade Arch 'constructed of ancient and modern appliances and manned by firemen clad in costumes of diverse periods'. Withington relates this type of display to the 'trade pageants' which were a common feature of the Lord Mayor's Show in London, and were found in other towns too (e.g. at Sandwich in 1573).[17]

Arches representing local trades were also erected for non-royal visitors. For the opening of a new technical school at Northwich, Cheshire, in 1897 an arch of salt was erected. The lower courses were of dark block salt, and the upper ones of white crystalline blocks. Battlements were the only decoration. Another salt arch welcomed the local MP, Sir John Brunner, after a parliamentary success. The Preston Guild of 1912 was celebrated with an arch made of bales of cotton. The Birmingham Fire Brigade Arch was emulated at Hastings in 1900, when Lord Brassey returned from Australia: four fire escapes were lashed together to support the word 'WELCOME'. Even more striking was the Fishermen's Arch, designed by Councillor Gallop 'after one at Boulogne'. The structure was of fish salesmen's barrels, decorated with nets, lobster pots,

18.5 Fettercairn, Aberdeenshire. John Milne, commemorating royal visit in 1861.

anchors, flags, crossed oars, and ships' coloured lanterns. At the bottom were blocks of ice with frozen ivy, flowers and reeds, on which rested two seals caught off Hastings.[18])

For the visit of the Prince and Princess of Wales to Truro in 1880 to lay the foundation stone of the new Cathedral, five arches were designed by the local architect Silvanus Trevail. They were in the 'Greco-Roman', Gothic, Tudor and Moorish styles. The first stood on Boscawen Bridge. The Moorish arch at the station imitated Siena marble, and had a cusped trefoil-headed opening and female statues on plinths in front of the piers.[19]

At Swansea in 1881 the Prince and Princess encountered an arch representing the medieval Swansea Castle 'as shown on the borough arms', and two arches representing local trades. The Tin Arch was clad in blue enamelled tin, with various devices 'worked out in bright tin', while the Wool Arch was composed entirely of wool and yarn. The piers 'consisted of bales of compressed wool, bound with gilded bands of iron', while the other decorations were of 'coloured yarns and raw wool, interspersed with a few evergreens'. On the cross-gallery sat two women in Welsh costume, knitting. A few days before the royal visit, huge gales damaged the arches, blowing down the Tin Arch, but they were repaired in time.[20]

For a visit to High Wycombe in 1884 an arch made of four hundred chairs was set up, chair-making being the local industry. The first such arch had been erected in 1877 for a visit by the Queen to Hughenden Manor (Disraeli's house). At the bottom in 1884 were Windsor chairs, then came 'drawing room, lounge, library, reading, rocking' and others, with the Mayor's state chair at the top. Another chair arch welcomed the return of Sir Edwin Dashwood in 1889, and yet another the Queen in 1962.

Even more bizarre was the Trades Arch erected in Donegall Square, Belfast, for a visit by the Prince and Princess in 1885. The soffit of the broad arched opening was lined with bales of cloth, its archivolt inscribed 'Man goeth forth unto his work and to his labour until the evening'. Above this were steps providing space for a weird assortment of machinery, bales, etc. The small side arches had pedimented aedicules over them, containing what looked like shop windows full of miscellaneous goods. One was inscribed 'Temperance is a girdle of gold', the other 'Employment is nature's physician'. On top of each was more machinery, including a beam engine.[21] At Leeds in 1894 the Duke and Duchess of York were greeted by an arch of bread. It was intended to give this to the poor afterwards, but rain spoiled it.[22]

The arch at Swansea was blown down in time for re-erection to be possible, and the weather on the day of the visit was 'faultless'. Much more alarming was the fate of one of the arches put up in Liverpool when Queen Victoria came to open the International Exhibition of Navigation, Travelling, Commerce and Manufactures in 1886. The visit was marred by torrential rain (which rendered one arch 'rather the worse for the moisture'), and a few days later a gale caused the arch at the corner of London Road, at a spot so windy that it was known as the 'Bay of Biscay', to collapse [18.6]. It was between 18 and 21m high; the 'embellishments' had been removed, but the timber structure remained. Its fall – dramatically illustrated

18.6 Liverpool, collapse of arch for royal visit, 1886.

in the *Penny Illustrated Paper* – injured four people, including the driver of a parcel-post van.[23]

The Gothic arch at Leicester has already been mentioned. It was an idea repeated on other occasions with the intention of emphasising the antiquity of the location. When the Prince of Wales visited York in 1866, the several arches included one at the Ouse Bridge in a peculiar Classical style, with a dome on top, designed by the City Architect, George Fowler Jones, and another at the Lendal Bridge which had battlements and turrets, and statues of soldiers with halberds.[24] When the Prince went to Chester in 1869, to open the new Town Hall, an elaborately Gothic arch was designed by the local architect John Douglas [18.7]. It stood in City Road, which leads to the railway station, at the approach to the canal bridge. Its half-timbered style (the timbering, of course, merely painted on) echoed the local vernacular, but its steep-pitched roof and fancy tourelles led the Chester press to compare it with a gateway in Prague. The arch was inscribed 'Welcome Earl and Countess of Chester' (the Earldom was one of the Prince's titles), but unfortunately the Princess did not come, and – worse still – the arch was not ready in time.[25]

When the Prince and Princess visited Sheffield in 1875, a number of arches went up. The most remarkable was built at the expense of the Duke of Norfolk on Lady's Bridge, which crosses the river Don just north of the city. Of wood and canvas, it was

18.7 Chester, arch in City Road, 1869. John Douglas.

18.8 Dublin, Leeson Street arch for Queen Victoria, 1900.

25 m high and 15 m wide, and looked like a substantial city gate, with three openings, a pyramidal roof, and tourelles on the corners linked by machicolated parapets. On these stood twelve youths in medieval armour (borrowed from the Opera House). The architects were M.E. Hadfield and Son. To hide the abattoir which stood west of the arch, they provided a battlemented 'town wall' 9 m high and some 107 m long.[26]

There was a particular reason for building the arch which welcomed the Queen to Dublin in 1900 in medieval style, as it was intended to represent Baggotrath Castle, which had stood nearby in the Middle Ages [18.8]. Set on Lower Bridge (over the Grand Canal) in Leeson Street, it had the look of a rugged stone gateway, with only one opening, and was tall in relation to its width. Authentically asymmetrical, it had two square turrets, the left-hand one larger and projecting slightly, arrow-slits, and crow-stepped battlements.[27]

A particularly remarkable series of eleven arches was put up in Leicester when the Prince and Princess of Wales came to open Abbey Park in 1882. Fortunately a detailed description exists, along with engravings and photographs of some of them [18.9].[28]

18.9 Leicester, arches for royal visit, 1882.

The first arch, at the railway station, was conventionally made of evergreens, flags and shields; it was designed by J.R. Sanders, architect to the Midland Railway Company. The next was in Renaissance style, designed by W. Howes. It had a semicircular opening, floral panels, and 'four Grecian statues'. Then, in Granby Street, came the first Gothic arch, designed by the well-known local firm Goddard and Paget. It was covered in scarlet and white awnings, and illuminated at night by 250 'obelisk lamps'. The arch at the entrance to the Market Place was set in a gap in the old town wall, and was designed by Isaac Barradale to represent a fourteenth-century gatehouse. It made no attempt to be 'authentic', but was half-timbered, with a steep tiled roof 'of the Neuremberg [sic] type' – in other words, much like Douglas's arch at Chester. It provided accommodation for spectators. The decoration was the work of 'Mr Frampton, artist at the Opera House'. The fifth arch, designed by Messrs Pigott Brothers of London, was covered in crimson cloth, with festoons of blue drapery, gold cords and tassels, and dark blue curtains. As well as the usual flags and banners, there was a 'large crystal device for illumination'. Then came another Gothic arch, designed by Stockdale Harrison of Leicester [18.10]. This had 'two Campanello

18.10 Leicester, 1882, arch by Stockdale Harrison.

18.11 Alfred Young Nutt (1847–1924), arch at Eton Bridge, from a collection of Christmas cards for his own use and from his own drawings, 1891–1910.

[campanile] castellated towers', nearly 50 feet (over 15 m) high. The turrets were illuminated, and there were crystal stars in the spandrels. The seventh was the most exotic arch of all, the 'Anglo-Japanese arch'. Its designer, H.W. Roberts of Leicester, had after his architectural training articled himself to Christopher Dresser 'to study colour and high-class decorative work'. Of lightly framed timber, and richly coloured, it had over seventy panels painted with Japanese flowers by Roberts and his assistants. At the corners of the central opening four Japanese figures climbed bamboo stems. After this the eighth arch, with its crimson cloth, gold lattice-work, vases of flowers, crystals, and so on, must have seemed tame, but the ninth, near St Mark's Church, was described as 'a strange design', mostly of Virginian cork, set with flowers and plants in bloom. The designers, Messrs Womersley & Co. of Leeds, were one of the firms which specialised in this type of work.[29] It had been intended that the tenth arch should be 'Moorish', to the design of Messrs Shenton and Baker, but because of lack of time a 'Venetian' one was substituted, with a large opening between smaller ones, and wooden pinnacles. The final

312 THE TRIUMPHAL ARCH

18.12 Eastham.

arch, by James Tait of Leicester, was again designed to look like an ancient tower, with battlements, though the light blue satin, trophies, flags and illuminated crystals must have cheered it up.

The royal Golden and Diamond Jubilees were naturally celebrated with many arches. For example, in 1887 Kensington erected one.[30] The royal visit to Birmingham in 1887 has already been mentioned. In 1897 Windsor, ever anxious to display its loyalty to its most famous resident, erected an arch at Eton Bridge, designed by Alfred Young Nutt, who was Office of Works architect at Windsor [18.11].[31] An arch built in Liverpool for the Diamond Jubilee had a curious fate. After the celebrations it was bought by the proprietor of the Ferry Hotel at Eastham, on the Cheshire side of the river Mersey, and re-erected as the entrance to the Ferry Gardens [18.12]. Easily reached by ferry from Liverpool, these were described in 1889 as 'the most popular pleasure resort on the Mersey'.[32] The arch was a large structure, comparatively simple in form, but with unusual decoration. In each pier a lifesize statue of the Queen (different from one another) was supported on a bracket, framed by a round-headed arch. Above these were relief panels showing men engaged in various occupations (one possibly intended to represent the digging of the tunnel for the Mersey Railway, opened in 1886). On the broad frieze winged putti held garlands. The arch was demolished in 1934, on the grounds that it was unsafe, but it turned out to be very difficult to destroy.[33] In 1897 the Queen visited Birmingham, where an arch had been made of twenty tons of brass, copper, and iron tubes, with a portrait of the Queen and the city arms made entirely of steel pens.[34]

Coronations were obvious occasions for arches. For Edward VII in 1902 there was a striking arch in Whitehall [18.13]. Erected by Canada, it was a rather cumbersome structure. The outer sides sloped in, and the upper stages were recessed and crowned with little concave-profiled roofs bearing spikes. In the centre was a tempietto with domed roof. The whole thing was 'covered with plaited straw fixed by red flowers'. Wheat, oat and barley sheaves were looped around the edges of the roofs. The arch itself was decorated with lines of twisted corn, and cherry red cloth. The inscription read 'CANADA BRITAIN'S GRANARY'. According to the *Building News*, the best feature was the 'harmonious colouring', but this cannot be appreciated from monochrome illustrations.[35]

For the royal visit to Leeds in 1908 an arch was erected at Moortown, the decoration based on Jacobean strapwork.

Twentieth-century Britain was not rich in temporary arches. When the Prince of Wales went to Ramsgate in 1926 to open the Promenade he was greeted by a rather squat arch, with square battlemented turrets on either side of a four-centred opening with pierced spandrels, all covered in greenery and bearing the word 'WELCOME'. Its naiveté has some charm.[36] For the coronation of Elizabeth II in 1953 simple metal 'arches' were set up along the Mall. Afterwards they were used for the construction of a factory. English Heritage decided to commemorate the centenary of Queen Victoria's Diamond Jubilee in 1997 by putting up an arch in the grounds of Osborne House in the Isle of Wight. A young sculptor, Stephen Page, was commissioned, and given a very small budget. The result, representing a curtained opening, with urns and a clock-turret above, all in red and yellow, was well-intentioned rather than really successful. One of the ideas for the commemoration of the Millennium put forward by the Millennium Commission was for the erection of arches in villages, but this seems not to have led to anything, and the only British 'Millennium Arch' known to the author is the 'Chair Arch' at High Wycombe (p. 431).

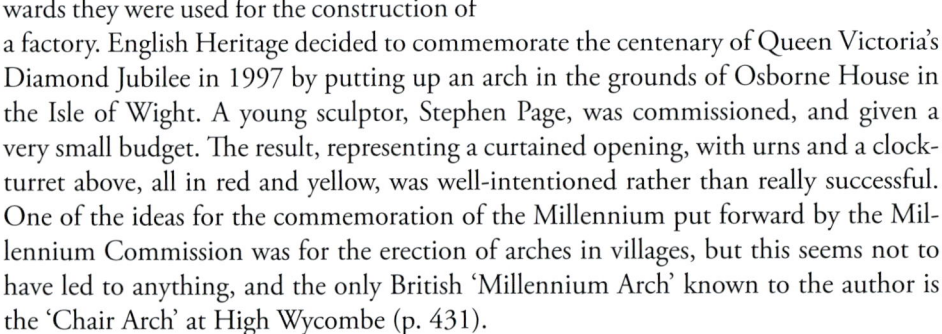

18.13 Whitehall, London, 'Canada Britain's Granary' arch for coronation, 1902.

Notes

1 John Champness, *Thomas Harrison: Georgian Architect of Chester and Lancaster 1744–1829* (Lancaster, 2005), 109–10. Harrison would have become familiar with the arches at Rome during his stay in 1769–76, and designs by him for arches of the Roman type survive.

2 Irish Architectural Archive, *The Architecture of Richard Morrison and William Vitruvius Morrison* (Dublin, 1989), 86–7. The Turner painting and Reilly engraving are in the National Gallery, Dublin. That the second picture is more accurate is suggested by the Countess of Glengall's comment on it as 'only fit for Jack-in-the-Green on a May day' (*The Creevey Papers*, ed. Sir Herbert Maxwell (London, 1904), II, 30).

3 John Dinkel, *The Royal Pavilion, Brighton* (London, 1983), 126–7.

4 *Morning Post*, 17, 22, 23 Aug. 1837; *Standard*, 23 Sept. 1837.

5 *Brighton Patriot*, 12 Sept. 1837; *Morning Post*, 13 Sept. 1837; *Morning Chronicle*, 29 Sept. 1837; *Brighton Patriot*, 3 Oct. 1837; *Morning Post*, 5 and 6 Oct. 1837; *Brighton Patriot*, 10 Oct. 1837; *Brighton Herald*, 17 Oct. 1837; *Brighton Patriot*, 24 Oct. 1837 (with ill.). Amphitheatre and arch had been declared safe by Captain Alderson of the Royal Engineers. Most of these references were supplied by Andrew Saint.

6 *Morning Post*, 23 Oct. 1837.

7 W.J. Loftie, *Kensington: Picturesque and Historical* (London/New York, 1888), 121.

8 *Illustrated London News*, 17 Sept. 1843, 297, 300–301; 24 Sept. 1842, 312–13.

9. Pauline Flick, 'Triumphant for a Day', *Country Life*, 26 Nov. 1987, 78–9; William Kelly, *Royal Progresses and Visits to Leicester* (Leicester, 1884), 589–93.
10. A parody of the arch was erected in 2016 as part of the Dundee Festival of Architecture.
11. *Aberdeen Journal*, 6 Sept. 1848; J.A. Henderson, *Twenty-One Aberdeen Events of the Nineteenth Century* (Aberdeen, 1912), 37–42; engraving in the RIBA.
12. Joseph Sharples et al., *The Buildings of Scotland: Aberdeenshire South* (New Haven/London, 2015), 485. Another arch near Fettercairn has no royal connection, but may be mentioned here. At Edzell, Angus, it was built in 1888 to commemorate the 13th Earl of Dalhousie and his wife. Designed by William Hay and George Henderson, a tall pointed arch with crowstepping stands over the High Street. It rises from rectangular towers with saddleback roofs, which have lower arches under stepped battlements at their sides. (John Gifford, *The Buildings of Scotland: Dundee and Angus* (New Haven/London, 2012), 445.)
13. *Illustrated London News*, 21 March 1863, 300–301, 321.
14. ibid., 312–13, 322.
15. *Illustrated London News,* 9 March 1872; A.J. Lewery, *Popular Art Past and Present* (Newton Abbot, 1991), 139.
16. Photograph in Ann Humphreys, *Royal Visits to Wolverhampton* (Wolverhampton, 1977).
17. R. Withington, *English Pageantry* (Cambridge, Mass./London, 1918), I, 257, n. 4.
18. Lewery (cit at n. 15), 140–41.
19. Ronald Perry and Hazel Harradence, *Silvanus Trevail* (London, 2008), 42–5.
20. *The Graphic*, 29 (1881), 435, 437. For the knitting women, Withington (cit. at n. 17) compares girls who spun and knitted in a Norwich pageant of 1578.
21. Photograph in the Irish Architectural Archive, Dublin.
22. James Lomax, *Victorian Châtelaine* (Leeds, 2016), 121.
23. *Penny Illustrated Paper*, 22 May 1886, 326.
24. *Illustrated London News*, 1 Sept. 1866, 220; 18 Aug. 1866, 165–6.
25. Edward Hubbard, *The Work of John Douglas* (London, 1991), 81–2.
26. H.C. Davidson and Mappin Art Gallery, *One Hundred Fifty Years of Architectural Drawings – Hadfield Cawkwell Davidson, Sheffield, 1834–1984* (Sheffield, 1984), 62; drawing in Sheffield City Record Office, HCD 124/15/1. For other examples of medieval-style arches, compare e.g. those erected at Hastings and Bradford in 1882 (*Illustrated London News* 81 (1 July 1882), 5, 9–10, 14).
27. Photograph in the Irish Architectural Archive, Dublin; watercolour by Percy French in the Royal Collection (Delia Millar, *The Victorian Watercolours and Drawings in the Collection of H.M. The Queen* (London, 1995), no. 2003).
28. Kelly (cit. at n. 9), 618–23; *Illustrated London News* 30 (1882), 541–2 (3 June); 573, 580 (10 June). An engraving showing two of the arches (Barradale's and Harrison's) is reproduced in Malcolm Elliott, *Leicester: A Pictorial History* (Chichester, 1983), pl. 141.
29. For example, they supplied the decorations, which included five arches, for the royal visit to Hastings in 1882 (*Illustrated London News* 81 (1 July 1882), 14. Their 1886 catalogue listed triumphal arches as a speciality.
30. Loftie (cit. at n. 7), 165.
31. Millar (cit. at n. 27), no. 4182.
32. Philip Sulley, *The Hundred of Wirral* (Birkenhead, 1889), 141–2.
33. Information from Mrs David Owen, of Eastham. On the arch, see I. and M. Boumphrey, *Yesterday's Wirral,* no. 9 (1999), 42–3. There is some doubt about the origin of the arch: descriptions of the Jubilee Day celebrations mention a procession, but not an arch. The Boumphreys say that it was erected 'for Queen Victoria's visit … in 1897', but she did not visit Liverpool that year. There may be confusion with the 1886 arch.
34. Lewery (cit. at n. 15). 140.
35. *Building News* 83 (1902), 143; *Illustrated London News* 121 (5 July 1902), 8 and 19. The latter illustration also shows a flimsy Gothic arch in Parliament Street, covered with heraldry.
36. Charles Busson, *The Book of Ramsgate* (Buckingham, 1985), 111, 120.

19
NAPOLEONIC ARCHES

The first great city that Napoleon entered on his Italian campaign was Milan, in 1796, where the Porta Romana was transformed by means of an inscription. In the next year the Porta Orientale was more elaborately decorated to celebrate the defeat of tyranny by France. In 1797 the French drove the papal troops out of Romagna. This was commemorated by the erection of a marble arch outside the Porta Imolese at Faenza, to the design of Giovanni Antolini. Of the Doric order, it had a single opening, with relief carving on the attic. Above this was a figure of the French Republic between genii. It was based on the Temple of Hercules at Cori, and was described by the art historian Gianni Mezzanotte as 'the first sign of an archaeological mentality in the North', though the Neoclassical architect Giuseppe Pistocchi attacked it as 'deforme' and 'pigmeo'. The arch soon showed signs of collapse, and it was demolished by the Austrian and Papal troops on their return in 1799. After the French in turn came back, Antolini was commissioned to build a new arch. His design was stronger than the previous one, but even so was described by Pistocchi as a *gran Credenzione da Sinagoga, abbellito nella sommità di parapeto da Balordo … in ogni parte insulso, ed un abuso lacrimevole di materia, di lavoro e di denaro* ('a great synagogue credence table, beautified at the top of the parapet by Fool … in every part idiotic, and a miserable abuse of material, work and money') It was never completed. Pistocchi himself produced a design which Mezzanotte described as showing *una violenza apparentemente ineducata* ('an obviously uneducated violence'), but in fact literate enough.[1]

In 1801 Paolo Pozzo designed an arch and a column for Mantua, when a festival was instituted by General Miollis.[2] In the same year Antolini produced his proposal for a vast Foro Bonaparte in Milan. It included almost everything except triumphal arches, but a rival project by Pistocchi had one on either side of the piazza in front of the Duomo, modelled on the Arch of Constantine.[3] Numerous projects for Rome included one of 1802 by Giuseppe Camporese, which had an arch linked to a pair of Trajanic columns by colonnades.[4] In 1804 Napoleon was welcomed at Cologne with arches. For his entry into Bologna in 1805 an arch was erected within the Porta Felice. Of the Ionic order, it was designed by Giovan Battista Martinetti, Giuseppe Turbertini and Giovanni Bassani, with paintings and bas-reliefs by Felice Giani.[5] In the same year, for his coronation as King of Italy an arch was erected at Monza, designed by Carlo Amati: Doric, and astylar, it had trophies on the piers and an eagle on top.[6] The first permanent arch erected at Milan by the Repubblica Cisalpina, for the entrance of Napoleon in 1807, was at the Porta Ticinese, designed by Luigi Canonica. Remarkably similar to the Arc de Triomphe de l'Étoile in Paris, but with trophies on the piers and a *sestiga* on top, much of its decoration was merely painted. It was destroyed at the end of the nineteenth century.[7]

In Paris itself, Napoleon at first rejected suggestions for arches from Quatremère de Quincy and others, though artists sometimes showed them in triumphal pictures. However, once he had been declared Emperor in 1804, his fondness for parallels with the ancient world, and especially Rome, together with his wish to remodel his capital in the manner of a great Classical city, caused him to change his mind. On the evening before the battle of Austerlitz, in 1806, he told his men that he wanted to lead them back home under triumphal arches. On his return after his victory, he decreed that a triumphal arch should be set up 'to the Glory of our Armies', between the palaces of the Louvre and the Tuileries. The architect was to be Pierre-François-Léonard Fontaine, and Vivant Denon was to supervise the artistic work.[8] Built in 1806–8, the arch is known as the Arc de Triomphe du Carrousel; the name dates back to the reign of Louis XIV, but the area was part of a new systematisation of the space between the Louvre and the Tuileries, which was cluttered with buildings [19.1]. It was based on the Arch of Septimius Severus in Rome, which Percier and Fontaine had asked permission to study in 1787, and even more closely on the Arch of Constantine, though it differs in having a passageway at right angles to the principal openings.[9] It is one

19.1 Paris, Arc du Carrousel, 1806–8. Pierre-François-Léonard Fontaine.

NAPOLEONIC ARCHES 317

of the richest arches ever erected. It is 15 m high, 20 m wide, and 9 m deep. The eight Corinthian columns of red Languedoc marble came from a seventeenth-century building (Fontaine had specified granite). Their bases and capitals are of bronze, and above stand statues of individualised soldiers. The six bas-reliefs, of Carrara marble, show the battle of Austerlitz and other military successes. The six sculptors included Clodion. The frieze is of reddish-brown Italian marble. On top were the horses of San Marco that Napoleon had taken from Venice in 1797, drawing a chariot in which Victory and Peace guided Napoleon, modelled by François-Frédéric Lemot in gilded lead. Napoleon disapproved of his statue, having expected one of Mars, and had it removed (it is now at Fontainebleau). He claimed to dislike the arch itself, preferring the Porte St-Denis. In fact he argued that triumphal arches were 'un ouvrage plus futile' ('a rather futile type of work'), and that he only had them set up to encourage French sculptors.

After the final defeat of Napoleon in 1815 the horses were returned to Venice, and the other figures and reliefs were removed. In 1827 a bronze group, by François-Joseph Bosio, was set up, representing Restoration leading Peace in a chariot drawn by four horses, based on casts of the San Marco ones.[10] In 1823 it had been decided that four new marble reliefs should be carved for the arch, to commemorate the success of the expedition led by the duc d'Angoulême in that year which put Ferdinand VII back on the throne of Spain. The four sculptors chosen were Louis Petitot, Jean-Baptiste-Louis Roman, Jean-Pierre Cortot and Nicolas-Bernard Raggi, and in 1825 Pierre-Jean David d'Angers and James Pradier were commissioned to do two more. In 1828 their plaster models were placed on the arch.[11] The marble versions were never completed, and in 1831, under Louis-Philippe, the original reliefs were put back.[12] Louis-Philippe also favoured the scheme that Percier and Fontaine had prepared for Napoleon, to add two wings to the Tuileries with a colonnade linking them to the Arc du Carrousel, but it came to nothing.[13]

In 1806 it was decided by the Consiglio Comunale of Milan to erect an arch in honour of Napoleon [19.2]. The architect was the Marchese Luigi Cagnola. It was to be called the Arco del Sempione, and to stand at the end of the Strada del Sempione (Simplon). By 1813 it stood as high as the imposts of the side arches. After Napoleon's fall, the Emperor Franz I of Austria visited the city in 1816, and it was decided to complete the arch in his honour, with the name Arco della Pace. Cagnola died in 1833, and was succeeded by Carlo Londonio. The arch was inaugurated by the Emperor Ferdinand I in September 1838. The structure is 24 m high, and is built of white marble from Lake Como, the carved parts of Carrara. Each side has four freestanding Corinthian columns. There is a great quantity of sculptural decoration, with reliefs representing victories over Napoleon, allegorical figures, and rivers (on the attic), by a variety of sculptors who included Pompeo Marchesi, Gaetano Monti, Camillo Pacetti and Luigi Acquisti. On top was a bronze *sestiga* driven by a figure of Peace, by Abbondio Sangiorgio. It was flanked by four Victories on horseback, by Giovanni Putti. The arch is described by Westfehling as 'the most complete example of North Italian Classicism'.[14]

There were also temporary arches erected in honour of Napoleon. These included one for the troops returning from Austerlitz in 1805 at La Villette on the edge of Paris, its piers decorated with trophies, and with a chariot drawn by six horses in

19.2 Milan, Arco del Sempione or Arco della Pace, 1806–38. Luigi Cagnola.

which Victory stood holding crowns.[15] Another welcomed the troops coming back from Prussia at the Porte de Pantin in Paris, in 1807. Large but fairly plain in structure, and richly decorated with sculpture, including a *quadriga* on top, it was designed by François Chalgrin.[16] Outside Paris, arches greeted Napoleon's entry into Strasbourg and Stuttgart (1806), Dresden, Milan, and Venice (all 1807).[17] The first, designed by P.-V. Boudhors, had pairs of columns set not on the corners but flanking the side openings, and an attic whose centre, supporting an equestrian statue, rose higher than its sides, which bore paintings of battles. The Stuttgart arch, designed by Nicolaus Friedrich Thouret, was very striking. It was a triple arch: over the side arches were rectangular openings in which stood *stelai*. The side arches were flanked by tall bases, supporting columns at the upper level, with pediments above. Over the attic was an immense trophy. The arch with illuminated parts in Dresden was a much more homely affair: on top were eagle, crown and sceptres within a huge halo. In Milan the arch at the Porta Romana was designed by Luigi Canonica: not dissimilar to the Arc de Triomphe de l'Étoile, it had a *sestiga* above the attic.[18] The principal Venice arch, designed by Giannantonio Selva (with the support of Canova), stood in the water at the entrance to the Grand Canal, and was a severe Doric structure, 35 m high, adorned with plentiful sculpture. A second arch was erected over the entrance to the Rio di Ca' Foscari, next to the Palazzo Balbi from which Napoleon presided over the regatta on the Grand Canal. Its rusticated base had a low opening, while the elegantly Neoclassical superstructure had a coffered niche in the centre containing a statue, with further statues in niches on the rusticated piers, while the plain surface above was decorated with flying Victories.[19] Before the Congress of Erfurt in 1808 three arches were erected, but Napoleon disapproved and they were demolished before his arrival.[20] Arches were sometimes set up to welcome rulers established by Napoleon, such as the one at Kassel in 1807 for Jérôme Bonaparte as King of Westphalia.

In 1806 Napoleon decided to build what would, after its lengthy gestation, become the Arc de Triomphe de l'Étoile in Paris [19.3].[21] The intention was to honour his 'Grande Armée'. Various sites were considered, but eventually it was decided to situate it at the 'étoile', the 'star' crossing of roads (now twelve), where there were two customhouses designed by Ledoux (demolished in 1860). It was an obvious site for a monument. In 1758 a proposal for a colossal elephant fountain had been made by

19.3 Paris, Arc de l'Étoile, 1806–37. Jean-François-Thérèse Chalgrin.

Ribart de Chaumont; in 1795 a competition for a triumphal arch to the revolutionary army was held; and in 1802, when a competition was held for an arch to celebrate the Peace of Amiens and the Law on Cults, Charles-Louis Balzac designed a bizarre specimen consisting of a semicircular structure decorated with 56 military standards, a huge keystone with an allegorical figure, and plinths bearing reliefs.[22] The architects appointed for the new arch were Jean-François-Thérèse Chalgrin and Jean-Arnaud Raymond. Each produced a design with columns, but Napoleon decided, after taking advice, that for such a vast structure there should be no columns. Chalgrin and Raymond failed to agree, and the latter resigned. The foundation stone of the arch as built was laid in 1806. In 1809 Chalgrin's project, close to the final one, was accepted. Chalgrin died in 1811, and was succeeded by his pupil L. Goust. By 1814, when work stopped, the building had only reached 20 m. In 1823 Louis XVIII ordered that work should begin again. It was directed by Goust, later associated with Jean-Nicolas Huyot. Each put forward several different proposals, some once again including columns.[23] Wilder schemes came from L. Bruyère (for a 'water-castle') and from the famous cook Marie-Antoine Carême. Naturally the various proposals were influenced by the political changes of these years. In 1825 Charles X ordered that Chalgrin's design should be followed, though in the end the arch was taller than he had intended. Goust carried on the work, but was replaced in 1828 by Huyot. Louis-Philippe, who became King in 1830, wished to emphasise the achievements of the Revolution and the Empire, in the interest of national reconciliation. In 1832 Abel Blouet took over the direction, and the arch was at last dedicated in 1836. It is 50 m high and 45 m wide. In February 1837 Victor Hugo published a celebratory poem.[24]

Apart from its size (the largest built to date), what makes this arch so impressive is its comparative simplicity, which sets off the fine sculpture. There are four great groups at the base of the piers. Most famous by far is *Le Départ des Volontiers (1792)*, also known as *La Marseillaise*, on the east side facing down the avenue de la Grande Armée, by François Rude; the other on the east side, *The Triumph of Napoleon*, is by Cortot. The two on the west face, *Resistance* and *Peace*, are by Antoine Etex. There are also six bas-reliefs, two on each front, and one on each side (that on the south by Carlo Marochetti). The spandrels of the great arches have Fames by James Pradier. The frieze on the entablatures (departure of the armies on the east, and return on the west), 137 m long, is by six sculptors, who include Rude. On the attic, between short pilasters, are round shields with the names of successful battles. On the inner walls of the piers are the names of ninety-four other battles, and of Napoleon's generals, beneath reliefs of Victories. As Westfehling writes, 'the monument was transformed into a gigantic picture-book of the patriotic cult of fame'.[25]

For Napoleon, the 'Temple de la Gloire' was the former church of the Madeleine, and this arch was simply another monument. However, it came to have great symbolic status. Various proposals were made for sculpture above the attic (the discussions involving Pradier, Rude, Barye, David d'Angers and Préault), but none was executed in permanent form. In 1834 Pradier made a design for a colossal group showing 'France distributing crowns', and in the same year he won a competition with a design for 'the Apotheosis of Napoleon', showing the Emperor carried up by an eagle, with a trophy below. Plaster models for it survive. Although highly praised by Victor Hugo, and despite a plea for its execution by Pradier in 1852, this never happened.[26] In 1838, for the celebration of the July Revolution of 1830, a *sestiga* driven by the figure of France was set up, made of wood and canvas: the sculptor was Bernard-Gabriel Seurre. In 1840 the procession translating the ashes of Napoleon passed through the arch. A large statue of the Emperor was put on top, with figures of Fame on horseback on the corners.[27] Hector Horeau was particularly distressed by the horizontality of the arch: in 1851 he proposed that it should be dedicated to 'universal peace', and produced several designs. One shows a statue on a heavy pedestal on top, flags at the corners, and garlands round the piers. Another shows enormous swags of drapery on the corners, linked by large banners, and a dancing Peace on top.[28] For the funeral of Victor Hugo in 1885, a huge sarcophagus was placed in the opening and vast black drapery hung down [19.4]. A *quadriga* had been set up in 1882, by Alexandre Falguière, though only in plaster and canvas.[29] The laying-out of the Place de l'Étoile is due to Baron Haussmann, while the twelve *hôtels* around it were designed by Jakob Ignaz Hittorff (1868). The arch finally achieved its national role in 1919, when the victorious armies passed through it after the end of the First World War. In 1921 the Unknown Soldier was buried there.

Napoleon wrote that he intended to build two more arches, one to Peace and one to Religion, but this never happened.[30] Another unexecuted proposal was for an arch at the Pont d'Iéna, surmounted by the *quadriga* from the Brandenburg Gate of Berlin.[31]

The final word on Napoleon's arches may be left to an old footsoldier from his army, as represented by Balzac. He claims that after Napoleon was crowned King of Italy 'le triomphe du soldat' began: *vous reveniez d'Espagne pour passer à Berlin; eh bien, vous retrouviez des arches de triomphe avec de simples soldats mis dessus en belle sculpture, ni plus ni moins que des généraux* ('you were coming back from Spain to go on to Berlin; well, you found triumphal arches with simple soldiers on top in fine sculpture, neither more nor less than generals').[32]

Some more temporary arches for Napoleon should be mentioned. At his coronation in 1807, 'Le Grand Trône' erected in Notre-Dame 'represented a triumphal arch, supported by eight columns decorated with trophies and bas-reliefs, and the armorials of the Empire' [19.5]. The decorations were designed by Percier and Fontaine.[33] In 1810 they designed the décor for the marriage of Napoleon and Marie-Louise, which included a triumphal arch erected in front of the Tuileries Palace, supporting a balcony. The arch was fairly plain, but on the spandrels were two very sexy winged females.[34] Percier and Fontaine also designed two arches set in colonnades at the entry to the Tuileries Gardens, one placed between the Chevaux de Marly. These were more richly decorated.[35] They were so much admired that Fontaine was ordered to construct one in marble, but this never happened.[36] At the Place de l'Étoile the unfinished arch was 'completed' with wood and canvas to the design of Chalgrin; on the piers were trophies, with paintings above by Louis Lafitte honouring the Emperor.[37] In the year of their marriage, the imperial couple made a tour of Holland and the newly created

19.4 Paris, Arc de l'Étoile, decorated for the funeral of Victor Hugo, 1885. Quadriga, 1882. Alexandre Falguière.

19.5 Coronation of Napoleon in Notre Dame, 1804. Decorations by Percier and Fontaine.

Grand Duchy of Berg. An arch was erected at Ghent in the Marché aux Grains. It was a curious affair, with a semicircular arch set between *stelai*, and a great deal of sculpture.[38] Another in Düsseldorf (1811) was simple in form but decorated with reliefs and inscriptions. There was also one at Duisburg.[39] What would no doubt have been a permanent arch honouring Napoleon was designed by Eustache de Saint-Far in 1807. He was 'Ingénieur en chef des ponts et chaussées' at Mainz, and it would have stood at the entrance to the Pont des Victoires over the Rhine.[40]

The defeat of Napoleon by the Italians and Austrians in 1814 led to a proposal for an arch at Trieste to be designed, with three other monuments, by Pietro Nobile.[41] In 1817 the Heger Tor in the walls of Osnabrück was replaced by the Waterloo Tor, in memory of the four hundred local soldiers who died at Waterloo. It has pairs of freestanding Ionic columns and an inscribed attic. The designer was Johann Christian Sieckmann.

A curious postscript: the short-lived Treaty of Amiens, signed in 1802, was celebrated by the French Ambassador to London by the illumination of his house in Portman Square. It represented a triumphal arch, with the word 'PEACE' above, and 'CONCORD' on the entablature over the door. The mob thought it said 'CONQUERED', and smashed all the windows. The word was replaced with 'AMITIÉ', but the mob read this as 'ENMITY'.[42]

Notes

1 Uwe Westfehling, *Triumphbogen im 19. und 20. Jahrhundert* (Munich, 1977), 30–31; Gianni Mezzanotte, *Architettura Neoclassica in Lombardia* (Naples, 1966), 240–42; Anna Ottani Cavina, ed., *L'età neoclassica a Faenza* (Bologna, 1979), cat. 273, 291–3; Aurora Scotti, *Il Foro Bonaparte: un'utopia giacobina a Milano* (Milan, 1989), 112, 116, 200. For a bizarre arch design (like a Roman town gate) of 1799, and a design for the Porta Orientale at Milan of 1811, with a pointed arch between Ionic columns, both by Pistocchi, see Cavina, *L'età*, cat. 270 and 285.

2 Mezzanotte (cit. in the preceding note), 215.

3 Scotti (cit. at n. 1), 201, 208–9.

4 Werner Oechslin, in Scotti (cit. at n. 1), 27.

5 Mezzanotte (cit. at n. 1), 398.

6 ibid., 293.

7 Anna Ottani Cavina, *Felice Giani (1758–1823) e la cultura di fine secolo* (Milan, 1999), 240.

8 Marie-Anne Dupuy, ed., *Dominique-Vivant Denon: L'œil de Napoléon* (Paris, 1999), 352–3, 356, 359, 362–3.

9 For a reconstruction drawing of the Arch of Septimius Severus, attributed to Percier, see P. F. L. Fontaine, *Journal 1799–1853* (Paris, 1987), 712. On the previous page a watercolour by Fontaine of the Arch of Titus is illustrated. He accompanied his presentation of a painting of the same arch to the duc d'Orléans with an essay on the arch (pp. 711–14), which cites Pirro Ligorio for the strange idea that the horses of San Marco stood above it. Fontaine called them 'les Chevaux de Corinthe' (*Journal*, 150), as that was thought to be their origin.

10 Marie-Louise Biver, *Le Paris de Napoléon* (Paris, 1963), 176–86; Westfehling (cit. at n. 1), 22–6; Eleanor Tollfree, *Napoleon and the New Rome: Rebuilding Imperial Rome in late 18th and early*

NAPOLEONIC ARCHES 323

19th century Paris (PhD, Bristol, 1999). A drawing by Louis-Pierre Baltard shows the chariot empty: Thierry Sarmant et al., *Napoléon et Paris: Rêves d'une capitale* (Musée Carnavalet, Paris, 2015), 192.
11 A detailed history and description was published in that year: *Arc de Triomphe des Tuileries... de MM. Percier et Fontaine – publié par Normand fils*.
12 Gérard Hubert, *Revue des Arts*, 4 (1955), 209–16; Westfehling (cit. at n. 1), 49–50. The unfinished marbles by Petitot, Pradier and Raggi survive in the Louvre. On Pradier's relief, see *Statues de chair: sculptures de James Pradier* (Geneva/Paris, 1985), 22–4, 388, no. 50; Claude Lapaire, *James Pradier (1790–1852) et la sculpture de la génération romantique* (Milan/Lausanne, 2010), 258–9 (cat. 35).
13 Fontaine (cit. at n. 9), 1080; Sarmant (cit. at n. 10), 205 (a drawing attributed to Percier).
14 Westfehling (cit. at n. 1), 32–4, 38–40; Giovanni Voghera, *Illustrazione dell'Arco della Pace in Milano* (Milan, 1838).
15 See the painting by Nicolas Antoine Taunay in the Musée du Château, Versailles: Sarmant (cit. at n. 10), 48–9.
16 Westfehling (cit. at n. 1), 21; Thomas W. Gaehtgens, *Napoleons Arc de Triomphe* (Göttingen, 1974), pl. 5a.
17 Strasbourg: Westfehling (cit. at n. 1), 21; Gaehtgens (cit. at n. 16), pl. 5b. Stuttgart: Westfehling, 21, pl. 19. Dresden: Westfehling, 21; Gaehtgens, pl. 4a.
18 Westfehling (cit. at n. 1), 30. For an engraving, see G. C. Bascapé, *I Palazzi de Milano* (Milan, 1945).
19 For the first arch, see Westfehling (cit. at n. 1), 30, pl. 49. For paintings of both arches by Giuseppe Borsato, see Claire Constans, *Musée national du château de Versailles: Les peintures* (Paris, 1995), nos 601–2. She attributes the design of the first arch to Borsato, saying that it was 'érigé par Selva'. See also Amable de Fournoux, *Napoléon et Venise* (Paris, 2002), 291, 299. For a design for a huge arch in honour of Napoleon by the Venetian architect Lorenzo Santi, see Eva Rita Rowedder Lehni, *Studien zu Lorenzo Santi (1783–1839)* (Venice, 1983), 225, pls 127, 128.
20 Westfehling (cit. at n. 1), 118, n. 144.
21 Gaehtgens (cit. at n. 16); Isabelle Rouge-Ducos, *L'Arc de Triomphe de l'Étoile: Panthéon de la France Guerrière – art et histoire* (Dijon, 2008). The museum which used to occupy the lower room in the upper part of the arch, with its fascinating collection of watercolours, engravings, etc., has regrettably been dismantled.
22 Westfehling (cit. at n. 1), 27, with pl. 37; Rouge-Ducos (cit. in the preceding note), 47–8.
23 A large plaster model of the design by Huyot including columns is in the Musée National des Monuments Français at the Palais de Chaillot. The bizarre reliefs on it are clearly based on those on the Arch of Septimius Severus at Rome. See Rouge-Ducos (cit. at n. 21), 150–54.
24 In November 1823 he had written his 'Ode huitième – À l'Arc de triomphe de l'Étoile', published in his *Odes et Ballades*, which regrets the 'monument inachevé'. In 1837 'À l'Arc de Triomphe' was published in *Les Voix intérieures*. At the end he regrets 'Phidias absent' – the failure to commission Hugo's friend David d'Angers – and 'mon père oublié' – the omission of his father's name from the arch, because of his military failure. He anticipates the eventual decay of the arch, its sculptures covered in moss. They have recently been cleaned.
25 Westfehling (cit. at n. 1), 54.
26 *Statues de chair* (cit. at n. 12), 180–83, 388, nos 58–9; *James Pradier* (cit. at n. 12), 275–6 (cat. 88–9); Rouge-Ducos (cit. at n. 21), 237–40.
27 Rouge-Ducos (cit. at n. 21), 255–9. An engraving by Verronnais in the Musée Carnavalet shows the arch in this state (TOPO PC 131 D).
28 Françoise Boudon and François Loyer, *Hector Horeau 1801–1872* (Paris, n.d.), 51.
29 Rouge-Ducos (cit. at n. 21), 297–301. Falguière's wax model is in the Musée d'Orsay (*Musée d'Orsay: Catalogue illustré sommaire des sculptures* (Paris, 1986), 153). It was shown in the Palais de l'Industrie in 1882. The plaster *quadriga* was taken down in 1886. Watercolours in the Musée Carnavalet show the arch in 1840 and 1885, both reproduced in an article on the arch's restoration in 1988–9 (Axelle de Gayneron, *Connaissance des Arts*, 444 (Feb. 1989), 111–15).
30 *Correspondance de Napoléon* (Paris, 1858–70), no. 10235 (14 May 1806).
31 Biver (cit. at n. 10), 96.
32 Honoré de Balzac, *Le médecin de campagne* (Paris, 1833), ch. III. I owe this reference to Andrew Saint.
33 *Description des cérémonies et des fêtes qui ont eu lieu pour le couronnement de leurs Majestés Napoléon ... et Joséphine...* (Paris, 1807).
34 Marie-Louise Biver, *Pierre Fontaine: premier architecte de l'Empereur* (Paris, 1964), pl. 27. A lavish and elegant design for an arch in honour of Napoleon and Marie-Louise is illustrated by Louis Hautecoeur, *L'art sous la Révolution et l'Empire en France* (Paris, 1953), 15.
35 Fontaine (cit. at n.9), 256; Westfehling (cit. at n. 1), 21; Sarmant (cit. at n. 10), 243.
36 Fontaine (cit. at n. 9), 1081.
37 Westfehling (cit. at n. 1), 21, pls 40 and 42.
38 Ill. in Fontaine (cit. at n. 9), 260.
39 Westfehling (cit. at n. 1), 21, pl. 18.
40 Philippe Prost, *Les forteresses d'empire* (Paris, 1992), 132.
41 Pietro Nobile, *Progetti di vari monumenti architettonici imaginati per celebrare il trionfo degi augusti alleati ... nell'anno 1814* (Trieste, 1814).
42 E. Walford, *Old and New London* (London, 1872–8), 413. The display is shown in an engraving by J.C. Stadler, after A.C. Pugin.

20

ARCHES IN FRANCE AFTER NAPOLEON I

During his brief reign in 1814–15 Louis XVIII was welcomed at the Hôtel de Ville in Paris in August 1814 with a very plain arch with attached Ionic columns surmounted by statues.[1]

Charles X was received with arches on his journeys, an example being the one at La Fère in 1827, which had on the piers pairs of attached columns flanking niches containing statues, more statues above, and reliefs, with trophies and flags on the attic.[2]

In 1830 the sculptor James Pradier made a design for an arch to honour the heroes of the July Revolution [20.1]. It was to stand in the Place de la Concorde, opposite the bridge. The structure is very plain. On top is a woman on a chariot drawn by lions, with genii offering her crowns. On pedestals at the base of the pilasters, at the front and sides, are statues of young men with *oriflammes* (banners) and guns.[3]

20.1 James Pradier, design for an arch for the Place de la Concorde, Paris, 1830.

The Porte d'Aix at Marseille was begun in 1825, and was intended to honour the duc d'Angoulême after his expedition to Spain, but after the change of regime in 1830 it celebrated the Napoleonic wars [20.2]. It is based on the Arch of Titus at Rome, but the order of the freestanding columns is Corinthian. The architect was Michel-Robert Penchaud. The arch is particularly remarkable for the fine sculpture by David d'Angers and Étienne-Jules Ramey. It was inaugurated in 1839. Hautecoeur states that there was a *sestiga* on top, but this is wrong. There were statues at attic level, but they decayed beyond repair. Eugène Guillaume made designs for a group of 'the Mediterranean spreading abundance' to go above it, but it was not executed.[4]

Shortly before claiming the title of Emperor, in October 1852, Louis Napoléon was welcomed with an arch by the men building the Cirque d'Hiver, on his passing along the boulevards. The arch, like the Cirque, was designed by Jacques-Ignace Hittorff. It had a pair of Corinthian columns on either side, a huge eagle on top, coats of arms, flags, and so on.[5]

In 1858 at least three arches were erected for visits by Napoleon III. One at Chatou had an attic which rose up in

20.2 Marseille, Porte d'Aix, 1825–39. Michel-Robert Penchaud.

a semicircle, and was lavishly decorated with sculpture. Another, based on the Roman model, was put up at St-Malo, and a third at Caen.[6] In 1860 he was greeted at Nice by an arch which had large statues above four pilasters on the piers, and on top one large eagle and four smaller ones.[7] A much grander arch was erected by the municipality of Paris in 1862 in the Place du Trône (now Place de la Nation) for the inauguration of the boulevard du Prince-Eugène (now the boulevard Voltaire). The competition for its design was won by Victor Baltard [20.3]. It was 30 m high. The inscription read: 'À Napoléon III Empereur des Français, aux armées victorieuses de Crimée, d'Italie, de Chine, Cochinchine, d'Algérie MDCCCLII-MDCCCLXII'. On top were a *quadriga*, and a Fame at each corner. On each face, including the sides, were pairs of detached columns supporting statues symbolising the various different types of soldier. It was hoped that the arch might be made permanent, but this was not to be.[8] Three years later Hector Horeau produced a design for an arch on the same site. The colossal and ungainly structure was to be 90 m high and 75 m wide. The opening is four-centred, with pairs of attached Corinthian columns on the piers, supporting trophies recalling the military achievements of the Empire. At the top the sides sweep up to a pedestal on which eagles would support four 'genii of civilisation' set around the national flag.

20.3 Arch for Napoleon III, Place de la Nation, Paris, 1862. Victor Baltard.

It is assumed that the arch would have been constructed of metal. A second drawing shows an arch similar in form but with much more lavish sculptural and architectural decoration, culminating in a dome with a huge statue on top.[9] In 1866 Horeau came up with a scheme for remodelling the setting of the Porte St-Denis, which included the provision of rather strange decoration to go on top of the arch, in the form of a tent with statues.[10]

Two architectural projects of the time of Napoleon III took the form of triumphal arches. One was the Fontaine St-Michel, of 1860, an elaborate façade designed by Gabriel Davioud for the corner on the south side of the Place St-Michel. The four freestanding columns support allegorical statues, while the central niche houses a bronze St Michael by Francisque-Joseph Duret, over the fountain cascade. Above is a fanciful gable in Renaissance style.[11] At Marseille the Palais Longchamp incorporates an even more lavish fountain with triumphal arch above. The complex, built in 1862–9 to the design of Henri Espérandieu (based on a sketch by Frédéric-Auguste Bartholdi), includes the museums of fine arts and of natural history. These are linked by a curving colonnade with, in the centre, the Château d'Eau which celebrates the aqueduct of 1847. Its arch is flanked by freestanding columns supporting allegorical statues. Over the opening is a frieze with marine motifs. The domical attic is crowned by a huge basket of fruit, and has the city arms on the front. The opening shelters a grotto which serves as backdrop to a sculptural group by Bartholdi representing the river Durance on a chariot. Further sculpture stands around, including a tiger and panther by Antoine-Louis Barye. The effect is lavishly Baroque.[12] Another building in Marseille by Espérandieu, the École des Beaux Arts, of 1864–9, has reliefs showing the principal schools of architecture, Roman being represented by the Arch of Constantine, and Modern by the Arc de Triomphe de l'Étoile.[13] Similarly the Grand Palais at

Paris (1897–1900, by Deglane, Louvet and Thomas) has a mosaic frieze of the great epochs of art, where Roman is represented by a triumphal arch.

In 1880 a design was published for a monument to the Countess of Caen, to stand in a museum to be established in her name at the Institut de France. She left money for scholarships in painting, sculpture and architecture, and the design was by the first *pensionnaire* architect, Émile Ullmann. It took the form of a marble triumphal arch in French Renaissance style, with pairs of Corinthian columns flanking an arched niche in which is a sarcophagus bearing a recumbent figure of the Countess. Above the opening smaller niches housed statues of the three arts.[14]

Notes

1. François Waquet, *Les fêtes royales sous la restauration* (Geneva, 1981), fig. 45.
2. Louis Hautecoeur, *L'architecture classique en France*, V (Paris, 1955), 5.
3. Claude Lapaire, *James Pradier (1790–1852) et la sculpture de la génération romantique* (Milan/Lausanne, 2010), 270 (cat. 68).
4. Hautecoeur (cit. at n. 2), VI, 6 ; Uwe Westfehling, *Triumphbogen im 19. und 20. Jahrhundert* (Munich, 1977), 50, 97; Musées de Marseille, *Marseille au XIXème: Rêves et triomphes d'une ville* (Paris/Marseille, 1991), 141–2, 213–14.
5. Thomas von Joest and Claudine Vaulchier, *Hittorff (1792–1867), un architecte du XIXe siècle* (Paris, 1986), 226.
6. The Chatou arch is shown in a watercolour by Pharamond Blanchard in the Musée National du Château de Compiègne; the St-Malo one was shown in an engraving in *L'Illustration* 32 (7 August 1858), 81; the Caen one appears on a commemorative plate in the Compiègne museum (also *L'Illustration* 32 (28 August 1858), 130).
7. This arch too was shown in *L'Illustration* 36 (22 Sept. 1860), 213.
8. Yvan Christ, *Paris des Utopies* (Paris, 1977), 202; Pierre Pinon, *Louis-Pierre et Victor Baltard* (Paris, 2005), 159–61; Alice Thomine-Berrada, *Victor Baltard: Architecte de Paris* (Paris, 2012), 76.
9. Christ (cit. in the preceding note), 202–3; Françoise Boudon and François Loyer, *Hector Horeau* (Paris, 1978), cat. 61.
10. Boudon and Loyer (cit. in the preceding note), cat. 54.
11. Westfehling (cit. at n. 4), 56.
12. ibid., 56–7.
13. Barry Bergdoll, *Léon Vaudoyer* (New York, 1994), 278–9.
14. *The Builder*, 39 (1880), 172.

21

LONDON – THE MARBLE AND WELLINGTON ARCHES

The Marble Arch

The Marble Arch now stands at the north end of Park Lane, but it was designed by John Nash in 1825 to stand in front of Buckingham Palace, where it formed the entrance to the courtyard [21.1]. When a new east wing was built in 1846–50 it had to be moved.[1]

In 1821 Sir John Soane had designed a new palace to be built in Green Park, on a vast scale. The courtyard would be entered by a huge arch, with open curved colonnades on the sides, a stepped podium on top bearing an equestrian statue, and much sculpture. A more conventional arch stood on either side beyond the gate piers. This related to his scheme for the western entrance to London, which included a group of four arches, or a pair on either side of a screen, at Kensington Gardens, and a triumphal arch at the Hyde Park Corner entrance to the park.[2] However, Nash was given the commission to reconstruct Buckingham House. His arch would be joined

21.1 John Buckler (1770–1851), Buckingham Palace with Marble Arch, 1835.

to the wings by railings. He worked on the design in collaboration with the sculptor John Flaxman, and a plaster model of about 1826 survives [21.2].[3]

It was to celebrate military victories. Nash summarised the proposed sculpture to the Duke of Wellington: 'One side and one end dedicated to the Army, and the other side to the Navy. The east front and north end to be a record of the Battle of Waterloo, and the west front and south end a record of the Battle of Trafalgar ... On the summit is an equestrian statue of the King'. Flaxman died in 1826. Sir Francis Chantrey refused to take responsibility for the sculpture, as he did not think marble would last in this climate. Three sculptors were commissioned, to base their work on Flaxman's designs, most of it being given to Richard Westmacott (assisted by his son), and the rest to E.H. Baily and J.C.F. Rossi.

It was first intended to build the arch of Bath stone, like the Palace, but in 1826 it was decided to clad it in marble. The marble dealer Joseph Browne was appointed agent for its supply, and he chose ravaccione, or 'Sicilian Carrara'. Work began in 1827, under the supervision of Browne, but progress was slow because of complaints about the King's extravagance, and after his death in 1830 work was stopped. By then the arch was almost complete, and the sculpture nearly ready. In 1831 Edward Blore was appointed to finish the job, and he proposed to omit the attic and equestrian statue. Some of the sculpture was put on the arch, while other pieces were set on the east and west fronts of the Palace. The bronze equestrian statue of George IV, by Sir Francis Chantrey, was later placed in Trafalgar Square, while other pieces were used by William Wilkins on the National Gallery (Baily's Britannia, altered to represent Minerva, Rossi's relief of Europe and Asia, and Victory figures from the attic pedestal corners). The commission for the gates had been given to Samuel Parker, but he went bankrupt in 1832, and the gates were completed by Bramah and Prestage, with the 'VR' cipher since they were hung at the time of Victoria's accession in 1837. The central ones are of 'mosaic gold', a type of bronze. The final cost of the Arch was estimated as £70.000.

Nash told the Duke of Wellington that his design was 'a plagiarism of the Arch of Constantine', and it is much the same size, though the slightly smaller Arc du Carrousel in Paris, about which Nash was kept informed by James Pennethorne, was a closer model. The columns are monoliths. What is now the north side would have been the military side, facing the Mall. On top would have been the equestrian statue of the King: on the front of the pedestal would been a relief by Rossi of Europe and Asia seated on a horse and camel, with Victories standing at the corners. Above the columns

21.2 Plaster model of Marble Arch, 1826 (Victoria and Albert Museum).

would be statues of military heroes. The attic frieze, by Westmacott, was to show the Battle of Waterloo. None of these were set on the arch, but the Victories in the spandrels, which were, are by Westmacott on the north side, and by Baily on the south. The reliefs set on the piers were to show scenes from the Waterloo campaign, but actually have females representing England, Scotland and Wales on one side, Peace and Plenty on the other. The present south side was to have been the naval side. On the attic pedestal would have sat Baily's Britannia, between a lion and a unicorn. The frieze would have shown three scenes from the life of Nelson. Above the columns would stand four naval heroes, by Baily. The reliefs on the piers show a naval warrior with a figure of Justice, and Peace with trophies. On the east and west sides were to be reliefs of Fame displaying Britain's recent triumphs, military on one side and naval on the other. Only the rows of laurel wreaths beneath these were executed. Under these were to have been lists of battles and commanders, in bronze letters.

When the time came for the moving of the Arch, various suggestions were made for a new site. It seems to have been Decimus Burton and W.A. Nesfield, who had been appointed to plan the new Palace forecourt, who decided to re-erect it at Cumberland Gate, the entrance to Hyde Park from Oxford Street and Park Lane. On either side were gateways, with Burton's lodge on the west. The work was done by Thomas Cubitt. He replaced the timber joists supporting the lead roof with iron girders and brick arches, and converted the three interior rooms into 'living rooms', to be used by the police.

In 1905 a Royal Commission on London Traffic recommended that the Arch should be moved further back, leaving space for a new road arrangement. The architect F.W. Speaight proposed that the arch should be left isolated within a 'Crescent of Peace', separated from the park by a simple screen. However, his comparison with the Arc de Triomphe in Paris was mocked, as the Marble Arch was on a much smaller scale. Eventually a modified version of this scheme was carried out, and the Arch was left on a traffic island. New railings and gates to the park were provided by H.H. Martyn, the piers bearing lamps by W. Bainbridge Reynolds. These disappeared in 1961–2 when Park Lane was doubled in width. The result was to provide the Arch with an even less satisfactory setting (not much helped by the 'framing' of it on the north by the hulking Cumberland Hotel and its matching block). Suggestions that it might be moved again to a better site have come to nothing.

The history of the arch is not a happy one, and the replacement of the attic by Blore's clumsy volutes was a disaster. The final humiliation has been the sale of the unused reliefs (a third of Westmacott's Waterloo relief, and one of the Nelson reliefs), discovered in Shepperton Film Studios in 1985: they were not bought for a public collection, and have left the country.

The Wellington Arch

The history of the Wellington Arch is not much happier [21.3].[4] The various projects for an arch as the western entrance to London, up to Soane's scheme of 1796, have been discussed (pp. 295–7). The idea was taken up again with enthusiasm at the end of the Napoleonic wars. In about 1825 Soane, as mentioned above, designed an arch for the entrance to the park: it had pairs of Corinthian columns standing against the channelled masonry of the piers, with pilasters on either side, both on the fronts and on the sides. A stepped podium on the attic bore an equestrian statue, flanked by sarcophagus-like aedicules. However in 1824 it had been decided that Decimus Burton, who was already working on lodges and railings for Hyde Park, should design entrances to the park, including a screen and a gateway at the head of Constitution Hill. In 1825 he presented his designs. That for the screen was as built, but the gateway would have repeated the centre of the screen, which takes the form of a triumphal arch with pairs of freestanding Ionic columns and a frieze on the attic. The committee wanted something grander, and Burton came up with a larger arch with Corinthian columns, projecting pilastered ends, and a tall attic. There were to be trophies on the piers, statues of guardsmen above the columns, a frieze of horsemen around the attic, and a gilt bronze *quadriga* on top. The sculptors would have been E.H. Baily and John Henning (who did the frieze on the park screen). By 1828 the screen and the carcass of the arch were almost finished, but estimates of the cost had risen, and in 1830 the Treasury called a halt. As a result most of the decoration remained unexecuted. The wide lintels over the openings (where on earlier arches the entablature would have been set back on the plane of the opening) are spanned with cast- and wrought-iron girders. The magnificent cast-iron gates were made by Joseph Bramah and Sons. As at the Marble Arch, the internal rooms were used as a police station, though here the southern pier was a park-keeper's residence.

In 1838 it was agreed that the monument should form the base for a memorial to the Duke of Wellington, close to his residence at Apsley House. The Duke of Rutland had the idea that a huge bronze equestrian statue should be erected, and ensured that the commission went to Matthew Cotes Wyatt. At 8.5 m high it was the largest equestrian statue ever made. Many thought it would look absurd on the arch, and permission was revoked in 1845, but it was then agreed that the statue could be put in place for a trial period of three weeks. This was done in 1846 (Wyatt having designed internal strengthening to support it). Loud criticism had to give way to Wellington's statement that taking the statue down would indicate royal displeasure, and that he would resign his commissions.

The statue certainly did look absurd, placed at a right angle to the arch. The increase of traffic at Hyde Park Corner led to the decision in 1882–3 to move the arch, so that instead of standing opposite the screen it would be at the head of Constitution Hill. This was the opportunity for the removal of the statue. When no site could be found, it was proposed that it should be melted down, but the army, whose officers had largely paid for it, was upset, and it was re-erected in 1885 at the Aldershot military town. In 1888 Sir Joseph Boehm made a new equestrian statue of Wellington to stand opposite

21.3 Wellington Arch, 1825–30. Decimus Burton, with equestrian statue by Matthew Cotes Wyatt.

21.4 Wellington Arch, quadriga, 1912. Adrian Jones.

Apsley House. In 1891 the Prince of Wales suggested that Captain Adrian Jones, who had exhibited a plaster *quadriga* at the Royal Academy, should make one for the Arch [21.4]. His magnificent *quadriga*, driven by Peace, was finally set up in 1912. It is 8.8 m high.[5]

In 1959–62 the area around the Arch became a large traffic island, and the piers and railings designed in 1907–8 by Sir Aston Webb were removed. The island is now also occupied by a number of war memorials, the finest being C.S. Jagger's Royal Artillery Monument and Derwent Wood's Machine Gun Corps Memorial.

Notes

1. The most recent account of the arch is David Robinson, *The Marble Arch: a Report on its Later History and Fabric* (English Heritage Historical Analysis & Research Team, Reports and Papers, 11 (1999). See also Andrew Saint, 'The Marble Arch', *The Georgian Group Journal*, 7 (1997), 75–93; Steven Brindle and David Robinson, *The Wellington Arch and the Marble Arch* (London, 2001).
2. Sean Sawyer, 'Sir John Soane's Symbolic Westminster: the Apotheosis of George IV', *Architectural History*, 39 (1996), 54–5.
3. In the Victoria and Albert Museum.
4. Steven Brindle, *The Wellington Arch, Hyde Park Corner: A History* (London, n.d.); *idem*, 'The Wellington Arch, Hyde Park Corner, and the Idea of a Western Entrance to London', *The Georgian Group Journal*, 11 (2001), 47–92; Brindle and Robinson (cit. at n. 1).
5. Adrian Jones, *Memoirs of a Soldier Artist* (London, 1933); Robert S. Burns, *Triumph: the Art and Life of Captain Adrian Jones* (Almeley, 2010).

22

GERMANY AND AUSTRIA FROM THE SIXTEENTH TO THE NINETEENTH CENTURY

Germany

One of the most remarkable triumphal arches ever created exists only on paper. This is the 'Ehrenpforte Maximilians I', a woodcut measuring 351 by 304 cm which Albrecht Dürer and his assistants created in 1512–17 [22.1]. It shows a triple arch, but the slender openings are subordinated to a vast display of figures and scenes. The whole is articulated by four columns standing forward on projecting bases, and rises to a central dome. Over the principal opening Maximilian's family tree is shown, with himself enthroned at the top. Over each side opening are twenty-four historical scenes from his reign. Round towers at the sides show his private history.[1]

The earliest known freestanding funerary monument is that to the Domdechant Christoph von Rheineck, formerly in the Liebfrauenkirche at Trier, which was re-erected in the Rheinisches Landesmuseum in 1993–9 [22.2]. It dates from 1530–32, though he did not die until 1535. Strikingly elegant, and made of sandstone, it is 4.6 m high. It has pairs of projecting Corinthian columns at the sides as well as on the front. At the back is a lower arched opening, while the sides have narrow rectangular ones. On the top the resurrected Christ stands on a sarcophagus, while four soldiers are seated before him. Within the opening there was originally a group representing the burial of Christ. Von Rheineck was a humanist with connections in South Germany and the Netherlands, and

22.1 Ehrenpforte for Maximilian, 1512–7. Albrecht Dürer and assistants.

it is considered that the monument is the work of a man from the South Netherlands, perhaps trained in France, with the assistance of sculptors from South Germany.[2]

A number of arches for the Emperor Charles V are mentioned elsewhere in this book. A particularly splendid example welcomed him to Nuremberg in 1541, and is shown in a woodcut by Peter Flötner [22.3]. Thirty painters and carpenters worked day and night on it and the other decorations. It had columns flanking the opening, which supported a projecting entablature, above which was a columned pavilion housing musicians. On the top an imperial eagle could be made to lower its head for the Emperor by means of ropes.[3]

An exceptionally fine portal, deserving its name 'Das schone Tor', was erected in the Grosse Schlosshof of the Dresden Schloss, as the entrance to the chapel, in 1555–6. It was designed by Giovanni Maria Mosca Padovano, and the sculptor was Hans Walther II. It has the form of a triumphal arch, with pairs of freestanding Corinthian columns on the piers, between which are two

22.2 Rheinisches Landesmuseum, Trier, tomb of Christoph von Reineck, 1530–2.

22.3 Arch for Charles V, Nürnberg, 1541. Woodcut by Peter Flötner.

tiers of niches containing statues. On the attic is a relief, and above stand figures with the resurrected Christ in the centre. The great art historian Wilhelm Lübke described it as 'the noblest portal-composition of the whole German Renaissance'. The portal has had a complicated history: in 1738 it was placed against the west end of the Evangelical Sophienkirche, from which it was removed in 1864; from 1872 until 2004 it stood in the Jüdenhof; and it has now been put back in its original position.[4]

One of the best-known German designers of the sixteenth century was Hans Vredeman de Vries. In 1589 he designed a gateway for the Heinrichstadt in Wolfenbüttel which incorporates, as its centrepiece, a rusticated triumphal arch which has banded columns on either side of the opening and banded pilasters at the ends, with a Doric frieze. Over the rectangular side openings are niches with statues. The attic is not at all Classical, apart from a broken pediment above the huge coat of arms.[5]

In 1613 Elizabeth, daughter of James I, married Frederick V, Elector Palatine of the Rhine. The first town she entered in the Palatinate was Oppenheim, and here she was greeted by an arch 'thickly painted with roses', to allude to her descent from the Houses of York and Lancaster. It was a single arch, fairly plain, except on top, where an attic panel had the arms of Britain and the Palatinate between obelisks. Rectangular side projections bore paintings, each showing four English gentlemen. When she entered the capital, Heidelberg, arches were erected by the faculties of the University. The arch of the Theology Faculty consisted merely of four posts holding up a gallery of musicians, the parapet decorated with portraits of the Fathers, Luther, Melanchthon and de Bèze. In the courtyard of the castle an arch 20 m high bore statues of former Palatinate rulers and their English wives. This was a more conventional affair, with pairs of freestanding Corinthian columns framing niches containing statues, pediments over the piers, and a tall attic over the central opening with statues of the royal couple.[6]

When the Kurfürst Max Emanuel returned to Munich from the Turkish War in 1683 an arch to welcome him was designed by Johann Baptist Gumpp, a member of the Innsbruck family of architects who then became civil and military engineers to the Bavarian rulers. It had freestanding columns, with obelisks above the cornice. On the attic was a figure of Fame, with an equestrian statue above. There were quantities of elaborate decoration.[7]

In the state of Brandenburg arches began to be built for rulers after the Thirty Years' War. They celebrated victorious campaigns by Friedrich Wilhelm, the Grosse Kurfürst, in 1677 and 1678. The latter, on the Lange Brücke at Berlin, was triple, Corinthian, with a pedimented aedicule above framing a trophy, and with a rearing equestrian statue on top of a pediment.[8] A permanent arch was erected as the Leipziger Tor in the fortifications in 1683 by Johann Arnold Nering to commemorate the battle of Fehrbellin, but it was demolished in 1736. On the death of Friedrich Wilhelm in 1688 two arches were set up. One had freestanding Corinthian columns on either side of the opening, and pairs at the ends, with reliefs on the piers and attic and much statuary, which included a female figure standing on a sarcophagus on the attic. It was re-erected on the hill at Golm.[9]

An altogether exceptional celebration marked the coronation of the first King of Prussia, Friedrich III, in 1701. The entry to Berlin took place on 6 May, and lasted four hours. Seven arches were erected along Jürgenstrasse, which was afterwards named Königstrasse. On the Schlossplatz stood the arch of the town of Cologne, a single arch imitating blue and white marble, with pairs of red pilasters and on top an eagle on a pedestal between statues. The arch of the towns of Friedrichswerder and Friedrichstadt had a column on either side, a fanciful attic with coat of arms, Fames, etc., and side pieces with obelisks. Within the opening were galleries for musicians. The Arch of the French Colony (or Refugees) was designed by the Huguenot Jean de Bodt. This elegantly Classical structure had pairs of pilasters on either side of the opening on a curved plan, in front of which statues stood at an angle. Beyond were projecting pairs of columns, with trophies above. Over the centre the attic had an inscription panel below a segmental pediment decorated with a relief. The reverse side had tall curved pedestals on the piers, with figures below and eagles on top, and the pediment on the attic was triangular. The principal colour was yellow; the columns and pilasters imitated porphyry, with capitals and bases of bronze; the consoles and frieze were gilded, and the metopes had a lapis lazuli ground. De Bodt also designed the Arch of the Court Servants. This triple arch was astylar, with channelled 'masonry'. On either side of the main opening broad piers stood forward, with sculpture groups at their bases. The side openings had reliefs set within them. The attic also bore reliefs, and a triangular pediment in the middle. Statues stood above the projections, and trophies at the ends. The arch of the town of Berlin, opposite the Rathaus, was designed by Martin Grünberg. It was a single arch with pairs of pilasters framing niches on two levels, and miscellaneous statues on top. Little is known of the other two arches. In December it was decreed that the arches should be taken down, but the Cologne arch was given to the King, and placed on the Golmer Berg at Potsdam, where the arch for the Grosse Kurfürst (by now decrepit) had stood. The other arches were sold off.[10] On the site of the arch of the Court Servants a Königstor was built, after the model of the Arch of Septimius Severus.[11]

It was in the reign of Friedrich III that the Berlin Stadtschloss received its immense portal, based on the Arch of Septimius Severus, but bigger.[12] The architect of the 'Neues Schloss' built in 1707–13 was Eosander Göthe. The arch had four freestanding Corinthian columns (the capitals with eagles on the corners), and pairs of rectangular reliefs over the side openings. There were also reliefs on the attic, which curved upwards in the centre as a broken segmental pediment over a cartouche. The portal is currently being rebuilt during the exterior recreation of the Schloss, which had been blown up in 1950.

De Bodt was also the architect of the charming Berliner Tor, the only surviving gate of the fortifications of Wesel. The structure is of channelled brickwork against which are placed pairs of Doric columns and an entablature of stone. Between the columns on the outer side are statues of Minerva and Hercules, with oval reliefs above. Within the opening is another relief. On the attic is a broad inscription panel, crowned by the royal coat of arms supported by female figures. The arch was built in 1718–22, and the sculptor was Guillaume Hulot, though his work was replaced by copies in the nineteenth century. The town side was destroyed in the Second World War. Another gate in the form of a commemorative arch was the Büchsentor at Stuttgart, rebuilt in stone in 1748 to celebrate the marriage of Herzog Karl Eugen and the Markgräfin Friederike Sophie von Brandenburg-Bayreuth. It was a simple single arch, with banded half-columns, and the ducal arms and trophies on top. It was demolished in 1855.

The Türkentor at Helmstedt, in Lower Saxony, was built in 1716 by the Abbot and Prior of St Ludger's Abbey to celebrate the victory of Prince Eugene of Savoy over the

Turks at Petrovaradin. Damaged in the Second World War, it was moved to its present site in 1986. Charmingly small-scale, it has pairs of pilasters, and a pediment with the Habsburg arms. Lower side-pieces have arched openings below scrolls.

It is not to be wondered at that Frederick the Great, who ruled from 1740 until 1786, should have been keen on triumphal arches. At Potsdam the Berliner Tor was built in 1753, its outer side in the form of a single arch, with a pair of three-quarter Corinthian columns. On the attic were four statues by Johannes Matthias Gottlieb Heymüller, representing Minerva and Bellona with a legionary and a centurion. The architect seems to have been Johann Boumann. Flanking the arch were curved, arcaded wings fronting guardhouses, but these were demolished in 1896. The gate itself was demolished in 1952.[13] Much grander, despite its modest scale, and still surviving, is the Brandenburger Tor, built in 1770 [22.4]. On the outer side this triple arch has four pairs of coupled Corinthian columns. Over these are trophies, and in the centre a cartouche flanked by Mars and Hercules. In the spandrels of the main opening Fames blow trumpets. The side openings originally contained the windows of guard-rooms, and were only later opened for pedestrians. The town side is simpler, with pilasters. There were flanking curved arcades, later removed. The design of the outer side seems to have been based by Georg Christian Unger on a sketch by Frederick himself, the model being mysteriously described as the 'Trojanische Triumphbogen zu Rom'. The

22.4 Potsdam, Brandenburger Tor, 1770. Frederick the Great and Georg Christoph Unger.

inner side was by Carl Philipp Christian von Gontard.[14] In about 1763 the French architect Jean-Laurent Legeay made designs for the colonnade of the Communs at the Neues Palais. One has freestanding Corinthian columns, and a pyramid above with much sculpture. In another the opening rises higher than the entablature of the colonnade and supports a fanciful dome with many more columns and a large urn on top. The colonnade was erected in 1765–6 to the second design, altered by Gontard.

Two gates at Berlin had the form of triumphal arches. The Oranienburger Tor of 1786–8 was designed by Carl von Gontard. It had Tuscan pilasters and bold rustication. The side openings were entrances to guardrooms, but (as at Potsdam) later opened for pedestrians. On the attic trophies flanked a curved pedestal supporting an obelisk. This gate was demolished in 1867–8. The Rosenthaler Tor, of 1781–8, was probably also designed by Gontard, but was executed by Unger. It had Tuscan columns on either side of the opening, and the projecting piers had pairs of columns with pediments above. On the attic was a curved pedestal with arms and a helmet on top. Here the side openings were entrances to curved, arcaded wings as at Potsdam. The gate was demolished in 1869.[15]

The Brandenburg Gate in Berlin does not have the form of a Roman triumphal arch, but with its crowning *quadriga* and symbolic function it has much in common with the type. It was built in 1788–91 for King Friedrich Wilhelm II, in the fashionable Greek Revival style, to replace an old gate. There are six Doric columns on each side. The architect was Carl Gotthard Langhans, and the *quadriga*, driven by Victory, is by Johann Gottfried Schadow. The arch stands at the entrance to Unter den Linden, the street leading to the royal palace. In 1806, after the battle of Jena, Napoleon made a triumphal entry through it. After his defeat, in 1814, the *quadriga* was redesigned by Karl Friedrich Schinkel, to designate it as the Prussian triumphal arch: to the figure of Victory were added the Prussian eagle and iron cross. The arch was damaged in 1945, but fully restored in 2000–2002.

Temporary arches were also erected in Potsdam during Frederick's reign. One greeted him in 1746 on his return from the Second Silesian War, and another in 1763 after the Seven Years' War. This was built by the magistrates, and was a triple arch with Ionic columns, and a balustraded attic with trophies on the corners and a seated female figure on a broad pedestal in the centre, inscribed 'Panthea Borussorum' (Goddess of the Prussians). For the entry of Grand Duke Paul Petrovich of Russia in 1776, a similar arch in the Doric order had a statue on either side of the central opening, and an obelisk on the attic surrounded with statuary.[16] For the entry of the Mecklenburg Princesses Luise and Friederike in 1793 an arch was designed by the Potsdam builder and engraver Andreas Ludwig Krüger. It was a triple arch with freestanding pairs of Corinthian columns flanking the main opening, and sculpture on top which included a Fame with trumpet. The garlanded columns also appear on a design of 1795 by Krüger, for an unknown purpose. This is larger and more elaborate, with an equestrian statue on the attic flanked by Victories leading horses.[17]

For the commemoration of the death of Friedrich Wilhelm II and the accession of Friedrich Wilhelm III in 1798 an up-to-date Neoclassical arch was designed by Aubert Parent. Two comparatively plain arches were linked by a much taller one, forming in effect a third arch. This was decorated with herms, reclining figures on each side of the opening, and a statue on top which Giersberg considers to be influenced

22.5 Potsdam, Alter Markt, arch for Princess Elisabeth, 1823.

by a design by Johann Gottfried Schadow for a monument to Friedrich II shown at the Berlin Academy in 1797. An extraordinary arch was built on the Alter Markt in Potsdam for the entry of the Bavarian Princess Elisabeth, bride of Crown Prince Friedrich Wilhelm, in 1823 [22.5]. Elaborately Gothic, it had three openings contained within a broad pointed arch. Between them rose tall pinnacles which framed the inscription. In the upper part a series of pinnacled Gothic aedicules culminated in a square pavilion.[18] For the coronation procession of Friedrich Wilhelm IV an 'arch' was built in the form of a tall square tent, with square piers at the corners, all decorated with flags and garlands. On top was a square 'tower' for musicians.[19]

In 1759, a year after the death of Wilhelmine, Markgräfin von Brandenburg-Bayreuth, her widower Friedrich married Sophie Karoline of Brunswick. To celebrate, Gontard designed a triumphal arch for the end of the canal in the garden at Bayreuth, for a firework display. It was a slender triple structure, the four Ionic columns decorated with twisted foliage. Over the rectangular side openings were reliefs, with chandeliers hanging below. The attic had statues and reliefs, and on top was a large sun. Balustraded steps led up to the arch.[20]

A splendid arch gateway was built in Heidelberg in 1775–81 to show the thanks of the town to Kurfürst Karl Theodor. Its cost led to complaints [22.6]. The architect was Nicolas de Pigage, and the sculptor Peter Simon Lamine. Four freestanding Doric columns support an attic above which are, on the inner side, the arms of the Kurfürst, and on the outer side portraits of him and his wife – on both sides with lions. What gives this large arch its great presence is the addition of curved pieces at the sides, of rusticated masonry, beyond which are further, lower extensions.

22.6 Heidelberg, 1775–81. Nicolas de Pigage.

The Napoleonic period saw designs made for arches. Eustache de Saint-Far proposed one for the entry to what was then called the Pont des Victoires at Mainz in 1807.[21] Another was built at Düsseldorf for the entry of Napoleon in 1811. It was a smaller version of the Arc de Triomphe de l'Étoile, with sculptural groups on either side of the opening, and smaller ones above.[22] The Königstor at Stuttgart, which had been built in 1807 for King Friedrich by Nikolaus Friedrich von Thouret, and dedicated in 1810, provided a setting for Crown Prince Wilhelm's entry after he had led the Württemberg troops against Napoleon. It had channelled masonry and a pair of Ionic columns. The trophies flanking the pediment on top came from the Baroque Esslinger Tor. After the Königstor was demolished in 1922 they were set up in the railway station, but they were destroyed in 1944.[23]

The plan for Munich by Fischer and Sckell envisaged the replacement of the medieval gates with triumphal arches. In 1812 Andreas Gärtner designed one as a new Schwabinger Tor at the northern entrance. It was a triple arch, with plenty of sculpture.[24] In 1816 King Ludwig I consulted Leo von Klenze about the erection of a Propylaion in Greek style at the northern end of the new Ludwigstrasse. By 1826 he had decided to build a 'Siegestor' in the form of a Roman triumphal arch. Already in 1819 Gustav Vorherr had designed one to honour the memory of Maximilian I, to stand at the eastern entrance to the town, but this remained unexecuted. Finally in 1840 the commission for the Siegestor was given to Friedrich von Gärtner (son of Andreas)

GERMANY AND AUSTRIA FROM THE SIXTEENTH TO THE NINETEENTH CENTURY

[22.7]. It was begun in 1843; by the time it was completed in 1852 Gärtner was dead and Ludwig had abdicated. The model was the Arch of Constantine, but the Siegestor is lighter and more slender. The sculptor was the elderly Johann Martin von Wagner. As he lived in Rome, he sent models to be executed in marble, or, in the case of the *quadriga*, iron, by local sculptors. The statues over the columns, and the reliefs in the spandrels, represent Victories. The rectangular reliefs over the side openings show battles from Bavarian history, while the circular reliefs on the attic bear emblems of the Bavarian provinces. On the *quadriga*, the four lions are driven by the figure of Bavaria. The arch was completed by Gärtner's pupil Eduard Metzger, who produced a design in 1852 for a 'Forum' to surround the arch, with a statue-crowned column and a low *quadrifrons* on either side. This was not executed. The south side of the arch was badly damaged in World War II, and was not fully restored, a new inscription being added: *Dem Sieg geweiht, im Krieg zerstört, zum Frieden mahnend* ('Dedicated to victory, destroyed in war, exhorting to peace').[25]

It is not surprising that imperial Berlin at the end of the nineteenth century should have seen proposals for arches. An example was an entry by an unknown architect for the competition for the Reichstagsgebäude held in 1882, which included a huge arch with pairs of Corinthian columns flanking equestrian statues, more statues over the columns, and a *quadriga* on top.[26] Another competition was held in 1888–9 for a National monument to Kaiser Wilhelm I. A number of entries included variations on the triumphal arch, including one by the sculptor Reinhold Begas. Several by Adolf

22.7 Munich, Siegestor, 1843–52. Friedrich von Gärtner.

Hildebrand included one with the statue enclosed within a huge arched opening in a square structure: on each side was a triumphal arch with pilasters and sculpture groups above. Three simpler designs had the statue framed in the central opening of a triple arch.[27]

Temporary arches were also erected. These included one at Karlsruhe for the jubilee of the Grossherzog in 1885. Designed by Götz, it was light yellow and gold, and had pairs of pilasters with very fanciful freestanding columns between them, a dome on the attic, and lavish decoration.[28] A large but not quite so fanciful one greeted the Kaiser at Düsseldorf in 1891. Designed by J. Kleesattel, it had groups of sculpture (by Buscher) in front of pedimented aedicules on the piers, and a dome on top bearing a crown, which was lit up. Although it got in the way of traffic, it remained standing for eight days.[29]

In 1912 Hildebrand designed a memorial to Kaiser Wilhelm I for Lübeck. He produced three drawings which he described as taking the form of a triumphal arch, with the Emperor shown on horseback in relief in a panel over the central opening. It remained unexecuted.[30]

Austria

It is not surprising that many arches were erected in Austria, mostly in honour of emperors. The earliest were six at Innsbruck and seven at Schwaz in the Tirol erected for Charles V in 1530.[31] Three greeted Maximilian II on his return to Vienna from his coronation at Frankfurt in 1563. Engravings, entries in accounts, and a description by Wolfgang Lazius, who was responsible for the programme (published in Vienna in 1563), give details. The iconography clearly derived from the engraved arch of Maximilian I by Dürer. A number at Graz included seven in 1571 for the marriage of Archduke Karl to Maria of Bavaria.

In 1577 the Emperor Rudolf II entered Breslau (now Wrocław) in Silesia. The triumphal arch erected for the occasion is shown in an engraving by Johannes Twenger. It was a triple arch, with pairs of Corinthian half-columns on each pier. Over the side openings were female figures in niches. On the attic were reliefs flanking the inscription, and on top was a pedimented pavilion for musicians, as well as a pair of armed men holding banners. Later that year Rudolf made his first entry into Vienna as emperor, and was greeted with two arches. They were supervised by Paulus Fabritius, the imperial astronomer and physician, who wrote an account of them. He tells us that the city fathers were excited by the Breslau example. The principal artists of the first arch were Mathias Monmacher, Hans Mont and Bartholomäus Spranger, all of whom had worked in Italy for the Pope. Spranger asked the Netherlandish painter Karel van Mander, who was working in Krems, to come and help. The first arch, on the Bauernmarkt, had statues of Maximilian II and Rudolf II flanking the opening. Below these were large stone globes which rotated to reveal inscriptions. There were also representations of the cardinal virtues, above which were scenes from ancient history exemplifying each. On top were statues of Pegasus, Neptune and Athena. On the back were statues of Jupiter and Hercules. There were coats of arms, inscriptions and poems. On the columns was a device (probably an armillary sphere with a clock) which showed the time in all the places lying on the same parallel as Vienna – just the sort of thing to appeal to Rudolf. The second arch was 'suburban'. It was made by the painter Jacob Maier, with the imperial carpenters Anton and Georg Haas, among others. On the Danube side were paintings of the Mediterranean and Europe, the latter able to bend her head and knees to Rudolf as he passed. On the back Austria, a maiden on whose body were shown the lands of Austria, could do the same. On top was the double-headed eagle. There were, again, poems and inscriptions. Thomas DaCosta Kaufmann considers that the arches' 'Copernican message and mechanisms usher in a new era', and that for Fabritius they represent 'the culmination or combination of many of his talents and interests'.[32]

Innsbruck put up three arches in 1582 for the marriage of Archduke Ferdinand with Katharina Gonzaga, and one in 1592 for the feast of Corpus Christi. When Archduke Ferdinand returned from university to Graz in 1595 to assume rule over inner Austria, the Jesuits erected an arch in front of their college. For the entry of King Matthias into Vienna in 1608, after extending his rule over Hungary and Bohemia, ten arches were built. The first was put up by the merchant Lazarus Henckl in his garden. Other towns erecting arches for imperial occasions in this period include Linz and Enns.

At Salzburg in 1612 an arch welcomed the new archbishop. Religious occasions predominated there, as when in 1624 two arches were built for the opening of the sarcophagus of St Erentrudis; on one stood a boy dressed as an angel, while the other had portraits of the founders of the Benedictine convent. Five were erected in 1628 for the translation of the relics of SS. Rupert and Virgilius. One was a triple arch with an attic which rose up to a pedimented aedicule: bishops stood in niches on either side of the central opening, and seven more stood on top. Similarly at Graz in 1640 six arches were put up for the centenary of the Jesuit college, but they were destroyed by a storm the night before the celebration.

An arch erected at Innsbruck to welcome Herzog Karl von Lothringen as governor in 1679 was still standing in 1686, when a painter altered the 'emblems' for a new occasion. The arch had an astonishing quantity of weapons and standards above the attic, with figures seated on cannons. In 1682 the eleventh centenary of the rule of St Rupert was celebrated at Salzburg with five large and lavishly fanciful arches and several smaller ones. The one for Archbishop Luipram had many columns, on two levels; such temple-like designs suited the ecclesiastical origin. For the return to Vienna of Leopold and Eleonor with the newly crowned King Joseph in 1690 two arches were built by the city and the foreign merchants. Both were designed by Johann Bernhard Fischer von Erlach. The former was a triple arch, with pairs of free-standing columns on either side of the main opening, while the side openings were recessed and had pairs of columns standing at their sides. Over the centre was another arched opening framing a *quadriga*, driven by Joseph, and flanked by piers with openings, the whole decorated with masses of sculpture and standards. The merchants' arch was also triple. Above the low side openings were tall columns decorated with reliefs. Between them was a large globe on which sat Joseph, as sun god, with statues of the imperial couple. In 1699 the wedding of Joseph I and Wilhelmina Amalia was celebrated with three arches at Vienna. Those of the city and the foreign merchants were again designed by Fischer von Erlach. The latter had openings supported on atlantes, with pairs of freestanding columns set at an angle beyond each. Within was a domed circular space. Above was a tempietto containing an equestrian statue among clouds and putti.[33] Haselberger-Blaha[34] sees the

22.8 J.B. Fischer von Erlach, Pons Milvius, *Entwurff*, 1721.

influence of Hagia Sophia, which Fischer had studied, and emphasises the Classicistic character, which shows an advance from the Roman Baroque arches of 1690. The third arch was attributed to J. L. von Hildebrandt.

In his *Entwurff einer historischen Architectur* of 1721 Fischer von Erlach illustrated reconstructions of the arches of Drusus, Septimius Severus and Domitian, and the arch at Orange, as well as an arch supposed to have been built on the Pons Milvius in honour of Augustus [22.8]: this is a *quadrifrons*, with a *quadriga* drawn by a pair of elephants facing the city.

Fewer arches were built in the eighteenth century. Most were again for imperial occasions, such as the entry to Innsbruck of Karl Philipp von Lothringen as governor in 1707. The grandest of the three was designed by Johann Martin Gumpp, an immensely rich affair with pairs of banded columns on the piers, and columned aedicules above these, which framed a large niche containing an equestrian statue. On top was a relief between obelisks. At the sides were curving walls with yet more elaborate sculpture.[35] There were also three to celebrate the sixth centenary of the monastery of Klosterneuburg in 1714.

When in 1736 Duke Franz Stephan of Lorraine married Maria Theresa, daughter of Emperor Charles VI, he recovered the imperial crown for the house of Habsburg-Lorraine. Vienna welcomed him after his election as Holy Roman Emperor in 1745 with three arches. One, erected by the merchants, was designed by Franz Rosenstingl, a second, erected by the 'artisans of the court', was designed by Giuseppe Galli Bibiena, and the third, that of the magistrates, was by Franz Anton Danne. This was 27 m high and astonishingly elaborate. At the top the imperial couple rode in a gilded chariot drawn by eagles.[36] Danne also designed the arch to welcome back Joseph II in 1764. This was surmounted by a circular tempietto sheltering a seated statue of the

GERMANY AND AUSTRIA FROM THE SIXTEENTH TO THE NINETEENTH CENTURY

22.9 Innsbruck, arch for Archduke Leopold, 1765. Konstantin Walter.

Emperor.[37] Two arches welcomed Leopold II to Vienna in 1790, though it was a sign of the times that he had the money collected for arches used for the dowries of forty poor peasant girls.

A particularly fine permanent arch was built at Innsbruck in 1765 [22.9]. It was intended to celebrate the marriage of Archduke Leopold, second son of Maria Theresa and Franz Stephan, but when the latter died during the festivities the arch was given a double function, the south (outer) side for the wedding, the north side mourning the deceased Emperor. Freestanding columns flank the central opening. The designer was the military architect Konstantin Walter, and the original sculptor was Johann Baptist Hagenauer, but his stuccoes were replaced in marble by Baltasar Ferdinand Moll. His elegantly Classical work recalls that of his master, Georg Raphael Donner. There are relief panels, and on top two females, one seated and one standing, hold reliefs with portraits of the bridal pair on one side and the dead man on the other.

At the Weltausstellung held in Vienna in 1873, the Industriepalast, designed by Karl Hasenauer (the ironwork by the naval architect John Scott Russell) had four gateways in the form of triumphal arches; the southern one was the grandest, with sculptural decoration designed by Ferdinand Laufberger.[38] An arch near the Kunstgebäude in the Prater was designed by Heinrich Ferstel and built by the Wienerberger Ziegelfabriks- und Baugesellschaft brick company. A conventional triple arch, it was decorated with much terracotta sculpture, including roundels over the side openings, a pediment over the central one, reliefs on the attic, and griffins supporting the imperial arms on an upper central attic.[39]

Notes

1. Rainer Schoch et al., *Albrecht Dürer: Das druckgraphische Werk* (Munich/Berlin/London/New York, 2002), II, 389–412 (cat. 238); Jochen Sander, ed., *Dürer: his Art in Context* (Munich/London/New York, 2014), 320–25.
2. Peter Seewaldt, ed., *Das Grabdenkmal des Christoph von Rheineck: ein Trierer Monument der Frührenaissance im Zentrum memorialer Stiftungspolitik* (Trier, 2000). For the use of the triumphal arch in tombs, see Hans-Christoph Dittscheid, 'Vom Heiligen Grab zur Anastasis: typologische, ikonographische und stylistische Aspekte zur Triumphbogenarchitektur des Grabdenkmals', ibid., 55–68.
3. Barbara Dienst, *Der Kosmos des Peter Flötner* (Munich, 2002), 403–4.
4. Fritz Löffler, *Das alte Dresden* (Dresden, 1955), 348–9, pl. 35. On Mosca Padovano, who was based in Krakow, see *Dictionary of Art*, 22, 167–8.
5. Werner Broda, *Dreiecks-Verhältnisse: Architektur- und Ingenieurzeichnungen aus vier Jahrhunderten* (Nuremberg, 1996), 28, 153.
6. Frances A. Yates, *The Rosicrucian Enlightenment* (London, 1986), 9–10. Engravings of these arches by Theodore De Bry were published in *Beschreibung der Reiss … des Herrn Friederichen dess Fünften … mit der Princessin Elisabethen* ([Heidelberg], 1613).
7. Michael Krapf, *Die Baumeister Gumpp* (Vienna/Munich, 1979), 25, 147, pl. 190.
8. Hans-Joachim Giersberg, *Friedrich als Bauherr* (Berlin, 1986), 194.
9. Giersberg (cit. in the preceding note), 193–4.
10. Günther Schiedlausky, 'Berliner Ehrenpforte 1701', *Jahrbuch der Preussischen Kunstsammlungen*, 56 (1935), 131–44. He discusses two designs for arches by De Bodt, but their destination is unknown; likewise a simpler design by an unknown hand, on top of which a statue of a king stands above seated figures.
11. Giersberg (cit. at n. 8), 195–6. He does not believe that the engraving of 1733 by J.B. Broebes can accurately represent the arch.
12. See the comparative engraving reproduced in ibid., 188.
13. ibid., 201–6.
14. ibid., 207–14.
15. ibid., 220–22.
16. ibid., 196–7.
17. ibid., 197–8.
18. ibid., 199–200.
19. Hans Martin von Erffa, 'Ehrenpforte', in *Reallexicon zur deutschen Kunstgechichte*, IV (Stuttgart, 1958), 1498. This article gives other examples of German arches (1445–1504).
20. Broda (cit. at n. 5), 144–5.
21. Philippe Prost, *Les forteresses d'Empire* (Paris, 1991), 132.
22. Julie Rosenthal, 'For Freedom's Battle': Heinrich Heine in England* (London, 1998), 42, ill. 6.
23. Gustav Wais, *Alt-Stuttgarts Bauten im Bild* (Stuttgart, 1951), 143–8.
24. Oswald Hederer, *Friedrich von Gärtner* (Munich, 1976), 252–3.
25. Hederer (cit. in the preceding note), 149–55; Ingeborg Kader, ed., *Das Münchner Siegestor – echt antik?* (Munich, 2000).
26. Elke Blauert et al., *Alfred Messel 1853–1909, Visionär der Grossstadt* (Berlin, 2009), 183.
27. Alfred Gotthold Meyer, *Reinhold Begas* (Bielefeld/Leipzig, 1901), 99–126; Sigrid Esche-Braunfels, *Adolf von Hildebrand* (Berlin, 1993), 473–5. See also the design by Wilhelm Rettig and Paul Pfann ill. in *Deutsche Bauzeitung*, 23 (1889).
28. J. Stübben, 'Der Städtebau', in *Handbuch der Architektur*, pt 4, 9 (Darmstadt, 1890), 431. He calls the arch 'an example of the best sort' of festal decoration. This chapter (430–38) is on 'Der Festschmuck'.
29. *Deutsche Bauzeitung*, 25 (1891), 317, 322. Other arches were erected by the guilds and the industrialists.
30. Esche-Braunfels (cit. at n. 27), 345–6.
31. A list of arches erected in Austria up to the year 1800 is given by Herta Haselberger-Blaha, 'Die Triumphtore Fischers von Erlach', *Wiener Jahrbuch für Kunstgeschichte*, 17 (1956), 72–85.
32. Thomas DaCosta Kaufmann, *The Mastery of Nature* (Princeton, 1993), 136–50.
33. The arch is illustrated in Fischer von Erlach's *Entwurff einer historischen Architectur* (Leipzig, 1721), bk IV, pl. I.
34. Haselberger-Blaha (cit. at n. 31), 81–2.
35. Michael Krapf, *Die Baumeister Gumpp* (Vienna/Munich, 1979), 313–14.
36. Danne's drawing is in the Albertina in Vienna.
37. Danne's drawing is in the Staatliche Museen zu Berlin. He also designed an arch for Joseph's wedding in 1760.
38. Renate Wagner-Rieger, *Wiens Architektur im 19. Jahrhundert* (Vienna, 1970), 152.
39. ibid., 187.

23

CENTRAL AND EASTERN EUROPE

Poland

In 1646 Marie-Louise de Gonzague-Nevers arrived at Gdansk on her way from France after marrying King Ladislaus IV Vasa, and was greeted with three arches. The single opening of the grandest had winged figures in the spandrels holding garlands, beneath a gallery. On the piers were pairs of elaborate columns projecting from double pilasters; between these were niches with royal figures [23.1]. Over the opening the attic had a term and a caryatid supporting a broken pediment. On the eastern side was a painting by Adolf Boy between a term and a caryatid, which showed the royal couple being crowned by Hymen. On top was a symbolic female with a winged child, and on the slopes of the pediment were a woman riding an elephant and another riding a horse. Two more symbolic statues stood at the ends of the cornice. On the gallery appeared figures representing Apollo, Diana and the Muses, who sang a Latin eulogy. The arch was made by G. Münch to the design of the Gdansk builder Wilhelm Richter and C. Roth.[1] The other two arches were designed by the engraver Jeremias Falck. One had a pair of obelisks linked by garlands supporting an eagle, while the other had a pair of beefy atlantes holding up a rocky base above which was a model of the city, encircled by a rainbow.

The coronation procession of kings of Poland, from the late sixteenth century, went through the old city of Cracow to the Cathedral on the hill of the Wawel, and the so-called 'Via Regia' was decorated with triumphal arches.[2] For the entry of Zygmunt III in 1587 an arch at the approach from Podgórze to the river Vistula was decorated with wreaths and tapestries. The Florianska Gate was enclosed within an arch of boughs, tapestries and paintings. In the city were 'several elegantly constructed arches in a

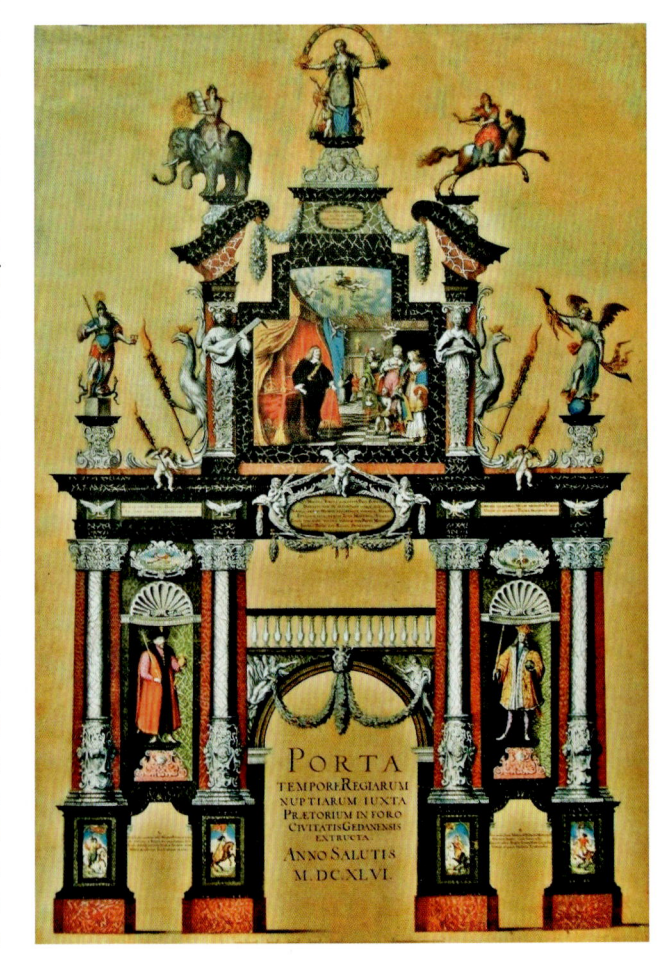

23.1 Gdansk, arch for Marie-Louise de Gonzague-Nevers, 1646. Wilhelm Richter and C. Roth.

row', displaying images of his Jagiellonian ancestors in reverse order, beginning with Zygmunt and ending with Jagiello, whose arch was at the entrance to the citadel. These portraits were taken from 'ancient monuments'. Inscriptions made it appear that the King was being advised by his ancestors.[3]

The powerful Polish nobility liked to adopt royal customs, and this included triumphal arches erected for their funerals, said to be in accordance with the traditions of ancient Rome. An example was that of the Crown Chancellor Jan Zamoyski, who died in 1605.[4]

The decline of Cracow was reflected in 1669, when Michal Korybut Wisiowiecki had been elected King; the guilds and citizens of Cracow asked the magistrate to build arches as cheaply as possible to show respect to the many poor people, even though the building of ephemeral structures could provide employment, and several of the arches were made of recycled materials. In Gdansk ephemeral architecture was stored in the arsenal.[5] The rich merchants of the city, especially the foreigners, helped to pay for the arches and fireworks.[6] An engraving of the entry of Jan III Sobieski into Cracow seven years later shows a triple arch.[7]

In 1677 Jan III Sobieski visited Gdansk for political negotiations, and his entry was marked with triumphal arches. One of these consisted of two pyramids, one with Turkish arms on it and one with Polish arms. In front of the King's House stood a triple arch with attached Corinthian columns, which had paintings between them, and oval ones above. On the keystone an angel lowered a crown. Side sections under the same entablature ended with obelisks. The central attic had an open arch framing a statue, with arms above.[8] A modest but permanent arch commemorating Jan III's victory of 1683 at Vienna stands at Podzamcze Chechinskie near Kielce. It has pairs of free-standing Corinthian columns, and an attic over the opening with smaller columns, a niche, and a broken pediment above. August II 'the Strong', elected King of Poland in 1697, came to Cracow for his coronation, and a 'small triumphal arch' was set up at the Skalka Church where he venerated the tomb of St Stanislas.[9] In 1734 August's son succeeded him, as August III. Elected in Cracow in January, in November he entered Warsaw, where a large but comparatively plain arch greeted him [23.2]. It was triple, and the broad pilasters had banded rustication. Over the central opening were coats of arms, and over the side ones paintings 'by a famous painter'. The attic had an inscription between garlanded panels. The top of the arch, crowded with spectators, had an eagle in the centre and four on each side. Within the central opening, below a 'golden ceiling', were two paintings, one showing the spirit of Warsaw, with other symbolic figures, and the other Neptune pouring out the water of the Vistula.[10]

The wings added in 1720–29 to the Palace of Wilanow by Elzbieta Sienieawska, to the design of Giovanni Spazzio, have triumphal arches in the centre of each.

In 1764 Stanislaw August Poniatowski was elected and crowned king. Along the side of the Castle Square in Warsaw a screen was erected, with a triumphal arch in the centre, which had pairs of columns on the piers, and an obelisk above with the King's portrait, and an eagle on top. There were two statues on either side.[11] In 1777 Efraim Schroeger (or Szreger) made a grandiose design for the same square in Warsaw, to be entered by a plain Neoclassical arch, with winged figures in the spandrels, oval portrait reliefs on each pier, and a central attic flanked by lions.[12] Another design for an arch in that square was made in 1781 by Jakub Kubicki, who in that year was appointed

CENTRAL AND EASTERN EUROPE   349

23.2 Warsaw, entry of August III, 1734. Painting by Johann Samuel Mock, Dresden.

23.3 Triumphal gate designed by Jakub Kubicki erected in 1809 in the Three Crosses Square in Warsaw.

architect to the King – an elaborate scheme with a screen on each side, and much sculpture, including an equestrian statue of the King over the attic. Above the screens were smoking urns, with smoking obelisks above the end sections.[13] It was also Kubicki who designed the arch with which the grateful citizens of Warsaw welcomed back the army after its successful campaign in support of the French in 1809 [23.3]. It stood on Trzech Krzyzy (Three Crosses) Square. Within the opening the archivolt was supported on Ionic columns. There were reliefs on the piers, and over the central attic an eagle with flags. On each side of this were trophies. Low walls linked the arch to columns topped with *fasces*.[14] Three years earlier four arches had been erected in Poznan to welcome Napoleon. The arch put up for him in Slesin survives, though damaged by a drunk crane-driver.

A watercolour of 1831 by Joseph Kornhäusel in the Cooper-Hewitt Museum in New York shows an arch for Jan Zygmunt Skrzynecki, Commander in Chief of the November Uprising in 1830.

The arches in the gardens of Jablonna, Powazki and Wilanow are described in the discussion of arches as garden features (p. 283).

The Hatzfeld Palace in Wrocław was largely destroyed in 1945, but the splendid porch survives, in the form of a triumphal arch [23.4]. The four freestanding Composite columns are matched by pilasters behind. The rectangular side entries have busts

23.4 Wroclaw, Hatzfeld Palace, 1764. I. Genevale.

above in circular frames. On top is a balustrade. The building was erected in 1764 to the design of I. Genevale.

Tsar Alexander II was welcomed to Warsaw in 1867 with a peculiar triple arch, in a kind of Gothic, largely transparent.

Polish independence in 1918 was celebrated in Warsaw with a rather amateurish arch with flags and inscriptions. A more sophisticated design (in the National Museum) was made in 1920–22 by the distinguished architect Stanislav Noakowski. It has statues around the base, while the upper parts of the piers are set back; the attic has a large cartouche in the centre.[15] (For Noakowski's design for an arch in honour of Marshal Foch, see p. 422.)

A large arch, the Brama Helenowna, was built as entrance to the new barracks at Molodeczno (now Maladzyechna in Belarus) in 1929. It commemorated the tenth anniversary of the 86th Regiment and the heroes fallen in defence of the Minsk region. It was a large triple arch, the side openings small, with reliefs of weapons above. Statues of soldiers flanked the opening at ground level. The attic had an inscription and more reliefs, and another statue on top. There was a colonnade on either side. Strangely, on the reverse of the attic was a semicircular opening, with a chapel within, where the chaplain said Mass for the troops below. The arch was demolished in the 1960s.

A triumphal arch formed part of Ivan Mestrovic's design for a monument to Marshal Jozef Pilsudski. On the Marshal's death in 1935 a committee was set up to plan the monument, which was to be sited in Plac na Rozdrozu, in southern Warsaw. A competition in 1936, open only to Polish artists, reached no conclusion, and a second limited competition ensued. Gustav Vigeland, Aristide Maillol and Mestrovic were invited to compete, but only Mestrovic did so, submitting a design in 1939. He proposed a bronze equestrian statue 25 m high, set in front of an arch 50 m high, which might have either one or three openings, decorated with statues of Victory. The War brought the project to a halt.[16]

Hungary

It is claimed that there is only one triumphal arch in Hungary, at Vác. Built to welcome Maria Theresa and her husband in 1764, it is fairly simple, but elegant. The attic has portrait reliefs of the imperial pair and the inscription *ETERNAE DOMUI* ('To the eternal house'). The designer was Isidor Canevale.[17] The Keleti Railway Station in Budapest (1881–4, by Gyula Rochlitz and János Feketeházy) has a huge arch on its façade, with niches on either side holding statues of James Watt and George Stephenson.[18]

Czech Republic

Hořice, in the north of Bohemia, is a town celebrated for its sculpture school. Its cemetery is entered by a magnificent triumphal arch of sandstone, 14.5 m high, built in 1892–1905, to the design of Antonín Cechner and Bohuslav Moravec [23.5]. Pairs of freestanding Composite columns flank the opening, within which the archivolt is supported on smaller columns. In the spandrels are flying angels. Above the columns are cartouches, while on the attic the Angel of Peace seated on a sarcophagus extends its arms in welcome. The sculptor was Moric Cernil. Projections at the sides

23.5 Horice, cemetery gateway, 1892–1905. Antonin Cechner and Bohuslav Moravec.

23.6 Johann Jelinek (1877–1918), 'Erection of a triumphal arch', presumably in his homeland, Moravia.

are surmounted by balustrades, with statues of Death and Resurrection by Quido Kocian at the corners.

The famous brewery at Pilsen (Plzen) is entered by a grand triumphal gateway, dated 1892. It has twin openings, and a coat of arms above.

The Moravian painter Johann Jelinek (1877–1918) painted a charming picture of children 'erecting a triumphal arch' on a country street [23.6]. A simple frame is decorated with greenery.

Ukraine

A very jolly porch was built as the entrance to the Cathedral of SS. Peter and Paul at Kamianets-Podilskyi in 1781, for a visit by the Polish King Stanislaw August Poniatowski. Of white stone, it was designed by the 'city masters'. There are pairs of pilasters, and above these are pedestals bearing statues of putti, while in the centre is a kind of Baroque tempietto with a statue of a saint above.

In 1821 Prince Victor Kochubey built an arch on his estate at Dykanka to celebrate the Russian victory over Napoleon, and for a visit by Alexander I. It has four attached Doric columns and an attic. The destroyed palace here was by Quarenghi.

An arch was built in Lviv for the visit by Franz Josef to the General Regional Exhibition in 1894. Opposite the station, on the site of the arch put up for his visit in 1880, it was of stone, but soon demolished. An elaborately decorated double arch, it had a bust of the Emperor in the centre.

CENTRAL AND EASTERN EUROPE 353

Notes

1. Konstanty Kalinowski, ed., *Teatr i Mistyka* (Poznan, 1993), III, 55–6. The arch is also shown in an etching by Jeremias Falck, who signed himself 'Polonus' or 'Gedanensis'. On him see E. Iwanoyko, *Jeremiasz Falck Polonus* (Poznan, 1952), which illustrates (pl. 45) an accompanying dedication, with a group of turbaned captives.
2. Karin Friedrich, ed.,'Festivals in Poland-Lithuania from the sixteenth to the eighteenth century', in J.R. Mulryne et al., eds, *Europa Triumphans* (Aldershot, 2004), 371–462; for the procession, see 376–8. From 1526 the Hapsburgs ruled Breslau (now Wrocław); an arch was erected there for Rudolf II in 1577: see p. 343.
3. ibid., 399–407.
4. ibid., 384.
5. ibid., 390.
6. ibid., 387.
7. ibid., 380.
8. ibid., 435.
9. ibid., 441.
10. ibid., 447–9, and pl. 17 (a painting in Dresden by Johann Samuel Mock).
11. A. Rottermund, ed., *Artes et humaniora* (Warsaw, 1998), 355.
12. ibid., 363. See also Stanislaw Lorentz, *Efraim Szreger Architekt Polski XVIII Wieku* (Warsaw, 1986).
13. Stanislaw Lorentz and Andrzez Rottermund, *Neoclassicism in Poland* (Warsaw, 1986), 22.
14. Krystyna Sroczynska and Zygmunt Vogel, *Rysownik Gabinetowy Staninslawa Augusta* (Wrocław/Warsaw/Cracow, 1969), cat. 259, fig. 264.
15. *The Builder*, 122 (1922), 100.
16. Ewa Ziembinska in *Monument: Central and Eastern Europe 1918–2018,* exhibition in the Xawery Dunikowski Museum of Sculpture, Warsaw (2019), 8–13.
17. G. Kelényi, in D, Wiebenson and J. Sisa, *The Architecture of Historic Hungary* (Cambridge, Mass.,1998), 142–3.
18. Two other stations with triumphal arches were the Gare du Midi at Brussels (1869, Auguste Payen, demolished 1949), based on the Arch of Constantine, with a sculptural group on top, and the Hauptbahnhof at Zurich (1871, Jakob Friedrich Wanner). The so-called 'Euston Arch' built as the entrance to Euston Station by Philip Hardwick in 1837, was not an arch but a huge Greek Doric propylaeum. It was demolished in 1961. At the other end of the line at Birmingham is the Curzon Street 'arch', which has four free-standing Ionic columns.

24

RUSSIA AND MOLDOVA

Russia

Although royal entries were known in Russia from the sixteenth century, there seem to have been no arches built for them.[1] The earliest arches were erected in Moscow in the reign of Peter the Great, who as well as being much involved in military exploits was notable for his Europeanising tendencies. On his return from Turkey in 1696 he ordered a triumph on Roman lines. A wooden arch celebrated the taking of Azov: the central opening, within which hung two trumpeting angels, was flanked by pairs of Corinthian columns [24.1]. Above were a broken pediment, and a tall 'attic' containing a painting, with a smaller one above. On each side were screen walls with arched openings, more paintings, and obelisks above. The arch is described by Dimitri Shvidkovsky as 'the first direct appeal to Antiquity in Russian architectural history'.[2] (Peter had in his library a manuscript translation of the book on imperial triumphal arches by Giovanni Pietro Bellori, Pietro Santi Bartoli and Giovanni Giacomo Rossi, published

24.1 Moscow, arch for Peter the Great, 1696. Iwan Sarudny.

in Rome in 1690.) On the inscriptions and pictures Peter compared himself with Julius Caesar and Constantine. The arch was designed by Iwan Sarudny, as were two of the four built in 1710 to celebrate Peter's victory over the Swedes at Poltava in the previous year. One of these had pairs of Corinthian pilasters on either side of the opening, with paintings both between and below them. There was another painting over the opening, in a pedimented frame on which stood three figures.[3] In 1721, after the Peace of Nystad, four more arches were erected for Peter's entry. Two were designed by Sarudny, and two by Iwan Ustinow (who had been in Holland).[4] Also built under Peter were two permanent gates in the form of triumphal arches. The one known as Peter's Gate in the Peter-Paul fortification of St Petersburg was erected in wood by Domenico Trezzini in 1708, then rebuilt in stone in 1717–18. The opening is flanked by doubled pilasters, and the whole is covered in banded rustication. Over the opening is a large relief, with segmental pediment above. The relief, by Hans Konrad Osner, shows St Peter causing the fall of Simon Magus, while the statues of Bellona and Minerva in the niches (two surviving from eight) are attributed to Nicolas Pineau.[5] At Moscow the gate of the Arsenal in the Kremlin, built in 1715 by Tschoglokow and Iwanow, has its lower part in the form of a triumphal arch, with pairs of banded attached Doric columns flanking reliefs of weapons on each pier. The upper part has pilasters, a central window, and a pediment above.[6]

A private commission was an arch opposite the mansion of Prince Menshikov in Moscow. The architect was Ivan Petrovich Zarudnyi. It is shown in an engraving of 1710.[7]

In 1742 four wooden arches were set up in Moscow for the coronation of Elisabeth Petrowna. The Twersk Gate was designed by Prince Dmitri Uchtomski (though officially Korobow was named as architect); the Synodal Gate was by Mitschurin; and the Jausa Gate and the Beautiful Gate were designed by Michail Semzow, but built by Iwan Blank. They are known from engravings. The first had three openings flanked by pairs of Corinthian columns. Over the side ones were paintings, and there were pairs of statues above. Over the central opening was a broken pediment from which rose a semi-octagonal 'pavilion' framing another painting, with dome and crown above. In 1748 the Beautiful Gate burnt down, and Uchtomski rebuilt it in stone between 1753 and 1757. The form of the arch was roughly similar, with pairs of Composite columns breaking forward on the piers, and a tall central attic rising to a curved pedestal, hung with curtains, above which stood a trumpeting Fame. The decoration was quite different. The remarkable side elevations had pairs of pilasters set close together and linked by an arch, above which the entablature also arched.[8] The Beautiful Gate was demolished in 1927. By 1753 the Synodal Gate had more or less collapsed, and it was decided to decorate the Woskressenie Gate in a similar fashion. Uchtomski produced instead a design for a gate-cum-belltower consisting of four diminishing arches, one above the other. The lowest stage had piers projecting at angles, with pairs of freestanding columns on each side, and rich sculptural decoration. The next stage was similar but smaller, while the upper two reduced the schema even further.[9]

In 1763–5 Savva Chevakinsky made designs for 'New Holland', a depot for shipbuilding timber in St Petersburg, but those for the façade were rejected, and Jean-Baptiste Vallin de la Mothe was commissioned to design it: his entrance took the

24.2 St Petersburg, New Holland, 1763–5. Jean-Baptiste Vallin de la Mothe.

form of a handsome Doric triumphal arch spanning the canal entrance [24.2]. Pairs of stout columns stand forward of the piers, and smaller columns support the arch in the opening. The brickwork remained unplastered.[10] The same architect designed St Catherine's Catholic Church, built in 1762–83: its façade takes the form of a triumphal arch, with pairs of pilasters framing the side doors, while the central one is recessed within an arched opening supported on columns. Above the powerful entablature are windows on either side, and statues on the parapet.[11]

The military and political successes of the reign of Catherine the Great were celebrated with arches. For the Gatchina Gates at Tsarskoe Selo, see the chapter on 'Arches as Features of Parks and Landscape Gardens' (pp. 281–2). After the Russian victory over the Turks in 1774, fourteen obelisks were set up at the southern edge of Moscow. From there the troops of Count Pyotr Rumyantsev marched through two triumphal arches to the city centre.[12] In 1776 Prince Potemkin made an inspection tour of Novgorod, and arches welcomed him everywhere.[13] In 1780 Catherine herself, on her way to meet Joseph II, entered Mozilev through an arch.[14] In 1787 Catherine and Joseph together entered Ekaterinoslav 'through an arch emblazoned with an unmistakable challenge to the Sublime Porte: "This is the road to Byzantium."'[15]

RUSSIA AND MOLDOVA

Meanwhile, back in St Petersburg, Catherine decided in 1780 to build an 'honorary gate' on the road to Moscow. She first intended to commission Charles-Louis Clérisseau, but then gave the job to Giacomo Quarenghi, who proposed a simplified version of the Arch of Titus. He then produced a design for a square propylaeum with sixteen equidistant columns, and a pavilion on either side. Neither design was executed.[16] When Potemkin returned to St Petersburg in 1787, Catherine realised that she had erected an arch to Orlov, and a monument to Rumysantsev, but nothing for him. Orlov had by now ceased to be her favourite, so she ordered that the Triumphal Gates at Tsarskoe Selo should be illuminated and decorated with naval and army arms, and a banner inscribed with verses from an ode by the court poet Petrov which told Potemkin 'You enter with splashing waves into Sophia's temple' – a reference to Hagia Sophia in Istanbul.[17] A more substantial tribute was an archway on the approach to Charles Cameron's Baths.[18] In 1792 Catherine was planning a Temple of Memory in the 'little forest' at Tsarskoe Selo, which would be approached 'through Triumphal Gates where all the previous actions in the current war will be represented on medallions'. A design by Cameron survives: the medallions, suspended from eagles and framed by garlands, are on the piers between pairs of fluted Doric columns. Above the plain attic are four statues. The arch was attached to an Ionic colonnade decorated with statues and reliefs.[19]

Quarenghi made yet more unexecuted designs for an arch to commemorate the Russian victory over Turkey, which included the annexation of the Crimea in 1783. One shows a standard type with pairs of attached Corinthian columns flanking panels with oval inscription tablets. The entablature projects over the end columns and the opening. On top is a double-headed eagle, and on either side is a rostral column. The inscription describes Catherine as entering 'the temple of Sofia'. A much more lavish design of 1791 for a rectangular *quadrifrons* has pairs of projecting columns on all four sides, those on the shorter sides linked, and pairs of columns flanking the shorter passageway. Beneath the columns on the short sides are equestrian statues, and the immensely tall attic bears seated statues and a *quadriga* driven by Catherine on top. A third design is for a triple arch decorated with reliefs.[20]

The 'Stone Island Palace' (Kamenoostrovskij Dvorec) in St Petersburg was built in 1776–81 for Catherine's son Paul. In about 1810 it was given a handsome gateway in the form of a simple but powerful triumphal arch. Pairs of stumpy Doric columns, their lower parts with square banding, stand against rusticated piers. The opening has emphatic keystones. The architect is thought to have been Jean-François Thomas de Thomon.[21]

Paul I wanted to commemorate the campaigns in Italy and Switzerland in 1799 under the command of General A.V. Suvorov, and several designs for arches by Quarenghi seem to relate to this idea. One drawing, at Bergamo, is for a broad structure which has a pedimented Doric aedicule, with rectangular opening, on either side of the central arched opening. Similar aedicules stand against the ends. Above each aedicule is a pair of roundels. Over the dentilled cornice is a gently sloping pyramidal roof. This design was approved, but yet again remained unexecuted because of the sudden death of the Emperor in 1814.[22] Two drawings by Quarenghi sold at Sotheby's New York in 2002 probably relate to the same commission. Both are Doric. One has pairs of columns with statues on bases between, and an attic with statues and reliefs,

24.3 St Petersburg, Narwa Gate, 1827–39. V.P. Stasov.

while the other is wider and has two free-standing columns in the broad rectangular opening. This one has a *sestiga* on top, driven by a Victory.[23]

Victory over Napoleon was celebrated in both St Petersburg and Moscow with great arches. The Narwa Triumphal Gate in St Petersburg was built in 1827–39 by V.P. Stasov, as a permanent version of the wooden arch built in 1814 by Quarenghi [24.3]. Stasov wrote that he did not think Quarenghi's design could be improved. Built of brick covered with metal plates, the arch has pairs of free-standing Corinthian columns on the piers and on the sides. In the niches are statues of ancient Russian warriors by S.S. Pimenow and W.I. Demut-Malinowski. Four statues stand on the attic, which is crowned with a *sestiga* by P.K. Klodt, driven by a Victory by Pimenow.[24] The Moscow arch, which stands near the Twer town gate, is remarkably similar. It was designed by O.I. Beauvais (or Bove). The columns, decoration and sculpture are all of cast iron, by I.P. Vitali and I.T. Timofejew, to the designs of Beauvais. Built in 1834, the arch was dismantled in 1936, but restored in 1966.[25]

Another triumphal gate at St Petersburg, the Moscow Gate, dates from 1834–8 and commemorates the Russian–Turkish War, but it is not an arch: it consist of two parallel ranks of Doric columns, of cast iron, with trophies on top.[26] Three grand public buildings in the same city incorporate arches. The Admiralty, by Andreyan Zakharov (1806–23) has as its centrepiece a triumphal arch beneath a tower and spire. The arch is decorated with flying Victories, and female figures holding heavenly and earthly globes, by Fyodor Shchedrin, and a long relief showing the creation of the Russian fleet by Ivan Terebenev.[27] The General Staff Building (Glavny Stab) of 1819–29 by Karl Rossi has a roadway running through the centre of its curved façade, which passes under a very broad archway, with winged figures in the spandrels [24.4]. The piers have pairs of Corinthian columns framing trophies and statues of warriors, while on top is a *sestiga* with a warrior holding the horse at each end. The statues and reliefs, in sheet copper, are again by Pimenow and Demut-Malinowski. Beyond stands another archway.[28] The Senate and Synod Building, also by Rossi, dates from 1829–34. Its façade is pierced by an archway which is flanked by freestanding pairs of Corinthian columns, and these in turn are flanked by windows, the upper ones arched, with further pairs of columns beyond. Above all the columns are winged figures, and the attic bears a long relief frieze. On top a stepped base supports figures of Justice and Piety. The same sculptors worked here, with several others.[29]

An earlier commemoration of the 'Patriotic War' at Novocherkassk, in 1817, took the form of a pair of identical arches, plastered and with bronze trophies on top. They were designed by Luigi Rusca.

The accession of Alexander I in 1801 was greeted at Irkutsk with a large arch. It was demolished in 1925 after earthquakes, but rebuilt a short distance away in 2011. It is rather overpowered by the elaborate attic.

24.4 St Petersburg, General Staff Building, 1819–29. Karl Rossi.

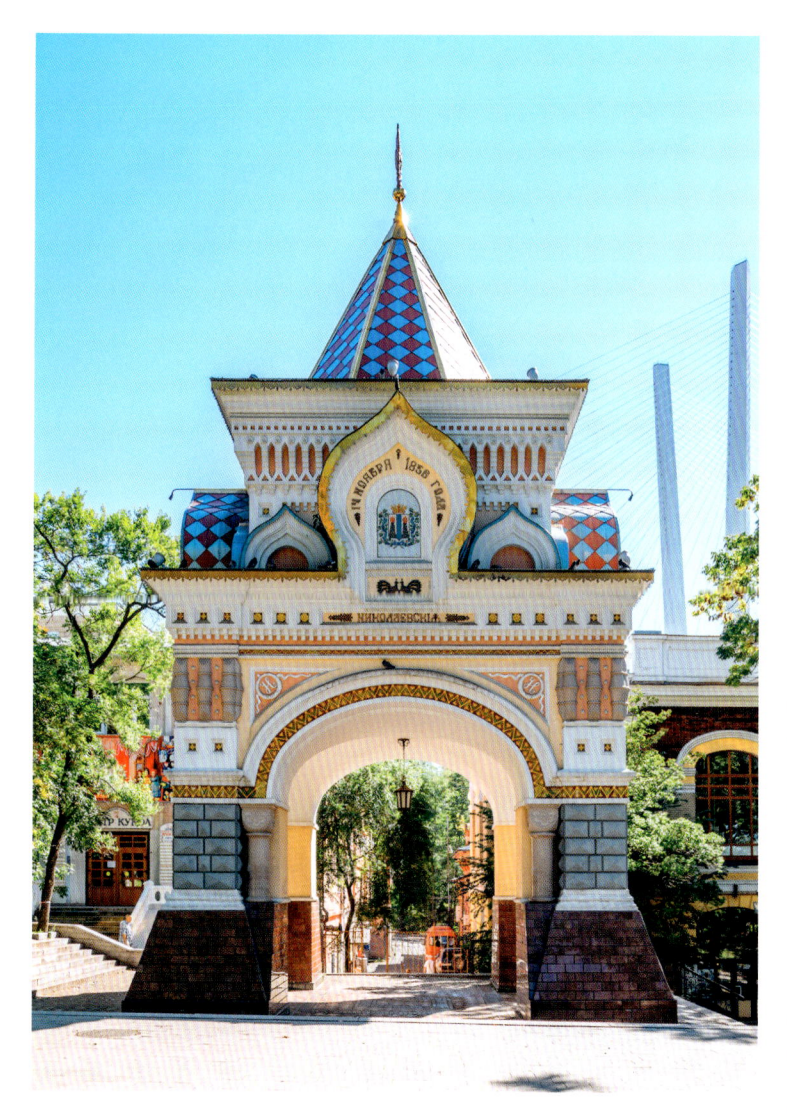

In 1821 Prince Sergei Galitzine built an elegant arch at Grebnevo, east of Moscow. It has four attached Doric columns and an attic.

An arch was built in 1859 as the entrance to the estate at Veskovo, northeast of Moscow, in honour of Peter the Great, who built his first boats on Lake Pleshcheyevo. The architect was Peter Campioni, of Moscow (others say Zherebtsov). The simple pilastered arch is surmounted by a trophy of arms.

Alexander III was welcomed to Krasnodar in 1888 with an elaborate brick arch in medieval Russian style. Demolished in 1928, it was rebuilt in 2008. Similarly three arches erected to welcome Crown Prince Nikolai in 1891 were destroyed under Communism. That at Blagoveshchensk, of familiar form, but with much fanciful decoration in 'Russian' style, was rebuilt in 2003–5. A jollier one at Vladivostok, in stone, was designed by Vladimir Konovalov [24.5]. Almost a parody of 'Russian' style, it was dismantled in 1936, and rebuilt in 1998–2003. The arch at Ulan Ude, in the Russian Far East, was rebuilt in 2006, in identical form, but larger. This was unfortunate as the arch is rather crude, with pairs of plain columns.

Simon Sebag Montefiore describes 'a hideous yellow triumphal arch of Soviet design' at the entrance to Potemkin Park in Dnieperpetrovsk (formerly Ekaterinoslav).[30] The Soviet attitude to the symbolism is shown by the decoration of a plate called 'Ride to Socialism', of 1927, by Zinaida Kobyletskaya. It shows factories with chimneys and Russian-style buildings in red, while at each side are buildings in Western styles, shown in grey, collapsing. One is a large triumphal arch.[31] The Propylaea built in Moscow as the entrance to the All Russia Exhibition Centre in 1935–9 take the form of a deconstructed triumphal arch. The central section, which projects slightly, has four square piers (which the side sections duplicate). In the middle is a plain arch, and above are a relief panel surmounted by bronze figures of a gesticulating couple. The opening of the Volga–Don Canal in 1952 was marked by the erection of a tall arch over the first lock at Volgograd. It has obelisk-shaped pilasters, and an attic crowned with trophies. As late as 1997–2000 an arch was built at Kursk to celebrate victory in the tank battle over the Germans in 1943. It bears statues of two Tsarist and two Soviet soldiers, and top is a flamboyant equestrian statue of St George.

24.5 Vladivostok, arch for Crown Prince Nikolai, 1891, demolished 1936, rebuilt 1998–2003.

Moldova

In the capital, Chisinau (Kischinjow), a bulky arch, known as the 'Holy Gates', stands at the entrance to the Cathedral Park. It was built in 1840 to commemorate the Russian–Turkish War: the designer is given as I.N. Sauschkewitsch, or Luca Zauschkevich. There are pairs of attached Corinthian columns on the piers on all four sides. The openings are rectangular. On the three sides above this the tall attic is pierced with an arch, while on the outer side there is a clock face. Within are three bells, the largest cast from trophy cannons. After the Second World War (the 'Great Patriotic War') marble tablets were set between the columns, the arch now being regarded as a symbol of that victory.[32] In the same city, the Republican Stadium, a Soviet structure, has a long façade with a triumphal arch-like centrepiece. The opening is rectangular, but is flanked by pairs of pilasters with pedimented panels of rustication framing niches. The tall attic has an inscription in the centre.[33]

Notes

1. Jean-Claude Roberti, *Fêtes et spectacles de l'ancienne Russie* (Paris, 1980), 75, 78.
2. Dimitri Shvidkovsky, *Russian Architecture and the West* (New Haven/London, 2007), 185.
3. I.E. Grabar, ed., *Geschichte der russischen Kunst*, V (Dresden, 1970), 36, 38.
4. ibid.
5. ibid, 68–9; *Bildhandbücher: Leningrad und Umgebung* (Munich, 1982), 2.
6. Grabar (cit. at n. 3), 25.
7. The engraving is in the Pushkin State Museum.
8. Shvidkovsky (cit. at n. 2), 199–202.
9. ibid., 203–5. There is some doubt about whether Uchtomski's scheme is really for this site.
10. *Bildhandbücher: Leningrad* (cit. at n. 5), 92; Shvidkovsky (cit. at n. 2), 233.
11. *Bildhandbücher* (cit. at n. 10), 145. After Vallin de la Mothe's return to France in 1775 the church was completed by Antonio Rinaldi.
12. D. Shvidkovsky, *The Empress and the Architect* (New Haven/London, 1996), 192.
13. Simon Sebag Montefiore, *Potemkin, Prince of Princes* (London, 2000), 177.
14. ibid., 248.
15. ibid., 410.
16. Sandro Angelini, ed., *Giacomo Quarenghi* (Bergamo, 1984), 164–5, figs 413, 431–2.
17. Shvidkovsky (cit. at n. 12), 103–4.
18. Dmitri Shvidkovskii, 'Cameron Discoveries', *Architectural Review*, 172 (Dec. 1982), 47.
19. Shvidkovsky (cit. at n. 12), 102–5. The building was demolished in 1797, on the order of Paul I. Isobel Rae (*Charles Cameron* (London, 1971), 63) claims that Cameron worked in the Crimea in the late 1780s, including the building of a triumphal arch, but Shvidkovsky states that Cameron never went there, and this shows a confusion with his assistant William Hastie.
20. Angelini (cit. at n. 16), 165–6, figs 413, 431–2.
21. *Bildhandbücher: Leningrad* (cit. at n. 5), 242.
22. Angelini (cit. at n. 16), cat. 218–9, figs 418, 419.
23. Sotheby's, New York, 25 Jan. 2002.
24. *Bildhandbücher: Leningrad* (cit. at n. 5), 227. Quarenghi's design is illustrated in Angelini (cit. at n. 16), fig. 77, together with a variant design almost identical with the second of the Sotheby drawings (fig. 79).
25. *Bildhandbücher: Moskau und Umgebung* (Munich, 1978), 178.
26. *Bildhandbücher: Leningrad* (cit. at n. 5), 225.
27. Shvidkovsky (cit. at n. 2), 299–301.
28. *Bildhandbücher: Leningrad* (cit. at n. 5), 64–8; Shvidkovsky (cit. at n. 2), 311-2.
29. Shvidkovsky (cit. at n. 2), 308–11.
30. Sebag Montefiore (cit. at n. 13), 306.
31. Tamara Kudryavtseva, *Circling the Square: Avant-Garde Porcelain from Revolutionary Russia* (London, 2004), cat. 46.
32. *Bildhandbücher: Ukraine und Moldawien* (Munich, 1985), 313.
33. A.L. Odud, *Kishinev* (Kishinev, 1964), 127.

25
SCANDINAVIA

The coronation of Christian IV of Denmark in 1596 was celebrated with a week of spectacles in Copenhagen. An arch was built in the Amager Market, concealed by boards until the great day. On each corner was a giant, two of them holding golden spears, and two flags. On the middle storey were trumpeters and drummers, while above were instrumentalists and singers. On the top were on one side a golden lion rampant, and on the other the arms of the Kingdom of Norway. Within the arch 'hovered a little angel with a gilt crown in his hands': as the King returned from the church the angel was lowered to present the crown to him.[1]

In Sweden, Eric XIV had an arch built in front of the Palace in Stockholm, after his coronation at Uppsala in 1560. It was designed by the French carpenter Cleophas Charon, and the painter was the Dutch Dominicus Verwilt. In summer 1568 two further temporary arches were built on the route to the Palace for his marriage to Karin Månsdotter. One one of them served for the arrival later the same year of his half-brother Johan III and Johan's wife Katarina Jagellonica.[2]

It was in the reign of Erik XIV that eight portals were set up at the royal castle of Kalmar, all the work of Roland Mackle, and dating from between 1562 and 1568. Two are reminiscent of triumphal arches. One has pairs of Ionic columns flanking the opening, and Corinthian columns above them, while the other (to the chapel) has pairs of Doric columns, and above the Doric frieze and entablature four armless herms supporting the cornice.[3] At Vadstena Castle, begun by Eric's father Gustav I in 1545, the entrance has a portal of 1563 with a Doric column on either side above each of which the entablature breaks forward, a Doric frieze, and a portrait roundel in each spandrel. It was designed by Pierre de la Roche from Brabant, and Konrad Ottenheym praises its 'extremely refined sculptural quality'.[4]

In the autumn of 1649 Queen Christina of Sweden was planning her coronation. Already in spring of that year the Stockholm magistrates had decided to erect two arches for the Queen's entry to the city. One, in Norrmalm, remained unfinished. The second was in Järntoget, designed by the stone sculptor Johan Wendelstam and painted by the Frenchman Nicolas Vallari. It had bas-reliefs of stucco and wax. It must be the one shown in an engraving of the celebrations by Johan Sasse, but that does not reveal much. The arch was greatly criticised.

Christina acquired several copies of the *Pompa Introitus Ferdinandi* (see p. 251), but her taste for ancient Rome would have ruled out its Baroque style. She had a passion for Italian culture, and had sent Mathias Palbitzki to Rome to buy drawings and antique marbles, and to bring back an Italian sculptor and the architect Jean de la Vallée, whose father had been royal architect in Sweden. He and Nicolas Cordier, son of a famous French sculptor who worked in Rome, but otherwise unknown, arrived by April 1650. Until then it was assumed that the coronation would be in Uppsala, as was traditional, but Christina now decided that it would be in Stockholm. De la Vallée's design for an arch, which he must surely have made in Rome, was approved at once. The materials were brought from Uppsala. As the coronation was to take place in October, time was short.

This, the principal arch, was much admired [25.1]. Made of wood and plaster, it cost well over twice as much as the Järntoget one, and was 25 m wide and 30 m high. The senate paid for it by imposing a tax on every horse-owner in the country. It stood on the mainland opposite the bridge leading to the Palace (on what is now Gustav Adolfs Torg). It was closely based on the Arch of Constantine, the chief differences being the addition of pairs of freestanding columns on the ends, the use of single circular reliefs over the side openings instead of pairs, and the addition of genii holding these reliefs, and garlands. It seems likely that de la Vallée was assisted in the elegant Classicism of the figurative sculpture by Cordier. The carpentry was by the court carpenter Louis Gillis, and the sculptor was Jost Schutze, whose assistants included Marcus Hebel. There were twenty-four allegorical statues, above the columns and on top of the attic. The circular paintings over the side openings, imitating bas-reliefs, represented Swedish victories in the Thirty Years' War, and were by Jakob Elbfas (Christina's old drawing master), Johan Assman and Adam Semler. They were surrounded with vines, crowns, and royal emblems including the Lion of the North with a thunderbolt in its paw and Christina's device of the sun. There were more paintings on the attic. The English ambassador, Bulstrode Whitelocke, wrote in May 1654: 'The whole building seems fair and stately and as of stone, but in truth is only

25.1 Stockholm, coronation of Christina, 1650. Jean de la Vallée.

364 THE TRIUMPHAL ARCH

wood plastered over; rather a show to please for a few years, than lasting.' Nevertheless, the arch still stood in 1660. It must have been demolished not long afterwards. Christina's pride in the arch led her to send back for the drawings from Rome in 1686.[5]

In about 1660 de la Vallée was employed by Magnus Gabriel de la Gardie to modernise his country house at Jacobsdal, and an arch decorated the garden. This is claimed to have been based on the Arch of Constantine, but the tiny view in Dahlberg's book suggests a single opening flanked by pairs of columns, no attic, and four pairs of statues on top.[6]

The accession of Karl XI in 1672 was celebrated with three days of festivities in Stockholm, culminating in a carousel. The knights entered the tiltyard through a triumphal arch in the antique style. The architect Nicodemus Tessin the Elder, the painter David Klöcker von Ehrenstrahl, and the sculptor Nicolaes Millich were in charge of the decorations. There was also an illuminated structure in the form of an arch, with a figure of Felicitas by Millich between two lions' heads from which wine poured.[7]

Karl was crowned at Uppsala in 1675, and for his entry into Stockholm an arch was built on almost the same spot as Christina's. It was designed by Tessin, and was less Classical than de la Vallée's. Tessin's son, Nicodemus the Younger, designed an arch for the same area early in his career.[8] Karl was also welcomed to Malmö in 1675 with an arch designed by Erik Dahlberg.[9]

In 1676 Karl won a decisive victory over the Danes, and was welcomed home to Stockholm with what is described as a triumphal arch, though it was really a screen in the form of an arch. It stood parallel to the bridge leading to the Palace. The freestanding columns flanking the centre and the pilasters on the corners were of the fluted Doric order. On the piers were niches with statuesca, and in the central 'opening' was a seated figure holding a cornucopia, between garlanded obelisks. Over the columns were statues of soldiers, and four more statues stood on top on the attic on each side. There were reliefs of armour on the base and above the side niches. The inscription commemorated *PAX OPTIMA*.[10]

In 1680 an arch in the middle of the Norrbro welcomed Ulrica Eleonora, the Danish princess who came to marry Karl XI. The elder Tessin started work on this and the other arches, but it was taken over by his son, who had just returned from Rome. The Norrbro arch was innovatively Roman Baroque in character, showing the influence of Bernini. The piers had paired Tuscan columns projecting on each of their four sides, with statues on pedestals between the columns. On top of the arch was an exedra, within which an obelisk rose from a rocky base, crowned with a sun. The exedra ended with pedestals supporting urns. Around were allegorical statues. A large cartouche with the inscription was placed over the opening. 'A memorandum … reveals that … the young Tessin was already an accomplished organiser and practitioner: he proposes some modifications intended to make the scenography more stable and weatherproof and also a way of building the triumphal arches indoors so that they could later be easily assembled *in situ*.'[11]

In 1726 Carl Harleman produced a design for a grandiose arch, shown in an engraving. The base is rusticated Doric, and diagonal projections have pairs of freestanding columns. Above each are a trophy and an obelisk. The upper storey also has diagonally placed columns, and a statue in the centre, presumably of King Frederik I. The shaped top has angels and a crown. The occasion for the design is unknown.

25.2 Stockholm, design by Louis Gustave Taraval, 1767.

In 1767 a design was made for an arch in Stockholm by Louis Gustave Taraval, the French 'inspecteur des bâtiments du Roi' (of Sweden) [25.2]. It is on a colossal scale. Each pier has pairs of freestanding Tuscan columns both in front and at the sides. The entablatures of these break forward and support groups of sculpture. On top of the stepped attic is a circular podium with a *quadriga* set at a rakish angle, driven by two figures. It is hard to see what in the reign of the feeble King Adolf Frederik could have inspired such a project.[12]

The Parliament Building in Stockholm (1897–1905, by Aron Johansson) incorporates a powerful rusticated triple arch at the entrance from Drotningsgatan.

Three of Copenhagen's gates took the form of triumphal arches.[13] The Norreport, dated 1673, had pairs of attached columns framing statues in niches, on either side of the opening. Over the Doric entablature was an attic with a bust in an oval niche surrounded by weapons, and a scrolled pediment above. The Vesterport (dated both 1663 and 1722) also had pairs of attached columns at the sides, framing obelisks, and a pedimented attic in the centre. The Osterport, dated 1703, with pairs of Doric pilasters and an attic with a coat of arms and garlands, was simpler. A lavish 'Temple of Honour' was designed in 1749 to stand in front of the City Hall, to commemorate the tercentenary of the Oldenburg dynasty. The engraved design by Johan Christoph Holtzbecher shows an octagonal structure with pairs of Corinthian columns on the corners, and statues on pedestals between them. The main elevation has a large arched opening with arms in relief above and a pediment.[14]

In 1835 Karl Johan III of Sweden was welcomed to Trondheim in Norway with a temporary arch in Kongens Gate. It had pairs of columns.[15]

In Copenhagen an arch was built in 1849 to welcome the troops returning after their victory in the First Schleswig War. It stood in Gammel Torv, and was astylar, with shields and swords on the piers and sides, which also had cannons and flags. Lions reclined on pedestals in front of the piers. The opening was coffered, and in the spandrels were wreaths and palm branches.[16] In the same year a small pedimented arch was erected at Fredericia framing a bust of General Frederik Rudbeck Henrik von Bülow, the Danish commander, by H.W. Bissen. The grand entrance to the Tivoli Gardens, of 1890, is a fanciful arch with dome above.

Notes

1 Frederick and Line-Lone Marker, *A History of Scandinavian Theatre* (Cambridge, 1996), 30-1; Mara R. Wade, 'The coronation of King Christian IV of Denmark, 1596', in J.R. Mulryne et al., eds., *Europa Triumphans* (Aldershot, 2004), II, 245–67.

2 Sten Karling, 'L'arc de triomphe de la Reine Christine à Stockholm', in Magnus von Platen, ed., *Queen Christine of Sweden, Documents and Studies* (Stockholm, 1966), 159–86. For the 1560s arches see p.163.

3 Martin Olsson, 'Kalmar slotts portaler och brunnsbyggnaden på slottets borggård', *Fornvännen* (1957), 137–83.

4 Konrad Ottenheym and Krista de Jonge, eds, *The Low Countries at the Crossroads: Netherlandish Architecture as an Export Product in Early Modern Europe (1480–1680)* (Turnhout, 2013), 60.

5 Karling (cit. at n. 2); Georgina Masson, *Queen Christina* (London, 1974), 123, 133–6; Veronica Buckley, *Christina Queen of Sweden* (London/New York, 2004), 173–5. There are two engravings of the arch by J. Marot in Erik Dahlberg, *Suecia Antiqua et Hodierna* (Stockholm, 1723), I, 15 and 29.

6 Karling (cit. at n. 2), 182; Dahlberg (cit. in the preceding note), I, 89.

7 Lena Rangström, '*Certamen equestre*: the carousel for the accession of Karl XI', in *Europa Triumphans* (cit. at n. 1), II, 292–323.

8 Karling (cit. at n. 2), 182.

9 ibid. The arch is shown in a painting in Malmö Town Hall.

10 Dahlberg (cit. at n. 5), I, 30.

11 Dahlberg (cit. at n. 5), I, 31; the quoted text is from Mårten Snickare, ed., *Tessin* (Stockholm, 2002), 60–63.

12 The drawing is in the Cooper-Hewitt National Design Museum, New York.

13 The gates are shown in Lauritz de Thurah, *Den danske Vitruvius* (Copenhagen, 1746). They have been demolished.

14 Birgitte Bøggild Johanssen, 'The King and his Temple', *Bulletin du centre de recherche du château de Versailles,* 3 April 2018, 16.

15 Shown in a painting by Mathias Anton Dalager (National Museum of Decorative Arts, Trondheim).

16 The arch is shown in a watercolour by Heinrich Gustav Ferdinand Holm.

26

SPAIN AND PORTUGAL

Spain

In sixteenth-century Spain portals based on the triumphal arch schema were common. An early example is the doorway to the 'Salon de los Marqueses' in the Castle of Calahorra, of 1509–12. The interiors are probably the work of Italians. This richly decorated portal has niches on the piers containing statues of Hercules, Ceres, Leda and Apollo.[1] Church doorways are often similar. The Puerta de la Pellejeria of the Cathedral of Burgos, of 1516, is the work of Francisco de Colonia. As at Calahorra there are statues in niches on the piers, and above is an attic with reliefs between pilasters and a semicircular relief above.[2] A more Italianate example is the portal of the El Salvador Chapel at Úbeda, which has pairs of freestanding columns on two levels, and much sculpture. Angels sit in the spandrels of the opening. It is the work of Andrés de Vandelvira.[3] The

26.1 Orihuela, Valencia, Cathedral, Portada de la Annunciacíon, 1588. Juan Inglés.

The Portal of the Annunciation of the Cathedral of Orihuela is even more Classical, with pairs of attached Corinthian columns, and flying angels in the spandrels, below a bold entablature and cornice [26.1]. It is attributed to Juan Inglés.[4] Also at Orihuela the portal of the Convent of Santo Domingo is a more elaborate version, with a pedimented centrepiece on the attic between urns.[5] The Portal of Pardon of the Cathedral of Granada, designed by Diego de Siloé, forms the entrance to the north transept. The lowest stage has pairs of freestanding Corinthian columns, the corner ones reduced to halves. Angels occupy the spandrels, and there is rich sculptural decoration.[6]

The triumphal arch motif was also used for tombs. The tomb of Archbishop Francisco Blanco (who died in 1581) in the University Church at Santiago de Compostela has pairs of columns flanking an open archway which frames the kneeling figure. Between the columns are niches with statues of saints on two levels, and above is a pedimented aedicule. The designer was Mateo López, and the sculptor possibly Pedro Fernández.[7] In the church of Nosa Señora da Antiga at Monforte de Lemos the tomb of Cardinal Castro, who died in 1600, has pairs of Corinthian pilasters framing the coffered opening, which houses the bronze statue of the kneeling Cardinal.[8] A curious use is for the freestanding Fuente de Santa Maria at Baeza, which dates from 1564, and was designed by Ginés Martínez [26.2]. The fountain has openings between freestanding columns in the centre and the sides. The columns support caryatid figures above impost level, and two more support the pedimented centrepiece.

41.2 Baeza, Fuente de Santa Maria, 1564. Gínes Martinéz.

Also at Baeza is the Arco de Villalar, a battlemented Gothic gateway built to commemorate the victory of Charles V in 1521 at the battle of Villalar. More Roman is the arch at Burgos built in 1592 by Philip II to honour the tenth-century conde Fernán González [26.3]. Pairs of freestanding Doric columns flank the opening, and support obelisks above, while in the centre is a rectangular panel with coats of arms, bearing a pedimented aedicule with more obelisks on top.

The screen of the trascoro or retrochoir of Burgos Cathedral dates from 1626. On either side of the central opening (which houses a painting) are two pairs of Corinthian columns. Between each pair is a niche containing a statue.

In Madrid in the seventeenth century royal processions were held several times a year, usually following a fixed route, with stops in the Plaza Mayor and Masses in various churches. Buildings were covered in garlands, and arches were erected with lavish decoration and texts and images in praise of the ruling dynasty. As the economy weakened, the splendour of these ceremonies increased. Later two permanent arches were built. The Puerta de Alcalá, in the Plaza de la Independencia, was built in 1774–8 to commemorate the entry of Charles III into the city [26.4]. The designer was

26.3 Burgos, arch for Conde Fernán Gonzaléz, 1542.

26.4 Madrid, Puerte de Alcalá, 1774–8. Francesco Sabatini.

Charles's Sicilian architect Francesco Sabatini, and the sculptors were the Frenchman Robert Michel and Francisco Gutiérrez. Very wide, it has five openings, the central one in a projecting pavilion which has a pedimented attic. This is flanked by semicircular openings, while at the ends are lower rectangular openings. These are separated by attached columns, each with a trophy above. The Puerta de Toledo was erected in 1813–17. It was originally intended to commemorate the Constitutional Congress of Cádiz, but Ferdinand VII changed it into a celebration of his reign. The architect was Antonio López Aguado, a pupil of the Neoclassical architect Juan de Villanueva, and the sculptors were Ramón Barba and Valentino Salvatierra. The triple arch has Ionic half-columns flanking the central opening, and pilasters at the ends. The attic bears trophies on either side of a raised inscription panel, over which is a large sculptural group, representing the power of the Spanish monarchy in medieval times.[9]

In 1852 the Real Academia de Bella Artes de San Fernando set as the test for approval as architect a design for a monumental bridge over a river in a rich city, with a triumphal arch at the entrance. The test was passed by Francisco de Paula del Villar y Lozano, who settled in Barcelona and was the first architect of the Sagrada Familia.[10] In 1888 Barcelona held an Exposició Universal in the newly laid out Parc de la Ciutadella. The entrance was through an arch 30 m high, designed by the Modernista architect Josep Vilaseca i Casanovas [26.5]. Built of reddish brick, with Mudéjar decoration, it

26.5 Barcelona, Parc de la Ciutadella, 1888. Josep Vilaseca i Casanovas.

has sculptured friezes in stone. That on the front, by Josep Reynés, shows Barcelona welcoming the nations, while that on the back, by Josep Llimona, shows 'Recompense' – the awards given to the participants. On one side are allegories of agriculture and industry by Antoni Vilanova, and on the other trade and art by Torcuat Tasso. The figures of Fame above the pairs of semicircular projections are by Manel Fuxà and Pere Carbonell. On top of each is a hemisphere with a spiky crown. These were some of the most important young Catalan sculptors: Reynés, for example, had worked in the studios of Carpeaux and Carrier Belleuse, and Llimona was influenced by Rodin.

The Fascist Arco de la Victoria at Madrid is dealt with in the chapter on twentieth- and twenty-first-century arches (p. 435).

Portugal

Temporary arches were erected in Lisbon for the visit of Philip III of Spain in 1619, and for the wedding of Pedro II to Maria Sophia in 1687. For the arrival of Maria Francisca to marry Afonso VI in 1666 the Italian merchants erected an arch by the church of Our Lady of Loreto, with sculptures of Roman emperors, and the liberal arts and sciences.

Lisbon has two permanent arches. The earlier was built in the Amoreiras district in 1740–44, in honour of King Joao V, to celebrate the start of the delivery of water by the new aqueduct known as the Aqueduto das Águas Livres. It stands over the street

26.6 Lisbon, Praça do Comércio, 1862–73. Veríssimo da Costa.

at right angles to the aqueduct, and has Doric pilasters and entablature below a pediment, above which is an attic crowned by a small aedicule. The architect was Carlos Mardel, a Hungarian who was engineer of the aqueduct.

The other arch forms the grand centrepiece of the Praça do Comércio, the great square which opens out to the river at the bottom of the Rua Augusta, the principal street of the new lower town built after the earthquake of 1755 by the Marqués de Pombal [26.6]. The initial design, of 1759, was by Eugénio dos Santos, architect of the square. By 1775 the first version of the arch had on the piers pairs of columns, with further pairs set back a little on either side. On top of these were statues. The plain attic had a pediment with a trumpeting Fame.[11] This arch was demolished in 1775. In 1843 a competition to replace it was won by Veríssimo José da Costa. Work began in 1862 to celebrate the marriage of Luis I, and was completed in 1873. The arch also has pairs of freestanding columns, with recessed sections on either side with further columns and outer pilasters. These sections link up with flanking arcades. Above the opening is a lavish coat of arms. The pairs of columns and detached columns bear statues of Portuguese heroes, by Vitor Bastos, who also carved the statues of the rivers Tejo and Douro on either side. On top is a large group by the French sculptor Célestin Anatole Calmels which represents Glory crowning Genius and Valour. The inscription reads *Virtutibus maiorum ut sit omnibus documento PPD* ('Dedicated at public expense to the virtues of our ancestors so that it may be a proof to all').

Notes

1 Fernando Chueca Goitia, *Arquitectura del siglo XVI, Ars Hispaniae*, XI (Madrid, 1953), 37.
2 ibid., 57–8.
3 ibid., 250–53.
4 ibid., 272.
5 ibid., 274–5.
6 Earl Rosenthal, *The Cathedral of Granada* (Princeton, 1961), 99–103.
7 Dolores Vila Jato, *Escultura Manierista* (Santiago de Compostela, 1983), 115–17, pl. 82.
8 ibid., 49–50, pl. 18. The statue is doubtfully attributed to Giambologna.
9 Ramón Guerra de la Vega, *Guia de Madrid: Siglo XIX*, I (Madrid, n.d.), 38–41.
10 *Tipologias arquitectónicas: Siglo XVIII e XIX, Real Academia de Bellas Artes San Fernando Museo*, (Madrid, 1999), 32.1.
11 Shown in a watercolour of 1775 by John Cleveley Jun., formerly with the dealers Abbott and Holder in London.

27
MALTA

It is hardly surprising that the Knights of Malta should have erected triumphal arches. From the time of the first Grand Master of the Sovereign Military Order of Malta, Philippe Villiers de l'Isle Adam, who made his ceremonial entry into his capital, Mdina, in 1530, Grand Masters held a *possesso* (like that of the popes – see pp. 169–79). In 1720 a wooden arch was put up for Grand Master Marc'Antonio Zondadari. The material was reused two years later for the entry of António Manoel de Vilhena. It was set up on the square inside the main gate. The design, as in 1720, was by Pietro Paolo Troisi; the structure was built by the master carpenter Andrea Cattari, and the painter was Aloisio Buhagiar. It was a triple arch. On each pier pairs of attached columns flanked rectangular openings: above one was a knight wrestling with a lion, and over the other a knight trampling enemies in a pile of trophies. On top a bust of the Grand Master was surrounded by captives, trophies, and figures of Fame.[1]

In 1725 several elaborate Rococo arches were erected in the Strada di San Giorgio in Valletta on the occasion of a procession for the presentation of an honour (the 'stoc et pilier') to Vilhena by the legate of Pope Benedict XIII.[2]

The Mdina arch must have provided the inspiration for the Altar of Repose designed for use on Maundy Thursday in the Cathedral of Mdina [27.1]. Troisi's design of *c.* 1750 was executed in 1755–6, by Francesco Zahra. The altar, which is still set up every year, is described by Hughes and Thake as 'the finest and largest Baroque ephemeral stage-set to have survived'. On each side is a pair of columns, only the outer ones of which, with their entablatures, project. On either side of these are statues of angels holding the symbols of the

27.1 Mdina Cathedral, Altar of Repose, designed *c.* 1750 by Pietro Paolo Troisi, executed 1755–6 by Francesco Zahra.

Passion. Within the tall opening pairs of receding Salomonic columns flank the silver tabernacle. Above that is a gallery, over which angels float against a blue sky. Above the outer projecting columns big brackets sweep up to triangular pilasters, which appear to support the angels on the broken pediment, which has a figure of Religion in the middle.[3]

A quite different type of arch was built long before these examples. In 1610 Grand Master Alof de Wignacourt decided to build an aqueduct to bring water to Valletta. The Bolognese engineer Bontadino di Bontadini was in charge. At Birkirkara the aqueduct crossed the road by a triple arch known as the Fleur de Lys Arch. On top were three large fleurs de lys, Wignacourt's heraldic symbol, and there were pairs of obelisks at the ends. A Latin inscription gave the date 1615. The arch was demolished in 1944 to make passage easier for military vehicles. A recent proposal for its reerection stalled.[4]

In 1798 it was intended to build two permanent arches to commemorate the elevation of the village of Zebbug to the status of Città di Rohan, in honour of Grand Master Emmanuel de Rohan-Polduc, who had died in 1797. Only one was built, to the design of Giuseppe Xerri. A severe structure, without sculpture, it has rusticated Doric pilasters on either side, the central ones slightly projecting. Above is a triangular pediment.[5] Also in 1798 an arch was erected at Zabbar in honour of the last Grand Master, Ferdinand von Hompesch zu Bolheim [27.2]. The designer is unknown. Not dissimilar to the Zebbug arch, the whole of the lower part is rusticated except for the inner pilasters and the 'buttress' on either side. The central attic has pairs of short pilasters and a triangular pediment.[6]

It is still the custom in Malta to erect temporary arches for the feasts of saints. At Floriana, for example, an arch is set up beside the church of St Publius [27.3].[7]

27.3 Temporary arch for feast of St Publius, Floriana.

Notes

1 Denis de Lucca, *Mdina: a History of its Urban Space and Architecture* (Valletta, 1995), 89; Quentin Hughes and Conrad Thake, *Malta: The Baroque Island* (Sta Venera, 2003), 34, 155. The drawing shows alternative treatments of the columns.
2 Victor F. Denaro, *The Houses of Valletta* (Malta, 1967), 125; Denis de Lucca, *Carapecchia: Master of Baroque Architecture in early eighteenth-century Malta* (Malta, 1999), 177.
3 De Lucca, *Mdina* (cit. at n. 1), 84–5; Hughes and Thake (cit. at n. 1), 34, 172; J. Azzopardi and M. Gauci, *Archivum Cathedralis Melitae Fons Historiae*, exhibition cat. (Mdina, 2018), 26–8.
4 Hughes and Thake (cit. at n. 1), 66–7.
5 ibid., 195.
6 ibid., 201.
7 Another example is the feast of St Agatha, patron of Catania, for which a huge and colourful arch is erected beside the Municipio, at the entrance to the Piazza del Duomo (*Guardian*, 7 Feb. 2020).

28

AMERICA, 1758–1939

Some arches erected before the United States came into existence are described first. An early use of the triumphal arch motif is at the Franciscan mission church of S. Antonio de Valero in Texas, better known as the Alamo. The church, begun in 1758 but never finished, has pairs of freestanding columns, of a rather barbaric Corinthian order, on projecting bases, with a niche, formerly holding a statue, between each pair. The upper parts of the columns are striated. Around the opening and the niches is equally barbaric decoration.

George Washington was honoured with a number of arches. In 1774 he was greeted at Boston with a broad triple arch across a street. Designed by Charles Bulfinch, it was rusticated and the openings were flanked by Ionic pilasters. On the balustrade was inscribed 'To the man who unites all hearts'. Above this was a bizarrely tall kind of tent, surmounted by a coat of arms and an eagle.[1] Another arch to Washington, en route for New York, was a crude one of 1789 on a bridge at Trenton, New Jersey.

In 1813 a competition was held for a monument to Washington at Baltimore. This was to be the first important civic memorial in the USA. Two of the designs produced were for elegant Neoclassical arches. That by Joseph Ramée shows a plain single arch, approached by steps up a tall plinth. Within the opening a recessed pair of Corinthian columns frame a bronze statue of Washington. They support a decorated entablature at the level of the springing, to which correspond bands of military ornament on the piers. Above these are reliefs of trophies. The plain attic bears the inscription. This highly original concept is a remarkable exercise in stereometry.[2] The design by Maximilian Godefroy has single columns attached to the piers, decorated with reliefs of trophies. In the spandrels are flying Victories, while on the tall attic is a large relief panel. In front of the opening is a statue on a pedestal.[3] In the event the monument took the form of a column, designed by Robert Mills.

For the visit of the Marquis de Lafayette to Philadelphia in 1824 William Strickland designed no fewer than thirteen arches. The final one, the Grand Civic Arch in front of Independence Hall, was decorated with statues of Wisdom and Justice by William Rush, which survive.[4]

Another arch in the USA was a public commemoration. In 1889 the centenary version, on the north side of Washington Square, on the axis of Fifth Avenue. White was again the architect. Built in 1890–95, and clad in marble, it is like a slimmed-down version of the Arc de Triomphe de l'Étoile. It is astylar, and has statues on pedestals set against the piers, added later. 'Washington in War' is by Hermon A. McNeil (1916), and 'Washington in Peace' by Stirling Calder (1918). The upper part of the arch is carved in relief; the Victories in the spandrels are by Frederick MacMonnies. On the keystones stand eagles.

Around the turn of the century, when Beaux Arts architecture was in fashion, the grandiose temporary buildings erected for exhibitions often incorporated triumphal arches. Their materials were timber and 'staff' (plaster). At the World's Columbian Exposition, held in Chicago in 1893, the long and tall Peristyle, which ran along the lake, had at its centre an arch 'resembling the famous Arc de Triomphe of Paris' [28.1]. This it did not do, having pairs of attached Corinthian columns, with statue groups between them, on each pier. Above the attic a stepped podium supported a *quadriga* driven by Columbus, the four horses led by two women. The architect was C.B. Attwood. The western entrance of the Manufactures and Liberal Arts Building, reached across a bridge, also took the form of an arch, in this case a triple one, with pairs of free-standing Corinthian columns, each topped by an American eagle on a golden globe. The architect was George B. Post.[5]

At the World's Fair held at St Louis in 1904 four buildings had arches as their entrances. The Palace of Varied Industries (by Van Brunt and Howe) had an arch with a single opening flanked by pairs of free-standing Ionic columns, on each of which stood a statue. The Palace of Manufactures (Carrère and Hastings) had Corinthian

28.1 Chicago, World's Columbian Exhibition, Peristyle, 1893. C.B. Attwood.

colonnades on either side of an arch, with pairs of free-standing Corinthian columns, which culminated in a *quadriga* with women and youths in front of it. The Palace of Liberal Arts (Barnett, Haynes and Barnett), lavishly decorated with columns and sculpture, had a much more fanciful arch, with a curious toothed archivolt, again crowned by a *quadriga* [28.2]. The Palace of Education and Social Economy (Eames and Young) had a simpler arch with lavish sculpture, including a *quadriga* driven by a standing female figure, the horses led by two women. Much less pretentious was the arch leading to 'Old St Louis', a rather clumsy composition with a broad opening with segmental top, and pairs of skimpy columns on either side, and on the ends.[6]

When the World's Fair was held at San Francisco in 1939, a triumphal arch was again included, though it was criticised as an inappropriate Beaux Arts intrusion. Its architect, Louis Hobart, had, however, avoided the use of columns and sculpture, and its faceted character is distinctly Art Deco, with octagonal projections on the corners. It stood between the Court of Flowers and the Court of Reflections, framing the view to the Federal Building. Shanken describes the arch and the Tower of the Sun as 'Latin interlopers in a Pacific fantasy'.[7]

Notes

1 Jane Holtz Kay, *Lost Boston* (Boston, 1980), 60–61.
2 Paul Turner, *Joseph Ramée* (Cambridge, 1996), 218. Turner suggests that Ramée might have got the idea of columns within the arch from the design by F.N. Pagot which won the Grand Prix in Paris in 1806, though the columns in that are not actually within the arch (331, n. 17). He compares Ramée's design with Pagot's arch proposed in 1793 to commemorate the Austrian recovery of Louvain (see p. 258).
3 ibid., 219. Godefroy made six designs, of which at least two took the form of arches, but only this one survives.
4 In the Pennsylvania Academy of the Fine Arts in Philadelphia.
5 *The World's Columbian Exhibition Reproduced* (Chicago, 1893).
6 Timothy J. Fox and Duane R. Sneddeker, *From the Palace to the Pike: Visions of the 1904 World's Fair* (St Louis, 1997), 54–5, 60–63, 72–3, 100–101, 227.
7 Andrew M. Shanken, *Into the Void Pacific: Building the 1939 San Francisco World's Fair* (Oakland, Calif., 2014), 102–3.

29

MEXICO, SOUTH AMERICA, CUBA

29.1 Mexico City, arch for Marquès de Laguna, 1680. Sor Juana Inés de la Cruz.

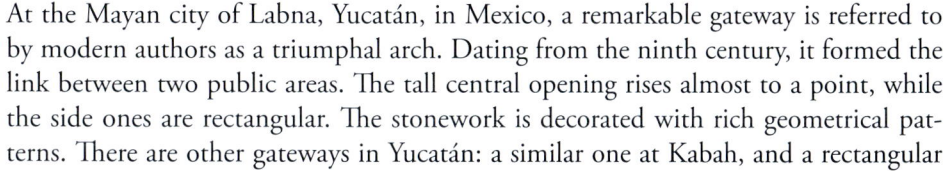

At the Mayan city of Labna, Yucatán, in Mexico, a remarkable gateway is referred to by modern authors as a triumphal arch. Dating from the ninth century, it formed the link between two public areas. The tall central opening rises almost to a point, while the side ones are rectangular. The stonework is decorated with rich geometrical patterns. There are other gateways in Yucatán: a similar one at Kabah, and a rectangular eighth-century entrance gate at Ek' Balam, which has only one opening on each of the four sides.

The colonial era led to the erection of arches by the Spanish, and the tradition was kept on after the countries' independence.

In Mexico, from the reign of the Emperor Charles V viceroys were welcomed to Mexico City with festivities lasting two months. The city council would erect an arch five storeys high, and the ecclesiastical authorities another in front of the Cathedral. On his way to Mexico City in 1680 the Marqués de la Laguna had been greeted by many arches. In the city itself the first arch was designed by Carlos Sigüenza y Góngora, and the second by Sor Juana Inés de la Cruz, a Hieronymite nun, who became well known as a writer. She published her description of it under the title *Neptuno alegórico*, as she compared Laguna with Neptune. Her one-sided arch was 75 feet (about 23 m) high, and had eight large paintings and several smaller ones [29.1]. These combined mythology with themes of local concern. The other arch had statues of the Aztec monarchs, whose virtues might provide models of statecraft as inspiring as those of Greeks or Romans.[1]

(about 18 m) high; they were linked along the street by balustrades with emblems, tapestries, mirrors and fountains. For the oath to Charles IV, who succeeded in 1788, the same arrangement was followed. The arches were designed by Don Antonio González Velázquez, director of architecture at the Academy of San Carlos. Between the balustrades was a temple containing a statue of the King, with a statue of Obedience on top. The balustrades were decorated with 102 silver panels and 40 silver chandeliers. The arches bore poems, illuminated by 7,600 candles. Entertainments included a dance by sixteen youths in red satin vests and sashes of silver thread. On their hats were letters, and at the end they spelt out *Viva Carlos Quarto*.[2]

In September 1821 the 'Ejército Trigarante' (Army of the Three Guarantees) made its 'solemn and peaceful entrance' to Mexico City, signalling the end of the War of Independence. A fairly plain arch was erected across a street, decorated with statues, coats of arms and flags. The lower side sections had paintings over rectangular openings.[3] The Heroes Causeway Arch in León, also called the Arch of Peace, dates from 1896. The lion on top was originally made of brick and cement, but was replaced in bronze in 1958 (sculptor Humberto Peraza Ojeda).

The Arco de la Independencia at Monterrey was erected in 1910 to celebrate the centenary of Mexico's declaration of independence. It was designed by an English architect, Alfred Giles. Built of red stone, 25 m high, it is a curious and not entirely happy design. Bulky piers are decorated with four pilasters on each, the middle two breaking forward under a curved pediment. The piers support a semicircular arch, on which stands a statue of Independence (known as Mona), made in the factory of W.H. Mullins in Salem, Ohio. Over the piers stand eagles. The setting of the arch has been horribly degraded.[4]

The 'Arcos' at Guadalajara in Mexico is a somewhat unusual monument, articulated with plain pilasters, and decorated with coloured tiles. It has two large and two small openings, and an attic with seven small windows. It was built in 1939–43, as the entrance to the city, to commemorate the 400th anniversary of its foundation.

Temporary arches were erected in Mexico in connection with triumphs performed by Indians, to recall events in Spanish royal history, or for viceregal or clerical entries. Routes were lined with arches 'like those in Spain'.[5] The Feast of the Assumption in 1617 was celebrated by the Jesuits with 'a great number of triumphal arches of flowers from their mountains and fields'.[6] A later example is the temporary arch erected in 1854 for the feast of St Anna in the Plaza Mayor of Mexico City. The architects were the Agea brothers, who had studied in Rome, carrying out archaeological work under the direction of Luigi Canina. They were responsible for parts of the Palacio Nacional. In 1878–9 Ramon Agea built the entrance gateway to the wooded park in Tacubaya (a suburb of the city), which surrounded the villa of Antonio de Mier y Celis, said to be the richest man in the country [29.2]. It was situated at the acute angle of two streets, and took the form of a triumphal arch, based on that of Constantine. It had freestanding Corinthian columns. Over the side openings were rectangular openings with balconies. The parapet broke forward over the columns, supporting urns. Within were the porter's lodge, the residence of the intendente, and two reception rooms. The building was demolished in 1929.[7]

In South America, at Lima in Peru an arch was built by 1682 on the bridge over the Rio Rimac near the Viceregal Palace [29.3]. In 1685 there was an arch at either

29.2 Tacubaya, Mexico City, 1878–9. Ramon Agea. Demolished 1929.

end of the bridge, but one was destroyed in an earthquake in 1687. In 1738 that arch was rebuilt to support a bronze equestrian statue of Philip V by Baltasar Gavilán. This arch, 18 m wide, had pilasters and a Doric frieze; above was a balustrade, and the pedestal for the statue was flanked with lions; at the ends were obelisks (it is suggested that these were inspired by the work of Juan de Herrera). The arch was destroyed in the great earthquake of 1746, but rebuilt in 1752. In 1771 two towers and a clock were added. It stood until the second half of the nineteenth century. The situation of the arch on a bridge recalls similar Roman arches, of which there were several in Spain (see pp. 14–16).[8]

From the sixteenth to the eighteenth century temporary arches were built at Lima to welcome viceroys. They seem to have been simple structures of wood, canvas and flowers, though in 1561 the Conde de Nieva's arch was made of adobe. The very Baroque arch erected in 1667 was covered in plates of white and gilded silver, paid for by the silver workers. The most expensive arch was that for the Conde de Castellar, in 1674, which was decorated with bars of silver. It was designed by Fray Cristóbal Caballero. Usually the architects and sculptors were the same as for church *retablos*. Arches were also erected on other occasions. In 1581 an arch attached to Lima Cathedral welcomed Archbishop Mogroviejo.

29.3 Lima, Peru, bridge with arch, 1682, rebuilt 1738, again 1752, towers added 1771.

MEXICO, SOUTH AMERICA, CUBA

For the proclamation of Charles II in 1666 a lavish arch-like structure framed a throne; the designer was again Caballero. Arches were erected on the plaza for the birth of Prince Baltasar Carlos in 1630. The inauguration of the church of the Desemparados in 1672 was celebrated with arches. The catafalques put up in the Cathedral for deceased royalty usually incorporated arch-like elements. That for Margarita of Austria in 1612 was similar to, but simpler than, that for Philip II at Seville of 1598. Later in the century they became even more elaborate, that for Philip IV in 1666 being like that put up in Mexico Cathedral. Those for Mariana of Austria (1697) and Charles II (1701) were both designed by Caballero, whose portal of the Church of La Merced in Lima has similar elements.[9]

A rare depiction survives of the arch built at Potosí in Peru for the entry of the Viceroy Archbishop Murcillo in 1716 [29.4]. It had twisted black and red columns, black panels with gold frames, a large statue on top, in native dress, holding a flag, with two smaller ones below, and miniature obelisks. In the opening hung a large flower.[10]

In 1800 a new avenue was laid out in Peru to link Lima with the port of Callao. In the city wall a splendid arch, designed by Luis Rico, was built to honour Charles IV of Spain. The central opening was flanked by pairs of Ionic columns, and surmounted by a pedimented attic, while the side openings, slightly set back, were flanked by single columns. Over each opening was an inscription panel. In front of the arch was the oval Plaza de la Reyna, with rows of columns above steps all round. A double colonnade ran out from this.[11] The arch was already deteriorating in 1822, and it was demolished in 1868. The Portada de Maravillas in Lima was built in 1807 on the site of a ruinous predecessor. It had pairs of Doric pilasters and a pediment with weapons above. It too was demolished in 1868. The entrance to the Parque de la Exposición, also in Lima, laid out by Manuel Atanasio Fuentes and Antonio Leonardi for the International Exhibition of 1872, had as its entrance a grand triple arch with attached Corinthian columns and plentiful decoration, culminating in a seated female figure above the attic. It was demolished for road widening in 1950, but has been replaced by a skeleton version.

29.4 Potosí, Peru, arch for Archbishop Murcillo, 1716. Diego Morcillo Rubio de Auñón, 1718.

The handsome Arco de Santa Clara at Cusco in Peru was built in 1835 to commemorate the founding of the Confederación Perú-Boliviana. It has pairs of attached Ionic columns. Pairs of obelisks flank the attic in the centre, which bears a statue of Liberty, between two condors. The sculptor was Ernesto Olazo Allende.

The centenary of Peruvian independence in 1924 was marked by two arches in Lima. The Arco de los Próceres de la Independencia had plenty of decoration. The sun of the Incas was on top, and there were pictures of battles and busts of significant figures. It was criticised for poor quality and blocking the view, and was destroyed. So also, in 1939, was the Moorish style arch in the Parque de la Amistad, given by the Spanish residents. It was rebuilt in 2001.

Brazil welcomed Don João, heir to the throne of Portugal, when he fled there in 1808 to escape Napoleon. He was acclaimed king in Rio de Janeiro in 1818. The ornamentation of the city was directed by the sculptor Auguste-Marie Taunay, the painter Jean-Baptiste Debret, and the architect Auguste-Henri-Victor Grandjean de Montigny. They had come out in 1816 as members of a French artistic delegation. Two arches were erected. One, said to have been based on the (then incomplete) Arc de Triomphe in Paris, had paintings in the form of transparencies by Debret. Another, 'in Roman style', had mythological statues and reliefs by Taunay; on top was a group representing the rivers Tejo and Rio de Janeiro reclining over the arms of the kingdom.[12]

In 1895 the popular Brazilian painter Pedro Américo Figueiredo e Melo produced a work called *Peace and Concord*, in the background of which is a huge building, the frontispiece of which is an elaborate triumphal arch.[13]

Ferdinand de Lesseps was welcomed to Panama City in 1886 with a rather clumsy arch, with his portrait at the top.[14]

In Venezuela, the Arco de la Federación at Caracas was built in 1895 to commemorate the Guerra Federal of 1859–63. It was designed by Juan Hurtado Manrique and his pupil Alejandro Chataing. It is a conventional single arch. The rusticated piers have statues on pedestals, and there is more statuary above the attic. In the spandrels are flying Victories, between coats of arms. Also at Caracas, the centenary of the battle of Carabobo, where Bolívar defeated the royalists, was celebrated in 1921 with an arch, like a taller but slimmed down version of the Arco de la Independencia at Monterrey in Mexico (the piers are 28 m high). Square piers with small statues on top support a semicircular arch on which is a bronze bust of the Republic by Pedro Basalo. The arch was designed by Alejandro Chataing, Ricardo Razetti and Manuel Vicente Hernández. Lorenzo Gonzáles executed the decorative sculpture.[15]

There is said to be only one triumphal arch in Cuba, and that is the one at Cienfuegos, built by the local workers' corporation in 1902 to celebrate the inauguration of the Republic of Cuba and the adoption of 'El Himno de Bayamo' as the national anthem. It stands in the park named after José Marti, who published the anthem in his newspaper, *Patria*, in 1892. The structure is rather unsophisticated – a triple arch with pilasters, and a curved attic projection in the centre with coat of arms.

In Chile (as in Mexico) an arch was erected in 1910 to celebrate the centenary of its declaration of independence. The Arco Británico in Valparaiso was given by the British community [29.5]. Designed by Alfredo Azancot, it is 10 m high, with a single opening and pairs of attached Doric columns. Clad in Italian marble, it has a large

29.5 Valparaiso, Chile, Arco Británico, 1910. Alfredo Azancot.

29.6 Coixtlahuaca, Mexico, San Juan Bautista, 1576.

bronze lion on top. On the piers are coats of arms, above circular portraits of four Britons who took part in the War of Independence.[16]

Church portals

The triumphal arch motif was often used in Spain for church doorways, and it is not surprising that it was also used in Latin America. In Mexico at Malinalco the doorway, of *c.* 1565, is flanked by pairs of curious pilasters with two tiers of niches between them. At Tecali there are pairs of attached Composite columns, again with pairs of niches between them, and a pediment over the opening. The source may be Serlio's design for an arch, or his plate of the Arco dei Gavi at Verona: his book was popular in Mexico. There are many examples of portals with pairs of columns flanking niches, often on two or even three levels. A bizarre version appears at

Coixtlahuaca, where between the pairs of columns are pairs of tiny niches which run up above the attic stage [29.6]. Here the source must be Serlio's plate of the Arch of Janus. It is also suggested that the arcades of two or three arches which often lead into the *atrio* or open-air church precinct may be intended to recall triumphal arches.[17] Similar examples of doorways in Peru include those of the Dominican Church at Cartagena (1580s), San Augustin in Potosí, and the Cathedral of Tunja, begun by Bartolomé Carrión in 1598.[18]

Notes

1 Linda A. Curcio-Nagy, 'Sor Juana Inés de la Cruz and the 1680 viceregal entry of the Marquis de Laguna into Mexico City', in J.R. Mulryne et al., *Europa Triumphans* (Aldershot, 2004), II, 352–7; Peter Davidson, 'Sor Juana's sources for *Neptuno alegórico*', ibid., 358–9; Peter Davidson, 'Mexico, 1680, summary of the first part of the festival: Carlos Sigüenza y Góngora's *Theatre of Political Virtues/Teatro de Virtudes Políticas*', ibid., 360–62; Sor Juana's text is reproduced at 364–428. Julie A. Boksel, 'Reading and writing Sor Juana's arch', *Rhetoric Society Quarterly*, 42.2 (2012), 144–63.

2 Linda Curcio-Nagy, *The Great Festivals of Colonial Mexico City: Performing Power and Identity* (Durham, N.C., 2005), 97–101.

3 Stanton Loomis Catlin and Terence Griedler, *Art of Latin America since Independence* (New Haven, 1966), pl. 6.

4 Edmundo Derbez García, *La estatua de la Independencia, esa desconocida* (Monterrey, 1997).

5 Antonio de Ciudad Real, *Tratado curioso y docto de las grandezas de la Nueva España* (1872, reprinted Mexico, 1976), I, 12.

6 Richard C Trexler, 'We think, they act: clerical readings of missionary theatre in 16th century Mexico', in *Church and Community 1200–1600, Storia e letteratura: Raccolta di studi e testi,* 168 (Rome, 1987), 581–99. This reference was kindly supplied by Dr Brenda Bolton.

7 Information from the website *Grandes casas de México*.

8 Rafael Ramos Sosa, *Arte Festivo en Lima Virreinal* (Seville, n.d.), 66–9; Francisco Stastny, 'From fountain to bridge: Baroque projects and Hispanism in Lima', in Henry A. Millon, ed., *Circa 1700: Architecture in Europe and the Americas* (*Studies in Art*, XLIII, Washington, 2005), 215–21; Francisco Stastny, *Estudios de arte colonial* (Lima, 2013), 273–9.

9 For all these see Ramos Sosa (cit. in the preceding note). He illustrates a number of them.

10 D.A. Brading, 'Civic festivals in Colonial Spanish America', in Mulryne (cit. at n. 1), II, 350, with pl. 20. The arch is shown in a painting by Pérez Holzuin in the Museo de América, Madrid.

11 Stastny, in Millon (cit. at n. 8), 220.

12 Afonso de E. Taunay, *A Missão artística de 1816* (Rio de Janeiro, 1956), 222, 231; Laurentino Gomes, *1808: The Flight of the Emperor* (Guilford, Conn., 2013), 214.

13 Catlin and Griedler (cit. at n. 3), pl. 51.

14 Darcy Grimaldo Grigsby, *Colossal: Engineering the Suez Canal, Statue of Liberty, Eiffel Tower and Panama Canal* (Pittsburgh, 2012), 116.

15 Rafael Pineda, *Francisco Narváez: El maestrazo* (Caracas, 1980), 143–4. In 1906 Chataing designed an Arco de la Restauración, but it remained unexecuted.

16 Suzanne Bosman kindly supplied information on this arch.

17 John McAndrew, *The Open-Air Churches of 16th-Century Mexico* (Cambridge, Mass., 1965), 152–5, 172–3, 228–31, 491; Richard C. Trexler, 'La vie ludique dans la Nouvelle-Espagne: l'Empereur et ses Trois Rois', in *Church and Community 1200–1600, Storia e Letteratura: Raccolta di Studi e Testi,* 168 (Rome, 1987), 502. A number of portals in triumphal arch form are illustrated in Joaquín Bérchez, *Arquitectura mexicana de los siglos XVII y XVIII* (Mexico, 1992).

18 Valerie Fraser, *The Architecture of Conquest: Building in the Viceroyalty of Peru 1535-1635* (Cambridge, 1990), 121-8.

30
AUSTRALIA

It is perhaps appropriate that the first arch in Australia was the entrance to the New Gaol of 1836–47 at Norfolk Island. Dated 1842, it is a shallow triple arch, with bold rustication.

The first royal visitor to Australia was Prince Alfred, Victoria's second son (later Duke of Edinburgh). For his visit in 1867–8 an arch was built in Adelaide, a pair of arches at either end of a bridge in Melbourne, and several more in Sydney and Hobart.[1] Later arches included one to welcome Australia's first cardinal to the church at Bega in 1886, one for the Governor, Lord Jersey, at Armidale in 1893, with Aborigines standing on it and King Malawangi and a 'piccanniny' on top, and a Coal Mining Arch at Newcastle in 1897, celebrating the centenary of the coal town [30.1].

There was a remarkable crop of 'Arches of Federation' erected to commemorate the inauguration of the Commonwealth on 1 January 1901 and the arrival of the Duke and Duchess of York for the opening of the first Australian Parliament in Melbourne on 9 May. There were twenty-one for the first occasion, and sixty-three for the second.

30.1 Newcastle, Coal Arch, 1897.

30.2 Sydney, Wheat Arch, Bridge Street, 1901.

Of those in Sydney, the most conventional was the Commonwealth Arch in Park Street, of triple form, designed by Varney Parkes (son of Sir Henry Parkes, 'the Father of Federation'), and covered in 'Bagasse fibrous plaster', imitating marble. Busts of the 'founding fathers' were set on the pedestals of the pilasters, and the arch was decorated with low reliefs, oil paintings and inscriptions. Above the parapet was a dome with an emu and a kangaroo. There was also a Coal Arch, which consisted of two great square piers made of blocks of coal, linked by a slender arch made of finer coal. On top of this was a small dome, with a mast above made of crossed picks and shovels. Framed photographs of collieries were set on the piers, and on top of one was a pithead, and on the other a ventilation fan. For the procession forty miners stood on stands halfway up the arch, in pit clothes with lamps, swinging their picks. A few days later some of the coal collapsed and almost buried a man and his daughter.

The Welcome Arch in Sydney was covered in native greenery, and lit up at night with coloured electric bulbs. The pyramidal Wool Arch was covered in bales of wool, with a merino sheep over the opening; on top was a crown. The Wheat Arch was covered in sheaves of wheat, with a plough on top [30.2]. The French Arch had an emu on one pier and a cock on the other, while the American Arch, covered in greenery with white plaster details, had an eagle above the entablature. So did the German Arch. These arches were erected by the residents of those nationalities. The Melbourne Arch in Sydney was decorated with greenery, flowers and flags.

Albury had one arch, and Perth two, including the Gas Company Arch, which had on top a star formed of gas jets. Brisbane had three arches of greenery, as well as an Agricultural Arch, with sheaves of wheat, pineapples, bananas and apples and agricultural equipment, and a Naval Arch, resembling a fortification, with naval guns on top of the piers, anchors and other nautical emblems, and carbines and cutlasses arranged in circular patterns. This celebrated the arrival of troops from various parts of the British Empire on 17 and 18 January.

It was suggested that some form of permanent memorial should be set up, and as one idea Varney Parkes proposed a permanent version of his Commonwealth Arch, to be built of concrete and sandstone and veneered with marble and bronze. There would be bronze portraits of public men and inscriptions recording the history of Federation. Nothing came of the proposal.

In May 1901 the visit of the Duke and Duchess of York to Melbourne was celebrated with nine arches. The grandest and most conventional was the Municipal Arch, a triple structure of rather squat proportions, designed by Harold Desbrowe-Annear [30.3]. The order was Doric. The keystone of the main opening took the form of the stern of a ship. As it was intended that the arch should stand for twelve months, it was covered with 'rubberoid' and waterproof paint, but after only a month a gale blew down some of the columns. The Chinese Arch had piers in the form of pagodas. The whole structure was draped with silks. Over the centre span rose a 'band house' where Chinese musicians played. The Butter Arch had square piers with projecting battlemented tops, and a straight bridge joining them, the whole built out of boxes of butter. It was, of course, painted yellow. The German Arch consisted of a pair of Corinthian columns, with lyrebird capitals, linked by a beam from which hung an oil painting of 'The Genius of Australia'. The Queen's Arch was of unusual design: pairs of arches crossed diagonally, with obelisks on their haunches. Above the shared keystone was a pavilion containing a statue of Queen Victoria. The other arches at Melbourne were more conventional, as were most of the six erected at Ballarat. In keeping with that town's botanical celebrity, two were decorated with greenery (in autumn tints). The rather weedy Marble Arch had on top a large painting of Edward VII reading a document, flanked by pictures of the Duke and Duchess. The clumsy Chinese Arch was much less effective than the Melbourne one, but it too was decorated with silks and costumed Chinese.

Brisbane erected two striking arches. The Royal Arch had piers like 'open minarets', while on top intersecting arches supported a crown. They were decorated with wool, the heads and horns of oxen, wheat and corn cobs. The bases of the piers were also covered with local produce – corn cobs, wheat stalks, palms and staghorns. The royal portraits on the piers were in the form of transparencies, framed in local shells.

30.3 Municipal Arch, Princes Bridge, Melbourne, 1901. Harold Desbrowe-Annear. Painting, Frederick McCubbin, *Arrival of the Duke and Duchess of York, Melbourne, 1901*, 1908.

30.4 Brisbane, Aboriginal Arch, 1901.

The inscription compared Desdemona's problem with that of the new nation – 'I do perceive here a divided duty'. Over the opening a standing figure of Britannia was flanked by figures of Aborigines. On the Aboriginal Arch the figures were real humans [30.4]. It had sloping piers forming a triangle over the arched opening. Their bases were covered with tea-tree bark, grass-trees, staghorns and bird's nest ferns. On top of each pier base was a 'typical Aboriginal gunyah' (hut). Beneath the opening hung shells, and above was a grass-tree. On the day of the procession Aboriginal women and children occupied the gunyahs, with emu and kangaroo skins, boomerangs, etc. Sixty Aboriginal men stood on the sloping piers, wearing emu feathers and carrying weapons, their bodies decorated in red and white. The Aborigines sang the song of welcome for a successful war party.

Newcastle put up a skimpy greenery arch. At Sydney only one new arch was erected, the King's Arch, with greenery and flags and the inscription 'Vivat Rex'. Two of the earlier arches were refurbished. Hobart set up a remarkable number of arches. The piers of the Lighthouse Arch, erected by the Marine Board, took the form of real lighthouses, complete with lights. Over the opening was a lookout tower with another light. The keystone showed a sailing ship passing a lighthouse, flanked on each side by three lifebuoys. The Tasmanian Fern and Floral Arch consisted of a single curved span, painted to resemble rocks, and decorated with ferns and plants. From the top a waterfall flowed down the sides. Water, along with electric lights changing colours, was the principal feature of the Fountain Arch, which was best seen at night. The nine Maypole Arches were as simple as the name implied. The Rustic Arch was made of loosely fitted rough stringybark timbers, and the piers had thatched domes. It gave the effect of a frontier fort, and advertised the Tasmanian timber industry. The Windsor Castle Rustic Arch had turreted piers and battlements, to represent that castle. The Apple Arch, inscribed 'Welcome to Appleland', was entirely covered in apples, used even to form a crown.

At Adelaide the Market Gardeners' Arch was decorated with carrots, turnips, parsnips and oranges. The only other arch requiring mention was the Fire Brigade Arch, where two ladders rose from fire engines, and were linked with a line of flags. For the procession firemen stood on the ladders, while the Fire Brigade Band played. At Perth, despite wind and rain eleven arches were prepared. The Railway Arch was surmounted by a globe with a winged wheel on top. It was intended to be either permanent or recyclable. First prize in the competition for designs was won by Mr Summerhayes with his Citizens' Arch, a rather bleak pedimented affair, enlivened by transparencies of the royal yacht, and of a gold prospector's camp with two camels. The Chinese Arch had somewhat squat pyramids as piers, with a surprisingly large pavilion perched over the opening. The decorations were much spoilt by rain, and the Chinese had to work hard to repair the damage. The Coal Arch had circular piers of coal, while the upper part had battlements in medieval style. The Timber Arch was a spidery construction of tree trunks, lit up at night to form a 'fairyland'. The Floral and Ducal Arches had the oddity of being octagonal. The only other arch worthy of remark was the Gold Arch, which had the same basic form as the Queen's Arch at Melbourne, with intersecting curved members, but was much sleeker: on top was a gold ball representing the entire output of gold from the state. Gold obelisks stood at the corners, while the spans were blue with gold stars.

In several places an Avenue of Honour was planted, the earliest commemorating those who fought in the Boer War. Most commemorate the First World War. They take the form of avenues of trees, each symbolising a dead citizen. At Ballarat the Avenue of Honour was planted from 1917 with 3,912 trees. In 1920 the Arch of Victory was built as its entrance. This clumsy structure has pairs of Doric columns against rusticated piers; above each pier is an octagon surmounted by a dome.

For the visit of Queen Elizabeth II in 1954 a Wool Arch was erected in Sydney, but it was a boringly rectangular affair.

Notes

1 I am grateful to the late Dr Joan Kerr for help with this section. She provided me with a copy of Tessa Milne, *Archways to Federation* (Sydney, 2000). See also Helen Irving, ed., *The Centenary Companion to Australian Federation* (Cambridge, 1999), 332–3.

31

INDIA

In 1344 Muhammad bin Tughluq, Sultan of Delhi, received Haji Said Sarsari, the envoy of the Egyptian Caliph al-Hakim II, with lavish honours. 'Triumphal arches' were erected in the city, and Muhammad (according to Sir Wolseley Haig) 'went forth to meet the envoy in a ceremony recalling the late Roman triumphal *adventus*'.[1] What these arches were like is unknown. Perhaps their form was like that of the *toruna*, a characteristic Buddhist archway derived from the bamboo gateways to temples, which seems to have originated around the turn of the pre-Christian and Christian eras. A *toruna* could mark the victory of a king. That building type spread with Buddhism further east, and may be the source for the Chinese *pai-lu* (see p. 396) and Japanese *torii*.[2]

Temple gateways in South India sometimes recall the triumphal arch; for example, at Trivandrum there is one with columns. A particularly curious one in a nearby village is a triple arch, with peculiar pilasters, on top of which is a chariot drawn by three horses, travelling at a right angle to the arch, driven by a Hindu deity – a bizarre parallel with the Classical *quadriga*.

It is not surprising that the British Raj liked to use the triumphal arch for grand gateways in the early years of the nineteenth century. Government House in Calcutta was built in 1799–1803 to the design of Lieutenant Charles Wyatt of the Bengal Engineers [31.1]. It was influenced by Robert Adam's Kedleston, but the four gateways were more similar to his gate-screen at Syon House. Each is of the Doric order, with pairs of free-standing columns. On top is a lion. At the sides are screens with columns and pilastered ends which are crowned with sphinxes.[3] The British Residency in Hyderabad, begun in 1803, to the design of Lieutenant Samuel Russell, was approached from the river by a very similar arch.[4] Government House at Mysore, built in

31.1 Calcutta, Government House, 1799–1803. Lieutenant Charles Wyatt. Engraving after James Baillie Fraser, *Views of Calcutta and its Environs*, 1826.

INDIA 393

31.2 Bombay, Gate of India, 1911. George Wittet.

1805 by Colonel Mark Wilks, has arches over the two approach roads which are much more individual: also Doric, they have a wide central opening flanked by pairs of pilasters. The balustraded attics are decorated with garlands and urns. There are smaller side openings for pedestrians.[5] Even private mansions might be approached through an arch: Davies illustrates an example with pairs of Ionic columns.[6]

When King George V and Queen Mary arrived for the Delhi Durbar in 1911, their landing at Bombay was commemorated by the Gate of India, a triple arch in Indo-Saracenic style, based on Gujarat architecture of the sixteenth century, designed by George Wittet [31.2]. Built of honey-coloured basalt, it was intended to form part of a larger scheme which was not executed.[7]

In front of the vast Victoria Memorial in Calcutta (now Kolkata), completed in 1921, stands a memorial to her son Edward VII [31.3]. It was presumably designed by the architect of the memorial, Sir William Emerson. It takes the form of a plain arch, on the attic of which is a bronze equestrian statue by Bertram Mackennal. Against the piers statues stand on bases; they represent the power of the British Empire (naval power, agriculture, civil government, and military power on land).[8]

Lutyens's India Gate, formerly the 'All India War Memorial', in New Delhi is discussed with arches as war memorials (p. 408).

31.3 Calcutta, Victoria Memorial, monument to Edward VII. (?) Sir William Emerson.

Notes

1 Sir Wolseley Haig, *Cambridge History of India,* III (Cambridge, 1928), 164.
2 Percy Brown, *Indian Architecture (Buddhist and Hindu Periods)* (Bombay, n.d.), 3.
3 Sten Nilsson, *European Architecture in India 1750–1850* (London, 1968), 101–4. One of the arches appears in a relief by William Goscombe John formerly on the base of the statue of the Earl of Minto (1913) and in the relief on the base of the statue of Baron Napier by J. E. Boehm. Both statues were at Calcutta (now Kolkata), but the second is now at Barrackpore (Mary Ann Steggles, *Statues of the Raj* (London, 2000), 137, 143).
4 Philip Davies, *Splendours of the Raj: British Architecture in India, 1660 to 1947* (London, 1985), 95–6.
5 ibid., 98–9.
6 ibid., 53.
7 ibid., 180–82; Thomas R. Metcalf, *An Imperial Vision: Indian Architecture and Britain's Raj* (London, 1989), 96. John Begg, whose assistant Wittet had been when he was government architect at Bombay, described the Gateway as 'just an Indianized version of a Roman triumphal archway' (Davies, cit. at n. 4, 265, n. 74).
8 Steggles (cit. at n. 3), 84–5.

32

THE FAR EAST

China

In his 'Memorie degli Architetti Antichi e Moderni', published in his complete works in 1827, Francesco Milizia writes that no country has so many arches as China, erected not only in cities but on mountains and in public streets, in memory of princes, generals, philosophers, mandarins, and others who have benefited the public. Over 1,100 are erected to the memory of illustrious men, among which are some 200 of extraordinary size and beauty. There are also some for women. Chinese annals name 3,636 illustrious men who had arches (a bizarrely precise figure). Some are of wood, but with pedestals of marble. The older ones are carved with flowers and animals.[1]

In the previous century J.B. Fischer von Erlach had illustrated a 'Chinese triumphal arch of which a great number can be seen in great cities' [32.1].[2] Sir William Chambers had written that 'the Päy-Leou, or triumphal arches, are very common in China', but in Canton he 'saw none that were fine'. He illustrates one 'which was the most tolerable

32.1 'Chinese triumphal arch', from J.B. Fischer von Erlach, *Entwurff einer historischen Architektur*, 1721.

I met with'.³ This has a taller central section with rectangular opening, with coving above, below a pitched roof with a dolphin at either end. At the sides are lower sections with round-headed openings, above which are fabric swags. Racine de Monville had a version of this (just the central part) built in the garden of his Chinese House in the Désert de Retz, *c.* 1777.⁴

The modern Romanisation of the name is 'pailou', 'pai' meaning 'tablet', and 'lou' meaning 'storey'. Less elaborate arches are called 'paifang'. These honorary gates are common all over China. The commonest type has four pillars, with a larger central opening and smaller side ones (like Chambers's), but some have twelve columns and some only two. The most important feature is the commemorative tablet. The arches combine simplicity of form with rich ornament. They were erected to public servants, those who died in war, local worthies or philanthropists, centenarians, literary figures, and women who were killed or committed suicide in defence of their chastity.⁵ Notable examples are the marble one at the thirteen Ming tombs in Beijing, built some time between 1409 and 1644, the four stone arches at a crossroads at Xixian (1527–96), and the nine arches at Tangyue [32.2].⁶ (Some fine timber pailou stand in Beijing on the road which runs in front of the Confucian temple, but many have been destroyed in the interest of traffic flow.⁷)

32.2 Beijing, pailou at the Thirteen Ming Tombs. 1540. Charles Bartlett, *c.* 1919, woodblock.

In recent years painted timber versions of the pailou have been erected to mark the Chinese quarters of Soho in London, Manchester, Newcastle upon Tyne and Liverpool. The last is the grandest, 50 m high, made in Shanghai and erected in 2000.

It hardly seems likely that there is any link between the Roman triumphal arch and the Chinese pailou, but the coincidence is remarkable.

Thailand

In 1897, as King Chulalongkorn was about to go to Europe on a diplomatic mission, an extraordinary arch was erected at Bangkok in his honour. Two huge elephants, ridden by figures in elaborate howdahs, held up a tiered crown with their trunks.

Vietnam

At Hue in 1864–7 the Emperor Tu Duc built himself a lavish mausoleum complex. Both the entrance and the main building take the form of triumphal arches, in black and red stone, with much orientalising ornament. The larger one is a *quadrifrons*, and has a smaller square structure on top. When Tu Duc died in 1883 he was buried elsewhere.

Laos

The huge Patuxai, or Victory Gate, in Vientiane, was built in 1957–68, as a war memorial for the independence struggle. Said to be inspired by the Arc de Triomphe in Paris, it was designed by Tham Sayasthsena. It was built with American funds and cement intended for an airport, so became known as the 'vertical runway'. It has five 'towers' representing the principles of coexistence and five Buddhist principles. The Laotian motifs include the bird-woman Kinnari.

Mangareva

Mangareva is one of the Gambier Islands in French Polynesia. The tyrannical Father Honoré Laval had an arch built as the entrance to the Rouro Convent at Rikitea [32.3]. It was designed by Frère Gilbert Soulié, and is 4 m high. Only the convent girls could go past beyond it. It is a plain single arch, with rusticated piers.[8] There

32.3 Mangareva, Rouro Convent entrance. Frère Gilbert Soulié.

was another arch at Rikitea, erected in 1864 to welcome the Bishop. It was designed by Frère Fabien 'à la façon de Vignola'.

The Philippines

The University of Santo Tomas at Manila was founded in 1611. In 1680 the 'Arch of the Centuries' was erected as its entrance. In 1927 the University moved to a new site, and in 1954 the arch was re-erected there. One face is original, and the other a replica. The arch has a certain crude charm, with pairs of stumpy fluted pilasters on the piers, and pedimented trefoil-headed niches between them. On the sides are panels showing scenes from the life of St Thomas Aquinas, and over the attic is a seated statue of the saint.

Another arch for Manila, to stand near the City Hall, was proposed in 1935 to celebrate the Tydings-McDuffie Act which established the Commonwealth of the Philippines [32.4]. The design by the Filipino sculptor Guillermo Tolentino showed, instead of piers, groups of Filipinos supporting the blocky upper part, on which were to be reliefs relating to the Act, and a statue on top. The Japanese invasion of 1941 put a stop to construction.[9]

The Visayas State University uses as the library of its Iloilo campus a building erected as the City Hall in 1931–5. Its front takes the form of a triumphal arch, and

32.4 Manila, design for Tydings-McDuffie Act arch, 1935. Guillermo Tolentino.

is distinguished for the large female figures in bronze in the spandrels, and the seated statues of Law and Order on plinths in front. The sculptor was Francesco Riccardo Monti, from Cremona. He was a friend of the architect, Juan Arellano.

At Naga City an arch was inaugurated in 2010 for the tercentenary of the devotion to Our Lady of Peñalfranca. Designed by Gian Paolo P. Prieta, it is 11 m high and 18 m wide. It has pairs of skinny attached columns both at lower and attic levels, and is decorated with framed panels.

Notes

1 Francesco Milizia, *Opere complete*, IV (Bologna, 1827), 91–2.
2 J.B. Fischer von Erlach, *Entwurff einer historischen Architectur* (Leipzig, 1721), III, pl. XV.
3 William Chambers, *Designs of Chinese Buildings, Furniture, Dresses, Machines and Utensils* (London, 1757), 7, with pl. XI 2.
4 Diana Ketcham, *Le Désert de Retz: a late 18th Century French Folly Garden* (Cambridge, Mass., 1994), 103, citing Georges Louis Le Rouge, *Jardins anglo-chinois*, Cahier XIII (Paris, 1785), ed. by Véronique Royet (Paris, 2004), 35, 197.
5 Samuel Couling, *The Encyclopaedia Sinica* (Shanghai, 1917), 417–18.
6 Laurence G. Liu, *Chinese Architecture* (London, 1989), 227, 243, 279. See also Ernst Boerschmann, *Baukunst und Landschaft in China* (Berlin, 1923), with photographs taken in 1906–9; and the list of 'Top ten ancient memorial archways in China', on the China Cultural Tours website.
7 I am grateful for assistance from Dr Frances Wood of the British Library.
8 Honoré Laval, *Mémoires pour servir à l'histoire de Mangareva* (Paris, 1968), CXVI, CXVII, pl. XII.
9 *Asociación filatélica de Filipinas*, 4 (1939), 5.

33

ARCHES AS WAR MEMORIALS

The erection of 'triumphal arches' to commemorate military successes is hardly surprising: this was their original function. What is much less easy to explain is their use as memorials to those who fell in war, in circumstances where 'triumph' would have been entirely out of place. The use of arches to commemorate the dead goes back to Roman times (e.g. Aix-les-Bains, Pula, Verona), but, so far as we know, none of those commemorated had any military connections. The arch form had often been used for funerary monuments, from the sixteenth century onwards, but almost exclusively as a mere formal motif.

A Crimean War arch

No war memorial arches seem to have been put up anywhere before the second half of the nineteenth century. The many arches erected in connection with the Napoleonic wars were all primarily intended to celebrate victory. The earliest strictly memorial arch seems to be the Royal Engineers' Memorial at the Brompton Barracks, Chatham, to commemorate members of the corps who died in the Crimean War [33.1]. It was built

33.1 Chatham, Kent, Royal Engineers Crimean Memorial Arch at Brompton Barracks, 1861. Matthew Digby Wyatt.

in 1860–61 to the design of Matthew Digby Wyatt. The site was chosen, on the vacant side of the barracks quadrangle, to form the gateway 'through which sappers might be marched on field days from their quarters to the lines on which their siege operations and other practical operations are carried on'. The Italianate style was selected 'to harmonise with the Barrack' by Wyatt's cousin James Wyatt ('probably the handsomest in the country', according to the *Illustrated London News*). The Portland stone structure has a tall central arch, with attic, and a lower arch on each side. There are winged victories in the spandrels, and panels with the names of battles. The principal sculptor was John Thomas. The bronze gates (cast by Potter) were made from Russian gunmetal.[1]

A contemporary arch at Halifax, Nova Scotia, was built both to commemorate the British victory in the Crimean War and in memory of the Nova Scotians who fought there. At the entrance to the Old Burying Ground (St Paul's Church cemetery), it was built in 1860 by the 'stone sculptor' George Lay. A plain astylar structure, it is crowned by a statue of a lion.

33.2 Hartford, Connecticut, Civil War memorial, 1884–6. George Keller.

American memorials to the Civil War and the Revolutionary War

The earliest memorial arches in the USA commemorate those who fell in the Civil War. It would be difficult to think of a war after which any kind of victorious boasting would have been less appropriate. The first is the Soldiers' and Sailors' Memorial Arch in Bushnell Park at Hartford, Connecticut; it is also the earliest permanent triumphal arch in the USA [33.2].

The idea of erecting an arch in honour of the 4,000 local men who served, and in memory of the 400 who died, came from the Revd Francis Goodwin, a member of the committee set up to decide on the memorial, who was an amateur architect. His idea was to have the arch on a bridge over the lake in the park, but when a competition was held this proved too costly, and the commission went to George Keller, who put the arch on land at the western end of the bridge. Keller was born in Cork in 1842; the family moved to New York in 1853, and Keller worked there with P.B. Wight. Built in 1884–6, the arch is in full-blown High Victorian Gothic, in the manner of William Burges (though the story that Keller was involved in the execution of Burges's Trinity College at Hartford seems to be untrue). Built of red stone, the piers are cylindrical towers with conical tops, 35 m high. Between them is a moulded arch, and at the top there are battlements between the turrets. A broad frieze runs all the way round. Made of terracotta (by the Boston Terracotta Company), this shows scenes from the War, on land and sea. The northern frieze was modelled by the English sculptor Samuel Kitson, while the southern one is by Caspar Buberl (who also modelled the frieze on the Pensions Building at Washington, D.C.). There are also six statues, supported on shafted corbels on the piers: these are by the German-born sculptor Albert Entress, and represent figures such as a schoolteacher, a mechanic and a black man. (On its restoration in 1988, the arch was 'rededicated' to the 128 black soldiers from Hartford 'who were not previously honoured'.) In the opinion of Henry-Russell Hitchcock, Keller here 'rather successfully emulated Burges': he describes the arch as 'one of the very few examples of such a Classical monument completely transformed into Gothic terms'.[2]

In 1888 a competition was held for the erection of an arch with the same purpose at Brooklyn, New York, and Keller entered with a Romanesque design.[3] However, the winner was John Hemingway Duncan, whose huge granite arch, 24 m high and wide, was built in 1889–92 [33.3]. Also known as the Soldiers' and Sailors' Arch, it

33.3 Brooklyn, New York, Soldiers and Sailors' Arch, 1889–92. John Hemingway Duncan, Frederick W. MacMonnies (sculptor).

ARCHES AS WAR MEMORIALS

is inscribed 'to the defenders of the Union, 1861/1865'. It is situated in the Grand Army Plaza, on the axis of Flatbush Avenue, and serves also as the gateway to Prospect Park. Architecturally it is rather clumsy. The piers are too broad for the height, and attached to each is a projection consisting of plinth and entablature, the latter oddly supported on three Corinthian columns. These serve as the bases for groups of sculpture. The excessively low attic is articulated by repeated stumpy pilasters. What gives the arch its distinction is the splendid sculpture by Frederick W. MacMonnies. On top, a *biga* (two-horse chariot) is drawn by America, with billowing drapery (1898), and on either side are rearing horses and Victories blowing trumpets. Yet more Victories appear in the spandrels. The large and crowded bronze groups on the piers (1901) represent the Army and the Navy. The former (which MacMonnies conceived as an 'explosion', inspired by Delacroix's *Liberty Leading the People*), has a winged Bellona (Roman goddess of war) at the back. The Navy group shows sailors below a helmeted female figure. Within the archway are plaques (1894) showing Lincoln and Grant on horseback, by Thomas Eakins in association with William R. O'Donovan.[4]

A third, very curious, arch is the Civil War Correspondents Memorial Arch at Crampton's Gap, Maryland, in what is now Gathland State Park [33.4]. The Civil War is the first in which there were war correspondents. The land was bought in 1884 by George Alfred Townsend, who had been the youngest war correspondent. He designed and built various structures there. The arch, erected in 1896, is a strange and colourful object. It looks as if Townsend had been inspired by medieval Italian castles. The large archway, of purple stone, has three smaller arches, of white limestone, above it, and battlements at the top. To one side is a taller battlemented tower. Over the upper arches are two horses' heads, and there are roundels of Electricity and Poetry. All these are of terracotta, but on the tower is a zinc copy of Thorvaldsen's *Mercury about to kill Argos*. There are many inscribed tablets, two with SPEED and HEED, some with the names of 157 war correspondents and artists.[5]

Clearly intended to resemble triumphal arches were the gateways erected at five National Cemeteries in the South. Each is of rusticated masonry, with a pair of Doric columns supporting a projecting entablature, and a low attic. The one at Nashville,

33.4 Civil War Correspondents Memorial Arch, Gathland State Park, Crampton's Gap, Maryland, 1896. George Alfred Townsend.

Tennessee, is the oldest (1870). The one at Arlington, Virginia, of 1879, is said to have been designed by the sculptor Lot Flannery. The others are at Chattanooga, Tennessee (*c.* 1880); Vicksburg, Mississippi (*c.* 1880); and Marietta, Georgia (1883).

In 1909–10 the Pennsylvania State Memorial was erected at the Gettysburg battlefield, to commemorate the 34,530 Pennsylvania soldiers who fought there in 1863 [33.5]. Designed by Liance W. Cottrell, of New York, it is a white granite *quadrifrons*, standing on a broad base faced with bronze tablets listing the soldiers' names. Pairs of freestanding Ionic columns, with bizarre diagonal fluting, flank the piers, against which stand eight bronze statues, added in 1913, of the military leaders (by Lee Lawrie, Cyrus Dallin, W. Clark Noble and J. Otto Schweizer). The attic has a relief in the centre of each side, by Samuel Murray, below an odd curved entablature. On top is a dome, with a statue of the Goddess of Victory and Peace, also by Samuel Murray, of bronze from cannons. The overall effect is not a happy one, as proportions and details are clumsy.

A later military arch in Pennsylvania commemorates an episode in the earlier, Revolutionary, War. The United States Memorial Arch, at Valley Forge National Historical Park, was built in 1914–17 to commemorate the arrival of General George Washington and his Continental Army. They encamped there for the winter of 1777–8. The arch was designed by the distinguished Beaux Arts architect Paul Cret, and is an elegant structure, based on the Arch of Titus at Rome. The opening is flanked by columns supporting a Doric entablature, which breaks forward along with the attic above. There are inscriptions, but little sculpture – just keystones with Athena, and Victories with trumpet and shield in the spandrels. The sculptor was Leo Friedlander. A second arch, to commemorate Washington's chief of staff, General von Steuben, had been proposed in 1907 for the opposite end of the park, but was not built.

33.5 Pennsylvania State Memorial, Gettysburg, 1909–10. Liance W. Cottrell.

ARCHES AS WAR MEMORIALS   **405**

The Boer War

The Boer, or South African, War, of 1899–1902, was commemorated by three arches – one in England, one in Ireland, and one in South Africa. In 1903 it was proposed to erect a memorial at the Brompton Barracks, Chatham, to the soldiers killed in the Boer War. At first it was suggested that this should take the form of an obelisk, but, despite the popularity of the idea, a copy of the existing Crimean Arch was proposed, to stand opposite it across the parade ground, in front of the Institute built in 1872–4. This idea was soon dropped in favour of an arch to a new design made by Ingress Bell, an architect 'for several years associated with the Corps'. This was inaugurated in 1904. It has a single opening, which the committee considered 'a great improvement on the other'. Also of Portland stone, it has pairs of pilasters on the piers, with panels for names of the dead between them, and reliefs above, showing 'Railways, Blockhouses, Pontoons Telegraphs and Balloons, and Entrenchments'. These were by W.S. Frith, and, like the spandrels (representing the South African War medals) and inscribed frieze, were to be of Istrian marble. Lack of money meant that only the frieze was marble, and the planned iron gates were omitted. It had been suggested that four huge bronze statues of Boer warriors, which had been presented to Lord Kitchener, might be incorporated, but this was impractical.[6]

Two other arches commemorate the Boer War.[7] The memorial to the men of the Royal Dublin Fusiliers takes the form of an arch set diagonally on the corner of St Stephen's Green, a large square in Dublin which is planted as a garden. It forms an entrance to the park, while occupying a prominent site in relation to the city's main shopping street. It is comparatively plain, with pairs of Doric pilasters on the rusticated piers, and an attic bearing inscription panels. On the frieze are the names of battles, and the soffit of the arch bears over two hundred names of the fallen. The monument, which was dedicated in 1907, was designed by John Howard Pentland, Chief Surveyor to the Dublin Board of Public Works, with Sir Thomas Drew as consultant.[8]

Another Boer War arch was in South Africa itself. In 1910 Edwin Lutyens travelled out there, primarily to design the Johannesburg Art Gallery, but also the Rand Regiments Memorial, to commemorate the men who died fighting for the British [33.6]. The foundation stone had been laid earlier in the year by the Duke of Connaught. Lutyens's design, sent out from Britain in 1911, was described by Christopher Hussey as 'the earliest demonstration of [Lutyens's] pure classicism: a triumphal archway, square in plan, with a lower arch in each flank, the whole surmounted by a flattened dome supporting a bronze figure of Victory'. He reproduces a drawing by William Walcot of the 'original full scheme', on a new site at the intersection of four avenues, with a setting of 'balustraded terraces, square pools, and flights of steps between groups of sculpture on pedestals'. Only the arch was executed. The figure of Victory on it was the work of Naoum Aronson, a Russian pupil of Rodin who lived in Paris.[9]

Gavin Stamp points out that in this Boer War arch Lutyens 'anticipated his later memorials, both in the employment of interpenetrating arches, springing from different heights, and by covering the sides of the arches with the carved names of the dead'. Sir John Summerson wrote that the 'relatively small monument … with its pedimented arches and winged figure seems to celebrate the glamour of victory rather than the tragedy of war. After 1918 Lutyens's memorials have more gravity.'[10]

33.6 Rand Regiments Memorial, Johannesburg, designed 1911 by Sir Edwin Lutyens, Naoum Aronson (sculptor).

The First World War

The First World War started on 28 July 1914 and ended on 11 November 1918. Immense casualties among the allies led to a widespread desire for memorials, and some of those in Britain, Italy, France and North America took the form of arches.

British memorials

As early as September 1914 an arch was proposed as a memorial to the Royal Engineers, to stand at the entrance to the Barracks opposite Brompton High Street, Chatham. Seven designs are preserved in the Royal Engineers Library. The only well-known architect is Maurice Webb (son of Ingress Bell's partner Sir Aston Webb). Nothing came of this, but in 1919 Sir Herbert Baker proposed an arch to stand at right angles to the earlier arches, to one side, with a statue of Kitchener on the other side. Only the plan survives. In the event, in 1922, the First World War memorial took the form of an obelisk between the two arches (designed by Hutton and Taylor of Glasgow).[11]

Another proposal made while the War was still in progress was put forward in 1916 by Sir Aston Webb. This was for a new Charing Cross Bridge, which could also serve as a war memorial. In 1921 Sir Herbert Baker pointed out that five years previously, with Webb and John Burns, he had suggested the line the bridge might follow, with '"Places" and a triumphal arch at either end'. He repeated that the bridge 'would provide for a fitting memorial *urbi et orbi*' of the Great War. In 1930 he produced a design for a suspension bridge with a huge arch at either end, though not as a war memorial.[12]

The first memorial designed by Lutyens was the All India War Memorial Arch (now the Delhi Memorial or India Gate), at New Delhi [33.7]. The idea went back to 1917, the proposed site being a crossroads at the eastern end of King's Way, the major axis from the Viceroy's House. Lutyens's design was approved in 1920, and the arch was built between 1921 and 1931. It commemorates 70,000 Indians who died in the War, and bears the names of 13,516 soldiers whose graves were unknown. Comparatively simple, the immense structure (42 m high) is articulated with amazing subtlety. There is a single opening on each side, those on the narrower sides reaching the height of the springing of those on the wider sides, and each stage is set back almost imperceptibly. There is no order as such, but tall pilaster-like projections are surmounted by disks. Above the bold entablature the attic

33.7 New Delhi, All India Arch, 1921–31. Sir Edwin Lutyens.

is set back much more emphatically. Panels bear the word 'INDIA'. On top is a shallow dome, the intention being that smoke would rise from it.[13]

The Arch of Remembrance in Victoria Park, Leicester, built in 1923, develops the theme of the All India Arch on a smaller scale, but here there is, as Summerson puts it, 'a slimming down and cutting away so that the actual arch-forms leap out of the mass and the play with proportional relationships is more intensive'. At the top, a shallow dome is supported on a vestigial attic with bold concavities on each of the main fronts. The piers are carved with wreaths suspended from ribbons. The arch is approached by an avenue, with lodges and gates also designed by Lutyens. At a public meeting Sir Jonathan North (Mayor of Leicester 1914–18) said that, while some might see it as a 'triumphal arch', 'it was possible to think of it as representing a spiritual triumph, which is why it was to be known as the "Arch of Remembrance."'[14]

The Imperial War Graves Commission was set up, under Fabian (later Sir Fabian) Ware, in 1917.[15] In that year Lutyens and Herbert Baker were sent to France to make recommendations. Lutyens was deeply moved by the 'pathetic' cemeteries: 'what humanity can endure, suffer, is beyond belief', he wrote to his wife. He subsequently wrote a memorandum in which he emphasised the importance of planting, and advised that each cemetery should have one large non-denominational monument. In 1918 Lutyens, Baker and Reginald Blomfield were appointed Principal Architects for France and Belgium, in charge of a team of Assistant Architects.

Lutyens's first use of the triumphal arch in a war cemetery was at Étaples, designed in 1919 and built in 1923–4. This was the largest of the earlier war cemeteries, with over 11,000 graves. Its chief features are twin cenotaphs, which take the form of comparatively small arches, supporting sarcophagi on tall bases, at the sides of which (on the arch's haunches) stand pairs of stone flags.[16]

Much the most remarkable use of the triumphal arch form by Lutyens was the Memorial to the Missing of the Somme at Thiepval, near Albert [33.8]. Indeed it is perhaps the most original and inventive transformation of the motif ever carried into execution. Precedents for it can be found in his unexecuted sketch designs for the Memorials to the Missing at Arras and St-Quentin. The Arras proposal, commissioned in 1924, took the form of a very tall and thin arch, 38 m high, stepped back on all sides, and penetrated by smaller arches in alternate levels. These arches were to contain bells. Unfortunately this scheme was rejected in 1925 as too expensive, and the memorial built in 1927–32 consists of a colonnaded cloister. The St-Quentin scheme, commissioned in 1923, had an arch almost 55 m high that would have stood over a road. However, in 1926 it was decided to erect that memorial at Thiepval instead. It was a suitable location: Edmund Blunden wrote, 'This name Thiepval began to have as familiar and ugly a ring as any place ever mentioned by man.'[17]

One of Lutyens's sketches for the Arras arch shows him calculating the space needed to inscribe the names of the missing. For the Thiepval arch, the total number was no less than 73,357, and this was the crucial factor in the design. The memorial was (uniquely) to commemorate both English and French dead. The layout was first discussed on a visit to Paris by Lutyens in 1922, and Hussey suggests that the rough sketch which he reproduces may date from then.[18]

Construction began in 1929, and the arch was inaugurated in 1932. Lutyens, wrote Hussey, 'may have been led to the basic conception … by the idea of multiplying the

33.8 Thiepval, Memorial to the Missing of the Somme, 1929–32. Sir Edwin Lutyens.

surfaces available for inscription by multiplying the number of arches. That is to say, by subdividing the four blocks, formed in plan by a greater and a lesser intersecting arch, by two smaller arched tunnels parallel to the greater, and two arched passages parallel to the lesser, forming sixteen squares in plan'. He adds: 'The two basic progressions followed throughout are that the arches are all of his favourite ratio of height to width (two and a half times); and that the block containing each set of arches rises to the height of the springing of the arch in the preceding block.' The faceting of the top section of the arch is, according to Stamp, 'reminiscent, if anything, of the top of an American Art Deco skyscraper. … Lutyens … developed a form of expression which was at once timeless and conspicuously modern.'[19]

The arch rises to a height of 43 m on a ridge above the rolling open country like an astonishing apparition of three-dimensional geometry. The materials are stone and brick. The stone is mostly Portland. The original bricks, of French manufacture, were small, of a pinkish colour, and delicate in texture. Unfortunately they weathered badly, and, after being replaced in 1952–5, they were replaced for a second time in 1973 with Accrington bricks of a harsh, darker colour and an ugly granular texture.[20]

On closer approach, the endless columns of names (the lettering designed by Macdonald Gill) are tragically moving. As usual in his war memorials, Lutyens avoided the use of sculpture. This seems to have been because he considered that developments in contemporary sculpture were making it less and less capable of playing the subordinate role to which it should be confined. His attitude towards the proposed completion of Alfred Stevens's Wellington Memorial in St Paul's Cathedral, in 1903, is revealing: he disapproved of John Tweed's scheme, because Tweed was a disciple of Rodin, and much as he admired Rodin Lutyens clearly thought that a style derived from his work was not capable of harmonising with the architectural elements in the way that Stevens's own sculpture had done.[21] Sensitive critics have justly praised the arch. They include Summerson:

> The Roman model is ruthlessly stripped, dissected and rebuilt, its massive shoulders cut away and their weight piled on top of the centre arch. Then, beneath the springing of this arch, the whole monument reproduces itself. It does so twice. Each of the lateral arches becomes the centre arch of a secondary monument, reproducing in its smaller arches the proportions of those of the first. The three monuments interlock with an appearance of innocent simplicity.

Roderick Gradidge wrote:

> The triumphal arch becomes a memorial cenotaph in one view, in another it is a solid memorial tower, its base pierced by arches in all directions. In fact it is all these forms, all interlocked in one building. For the first time in two thousand years an architect has found something new to do with the triumphal arch, and he was in a position to do this because he was brought up within the tradition of the Gothic Revival with a Gothic revival sense of form.[22]

Arches also appear in the work of other designers of First World War memorials. The most remarkable is the Menin Gate at Ypres, whose site was chosen by Reginald Blomfield in 1919 [33.9]. It takes the form of a new gate (a colonnade with an arch at each end) in the fortifications erected in the seventeenth century by Vauban, whose gate had already been demolished before the War. Blomfield's admiration for the great military engineer was to lead him to publish a biography in 1938. The road to Menin was the one used by the Allied soldiers en route for the German lines. Blomfield liked the idea of the arch being reflected in the wide moat. Like Lutyens at Thiepval, he had to provide spaces for the names of the missing who had died on the Ypres Salient.

The Gate faces out to a bridge over the moat. Blomfield had hoped that on the town side there would be a widened road leading to a 'place', but the citizens wanted Ypres rebuilt exactly as it was before the War, and it leads to a narrow street. On both inner and outer faces the central motif is a triumphal arch of ashlar, with a high arched central opening for the roadway flanked by lower rectangular openings for pedestrians, framed by Doric columns with projecting entablatures. The central part of the attic is taller than the side pieces, and recessed, bearing on the outer side a recumbent lion – 'not fierce and truculent, but patient and enduring … a symbol of the latent strength

33.9 Ypres, Menin Gate, 1923–7. Sir Reginald Blomfield.

and heroism of our race', as Blomfield wrote – carved by one of the best sculptors of the time, William Reid Dick.[23]

On the town side the attic supports a sarcophagus draped with a flag and surmounted by a wreath. Flanking the triumphal arch on both sides are panels of brick, with stone plinths and entablatures, which form the ends of colonnades at rampart level reached by stairs from within the spacious 'Hall of Memory', 35 m wide and 18 m high, through which the roadway runs. This has a coffered vault of reinforced concrete, designed, with the foundations, by Dr Oscar Faber. On the walls the 1,200 stone panels bear 54,896 names of the missing (though Blomfield says 58,600).

There were many problems in the building of the Gate, and, although begun in 1923, it was not opened until 1927. In it Blomfield sought 'to symbolise the enduring power and indomitable tenacity of the British Empire'.[24] He described it as 'perhaps the only building that I have ever designed in which I do not want anything altered'.[25] It soon became far the best known of all the British war monuments.

The Gate has attracted mixed criticism. Sir Charles Reilly considered it 'the most impressive of all our war memorials'.[26] Blomfield quoted in his *Memoirs* from a eulogistic article of 1920 by Stefan Zweig, who wrote: 'The broad gate is vaulted in plain Roman masses, more mausoleum than triumphal arch … In this truly Roman simplicity, this gravestone of the 56,000 has a more moving effect than any triumphal arches or victory monuments that I have ever seen.'[27]

However, one unidentified critic quoted by Longworth denounced it as 'made up from the stock of architectural commonplaces … lacking power and significance'.[28]

Criticism of a more poignant kind came in Siegfried Sassoon's poem 'On Passing the New Menin Gate':

> Crudely renewed, the Salient holds its own.
> Paid are its dim defenders by this pomp;
> Paid, with a pile of peace-complacent stone,
> The armies who endured that sullen swamp.
> Here was the world's worst wound. And here with pride
> 'Their name liveth for ever', the Gateway claims.
> Was ever an immolation so belied
> As these intolerably nameless names?
> Well might the Dead who struggled in the slime
> Rise and deride this sepulchre of crime.[29]

Some of the smaller war cemeteries used a form of triumphal arch as their entrances. A striking example was another Memorial to the Missing of the Somme, at Pozières, close to Thiepval. Designed by William Harrison Cowlishaw, a rather eccentric architect with Arts and Crafts leanings, this very broad arch has groups of three Doric columns, with projecting plinths and entablatures, on either side (a curious parallel with Brooklyn in New York: p. 403), and a large attic above, with the royal arms carved over the plain central opening, and sarcophagi on the haunches. The sculptor was Laurence Turner.[30]

There are four British municipal war memorials in the form of arches. In the War Memorial Gardens on Trent Embankment in Nottingham stands a large triple arch, with freestanding Doric columns and projecting entablature. Very plain, it has the city arms on the attic and inscriptions, and a curving colonnade on either side. It was erected in 1927 to the design of the City Engineer, T. Wallis Gordon. Another Memorial Park with a triumphal arch gateway is at Fleetwood in Lancashire. The 'stiffly Baroque triumphal arch with three unequal arched openings, coupled engaged columns etc.' was 'recycled from the Raikes Pleasure Gardens in Blackpool and erected in 1926'.[31] Much smaller is the War Memorial Gateway to the cemetery at Wainfleet All Saints in Lincolnshire, unveiled in 1920, and apparently designed by the stonemason H.C. Wood. It is an ungainly structure with pairs of skinny columns and too small an attic. A much more up-to-date memorial is at Greasbrough, near Rotherham in Yorkshire. Designed by James Totty, of Rotherham, it dates from 1925, and consists of a tall, narrow and plain arch, on a high base. Within the opening attached columns supporting an entablature frame a large urn.

Guy's Hospital in London has a memorial arch unveiled in 1921. It used to have a colonnade on either side, but in 1992 it was moved and is now freestanding. Designed by William Walford, it is a simple structure, decorated with raised panels, with a coat of arms at the top of each pier. The Clifton College (Bristol) war memorial of 1922 takes the form of a striking though quite simple Gothic triple arch, of limestone and red rubble. It was designed by Charles Holden.

An Australian memorial

It was proposed to build a memorial arch at Wagga Wagga, New South Wales, as early as 1916, and one was built in 1926–8 in the Victory Memorial Gardens. A competition was won by Thomas Kerr. The very plain sandstone arch has a stepped pedestal above with a date panel, and side walls with panels bearing the names of the dead.

Italian memorials

The arch at Asiago, designed by Orfeo Rossato of Venice and finished in 1936, makes an interesting comparison with Thiepval [33.10]. Asiago is high up on the remarkable mountain plateau – the Altopiano dei Sette Comuni – between Bassano and Trento in the north of Italy. The area saw bitter slaughter in the First World War. Situated at a height of 1,058 m, the monument is a *quadrifrons*, identical on all four sides, 47 m high. The arched openings are slightly recessed behind the piers, each of which has two niches, one above the other. Over the cornice, the attic bears on each corner (above the piers) a low relief of a winged figure in flight. The attic 'cornice' is decorated with lions' heads. Within the arch is an altar. The arch stands on a huge podium, 80 m square, within which is a crypt where 54,286 dead from the First World War (and three from the Second, added later) are buried. Over the doors leading into the crypt are helmeted soldiers' heads. In its centre is an octagonal votive chapel. The podium has stumpy obelisks, decorated with reliefs of swords, on the corners. A long avenue, and a shallow flight of steps, lead up to the monument. The whole structure is built of beautiful creamy stone. Its vast size, and symmetry, make it a striking landmark from far away on the Altopiano.[32]

33.10 Asiago, Veneto, 1936. Orfeo Rossato.

Asiago was not the first Italian war memorial for which the form of an arch was proposed. Several of the entries did so in a competition of 1924 for a 'Monumento ai Caduti', a monument to the fallen, in Milan. The design of Ottavio Cabiati and Alberto Alpago Novello was based on the Arch of Janus at Rome: it was a *quadrifrons*, with six niches in two tiers on each broad pier. The central niche of each trio held an urn, while the others held sculpture. The project of Giovanni Muzio was more original: the pairs of Ionic columns on each pier were surmounted by the two halves of a broken pediment, on either side of the arch, and between the columns were tall rectangular openings. There was a great quantity of sculpture. Marcello Piacentini reviewed the designs at the time, and characterised this one as *ricco e sonoro come un'arpa* ('rich and sonorous as a harp'). Aresi and Baciocchi proposed a huge and severe arch: the lower halves of the piers had blank porticoes attached, each with three Doric columns squeezed in between pilasters. Other entries diverged even further from the normal type of arch. Giuseppe Vaccaro and G. Tonnini proposed a rectangular structure with three equal arches on each side, all supported on columns. The rusticated attic bore a *quadriga*. This was described by Piacentini as 'Donatellian'. Even more bizarre was that of Enrico Mariani, who designed three vast, shallow slabs set parallel to each other, pierced by arches, and subdivided into innumerable squares. The project was named *le tavole della storia* ('the tablets of history'). In the event none of these designs was used: the monument built in 1927–30, to the design of Giovanni Muzio, takes the form of an octagon.[33] It seems that a design by Armando Brasini for *un arco di trionfo da erigersi a Milano a commemorazione della vittoria* ('a triumphal arch to be erected at Milan in commemoration of the victory') was not submitted to the competition. It is an astonishingly grandiose affair, in which the arch in the centre, with pairs of columns and a troop of soldiers on top, was dwarfed by immense wings with arches one above the other, and innumerable columns and sculpture groups, each crowned by *quadrigae*.

Another project for a memorial, for Palermo, also dating from 1924, took the form of a curving arch which was comparatively plain on the underside, but whose upper side writhed with elaborate sculpture. It was the joint work of Francesco Fichera and (surprisingly) the normally more austere sculptor Arturo Dazzi. It was not executed.[34]

Dazzi was to get his opportunity with another Monumento ai Caduti, at Genoa, to be sited on the 'spianata del Bisagno', the flat ground to the west side of the river Bisagno, in front of the Stazione Brignole [33.11]. Here again a competition was held in 1924, and in this case it was specified that the monument must take the form of a triumphal arch. Oriolo Frezzotti came up with an arch with piers whose sides sloped steeply up to a square attic, on which stood a huge statue. Felice Nori and Giuseppe Tonnini produced an indigestible effort, in which a fairly conventional arch was given bizarre decorative treatment, and vast sculptural groups stood on cylindrical bases in front. Enzo Bifoli's design was weirdest of all: a fairly basic arch structure was virtually 'deconstructed' by Art Nouveau-ish excrescences, wild sculpture, and pairs of columns completely detached from the piers and supporting nothing.

The judges made a shortlist of three. The project of the architect Alessandro Limongelli and the sculptor Giovanni Prini was comparatively simple, with each pier articulated by three tiers of aediculed niches. Much more original was the project of the architect Angiolo Mazzini, with the sculptors Eduardo De Albertis, Guido Galletti and Francesco Messina: two clusters of six Doric columns each support a large

33.11 Genoa, Monumento ai Caduti, 1927–31. Marcello Piacentini and Arturo Dazzi (sculptor).

rectangular attic, looking alarmingly top-heavy. Above are dancing Victories. The third design selected was by the architect Marcello Piacentini and the sculptor Arturo Dazzi. The judges postponed their final decision, considering that none of the three designs showed complete harmony with the site, or a perfect combination of architecture and sculpture, and their authors were asked to produce revised designs.

Meanwhile, another competition was launched for the layout of the proposed site. This was won by Piacentini. His triumphal arch would have stood within a horseshoe of trees and shrubs.[35] In the same year a second competition for the 'spianata' was held, sponsored by the *Corriere mercantile* as a counterblast to the official Comune competition, and Piacentini entered two schemes.[36] In 1925 his design for the arch itself was selected, and in 1926 he made yet another scheme for what was now called 'il Foro Littorio di "La Grande Genova"' (*littorio* – 'lictorial' – was a favourite Fascist term, recalling the attendants of Roman magistrates and their *fasces*, a bundle of rods with an axe, which symbolised the right to kill), which served as the basis for the project of 1928, itself worked up in detail in 1935.[37]

Piacentini's arch, built in 1927–31, stands in the middle of the Piazza della Vittoria – a vast rectangle, laid out as a park, surrounded by eight blocks of buildings. The earliest of these was begun in 1929. The only one by Piacentini himself, the Palazzo dell'INPS, on the north-east corner, dates from 1936–8.[38] Piacentini was the outstanding Roman architect of the 1920s and 1930s, producing a type of monumental classicism, severe in the details, but making telling use of sculpture, which was very much to the taste of the Fascists in power. He said that for the monument at Genoa he and Dazzi wished to combine triumphal arch and temple, more in the spirit of Palladio

416 THE TRIUMPHAL ARCH

than of ancient Rome. This 'Palladian spirit' is evident perhaps in the proportions, and in the overall simplification of forms. On the broad sides freestanding Doric columns are placed against the piers, flanking tall rectangular openings; on the narrower ends there are four evenly spaced columns, also framing tall rectangular openings. The effect is one of transparency. Each column has a projecting entablature bearing a statue. Broad friezes, one above the other, run along all four sides of the arch. At the corners are diagonally projecting rostra. The low attic bears inscription tablets on all sides. (In the competition design, the attic was taller, and decorated with some relief sculpture.)

Arturo Dazzi's sculpture here is very unlike that on the crazily 'Floreale' project for Palermo. He had in fact collaborated with Piacentini since 1917. Piacentini said that the sculpture on the arch was intended to speak 'directly to the people', representing actions and gestures in the same way as Roman sculpture did. The friezes, 105 m long, which show scenes of warfare, are indeed exceptionally easy to read. The final scene (on the east side) shows Piacentini holding a model of the arch, and Dazzi stretching out his arms to touch it in a gesture of cooperation. The critic Ugo Ojetti characterised the whole as *pura architettura e obbediente scultura* ('pure architecture and obedient sculpture'). Beneath the arch is a crypt, in which the sculpture is by Eduardo De Albertis. The arch's setting adds to its effect: on its axis to the south broad flights of stairs lead up to a curving wall pierced with arches (the 'Mura delle Cappuccine'), and the buildings around the piazza are satisfyingly homogeneous.[39]

In 1924 Piacentini had designed an arch for Genzano, which remained unrealised. The model shows a simple astylar structure, decorated with low relief sculpture above the springing of the arch, and with a statue standing on the keystone. The 'archetto di trionfo' would have been built of peperino, with the frieze in travertine, and the statue in bronze.[40]

33.12 Bolzano, Alto Adige, 1926–8. Marcello Piacentini.

Piacentini was responsible for another arch whose purpose was, at least initially, to commemorate men who had died heroically, but which represented a powerful political symbol. This was at Bolzano, capital of the Alto Adige, in the South Tirol, which had been 'taken back' from the Austrians by Italian troops in 1918, and officially handed over to Italy in the next year [33.12]. In 1926 Mussolini announced the intention to build a monument to three martyrs of 'Irredentismo', the movement to recover Italy's lost territories: Cesare Battisti, Damiano Chiesa and Fabio Filzi, all executed by the Austrians in 1916. The commission was at first to be given jointly to Piacentini and the sculptor Pietro Canonica, but Piacentini soon elbowed Canonica out of the way. Mussolini is said to have made a sketch to show what he wanted. The foundation stone was laid in the same year, and the monument was inaugurated in 1928. It was hailed as the beginning of a new age for Italian architecture.

The form of the Arco della Vittoria at Bolzano is comparatively simple: the three narrow openings in the centre are rectangular in shape, while the solid piers each have three small niches, one above the other. The articulation is by means of a so-called 'ordine littorio': the attached and freestanding 'columns' on each front, and one in the centre of each side, take the form of *fasces*, and from the upper part of each projects an axe. The attic is plain, apart from the sculpture (see below). The cornice has Latin inscriptions on front and back. The former reads: *Hic patriae fines. Siste signa. Hinc ceteros excoluimus lingua legibus artibus* ('Here is the boundary of the fatherland. Set up the standards. From here we have civilised others in language, laws and arts'). On the back is inscribed: *In honorem et memoriam fortissimorum virorum qui iustis armis strenue pugnantes hanc patriam sanguine suo paraverunt Itali omnes aer. coll.* ('To the honour and memory of the most brave men who, fighting energetically with just arms, established this fatherland with their own blood, all Italians [erected this] with their contributions of money'). Originally there were inscriptions on the sides, commemorating King Vittorio Emanuele and Benito Mussolini, but these have been removed. The columns are clad in Zanobbio marble, and the axes and walls in Botticino. The steps are of granite.

The sculptural decoration was an integral part of the scheme, and was carried out by the leading Italian sculptors of the time. Canonica himself modelled a rectangular frieze for the front in 1926, but this was rejected by Piacentini. He did execute three circular reliefs for the rear attic, representing Icarus studying the flight of eagles, Victorious Italy, and Prometheus. For the front attic, Arturo Dazzi carved a Victory – a winged female shooting with a bow. Giovanni Prini carved the eight helmeted heads for the cornice, and the heads of eagles, lions and wolves which surmount the axes. Libero Andreotti proposed to make an altar with figures of Christ and the four cardinal virtues, but in the end executed only a large and powerfully moving bronze figure of the risen Christ, which occupies a porphyry niche in the centre of the monument.[41]

On the inner walls of the arch, left and right, are texts and busts on pedestals, on one side of Cesare Battisti, and on the other of Fabio Filzi and Damiano Chiesa. These are by the remarkable sculptor Adolfo Wildt (born in Milan of Swiss parents). His work always has a dramatic intensity, and these busts are no exception. Unfortunately, the political implications of the monument have caused them to suffer damage on two occasions: in 1943 all three were damaged (Battisti worst) by an attack with a lorry, and in 1978 an explosion smashed the bust of Chiesa. After the first disaster, the busts were restored by Wildt's son Francesco. After the second, Chiesa's was inaccurately restored. Beneath the arch is a crypt, decorated with frescoes by Guido Cadorin representing the guardians of history and victory. Its furnishings included an urn containing earth from the place where Battisti fell from his scaffold, but they are no longer there. The monument continues to be a political embarrassment, and a fence prevents close access.

The setting of the arch was, as at Genoa, carefully considered. It is placed on the axis of the important street which leads from the old town across the river Talvera towards the suburb of Gries. In 1930 a competition was held for a *piano regolatore* (regulatory plan), and the three judges, who included Piacentini, chose three projects by well-known architects – Adalberto Libera (with Giuseppe Pollini), Giovanni Muzio and Ettore Sotsass. However, in 1933 Piacentini again got the job for himself. Between 1935 and 1940 the western part of the scheme was executed, the actual buildings being designed by Paolo Rossi de Paoli. Large plain blocks, with colonnades along their ground floors, are arranged more or less symmetrically, the side streets screened by double arches. The eastern part of the scheme, including two symmetrical blocks, a pair of columns, and a new bridge, remained unexecuted.[42]

Pietro Canonica did carry out one memorial in the form of an arch in his own right – the Arco in onore all'Artigliere (the Artillery) d'Italia in Turin [33.13]. It stands at the eastern end of Corso Vittorio Emanuele, at the approach to the Ponte Umberto I, and at the top end of the Parco Valentino. Erected in 1930, though Canonica had worked on the project since 1922, it makes up for its comparatively small size by its richness. The four corners are canted, and are flanked by Corinthian columns of purple marble, which is also used for the entablature, whereas the basic material of the structure is grey stone. Panels of white marble add further diversity. There is much sculpture, including cannons, equestrian statues, the prows of boats and reliefs all in bronze, and other reliefs in marble. The inventive and characterful sculpture repays close inspection. The rhetorical tone and the dissonance between the classical citations and naturalistic elements gave rise to much criticism, one critic suggesting that the artillery of Italy should destroy it with their cannons.[43]

33.13 Turin, Arco in onore all'Artigliere d'Italia, 1930. Pietro Canonica.

A rather belated memorial arch closes the view down the main street at Caserta, near Naples. Built in 1935, it bears the words *CASERTA AI NOSTRI EROI* ('Caserta, to our heroes'). On a broad stepped podium, the 'stripped classical' arch, of marble, has at attic level a bronze statue of 'Liberty and Victory' set in a curved niche.

A French memorial

South-east of the centre of Marseille a very individualistic arch stands on a terrace above the sea [33.14]. In 1924 a competition for a 'national monument to the heroes of the army of the East and of distant lands' was won by the Provençal team of Gaston Castel (architect) and Antoine Sartorio (sculptor). The monument was inaugurated in 1927. A tall oblong block with slightly tapering sides is pierced by a single arched opening, surrounded by a broad band. The plinths are extended sideways to bear the figures of soldiers marching behind Victories (Bellona and Amphitrite) who protect them with their wings. Above are the names of the places where they fought. In the centre is a female figure, with arms raised, representing 'La Patrie', giving the first cry of joy at victory, on the announcement of the armistice. At the crest of the arch is the Muslim symbol of crescent and star; it is below an inscription saying *AUX HÉROS*

33.14 Marseille, 1927. Gaston Castel and Antoine Sartorio.

DE L'ARMÉE D'ORIENT ET DES TERRES LOINTAINES. Behind, a monumental staircase descends towards the sea.[44]

North American memorials

Five arches in North America commemorated the First World War. The one at Newport News, Virginia, the port of embarkation for the American Expeditionary Force, was built in 1919 in a temporary form, of brick, wood and stucco, but was rebuilt in stone in 1962. It is comparatively plain, with a pair of pilasters on each pier, and some carved decoration at the upper level. The arch at Rosedale stands on a height with a fine view of Kansas City. Built in 1923, to the design of John Leroy Marshall, it is even plainer, but taller and leaner.

Much more elaborate is the Canadian National War Memorial at Ottawa [33.15]. A competition was won in 1926 by the English sculptor Vernon March, who had been the youngest artist ever to exhibit at the Royal Academy. His theme was 'The Great Response of Canada', 'symbolised by service people from all disciplines marching through a triumphal arch, but with a deliberate aim to avoid the glorification of war'. Ironically, the arch was unveiled in May 1939. This was after March's death (he had been helped by his seven artist siblings). The tall, plain arch, of Quebec granite, tapering inwards, is surmounted by a large bronze group of Peace and Freedom, while

420 THE TRIUMPHAL ARCH

through it twenty-two bronze figures emerge, journeying from war to peace. The powerful sculpture dominates the monument.

Another memorial stands at the Royal Military College, Kingston, Ontario. Erected in 1923–4, to the design of John M. Lyle, it is simple but elegant, in the Beaux Arts style. The quoins at the corners and round the opening are of vermiculated rustication, and above the Doric frieze the attic bears the inscription. Sculptural decoration is discreet.

A fifth arch only had a short life. The 1912 entrance to the New York State Fairgrounds at Syracuse consisted of four gatepiers set between tall square pavilions. In 1918 a new 'memorial arch' with three equal openings, and a frieze inscribed 'To New York's hero defenders of liberty and the flag', was set between the pavilions. The arch, 15 m high and 21 m long, was built by J.C. Nugent, 'representing State Architect L.F. Pilcher'. By 1940 it had gone, and the piers and pavilions were dressed up for 'Polish Relief Day'.[45]

33.15 Ottawa, Canadian National War Memorial, 1926–39. Vernon March.

ARCHES AS WAR MEMORIALS 421

A privately proposed arch was never erected. It was the idea of the remarkable sculptor George Grey Barnard, best known for *The Struggle of the Two Natures in Man* in the Metropolitan Museum. He was so distressed by the First World War that he decided to build an 'Arch of Peace', to stand in Fort Tryon Park on Hudson Heights. He began the design on Armistice Day in 1918, and the plaster model was ready for display in 1933. The arch, to be executed in Carrara marble, was to be 100 feet (about 30 m) high. Fifty-three figures were arranged on either side. On the left were the dead soldiers, groping upwards, while on the right were the grieving mothers and widows. The arch at the top would represent a rainbow, in coloured mosaic – 'a door to the future'. The arch would have formed part of a larger 'Monument to Democracy'. Barnard spent $240,000 of his own money on the scheme, and reckoned that the finished work would cost half a million. The Depression put paid to the proposal.[46]

Arches for returning troops

The 1919 victory parade in Paris made use of the Arc de Triomphe, but a design for an arch in honour of Maréchal Foch was made by S. Noakowski. The many columns were all set within the rectangular opening, and there was much sculpture on the top.[47]

A very large arch was erected immediately after the Armistice for the return of American troops to New York. Designed by Thomas Hastings, it was based on the Arch of Constantine, with very similar sculptural decoration, but used the Doric order. Freestanding fluted columns, with statues on top, flanked the opening. Above the central attic was a lavish sculptural *quadriga*, crowned by a winged Victory. Hastings described the arch as 'naturally a hurried undertaking executed in plaster'. It was intended to erect a permanent version on 5th Avenue, but this did not happen.[48]

The Second World War

The Second World War, of 1939–45, only received its national memorial at Washington, D.C., in 2004. Designed by Friedrich St Florian, it consists of two semicircles, each of twenty-eight pillars, flanking the approach to the Lincoln Memorial. Each semicircle has at its centre a *quadrifrons*, 13 m high, one inscribed 'Atlantic', the other 'Pacific'. They 'celebrate America's victory – the victory of light over darkness', and each contains a bronze 'baldacchino', by the sculptor Ray Kaskey, consisting of a laurel wreath held in the beaks of eagles perched on columns. The stripped classicism of the arches is reminiscent of Fascist arches such as the one at Caserta.[49]

A final word may be added on the use of arches as war memorials. This had already been ruled out by the Syracuse, New York, architect and planner A.L. Brockway in 1919: 'the Triumphal Arch invariably commemorated … wars of aggression and conquest … I cannot see the appropriateness of the Triumphal Arch … commemorating events of fundamentally different character.'[50]

Bertold Brecht would have agreed. In his *Berliner Requiem*, set as a cantata by Kurt Weill in 1928, are two *Berichte über den Unbekannten Soldaten unter dem Triumphbogen* ('Poems on the unknown soldier under the triumphal arch'). In the first, the soldier is killed and rendered unrecognisable:

Und [wir] gruben ihn aus unter dem Erz,
Trugen ihn heim in unsere Stadt und
Begruben ihn unter dem Stein, und zwar unter einem Bogen, genannt
Bogen des Triumphs,
Welcher wog tausend Zentner, dass
Der Unbekannte Soldat
Keinesfalls aufstünde am Tag des Gerichts
Und unkenntlich
Wandelte vor Gott,
Dennoch wieder im Licht,
Und bezeichnete uns Kenntliche
Zur Gerechtigkeit.

('And we dug him out from under the metal, carried him home to our city, and buried him under the stone, indeed under an arch, called a triumphal arch, which weighed one thousand hundredweight, so that the Unknown Soldier should under no circumstances rise up on Judgement Day and, unrecognisable, walk before God, once more in the light, and call us recognisable ones to justice.')

Brecht is obviously referring to the Tomb of the Unknown Soldier beneath the Arc de Triomphe de l'Étoile in Paris.

A succinct comment is provided by a cartoon by Rube Goldberg of 28 August 1944 in the *New York Sun* showing the returning troops marching under an arch formed of the word 'JOBS'.[51]

Notes

1 *The Times*, 2 March 1860, 12; *Illustrated London News*, 10 March 1860, 225, 237–8; *The Builder*, 19 (1861), 615. The original design is shown in a watercolour of which there is a photograph in the Royal Engineers Library, London: see the *Royal Engineers Journal*, 1 Sept. 1903, 191. It is shown in the *Illustrated London News* (as above), 225.

2 H.-R. Hitchcock, *Architecture: Nineteenth and Twentieth Centuries* (3rd edn, Harmondsworth 1971), 266; David F. Ransom, *Geo. Keller, Architect* (Hartford, 1978), 128–35. Keller made an unexecuted design for a bridge over the Potomac at Washington, on the line of New York Avenue, with a triumphal arch in a circular piazza at one end (*American Architect* (1900), 77–9; A. Hofmann, *Denkmäler, Handbuch der Architektur*, IV 8.2 (1906); Ransom 32–5.

3 Ransom (cit. in the preceding note), 146–7.

4 F. Fried and E.V. Gillon, *New York Civic Sculpture* (New York, 1976), 155. On MacMonnies, see Mary Smart, *A Flight with Fame* (Madison CT, 1996).

5 Ruthanna Hindes, *George Alfred Townsend* (Wilmington, Del., 1946).

6 *The Royal Engineers Journal*, 1 March, 1 May, 1 Aug., 1 Sept., 2 Nov., 1 Dec. 1903; 1 Feb., 1 March, 1 July, 1 Aug., 21 Oct. 1904; *Builders' Journal and Architectural Record*, 22 (1905), 107. Contract drawings in the Royal Engineers Library, London.

7 The proposal to use Admiralty Arch as a Boer War memorial is mentioned on p. 426.

8 M.J. McDermott, *Dublin's Architectural Development 1800–1925* (Dublin, 1988), 74; Christine Casey, *Buildings of Ireland: Dublin* (New Haven/London, 2005), 533. Ironically, the arch was damaged in the 1916 Easter Rising.

9 C. Hussey, *The Life of Sir Edwin Lutyens* (London, 1953), 207–8, 271, pl. 62. Walcot's drawing is also reproduced in A.S.G. Butler, *The Architecture of Sir Edwin Lutyens* (London, 1950), III, pl. 98, with p. 40. Lutyens had apparently thought of giving the job of the Victory to Jacob Epstein (Hussey, 231).

10 G. Stamp, *Lutyens* (Hayward Gallery, London, 1981), 148; J. Summerson, *Lutyens* (Hayward Gallery, London, 1981), 45; G. Stamp, *The Memorial to the Missing of the Somme* (London, 2006) 34, 131. Preliminary drawings are reproduced in the *Catalogue of the RIBA Drawings Collection: Lutyens* (Farnborough, 1973), fig. 41, see no. 112.

11 Thanks are due to Rebecca Nash of the Royal Engineers Library for her assistance.
12 *RIBA Journal*, 3rd ser., 23 (1916), 278; R. Blomfield in A. Webb, *London of the Future* (London, 1921), 114; Richard A. Fellowes, *Sir Reginald Blomfield* (London, 1985), 138–40.
13 Hussey (cit. at n. 9), 406–7; Butler (cit. at n. 9), III, pls 98–100; *RIBA: Lutyens* (cit. at n. 10), no. 38; Stamp (Hayward, cit. at n. 10), 180; Summerson (cit. at n. 10), 45; Stamp, *Memorial* (cit. at n. 10), 131; Tim Skelton and Gerald Gliddon, *Lutyens and the Great War* (London, 2008), 98, 100.
14 Summerson (cit. at n. 10), 45; Butler (cit. at n. 9), III, pls 101–3; *RIBA: Lutyens* (cit. at n. 10), no. 123; Stamp, *Memorial* (cit. at n. 10), 132; Skelton and Gliddon (cit. in the preceding note), 65–70.
15 Philip Longworth, *The Unending Vigil: A History of the Commonwealth War Graves Commission 1917–1967* (London, 1967).
16 Hussey (cit. at n. 9), 473–4, pl. 142; Butler (cit. at n. 9), III, pls 114–6; *RIBA: Lutyens* (cit. at n. 10), fig. 56; Stamp, *Memorial* (cit. at n. 10), 92–5, 132, 182; Skelton and Gliddon (cit. at n. 13), 194. Lutyens's first design for the Southampton Memorial, also of 1919, included a pair of arches with sarcophagi on top (Skelton and Gliddon, 37–8).
17 Stamp, *Memorial* (cit. at n. 10), 106–7, 109, 111, 114, 133, 146 (Arras); 58, 106–7, 109, 111–12, 130–38, 144 (St-Quentin); *RIBA: Lutyens* (cit. at n. 10) no. 5, figs 71–2; Skelton and Gliddon (cit. at n. 13), 133–9; E. Blunden, *Undertones of War* (London, 1928), 108.
18 Hussey (cit. at n. 9), 479.
19 ibid., 474–5; Stamp, *Memorial* (cit. at n. 10), 144.
20 Longworth (cit. at n. 15), 137.
21 Hussey (cit. at n. 10), 121.
22 Summerson (cit. at n. 11), 45–6; R. Gradidge, in J. Fawcett, ed., *Seven Victorian Architects* (London, 1976), 134. Other memorials by Lutyens which use types of arch include those at Serre Road No. 2, Villers-Bretonneux, Brown's Copse, Grévillers, Monchy, Pernes and Quéant Road (see Skelton and Gliddon, cit. at n. 13).
23 The quotation is from R. Blomfield, *Memoirs of an Architect* (London, 1932), 189.
24 Longworth (cit. at n. 15), 102.
25 Blomfield (cit. at n. 23), 189.
26 *Representative British Architects of the Present Day* (London, 1931), 61.
27 *Begegnungen mit Menschen, Büchern, Städten* (Berlin/Frankfurt, 1955), 251; Blomfield (cit. at n. 23), 190.
28 Longworth (cit. at n. 15), 105.
29 *The Heart's Journey* (1928), *Collected Poems* (London, 1961), 188.
30 G. Stamp, *Silent Cities* (London, 1977), 14; Stamp, *Memorial* (cit. at n. 10), 109, 168, 189.
31 Clare Hartwell and Nikolaus Pevsner, *Buildings of England: Lancashire North* (New Haven/London, 2009), 295.
32 For Rossato, see the website 'Architettura del Lido'.
33 For illustrations, and a critical review by Marcello Piacentini, see *Architettura e arti decorative*, IV (1924–5), 410–31.
34 C. Cresti, *Architettura e Fascismo* (Florence, 1986), 69.
35 *Architettura e arti decorative*, III (1923–4), 363–70. The scheme by O. Frezzotti which came second included a more conventional arch than his entry in the Monumento ai Caduti competition.
36 M. Lupano, *Marcello Piacentini* (Rome/Bari, 1991), 194 and figs 59–60.
37 ibid., 195.
38 L. Capellini and E. Poleggi, *Guide di Architettura: Genova* (Turin, 1992), 174.
39 On the competition, see *Architettura e arti decorative*, III (1923–4), 319–33 (text by Gustavo Giovannoni). For further illustrations of Piacentini's design see ibid., V (1925–6), 74–7. On the sculpture, see Guglielmo Matthiae, *Dazzi* (Rome, 1979), 28–30, 141–3; Flavio Fergonzi, *La Scultura monumentale negli anni del Fascismo* (Turin, 1992), 177–8; Anna Vittoria Laghi, ed., *Il Primato della scultura: Il Novecento a Carrara e dintorni* (Montespertoli, 2000), 44–5.
40 *Architettura e arti decorative*, V (1925–6), 78.
41 On it see Laghi (cit. at n. 39), 52–3; Silvia Lucchesi in Penelope Curtis, ed., *Scultura Lingua Morta* (Leeds, 2003), 54–5; *Dazzi* (cit. at n. 39), 28–30; Dario Durbé et al., *Canonica scultore e musicista* (Rome, 1985), 222.
42 Ugo Soragni, *Il monumento alla Vittoria di Bolzano* (Vicenza, 1993). See also M. Piacentini in *Architettura e arti decorative*, VIII (1929), 255–63; Lupano (cit. at n. 36), 71, figs 62–4 and 165–6; Fergonzi (cit. at n. 39), 177. The latter reprints an important article by the critic Ugo Ojetti from the *Corriere della Sera* of 13 July 1928, on pp. 210–11.
43 Durbé (cit. at n. 41), 224–8.
44 Westfehling 1977, 77; Violaine Menard-Kiener, *Antoine Sartorio* (Le Tholonet, 1996), 48–51. Sartorio was also responsible for the cenotaph erected in the Champs Élysées for the 1919 victory parade.
45 *Syracuse Herald*, 23 July 1918: information provided by Barbara Scheibel of Onondaga County Public Library.
46 Barnard gave the plaster models to the County Museum in Kankakee, Ill. Veronica Featherstone, of the Museum, gave me invaluable help. See also P. Pruchnicki, *Barnard* (Manteno, Ill., 1982, reprinted 2015 by the Kankakee Historical Society); Timothy Husband, 'Creating the Cloisters', *Bulletin of the Metropolitan Museum of Art*, 70, 4 (2013), 4–48. I have not seen Brian Hack's PhD thesis, 'American Acropolis: George Grey Barnard's "Monument to Democracy, 1918–38"' (City University of New York, 2008).
47 *The Builder*, 122 (1922), 100.
48 *Building News*, 122 (1922), 273.
49 Thomas B. Grooms, *World War II Memorial, Washington, D.C.* (Washington, 2004)
50 *American Architect*, April 1919, 511–14.
51 This reference is owed to Professor Andrew M. Shanken. See also his 'Planning Memory: Living memorials in the United States during World War II', *Art Bulletin*, 84 (2002), 134.

34

TWENTIETH- AND TWENTY-FIRST-CENTURY ARCHES

A number of twentieth-century arches have been dealt with in earlier chapters, but others find their place here.

The use of arches as war memorials has been discussed. Arches could also be used as memorials to people who did not die in war. When Queen Victoria died in 1901, a committee decided that her memorial should be architectural, and include an effigy. The *Architectural Review* later expressed the opinion that the 'logical solution' would have been a triumphal arch with statue above in the forecourt of Buckingham Palace (recalling the original position of the Marble Arch), but the committee ruled that out, and adopted a plan drawn up by Richard Allison, a 'young and talented' draughtsman in the Office of Works, which proposed to move the carriageway in the Mall towards the south, to form a piazza in front of the palace, with a seated statue of the Queen in its centre, and build a triumphal arch at the eastern end of the Mall, which would represent the progress made in the arts and sciences during Victoria's reign. Allison later suggested that the arch should be at the Trafalgar Square end: it would provide a grand entry where the way was blocked by a group of buildings through which there was only pedestrian access.

Sir Thomas Brock received the commission for the memorial statue, and a limited competition was held for the Mall project. Five architects were asked to provide designs. Sir Thomas Drew placed a tall, narrow arch, with paired columns and plentiful sculpture on the attic, at the western end of a rectangular 'court' placed between the end of Carlton House Terrace and Trafalgar Square. It included office accommodation. R. Rowand Anderson set his arch in much the same position; a 'two-tier' arch, apparently based on Temple Bar, had an equestrian statue within the upper arch, though it was not clear whom it represented. Ernest George's proposal was unconventional: at the centre was a tall arch flanked by paired columns, and with a pediment above bearing lively statues. On each side were pairs of arches, with balustrades above, and at each end were piers which replicated the pairs of columns on the central arch, and also bore sculpture. T.G. Jackson set his arch even further west, by York Steps. Very French in character, its plain piers had broad, shallow projections, with bands of relief sculpture running around them above the plinth. The arched opening was supported on fluted columns set within the piers. Above the narrower attic was a figure of Britannia, above symbolic females. The *Architectural Review* considered it 'the most impressive piece of design shown'[1]

The accepted scheme was that of Aston Webb, who put his 'Admiralty Arch' on a curve so as to disguise the change in axis from the Mall towards the opening to Trafalgar Square.[2]

Brock's contract was signed in 1902, and Webb's work began in 1903. His first design, of late that year, showed a huge arch, similar to the Arch of Constantine, with relief sculpture and inscriptions all over it, and a large sculptural group on top. On either side were office blocks, whose cornices continued those of the arch. Each had a tower crowned with a cupola. These would provide additional accommodation now required for the Admiralty. Two further designs approximated more closely to what was built. Alex Bremner sees Webb as moving away from seventeenth- and eighteenth-century British influence to the new Beaux Arts ideas. He points out the resemblance of Webb's later designs to the Arc du Cinquantenaire in Brussels, of 1904–10 (see below) – an imperialist erection if ever there was one.[3]

Meanwhile, between June 1904 and November 1905 the idea was proposed of using the arch as the 'Imperial Peace Memorial', to commemorate the 25,000 men killed in the Boer War of 1899–1902. Their names would be inscribed on it. The impracticality of the idea was one of several motives leading the Office of Works to drop it. At the Royal Academy of 1905 Webb showed a design whose attic bore large reliefs and a *quadriga* driven by Britannia on top. When work began in 1906 a more utilitarian scheme was adopted. It has three tall openings, set with banded rustication between Corinthian columns. Much lower arches on either side take pedestrian traffic. Beyond these are office buildings for the Admiralty and a house for the First Sea Lord, each of three storeys and six bays. A continuous entablature and cornice run all round, and above is a row of windows lighting rooms over the arches. On top is a tall attic with more windows below a Latin inscription. On the Mall side, at ground level, there are seated figures of Gunnery and Navigation, by Sir Thomas Brock (1911). It is easy to see why the Government would have liked a scheme that provided useful accommodation as well as architectural display, but the result was not universally approved. Charles Reilly mocked 'an Arc de Triomphe with ninety-six domestic windows in its front', suggesting that 'if we are ever to put up a great memorial to King Edward VII, I imagine it will be another triumphal arch, devoted this time, perhaps, to a lingerie store'. The arch is, however, grand and 'scenographic', and is perhaps too much taken for granted to be properly appreciated.[4]

The monument to Giuseppe Verdi in front of the Palazzo della Pilotta in Parma is sadly not what it was. It consisted of a large triumphal arch with a curving colonnade on either side, in which stood twenty-eight statues representing his operas. Each colonnade ended in a *quadrifrons*. Above the arch was a *quadriga* drawn by lions. All the sculpture was the work of Ettore Ximenes, and he provided the sketch for the whole, which was developed by Lamberto Cusani. Erected for the centenary of Verdi's birth in 1913, it was inaugurated in 1920. In 1944 it was slightly damaged by bombing, and then destroyed in 1945 so that only the reliefs on the 'altar', which stood in front, and the statue of the seated Verdi survive. The representation of Vittorio Emanuele II disgusted antimonarchists. The *quadriga* was a reworking of Ximenes's huge one, dating from 1904–5, which was put on top of Guglielmo Calderini's Palazzo di Giustizia in Rome in 1926.[5]

Another arch in memory of a deceased person was erected at Bridgeport, Connecticut, although in this case the deceased was not a Queen Empress but a sewing

34.1 Bridgeport, Connecticut, William Hunt Perry arch, 1918. Henry Bacon.

machine manufacturer [34.1]. William Hunt Perry (1820–99) was superintendant of the Wheeler and Wilson Manufacturing Co. He was also a commissioner of Seaside Park, established in 1865 and laid out by Calvert Vaux and Frederick Law Olmsted. (The idea came from Bridgeport's best-known citizen, P.T. Barnum.) After Perry died, his widow decided to erect a memorial in the form of an arch, to serve as the main entrance to the park. She wanted her friend Paul Winters Morris to do the sculpture, and even to design the arch. Morris chose the site, on the axis of Park Avenue, but insisted that an architect should design the structure. This was Henry Bacon, who had worked with McKim, Mead and White, and was to design a number of First World War memorials. Mrs Perry died in 1914, leaving $75,000 for the project. The Perry Memorial Arch was dedicated in 1918. Built of Woodbury granite, it is severe and imposing, with a pair of equal openings. Astylar, it has sparing decoration – lion masks on the cornices, a central panel with garlands, and lozenge-shaped coffering on the archivolts. A pedimented aedicule at ground level on the principal front contains a bronze relief – not by Morris, who died before his first sketch was completed, but by Adolph A. Weinman. It shows Perry, with a woman holding a cornucopia and oak leaves above.[6]

Another arch in the USA was a public commemoration. In 1889 the centenary of George Washington's installation as president was celebrated with a procession in New York, for which a wooden arch was erected on Fifth Avenue. Designed by Stanford White, it was a plain affair, on whose balustrade top stood a wooden statue of Washington. The arch was so much admired that it was decided to build a permanent version, on the north side of Washington Square, on the axis of Fifth Avenue. White

TWENTIETH- AND TWENTY-FIRST-CENTURY ARCHES   427

34.2 Boldt Castle, New York State, landing arch, 1900–04. G.W. and W.D. Hewitt.

was again the architect. Built in 1890–95, and clad in marble, it is like a slimmed-down version of the Arc de Triomphe de l'Étoile. It is astylar. The statues on pedestals set against the piers were added in the twentieth century. 'Washington in War' is by Hermon A. McNeil (1916), and 'Washington in Peace' by Stirling Calder (1918). The upper part of the arch is carved in relief; the Victories in the spandrels are by Frederick MacMonnies. On the keystones stand eagles.

A very curious arch, entirely a private commission, is at Boldt Castle, on Hart Island in the St Lawrence River, in New York State [34.2]. George Boldt, born at Rugen in the Baltic, was manager of the Waldorf-Astoria Hotel in New York. In 1900 he began to build a six-storey granite castle on the island. The architects were G.W. and W.D. Hewitt of Philadelphia (who designed the Bellevue-Stratford Hotel in that city for him). The castle was intended as a present for Boldt's wife, but after she died in 1904 construction stopped, and he never revisited the site. The landing stage takes the form of a triumphal arch, built of rough stone blocks, rising out of the water, with causeways linking it to the land. Pairs of columns flank the opening, and the openings at the sides are also flanked by columns.[7]

For 'Old Home Week' in Harrisburg, Pennsylvania, in 1905 an arch was erected, with pairs of attached columns and a big eagle on top.

A great public commemoration was the exhibition held in Brussels in 1880 to celebrate the fiftieth anniversary of the founding of the state of Belgium. The site was a sloping piece of ground on the axis of the road to Tervuren. Two large exhibition

34.3 Brussels, Cinquantenaire, 1904–5. Charles Girault.

halls were linked by a curving colonnade, in the centre of which was set a wooden arch, with a *quadriga* on top [34.3]. It was intended that this should be replaced by a permanent arch, but it was not until 1904 – the year before the seventy-fifth anniversary – that King Leopold finally got his way. The arch was built with frenzied speed, and was duly inaugurated in 1905. The architect was the Frenchman Charles Girault, who also designed the Petit Palais in Paris and the Museé du Congo Belge at Tervuren. The enormous structure, 42 m high and 58 m broad, built of grey stone from Soignies, has three tall arched openings of equal height. Each is flanked by Ionic columns, and projections at the ends each have pairs of columns, producing a rhythm of 3-2-2-3. Architecturally rather undistinguished, the arch has a great deal of sculpture by some of the leading Belgian sculptors of the time. The raised central attic provides the pedestal for a copper *quadriga*, on which stands the figure of Brabant, holding a flag and accompanied by a Victory. The sculptors were Thomas Vinçotte and Jules Lagae. Against the pedestal is a cartouche of the arms of Belgium, by Julien Dillens, and over the inner pairs of columns on each side are pairs of allegorical figures. The pedestals on the four outer corners originally bore winged Victories. The four main plinths on either side are raised up on rusticated bands; against these are semicircular pedestals, supporting bronze figures representing the provinces of Belgium with their attributes (the sculptors include Charles van der Stappen and Jef Lambeaux). The spandrel reliefs represent the arts and industries. Within the central arch is a panel with portraits of the five Belgian kings to date and the inscription *HOMMAGE À LA DYNASTIE LA BELGIQUE ET LE CONGO RECONNAISSANTS*. In fact, the King had paid for it himself, but had created the impression that it was a public offering. Its rather vapid pomposity and deceitful origin make it an appropriate monument to a loathsome tyrant.[8]

The Hartbeestpoort Dam in South Africa was constructed in 1916–25. Over the approach road is a plain triumphal arch, designed by Thomas Graham Ellis. It has a functional purpose, 'to provide structural mass to the wall's water-restraining strength'.

Another arch erected to commemorate the foundation of a state is the one at Bucharest. This was first put up in 1922 to mark the establishment of the Romanian state after the First World War. The architect Petre Antonescu was responsible both for this initial version and for the permanent rebuilding of 1933–6. The Arc de Triomphe again provided the model for a simple arch, whose severity is relieved by subtle projections and recessions, a mild flavour of Art Nouveau, and a restrained use of idiosyncratic relief sculpture (by I. Jalea, C. Baraschi, Mac Constantinescu and A. Calinescu).[9]

The 'Independence Arch' in Accra is inscribed 'Freedom and Justice AD 1957', and marks the independence of Ghana. It is a wide rectangular structure, with a broad opening flanked by narrow ones, all with flat lintels. A large black star stands on top.

National identity is responsible for the Porta Makedonija inaugurated in the capital, Skopje, in January 2012 [34.4]. Since the formerly Yugoslav state declared independence in 1991, the Greek Government has disputed its right to use the name Macedonia. The government of Prime Minister Gruevski is seeking to counter this by a building programme including a statue of a warrior on horseback, 22 m high, which is clearly intended to resemble Alexander the Great, an Orthodox church, and a triumphal arch. This rather crude structure, 21 m high, is the work of Valentina Stefanovska (also responsible for the warrior statue). It has pairs of Corinthian columns on the piers, with reliefs of scenes from Macedonian history between them. The recessed attic also has columns at the corners, with a statue in front of each, and more reliefs. The

34.4 Skopje, Porta Makedonija, 2012. Valentina Stefanovska.

arch project met with opposition from critics, who demanded to know what triumph was being celebrated, and denounced the whole 'Skopje 2014' project, estimated to cost €500 million, as 'retarded nationalism'.

Royal commemoration, though less common than in previous centuries, has continued to take the form of temporary arches. For the coronation of Edward VII in 1902, the Canadian Government built a large arch across Whitehall, inscribed 'Canada Britain's Granary' (see pp. 313–14). It was decorated with sheaves of corn, and with 'tinkling gewgaws', which caused the cab-horse of Joseph Chamberlain, the Colonial Secretary, to shy. He suffered a serious accident.[10]

For a visit by King George V and Queen Mary to Aberdare in 1912, an arch of coal was built, a plain tripartite structure, celebrating the fact that for half a century over two million tons a year had been mined in the parish. When they went to the Dowlais ironworks there were two more arches – the Coal Arch, made to resemble stone, with a painting of a loaded coal wagon over it, and the Steel Arch, which had square piers supporting fancy metalwork with three crowns.[11]

When the Prince of Wales went to Ramsgate in 1926 to open the Promenade, a broad arch was inscribed WELCOME. The four-centred arch and battlemented turrets were covered in greenery. In the next year he and Prince Albert opened the Canadian National Exhibition in Toronto. The 'Princes' Gate' is a tall triumphal arch, designed by Chapman and Oxley. Freestanding columns on the piers are topped by statues, while the attic is crowned by the Goddess of Winged Victory holding a maple leaf (originally concrete; replaced in GRP in 1987). The sculptor was Charles McKechnie. On either side long colonnades link the arch to pavilions.

At the Coronation of Elizabeth II in 1953 the Mall was spanned by a series of decorated steel arches, which were later used to build a warehouse.[12]

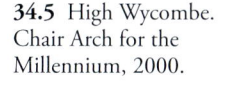

34.5 High Wycombe. Chair Arch for the Millennium, 2000.

The centenary of Queen Victoria's Diamond Jubilee was commemorated at Osborne House in 1987, where English Heritage commissioned the young sculptor Stephen Page to design an arch, to be constructed 'on a very minimal budget'. The result was indeed minimal. Equally disappointing was the 'chair arch' erected at High Wycombe to commemorate the Millennium in 2000 [34.5]. It was intended to recall the 'chair arch' put up for the Prince of Wales in 1880 (see p. 309), and was on the same site, but it was a sad travesty, consisting of shelves of scaffolding on which sat upholstered chairs and sofas [34.6]. The authorities responsible for Millennium commemoration had suggested that villages might erect arches, but the suggestion was not taken up elsewhere.

34.6 High Wycombe, Chair Arch for the Prince of Wales, 1880.

Much more spectacular than any royal commemorations have been the arches erected by or in honour of dictators, often Fascists. Of these the most grandiose was the colossal arch designed in about 1925 by Adolf Hitler himself to span the north–south axis, 120 m wide, of Albert Speer's plan for Berlin [34.7]. Comparatively plain, but 117 m high, it was to have rectangular projections on either side of the opening, with a pierced balustrade above, and some sculpture (two men holding horses) in the centre.

34.7 Berlin, design for an arch for the North-South Axis. Adolf Hitler and Albert Speer.

On the attic would be carved the names of all the German soldiers who fell in World War I. In April 1939, for Hitler's birthday, Speer commissioned a wooden model of the arch, 3 m high. A circular concrete block weighing over 12,000 tons was placed in the Tempelhof district to find out whether the sandy soil would bear the arch; it survives.[13]

It is not surprising that Gerdy Troost's *Das Bauen im neuen Reich* contains a design by Wilhelm Kreis for a huge memorial in the form of a plain arch whose four corner piers bear flaming urns, while within the opening an altar bears a vertical sword.[14] It was intended for Kutno in Poland, where the invading Germans fought an important battle in 1939.

The various arches erected in Fascist Italy as war memorials are described in that chapter. Other arches were merely commemorative. The earliest seems to have been the one at Mogadishu, in Somalia, in honour of King Umberto. An attenuated version of the Arch of Titus, its piers have very thin pilasters at the corners. Their upper parts are carved with crowns, while the attic bears the inscription UMBERTO DI SAVOIA ROMANAMENTE ('in the manner of Rome'). It must presumably be the arch 'raised in the name' of General Antonino di Giorgio in 1924. The arch is now very battered.[15]

A more original arch was made to welcome King Vittorio Emanuele to Mogadishu in 1935. Designed by Carlo Enrico Rava, it had tall round towers linked by a rectangular 'lintel', and was faced with local stone.[16]

34.8 Ras Lanuf, Tripolitania, Arco dei Fileni, dedicated 1937. Florestano di Fausto.

Rava had designed a temporary arch for Tripoli in 1931, a curiously boxy structure. It was far simpler than the fantastically elaborate one designed for a royal visit to the city in 1928 by Alessandro Limongelli: executed in stucco by Mirko Vucetich, this had huge statues on projections around the base, and attics set back in four stages with sculpture and inscriptions.[17]

An even more remarkable arch built to celebrate Italian colonialism was the Arco dei Fileni, in the desert at Ras Lanuf in Tripolitania [34.8]. This was intended by the Governor of Libya, the aviator Italo Balbo, to commemorate the building in 1935–6 of the road between the Egyptian and Tunisian frontiers of the province. It was designed by Florestano di Fausto, an architect favoured by Mussolini who did much work in Libya and Rhodes, as well as in Italy. The arch, built of concrete faced with travertine from Tivoli, was 31 m high. Steeply tapering piers flanked the arched opening, and the attic had four setbacks, with an altar on top. Between these were inscribed words from Horace's *Carmen Saeculare* – ALME SOL, POSSIS NIHIL URBE ROMA VISERE MAIUS ('Nurturing sun, may you see nothing greater than the City of Rome'). Between the opening and the attic, on each side, was a horizontal recess containing a bronze figure of a writhing man by Ulderico Conti. These referred to the legend of the Philaeni (Fileni). In the fourth century BC the Phoenicians of Tripolitania and the Greeks of Cyrenaica were in dispute about their boundary, and it was agreed that two pairs of runners would start at the same time from Carthage and from Cyrene, the boundary to be fixed where they met. The Carthaginian Philaeni ran more than three times as far as the others, and were accused of cheating. To prove their good faith they offered to be buried alive at the meeting place (which was in fact 30 km west of Ras Lanuf), and it became known as the Arae Philaenorum (altars of the Philaeni). Within the opening were tall reliefs showing the construction of the road (by Quirino Ruggeri) and the foundation of the new Roman Empire (by Ercole Drei). The latter showed Mussolini, who flew in to dedicate the arch in 1937. In the Second World War it was known to British troops as 'Marble Arch'. In 1972 it was demolished, though the bronze statues and parts of the reliefs survive.[18]

At Rome itself, the only 'arches' were two transformations of the façade of the Palazzo delle Esposizioni in the Via Nazionale. Built by Pio Piacentini in 1883, it had a front based on a triumphal arch. For the Mostra della Revoluzione Fascista in 1932 this was covered by a stark Modernist façade, with three enormous fasces, designed by Adalberto Libera and Mario di Renzi.[19] Five years later it was transformed again for the Mostra Augustea della Romanità, by Alfredo Scalpelli (one of the architects of the new town Sabaudia). Again very plain, it had four tall attached piers, each bearing a statue of a barbarian prisoner. On the keystone was 'the Victory of Metz'. The arch was said to reproduce 'the Arch of Domitian at Philae', a mysterious source. On either side of the arch were passages translated from classical authors praising Roman patriotism, with the word *DUX* repeated along the balustrade. On entering, the visitor was confronted with representations of the Arch of Constantine, the war memorial arch at Bolzano, and the Arco dei Fileni.[20]

In 1937 the centenary of the death of the poet Giacomo Leopardi was commemorated in his birthplace, Recanati, in the Marche. Rather surprisingly, a triumphal arch was erected in the main square. Even more oddly, none of the decoration of the fairly plain structure referred to Leopardi. On the piers were standards with wreaths and panels inscribed *ROMA*, and eagles on top. In the spandrels were crowned lions, and on the attic an eagle between swords. On the cornice the word *DUCE* was repeated four times.[21]

Adalberto Libera was also responsible for the design of an arch which remained unbuilt. This was the 'Great Monumental Arch' which would have spanned the Via Imperiale as it left the Porta del Mare en route for the Esposizione Universale to be held in 1942 (known as EUR). A huge semicircle, tapering towards the centre, it would have been the largest reinforced concrete arch in the world, with a span of 200 m and a height of 100 m. Lifts and trains would have taken people to the top, where there would be a restaurant. The architect himself described it as a triumphal arch.[22]

The similarity between that scheme and that for the Gateway Arch at St Louis was noted by a citizen of that town, who brought a prosecution against Eero Saarinen for stealing Libera's design, the real motivation being the Fascist origin of the scheme. Libera, however, supported Saarinen, so the matter was dropped. The amazingly convoluted story of the competition held in 1947 for the building of what was conceived as a Jefferson National Expansion Memorial is told by Tracy Campbell [34.9].[23] In

34.9 St Louis, Missouri, Gateway Arch, 1947–68. Eero Saarinen.

settling on the idea of an arch parallel to the river, Saarinen considered that 'it seemed like sort of a modern adaptation of a Roman triumphal arch'. After a building history marked by bizarre political and financial shenanigans, it was finally dedicated in 1968. Saarinen had died in 1961. The arch, built of stainless steel, is 192 m high. It was the Swedish sculptor Carl Milles who suggested that the cross-section should be an equilateral triangle.[24]

The symbolic significance of the triumphal arch in Fascist ideology is borne out by the appearance of one in Mario Sironi's fresco in the Aula Magna of the Palazzo del Rettorato of the Città Universitaria in Rome (1932–5, by Marcello Piacentini).

Spain has one grandiose Fascist arch – the Arco de la Victoria, on Plaza de la Moncloa, Madrid. Built in 1956, this was Franco's tribute to his Nationalist army, and stands over the route to his palace at El Pardo. It is a slim and elegant structure, 39 m high, with a single opening. On top is a bronze *quadriga* driven by a helmeted goddess holding a wreath. It bears the date 1937, the 'year of victory'. Latin inscriptions on the attic on one side dedicate the arch to the memory of the troops, and on the other celebrate the nearby University, 'restored by the Leader of the Spanish'. These are linked by low reliefs. The arch is attributed to the architects 'Lopez Knoll, Arregui, and Paschal Bravo', and to the sculptor Jose Ortells, who did the Victory on the keystone.

A surprising number of arches have been erected over the last fifty years or so. Obviously their symbolic function is still regarded as potent, not least by autocratic rulers and totalitarian states. In 1966 Hossein Amanat, at the age of twenty-four, won the competition to design a monument in Tehran for the 2,500th anniversary of the foundation of the Persian Empire. Inaugurated in 1971, it was called the Sahyad, the Shah's Memorial, but after the 1979 revolution and the fall of the Shah it was renamed the Azadi – 'Independence' or 'Freedom' – Arch. It is said to combine elements of Sassanid and Islamic architecture. It is built of Isfahan marble. Its piers, 50 m high, flare outwards like pleated skirts; the sides, 45 m high, swoop upwards.

One of the many extravagances of Jean-Bedel Bokassa, self-declared Emperor of Central Africa, is said to have been 'triumphal arches', but there seems to have been only one, in the capital Bangui, and that a very feeble effort, with two Doric

TWENTIETH- AND TWENTY-FIRST-CENTURY ARCHES 435

columns supporting a skinny pediment. Much bigger, but equally clumsy, is the 'Arch of Triumph' built in 1982 at Pyongyang, the North Korean capital, 'to glorify President Kim Il-sung's role in the resistance against Japanese rule' [34.10]. It was deliberately built to be slightly larger than the Arc de Triomphe in Paris, on which it is (implausibly) said to be based, and at 60 m claims to be the tallest arch in the world. The 25,500 blocks of granite represent the days in the life of the President up to his seventieth birthday, when the arch was opened. The hideous structure is like a parody of a typical arch, with three crude slabs diminishing on top. The openings are carved with azaleas, and the inscription is the 'Song of General Kim Il-sung', his revolutionary hymn.

Much more original are the two 'arches of triumph' built as the entrances to Great Celebrations Square in Baghdad, to commemorate Iraq's so-called 'victory' over Iran. 'Based on a concept sketch by Saddam Hussein', they were designed by Adil Kamil, 'Iraq's leading sculptor', and were dedicated in 1990. Each consists of two arms holding swords, meeting in the centre of the road. Each sword is 43 m long. The swords were cast in Iraq, the arms at the Morris Singer foundry in Basingstoke. Each plinth held 2,500 helmets, said to be from dead Iranians. Demolition was begun in 2007, but halted, and restoration 'as a sign of reconciliation' commenced in 2011.[25]

Prize for ugliness has to go to the 'Arch 22' built in 1996 at Banjul in The Gambia to mark the coup of 22 July 1994 which brought President Jammeh to power. Designed by the Senegalese architect Pierre Goudiaby, it is 35 m high: eight fat columns support an entablature above which is a huge pediment pierced by a large arch.

34.10 Pyongyang, Arch of Triumph, 1982.

In 2011 an arch called Mangilik El ('the Eternal Land') was inaugurated in Astana, capital of Kazakhstan, to mark twenty years of independence. The initiative came from President Nazarbaye, and the designers were 'Astana chief architect Sagyndyk Dzhambulatov and architect Kanat Kurganov'. It is a fairly conventional arch, with deep niches on the piers and sides containing bronze statues of warriors, a mother, and an 'aksalal-wiseman'. The semicolumns on the corners and other parts have shallow Kazakh ornament.

In view of the militaristic associations of arches, it may seem surprising that some have been erected to commemorate peace. The 'Peace Arch' at Blaine, Washington, is placed on the boundary between the USA and Canada [34.11]. One of the projects of the entrepreneur Sam Hill, it was dedicated in 1921 to commemorate the Treaty of Ghent, signed in 1814, which ended the war of 1812 between the USA and Great Britain. Designed by Harvey Wiley Corbett, it is a severe but elegant structure, 20.5 m high, with a tall rectangular opening beneath a pediment. It contains iron gates, with an inscription saying 'May these gates never be closed'. Inevitably various demonstrations have taken place at the arch. A notably ironic event took place in 1952, when Paul Robeson, who was banned from international travel, sang from the American side to a Canadian audience.

34.11 Peace Arch, Blaine, Washington, dedicated 1921. Harvey Wiley Corbett.

Even more ironic is the 'People's Friendship Arch' at Kiev, opened in 1982 to commemorate the 'unification' of Russia and Ukraine. Standing on the bank of the Dnieper, it consists of a striated semicircle of titanium, 50 m in diameter, beneath which is a huge bronze group of Russian and Ukrainian workers. The sculptor was Oleksandr Skoblikov, and the architects were Serhiy Myrhorodsky, Kostyantyn Sydorov and I. Ivanov.

Some recent arches have very vague symbolic functions. The Grande Arche at La Défense in Paris was built to provide a third arch on the axis of the Arc du Carrousel and the Arc de Triomphe de l'Étoile, and it seems that, although 'intended from the very beginning as a monument to be built in the name of hope', it was only later that it 'has become the symbol of the defence of human rights and of freedom'. A competition, held in 1982–3, was won by the Dane Johan-Otto von Spreckelsen. The 'arch' was opened in 1989. It is almost a perfect cube, 108 m wide, 110 m high, and 112 m deep, faced in Carrara marble. The rectangular opening is like a giant frame, with the surrounding elements canted inwards. The sides contain offices, and the top houses the Fondation L'arche de la fraternité.[26]

The United Kingdom Millennium Commission suggested to parish councils that they might mark the occasion by erecting temporary arches, but they do not seem to have taken up the idea. However, in the USA Rodney Cook Jr built an arch as the centrepiece of his $2 billion development in Atlanta, Georgia [34.12]. He had intended in 1999 to build an arch in Washington, D.C., to celebrate peace, but the 2001 disasters put paid to that. The architect in Atlanta was the English Hugh Petter, of Adam Architecture.[27] The arch is 70 feet (just over 21 m) high, and resembles a plainer and slimmer Arc de Triomphe. A panel in the centre of the attic has crossed palm branches, below a vestigial pediment. On top is a glass pavilion providing an office for Mr Cook, and within the arch is a museum. At the front of the piers and at the sides there were to be bases on which were to stand sculptures by the Scot Alexander Stoddart, representing Peace and Justice at the sides, and 'peaceful accomplishments throughout the ages' on the fronts. On one side at a lower level there are curving colonnades. The 'Millennium Gate', which cost $18 million, was inaugurated in 2008. Inevitably it has attracted criticism, being called 'a kitschy McMonument' or 'Arc d'Ikea', but it is a powerful building, though somewhat let down by the setting and the absence of the sculptures.

34.12 Atlanta, Georgia, Millennium Gate, inaugurated 2008. Hugh Petter.

Notes

1. *Architectural Review* 10 (1 Dec. 1901), 208–9.
2. Ian Dungavell, *The Architectural Career of Sir Aston Webb (1849–1930)* (PhD, London, 1999), 258–76. See also Neil Bingham, *Victorian and Edwardian Whitehall: Architecture and Planning 1865–1918* (PhD, London, 1985), 288–308.
3. G. Alex Bremner, '"Imperial Peace Memorial": The Second Anglo-Boer War and the origins of the Admiralty Arch, 1900–05', *British Art Journal*, 5, no. 3 (2004), 62–6.
4. C.H. Reilly, *Country Life*, 55 (9 Feb. 1924), 194. See also M.H. Port, *Imperial London* (New Haven/London, 1995), 24–5, 192–3; and for the competition entries *Architectural Review*, 10 (1901), 199–212; *British Architect*, 56 (1901), 309–19, 328–9.
5. Ugo Fleres, *Ettore Ximenes – sua vita e sue opere* (Bergamo, 1928), 66–7, 126–8, 134–46, 217–18. His last scheme, in 1926, was for an arch commemorating the March on Rome, with much sculpture (ibid., 243).
6. Information from newspaper cuttings file in Bridgeport Public Library. Curiously, there is an earlier arch in Bridgeport: the monument in the Mountain Grove Cemetery to Alfred and Mary Bishop is a sizable but plain arch, apparently dating from after 1880. Like many of the monuments there, it shows off the local granite admirably.
7. Julian Cavalier, *American Castles* (South Brunswick/New York, 1973), 74–82.
8. Uwe Westfehling, *Triumphbogen im 19. und 20. Jahrhundert* (Munich, 1977), 71–2.
9. Virgil Vatasianu, *Kunstdenkmäler in Rumänien* (Darmstadt, 1986), 76, 411.
10. J. Amery, *The Life of Joseph Chamberlain*, IV (London, 1951), 449; R. Quinault in T.R. Gourvish and A. O'Day, *Later Victorian Britain 1867–1900* (Basingstoke, 1988), 86–7. Information kindly supplied by Richard Wallington.
11. R.I. Parry and T. Whitney, *Old Aberdare and Merthyr Tydfil in Old Photographs* (Barry, 1976), 6, 127–8.
12. *Building Design*, 28 May 1976, 11. The quarter-size prototype was on loan from a private collection to the Pitt Rivers Museum in Oxford from 1994 to 2009.
13. L.O. Larsson, *Die Neugestaltung der Reichshauptstadt: Albert Speers Generalbebauungsplan für Berlin* (Stockholm 1978), 52, with ills 35 (the plan of the axis) and 92 (the model); Alex Scobie, *Hitler's State Architecture: The Impact of Classical Antiquity* (University Park, Pa./London, 1990); Dawn Ades, ed., *Art and Power: Europe under the Dictators, 1930–45* (London, 1995), 258, 285, 328–9; Chris Hall, reviewing T. Friedrich, *Hitler's Berlin: Abused City* (New Haven/London, 2012) in the *Guardian Review*, 9 June 2012.
14. Gerdy Troost, *Das Bauen im neuen Reich*, II (Bayreuth, 1943), 10.
15. R. Trevelyan, *Princes under the Volcano* (London, 1972), 393.
16. *Architettura*, XIV (1935), 26–7; Carlo Cresti, *Architettura e Fascismo* (Florence, 1986), 318.
17. Cresti (cit. in the preceding note), 316–20.
18. Italo Balbo, 'La Litoranea Libica', *Nuova Antologia*, 390 (1937), 11–13; Martin Moore, *Fourth Shore: Italy's Mass Colonization of Libya* (London, 1940), 206–9; Paul Schmidt, ed., *Revolution im Mittelmeer: Der Kampf um den italienischen Lebensraum* (Berlin, 1940), 99; Ugo Ogetti, *Cose Viste (1921–43)* (Florence, 1960), 1457–62; Claudio G. Segré, *Italo Balbo: A Fascist Life* (Berkeley, 1987), 308–9; Philip Kendrick, *Libya Archaeological Guides: Tripolitania* (London, 2009), 154–6. Information kindly supplied by Dr David Atkinson.
19. Cresti (cit. at n. 16).
20. *Architettura*, XVII (1938), 657: Cresti (cit. at n. 16), 324–6; Jobst Welge, 'Fascism *Triumphans*', in Claudia Lazzaro and Roger J. Crum, eds, *Donatello among the Blackshirts: History and Modernity in the Visual Culture of Fascist Italy* (Ithaca, NY, 2005), 86–7. Welge discusses the triumphal arch in Fascist iconography.
21. *Leopardi: Primo Centenario della Morte* (Recanati, 1937), 23; Benjamin George Martin, 'Celebrating the Nation's Poets: Petrarch, Leopardi, and the Appropriation of Cultural Symbols in Fascist Italy', in Lazzaro and Crum (cit. in the preceding note), 187–202.
22. *Architettura*, XVII (1938), 821.
23. Tracy Campbell, *The Gateway Arch: a Biography* (New Haven/London, 2013).
24. ibid., 78.
25. Samir al-Kalil, *Monument: Art, Vulgarity and Responsibility in Iraq* (Berkeley, 1991).
26. Jérôme Coignard, ed., *La Grande Arche* (Paris, 1990).
27. Hugh Petter kindly supplied information.

BIBLIOGRAPHY

This list contains only works which are referred to by abbreviations.

Cancellieri 1802 Francesco Cancellieri, *Storia de' solenni possessi de' sommi pontifici* (Rome, 1802)
Claridge 2010 Amanda Claridge, *Rome: An Archaeological Guide* (Oxford, 2nd edition, 2010)
De Maria 1988 Sandro de Maria, *Gli archi onorari di Roma e dell'Italia Romana* (Rome, 1988)
Dictionary of Art 1996 *The Grove Dictionary of Art*, ed. Jane Shoaf Turner (London, 1996)
Europa Triumphans 2004 J.R. Mulryne and Helen Watanabe-Kelly (edd.), *Europa Triumphans: court and civic festivals in early modern Europe* (Aldershot, 2004)
Fagioli 1997 Marcello Fagioli, *La Festa a Roma, dal Rinascimento al 1870* (Turin, 1997)
Fagioli dell'Arco 1997 Maurizio Fagioli dell'Arco, *La Festa Barocca* (Rome, 1997)
Fähndrich 2005 Sabine Fähndrich, *Bogenmonumente in der römischen Kunst* (Rahden, 2005)
Fêtes 1956–75 Jean Jacquot and Elie Konigson (edd.), *Les Fêtes de la Renaissance* (Paris, 1956–75)
Grove Dictionary of Art (London, 1996)
Kähler 1939 Heinz Kähler, in A.F. von Pauly and G. Wissowa (edd.), 'Triumphbogen', *Real-Encyclopädie der classischen Altertumswissenschaft* (Stuttgart, 1939)
Kleiner 1985 F.S. Kleiner, *The Arch of Nero at Rome* (Rome, 1985)
Küpper-Böhm 1996 A. Küpper-Böhm, *Die römischen Bogenmonumente der Gallia Narbonensis in ihrem urbanen Kontext* (Espelkamp, 1996)
Giuseppe Mazzilli *L'arco di Traiano a Leptis Magna* (Rome, 2016)
Nash Ernest Nash, Pictorial Dictionary of Ancient Rome
Roehmer 1997 Marion Roehmer, *Der Bogen als Staatsmonument* (Munich, 1997)
Von Erffa 1958 Hans Martin Freiherr von Erffa, 'Ehrenpforte', *Reallexicon zur deutschen Kunstgeschichte IV* (Stuttgart, 1958), 1443–1504
Westfehling Uwe Westfehling, *Triumphbogen im 19. und 20. Jahrhundert* (Munich, 1977)

PICTURE CREDITS

Thank you to the following sources for providing the images featured in this book:

Alamy/AA World Travel Library: 17.4; PWB Images: 14.9; Ivan Vdovin: 8.3

ARCA, Arte Colonial Americano: 29.1

Biblioteca di Archeologia e Storia dell'arte di Roma: 10.1, 10.2

Bibliotheque national de France: 8.1, 14.10, 14.11

Bildarchiv Ostpreussen: 15.3

Cooper Hewitt, Smithsonian Design Museum: 4.12, 25.2

Cornell University Library: 22.8, 26.3

D.R. Instituto Nacional de Antropología e Historia, México: 29.6

Edward Diestelkamp: 9.4.

Flickr/Chris Dawkin: 17.9; Bruce Guenter: 33.15; Jasperdo: 34.11; Dan McKay: 19.1; Neil Alexander McKee: 17.3; Mario Micklisch: 34.10; Nairnbairn: 18.5; Daniel and Kate Pett: 7.3; Carole Raddato: 2.10; Dan Sloean: 7.6; Triplefivedrew: 17.7; Billy Wilson: 17.8

Fondo Antiguo de la Biblioteca de la Universidad de Sevilla: 29.3

Geograph/David Hillas: 34.5

The J. Paul Getty Museum. Digital image courtesy of the Getty's Open Content Program: 20.3

Houghton Library, Harvard University: 14.1

Peter Howell: 1.1, 2.4, 2.5, 2.8, 2.9, 2.13, 4.1, 4.5, 4.9, 4.10, 4.15, 4.18, 5.7, 9.2, 9.3, 9.9, 9.15, 9.16, 10.11, 12.3, 13.4, 14.6, 16.5, 16.7, 16.14, 27.3, 33.2, 33.10, 33.11, 33.12, 34.1, 34.9

iStock/Vladone: 34.2

Library of Congress, Washington, DC: 6.8, 7.5, 28.1, 28.2, 32.2, 33.1, 33.5

Margo Malcolm, romanfootsteps.com: 5.5

Courtesy: Metropolitan Cathedral of Mdina, Malta. Photo: Joe P. Borg: 27.1

Metropolitan Museum of Art: 4.7, 11.1, 22.1

National Gallery of Victoria, Melbourne: 30.3

New York Public Library: 7.9

Hugh Petter: 34.12

Picfair/Mark Hutchinson: 16.9

Rijksmuseum: 14.2, 17.1

Rheinisches Landesmuseum, Trier: 22.2

Shutterstock/Agsaz: 26.2; Franck Camhi: 9.5; ChiccoDodiFC: 9.10; Chrislofotos: 33.9; Clearlens: 22.6; Diagram: 24.2; Vladislav Gajic: 2.12; Man Hurt: 33.3; Alexander Ingerman: 5.6; Anton Ivanov: 7.8; Petr Jilek: 11.3; Jorgedasi: 26.4; Jorisvo: 34.3; Mariusz S. Jurgielewicz: 23.4; Lev Levin: 7.2; Felix Lipov: 14.3; Mark2481: 7.7; Mistervlad: 16.12; Ryzhkov Oleksandr: 6.1; Olrat: 20.2; Joaquin Ossorio Castillo: 33.8; Sanga Park: 24.5; Soumitra Pendse: 31.2; Jeafish Ping: 33.14; Geraldo Ramos: 29.5 Redchanka: 33.7; Rmichev: 9.11; Andrei Rybachuk: 4.11; Saiko3p: 31.3; Siaath: 5.9; Gennadiy Solovyev: 24.4; Ruth Swan: 4.4; S. Tatiana: 11.2; ValeStock: 9.7; Mishakov Valery: 24.3; Guido Vermeulen-Perdaen: 14.8; Timofey Zadvornov: 2.2

SLUB, Dresden/Deutsche Fotothek: 10.4, 10.5

State Library of New South Wales: 30.2

State Library of Queensland: 30.4

Stockholmskällan: 25.1

Victoria and Albert Museum, London: 10.7, 12.1, 12.8, 12.9, 12.12, 21.2, 31.1

Wikimedia Commons/Rehman Abubakr: 26.6; Acroterion: 33.4; Alvesgaspar: 19.3; Maurizio Beatrici: 16.15; Benutzer: 14.4; Bill Boaden: 16.3; Eric Borda: 33.13; W. Bulach: 15.2; Camster2: 4.14; Marianne Casamance: 2.7; Classical Numismatic Group, Inc. www.cngcoins.com: 3.2; Decan: 4.13; DeFacto: 16.2, 16.8; Didier Descouens: 9.6, 9.14; Deshrnndzz: 26.1; James F.: 12.4; Bernard Gagnon: 6.9; Giogo: 13.2; Jean-Pol Grandmont: 15.4; Michael Gunther: 6.6; Jakub Hałun: 19.2; Jebulon: 4.2; Jirka23: 23.5; Judgefloro: 32.4; Kamée: 5.3; Kokin: 3.1; Kuebi – Armin Kübelbeck: 8.2; Simon Legner: 22.9; Mister No: 34.4; MM: 4.17; Reinhold Möller: 21.4; Wolfgang Moroder: 10.3; Burkhard Mücke: 9.13; Belaloui Nacer Eddinev: 7.1; Nilfanion: 5.4; Panairjdde: 4.8; Patche99z: 16.6; Peter1936F: 9.12; Poliphilo: 12.6; Prosopee: 14.7; Rheins: 2.11; Enrico Robetto: 2.3; Hans A. Rosbach:

441

17.6; A. Savin: 5.8; Hendrik Schöttle: 22.7; Andy Scott: 12.5; Selbymay: 26.5; Klaus-Peter Simon: 6.2, 6.3; Nadine Spires: 33.6; Matthias Süßen: 11.4; Marcin Szala: 16.13; Arild Vågen: 22.4; Velela: 18.1; Victorgrigas: 5.2; Frank Vincentz: 27.2; Renardo la Vulpo: 10.10; Hermann Wendler, www.hermannwendler.com: 13.3; Wernervc: 14.5; Wikipedro: 5.1; Zairon: 9.8

Christopher Wilson: 6.4, 6.5, 6.7, 7.4

Wolverhampton Arts and Culture owned and managed by City of Wolverhampton Council © David Brangwyn: 4.16

Yale Center for British Art: 12.7

Every effort has been made to trace copyright holders and acknowledge the images. The publisher welcomes further information regarding any unintentional omissions.

ACKNOWLEDGEMENTS

During the long gestation of the book, many people have given generous help. It is impossible to list all their names, but some should be mentioned.

First of all must be the godfather of the book, Sir Howard Colvin. His own interest in the triumphal arch is attested by his writings, He gave generous encouragement for this work, and I can only regret that it did not appear in time for him to see it.

It was thanks to his support that I obtained a grant from the Arts and Humanities Research Council to fund an extensive arch-hunt in France, Germany and Italy. This was made possible by a sabbatical term from the Classics Department of Royal Holloway, to which college I had been banished after the unforgivable suppression of Bedford College.

My publisher Ian Strathcarron nobly took the book on when many others had turned it down. Emily Lane has lived up to her reputation as the queen of editors. Her eagle eye and perceptive criticisms have saved me from many an error. Katie Greenwood did a first-rate job as picture researcher, and her endurance and ingenuity were most helpful. Lucy Duckworth has been a sympathetic editor, and Nick and George Newton have shown remarkable care, skill, and patience in the design of the book. Nicola King gave perceptive assistance as the indexer.

I am particularly grateful to Christopher Wilson for allowing me to use some of his photographs.

Edward Diestelkamp has been an invaluable ally, whether as travelling companion, photographer, or provider of moral support.

Others who have assisted are:

Brenda Bolton; Mosette Broderick; Ian Campbell; Amanda Claridge; Michael Hall; John Harris; Charles Hind; the late Joan Ker; Sir Jonathan Marsden; John Nicoll; Andrew Saint; Sally Salvesen; Andrew Shanken; the late Ian Sutton; Adam White; Peter Wiseman; Geert Wisse.

INDEX

Numbers in *italic* denote pages with figures.

Aalst, Belgium 258
Abad Casal, L. 81, 82
Aberdare, Wales 431
Aberdeen, Scotland 307
Acaja, Gian Giacomo dell 152
Accra, Ghana 430
Ackerman, J.S. 187
Acquisti, Luigi 179
Actium, Greece 7
Adam, John 294
Adam, Robert 265, 275, 276–7, 294–8, *296*, *298*
Adam, William 294, *294*
Adelaide, Australia 388, 392
Admiralty Arch, London 426
Adrian VI, pope 156
Agea, Ramon 382, *383*
Aïn el Bordj, Algeria 113
Ain Golea, Tunisia 109
Ain Melluk, Algeria 124
Aix, France 227, 235
Aix-les-Bains, France 24
Alamo, Texas, USA 377
Albert VII, Archduke of Austria 249
Alberti, Leon Battista 137, 138–41, *139–40*, 142, 144, 291
Albicante, Giovanni Alberto 193
Albrecht, Duke of Brandenburg 250, *251*
Alcántara, Spain 80–1, *80*
Aldrovandini, Pompeo 177, *177*
Aleandri, Ireneo 186
Alessandria, Italy 197
Alexander I, Tsar 353, 360
Alexander II, Tsar 352
Alexander III, Tsar 361
Alexander VII, pope 56, 174
Alexander Severus *see* Severus Alexander
Alexandria, Egypt 126
Alexandria Troas, Turkey 95
Alfonso I, K. of Naples 141, *141*

Alfred, Duke of Edinburgh 388, *388*
Algeria 108–14, 116–18, 120–5
Allason, Edward 26
Allison, Richard 425
Allori, Alessandro 195
Almeyda, Giuseppe Damiani 199, *199*
altarpieces 153, *153*, 175, *175*
Altobelli, Gioacchino 181
Alton Towers, Staffs. 267–8, 268
Amadori, Federico 187
Amanat, Hossein 435
Amati, Carlo 316
Américo Figueiredo e Melo, Pedro 385
Ammannati, Bartolommeo 279, *279*
Ammianus Marcellinus 1, 75
Amsterdam, Netherlands 248, 255–6, 258
Anazarbos, Turkey 94–5, *94*
Ancona, Italy 61, *62*, 63, *64*, 184, 186
Ancy-le-Franc, France 147, *148*
Anderson, R. Rowand 425
Andreasi, Gerolamo 158, *158*
Andreotti, Libero 418
Androuet du Cerceau, Jacques 222, *222*
Anet, France 224, *224*
Angelicoussis, E. 44–5
Angers, David d' 325, *326*
Anguier, François 229
Anguier, Michel 231
Anne Boleyn 203
Annouma, Algeria 121, 122, 123
Anonymus Einsiedlensis 37, 56
Antalya, Turkey 92, *93*
Antinoe, Egypt 126, *126*
Antioch, Turkey 23, 92, 96
Antiochia ad Maeandrum, Turkey 95
Antipatris, Israel 105
antiquities, early medieval interest in 132–3, 135–6
Antolini, Giovanni 316
Antonescu, Petre 430

Antoninus Pius 44, 64–5, 85, 109–11, *110*
Antwerp, Belgium 203, 204, 207, 246–7, 249, *249*, 250–5, *252–4*, 256, *257*, 259
Aosta, Italy 11–12, *11*
Apamea, Syria 102
Aphrodisias, Turkey 94
Apollodorus of Damascus 83
Appuldurcombe, Isle of Wight 264
aqueducts 33, 184, 372, 375
Aquino, Italy 3–4, *4*
Arasa i Gil, F. 81
Arc de Triomphe de l'Étoile, Paris 319–21, *320*, *322*
Arc de Triomphe du Carrousel, Paris 317–18, *317*
Arcadius 56, 97
Arce, J. 82
Arcevia, Italy 153
architectural competitions 238, 240–1, 241–4, 320, 321, 342–3, 352, 377, 415–16, 425
Arçon, Jean-Claude Éléonor le Michaud d' 238
arcus triumphalis 1, 75, 112, 118, 131
Argomenti, Giuseppe 179
Ariassos, Turkey 92
Arles, France 17, 19
Arlington, USA 405
Armidale, Australia 388
Arques-la-Bataille, France 248
Asiago, Italy 414, *414*
Aspertini, Amico 163–4
Asselyn, Jan 165
Assos, Turkey 96
Astana, Kazakhstan 437
Aston, Sir Roger 216
Athens, Greece 5, 83–5, *84*
Atlanta, USA 438, *438*
Attingham Park, Shrops. 268
Attwood, C.B. 378, *378*
Aubry, Claude-Guillot 238
August II & III, Ks. of Poland 349
Augustus 7–11, *8*, 12, 23, 125

Australia 388–92, 413–14
Austria 75, 254, 284–5, 343–6
Avignon, France 227
Aviler, Augustin-Charles d' 234
Avitta Bibba, Tunisia 109, 112
Azancot, Alfredo 385–6, *386*
Azzurri, Francesco 182

Bacchielli, L. 117
Baccio d'Agnolo 153
Bacon, Henry 427, *427*
Baeza, Spain 369–70, *369*
Baghdad, Iraq 436
Baily, E.H. 330, 331, 332
Baini, Giuseppe 181
Baker, Sir Herbert 408
Bal Kiz, Turkey 33
Balbo, Italo 433
Ballarat, Australia 390, 392
Ball's Grove, Co. Louth 277
Ballu, A. 120–1
Baltard, Louis-Pierre 244
Baltard, Victor 326, *327*
Baltimore, USA 377
Balzac, Charles-Louis 320
Bangkok, Thailand 398
Banjul, Gambia 436
Bantry House, Co. Cork 278
Barba, Ramón 371
Barbaro, Daniele 187
Barberi, Francesco 179
Barberi, Giuseppe 178
Barcelona, Spain 371–2, *371*
Barnard, George Grey 422
Baronscourt, Co. Tyrone 278
Barradale, Isaac 311
Bar-sur-Seine, France 238
Barye, Antoine-Louis 327
Basalo, Pedro 385
Bassani, Giovanni 316
Bassano, Alessandro da 194
Bastos, Vitor 373
Battaglia, Pier Paolo 151
Battisti, Antonio de' 173
Battisti, Cesare 417, *417*, 418
Baudeloo, Belgium 258
Baur, P.V.C. 100
Baybay, Philippines 399–400
Bayramli, Turkey 95

Bayreuth, Germany 340
Beard, Mary 3
Beaubrun, Charles & Henri 229, 230
Beauvais, O.I. 359
Bêdja, Algeria 122
Beeckestijn, Netherlands 281
Beeckmans, F. 259
Begas, Reinhold 342
Beijing, China 397, *397*
Béja, Tunisia 113
Bélanger, François-Joseph 264
Belarus 352
Belfast, N. Ireland 309
Belgium
  celebratory arches 137, 203–4, 207, 246–8, 249–55, *249*, 256–8, 306, 323
  garden features 283, 284
  monuments 250
  20th cent. 428–9, *429*
  war memorials 411–13, *412*
Bell, Ingress 406
Bellange, Jacques 227
Bellini, Jacopo 159–60, *159*
Beloch, J. 65
Bénard, Charles-Jean 240–1
Benedetto da Maiano 153
Benedict XIV, pope 178, *178*, 184–5
Benevento, Italy 59–60, *59, 61*, 64
Berenson, Bernard 54
Berlin, Germany 336–7, 339, 342, 432–3, *432*
Bernini 184, 187
Berrington Hall, Herefs. 265–6
Besançon, France 71–3, *72*
Besseriani Negrin, Algeria 121–2
Bevingon, Michael 275
Bevis Mount, Hants. 262–3, *262*
Bible illuminations 132
Bifoli, Enzo 415
Binche, Belgium 248
Birkirkara, Malta 375
Birmingham, West Mids. 308, 313
Bizya, Turkey 85
Blackburn, Lancs. 268
Blagoveshchensk, Russia 361
Blaine, USA 437, *437*
Blanco, Francisco, archbishop 369
Blenheim Palace, Oxon. 263–4, *263*
Blomfield, Reginald 233, 411–13, *412*
Blondeel, Lancelot 248
Blondel, François 231, 232, *232*
Blondel, Georges-François 241
Blondel, Jacques-François 239, *239, 242*
Blore, Edward 330, 331
Blouet, Abel 321
Blundell, Henry 266
Blunden, Edmund 409
Blunt, Anthony 224, 225

Boccadiferro, Lodovico 158
Bodt, Jean de 337
Boffrand, Germain 238
Bokassa, Jean-Bedel 435–6
Boldt, George 428, *428*
Bollani, Domenico 148
Bologna, Italy 158, 182–3, 316
Bolzano, Italy 417–18, *417*
Bombay, India 394, *394*
Bontadino di Bontadini 375
Borch, Gerard ter, the Elder 165
Bordeaux, France 221, 238, 244
Bordiau, Gédéon 259
Bordj el Arbi, Tunisia 112
Boringdon Arch, Devon 276–7
Bosio, François-Joseph *317*, 318
Boson, John 293, *293*
Bostra, Syria 100, 102, 105
Botticelli, Sandro 54, 161, *161*
Boudhors, P.-V. 319
Boullée, Étienne-Louis 241
Boulogne, France 33
Boumann, Johann 338
Bowood, Wilts. 275
Boy, Adolf 348
Boyle, Richard, Earl of Cork 216
Bracci, Pietro 52–3
Bramante, Donato 143–4, 156
Brangwyn, Sir Frank 63, *64*
Brasini, Armando 415
Brazil 385
Brecht, Bertold 422–3
Breda, Netherlands 257
Bregno, Andrea 153, *153*
Bremner, Alex 426
Brézé, Louis de 222, *223*, 224
Bridgeport, USA 426–7, *427*
Bridges, James 299
Brie, Adriaen de 251
Brighton, E. Sussex 305, *305*, 306
Brindisi, Italy 7
Brindle, Steven 295, 296
Brisbane, Australia 389, 390–1, *391*
Bristol, England 299, 306, 413
Brock, Sir Thomas 425, 426
Brockway, A.L. 422
Brongniart, Alexandre-Théodore 241–2, 243
Brooklyn, New York 403–4, *403*
Brown, Fortini 143
Brown, Lancelot (Capability) 266
Browne, John 202
Browne, Joseph 330
Bruges, Belgium 137, 246, 248, 306
Brunette, Narcisse 73
Bruschi, Arnaldo 143, 144
Brussels, Belgium 247, 248, 249, 259, 428–9, *429*
Bryanston, Dorset 265
Bryant, Lawrence 230
Buberl, Caspar 403
Bucharest, Romania 430
Buckler, John 262–3, *262*

Budapest, Hungary 352
Buhagiar, Aloisio 374
Bulfinch, Charles 377
Bullant, Jean 222–3
Bullet, Jean-Baptiste 234
Bullet, Pierre 232, *233*, 234
Buontalenti, Bernardo 155, 173
Burford, Oxon. 216
Burghley, Mildred, Lady 208–9, *209*
Burgos, Spain 368, 370, *370*
Burton, Decimus 331, 332
Butler, H.C. 102

Caballero, Cristóbal 383–4
Cabanes, Spain 81
Cabiati, Ottavio 415
Cadeleigh, Devon 216
Cadorin, Guido 418
Cagnola, Luigi 286, 318, *319*
Cailleau, Hubert 221
Caius, John 204, 206, *206*
Calahorra, Spain 368
Calcutta, India 393, *393*, 394, *395*
Calder, Stirling 378, 428
Caledon, Co. Tyrone 277–8
Caligula 32, 107–8
Callixtus II, pope 133, 169
Callot, Jacques 228
Calmels, Célestin Anatole 373
Cambridge, Cambs. 204, 206–7, *206*
Cameron, Charles 282–3, 358
Campbell, Colen 264
Campbell, Ian 165, 217
Campen, Jacob van 255
Campioni, Peter 361
Camporese, Giulio 186, *186*
Camporese, Giuseppe 47, 316
Canada 402, 420–1, 431
Canaletto, Antonio 279, 280
Canevale, Isidor 352
Canina, Luigi 285–6
Canonica, Isidor 319
Canonica, Pietro 417, 418, 419, *419*
Canova, Antonio 39
Canzio, Michele 286, 287
Cáparra, Spain 79–80
Caprarola, Italy 144
Capua, Italy 65, 133, 135, *135*
Caracalla 1, 45, 48, 65, 116–17, 119–20, *119*, 121, 124, 125
Caracas, Venezuela 385
Caraffe, Armand-Charles 242–3
Carbonell, Pere 372
Carden Hall, Ches. 267
Caristie, Auguste 21
Carlone, Taddeo 197
Carnevale, Fra 160
Caroto, Giovanni Francesco 165
Carpaccio 163
Carpentras, France 17–18, *17*
Carrickglass, Co. Longford 277
Caselli, Giuseppe 197

Caserta, Italy 419
Cassius Dio 11, 23, 33, 36, 40, 43
Castagno, Andrea del 160
Castel, Gaston 419–20, *420*
Castle Coole, Co. Fermanagh 278
Castle Hill, Devon 269
Catania, Italy 197, *198*
Catherine of Austria 194
Catherine the Great 281–3, *282*, 357–8
Cattari, Andrea 374
Cavaillon, France 18, *18*
Cechner, Antonín 352–3, *353*
celebratory arches
  Australia 388–92, *389–90*
  Austria 343–6
  Belgium 137, 203–4, 207, 246–8, 249–55, *249*, 256–8, 306, 323
  England 305–14, *305, 309–14*, 431, *431–2*
  France 217, 225–7, 229–30, *229*, 235, 239–40, *239*, 241, *242*, 325–6, *327*
  Germany 335, *335*, 336–7, 339–40, 341, 343
  Italy 191–9, *195, 198–9*
  London 202–3, 203–4, 209–16, *210, 212–15*, 302, 306, 308, 313–14, *314*, 431
  Malta 374, 376, *376*
  Mexico 381–2, *381*
  Netherlands 248–9, 255–6, 257, *257*, 258
  Peru 383–4
  Poland 343, 348–9, *348, 350*, 351, 352
  Portugal 372
  Russia 355–6, *355*, 357
  Scandinavia 363–5, *364*, 367
  Scotland 217–18, 306, 307, *307–8*
  Spain 370
  United States of America 377
  Wales 431
Celenderis, Turkey 96
Cellerier, Jacques 241, *242*
Central African Republic 435–6
Cernil, Moric 352–3, *353*
Cesarini, Gabriele 172
Cevasco, Giovanni Battista 286, 287
Chalgrin, François 319
Chalgrin, Jean-François-Thérèse 320, *320*
Challe, Charles Michel-Ange 240
Châlons-en-Champagne, France 238
Chambers, Sir William 264, 272, *273*, 299, 396–7
Chantrey, Sir Francis 330
Chapelain, Jean 230
Chapman and Oxley 431
Charlemagne 130, 132
Charles I 212–13, *213*, 217–18

Charles II 214–16, *214–15*, 255–6
Charles III, K. of Spain 197, 370–1, *370*
Charles IV, duc de Lorraine 227
Charles V, Emperor 152, *152*, 165, 182–3, 191, 193, 196–7, 221–2, 246, 248, 335, *335*, 343
Charles VI, Emperor 256
Charles VIII, K. of France 192
Charles IX, K. of France 226
Charles X, K. of France 319, 325
Charles the Bald 132
Charon, Cleophas 363
Chataing, Alejandro 385
Chatham, Kent 401–2, *401*, 406, 408
Châtillon-sur-Seine, France 238
Chatou, France 325–6
Chatsworth, Derbys. 299, *299*
Cheesman, George Jun. 306
Chehab, M.-H. 100
Chelli, Carlo 181
Chelsea, London 207, *208*
Chester, Ches. 310, *310*
Chicago, USA 378, *378*
Chieri, Italy 151
Chiesa, Damiano 417, *417*, 418
Chile 385–6
China 396–8
Chinea festival, Rome 192
Chippenham Park, Cambs. 266
Chisinau, Moldova 362
Christ Church, Oxford 300, *300*
Christian IV, K. of Denmark 212, 363
Christina, Queen of Sweden 191–2, 363–5, *364*
Christina of Denmark 193
Christina of Lorraine 195
Christmas, Gerard 212, 216
Chrysoloras, Manuel 135–6
church furnishings and monuments
 England 207–9, *208–9*, 216
 France 224–5
 Germany 334–5, *335*
 Italy 133, *134*, 153–9, *153–5*, *157–8*
 Low Countries 248, 250, *250*
 Mexico 386–7, *386*
 Russia 250, *251*
 Spain 369, 370, *370*
Cicero 2, 3, 5
Cienfuegos, Cuba 385
Cingoli, Italy 186
Civiletti, Benedetto 199, *199*
Città Castellana, Italy 133
Clarke, George 293
Claudian 56
Claudius 32–3, 50
Claussen, P.C. 133
Clement VII, pope 156–8, 171, 182–3
Clement VIII, pope *154*, 155, 183

Clement X, pope 63, *174*, 175–6
Clement XI, pope 176, *177*
Clement XIV, pope 178, 185–6, *185*
Cleyn, Francis 212
clocks 179
Clumber Park, Notts. 266
Coarelli, F. 55, 56
Coccetti, Liborio 179
Codex Coner 164
Coecke van Aelst, Pieter 247, 248
coins
 of Domitian 40, *41*
 of Maximinus 87, 95
 of Nero 34–5, *34*
 Parthian arch 7–8, *8*
Coixtlahuaca, Mexico 386–7, *386*
Colbert, Jean-Baptiste 230
Colchester, Essex 76
Colebrook, Co. Fermanagh 278
Coli, Giovanni 191
Cologne, Germany 316
Colonia, Francisco de 368
Colonna, Francesco 137–8
Colonna, Marcantonio 191
Colt, Maximilian 216
Coltellini, Girolamo 158
Colvin, Howard 203, 269, 299
Colyton, Devon 216
Combe Abbey, Warwicks. 266
Commodus 44–5, 85, 102, 113
Conant, J. 132
Constanta, Romania 87
Constantine 41, *42*, 44, 45, 50–5, *51*, *53*, 65–7, *66–7*, 96, 97
Constantine, Algeria 1, 120, 122, 125
Constantinople, Turkey 97–8, *97*
Constantius 75
Constantius II 75, 121
Conti, Ulderico 434
Cook, Rodney Jr 438
Cool, Jacob 211, 212
Copenhagen, Denmark 363, 366, 367
Corbett, Harvey Wiley 437, *437*
Cordier, Nicolas 364
Corinth, Greece 82–3, 85–6
Corio, Bernardino 170
Cornacchini, Agostino 184
Cornaro, Alvise 144
coronation arches *see* celebratory arches
Cosa, Italy 4, 6
Cosimo I de' Medici, Grand Duke 194
Costa, Veríssimo José da 373
Cottius 12–13
Cottrell, Liance W. 405, *405*
Cousin, Jean 226
Coutu, Joan 275
Couture, Guillaume-Martin 240
Cracow, Poland 348–9
Crampton's Gap, USA 404, *404*
Cranford, Middlesex 216
Cremona, Italy 192, 194

Cressant, Jacob 281
Cret, Paul 405
Croatia 24–6, 83, 87
Cromois, Jean de 248
Croome Court, Worcs. 265
Croy, Wilhelm von 250
Cuba 385
Cubitt, Thomas 331
Cumae, Italy 58
Cusani, Lamberto 426
Cusco, Peru 385
Cuypers, P.J.H. 258
Cyrene, Libya 112
Cyriacus of Ancona 96
Czech Republic 283–4, 352–3

Dacres, Andrew 215–16
Dahlberg, Erik 365
Dal Pozzo, Cassiano 164, 165
damnatio memoriae 34
Damotte, Jean 226
Dandolo Priuli, Zilia, Dogaressa 194
Danne, Franz Anton 345–6
Dashwood, Sir Francis 272–3
Dativius Victor 75
Davioud, Gabriel 327
Davis, Charles 159
Dazzi, Arturo 415, 416–17, *416*
De Albertis, Eduardo 415, 417
De la Vallée, Jean 364, *364*, 365
De Maria, Sandro 2, 5, 9, 58, 126
Debret, Jean-Baptiste 385
Decius 95
Delafosse, Jean-Charles 240
Delft, Netherlands 250, *250*, 255
Delhi, India 393
Della Porta, Gian Giacomo 197
Della Rovere, Federigo Ubaldo 196
Della Rovere, Girolamo Basso 156, *157*
Delphi, Greece 85
Demetrios Poliorketes 5
Demut-Malinowski, W.I. 359, *359–60*, 360
Denmark 363, 366, 367
Denon, Vivant 317–18
Der Sim'an, Syria 104
Déruet, Claude 227
Desbrowe-Annear, Harold 389, *390*
design competitions *see* architectural competitions
Desio, Italy 286
D'Este, Ippolito 151
D'Este, Lionello 139
D'Este, Niccolò III 139
Détournelle, Athanase 242–3
Diadumenianus 86, 121
Dick, William Reid 412, *412*
Didier, Robert 248
Dijon, France 226, 239
Dillens, Julien 429
Diocletian 50, 121–2
Disraeli, Benjamin 306

Djebel Halaka, Syria 104
Djemila, Algeria 1, 110–11, 117–18, *118*
Dnieperpetrovsk, Russia 357, 361
Dodington Park, Gloucs. 265
Doisy, H. 121
Domergue, C. 119
Domitian 40–3, *41–2*, 57–8, 76, 77, 79, 125, 126
Dondi, Giovanni 135
Donowell, John 272–3
Dorat, Jean 226
Doriny, Charles 226
Doriny, Michel 230
Dosio, Giovanni Antonio 165
Dougga, Tunisia 32, 107–8, 113, 121
Douglas, John 310, *310*
Dowlais, Wales 431
Downes, Kerry 264
drawings of and designs for arches
 Belgium 258, 283
 England 264, 265, 269, 291–3, *291*, 295, 300, 301
 France 236, 238, 240–1, 241–4, *243*, 320, 321, 326–7
 Germany 334, *334*
 Ireland 278
 Italy 164–6, *279*, 280, 286
 Russia 358
 Scotland 294, 297
 Sweden 366, *366*
Dresden, Germany 319, 335–6
Drew, Sir Thomas 278, 425
Drusus (son of Germanicus) 31–2
Drusus Minor (son of Tiberius) 12, 29, 30, 31, *31*
Du Broeucq, Jacques 247
Dublin, Ireland 300, *301*, 305, *305*, 310, 311, 406
Duca, Giovanni del 151
Ducros, Louis 183
Dugdale, Gilbert 211
Duncan, John Hemingway 403–4, *403*
Duncombe Park, Yorks. 267
Dundee, Scotland 307, *307*
Dupré i Raventos, Xavier 16
Duquesnoy, Jerome 250
Dura Europos, Syria 100
Durand, Nicolas 238
Dürer, Albrecht 334, *334*
Duret, Francisque-Joseph 327
Düsseldorf, Germany 323, 341, 343
Dykanka, Ukraine 353
Dzhambulatov, Sagyndyk 437

Eakins, Thomas 404
Earnshaw, Brian 267
Eastbury Park, Dorset 269, 292
Eastham, Ches. 313, *313*
Écouen, France 222–3
Edinburgh, Scotland 217–18, 294, 297

446 THE TRIUMPHAL ARCH

Edward VII 308, 309, 310, 313–14, 394, *395*, 431
Edward VIII 314, 431
Edwards, C.M. 83
Egypt 126, *126*
Ehrenstrahl, David Klöcker von 365
Einhard 130–1, *130*
Eisler, William 247
Eleonora of Toledo 194
Eléonore, Queen of France 221
Eleusis, Greece 85
Elisabeth of Austria 226, 227
Elisabeth Ludovika of Bavaria 340
Elisabeth Petrowna, Empress of Russia 356
Elizabeth I 203–4, 207, 216
Elizabeth II 314, 392, 431
Elizabeth Stuart, Queen of Bohemia 255, 336
Ellis, Thomas Graham 430
Elsner, Jas 48
Emerson, Sir William 394, *395*
Enghien, Belgium 250, 283
England 76–8, 202–16, 262–77, 305–14
  celebratory arches 305–14, *305, 309–14*, 431, *431*–2
  church monuments 207–9, *208–9*, 216
  drawings of arches 264, 265, 269, 291–3, *291*, 295, 300, 302
  garden features 268–77, *270–1, 273–6*
  gateways 204–7, *204–6*
  park entrances 262–8, *262–3*
  Roman period 76–8, *76–7*
  Romanesque 132
  war memorials 401–2, *401*, 406, 408, 409, 413
  see also London
Enkhuisen, Netherlands 257
Entress, Albert 403
entries *see* celebratory arches
Ephesus, Turkey 22, *23*, 91–2
Erffa, Hans Martin, Freiherr von 171, 173, 176
Erfurt, Germany 319
Eric XIV, K. of Sweden 363
Erlach, J.B. Fischer von 396, *396*
Ernst, Archduke of Austria 249
Espérandieu, Henri 327
Espiel, Spain 82
Este, Italy 280
Étaples, France 409
Etex, Antoine 321
Ettlingen, D. *161*, 163
Evelyn, John 216, 281
Everard, William 266
Eyck, Jan van 255

Faber, Oscar 412
Fabian, John 306
Q. Fabius Maximus 2, 3
Fabritius, Paulus 343

Facio, Attilio 196
Faenza, Italy 316
Fagiolo, M 170, 171
Fairbairn, Lynda 159, 165
Falck, Jeremias 348
Falcone, Giovanni Angelo 197
Falconetto, Giovanni Maria 144, 280
Falda, Giovanni Battista 175
Falerii Novi, Italy 5
Falguière, Alexandre 321, *322*
Fano, Italy 66–7, *67*
Farrell, William 278
Fascist arches 432–4, *432–3*, 435
Fausto, Florestano di 433, *433*
Fea, Carlo 47
Ferdinand I, K. of the Two Sicilies 197, *198*
Ferdinand II, Archduke of Austria 344
Ferdinand II, K. of Spain 192
Ferdinand VII, K. of Spain 371
Ferdinand of Austria, Cardinal-Infante 197, 250–5, *252–4*
Ferdinando I de' Medici, Grand Duke 195
Fernández, Pedro 369
Ferrante, K. of Naples 142–3
Ferrara, Italy 139–41, *140*, 183, 196
Ferroni, A.M. 51
Ferrucci, Andrea 153
Ferry, François 234
Ferstel, Heinrich 346
Fettercairn, Scotland 307, *308*
Fiasella, Domenico 197
Fichera, Francesco 415
Fiesole, Italy 153
Filiberto, Emanuele, Duke of Savoy 151
Filzi, Fabio 417, *417*, 418
Fischer von Erlach, Johann Bernhard 344–5, *345*
Flannery, Lot 405
Flaxman, John 330
Fleetwood, Lancs 413
Florence, Italy 153, 155, 162–3, 182, 192, 193–4, 195, 197, *198*
Floris, Cornelis 250, *251*
Floris, Frans 247
Flötner, Peter 335, *335*
Foch, Ferdinand 422
Fogari, Bernardo 196
Foggini, Vincenzo 197
Folchi, Clemente 179
Fontaine, Pierre-François-Léonard 317–18, *317*, 322, *323*
Fontana, Carlo 56, 57, 176, *176–7*
Fontana, Giacomo 63
Fonthill, Wilts. 264
fornix 2, 6
Forssmann, Erik 250
Fowler, Charles, Junior 268

Francavilla Fontana, Italy 152
France
  Ancien Régime 147, *148*, 221–8, *223–5*, 229–44, *234–5, 237*
  antiquity 14–15, *15*, 17–22, *17–19, 21*, 24, 30–1, *31*, 33, 71–4, *72–3*
  Bourbon Restoration 325, *326*
  celebratory arches 217, 229–30, *229*, 235, 239–41, *239, 242*
  drawings of arches 236, 238, 240–4, *243*
  Napoleonic arches 319
  Second Empire 325–6
  war memorials 409–11, *410*, 419–20, *420*, 422
  see also Paris
Francesco I de' Medici, Grand Duke 195
Francini, Alessandro 280
Francini, Tommaso 280
Francis I (Franz Stephan), Emperor 197, *198*, 345, 346
Francis II, Emperor 258
Francis, Duke of Anjou 249
Francken, Frans 249
Franco, Battista 165
Franco, Francisco 435
François I, K. of France 221, 224–5
Franz Josef I, Emperor of Austria 353
Frederick II, Emperor 133, 135
Frederick the Great 338, 339
Frederik Henrik, Prince of Orange 255
Frere, S.S. 78, 83
Frezzotti, Oriolo 415
Friederike of Mecklenburg 339
Friedlander, Leo 405
Friedrich III, K. of Prussia 336–7
Friedrich, Margrave of Brandenburg-Bayreuth 340
Friedrich Wilhelm II, III & IV, K.s of Prussia 339, 340
Friedrich Wilhelm, Elector of Brandenberg 336
Frith, W.S. 406
Frommel, C.L. 142
Frommel, Sabine 147
Frontinus 91
Frosini, Donato 172, *172*
Frothingham, A.L. 51, 95, 109, 113, 122, 124, 125
Fuga, Ferdinando 178, *178*
furniture 293, *293*
Fuxà, Manel 372

Gaasbeek, Belgium 284
Gabelmann, Hanns 151
Gabriel, Ange-Jacques 238
Gadara, Jordan 103–4
Gafsa, Tunisia 109
Gaius Caesar 14

Galaup de Chasteuil, Jean de 227
Galaup de Chasteuil, Pierre de 235
Galba 125
Galerius 87–8
Gall, H. von 75
Galletti, Stefano 181, 183
Galli, Edoardo 63
Galli Bibiena, Giuseppe 345
Gallienus 49–50, *49*, 95, 108
Galvani, Alberto di 151
Gambia 436
Gandon, James 277, 300, *301*
Garcia y Bellidos, A. 80, 81
garden features
  Britain and Ireland 268–78, *270–1, 273–6*
  other countries 278–87, *279–80, 282, 284–6*
Garendon, Leics. 270–1, *271*
Garrett, Daniel 271
Gärtner, Friedrich von 341–2, *342*
Gatchina, Russia 281–3, *282*
Gatti, G. 44
Gavilán, Baltasar 383
Gdansk, Poland 348, *348*, 349
Geneva, Switzerland 75
Genevale, I. 351–2, *351*
Genoa, Italy 196–7, 203, 286–7, *286*, 415–17, *416*
Genzano, Italy 417
George I 291, *291*
George II 292, 302
George III 302
George IV 302, 304–5
George V 388–92, *389–91*, 394, 431
George, Ernest 425
Gerbier, Sir Balthasar 214
Germaine of Foix 192
Germanicus 12, 29–30, *31*
Germany
  antiquity 30, 71, 74–5, 131–2
  celebratory arches 335, *335*, 336–7, 339–40, 341, 343
  garden features 281
  Napoleonic arches 316, 319, 323
  16th to 19th cent. 334–43, *334–5, 338, 340–2*
  20th cent. 432–3, *432*
Geta 45–6, 48
Gettysburg, USA 405, *405*
Gevaerts, Jan Casper 251, 254
Ghana 430
Ghardimaou, Tunisia 123
Ghent, Belgium 137, 246, 249, 250, 256–7, 258, 323
Gherardi, Filippo 191
Ghirlandaio, Dominico 162
Giani, Felice 316
Gibbs, James 264
Giersberg, Joachim 339–40
Gigli, Giacinto 173
Gigthis, Tunisia 123

INDEX 447

Giles, Alfred 382
Gillis, Louis 364
Gilpin, William 272
Giovanni da Maiano 202
Girardon, François 235
Giraud, Antoine 226
Girault, Charles 429, *429*
Girouard, Mark 204, 207, 210, 267, 271
Giulio Camillo dell'Abbate 227
Godefroy, Maximilian 377
Goldberg, Rube 423
Gomme, Andor 216
Gontard, Carl von 338–9, 340
Gonville and Caius College, Cambridge 204, 206–7, *206*
Gonzaga, Francesco 194
Gonzaga, Margherita 227
Gonzáles, Lorenzo 385
González, Fernán 370, *370*
González Velázquez, Antonio 382
Goodwood House, W. Sussex 299
Gordian 121
Gordian III 49, 87
Göthe, Eosander 337
Goudiaby, Pierre 436
Goujon, Jean 222, 223, *223*, 226
El Gouléa, Algeria 109
Goust, L. 319–20, *320*
Gradidge, Roderick 411
Graham, Gillespie 268
Granada, Spain 369
Grandi, Francesco 181
Grandjean de Montigny, A.-H.-V. 385
Grapheus, Cornelius 246
Gratian 56, 67–8, 123, 124
Graz, Austria 343, 344
Greasbrough, Yorks. 413
Grebnevo, Russia 361
Greece 5, 7, 22, 82–8, 96
Gregorius, Magister 133
Grell, Peter 212
Grenoble, France 235
Grimani, Marino, Doge 196
Grünberg, Martin 337
Guadalajara, Mexico 382
Guénepin, Auguste-Jean-Marie 39
Guercio, Gaspare 152
Guillaume, Eugène 325
Guillaumot, Charles-Axel 238
Gumpp, Johann Baptist 336
Gumpp, Johann Martin 345
El Gussa, Algeria 123
Gustav I, K. of Sweden 363
Gutiérrez, Francisco 370–1, *370*
Gwynn, John 295

Haas, Anton and Georg 344
Hack, Jean 248
Hadlow Castle, Kent 268
Hadrian 43–4, 64, 83, 85, 90, 91, 92, 100, 102, 108–9
Hague, The, Netherlands 248–9, 256, 257, *257*
Haïdra, Tunisia 113, 124
Halifax, Canada 402
Hardtmuth, Joseph 283–4, *284*
Harewood, Yorks. 266–7
Harleman, Carl 365
Harleyford, Bucks. 293
Harris, John 213, 214
Harrisburg, USA 428
Harrison, Stephen 209, 210, *210*, 211, 212, *212*
Harrison, Stockdale 311–12, *312*
Harrison, Thomas 304, *304*
Hart Island, USA 428, *428*
Hartbeespoort Dam, South Africa 430
Hartford, USA 402–3, *402*
Hartwell House, Bucks. 275–6
Haselberger-Blaha, Herta 344–5
Hasenauer, Karl 346
Hassel, J. 61
Hastings, E. Sussex 308–9
Hastings, Thomas 422
Haveus, Theodore 206, *206*, 208, *208*
Hawksmoor, Nicholas 263–4, *263*, 292–3
Haynin, Antoine de 250
Hearne, Thomas 272
Heaton Park, Manchester 267
Heemskerck, Maarten van 165
Heere, Lucas de 249
Heidelberg, Germany 336, 340, *341*
Helmstedt, Germany 337–8
Henchir Aïn Bez, Tunisia 116
Henchir Bu Arada, Tunisia 123
Henchir Bu Ftîs, Tunisia 109, 112
Henchir ed-Douâmis, Tunisia 121
Henchir el Ust, Tunisia 113
Henchir Gasrîm, Tunisia 122
Henchir Kissa, Algeria 123
Henchir Mest, Tunisia 121
Henchir Midid, Tunisia 122
Henderson, William 268
Henri II, duc de Lorraine 227
Henri II, K. of France 225, 226
Henri III, K. of France 195–6, *195*, 227
Henri IV, K. of France 227
Henry VIII 203, *203*
Herbert, Henry, 9th Earl of Pembroke 269, 270, *270*
Héré, Emmanuel 237–8, *237*
Herodes Atticus 85
Herodian 46
Hesberg, Henner von 12
Hesdin, France 225, *225*
Heveningham, Suffolk 293
Hewitt, G.W. & W.D. 428, *428*
Hewlings, Richard 291
Heymüller, J.M.B. 338
Hierapolis, Turkey 91
Higgott, Gordon 213, 214
High Wycombe, Bucks. 309, 431, *431–2*
Highclere, Hants. 267, 270, *270*

Hildebrand, Adolf 342–3
Hill, Sam 437
Hills, Alexander 216
Hiort, William 302
Hitchcock, Henry-Russell 403
Hitler, Adolf 432–3, *432*
Hittorff, Jacques-Ignace 325
Hoare, Henry 293, *293*
Hobart, Australia 388, 391–2
Hobart, Louis 379
Hoecke, Jan van den 253
Holbein, Hans 202–3
Holden, Charles 413
Holkham Hall, Norfolk 264
Holl, Pietro 180
Holland, Henry 265–6
Holyhead, Wales 304, *304*
Hompesch zu Bolheim, F. von *375*, 376
Honorius 56, 97
Hooghe, Romeijn de 256
Horeau, Hector 231–2, 321, 326–7
Hořice, Czech Republic 352–3, *353*
Horton, Northants. 274
House of Dun, Scotland 294, *294*
Howard, Deborah 146
Howley, James 277
Hughes, Quentin 374
Hugo, Victor 321, *322*
Hulot, Guillaume 337
Hülsen, C. 55, 124
Hungary 352
Hunt, T.F. 277
Hussey, Christopher 406, 409–10
Huygens, Louis 281
Huyot, Jean-Nicolas 319–20, *320*
Hyde Park, London 295–7, *296*, 306
Hyderabad, India 393

iani 5–6, 54
Il Tribolo 194
Imola, Italy 186
Ince Blundell Hall, Lancs. 266
India 393–5, 408–9
industry pageants and arches 308–9
Ingatestone, Essex 216
Innocent XII, pope 176, *176*
Innocent XIII, pope 176–7, *177*
Innsbruck, Austria 254, 343, 344, 345, 346, *346*
Iran 435
Iraq 436
Ireland 216, 277–8, 295, 300–1, 305, 309–11, 406
Irkutsk, Russia 360
Isabella Clara Eugenia of Austria 249, 250
Isaura, Turkey 92–3, 95
Israel 102, 105
Istanbul, Turkey 97–8, *97*
Isthmia, Greece 82
Itálica, Spain 81

Italy
  antiquity 3–7, *4*, 10–14, *10–11*, *13*, 26–7, *26*, 31–2, 57–68, *59*, 61–2, *64*, 66–7
  celebratory arches 191–9, *195*, *198–9*
  Napoleonic arches 316–17, 318, 319, *319*, 323
  other arches 426, 434
  park gates and garden features 278–80, *279*, 286–7, *286*
  Renaissance 137–66
    arches 137–52, *138–41*, *143*, *145*, *147–50*, *152*
    church furnishings 153–9, *153–5*, *157–8*
    drawings of arches 164–6
    paintings, arches in 159–64, *159–62*, *164*, 183
  Romanesque 133, *134–5*, 135
  war memorials 414–19, *414*, *416–17*, *419*
  see also Rome; Vatican City; Venice
M. Iulius Cottius 12–13
Ivanov, I. 438
Ivry, Pierre Contant d' 240
Iznik, Turkey 90, 96

Jablonna, Poland 283
Jackson, T.G. 26, 425
Jacobs, Philip 212
Jacobsdal, Sweden 365
Jacquet, Alexandre 229
Jadot, Jean-Nicolas 197, *198*
James I 209–12, *210*, *212*, 217
James II 302
James IV, K. of Scotland 217
James V, K. of Scotland 217
Jamesone, George 218
Jammeh, Yahya 436
Jan III Sobieski, K. of Poland 349
Jansen, Conraet 211
Janssen, Bernard 212
Janus 5–6
Jean de Boulogne 247, 248
Jefferson, Thomas 274
Jelinek, Johann 353, *353*
Jerash, Jordan 100–1, *101*, 104, 105
Jérica, Spain 81–2
Jerusalem, Israel 102, *102*
Jervoise, Richard 207, *208*
Jesi, Italy 184
Joanna of Austria 195
Joao V, K. of Portugal 372, *372*
Joao VI, K. of Portugal 385
Johannes von Crema 133
Johannesburg, South Africa 406, *407*
John of Salisbury 133
Johnston, Francis 300
Jones, Adrian 333, *333*
Jones, George Fowler 310

Jones, Inigo 212, 213–14, *213*, 264, 269, 292, *292*
Jones, Mark Wilson 52
Jonson, Ben 210, 212
Jordaens, Jacob 251–2
Jordan 99–105
Joseph I, Emperor 344
Joseph II, Emperor 345–6, 357
Josephus 3, 36
Josselin, Ralph 216
Juana Inés de la Cruz, Sor 381, *381*
Julius II, pope 144, 156, 170, 182

Kader, Ingeborg 98, 99, 100
Kähler, Heinz 1, 64, 76, 78, 82
Kaliningrad, Russia 250, *251*
Kalmar, Sweden 363
Kamianets-Podilskyi, Ukraine 353
Kamil, Adil 436
Kansas City, USA 420
Karl XI, K. of Sweden 365
Karl Johan III, K. of Sweden 367
Karl Theodor, Elector of Bavaria 340, *341*
Karlsruhe, Germany 343
Kaskey, Ray 422
Kassel, Germany 319
Kaufmann, Thomas DaCosta 344
Kazakhstan 437
Kedleston, Derbys. 265, 298, *298*
Keller, George 402–3, *402*
Kenilworth Castle, Warwicks. 207
Kent, William 264, 269, 292, *292*, 298–9, 302
Kerr, Thomas 413–14
Kew, London 272, *273*
Keyser, Hendrick de 250, *250*, 255
Khamissa, Algeria 113, 123
Kidson, Peter 132
Kiev, Ukraine 438
Kilikiai Pylai, Kodregai, Turkey 94
Kim Il-sung 436, *436*
Kingston, Canada 421
Kirby, Joshua 301
Kirby Hall, Northants. 204, *205*
Kitson, Samuel 403
Kleesattel, J. 343
Kleiner, Diana 54
Kleiner, F.S. 22, 34, 35, 36, 125
Kleinwetzdorf, Austria 284–5, *285*
Klieber, Joseph 283, *284*
Klodt, P.K. 359, *359*
Kobyletskaya, Zinaida 361
Kochubey, Victor, Prince 353
Konovalov, Vladimir 361, *361*
Korykos, Turkey 93–4
Kraat, Cor 258
Krasnodar, Russia 361
Kraus, Theodor 72
Krauthaimer, R. 132
Kreis, Wilhelm 433
Krüger, Andreas Ludwig 339
Krzyztopór, Poland 283

Ksûr Abd el Melek, Tunisia 120, 125
Ksûr el Ahmar, Algeria 122–3
Kubicki, Jakub 349, *350*, 351
Kuch Batia, Tunisia 123
Küpper-Böhm, Annette 14, 18, 19, 22, 24
Kurganov, Kanat 437
Kursk, Russia 361
Kutno, Poland 433

La Fère, France 325
La Roche, Pierre de 363
La Rochelle, France 234
Labna, Mexico 381
Labraynda, Turkey 96
Lafayette, Gilbert du Motier, Marquis de 377
Lafitte, Louis 322
Lafréry, Antoine 165
Lagae, Jules 429, *429*
Lageirse, Marcel 248
Lahure, Jean-Baptiste 243
Lallemand, Jean-Baptiste 240
Lambaesis, Algeria 108, *109*, 113, 114, 125
Lamine, Peter Simon 340, *341*
Langhans, Carl Gotthard 339
Langley, Batty 269, 272
Laos 398
Lasalle, Philippe de 242
Latakia, Syria 98, *98*
Laufberger, Ferdinand 346
Laval, Honoré 398, *398*
Lay, George 402
Le Boucq, Noel 221
Le Brun, Charles 230
Le Nôtre, André 235–6
Le Sueur, Hubert 272
Leach, Sir Simon 216
Lebanon 99–100
Lecce, Italy 152, *152*
Lednice, Czech Republic 283, *284*
Ledoux, Claude-Nicolas 241
Leeds, Yorks. 309, 314
Legeay, Jean-Laurent 339
Legendre, Jean-Gabriel 236–7, *237*
Leicester, Philip Sidney, Earl of 248–9
Leicester, Leics. 307, 311–13, *311–12*, 409
Leiden, Netherlands 248
Lemaire, Jean 280, 281
Lemot, François-Frédéric 318
Leo X, pope 53–4, 156–8, 170–1, 182
Leo XI, pope 172–3, *172*
León, Mexico 382
Leoni, Giacomo 291–2, *291*
Leopardi, Giacomo 434
Leopold I, K. of Belgium 259
Leopold II, Emperor 346
Leopold II, K. of Belgium 429
Leopold Wilhelm, Archduke of Austria 255

Lepcis Magna, Libya 32, 107, 108, 110, 112, 114–16, *114*
Lepper, F. 83
Lequeu, Jean-Jacques 243, *243*
Lescot, Pierre 222
Lesseps, Ferdinand de 385
Leverton, Thomas 276, *276*
Leys, Henri 259
Libera, Adalberto 434
Libya 32, 107–8, 110–12, 114–16, 433–4
Lichfield, Staffs. 306
Licht, Margherita 166
Licinianus 96
Liège, Belgium 248
Lightfoote, William 215–16
Ligorio, Pirro 33, 44, 151, 165
Lille, France 233, *234*
Lima, Peru 382–5, *383*
Limongelli, Alessandro 415, 433
Lincoln Cathedral, Britain 132
Liria, Spain 81
Lisbon, Portugal 372–3, *372*
Liverpool, Lancs. 309–10, *309*, 313
Livy 1, 2, 6
Llimona, Josep 372
Locke, Matthew 215
Lombardo, Pietro 155, 156
London, England
 Admiralty Arch 426
 celebratory arches 202–3, 203–4, 209–16, *210*, *212–15*, 302, 306, 308, 313–14, *314*, 431
 church monuments 207, 208–9, *208–9*, 216
 garden features 272, *273*
 Marble Arch 329–31, *329–30*
 Napoleonic arch 323
 proposed arches 291–2, *291*, 293
 Robert Adam, work of 294–7, 298
 Royal Mews 298–9
 war memorials 408, 413
 Wellington Arch 331–3, *332–3*
Londonio, Carlo 318
Longleat, Wilts. 267
López, Mateo 369
López Aguado, Antonio 371
Loriny, F. de 236
L'Orme, Philibert de 224–5, *224*, 226
Lorrain, Claude 227–8
Lorsch, Germany 131–2, *131*
Lothringen, Karl von 344
Lothringen, Karl Philipp von 345
Louis XII, K. of France 192, 196
Louis XIII, K. of France 227
Louis XIV, K. of France 229–36, *229*, *231–5*
Louis XV, K. of France 236–8, *237*, 239, *239*, 241
Louis XVI, K. of France 238–9, 241, *242*

Louis XVIII, K. of France 320, 325
Louis, dauphin of France 239
Louis Joseph, prince de Condé 239
Louis-Philippe I, K. of France 318, 321
Louvain, Belgium 258
Lovekin, George 202
Lovell, Humfrey 207
Lübeck, Germany 343
Lübke, Wilhelm 336
Lucius Caesar 9
Lucius Septimius Geta *see* Geta
Lucius Verus 44, 111, 112
Ludwig I, K. of Bavaria 341–2, *342*
Luise of Mecklenburg 339
Luton Hoo, Beds. 298
Lutyens, Edwin 406, 408–11, *408*, *410*
Lviv, Ukraine 353
Lyle, John M. 421
Lyngby, Helge 41
Lyon, France 221, 225, 226, 227
Lysias 8, 9

Mackennal, Bertram 394, *395*
Mackle, Roland 363
MacMonnies, Frederick W. 378, *403*, 404, 428
Macrinus 86, 95, 121
Mactar, Tunisia 108
Madonna, M.L. 170, 171
Madrid, Spain 370–1, *370*, 435
Maggi, Giovan Paolo 173
Magni, Giovan Battista 175
Maier, Jacob 344
Mainz, Germany 30, 74–5, *74*, 323, 341
Málaga, Spain 81
Malatesta, Sigismondo 138–9
Malborghetto, Italy 65–6, *66*
Malinalco, Mexico 386
Malmö, Sweden 365
Malta 374–6
Mancini, Giacomo 197
Mander, Karel van 343
Manetti, Gianozzo 141
Mangareva 398–9
Manila, Philippines 399, *399*
Manrique, Juan Hurtado 385
Mantegna, Andrea 160–1, *160*
Mantova Benavides, Marco 278–9, *279*
Mantua, Italy 138, *139*, 158, *158*, 163, 165, 193, 194, 196, 316
Marble Arch, London 329–31, *329–30*
Marc, Jean-Yves 86
Marcattili, Francesco 2
March, Vernon 420, *421*
Marchionni, Filippo. the Yngr 186
Marconi, Henryk 283

INDEX 449

Marcus Aurelius 41, 44–5, 93, 102, 111, 112
Mardel, Carlos 372–3
Maret, Jean-Philippe 239
Margaret of Austria, Duchess of Savoy 221
Margaret of Austria (Margaret of Parma) 193–4
Margaret of Austria, Queen of Spain 197
Margaret Tudor, Queen of Scotland 217
Maria of Austria 194
Maria de' Medici, Queen of France 227, 255
Maria Carolina of Austria 197, *198*
Maria Theresa, Empress 256–7
Mariani, Enrico 415
Marie Antoinette, Queen of France 238, 240
Marie-Louise de Gonzague, Queen of Poland 348, *348*
Marie-Thérèse, Queen of France 229–30
Markouna, Algeria 111
Marlier, Georges 247
Marnotte, P. 71
Marot, Daniel 236
Marseille, France 325, *326*, 327, 419–20, *420*
Marshall, John Leroy 420
Martial 33, 40
Martin, Jean 226
Martin, John Rupert 252, 253, 254
Martinetti, Giovan Battista 316
Martínez, Ginés 369, *369*
Martini, Francesco di Giorgio 163, *164*, 165
Martino, Pietro di 141–2, *141*
Martinucci, Filippo 182
Martorell, Spain 15–16, *16*
Mary I 203
Mary, Queen of Scots 217
Mary of Hungary, Queen 248
Matthias, K. of Hungary 344
Maucord, Jean 236
Max Emanuel, Elector of Bavaria 336
Maximian 82, 121–2
Maximilian II, Emperor 343
Maximinus 87, 95, 96
Maynard, Alan 207, *208*
Mazeline, Pierre 235–6
Mazzini, Angiolo 415–16
McGrath, Elizabeth 254
McKechnie, Charles 431
McNeil, Hermon A. 378, 428
McParland, Edward 300
Mdaurusch, Algeria 124
Mdina, Malta 374–5, *374*
Medeina, Tunisia 108, 123
Medici, Alessandro de' 193–4
Medici, Claudia de' 196
Medici, Lorenzo de' 137

Medinaceli, Spain 78–9, *79*
Melbourne, Australia 388, 389–90, *390*
Mélin, Didier-Joseph-François 238–9
Mélin, Pierre 229
Mellucco Vaccaro, A. 51
Melton Mowbray, Leics. 306–7
Mengíbar, Spain 15
Mereworth, Kent 269–70
Mérida, Spain 81, 82
Messina, Italy 193
Mestrovic, Ivan 352
Metz, France 227
Metzger, Eduard 342
Mexico 381–3, 386–7
Mexico City 381–2, *381*, *383*
Mezzanotte, Gianni 316
Michael, Johann Georg 281
Michel, Robert 370–1, *370*
Michelangelo 187
Milan, Italy 67–8, 143–4, 192–3, 194, 286, 316–17, 318, 319, *319*, 415
Milizia, Francesco 178, 396
Millennium Arches 314, 431, 438
Milles, Carl 435
Millich, Nicolaes 365
Mills, Peter 214
Milne, John 307, *308*
Minturno, Italy 57–8
Mocenigo, Ludovico 155
Mocenigo, Pietro 155, *155*
Mogadishu, Somalia 433
Moitte, Philibert 242
Moldova 362
Molin, Nicolo 211
Moll, Baltasar Ferdinand 346, *346*
Momper, Joos de 249, *249*
Mona, Domenico 183
monastery gateway 131–2, *131*
Mone, Jean 250
Moneypenny, George 267
Monforte de Lemos, Spain 369
Monmacher, Mathias 343
Mons, Belgium 247
Mons Amanus, Syria 29, 30
Mont, Hans 343
Montalto, Co. Down 278
Montano, Giovanni Battista *154*, 155, 164–5
Monte Oliveto Maggiore, Italy 163
Montelupo, Raffaello da 157–8
Monterrey, Mexico 382
Montesa, Francisco 247
Monti, Francesco Riccardo 399–400
Montmorency, Anne de 222–3
Montpellier, France 234–5, *235*
Monville, Racine de 397
Monza, Italy 316
Mopsuestia, Turkey 95
Moravec, Bohuslav 352–3, *353*
Moreau, J.-C.-A. 240
Morelli, Cosimo 185

Morocco 110, 118–20
Morosini, Morosina, Dogaressa 196
Morris, Paul Winters 427
Morris, Roger 264, 269, 292
Morrison, Richard 305, *305*
Morrison, William Vitruvius 278
Mosca Padovano, Giovanni Maria 335–6
Moscardi, Agostino 173
Moscow, Russia 355–6, *355*, 357, 359, 361
Mote Park, Co. Roscommon 277
Mowl, Tim 267
Mozilev, Russia 357
Mses el Bab, Tunisia 124
Muhammad bin Tughluq 393
Munich, Germany 336, 341–2, *342*
Murray, Samuel 405, *405*
Muschamp, John 266
Mussolini, Benito 61, 417
Muzio, Giovanni 415
Myrhorodsky, Serhiy 438
Myriandos, Turkey 95–6
Mysore, India 393–4
Mytilene, Lesbos, Greece 96

Naga City, Philippines 400
Nancy, France 227, 237–8, *237*, 238–9
Nanni di Baccio Bigio 157–8, 184
Naples, Italy 141–3, *141*, 153, 192, 193
Napoleon 179, 316–23, *317*, 319–20, 322–3, 339, 341, 351
Napoleon III 325–7, *327*
Nash, John 277–8, 329–31, *329–30*
Nashville, USA 404–5
Naumann, R. 98
Nazarbayev, Nursultan 437
Nedergard, Elisabeth 7
Nering, Johann Arnold 336
Nero 31–2, 33–5, *34*, 82
Nero Claudius Drusus 9
Nerva 43
Nesfield, W.A. 331
Netherlands 248–9, 255–6, 257, 258, 281
Neuf Brisach, France 234
Neufforge, Jean-François 240
Nevers, France 236
New Delhi, India 408–9, *408*
New York, USA 377–8, 422, 427–8
Newcastle, Australia 388, *388*, 391
Newman, John 270
Newport News, USA 420
Niccolò dell'Abbate 226
Nice, France 326
Nicholas II, Tsar 361, *361*
Nicholas V, pope 141, 159, 169–70

Nickson, Tom 207
Noakowski, Stanislav 352, 422
Nobile, Pietro 323
Nonnius, Ludovicus 251
Noort, Lambert van 247
Norfolk Island 388
Nori, Felice 415
North, Sir Jonathan 409
North Korea 436
North Macedonia 430–1
North Mymms, Herts. 264
Northwich, Ches. 308
Norway 367
Nostell Priory, Yorks. 265
Nottingham, Notts. 300, 413
Novello, Alberto Alpago 415
Novgorod, Russia 357
Novocherkassk, Russia 360
Nugent, J.C. 421
Nuremberg, Germany 335, *335*
Nutt, Alfred Young *311*, 313

Oak Park, Co. Carlow 278
Ogilby, John 214, 215
Ojetti, Ugo 417
Olazo Allende, Ernesto 385
Olympia, Greece 82
Oppenheim, Germany 336
Opstal, Gérard Van 229
Oram, William 302
Orange, France 20–2, *21*
Orbay, François d' 234, *235*
origins of triumphal arches 1–6
Orihuela, Spain 368–9, *368*
Orléans, France 221, 227
Orley, Bernard van 248
Orosius 2
Ortells, Jose 435
Orvieto, Italy 145
Osborne House, Isle of Wight 314, 431
Osnabrück, Germany 323
Osner, Hans Konrad 356
Oste, Jan 246
Ostia, Italy 58, 65
Otacilia Severa 95
Ottawa, Canada 420–1, *421*
Ottenheym, Konrad 363
Oxford, Oxon. 292–3, 300, *300*, 301

Padua, Italy 144, 160, *160*, 194, 196, 278–80, *279*
Page, Stephen 314, 431
Pagni, Giovanni 111
Paine, James 299, *299*
Painshill, Surrey 273
paintings including arches
  Belgium 248
  Brazil 385
  England 63, *64*, 214, *214*, 272
  France 227–8
  Ireland 305, *305*
  Italy 156, 159–64, *159–62*, *164*, 183, 435

Palagi, Pelagio 286
Palermo, Italy 152, 197, 199, *199*, 415
Palladio, Andrea 59, 147–51, *149–50*, 155, 158, 194, 195–6, *195*
Palma, Niccolo 197
Palmyra, Syria 102–3, *103*, 105
Panama City 385
Panella, Clementina 51
Panini, Giuseppe 178
Panvinio, Onofrio 8
papal arches 169–87
　outside Rome 182–3
　permanent 183–7
　processional 133, 169–82, *172*, *176–8*, *180–1*
Papworth, J.B. 267–8, *268*
Parent, Aubert 231, 339
Pargfrieder, Joseph 284–5, *285*
Parion, Turkey 96
Paris, France
　Ancien Régime 221, 222, 229–32, *231–3*, 241, *242*
　Arc de Triomphe de l'Étoile 319–21, *320*, 322
　Arc de Triomphe du Carrousel 317–18, *317*
　Bourbon Restoration 325, *325*
　celebratory arches 217, 226–7, 229–30, *229*, 235, 239–40, *239*, 241, *242*, 326, *327*
　drawings of arches 238, 240–1, 241–4, *243*
　garden features 280–1, *280*
　Napoleonic arches 317–18, *317*, 318–19, 319–22, *320*, *322–3*
　Republican period 241–4, *243*
　Second Empire 325–8, *327*
　20th cent. 438
　war memorials 422
park entrances
　Britain and Ireland 262–8, *262–3*, *268*, 277–8
　in other countries 280, 281–2, *282*
Parker, Samuel 330
Parkes, Varney 389
Parlington Park, Yorks. 276, *276*
Parma, Italy 426
Partridge, Loren 172
Pascoli, Lione 177–8
Pasquier, Antoine Léonard 238
Patara, Turkey 91
Patras, Greece 85
Patte, Pierre 238
Paul I, Emperor of Russia 339, 358
Paul II, pope 159
Pausanias 5, 82, 85
Pavia, Italy 14, 192, 194
Pecksall, Sir Richard 209
Pegli, Italy *286*, 287
Pèlerin, Jean 221
Pellone, Rocco 197

Penchaud, Michel-Robert 325, *326*
Pennethorne, James 330
Penni, Giovanni Giacomo 170
Pensabene, Patrizio 51
Pentland, John Howard 406
Pepys, Samuel 216
Percier, Charles 317, 318, 322, *323*
Perge, Turkey 90, 91
Perino del Vaga 196–7, 203
Perrault, Claude 230–1, *231*
Perry, William Hunt 427, *427*
Perth, Australia 389, 392
Perth, Scotland 306
Peru 382–5, 387
Perugino, Pietro 54, 161–2, *162*, 192
Peruzzi, Baldassare 156, 171
Peter the Great 355–6, *355*
Petra, Jordan 99, *99*
Petre, John, Baron 216
Petronell, Austria 75
Petter, Hugh 438, *438*
Pevsner, Nikolaus 208, 265, 295
Peyssonel, I.A. 121
Philadelphia, USA 377
Philip II, K. of Spain 194, 197, 204, 207, 246–7, 248, 370, *370*
Philip IV, K. of Spain 251, *252*, 384
Philippi, Greece 22
Philippines 399–400
Philippopolis, Syria 105
Philippus 92
Phillipps, Ambrose 270–1, *271*
Piacentini, Marcello 415, 416–19, *416–17*
Picard, G. 73, 74
Piernicoli, Benedetto 179, 186
Pierretz, D.A. 236
Pieve del Cairo, Italy 151–2
Pigage, Nicolas de 340, *341*
Pilon, Germain 221
Pilsen, Czech Republic 353
Pilsudski, Jozef 352
Pimenow, S.S. 359, *359–60*, 360
Pineau, Nicolas 356
Pinelli, A. 163–4
Pinturicchio 161, 170
Pisa, Italy 14, 192
Pistocchi, Giuseppe 316
Pitt, Thomas 274–5, *275*
Pius V, pope 66, 171
Pius VI, pope 186, *186*
Pius VII, pope 39, 179, *180*
Pius IX, pope 180–2, *181*, 183, 186–7
Pliny the Elder 1, 8
Pococke, Richard 270
Podgrade, Croatia 83
Podzamcze Chechinskie, Poland 349
Poggibonsi, Italy 153
Poitiers, Diane de 224

Poitiers, France 221
Poland 283, 343, 348–52, 433
Pole, Elizabeth, Lady 216
Poletti, F. 163
Poletti, Luigi 180, 181, 183
Polidoro da Caravaggio 193
Pollaiuolo, Antonio & Piero 163
Pompeii, Italy 31–2
Poniatowski, Jozef, prince 283
Pont du Chelif, Algeria 108
Pontarlier, France 238
Ponte, Nicolò da, Doge 159
Pope, Alexander 262, 263
Popham, A.E. 247
Pordage, Samuel 215
Portier, Nicolas 238
Portugal 82, 372–3
Posi, Paolo 192
Post, A. 84
Post, George B. 378
Potemkin, Grigory, Prince 282, 357, 358
Potocki, Anna 283
Potosí, Peru 384, *384*
Potsdam, Germany 338–9, *338*, 339–40, *340*
Pourbus, Pieter 248
Poyet, Bernard 241, *242*
Poznan, Poland 351
Pozzo, Paolo 316
Pradier, James 321, 325, *325*
Prawady-Devno, Serbia 86, 87
Prieta, Gian Paolo P. 400
Prini, Giovanni 415, 418
Priuli, Matteo, bishop 194
processional arches *see* celebratory arches; papal arches
Provinciali, Paolo 179, *180*
Pula, Croatia 24–6, *25*
Puteoli, Italy 58, 63–4, 64–5
Putti, Giovanni 318, *319*
Puyvelde, Leo van 248
Pyongyang, North Korea 436, *436*
Pyte, Robert 203, *203*

Quarenghi, Giacomo 282, *282*, 358–9
Quellinus, Erasmus I 251
Quellinus, Jerónimo 255, 256
Quijano, Jerónimo 368, 369
Quiney, Anthony 132
Quiza, Algeria 108

Radetzky, Joseph Graz von 285, *285*
Raffaelli, Giacomo 179
Rainaldi, Carlo 174, *174*, 175, 176
Rainaldi, Girolamo 174
Ramée, Joseph 258, 377
Ramey, Étienne-Jules 325, *326*
Ramsgate, Kent 305, 314, 431
Rangone, Tommaso 146
Raphael 53–4
Ras Lanuf, Libya 433–4, *433*

Rathfarnham Castle, Dublin 277
Rava, Carlo Enrico 433
Recanati, Italy 434
Reijsschoot, Emmanuel van 258
Reilly, Sir Charles 412, 426
Reims, France 73–4, *73*
reliquaries 130–1, *130*
Remigius, bishop of Lincoln 132
Renzi, Mario di 434
Repton, Humphry 266–7
Retti, Lionardo 176
Revese, Ottavio Bruto 151
Revett, Nicholas 83, 273
Reynés, Josep 372
Rezi, Martino 197
Rheineck, Christoph von 334–5, *335*
Ricci, Sebastiano 266
Richborough, Kent 76–7, *76–7*
Richelieu, Cardinal 280–1, *280*
Richter, Wilhelm 348, *348*
Rico, Luis 384
Ridolfi, Nicolò 194
Rikitea, Mangareva 398–9, *398*
Rimini, Italy 10–11, *10*, 138
Rinaldi, Antonio 281–2, *282*
Rio de Janeiro, Brazil 385
Ripoll, Spain 132
Riva, Giovanni Battista 151
Rizzo, Antonio 156
river crossings 5–6, 11
road-building 9, 11, 14–16, 57–8, 64, 81
Robbia, Giovanni della 153
Robbia, Girolamo della 221
Robert, Louis 95
Robertson, Daniel 301
Robinson, Thomas 295
Rochead, John Thomas 307, *307*
Rockox, Nicolaes 251
Roda de Berà, Spain 16
Rodriguez Almeida, E. 30
Roehampton, Surrey 264
Roehmer, Marion 17, 23
Romania 87, 430
Romano, Giulio 146, *147*, 158, *158*, 163, 193
Rome, Italy
　antiquity 1–3, 5–9, 29–30, 32–57, 125, 126
　arch of Gallienus 49–50, *49*
　arch of Janus 54, *55*
　arch of Nero 33–5, *34*, 125
　arches of Constantine 41, *42*, 44, 45, 50–5, *51*, *53*
　arches of Domitian 40–3, *41–2*, 126
　arches of Septimius Severus 45–8, *45–7*
　arches of Titus 36, 37–9, *38–9*
　arco di Portogallo 56–7, *57*
　Parthian arch of Augustus 7–8, *8*

INDEX　　451

(Rome, Italy, continued)
  Fascist arches 434, 435
  garden features 285–6
  medieval and Renaissance 133, 144, 153, *153*, 156–8, *157*
  other arches 175, *175*, 191–2, 316
  papal arches 169–87
    permanent 183–7
    processional 133, 169–82, *172*, *176–8*, *180–1*
  see also Vatican City
Ronsard, Pierre 226
Rosenstingl, Franz 345
Rossato, Orfeo 414, *414*
Rossellino, Antonio 153
Rossi, Alessandro 185
Rossi, J.C.F. 330
Rossi, Karl 360, *360*
Rosso, Giulio Raviglio 203
Rosso Fiorentino 182
Rothman, Margret S. Pond 87–8
Rothschild Collection, Louvre 166
Rotili, M. 61
Rotterdam, Netherlands 258
Rouen, France 222, *223*, 226, 227
Rousseau, Pierre 241
Rousset, Pierre-Noel 238
Royston, Herts. 306
Rubens, Peter Paul 251, 252, *252–4*, 253–4, 259
Rude, François 321
Rudolf II, Emperor 343–4
Rueil-Malmaison, France 280–1, *280*
Rumyantsev, Pyotr, Count 357
Rusca, Luigi 360
Rush, William 377
Russell, Sir John 208–9
Russell, Samuel 393
Russia 250–1, 281–3, 355–61
Rutelli, Mario 199, *199*
Rutter, John 264
Ryckaert, David III 255

Saarinen, Eero 434–5, *435*
Sabatini, Francesco 370–1, *370*
Sádaba, Spain 81
Sagalassos, Turkey 96
Saint, Andrew 233
Saint-Far, Eustache de 323, 341
Sainte-Croix, Bruno Nègre de 236
Saintes, France 30, *31*
Sala, Morocco 110
Salerno, Italy 133, *134*
Saltram, Devon 276–7
Salvatierra, Valentino 371
Salvi, Nicola 177
Salviati, Francesco 191
Salzburg, Austria 344
Sambin, Hugues 226
San Benedetto Po, Italy 146, *147*
San Francisco, USA 379–80
Sangallo, Antonio da, the Yngr 156–7, 184, 191

Sangallo, Giuliano da 61, 66, 163, 165
Sangallo, Raffaello 151
Sangiorgio, Abbondio 318, *319*
Sanmicheli, Michele 144–5, 194
Sannelli, Scipione 135
Sansovino, Andrea 153, 156, *157*
Sansovino, Jacopo 145–6
Santarcangelo di Romagna, Italy 185–6, *185*
Santiago de Compostela, Spain 369
Santos, Eugénio dos 373
Sartorio, Antoine 419–20, *420*
Sarudny, Iwan 356
Sassoon, Siegfried 413
Sauschkewitsch, I.N. 362
Savigliano, Italy 151
Saxl, F. 162–3
Sayasthsena, Tham 398
Sbeitla, Tunisia 109, *110*, 113–14, 122
Scalpelli, Alfredo 434
Scamozzi, Vincenzo 158–9, 194
Scève, Maurice 225
Schadow, Johann Gottfried 339
Schauwasch, Tunisia 111, 124
Schiappalari, Stefano Ambrosio 247
Schinkel, Karl Friedrich 339
Schroeger (Szreger), Efraim 349
Schutze, Jost 364
Schwaz, Austria 343
Schwetzingen, Germany 281
Scipio Africanus 2, 3, 5
Scotland 217–18, 268, 294, 297, 306–9
Scott, William Alphonsus 278
Scriptores Historiae Augustae 85
Sebag Montefiore, Simon 361
Seghers, Gerard 253
Seigne, J. 101
Selva, Giannantonio 319
Semzow, Michail 356
Seneca 2
Senigallia, Italy 184–5
Sens, France 238
Septimius Severus 45–8, *45–7*, 65, 85–6, 92, 94, 100, 112, 113, 114–16, *114*, 121, 123
Serbia 86, 87
Serlio, Sebastiano 146–7, *148*, 204, 207
Servandoni, Giovanni Niccolò 239–40, 272
Seurre, Bernard-Gabriel 321
Severus Alexander 1, 95, 104, 121
Sextus Julius Frontinus 91
Sforza, Ascanio 156
Sforza, Bona 194
Sforza, Francesco 193
Sforza, Ludovico (Il Moro) 143, 192
Sforza, Massimiliano 192–3
Shaba, Syria 105
Shanken, Andrew M. 380

Shchedrin, Fyodor 359–60
Sheffield, Yorks. 268, 310–11
Shugborough, Staffs. 274, *274*
Shvidkovsky, Dimitri 355
Sî, Syria 104
Side, Turkey 97
Sidi Amara, Tunisia 123
Sidi Bellater, Algeria 108
Sieckmann, Johann Christian 323
Siena, Italy 155, 163, *164*, 192, 193
Sigüenza y Góngora, Carlos 381
Siloé, Diego de 369
Sinuessa, Italy 6
Sironi, Mario 435
Sistine Chapel, Vatican City 54, 161–2, *161–2*
Sixtus V, pope 63, 184, 187
s'Jacob, Henriette 250
Skoblikov, Oleksandr 438
Skopje, North Macedonia 430–1, *430*
Skrznyecki, Jan Zygmunt 351
Slaugham Place, W. Sussex 207
Slesin, Poland 351
Smith, John 307
Smith, Joseph 195, 269, 292, *292*
Soane, Sir John 54, 265, 297, 329, 331–2
Sobre, Jean-Nicolas 240, 242
Sodoma 163
Somalia 433
Somerset House, London 204, *204*
Söntgen, Johann Joseph 238–9
Soulié, Gilbert 398, *398*
South Africa 406–7, 430
Spain 14–17, 78–82, 132, 368–72, 435
Spazzio, Giovanni 349
Speaight, F.W. 331
Specchi, Alessandro 176–7, 192
Speer, Albert 432–3, *432*
Spello, Italy 12
Spiddal, Co. Galway 278
Spinelli, Gasparo 202
Spoleto, Italy 12
Spranger, Bartholomäus 343
Spreckelsen, Johan-Otto von 438
Springwood Park, Scotland 268
St Albans, Herts. 78
St Chamas, France 14, *15*
St Florian, Friedrich 422
St Louis, USA 378–9, *379*, 434–5, *435*
St Petersburg, Russia 356–7, *357*, 358, 359–60, *359–60*
  stables 298–9, *299*
  stage designs 236, 241, 255
  stained glass windows 248
Stamp, Gavin 406, 410
Stanislas, K. of Poland 237–8, *237*
Stanislaw August, K. of Poland 349, *350*, 351, 353
Starn, Randolph 172

Stasov, V.P. 359, *359*
Statius 57–8
Stefanovska, Valentina 430, *430*
Stern, Raffaele 39
L. Stertinius 1, 5
Stilicho 56
Stirling Castle, Scotland 217, 218
Stockholm, Sweden 363–6, *364*, 366
Stöpfel, W. 178, 185
Stourhead, Wilts. 293, *293*
Stowe, Bucks. 274–5, *275*
Strasbourg, France 234, 239, 240, 319
Streater, Robert 302
St-Rémy, France 19–20, *19*
Strickland, William 377
Strocka, M. 115, 116
Strong, Donald 77
Strong, Roy 246
Stuart, James 'Athenian' 83, 85, 274, *274*
Studley Royal, Yorks. 264
Stuttgart, Germany 319, 337, 341
Subiaco, Italy 186, *186*
Suetonius 32, 40
Summerson, Sir John 137–8, 204, 406, 409, 411
Susa, Italy 12–13, *13*
es-Suweda, Syria 104
Swansea, Wales 309
Swart, Pieter de 257, 258
Sweden 363–6
Switzerland 71, 75
Sydney, Australia 388, 389, *389*, 391, 392
Sydorov, Kostyantyn 438
Syon, Middlesex 265
Syracuse, Sicily, Italy 3, 5, 6, 12
Syracuse, USA 421, 422
Syria 30, 98, 100, 102–5

Tabley Hall, Ches. 267
Tacitus 29, 33, 34
Taillebert, Urbain 250
Tamworth, Staffs. 306
Tanfield, Sir Lawrence 216
Taraval, Louis Gustave 366, *366*
Tarragona, Spain 16–17
Tarsos, Turkey 93
Tasso, Torcuat 372
Tatham, Edward 301
Tatton Park, Ches. 267
Taunay, Auguste-Marie 385
Taylor, Benjamin Broomhead 268
Taylor, George Ledwell 268
Taylor, Sir Robert 293
Tebessa, Algeria 116–17, *116*, 124
Teboursouk, Tunisia 113
Tecali, Mexico 386
Tehran, Iran 435
Temple Bar, London 213–14, *213*, 292, *292*
Templepatrick, Co. Antrim 295
Terebenev, Ivan 360

Tessin, Nicodemus, the Elder and Younger 365
Thailand 398
Thake, Conrad 374
Thasos, Greece 86
Thebursuk, Tunisia 122
Theodosius I 56, 97–8, *97*, 123, 124
Theodosius II 56
Thessalonika, Greece *86*, 87–8
Thiepval, France 409–11, *410*
Thomas, John 402
Thomon, Jean-François Thomas de 358
Thornhill, James 250
Thornton Hall, Yorks. 265
Thouret, Nicolaus Friedrich 319
Thuburbo Maius, Tunisia 124
Thulden, Theodor van 251
Tiberius 21, 22, 23, 24, 29, 30, *31*, 32, 107
Tiberius Gracchus 2
Tiddis, Algeria 125
Timgad, Algeria 109–10, 112, 120–1, *120*
Timofejew, I.T. 359
Tipasa, Algeria 125
Titus 36, 37–9, *38–9*, 108
Tivoli, Italy 151
Tolentino, Guillermo 399
Tonnini, Giuseppe 415
Torelli, M. 45, 57
Toronto, Canada 431
Tortebat, François 230
Totty, James 413
Toul, France 227
Toulon, France 236, 244
Tournai, Belgium 247–8
Townsend, George Alfred 404, *404*
trade pageants and arches 308–9
Trajan 43, 59–61, *59*, 61–2, 63–4, *64*, 81, 83, 91, 100, 108, 125
Trajan's Column 63, 83
Trent, Italy 194
Trenton, USA 377
Trevail, Silvanus 309
Treviso, Italy 196
Trezzini, Domenico 356
Tribolo, Niccolò 194
Trier, Germany 71, 334–5, *335*
Triest, Antonius 250
Trieste, Italy 323
Tripoli, Libya 111–12, *111*, 433
triumphal arches
 definition of viii–ix
 origins of 1–6
 use of the term, earliest 112
Troisi, Pietro Paolo 374–5, *374*
Tron, Nicolò, Doge 156
Trondheim, Norway 367
Troost, Gerdy, *Das Bauen im neuen Reich* 433
Troyes, France 227
Truro, Corn. 309

Tsarskoe Selo, Russia 281–3, *282*, 358
Tuby, Jean-Baptiste 229, 232
Tunisia 32, 107–9, 111–14, 116, 120–5
Turapilli, Ventura di ser Giuliano 155
Turbertini, Giuseppe 316
Turin, Italy 196, 419, *419*
Turkey 22–3, 33, 85, 90–8
Turner, Thomas 278
Turner, William 305, *305*
Turvey, Beds. 208, *208*
Twining, Thomas 258
Tyre, Lebanon 99–100
Tyringham Hall, Bucks. 265

Úbeda, Spain 368
Uchtomski, Dmitri 356
Udine, Italy 148
Ukraine 353, 438
Ulan Ude, Russia 361
Ullmann, Émile 328
Ulrica Eleonora of Denmark 365
Um el Abuab, Tunisia 124–5
Umberto I, K. of Italy 433
Umm Quais, Jordan 103–4
Umm-el-Jimal, Jordan 102
Unger, Georg Christian 338, *338*, 339
Unghero, Nanni 155
United States of America 377–80, 402–5, 420, 421–2, 426–8, 437–8
Urbino, Italy 196
Ustinow, Iwan 356
Utrecht, Netherlands 248
Uzuncaburç, Turkey 95, 96–7, *96*

Vác, Hungary 352
Vaccaro, Giuseppe 415
Vadstena, Sweden 363
Valadier, Giuseppe 39, 54–5, 179, 186
Valenciennes, France 221–2, 249
Valens 55–6, 123
Valentinian I 55–6, 123, 124
Valentinian II 56
Valeri, Domenico 184
Valerian 197
Vallari, Nicolas 363
Valletta, Malta 374
Valley Forge National Historical Park, USA 405
Vallin de la Mothe, Jean-Baptiste 356–7, *357*
Valparaiso, Chile 385–6, *386*
Valtice, Czech Republic 284
Vanbrugh, Sir John 269, 275
Vandelvira, Andrés de 368
Vanvitelli, Luigi 184
Vasari, Giorgio 54, 157, 158, 171–2, 191, 193
Vasari, Giorgio, the Yngr 155
Vatican City 54, 144, 161–2, 170

Vauban, Sébastien Le Prestre de 233, 234
Vauxhall Gardens, London 272
Veere, Netherlands 257
Velde, Franciscus van de 246
Vendramin, Andrea, Doge 156
Venezuela 385
Venice, Italy 143, 145, 146, 151, 155–6, 158–60, 178, 194–6, 319
Vennekool, Steven 256
Venner, Thomas 216
Venturi, Adolfo 141
Verdi, Giuseppe 426
Verona, Italy 26–7, *26*, 58–9, 144, 145
Verres 3, 5, 6
Versailles, France 235–6
Verwilt, Dominicus 363
Verzone, P. 95
Veskovo, Russia 361
Vespasian 36, 42, 108
Vespignani, Virginio 180, *181*, 182, 183, 187
Vicenza, Italy 148–51, *149–50*, 194–5
Victoria, Queen 306–13, *307–13*, 425, 431
Vienna, Austria 343–4, 344, 345–6
Vietnam 398
Vigevano, Italy 143, 144
Vignola, Giacomo 144
Vilanova, Antoni 372
Vilaseca i Casanovas, Josep 371–2, *371*
Villa Borghese, Rome 285–6
Villa d'Este, Tivoli, Italy 151
Villa Giulia, Rome, Italy 144
Villar y Lozano, Francisco de Paula del 371
Vinçotte, Thomas 429, *429*
Visentini, Antonio 195, 269, 292, *292*
Vitali, I.P. 359
Viterbo, Italy 183
Vitry le François, France 236–7, *237*
Vittoria, Alessandro 158–9
Vittorio Amedeo III, K. of Sardinia 197
Vittorio Emanuele, K. of Italy 433
Vladivostok, Russia 361, *361*
Voinier, Antoine 243
Volgograd, Russia 361
Vollant, Simon 233, *234*
Volpaia, Bernardo della 164, 165
Volpe, Vincent 202
Volubilis, Morocco 118–20, *119*
Vos, Daniel de 211
Vos, Marten de 249, *249*, 251–2, *252*
Vredeman de Vries, Hans 336
Vries, N. de 255
Vucetich, Mirko 433

Wagga Wagga, Australia 413–14
Wagner, C. 101
Wagner, Johann Martin von 342, *342*
Wailly, Charles de 240, 244, 283
Wainfleet, Lincs. 413
Wales 304, 309, 431
Walford, William 413
Wallington, Northumbs. 271–2
Walnaeffer, Jean-Baptiste 238
Walpole, Horace 269, 273
Walter, Konstantin 346, *346*
Walther, Hans II 335–6
war memorials 401–23
 American Civil and Revolutionary Wars 402–5, *402–5*
 Boer War 406, *407*
 Crimean War 401–2, *401*
 First World War 408–22, *408*, *410*, *412*, *414*, *416–17*, *419–21*
 Second World War 422–3
Warburg, Aby 162
Ward-Perkins, J.B. 84–5
Warsaw, Poland 283, 349, *350*, 351, 352
Washington, George 377, 405, 427–8
Washington, D.C., USA 422
Waterford, Co. Waterford 300
Waugh, Evelyn, *Helena* 50–1
Webb, Sir Aston 408, 426
Webb, John 213–14
Webb, Maurice 408
Weinman, Adolph A. 427
Wellington Arch, London 331–3, *332–3*
Wendelstam, Johan 363
Werner, Samuel 240
Werrington, Cornwall 270
Wesel, Germany 337
Westfehling, Uwe 318, 321
Westmacott, Richard 330, 331
Westminster Abbey, London 208–9, *209*, 216
Westwood, Worcs. 216
White, Adam 207, 209, 216
White, Roger 293
White, Stanford 377–8, 427–8
Whitelocke, Bulstrode 364–5
Wignacourt, Alof de 375
Wilanow, Poland 283, 349
Wilde, Bernard de 257
Wildt, Adolfo 418
Wilhelm I, K. of Württemberg 341
Wilhelm I, Kaiser 342–3
Wilhelm II, Kaiser 343
Wilks, Mark 393–4
William II & III, Ks. of the Netherlands 258
William III (of Orange) 248, 249, 256, 302
William IV 305

INDEX   453

William IV of Orange-Nassau 257
William V, Prince of Orange 257
Wilson, Jean 216
Wilson, Richard 272
Wilton, Wilts. 272
Windisch, Switzerland 71
Windsor, Berks. 306, 308, 313
Winwick Manor, Northants. 207
Wiseman, T.P. 3
Withington, R. 308
Wittet, George 394, *394*
Wittkower, Rudolf 138
Woburn Abbey, Beds., 266
Wolfenbüttel, Germany 336
Wolsey, Thomas 202
Wolverhampton, West Mids. 308
Woodbridge, Kenneth 280
Worksop Manor, Notts. 299
Worsley, Giles 299
Wright, Stephen 266
Wright, Thomas 274
Wrocław, Poland 343, 351–2, *351*
Wyatt, Charles 393, *393*
Wyatt, James 264, 265, 266, 272, 300, *300*
Wyatt, Lewis 267
Wyatt, Matthew Cotes 332, *332*
Wyatt, Matthew Digby 401–2, *401*
Wyatville, Sir Jeffry 267, 297

Xanthos, Turkey 90
Xerri, Giuseppe 376
Ximenes, Ettore 426

Yonge, John 217
York, Yorks. 308, 310
Youghal, Co. Cork 216
Young, Arthur 273
Ypres, Belgium 250, 411–13, *412*

Zabbar, Malta *375*, 376
Zadar, Croatia 87
Zagarolo, Italy 151

Zahra, Francesco 374–5, *374*
Zakharov, Andreyan 359–60
Zama Maior, Tunisia 108–9
Zana, Algeria 112, 121, 123–4
Zanfour, Algeria 117
Zappati, T. 47
Zarudnyi, Ivan Petrovich 356
Zebbug, Malta 376
Zijdebalen, Netherlands 281
Zoppo, Marco 160
Zorzi, G. 194
Zuccarelli, Francesco 269, 292, *292*
Zweig, Stefan 412
Zygmunt III, K. of Poland 348–9